AF569597

Old American Prints for Collectors

Old American Prints for Collectors

JOHN & KATHERINE EBERT

Charles Scribner's Sons New York

Library of Congress Cataloging in Publication Data

Ebert, Katherine.
Old American prints for the collector.

Bibliography: p.
1. Prints, American. 2. Prints—Collectors and collecting. I. Title.
NE505.E23 769′.973 73-19685
ISBN 0-684-13635-X

This book published simultaneously in the United States of America and in Canada—
Copyright under the Berne Convention

1 3 5 7 9 11 13 15 17 19 MD/C 20 18 16 14 12 10 8 6 4 2

Printed in the United States of America

ACKNOWLEDGMENTS

Generous help in the preparation of this book was provided by a number of individuals and institutions. Our daughter Ellen Catherine Ebert typed most of the manuscript in addition to working for weeks in various libraries on the preliminary compilation of Appendix II, "Names in American Printmaking 1670 to 1880." Mr. Ladd MacMillan was also especially helpful in allowing us to photograph some of the Currier and Ives prints in his outstanding collection. Miss Ann Serio, Curator of the Harry T. Peter's Collection of the Smithsonian Institution and Mr. H. R. Bradley Smith of Heritage Plantation of Sandwich, Massachusetts, were especially kind in making photographs available to us. The many other institutions and individuals who lent assistance are acknowledged throughout the book.

Table of Contents

INTRODUCTION

Prints made in America form a vast body of material from the late seventeenth century to the present. Extending the field to include prints related to America but printed in other countries pushes its beginnings back to the voyages of Columbus. American prints are a rich resource abounding in information of all descriptions. Prints lend themselves more readily than painting to representation of the ordinary and everyday and to the newsworthy event of immediate interest, areas now commanded by photographs. In addition to their informational content many of these prints have artistic merit and decorative appeal.

This book seeks to chart the ocean of American printmaking from its beginnings to about 1880 with emphasis on periods and types roughly in proportion to existing material. Thus the nineteenth-century lithographs which include those by Currier and Ives are treated expansively since they are relatively abundant as compared with most other types of prints. The very early and rare historical prints are not covered in depth and, furthermore, are discussed in various scholarly works devoted to them. Prints such as those of J. J. Audubon which were printed in England are included for their American subject matter and close connection with this country. The chapter on miscellaneous prints includes the widely collected and influential Bartlett views, also printed in England. The appendix listing of color plate books contains some with handsome plates brilliantly hand-colored. Since not every artist, printmaker or publisher could be covered in a book of this length, an appendix of selected names identifies some of the most significant. A chapter on techniques serves as an aid to the identification and appreciation of the various methods for making prints used in this country.

It is hoped that this book, abbreviated though it is, will serve to provide stimulus for further study of American prints and their influence, and for the formation of collections of the valuable material still available.

CHAPTER ONE Historical Background

The Role of the Print

The print has had a profound effect on Western civilization. A print is an exactly repeatable picture and has played an ambidextrous role in art and commerce. The essence of a print, its exact repeatability, has been a fundamental factor in the development of science and technology. The Greek botanists wrote books classifying and describing plants which were then illustrated by drawings. As the books were copied and recopied the drawings varied so widely from the originals, that this approach was abandoned and they fell back upon purely verbal descriptions. The inadequacy of words alone to describe a particular plant, the shape of its leaves, texture, color, and other features limited the development of Greek botany as it did other areas of science and technology. The print as a conveyor of information is so essential to modern life that medicine, botany, physics, anatomy, biology, electronics, architecture, transportation, and manufacturing processes would all break down if confined to words alone.

The illustrated book was an important democratizing influence. For the first time a craft could be learned at home from a "how to" book instead of from a master. In the first half of the sixteenth century the first practical book on metallurgy appeared as well as a volume detailing the use of the astrolabe and the equatorium, both illustrated with

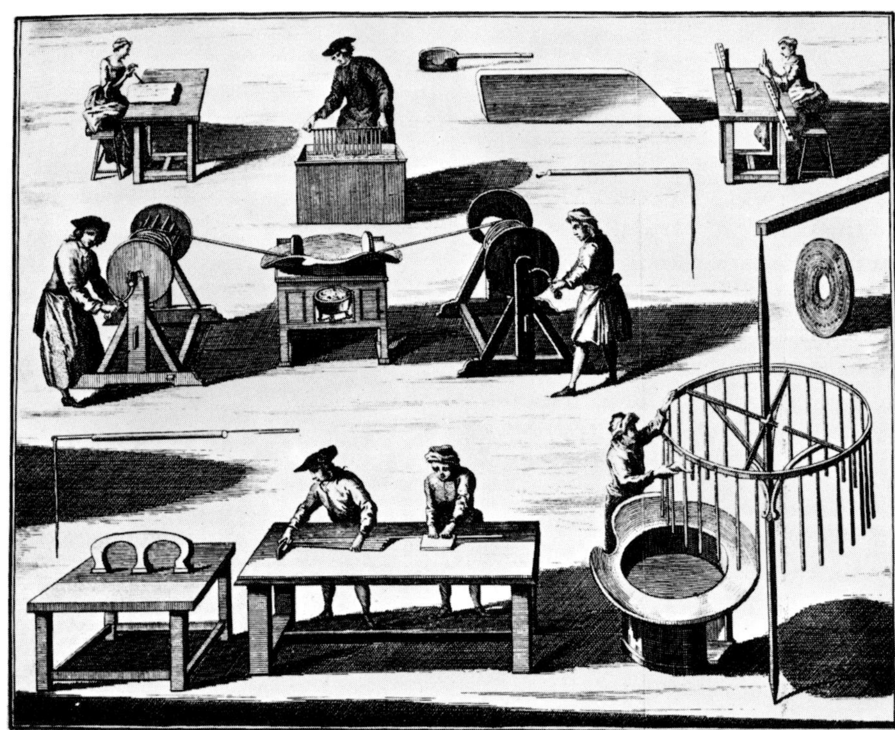

The Art and Mystery of Making Wax and Tallow Candles, engraved for the *Universal Magazine,* London 1749

woodcuts. In 1645, Abraham Bosse wrote a treatise describing the processes of etching and engraving with illustrations of the tools and their use. Some thirty-five years later the Englishman, John Moxon, published instructions for smithing, woodworking, and printing. Intended as a monthly series it was discontinued probably due to pressure from the still powerful guilds. The two-volume *Cyclopedia of Arts and Sciences* written in 1728 by Ephraim Chambers described various trades and was the point of departure for Denis Diderot's thirty-three volume *Encyclopédie* which took the "mystery" out of the "art and mystery" of many of the crafts. The invention of a paper-making machine around 1800 which produced paper by a continuous process and the invention of wood engraving enabled the mass production of cheap illustrated books. In England, during much of the nineteenth century, many of the inventions were made by the self-educated rather than by the classically educated upper classes.

In 1511, the book on architecture and building methods, written by the Roman Vitruvius during the reign of Augustus, was printed in Italy with illustrations. Andrea Palladio's designs for the Venetian patricians of the last quarter of the sixteenth century were studied by Thomas Jefferson, who gave a Palladian accent to Monticello and other buildings he designed. Furniture designs were printed in Nuremberg in the first half of the sixteenth century. Paris set the styles for France and exported them all over Europe by prints. Chippendale published his *Director* in 1754, a book of furniture designs which could be ordered from the Chippendale workshop. This and the later book by Hepplewhite provided a design source for the American cabinetmaker. The elegance of the palace of Versailles was shown as the pinnacle of interior harmony and demonstrated interior decoration in thousands of etchings. Robert Adam's etchings in England made neoclassical interior decor the fashion. Designs for embroidery, lace, jewelry, clothing, and all kinds of household goods were spread in prints. Prints, themselves, were used on wallpaper, cloth, china, enamel, and even by American sailors who copied them when carving their whales' teeth.

Prints transmitted information about all manner of things, easily crossing national boundaries. The voyages of Columbus with his trophies of the New World were put into prints. Travelers brought back prints as souvenirs of their journeys as travelers bring back photographs and postcards today. Prints about the variety of the earth and its peoples stimulated curiosity which led to exploration, conquests, and migrations. Interest in geography was also fostered by maps which only became widely available after they were made into prints.

Prints were used as substitute paintings and tacked on the wall as decoration, but the most important kind of popular image was the religious print. It was put on the wall, pasted into bibles and prayer

Manufacture of playing cards. The layers of paper were stiffened with paste and laminated in a press. The printing was done in the tax office and the cards were then hand-colored, using stencils, a different one for each color. From Diderot's *Encyclopedie,* (1751–1772)

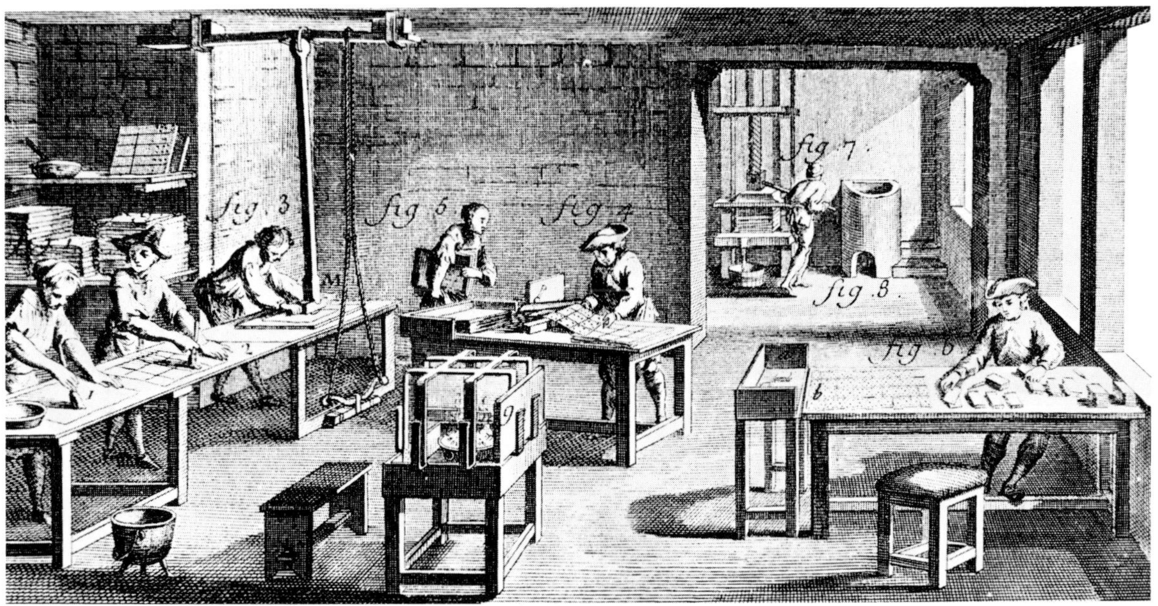

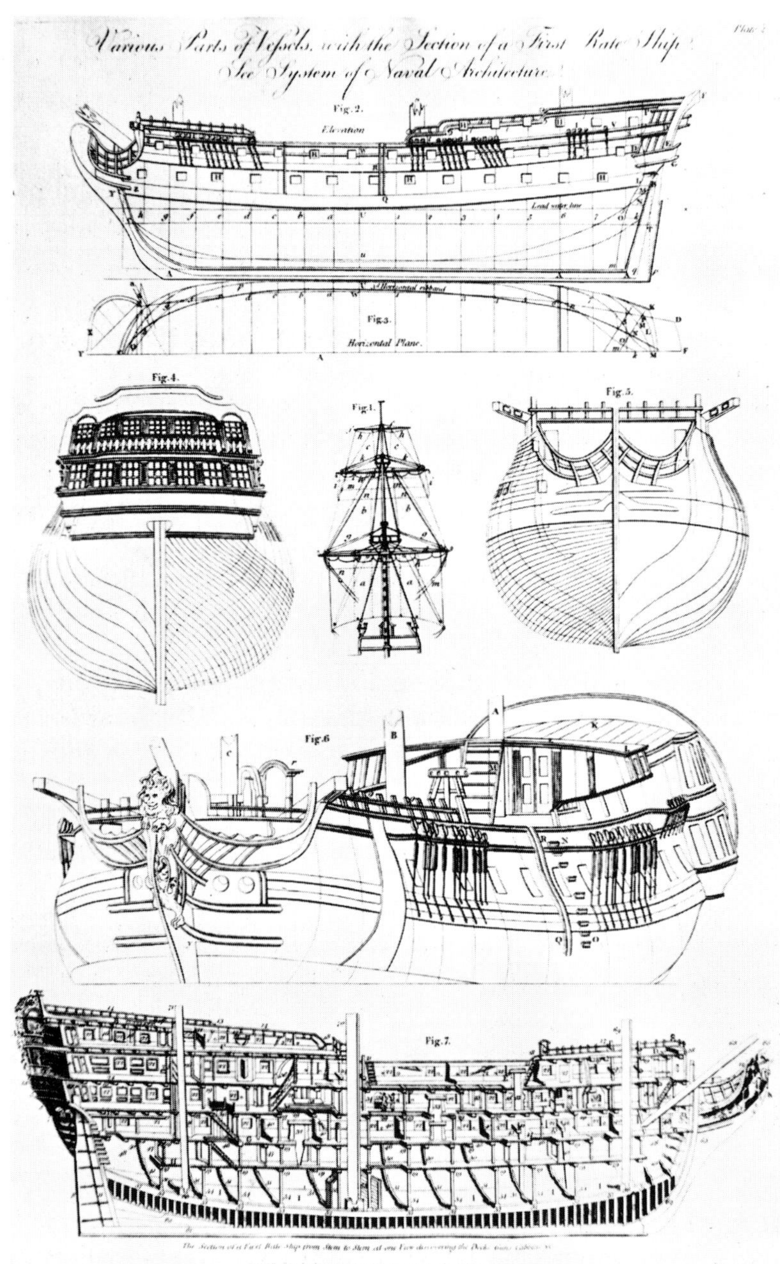

Various Parts of Vessels with the Section of a First Rate Ship, engraved by Page for the *Royal Encyclopedia,* London 1790

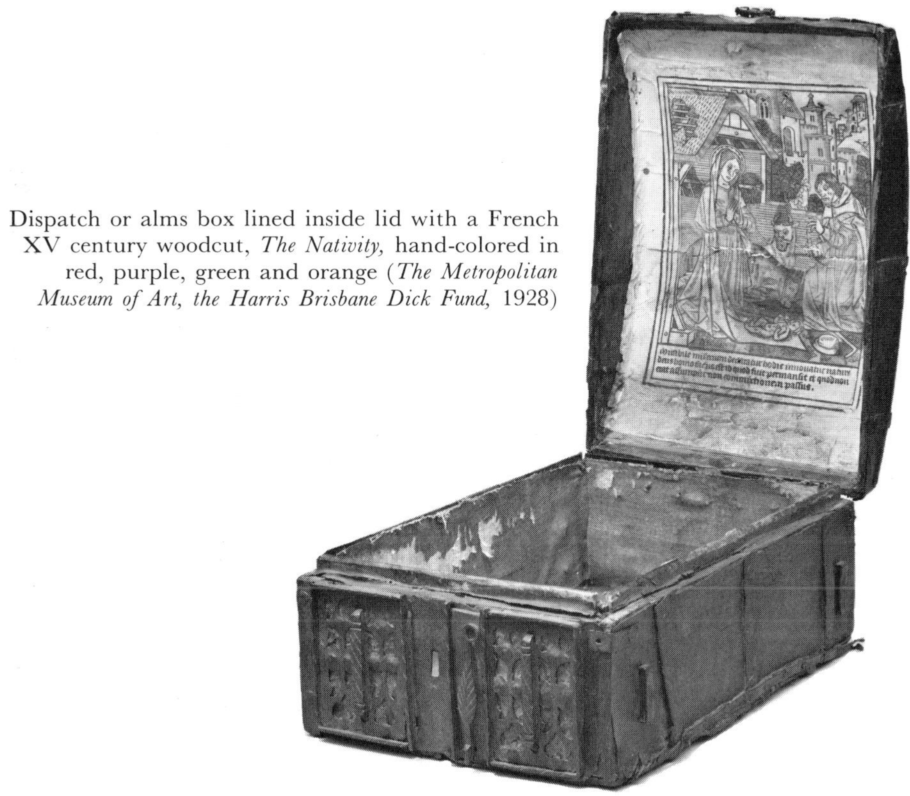

Dispatch or alms box lined inside lid with a French XV century woodcut, *The Nativity,* hand-colored in red, purple, green and orange (*The Metropolitan Museum of Art, the Harris Brisbane Dick Fund,* 1928)

books, and inside the tops of boxes. Albrecht Dürer made large numbers of these to be sold at fairs or to religious pilgrims. Artists also used prints to advertise their paintings. Like an author who sells the motion picture rights to his book, artists sometimes made more money from selling the prints of their paintings than from the paintings themselves.

The art of the great Italian Renaissance was brought to the North by means of prints. The introduction of perspective drawing made all kinds of diagrams spatially legible. Artists made collections of prints for use as source material. Rembrandt had a large collection, and though he never left Holland, was well aware of the developments to the South.

So much of art has been studied through the medium of the print that it has had a kind of homogenizing effect on art values. Prints emphasize subject and composition, substitute line and tonal blacks and whites for color, and interpose their own patterns for the textures of paintings and sculpture. During the nineteenth century most art history books contained prints as ours today contain photographs. Modern vivid color photographs, often bigger and better than life, leave one disappointed when encountering an impressionist painting for the first time since it may not be nearly as bright as its color slide. The reality is dimmed by the expectation. Scale distortions by both print and photo-

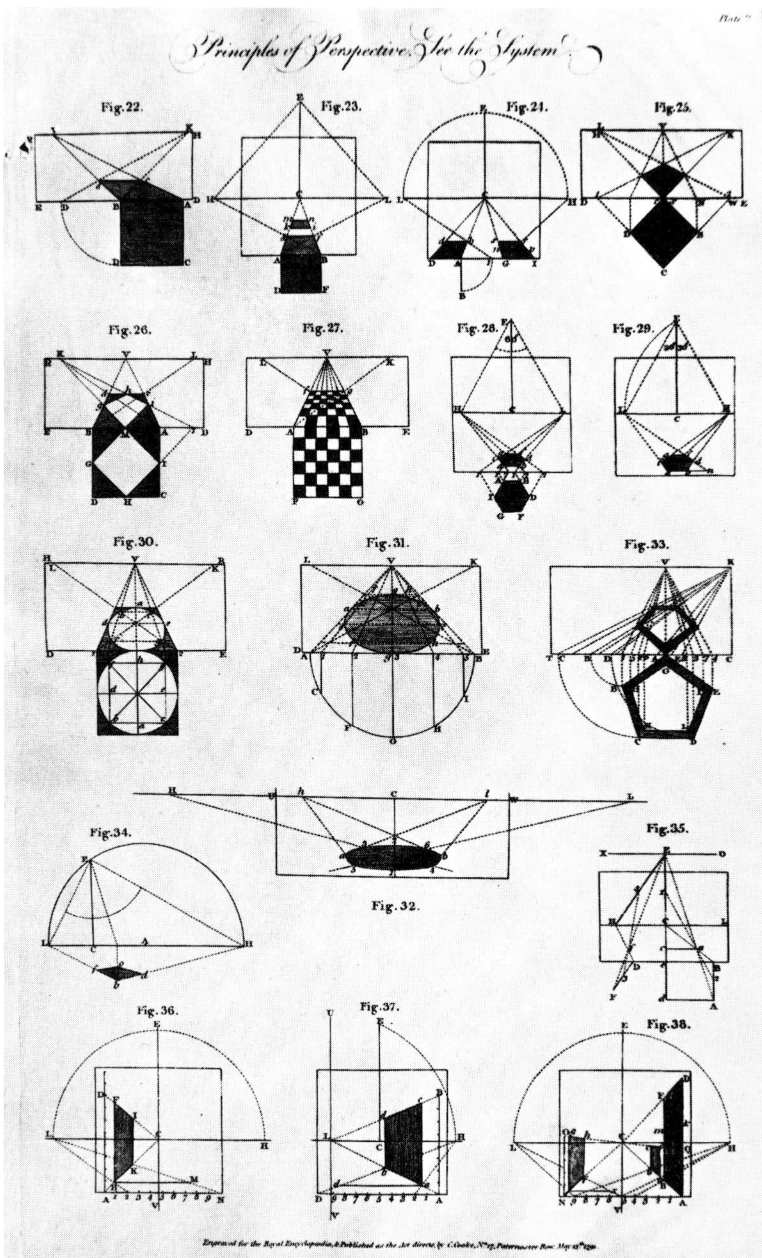

Principles of Perspective, engraved for the *Royal Encyclopedia,* London 1791

graph can impart dimensions of grandeur far beyond actuality. Goethe was disappointed by his first trip to Rome when it failed to measure up to Piranesi's melodramatic etchings. The first artists in our country rarely saw a painting first hand. Their main contact with art was by way of prints of English paintings.

Prints served as propaganda, political protest and satire. Savonarola had his writings illustrated. Paul Revere's *Boston Massacre* inflamed the colonials against the British soldiers. William Hogarth's engravings satirized the manners and morals of English society. Daumier's caricatures have left some unforgettable images.

Prints have served as a vital form of storage and communication of information with a concreteness not possible with the printed word alone. Although starting as an accessory to prayer books, separate prints grew from religious images to become works of art themselves. The aim of printmakers was to make as large a number as they could sell. Multiplication was their goal. The limited, numbered edition is a relatively modern notion.

Paper

The history of prints is inextricably bound up with the history of paper. The Chinese invented paper shortly after 100A.D. but it took a thousand years more before paper was made in Europe. Papermaking was brought to Spain by the conquering Moors in the middle of the twelfth century. From there it spread to Italy some twenty-five years later, and reached Germany near the end of the fourteenth century.

A Chinese court official, Ts'ai Lun, worked out the process which is still the basis for modern paper. Wet cloth clippings were beaten by hand into a mass of fibers which was then mixed with water. This slurry was poured onto a cloth or bamboo screen and after draining and drying left a matted sheet of vegetable fibers, or paper.

The Europeans developed water-powered hammers for separating the fibers. The Chinese bamboo mold was supplanted by a hardwood frame with a series of parallel wooden ribs across which were laid closely spaced wires. These wires left impressions on the paper called "laid lines"

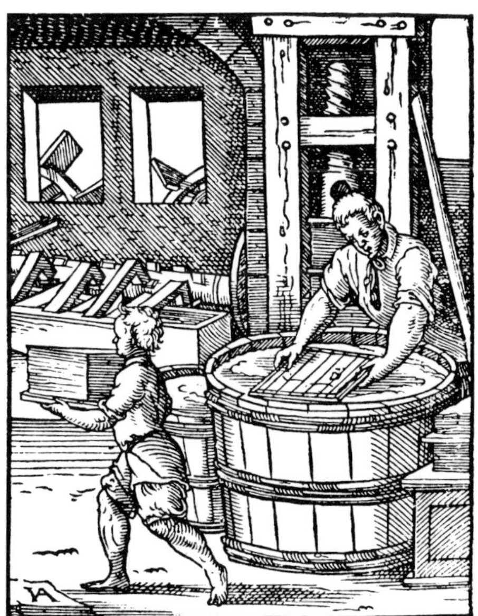

Sixteenth-century woodcut of papermaking

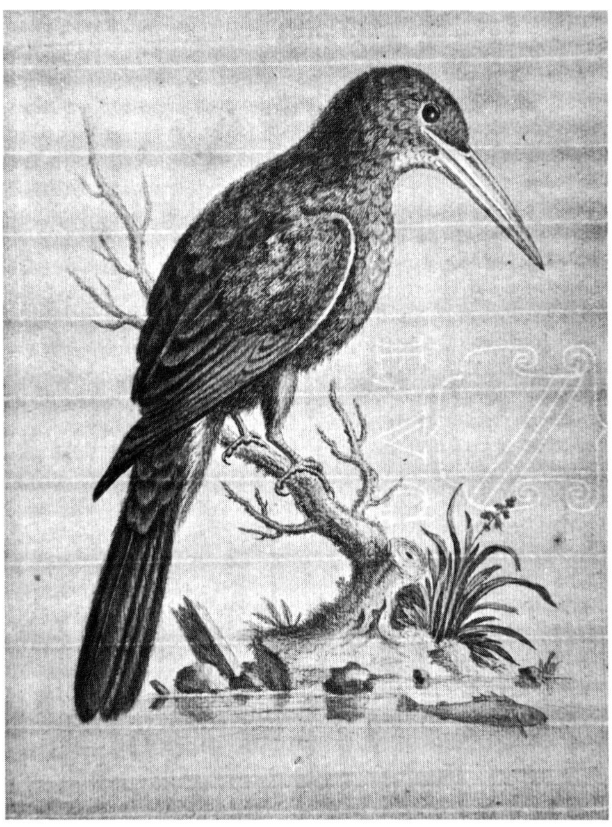

Print of a bird on laid paper. The vertical lines are the laid lines and the horizontal ones the chain lines which are spaced at about one inch intervals on the original. A watermark appears under the bird's beak. Note the greater density of the paper along the chain lines where the fibers piled up in the mold. Hand-colored engraving and etching, $9\frac{1}{4}$ x $7\frac{1}{4}$ inches, George Edwards, England *c.* 1750

and paper made in such a mold is called "laid paper". The laid wires were secured by sewing them to the wooden ribs underneath. The lines of sewing are perpendicular to the laid lines and are called chain lines. A removable frame called a deckle fitted over the mold to keep the watery pulp from running off.

Papermaking involved a series of operations which had to be performed skillfully in order to produce reasonably uniform sheets. After the rags were reduced to a slurry of fibers, a mold was dipped into the vat to scoop up enough for one sheet of paper. The mold was then shaken back and forth to eliminate excess water, mat the fibers, and distribute them evenly. The sheets were then piled up between felts and placed in a press where water was squeezed out and the paper compressed and made denser. As a surface finish the paper was sized with animal gelatin. After sizing the sheets were draped over long poles to dry. The sizing added stiffness and crackle to the paper and lessened its blotter-like absorbency. The amount depended on the ultimate use of the paper.

The lines and ridges left by the molds of laid paper were found undesirable and in order to minimize them, an improved mold was made in which the wires were woven into a loose mesh. Paper made this way is called "wove" paper and is the modern type. It was first introduced into England in 1757. However, laid paper continued to be made for some time after that. In 1819, Ree's *Cyclopedia* stated that:

> The wove paper is a very superior article to the old paper, particularly for books but a prejudice still prevails in favor of the old paper with lines, which obliges manufacturers still to make it, though by no means so fine or good as wove.

Around the end of the eighteenth century a machine was invented which made wove paper in a continuous roll. The preference of some for the old laid paper was satisfied in 1825 by the invention of the dandy roll, which imitates the laid patterns and watermarks of handmade papers.

The demand for paper triggered by Gutenberg's invention of moveable type outdistanced the supply. Various innovations such as the Hollander machine for mincing the rags shortened the process, but the quantity of rags was totally inadequate. Finally, in 1840, a German named Keller made paper from ground wood pulp and in 1867, an American, Tilghman, separated wood fibers using sulfurous acid.

The properties of paper govern the kinds, qualities, and durability of the prints made on it. The uneven surface of early handmade papers made it impossible to print fine details since they were lost in the surface ridges and hollows. Some of the later innovations in papermaking produced excellent uniform surfaces but also introduced destructive chemicals which are still plaguing library and museum conservators.

European Background

First European Prints

Since the survival of early prints has been largely a matter of accident, it is impossible to be positive about the place of origin of prints in Europe. The earliest ones in existence are religious prints whose makers are unknown. A hand-colored woodcut, *Mary at Rest on the Flight into Egypt,* was made in Bohemia around 1410. A Dutch Madonna bears the date 1418, and a south German St. Christopher, 1423. The date of the earliest Italian print, *The Madonna of the Fire,* is 1428. Religious woodcuts were bought in large numbers as holy pictures by pilgrims to the various shrines. Martin Luther criticized the monasteries for being deserted except for a friar who sat in church all day to sell souvenirs and little pictures to the pilgrims. Later on, these became engravings rather than woodcuts.

Not all concerns were holy ones during the fifteenth century. Playing cards were made in large numbers. The earliest ones were woodcuts, but later woodcuts were used on the cheaper cards, while the more expensive ones were engraved.

Early Books with Prints

The earliest books with printed pictures were blockbooks where words and illustrations were carved out of one block of wood. To make these, the words and pictures were drawn on a thin piece of paper and pasted face down on the wood. The cutter then gouged out the wood between the lines leaving the pictures and letters in relief. At the same time this reversed the image so that when printed it appeared as drawn.

The manuscript, *The Bible of the Poor,* which was illustrated with drawings of the life of Christ matched with prophetic events in the *Old Testament,* was published in blockbook form around 1450. Another popular life of Christ was *The Mirror of Man's Salvation* which was copied and recopied in many versions. The short version of the manuscript book, *The Art of Dying,* was printed in over twenty blockbook editions. It shows how to make one's exit from this world on the side of the angels and was studied earnestly during the Middle Ages. The sudden, unexpected, unexplainable, irrational, and universal presence of death for young and old made it a subject for popular prints and folk art of all kinds well into the nineteenth century. Blockbooks continued to be published after the invention of moveable type. A block, once carved, could be readily

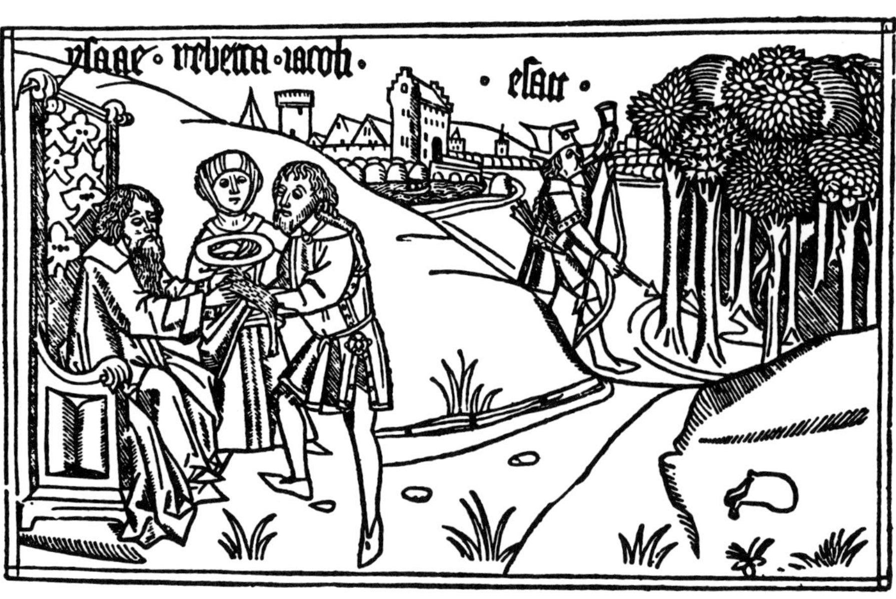

Isaac and Jacob, woodcut from the Cologne Bible, 1478–1480

used to run off a small number of copies, whereas it was not worthwhile to reset type for a short run. The first printed Bible with a generous number of illustrations was printed at Cologne about 1478. These hand-colored woodcuts were relatively crude but as part of the Bible exerted tremendous influence.

So much effort was expended on producing recognizable religious images, that the informational potential of illustrated books was not appreciated at first. In 1472, Valturius' *Art of War,* as always a high-priority subject, appeared in an edition illustrated with many woodcuts of specific machines and their uses. It is the first datable, technical, how-to book. Several books on nature and botanical subjects were printed prior to the herbal, *Gart der Gesundheit,* published in Mainz in 1485, but this is the first with drawings done directly from nature. Breydenbach's *Travels,* published the next year, is the first illustrated travel book. The famous *Nuremberg Chronicle* of 1493 is an encyclopedia of world history and geography with many woodcut illustrations. When the *Chronicle* was short of an illustration here or there, it merely appropriated a city view or portrait it had previously used and ran the same illustration with another title.

Early Engraving

Although crude, brightly-colored woodcuts continued to be sold as popular images, the limits of the woodcut, under the conditions imposed by the paper and ink available, were being reached by those who strove for ever more delineation, finer lines and shading. The information that could be contained in a block of wood was limited by the nature of the wood,—fine lines would splinter or break when printed—by the inking process which clogged fine lines, and by the presses which could not print fine detail easily on the ridged paper. More printmakers turned to engraving, a centuries-old craft practised by goldsmiths and silversmiths. With the invention of the new oily ink that made Gutenberg's press practical, someone thought to make intaglio prints by inking an engraved metal surface, wiping it, and pressing paper into the inky engraved lines. Its association with silversmithing lent an aura of high status to engravings not shared by woodcuts. They were also more expensive because the technique took longer to learn and the necessary equipment—copper plate and engraving press—were more expensive. Dürer charged four and a half times as much for an engraving as for a comparable woodcut.

By 1450, in the Upper Rhine, the Master of the Playing Cards, an engraver whose name is unknown, was making prints with delicate hatching. His pupil, E. S., carried the technique further, reveling in portraying flowers and plants. Martin Schongauer added a new dimen-

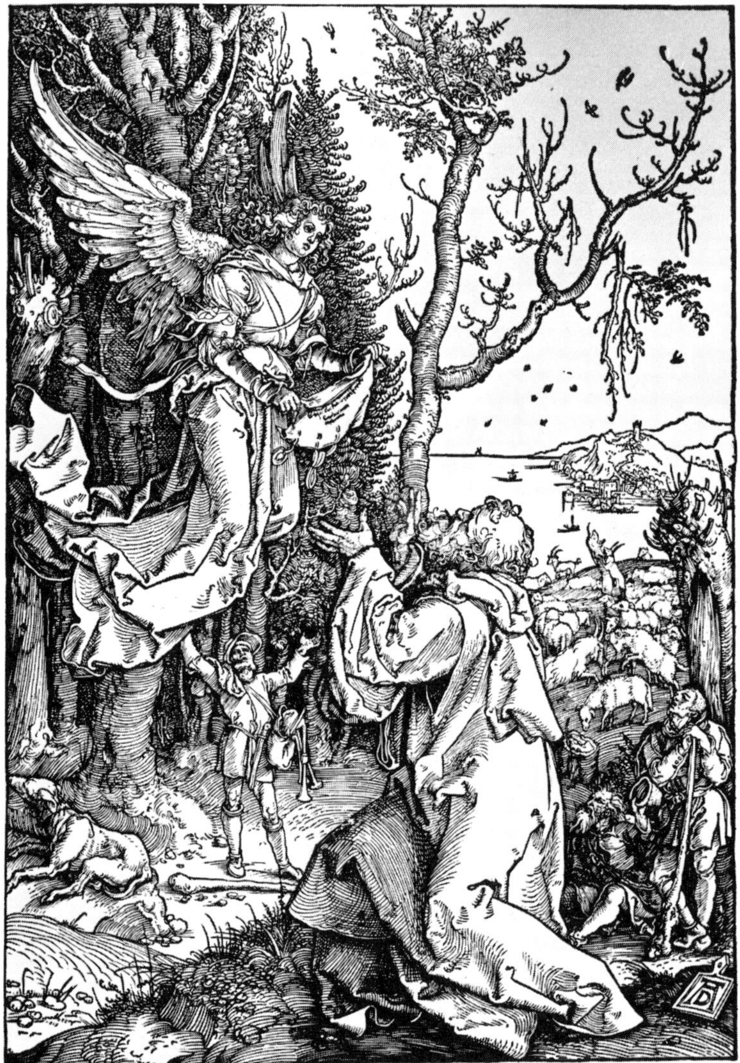

Albrecht Dürer, *Joachim and the Angel* from the *Life of the Virgin,* Woodcut *c.* 1504

sion by using the engraving tool to incise deep lines which printed boldly and shallow lines which printed lightly. In Italy during this period, painting, sculpture and architecture were claiming the energies of the artists of the Renaissance. Copper engraving was treated as a cheap method of reproducing popular works, with a few exceptions. Antonio Pollaiuolo delineated the study of the human body and Andrea Mantegna spread the images of antique sculptures throughout Europe. Mantegna's engravings were copied as models for their composition and influenced Dürer and Rembrandt.

Albrecht Dürer is the towering figure of woodcut and engraving. He became a virtuoso in the techniques and used them with expressiveness and individuality. During his visits to Italy he absorbed the developments of the Italian Renaissance and brought them to the North with his prints and engravings. He was a keen observer of nature and his prints included finely detailed animals and plants with their northern setting. Dürer was also a pioneer in etching, producing six plates between 1515 and 1518.

By the early 1600's woodcut illustration was no longer important. The trend continued away from bold lines toward a more tonal effect. Lucas of Leyden introduced copper for etching and developed a technique for speeding up his work. The plate was first quickly etched and then finished by engraving. This mixed technique became widespread for reproductive copper plates and after 1700 there were very few "pure" engravings.

Albrecht Dürer, *St. Jerome in his Study,* engraving 1514

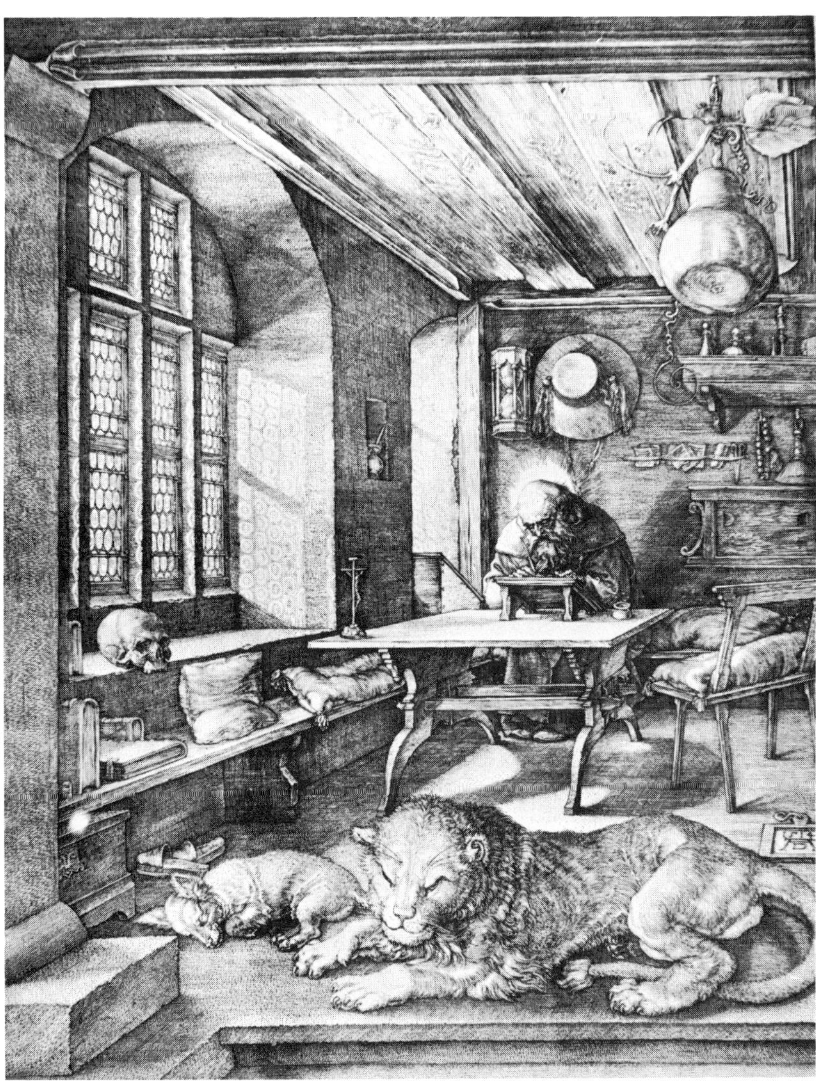

Engraving Becomes an Industry

The first engraver's shop of international importance was organized by Marcantonio Raimondi. He understood Dürer's masterly rendering of rounded shapes, textures, light and shadow and the techniques of other engravers and of painters, and synthesized these into an organized method for interpreting paintings into prints. This system made possible a large workshop in which engravers collaborated interchangeably. From his workshop in Rome he spread the style of the Italian Renaissance throughout Europe. After the sack of Rome in 1527, the workshop dispersed and Marcantonio's system was taken wherever members of his workshop alighted. His system was refined by the various engraving centers into a syntax of cross-hatching, with lozenge, line and dot as the elements which evolved into the artificial convention used in bank-note engraving. These linear systems were accepted as placidly as we accept photomechanical screening. With time, engraving became even finer and more tonal, approaching the effect of a photograph.

Antwerp became a manufacturing center for engravings after 1510 when it became a great commercial seaport for the new sea route around

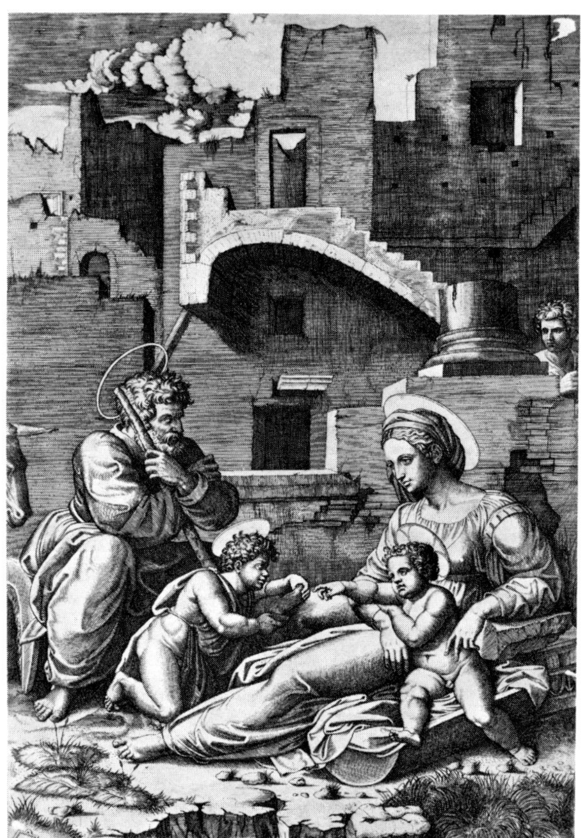

Marcantonio (*c.* 1488–1530), engraving after Raphael's *La Vierge à La Longue Cuisse* (*The Metropolitan Museum of Art, the Joseph Pulitzer Bequest,* 1917)

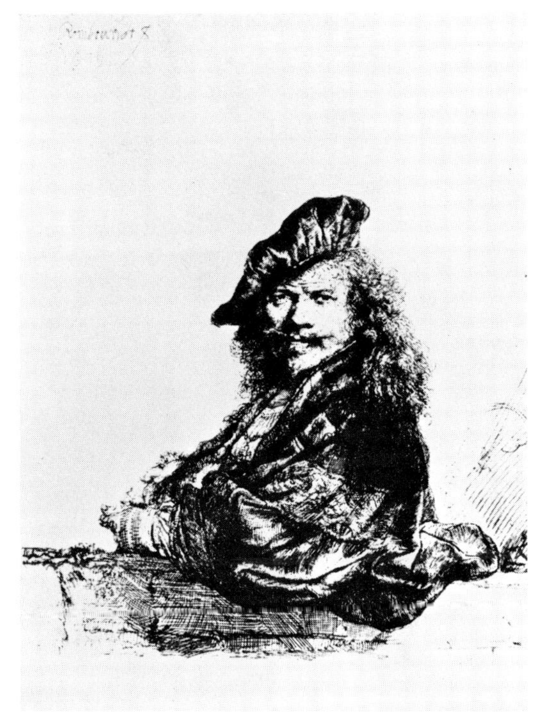

Rembrandt, *Self-portrait leaning on a stone sill,* etching and drypoint, 1639

Africa, which bypassed Venice, and for trade with the New World. Hendrick Goltzius of Haarlem perfected an engraving style of tapering curves which intersect in lozenges and follow contours in a grid which shrinks and stretches, giving the effect of shimmering taffeta. Rubens, dissatisfied with the Antwerp workshop, imported engravers trained by Goltzius. He developed a flourishing workshop which reproduced the heroic style of his paintings. In 1626, when Anthony Van Dyke returned from Italy, he began publishing his portraits of artists and writers by hiring some of Rubens' engravers.

Etching

Jaques Callot made technical advances in copperplate engraving and etching which had far-reaching effects. He substituted the tough varnish for making lutes for the waxy etcher's ground, which resulted in making the acid biting more controllable. His invention of the échoppe, a new etching tool, made it possible to draw lines on copper that swelled and diminished in thickness like engraved lines. He refined the process of biting in acid to selectively deepen and widen lines. In 1645 Abraham Bosse, a pupil of Callot, published these innovations in a treatise on engraving in which he states that "the etcher's chief aim is to counterfeit engraving."

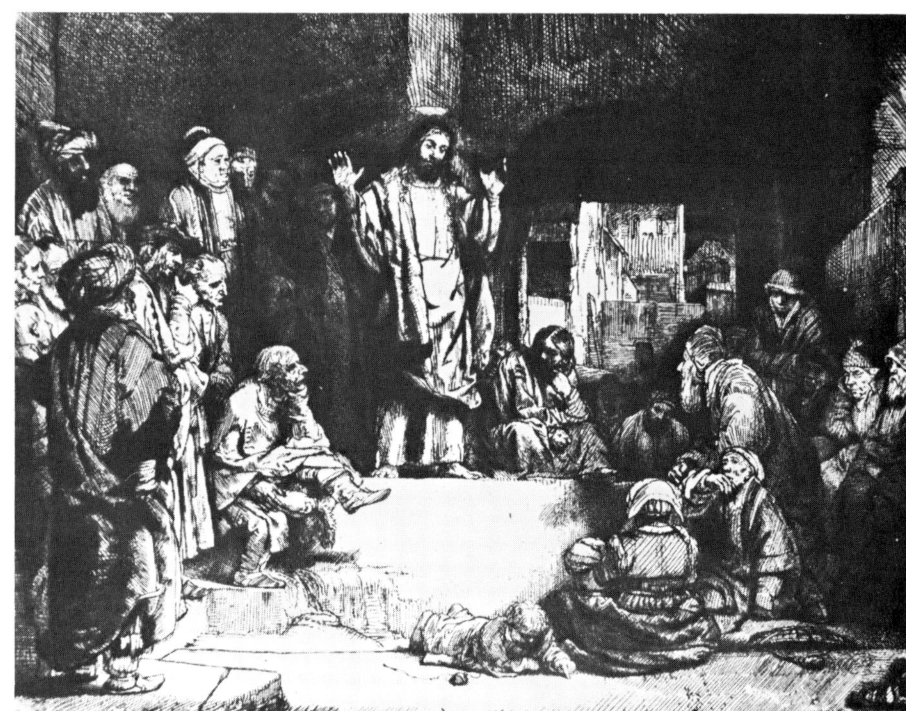

Rembrandt, *Christ Preaching,* etching and drypoint, 1652

Unlike Rubens or Callot, Rembrandt showed little interest in the commercial aspects of printmaking. He explored and developed the techniques of engraving, etching and drypoint for their artistic possibilities and his achievements are consistent with his greatness as a painter. He followed no formula. Sometimes his lines were laid densely with a few dim figures emerging from the shadows and other times a few economical lines conveyed a landscape. His idiosyncratic scribbles and doodle-like lines are diametrically opposed to the systems used by others, and their individuality started no trend or movement until the nineteenth century. The notion of the *state* began with Rembrandt since he worked and reworked his plates, changing tonality and compositions. Rembrandt made a fine art of etching, reaching unprecedented heights.

In the 1700's Venice produced an innovative etcher in Antonio Canal, known as Canaletto. His etchings of sunlight shimmering on water remind one of French impressionism of more than a century later. Giovanni Domenico Tiepolo, and his father Giovanni Batista Tiepolo, with their fresh scribble approach to cross hatching, inspired Piranesi to become an etcher. Centering his talents on architectural views, especially of Rome, Piranesi's nearly one thousand etchings became the view of Rome envisioned by most people—dramatized, romanticized, and in colossal scale.

Eighteenth-century Europe was flooded by prints after Watteau and Boucher when an avid collector of Watteau's works undertook to have his entire output reproduced. Boucher's etchings after Watteau's drawings, as well as his own, became popular home decorations. The dazzling life of the French aristocrats was portrayed by Fragonard and Moreau Le Jeune until this life was sobered by the French Revolution.

Giovanni Battista Piranesi (1720–1778), *Piazza Navonna* from *Views of Rome,* etching (*The Metropolitan Museum of Art, the Harris Brisbane Dick Fund,* 1937)

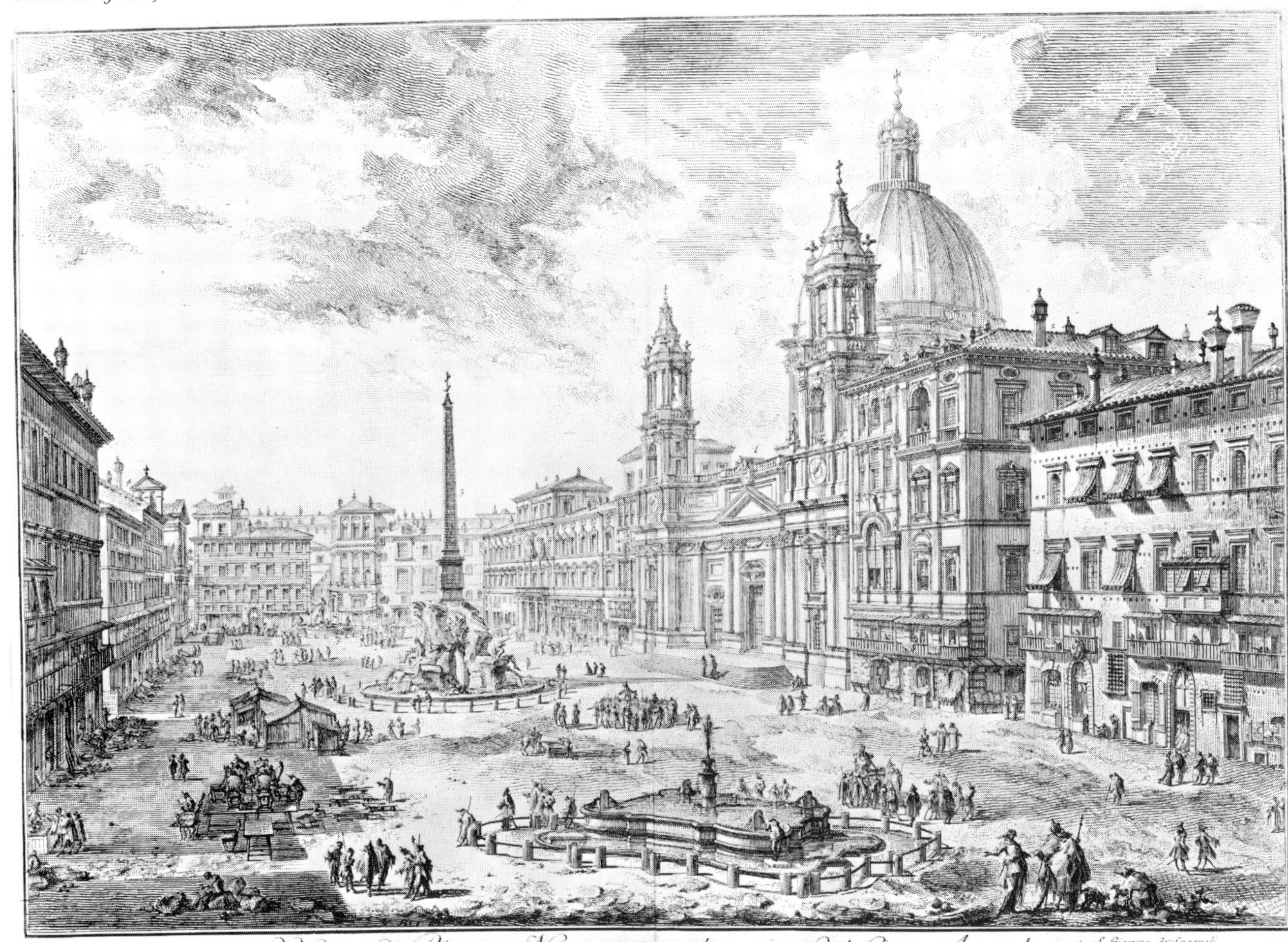

Mezzotint

The search for ways to render the tonality of seventeenth-century painting in reproductive prints led to the invention of the mezzotint process, perfected by Prince Rupert of the Palatinate in 1657. This method of making prints in which the whole plate is roughened and then the highlight areas smoothed out, prints only tones, not lines. It is the process that most resembles the photograph in its effect and is ideal for portraits. Upon being introduced into England, it became so popular that it was known as the English Manner. The English used mezzotints to decorate their rooms and they were brought to America where they served the same purpose.

Aquatint

Spain's first important printmaker, Francisco Goya, published his satirical *Caprichos* in 1799, followed some years later by the emotion-charged *Disasters of War.* Goya made dramatic use of the process of aquatint. Although the process had been invented in the 1650's in

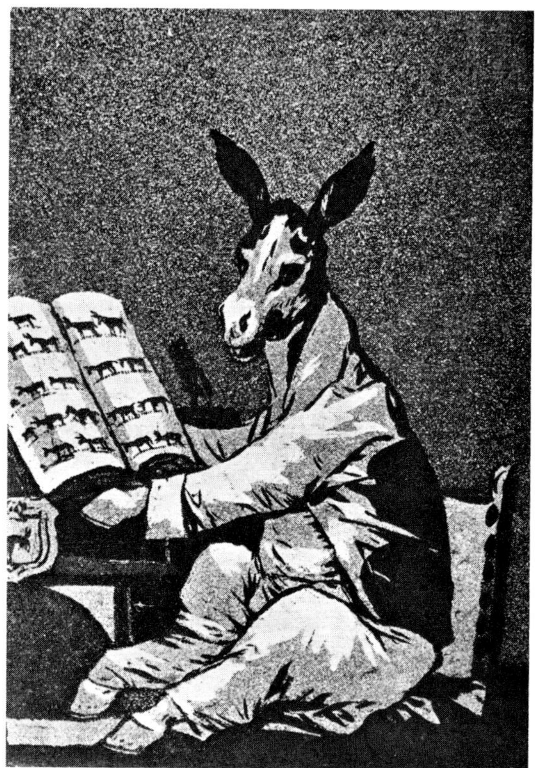

Francisco de Goya, "As far back as his grandfather" from *The Caprichos,* aquatint 1799

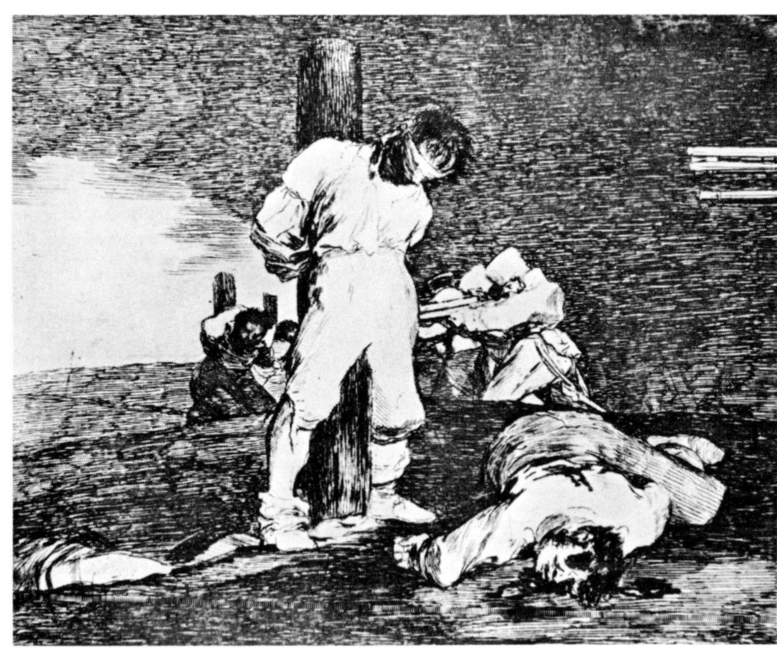

Francisco de Goya, "And there is no remedy" from the *Disasters of War,* etching *c.* 1810

Amsterdam, descriptions of the procedure were not published until 1773 and 1780. Aquatint approximates the continuous tone of a water-color wash although it is a grainy rather than a uniform tone. Aquatints were used by the English to reproduce views which were then hand-colored by assembly line methods. Many views of America were done this way. Audubon had his *Birds of America* etched, aquatinted, and hand-colored in England. By about 1840 the aquatint was supplanted by the cheaper lithograph.

Lithography

Lithography was patented by its inventor, Alois Senefelder, in Munich in 1799 and it was introduced in London in 1800 by Benjamin West, the American-born president of the Royal Academy. "Lithography," from the Greek "stone drawing" or "writing," begins with drawing on a specially prepared stone with a greasy crayon. When the stone is soaked in water, prints can be made by inking the stone with a greasy ink which is repelled by the wet surface but adheres to the greasy crayon design, and then using this inked surface to print the design. Lithography was quickly adopted as a parlor game by fashionable ladies and gentlemen for whom drawing was a routine accomplishment. After a slow start, lithography went on to become a huge commercial success. When lithography began to make inroads on aquatinting, British aquatinters were influential in obtaining a heavy import duty on the essential Munich stone.

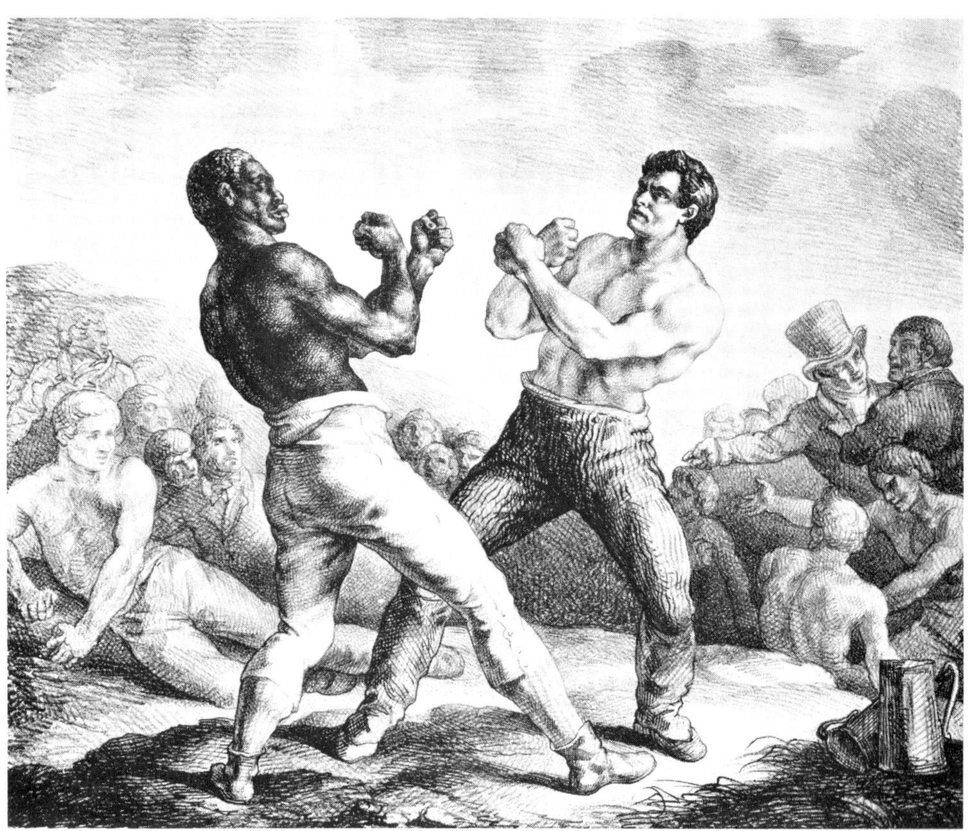

Théodore Géricault (1791–1824), *Boxeurs,* lithograph (*The Metropolitan Museum of Art, the Schiff Fund,* 1922)

In France, lithography was taken up by serious artists who recognized the advantages of a medium where the artist can draw directly on stone or transfer paper without learning a new technique or trusting an intermediary with the execution of his work on wood or metal. Théodore Géricault was the first major artist to produce a substantial number of lithographs, followed by Eugéne Delacroix. Daumier drew thousands of satirical lithographs which appeared in the Parisian periodical *Le Charivari.* Manet, Degas, Whistler all tried their hand at lithographs but Henri de Toulouse-Lautrec made a new art form of the poster with color lithography. The color lithographs by Paul Cézanne, Vuillard, and Bonnard at the end of the century set the stage for renewed interest in the twentieth.

Wood Engraving

Although copperplate could render fine detail, it had the serious drawback that it could not be printed in the same press with type. When used for book illustrations the plates had to be run off separately. About

1780 Thomas Bewick developed wood engraving which used engraving tools on the end grain of wood. This opened up the whole field of illustrated newspapers and magazines. It supplied pictorial journalism in the *Penny Magazine* in 1832, *Punch* in 1841, and the *London Illustrated News* in 1842. Other countries soon followed England. With machine-made paper the steampresses could spew out large issues with great speed.

Photography

Just as wood engravings were making inexpensive illustrated periodicals available, photography was invented. In 1839 Daguerre announced his daguerreotype and Fox Talbot his calotype. Talbot's process was based on a paper negative which led to modern photography. Photographs for publication were mainly reproduced by wood engravings until the half-tone screen was invented in 1885. The development of photomechanical means for the reproduction of illustrations gradually pushed aside printmaking as a means of conveying information and news. Printmaking developed into two separate avenues, that of commercial and advertising art; and that of fine art, often signed and restricted in number.

History of Printmaking in America

American prints were primarily colonial in character until well after the Revolution. The first prints in North America were made in Mexico, long before Europeans established permanent settlements in the present United States. Juan de Zumarraga, the first bishop of Mexico, requested papermakers and printers from Spain in 1533. The first known print in North America is the woodcut frontispiece by Juan Pablos for a religious work of 1544. Woodcuts resembling the late medieval German ones were used as illustrations for religious books but separate prints were not common until the nineteenth century. It was well over a century before prints were made in the English-speaking colonies to the north. Here, they were strongly influenced by England, where the Puritan and Protestant traditions rejected holy pictures.

The Use of Prints

Prints imported from England were framed and used as home decorations, especially in hallways and along stairs. In 1690 the inventory of the estate of David Fox of Lancaster, Virginia, lists twenty-five pic-

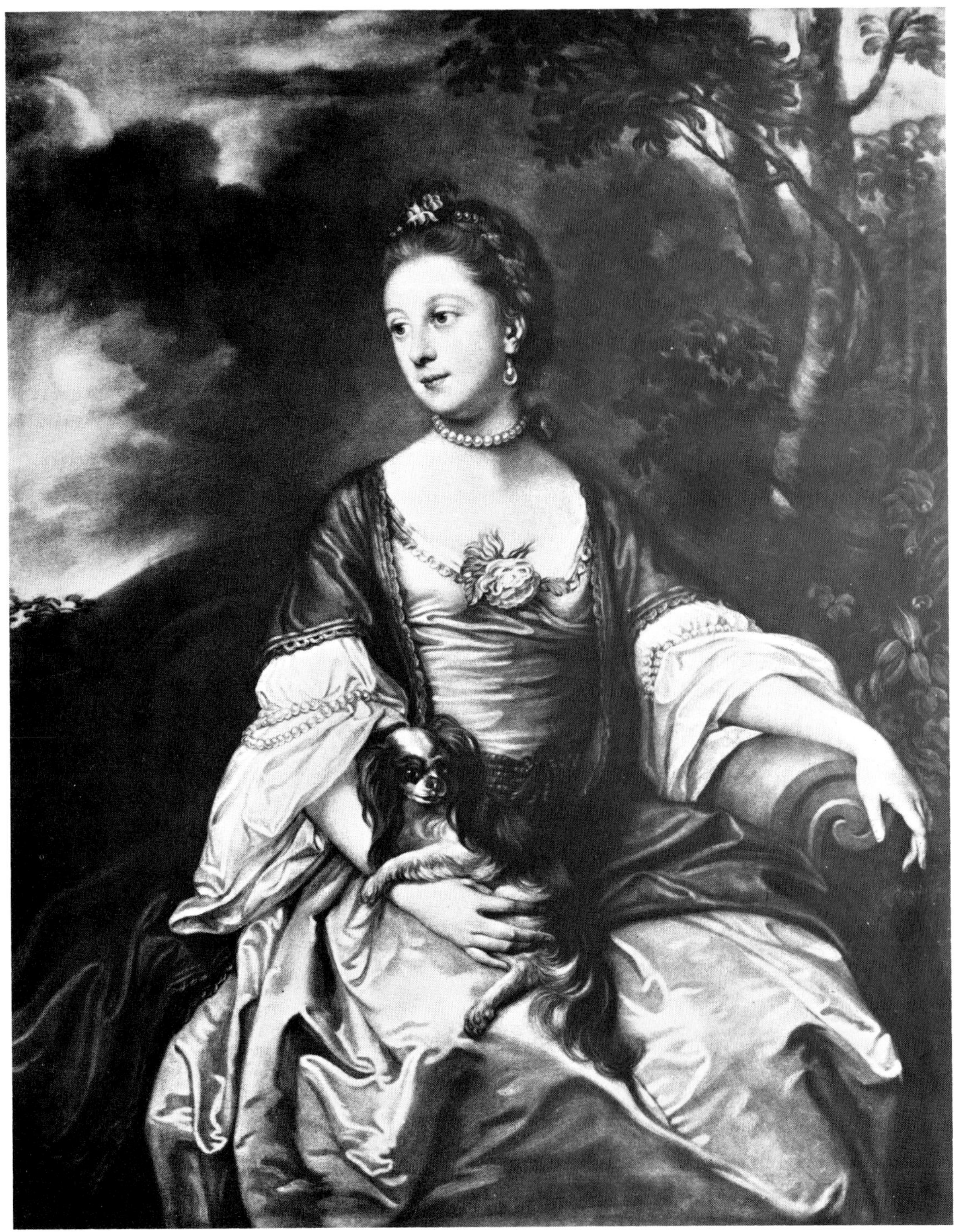

James McArdell, *Lady Caroline Russell,* mezzotint after J. Reynolds 1759. An English mezzotint copied in exquisite detail by John Singleton Copley. The use of English mezzotints as models for portraits was a widespread practise among our colonial artists (*Prints Division, The New York Public Library, Astor, Lenox and Tilden Foundations*)

tures in his hall. In the Massachusetts Bay Colony, the first mention of prints occurs in 1716 in the inventory of Capt. Samuel Ruggles who left "Pictures and Glasses." An advertisement in the *Boston Gazette,* April 4 and 11, 1720, offers "a Collection of choice Pictures, fit for an Gentleman's Dining-room or Staircase." In the issue of August 14, 1721, "a Choice parcel of the best sort of Prints & Maps lately brought from London, all in Good Frames well black'd." By 1749, a wealthy man like the Honorable Wm. Dudley Esquire of Roxbury, left twenty-nine pictures and some old maps including "4 Metsotinta Pictures of Indian Kings" in the hall and "4 Caesar Pictures" in the back room. Col. Robert Oliver Esquire of Dorchester left "12 Metzitens pictures Glaz'd" in the "Setting Parlour" and seventeen pictures "In the Entry and Stair Case." "Heads," or portraits, were very popular and served as models for many of our portrait painters including John Singleton Copley. Maps, flowers,

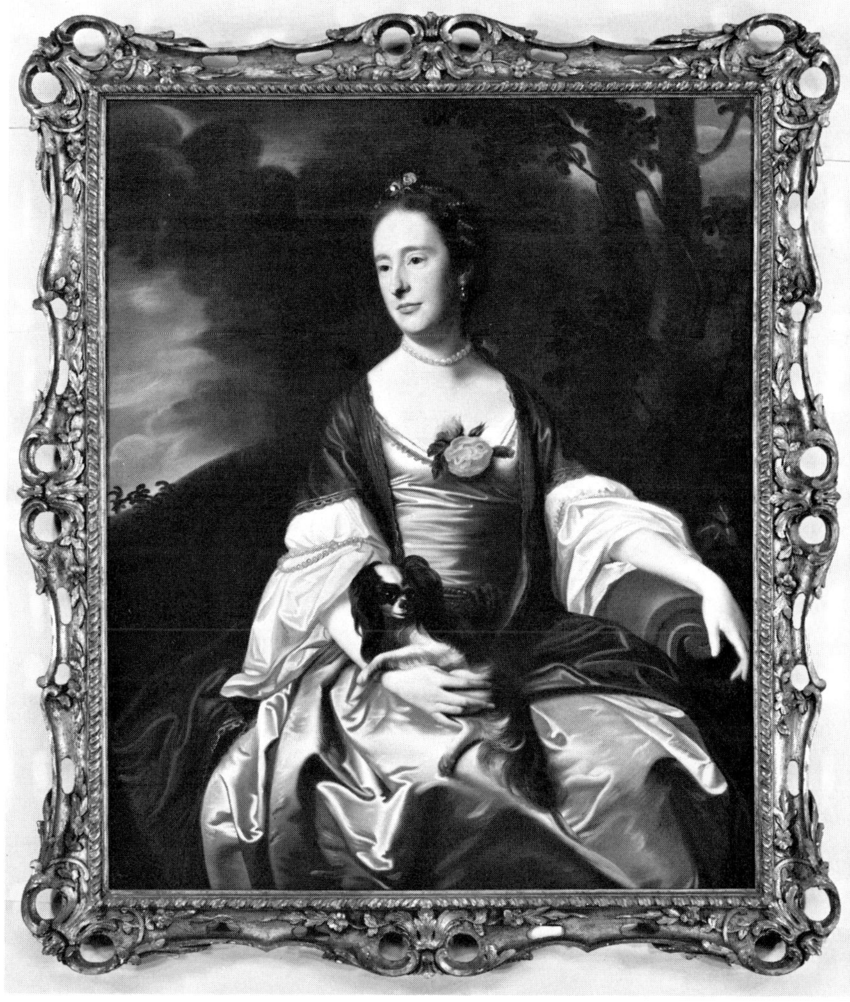

John Singleton Copley, *Mrs. Jerathmael Bowers,* oil on canvas, painted about 1767 (*The Metropolitan Museum of Art, the Rogers Fund,* 1915)

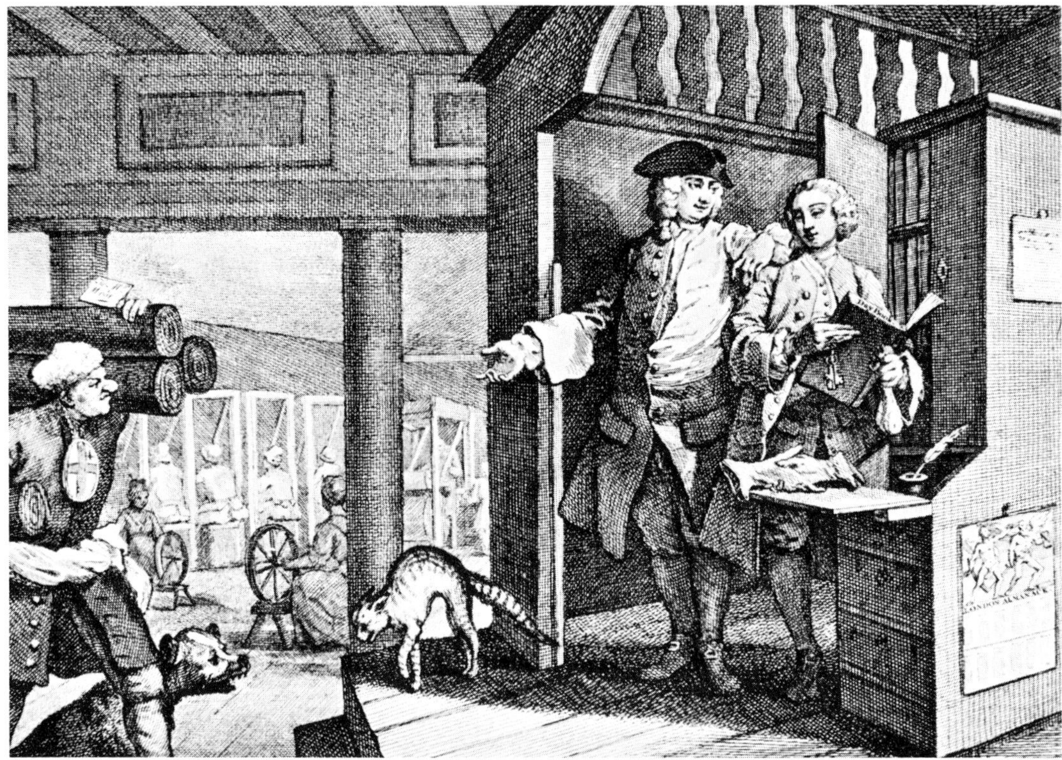

William Hogarth, *The Industrious Prentice, a Favourite, and Entrusted By the Master,* Plate IV of a set of twelve engravings extolling the success and good fortune of the industrious and the downfall of the lazy

fruits and views were also popular. Hogarth's prints were especially sought after with *The Idle and Industrious Prentice* a favorite. This set was repeatedly advertised from its publication in 1747 until after Hogarth's death. Biblical stories or "scripture pieces" also found a ready market. In addition to being framed and hung, prints were used for paintings on glass and as sources for embroidery.

Papermaking in America

Until 1700 almost all the paper came from Europe, mainly England. The first American papermill was built by the German immigrant, William Rittenhouse, near Germantown, Pennsylvania in 1690. Twenty years later a second mill was established by William De Wees, brother-in-law of Rittenhouse's son Klaus. A third mill, The Ivy Mill, was founded on Chester Creek near Philadelphia in 1729 by Thomas Wilcox. Wilcox was a friend of Benjamin Franklin and supplied him with large quantities of paper. Franklin had a keen interest in papermaking and helped in the establishment of about eighteen papermills.

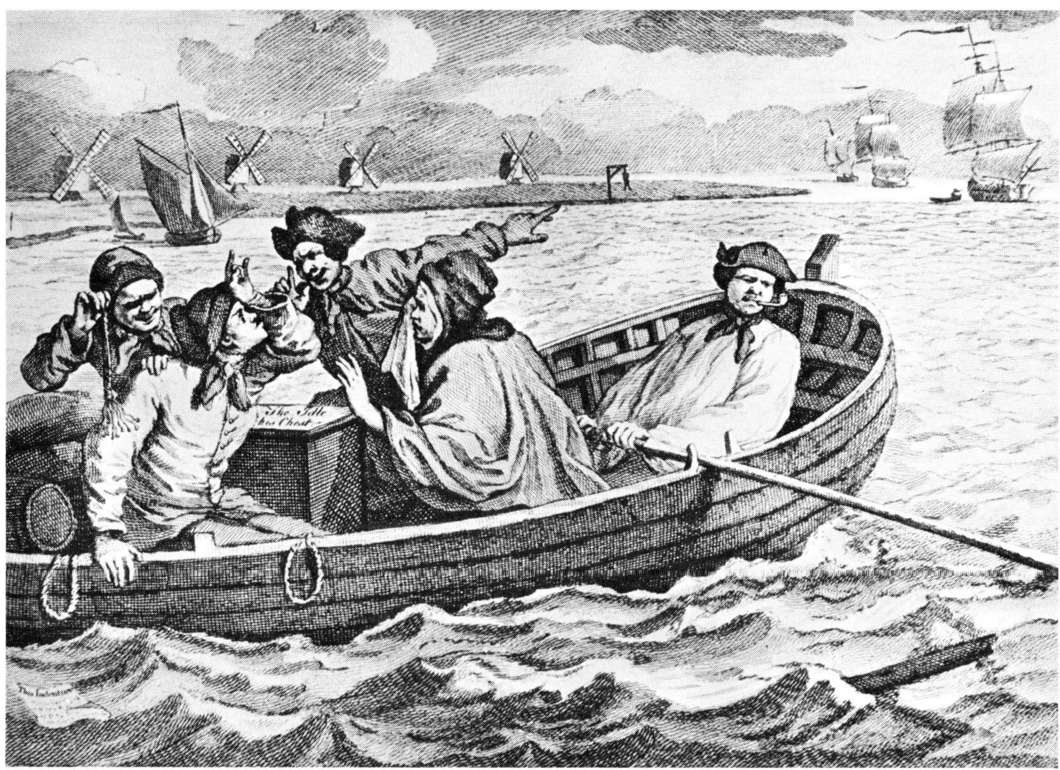

William Hogarth, *The Idle Prentice Turn'd Away, and Sent to Sea,* Plate V from *The Idle and Industrious Apprentice*

Nevertheless the colonies continued to be dependent upon England for paper as well as other supplies until well after the Revolution when there was a great push to become self-sufficient. The Gilpin brothers, Joshua and Thomas, established their papermill on Brandywine Creek near Wilmington, Delaware, after the war. They produced high quality handmade papers but aggressively sought improved techniques, especially the advances made in England. By various devious tactics including the hiring of agents to get drawings of machinery and patent specifications, the Gilpins were able to develop a papermaking machine by 1816 similar to the top-secret one of the Englishman John Dickinson. But the Gilpins could not keep their secret long, either, for they were victims of similar plots, and machine-made paper was made by more and more firms.

The limiting factor in the production of paper was the shortage of rags. In 1854 two English immigrants, Hugh Burgess and Charles Watt, took out a patent for a chemical process developed by them in England for making paper from wood pulp. Several factories were established in the Philadelphia area to produce the paper. By 1860 there were five hundred fifty-five papermaking companies in the United States employing eleven thousand workers. In 1867 grinding machines were imported which made large scale production of groundwood pulp, the principal constituent of newsprint, commercially practical. The availability of inexpensive paper helped bring printed materials of all kinds within the reach of almost everyone.

Early Prints

Most American prints of the seventeenth and eighteenth centuries were not intended primarily as works of art. They were utilitarian, informative, or records of events and personalities. For most printers it was a part-time occupation carried on in addition to some more reliable trade. Printmaking started slowly although there was a need for such items as seals, crests, paper currency, playing cards, coats of arms, book plates, shop bills, bills of exchange, bills of lading, maps, portraits, and frontispieces for books. During the period from 1683–1735 there was never more than one engraver listed in New York City each year. From 1756–1773 the number varied from one to three and in the year 1774 there were ten. In Philadelphia the situation was similar with the number of engravers varying from one to three for the years 1663–1768 and increasing to five in 1769. After the Revolution the number increased steadily with Philadelphia pulling well ahead. In 1800 there were thirty-five engravers working in Philadelphia but only fourteen in New York City. Twenty years later Philadelphia increased the lead with sixty-three to only twenty-four for New York City. It is not known how many of these actually made prints.

The earliest surviving print is from the Massachusetts Bay Colony, a woodcut portrait of the Reverend Richard Mather made by John Foster about 1670. Foster is also credited with the first American map, the *White Hills Map,* which appeared as an illustration in the Boston edition of Reverend William Hubbard's narrative of King Philip's War. John Coney became our first copperplate engraver when he engraved the plates for the Massachusetts Colony Bills of 1690. The speed with which these bills were counterfeited indicates that some alternate but anonymous engraving talent was available.

Very few woodcuts were made. Engraving was a natural side line for silversmiths and, furthermore, was in the British tradition. Among the continually arriving new settlers who brought their skills with them was Peter Pelham. He introduced the mezzotint process with a portrait of Cotton Mather, and with his son Henry ran a flourishing engraving shop in Boston. Peter Pelham married the widowed mother of John Singleton Copley, who became one of our most important portrait painters. Paul Revere, mainly a craftsman and manufacturer, issued some engravings which were politically influential and are of great historic interest. Copperplate engraving was the most widely used medium for book illustrations, especially technical works. Revere engraved a plate of a hemp mill for a treatise on hemp husbandry and the *Transactions of the American Philosophical Society* include plates on astronomy and other subjects.

After the war printmaking gradually gained momentum. There was a demand for engravers to make paper money for the new country. The eighteen-volume English Dobson *Encyclopedia* was reprinted in Philadelphia from 1790–1797 with all of the plates re-engraved. The publish-

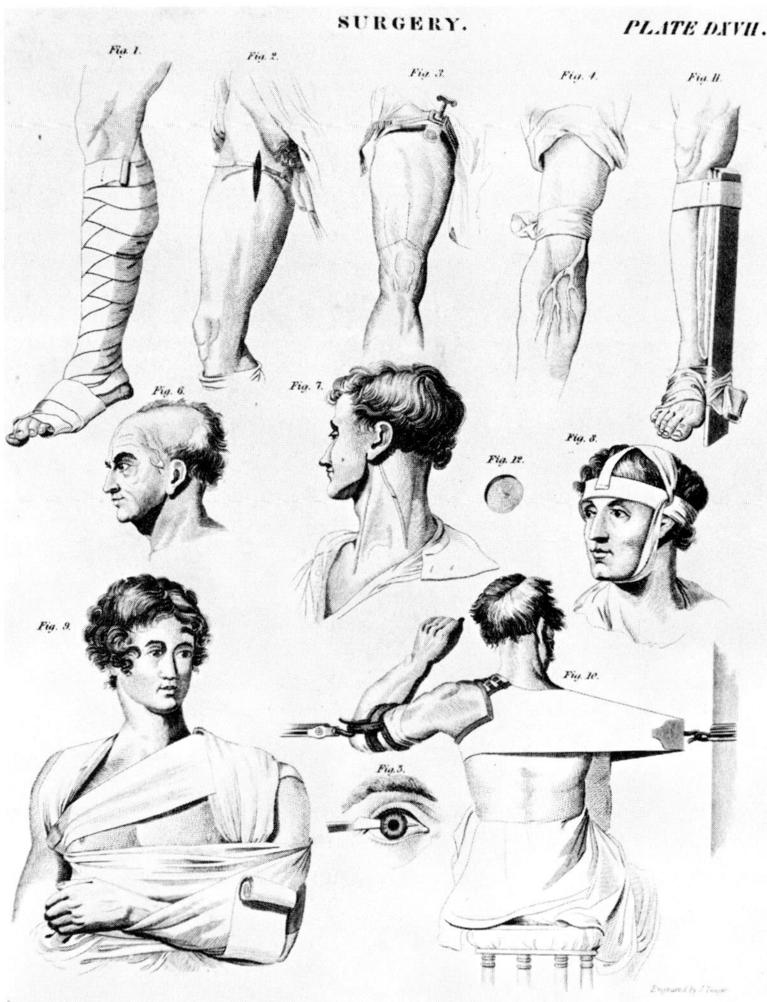

Engraving by J. Yeager (*c.* 1792–1859) for *Rees' New Cyclopedia*, Philadelphia. Alexander Wilson was employed in 1806 as assistant editor for the *Cyclopedia*

ing of these books with over five hundred plates gave impetus to the printing trades in that city and marked the end of printing as a household craft. The fact that the American engravers lacked the sophistication of their English counterparts was commented upon by Alexander Lawson, an engraver of Wilson's *American Ornithology:*

> "Thackara and Valance were partners when I came to Philadelphia. I engraved with them two years. They thought themselves artists, and they knew every part of the art; and yet their art consisted in copying, in a dry, stiff manner with the graver, the plates for the Encyclopedia, all their attempts at etching having miscarried. The rest of their time, and that of all others of this period, was employed to engrave card-plates, with a festoon of wretched flowers and bad writing—then there was engraving on type metal—silver plate—watches—door-plates—dog-collars and silver buttons, with an attempt at seal cutting. Such was the state of engraving in 1794."

One of the earliest books with fine botanical and zoological illustrations is William Bartram's *Travels through North and South Carolina* published in Philadelphia in 1791. Many European artists came to America attracted by the wilderness and the exotic Indians. Alexander Wilson came from England to draw the birds for *American Ornithology,* one of the first great American colorplate books. Audubon's later work, the *Birds of America,* a magnificent wedding of drawing, painting, aquatint, and etching, overshadowed Wilson's pioneering effort.

Lithography

Some twenty years after its invention in Europe, lithography was introduced into the United States. It was made a commercial success by the Pendleton brothers of Boston. Pendleton's 1828 lithograph of George Washington after a Gilbert Stuart portrait was widely circulated. Popular lithographs were produced by numerous firms but the biggest and most successful by a large margin was Currier and Ives. Their prints, more than seven thousand different ones, provided concrete images of personalities, places, events, and social, cultural, and technological progress to even the most isolated communities.

Wood Engraving

After the introduction of lithography, engraving continued to be used for the reproduction of paintings. The artist, Asher B. Durand, worked as a copperplate engraver before becoming a painter. Dr. Alexander Anderson introduced wood engraving into this country about 1794 for book illustrations. He closely copied Bewick's style and was called

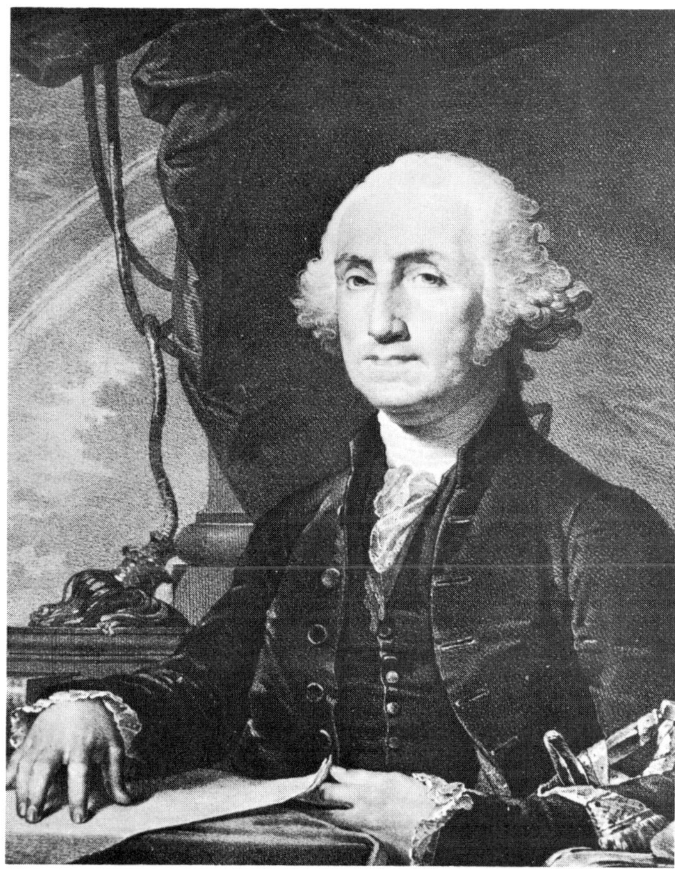

George Washington after the painting by Gilbert Stuart. One of the series called the "American Kings," lithograph by Pendleton, 1828

"The Bewick of America." Abel Bowen was the first wood engraver in Boston in 1812. Wood engraving, being congenial with the presses for printing type, was used for illustrating books, periodicals and newspapers. The most notable of these was *Harper's Weekly* with wood engravings after drawings by Winslow Homer and other artists.

By mid-century photography had become a serious competitor to lithography, especially in the area of portraits. In the census of 1860, in New York and Brooklyn, there were twenty-nine wood engraving establishments employing one hundred forty-seven; twenty-three lithography firms employing three hundred twenty-one; and thirty photographers employing one hundred thirty-nine. When a photomechanical method was developed for reproducing photographs, wood engraving and lithography were replaced for this use. After this, lithography flourished mainly as chromolithography for color printing.

CHAPTER TWO Mechanics of Printmaking, Including Reproductions

In the animal, vegetable, and mineral sense there are only four basic techniques for making prints. There are, however, dozens of variations usually intended to produce some specific effect.

The important variations used in the eighteenth and nineteenth centuries are discussed, but a description of the more recent innovations is outside the scope of this book. Also, as in other parts of this book, the techniques are described and discussed only in terms of printing on paper.

In brief, the four basic techniques are:

1. Stencil—the ink or color is applied to the paper through an opening in a mask or stencil.
2. Relief—the ink is applied to the paper from the raised inked surface of the printing block.
3. Intaglio—the ink is applied to the paper by pressing the paper (usually moistened) into inked crevices on the printing plate.
4. Planographic—the ink is applied to the paper from an inked flat plate, the print part of which has an affinity for ink while the blank part repels ink.

Stencil

Stencil techniques were seldom used for making prints but they were widely used for coloring lithographs and other prints. The stencil itself is usually a thin sheet of metal or heavy paper with a cutout design or pattern. The stencil is placed on the surface to be printed or colored and an inked sponge, brush, or roller is passed over the back allowing the ink to go through the opening of the stencil and on to the paper.

Stencil printing is a very old technique used in China and Europe to color prints, to print designs on cloth and to make very simple printed designs on paper, the walls of houses and on furniture. Modern 20th century technology, however, has taken this rather crude technique and in the mimeograph printing machine and the silk screen has created relatively refined printmaking processes. The silk screen is just that, a screen or stencil of thin silk or other cloth stretched over a frame. The areas that are to print are untreated while the rest is coated with a varnish-like coating that keeps the ink from penetrating through to the paper. Often the design is applied photochemically. Because the entire pattern is suspended on the silk mesh it is possible to have islands with no ink in the middle of solidly printed sections. This is impractical with regular paper or metal stencils.

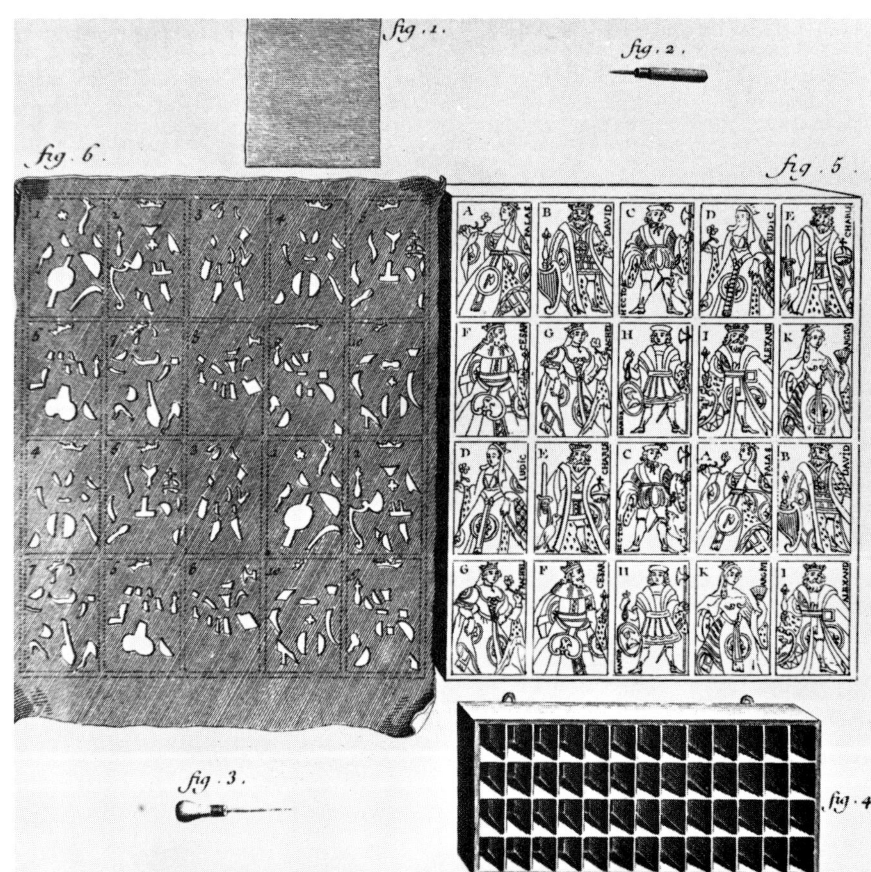

Stencil for use in hand-coloring playing cards. Engraving from Diderot's *Encyclopédie,* (1751–1772)

Relief

The rubber stamp used in the office is a relief printing device familiar to everyone, as is the conventional cast metal type used by printers. Among the relief techniques used in making old prints are woodcut and wood engraving and some secondary processes such as relief etching. The latter did not become important until late in the nineteenth century.

Woodcuts were used as early as the ninth century in China to print pictures and words on paper. The earliest European prints were made using woodcuts. The earliest woodcut block found so far is dated about 1380. America's first print, a portrait of Richard Mather by John Foster, is a woodcut done in 1670. This medium was only sparingly utilized in this country.

A woodcut is made on the soft sidegrain or plank side of a one inch thick block of apple, pear or sycamore wood. The design is either drawn directly on the wood, or a sheet of paper with the design is pasted on the block. The areas to be printed are left untouched while all other sections are carefully cut away to a depth of about ⅛ inch. The fine cuts are usually made with a knife and large areas are cleared using chisels and gouges. Great care must be taken when cutting across the grain; otherwise the printing ridge splits and breaks off. These projecting ridges are the black lines of the print.

To print from a woodcut, the projecting pattern is inked, using a leather ball or roller that has been dipped in a thick sticky ink formulated to resist running into the crevices of the design. Damp paper is then placed in contact with the inked block and sufficient pressure is applied to make sure that contact is made in all areas. For new blocks the required pressure is usually light and little distortion can be noticed on the paper. With a worn block on a surface that is not a perfect plane, heavier pressure must be applied. As a result, old woodcuts may have the black lines in valleys below the surface of the paper. The resulting print is usually a simple picture in firm clear outlines. Due to the physical limitations of the wood the design is usually not complex. Since the lines are made by a ridge that has had its neighborhood cut away, woodcut lines have characteristics reflecting this. The lines are often not symmetrical and have varying shapes. The lines are furthermore uniform in blackness and there are often areas of solid black. These identifying properties of a woodcut, while desirable for certain artistic effects, also point out the weaknesses and limitations of the technique.

The serious limitations of the woodcut led to the search for other printing techniques. About 1500 some of the print masters began using copper engraving and etching to produce prints with finer detail and expression than could be achieved with woodcuts. Then, in the beginning of the eighteenth century some workers in England experimented with techniques using the end grain of wood rather than the flat plank side used in woodcuts. The polished end grain offered no directional resistance to cutting and did not split off, as many of the cross cuts did while making woodcuts. This permitted the use of finer lines and easy gradations of shading using techniques similar to those used in engraving. Since the burin or graver, the engraver's tool, was used, and the resulting picture often superficially resembled the copperplate engravings, this new end grain technique was called wood engraving. It is fundamentally different from engraving, however, in that the printed line is in relief as it is for the woodcut. There is no platemark and the printing is done with the same light pressure used for the woodcut.

Thomas Bewick, an Englishman, should be credited for much of the development of wood engraving although he did not invent the process. In 1775 he won the prize offered by the Society of Arts for the best "engraving on wood or type capable of being worked off with letterpress." There was a great need for a technique that would provide a high quality illustration from some sort of plate that could be set together with the cast type. Printers were called upon to produce large numbers of books for the growing demand of a literate populace. During the nineteenth century a high percentage of the books, catalogues and weeklies were illustrated using wood engravings. *Harper's Weekly,* first published in New York in mid-century, used many wood engravings, some by Winslow Homer.

Many of the illustrations were too large in size to be made from a single block of wood. The boxwood tree, whose wood was found best for this purpose, had a limited diameter of five or six inches. For these large illustrations, two or more pieces were fitted together and frequently this joining can be seen as white or black grid lines in the finished print. Parts of the print were farmed out to different engravers working simultaneously in order to rush newsworthy pictures into print.

Relief etching is one of the secondary techniques for relief printing, mentioned above, that was used in the eighteenth and early nineteenth centuries. In this technique a design is painted on a copper plate using an acidresisting varnish. The plate is then immersed in an acid bath which eats away the surface on all areas except that of the design. After etching, the varnish is removed from the design which now stands above the background surface. The design is inked and an impression made as with the other relief techniques. The method is limited, however, because the etched area is so shallow that portions are inadvertently inked. This misplaced ink must be wiped out frequently in order to keep the prints clean. The extra work prevented the process from being widely used until better printing machinery was developed late in the nineteenth century.

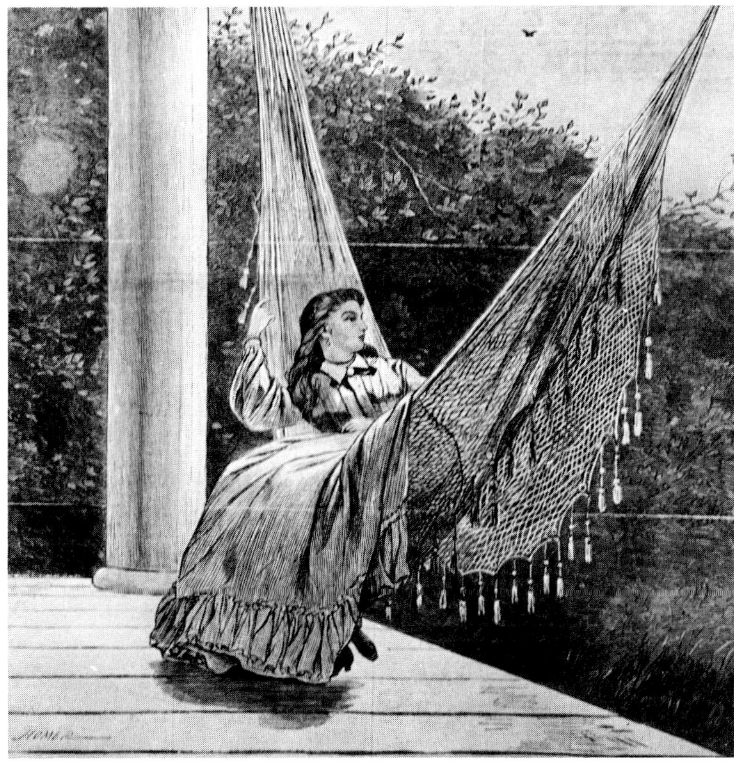

Wood engraving, *The Robin's Note,* showing lines where blocks were joined to make one large print. After drawing by Winslow Homer published in *Every Saturday,* August 20, 1870, $8\frac{7}{8}$ x 9 inches

Intaglio

Line engraving, the first of the intaglio processes, was used extensively by the old print masters. Probably because of this association, any of the various types of intaglio engravings became the accepted professional "quality" print techniques until this bias was broken in the late nineteenth century.

In all of the intaglio processes, the design is created by making engraved or incised lines and crevices into a copper or other metal surface. These crevices are filled with a thick ink and the plate surface then wiped clean of ink except for the incised lines. Next, damp paper is pressed against the plate with enough pressure to force the paper into the inked grooves. Due to the great pressure required, the side edges of the printing plate were also forced into the paper creating a ridge or "plate mark." Viewed in a raking light, the inked lines can be seen to stand in relief above the paper.

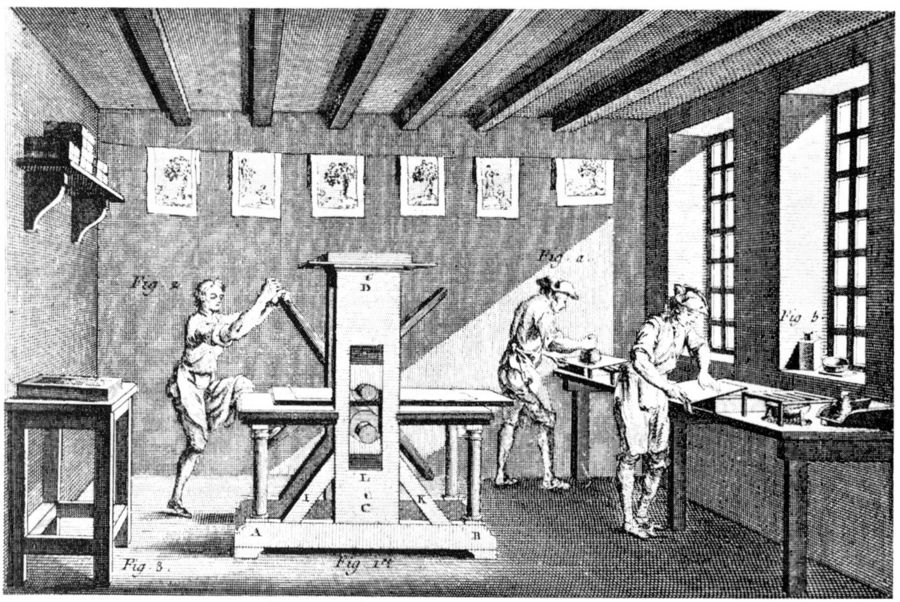

Copperplate printing: Fig. 1a) Inking the plate, b) Wiping ink off flat surface of plate; Fig. 2) Printing by passing plate and paper between rollers. Vol. VIII, Diderot's *Encyclopédie,* (1751–1772)

Intaglio print making is an old technique with innumerable variations that were developed over the years for creating special effects. However, there are only two fundamental classifications—linear and tonal. In the linear process the entire picture is formed using lines. Shading is created by a series of closely spaced lines or crosshatching. In the tonal technique the entire picture, or most of it, is created by light and dark shaded areas on the paper. The degree of shading is controlled by the number of very small ink spots in a particular area. In the nineteenth century several of the linear and tonal techniques were often combined on the same print.

The principal techniques in both categories are:

1. Linear
   a. Line engraving
   b. Drypoint
   c. Etching
2. Tonal
   a. Mezzotint
   b. Aquatint
   c. Stipple

The notation "Engraved by . . ." at the lower corner of a print should not be taken too literally. This designation is attached to etchings, aquatints, mezzotints and even lithographs.

Line engraving

The cut in the copper or metal plate is made using a tool called a graver or burin. This sharp tool is pushed into the metal, thereby creating a taper at the start of the line which in most cases is also repeated at the end of the line as the tool is withdrawn. The tool gouges a sliver of metal from the copper plate and leaves a ravine for the ink. Any burr of metal thrown up along the sides of the cut is usually taken off.

As with many things in life the first impressions are the best. With use the print quality quickly decreases as the engraved lines lose their clarity so that a copper plate is worn out or ready for rework after only 1000 to 4000 impressions. To remedy this, in the 1820's, the copper was replaced for long print runs by a steel plate which sometimes was fire-hardened after being engraved. Then in 1857 an improvement was made when steel facing was invented. This process enabled the engraver to go back to executing his work on a soft copper plate to which a long-wearing steel surface was later added by electroplating.

Because every line must be planned and executed with great care, line engravings have a tendency to be stiff and cold. These tendencies were exaggerated in the steel engravings because of the increased hardness and consequent difficulty in working the plate. In some late prints the stiffness of the steel engraving was further intensified when at mid-century less talented engravers were hired to run machines for mechanically ruling-in the sky and similar areas.

The first American line engraving, a portrait of Increase Mather, was made in 1702 by Thomas Emmens. Line engraving was the principal intaglio technique used in the United States in the eighteenth century.

Drypoint

Drypoint is similar to line engraving and originated about the same time. A drypoint plate has the lines scratched in by the engraver using a hard steel or diamond point. This grooves the metal forcing a burr or ridge on one or both sides of the line. Little or no metal is removed; it is only displaced. The cut is usually shallower than for line engraving and the burr is quickly flattened by the pressure of printing. Much of the ink is held by the burr so that it must by protected if the plate is to last. Without a protective covering of electrochemically deposited steel only 100 or so good impressions can be taken from a copper plate.

The burr on the incised drypoint line produces a fuzziness in the printed line which gives the impression a velvety richness. Drypoint engravings are usually less stiff and cold but the short life of the plate makes it an artistic rather than a commercial technique.

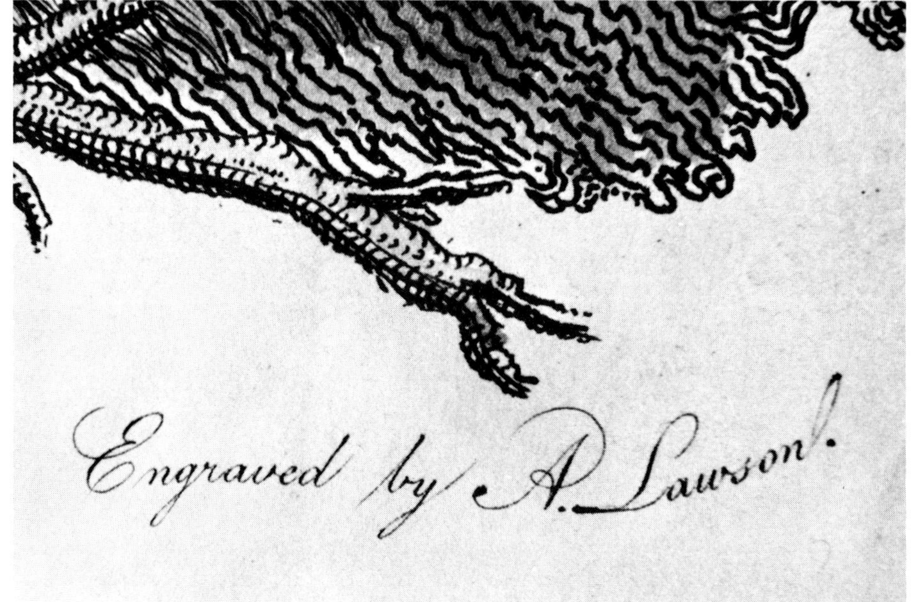

Detail of etching and engraving showing characteristic blunt etching lines with their nervous movement in upper part and the controlled tapered line of line engraving in the writing below. *Great-Footed Hawk,* drawn from Nature by A. Wilson, engraved by A. Lawson. Hand-colored. Size of detail on original approximately $\frac{7}{8}$ x $1\frac{5}{8}$ inches

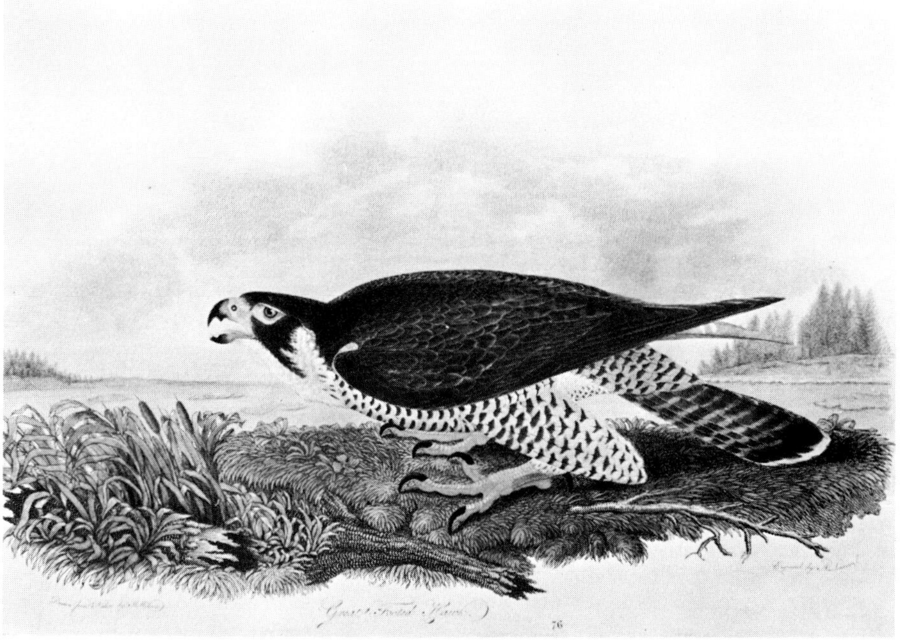

Great-Footed Hawk, drawn by A. Wilson, engraved by A. Lawson. Detail shown above is at the end of the branch at lower right and includes writing below

Etching

Etching is another technique first employed by the old print masters. The line is eaten into the copper plate by acid. To prepare the plate it is first coated with a thin layer of acid-resisting material such as wax. The artist then draws his design using a sharp tool or needle which penetrates the wax and exposes the copper. When he is finished the plate is dipped in acid which goes through the cuts and scratches in the protective coating to eat out the design in the exposed copper. The resulting line has no burrs and can be made deep if immersed in the acid etch long enough. In these physical respects the line resembles that engraved by the burin. Under close examination, however, the etched line has a blunt start and finish as compared to the tapered start and finish of line engraving. Etching is a quick and easy way to prepare a plate compared to line engraving. Because the artist can draw with ease, the compositions are freer, with works sometimes resembling pencil sketches.

A variant of the above hard-line etching process is soft-ground etching, a technique which uses a soft rather than a hard acid resist on the copper. A paper is placed on the surface of the resist and the design is then drawn on the paper. Each stroke of the pencil causes a corresponding line of the acid resist ground to attach itself to the back of the paper. When the drawing is complete the artist pulls off the paper, including the attached pieces of acid resist, and then etches the copper plate in the same way as the hard line etching technique. Since the resulting prints resemble crayon sketches, this is often called "the crayon manner."

Etching was not used until about 1800 in the United States. It is probable that the early engravers, many of whom were silversmiths, felt more comfortable using line engraving rather than etching.

Mezzotint

The German engraver Ludwig Von Siezen is credited with devising the mezzotint process in 1642, but it was the English who so firmly embraced it that it was sometimes called the English Manner. Since mezzotint produces tones of gray, not lines, it is an especially suitable technique for portraits where softness is desired, rather than for work that requires sharp outlines.

As is the case for most print techniques there are different methods of implementation. In the one most commonly used, the preparation of the mezzotint plate is the reverse of engraving. First, the copper plate is roughened uniformly with a toothed tool called the rocker. If the plate is inked and a print taken at this time, a solid black results. Then, in

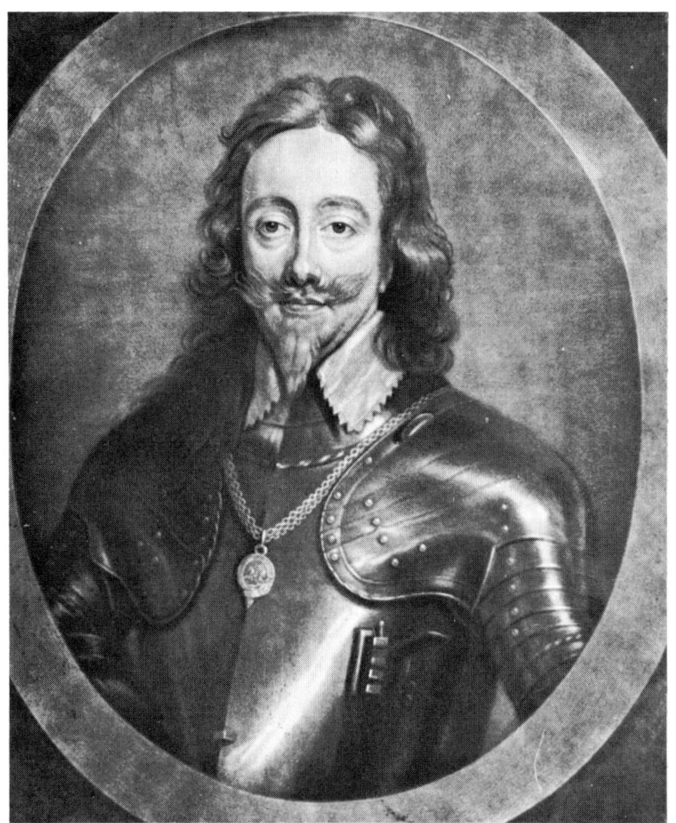

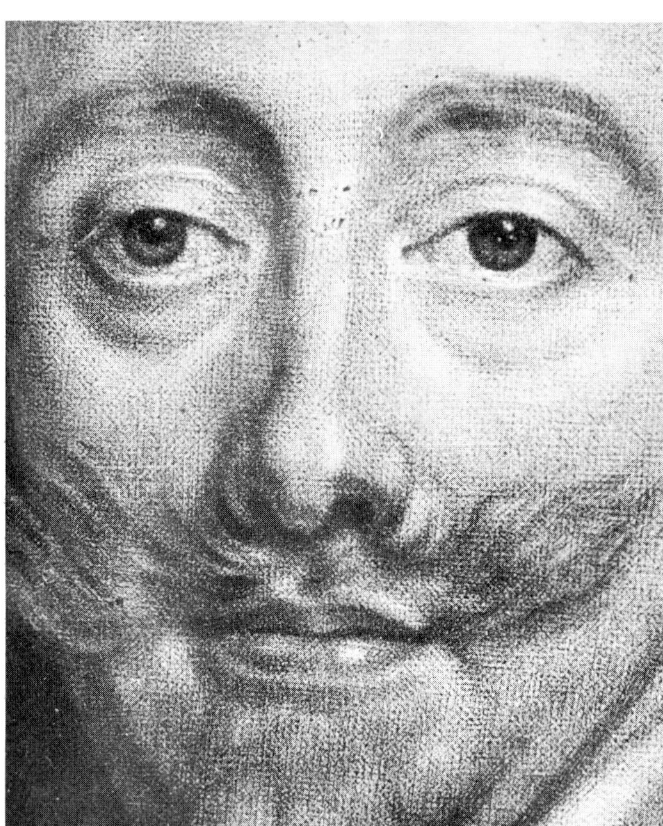

Mezzotint. Detail of face at right shows cloth-like texture of the roughened ink-holding surface. *Charles I* after Van Dyke, engraved by I. Beckett, English, $11\frac{3}{8}$ x $9\frac{3}{4}$ inches

order to create a picture, some of the roughness is scraped and polished away until the design or portrait emerges from the black background. A full and rich gradation of black to white can be created in this way. Prints are made from the plate as in the other intaglio methods.

Some artists did not start with a completely roughened plate but rather confined the toothed wheel to areas that were to be gray or black. Also, in some prints line engraving and mezzotint were combined. In any event, the characteristic pattern produced by the toothed wheel can usually be seen by close examination of most mezzotints.

The mezzotint has been called the noblest of the prints, in part because of its beautiful tone and texture, but also because only a few hundred prints can be made from a copper plate. In the 1820's some plates in England were made of steel to add life. But even in England the use of mezzotint died out early in the nineteenth century except for special and limited new artistic prints.

In America, the Mather family again takes a bow. This time a portrait of Cotton Mather by Peter Pelham produced in 1728 is credited with being the first mezzotint engraved in the colonies. It never became a common American print technique and was confined mainly to portraits of important individuals in the eighteenth and early nineteenth centuries.

Aquatint

This second tonal method of engraving has no connection with watercolor as the name might imply. The aqua comes from aqua fortis, nitric acid, which is used to etch the design. The process was developed in the mid-eighteenth century in France and the technique was introduced in England about 1775.

To prepare an aquatint, a copper plate is first coated with an even dusting of rosin which must then be fixed in position. This is done by heating the plate until the rosin softens enough to stick. Alternatively, the rosin is applied by first dissolving it in alcohol and then painting the copper surface with the mixture. When dry the rosin reappears as small, irregular islands. These procedures are called "laying the ground." In either case the rosin resists the etch acid which attacks the plate in the spaces between the islands. This etching action leaves a characteristic grain effect on the finished print.

The first step in creating the picture is to "stop" paint the areas that are to remain white with an acid-resist varnish. The first etch is then made. The plate is removed and areas that are to have the lightest tone are painted out with varnish and the plate is then etched again. This process is repeated sometimes twenty or thirty times until the darkest tones, which are the most deeply etched areas on the plate, are reached.

In practice most aquatint plates were first set up using a line etch to outline the picture. This is an enormous help as a guide in laying the tones and in sharpening the edges of the design.

Aquatint was used in America from about 1780, but sparingly. In the 1820–1825 period John Hill made twenty aquatints of paintings by W. G. Wall called the *Hudson River Portfolio.* Another important series, *Views of American Cities,* was put out in 1836 by W. J. Bennett. Probably the most familiar American aquatints are J. J. Audubon's *Birds of America.* They are of an American subject by an American artist but were in fact aquatinted and hand colored in England.

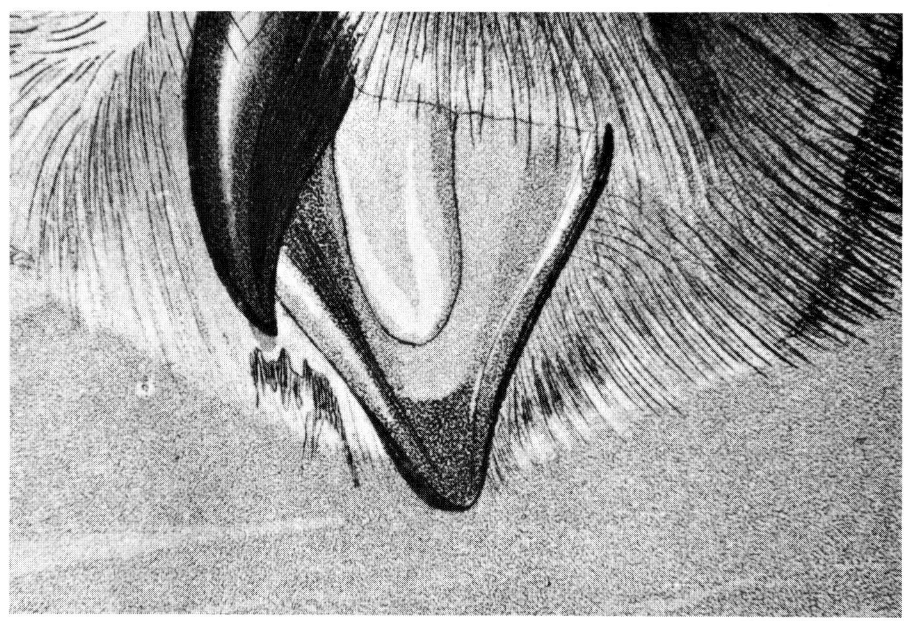

Detail showing engraved or etched outlines with grainy shading produced by aquatint. Length of tongue is approximately ½ inch on the largest owl in lower right of *The Burrowing Owls,* Plate 383 of the *Birds of America,* drawn by J. J. Audubon, engraved and printed by Robert Havell, London 1838

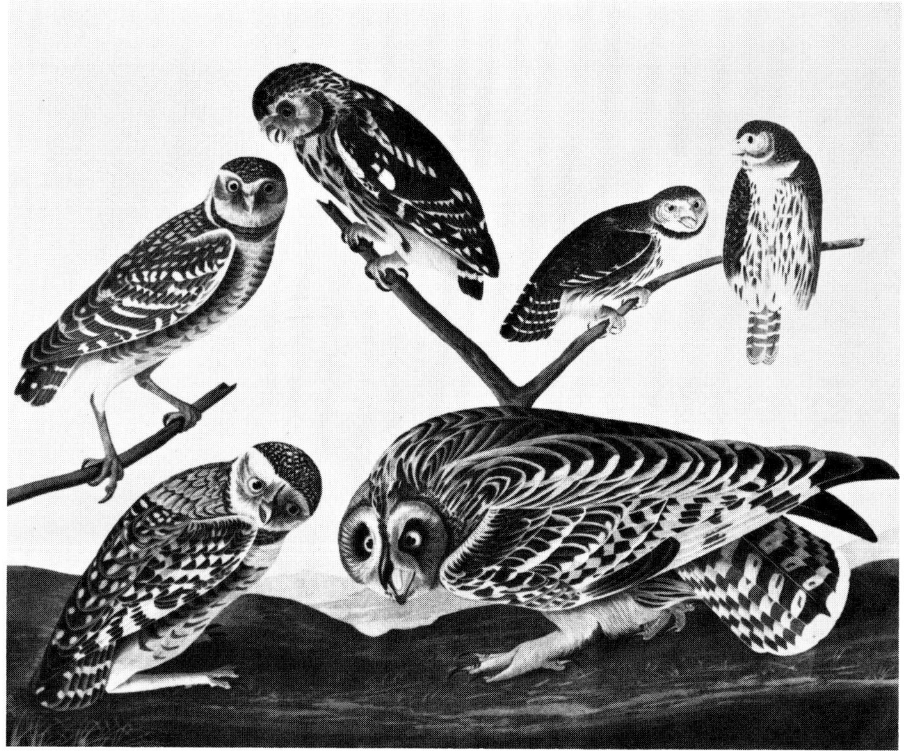

Stipple

Stipple engraving builds the image out of thousands of very small dots which the eye reassembles into tonal gradations. The French impressionist painter Seurat applied this principle to color with his pointillism style of painting. The method was developed in England in the late eighteenth century where it was used for portraits, scenes and other print work.

The stipple copper plate was originally prepared by punching each of the dots and then removing the burr. This was too laborious so that most stippling was done using the etching process with the dots produced by hand using a needle, or by a roulette, spur wheel or similar device. After the plate is etched the print is made from it as in intaglio methods. In most prints, stipple is combined with line etching.

Stipple engraving was used sparingly in America beginning about 1780.

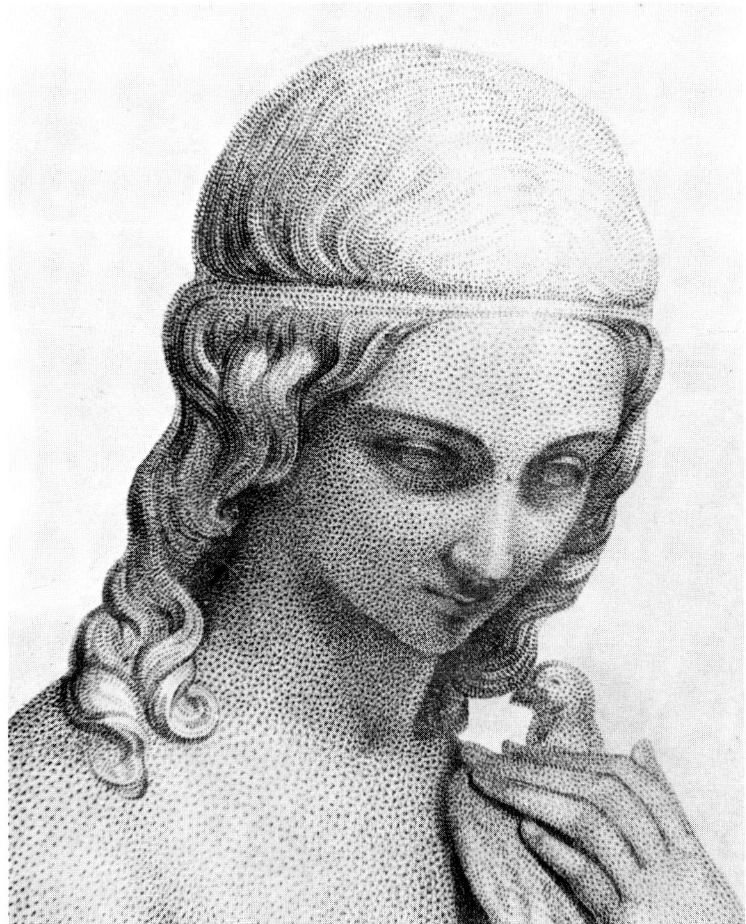

Stipple detail from a nineteenth-century book illustration of the statue, *Innocence.* Headband is approximately one inch across on the original

Planographic (Lithography)

About 1798 Alois Senefelder, an unsuccessful Bavarian playwright, invented the first totally new method of printing since the development of intaglio techniques around 1500. Senefelder used a flat block of Kelheim limestone as a plate and based his technique on the fact that grease and water do not mix. In 1819 an English edition of Senefelder's book, *Complete Course of Lithography,* was published and within a few years the method was in commercial use both in England and America.

A typical procedure uses a 2 to 4 inch thick slab of polished Kelheim or Solenhofen limestone from Bavaria as the plate. The design is drawn on the flat surface with a greasy crayon made of wax, tallow, soap and shellac. Lamp black is added so that the design is visible on the stone. Sometimes fine lines are drawn with a steel pen using special lithographic ink. After the design is drawn it must be "fixed" to keep it from spreading and smearing as the prints are made. This "fix" or "etch" uses a mild syrupy bath of nitric acid and gum arabic. The "etch" also keeps the design from spreading by making the stone more open and receptive to water.

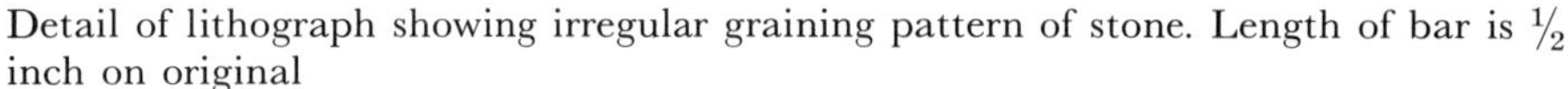
Detail of lithograph showing irregular graining pattern of stone. Length of bar is ½ inch on original

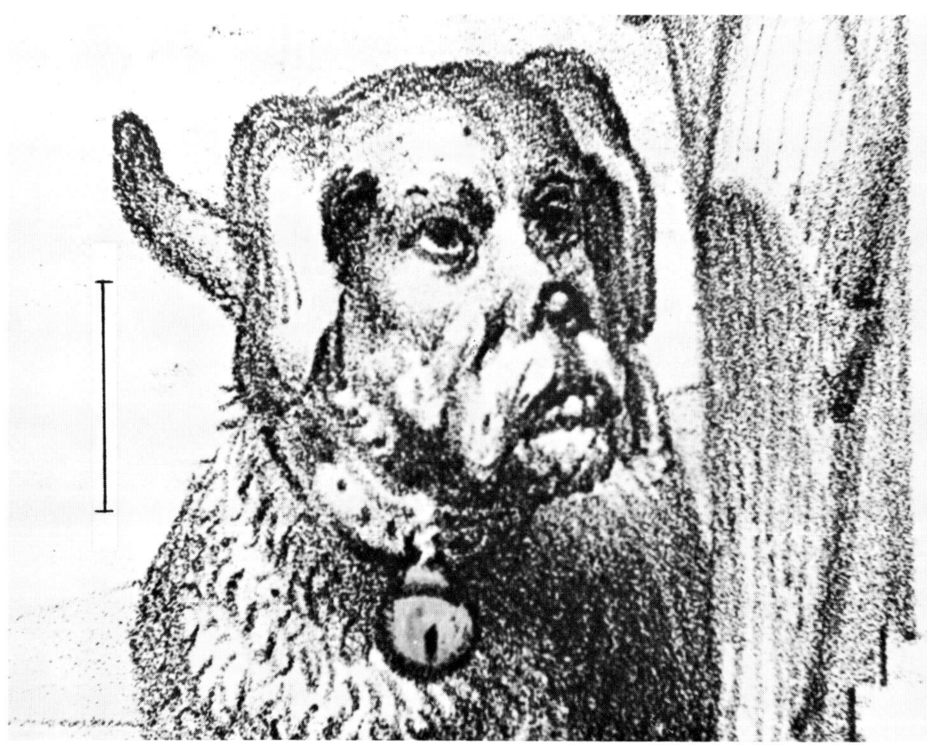

The surface is next washed with turpentine to remove the remains of the crayon. The stone is then wet and inked with a greasy ink that adheres to the design but is repelled by the wet stone. A piece of paper is put on top and the ink transfer from stone to paper is made using light pressure. No depressed plate mark is produced on the paper. Damp paper is sometimes used so that it will lie flat and take the best transfer.

A properly prepared and cared for stone can produce an extremely large number of prints. Modern lithography on metal plates can make millions of copies from the same plate. The early output was limited by the speed of the pressmen who could typically turn out only 200 to 250 prints in a twelve hour day.

Lithography quickly became a commercial printmaking process, although in Europe there were some artists who used the medium to create original works which exploited the versatility of the medium. Many of the commercial houses had special formulas for ink, lithographic crayon, etc., but the basis for the industry was Senefelder's book on lithography. Special techniques were worked out by the lithographers, the men who put the design on stone, but they never attained the prominence that comparable technicians in intaglio printing had achieved.

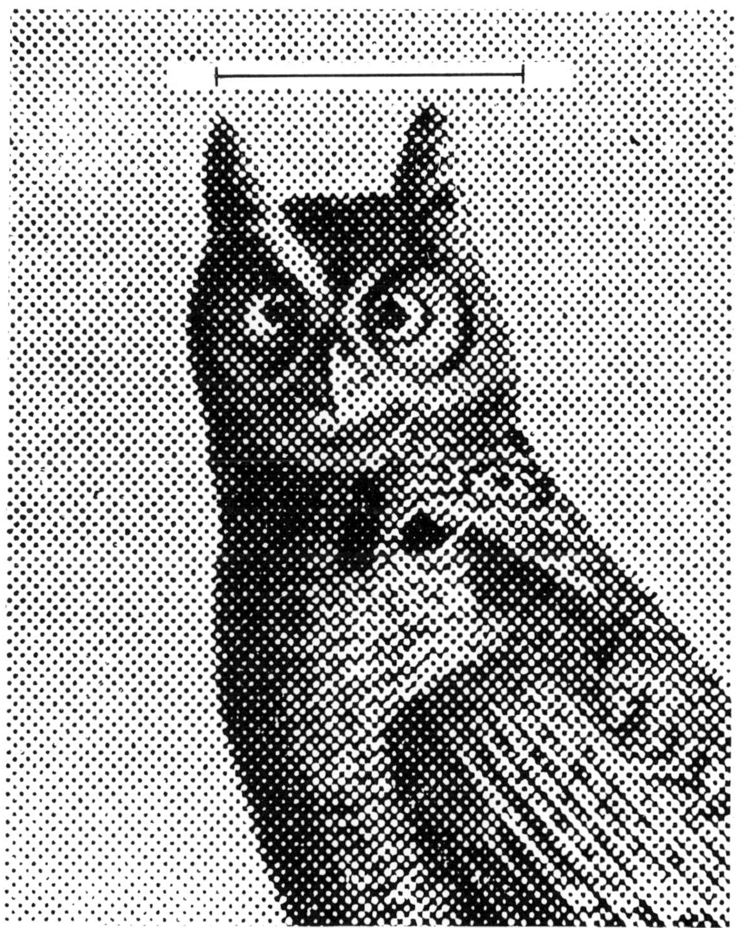

Detail of newspaper illustration showing halftone pattern produced on a black and white illustration. Bar is ½ inch long on original

The first commercially successful American lithographic house was founded in Boston by William and John Pendleton in 1825. A few years later they took on Nathaniel Currier as an apprentice and there he acquired the background for his own business. After Currier's news print in 1840 of the "Lexington" steamship disaster, the lithograph dominated American commercial decorative printmaking for the rest of the century. Lithography failed to achieve the high esteem of the tradition-minded of the art and society circles so that Currier found it good business to advertise his prints as *"Engravings for the People."*

Colored and Color Prints

Color prints are printed in color whereas colored prints have color applied after printing. In America some of the eighteenth and early nineteenth-century black and white engravings were hand colored with water color and gouache. Also some of the aquatints and mezzotints were colored using different copper plates, carefully registered, for the different colors. The big drive to color, however, came with the decorative lithographs made after 1840. These were often colored using a production line technique by women and girls putting on one color at each station. Colors were applied between the black lithographed outlines—or approximately so. Some of this work was also done at home by colorists and also by unsuccessful or student artists. Since they were paid typically one cent each for the small folio prints (about 8 inches × 12 inches), it was necessary to cut corners. Stencils and wood blocks were sometimes used for filling in areas of flat color. Later, lithographic stones were used for this purpose, the start of chromolithography. Prints partially colored by stone often have two pinholes in the paper along the edge of the print which are used to align the paper and stone for proper register.

During the 1840's and 50's lithographers in different countries were working on the chromolithograph where, in its most developed form, the picture is printed entirely in color without the black outlines of the older lithographic technique. The colors were also changed to opaque oils so that the colors put down by each of as many as twenty or thirty stones could be used without interference from an underlying color. This was an expensive and long printing process often requiring months of printing and drying before the print was complete. A contemporary description is given in the New York *Tribune* of May 25, 1866:

> Upon the first stone a general tint is laid, covering nearly the whole picture and as many sheets of paper as there are copies of the picture are printed from it. A second stone is then prepared, embracing all the shades

of some other color, and the sheets already printed with the first color are worked over this stone. A third, fourth, fifth, and sixth follow, each one repeating the process and adding some new color, advancing the picture a step further until the requisite number of colors have been applied.

P. S. Duval of Philadelphia and Louis Prang of Boston were pioneers of chromolithography in the United States. Prang put out his first "chromo" soon after the Civil War. During the 1870's he introduced the Christmas card and began to issue realistic color reproductions of famous paintings. This spelled the death of old line concerns such as Currier and Ives who could not meet this competition.

Photo-mechanical Printing Methods

Photography is used in most modern printing methods to transfer the image to the metal printing plate. Photosensitive coatings are selected which act as a shield against ink, act to protect the metal plate from an acid etch, or act as an ink holding surface, depending on the application. The basic types of photomechanical printing correspond exactly to the basic hand methods but, of course, have different names.

- Photostencil—a stencil technique usually using the silk screen principle
- Photoengraving—a relief process where the background is etched away
- Photogravure—an intaglio process where the lines to be printed are etched into the plate
- Photo-Lithography—a lithographic process where the ink-holding surface is photographically fixed on an otherwise ink-repelling metal surface.

Work on photography was carried out in the 1830's by L. J. Daguerre in France and W. H. Fox Talbot in England. In 1852 Talbot patented the photogravure process although some work along similar, but not truly photographic, lines was done as early as 1826 in France. Photogravure was the first photochemical method developed.

Photographs in modern books, magazines and newspapers have the gray tones produced using large numbers of closely-spaced dots which the eye then integrates as an average tone over a particular area. If these dots cover fifty percent of a $\frac{1}{2}$ in $\times$ $\frac{1}{2}$ inch square then the tone as the eye sees it will be darker than if the dots covered only ten percent of the same area. Paul Pretsch of Austria was the first to use halftone plates and in 1882 G. Meisenbach of Germany was the first to make commercial use of halftone.

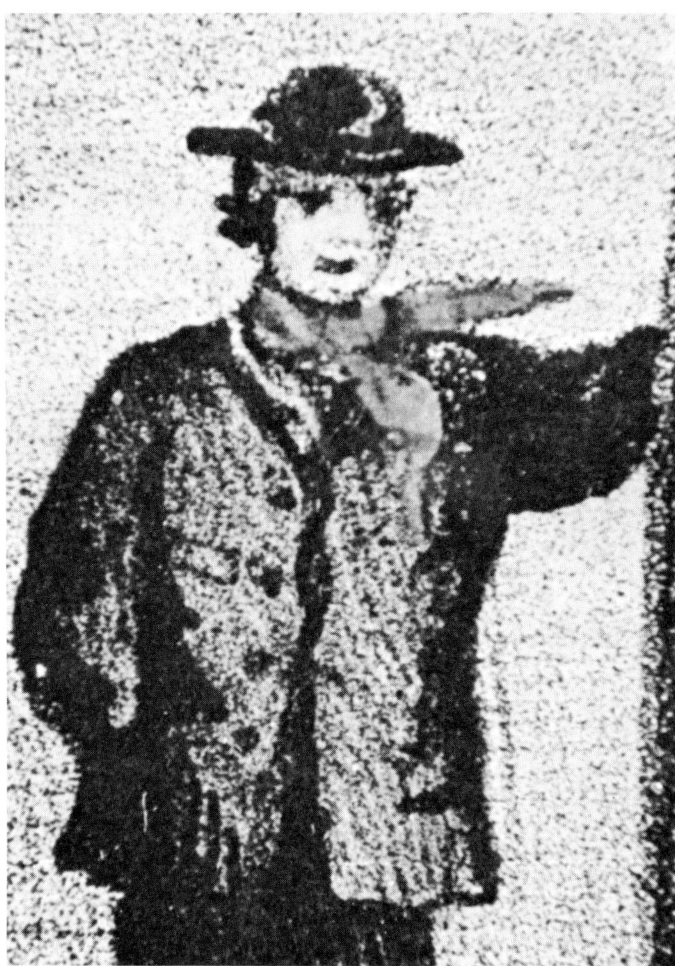

Detail of hand-colored lithograph showing random pattern of stone. Uniform shading is the hand-coloring, especially noticeable in the scarf. *Ice-Boat Race on the Hudson,* by Currier and Ives. See Chapter on Currier and Ives, page 161, for illustration. The height of figure in this detail is about one inch on the original.

In essence, modern halftone printing uses an image that is projected on to the photo-sensitized printing plate through a halftone screen. These screens are made of two sheets of glass each covered with rows of equally-spaced black lines forming a grid. The screens are aligned at right angles to each other. The fineness of the grid can range from about fifty to 300 or 400 lines per inch depending on the desired quality and the printing surface of the finished print. The screen breaks the print projected onto the sensitized plate into a matrix of small squares which when developed will have a printing area in inverse proportion to the amount of light hitting that particular block.

A high quality photograph printed in a magazine with glossy paper will typically use a screen with 100 lines to the inch. A newspaper might use a sixty lines per inch screen. At that level the screening is readily visible even without magnification. Art reproductions often use screens so fine that it is nearly impossible to see the screening except in a few areas where the dots have not blended or blurred into each other or into the surface texture of the paper.

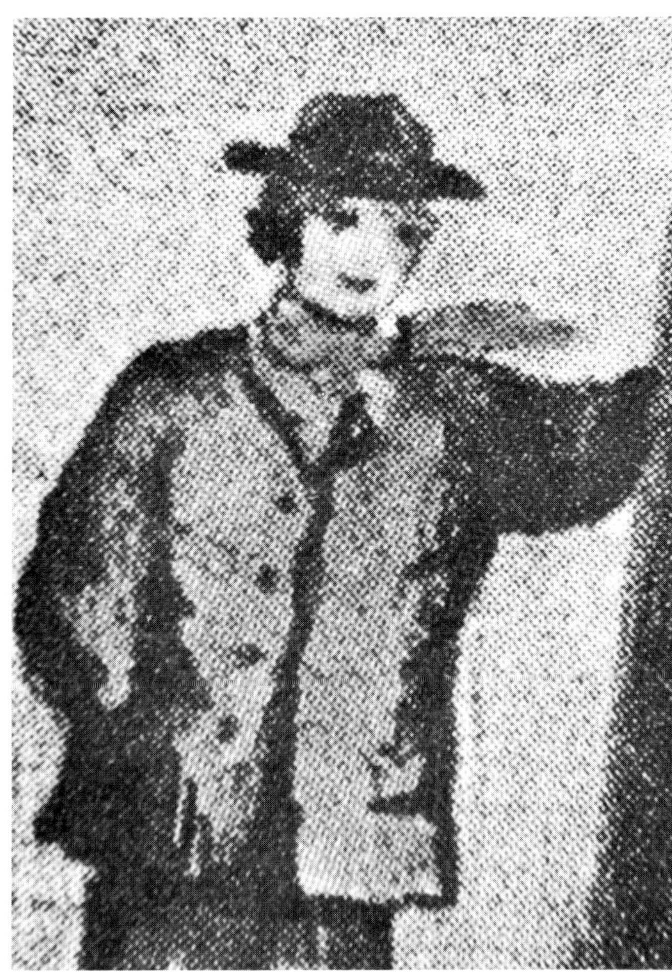

Same detail from a modern color reproduction printed by modern photolithography showing halftone rosette pattern of color printing. Height of figure in this detail is about one inch on original.

Reproductions

Reproductions of American prints ordinarily should be hailed and regarded by a collector as a sign of acceptance of the print and as confirmation of his good judgment in starting his collection. However, there is always the possibility of buying a clever reproduction, and at a high price. Fortunately, many reproductions are not made the exact size as the originals so that the discrepancy in size is a quick give-away. Those that are the correct size or nearly so can occasionally be troublesome. The unwary are most often trapped by some reproductions of the large folio Currier and Ives prints and certain of the engravings such as Paul Revere's *The Bloody Massacre.*

Reproductions can be divided into four categories:

1. Those made for decorative or educational purposes but not the same size as the original.
2. Prints made the exact size as the original using a modern plate but with obvious screening dots, or those sometimes thoughtfully labeled as reproductions in a spot that cannot be cut off without destroying the print.

3. Those made the same size as the original using modern plates without obvious halftone screening and not marked as reproductions.
4. Restrikes from the original plates, or stones—not strictly a reproduction but of great interest to the collector since they usually lack the value of prints pulled at the time of the preparation of the plate, block or stone by the firm or individual who prepared it.

It is impossible to describe in writing how to detect the third and fourth categories, both of which can fall into a classification that borders on fraud. There are, however, certain guidelines that can help.

1. Measure the print size very carefully and compare the dimensions with those published of a known original.
2. Using a ten or twenty power magnifier check at least five or ten areas for the regular grid-like pattern of photographic halftone screening. This is not a sure test since some prints can be reproduced using non-screening techniques and some screening is so fine that the grid pattern blurs out.
3. If possible, compare the paper with the paper of an original for thickness, texture and surface finish.
4. Colored prints should have the same color tones as a genuine print or a similar print of the period. Hand-colored prints are most often reproduced by printing in colors. The color areas may show the screening grid. This must not be confused with the color sometimes printed in old lithographs where the color will show the graining of the stone.
5. Since genuine eighteenth and nineteenth century prints are 100 to 200 years old some indication of age is usually present even on most prints that have been cleaned and restored. Check for discoloration on the back of the paper that may have been caused by the pine board often used in early framing. The paper is usually time-toned in some way, such as dirt, yellowing or a fade line where the sides or bottom were protected from light by the frame.
6. Keep an open mind both to the possibility that the print might be a reproduction as well as to the possibility that it might be genuine.

Convincing reproductions are scarce enough so that a collector following normal precautions has a very small likelihood of being fooled. But do take the precautions, and even better seek expert advice.

CHAPTER THREE American Engravings

Bits and scraps is a harsh but reasonably accurate description of the half-dozen or so American prints that have come down to us from the seventeenth century. American output in the eighteenth century was somewhat greater but the vast majority of prints were still imported from England and the Continent. Most of the important eighteenth-century American prints are now in permanent collections and the few that are still in private hands are carefully tracked. In the nineteenth century, particularly after the War of 1812, there was a rapid increase in the output of prints as with almost everything else in America. Between 1840 and 1870, engravings were produced in large numbers, mostly copies of paintings intended for use as framed decoration. Engravings were esteemed as high art as compared to the common Currier & Ives lithographs. By the 1880's and 90's, however, the colors of the chromolithograph won out over both the engravings and the old hand-painted lithographs. Photographic reproductions for books also became practical, a further blow to metal plate and wood engraving.

Seventeenth-Century Prints

All of the surviving seventeenth-century American prints come from the Massachusetts Bay Colony. If prints were made in other sections of America there is no record of them and if any have survived they have not been identified.

John Foster is credited with being America's first printmaker. He was born in Dorchester, close to Boston, in 1648 and went to Harvard where he graduated third in a class of seven in 1667. It should be noted that until 1773 class ranking was done on a social rather than an academic basis. Two years after graduating he went to work as a school teacher in Dorchester but in 1675 he left for Boston where he set up the first printing press in that city. In 1670, while still a teacher, he made his and America's first print, a half-length woodcut portrait of Richard Mather, progenitor of one of New England's most famous families. Foster was a friend of Increase Mather, a well-known clergyman, and this friendship was probably the basis for the portrait of Richard Mather which was done a year after his death. It is not known how many were printed, why they were printed or for whom they were printed. At present five copies are known to have survived.

Other surviving seventeenth century woodcuts include:

A book ornament—John Foster, 1672
A map of New England, *White Hills Map*—John Foster, 1677 which appeared as an illustration in the book *A Narrative of the Troubles with the Indians in New England,* by William Hubbard
The Copernican System (an astronomical chart as an illustration in a book)—John Foster, 1681
A Harp Player—probably by Richard Pierce in the 1680's
Seal of the Massachusetts Bay Colony—Richard Pierce, in the 1680's

The first copperplate engraving was cut by John Coney for the Colony Bills of 1690, the first paper money in America. Coney, a silversmith, is the first of the colonial silversmith engravers that in the eighteenth century included Nathaniel Hurd and Paul Revere.

Eighteenth-Century Prints

The scope of the repeatable image was enlarged in the eighteenth century to include views or scenes, battles, political and patriotic prints, marine subjects, copies of paintings and some minor engravings for bookplates, trade cards and embellishments on certificates. However, the number of prints produced was small partly because there were only a dozen or so significant engravers working in America throughout the

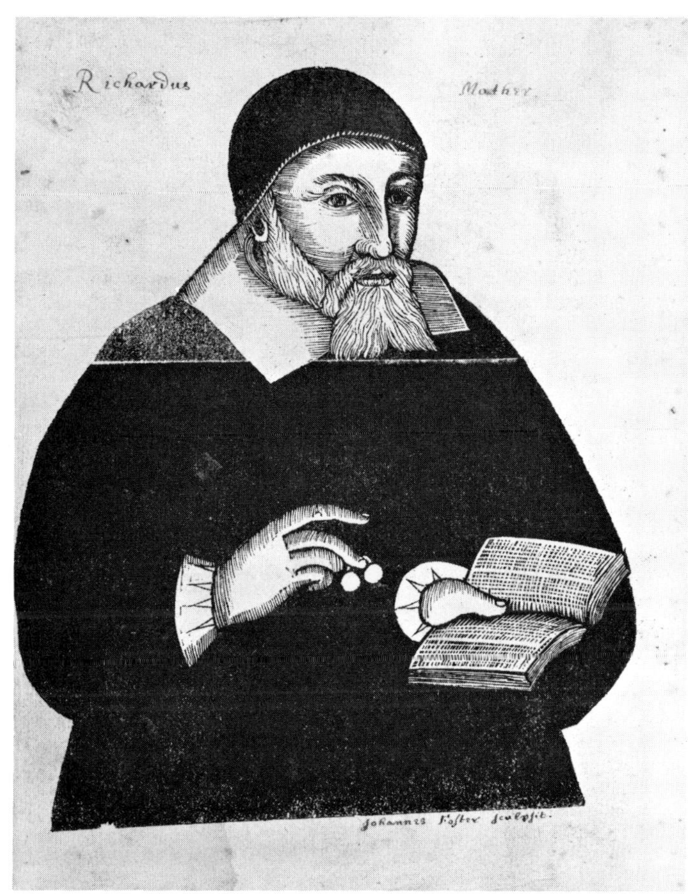

First print made in America. Woodcut, $6\frac{1}{8}$ x $4\frac{7}{8}$ inches, of Mr. Richard Mather by Fohn Foster, 1670 (*By Permission of the Harvard College Library*)

entire one-hundred year period. The print century started in 1702 with America's first copperplate portrait engraving. The subject was Increase Mather, engraved by Thomas Emmens of Boston, and used as an illustration is several books. About a half-dozen copies are known.

Decorative prints from England, the principal source, were advertised as early as 1713 in Boston papers. A typical advertisement in the *New England Courant* for August 13–20, 1722 reads:

> "Prospect of New York To be sold at the Picture-Shop over against the Town-House in Boston, an exact Prospect of the City of New York, with all Sorts of Prints and Maps, lately come from London, in Frames, or without, by Will Price."

Later, notices in the *Boston Gazette* in the 1750's announced that Nathaniel Warner regularly carried a supply of Mr. Hogarth's works from London including *The Harlot's Progress* and *The Rake's Progress.*

The view of New York that Mr. Price advertised in 1722 was probably *A South Prospect of ye Flourishing City of New York* . . . drawn by William Burgis and engraved and published in four sections in London

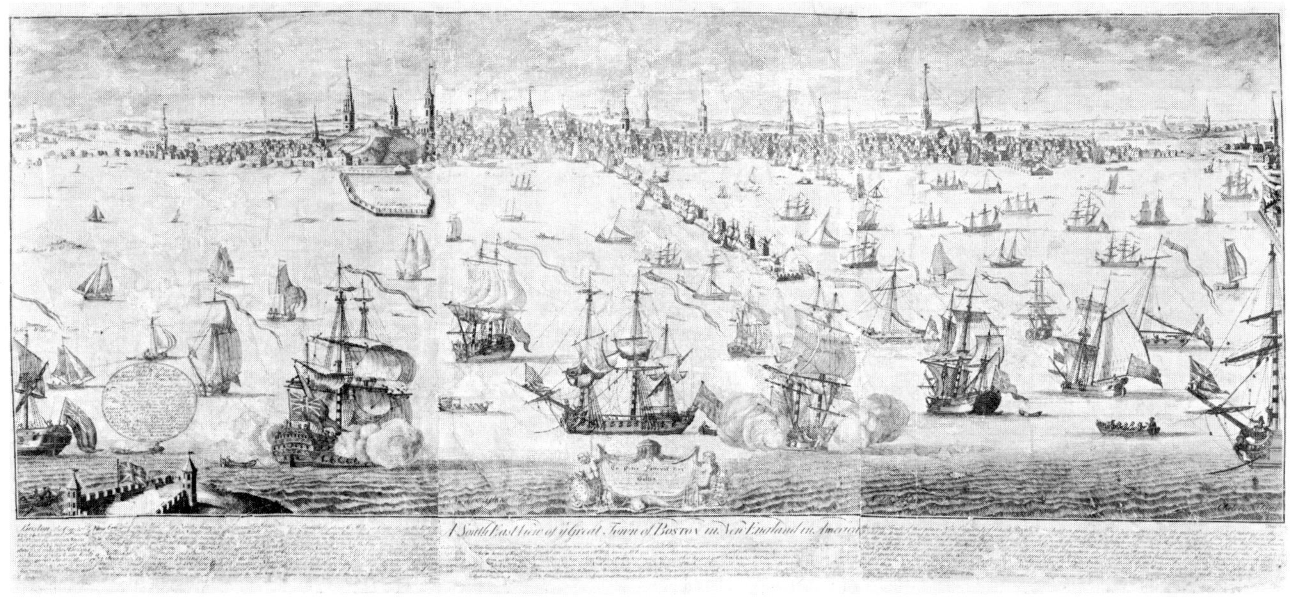

A South East View of ye Great Town of Boston in New England in America, drawn by William Burgis and engraved by I. Harris in London. This issue, *c.* 1743, was published by William Price, 23½ x 52 inches (*The Henry Francis du Pont Winterthur Museum*)

between 1719 and 1721. Such views were usually offered by subscription as was the Boston view advertised in the *New England Courant,* October 1–8, 1722:

> "View of Boston. A View of the Great Town of Boston, taken from a Standing on Noddles-Island, and designed to be cut on Copper, will be carried on by Subscription, as such expensive Works generally are. Those Gentlemen that would encourage such a Design, may see the View at Mr. Price's, Print and Mapseller, over against the Town-House, where Proposals are to be had, and Subscriptions taken in."

A short time later, November 5–12, 1722, also in the *Courant,* William Burgis, the artist, pleaded:

> "View of Boston. Whereas there has been an Advertisement lately publish'd of a Design to print a View of this Town of Boston, taken from Noddles Island. This is to certify, that the Undertaker William Burgis, desires all Gentlemen to be speedy in their Subscription, in order to send the Drawing to England this Fall, that he may conform to the Proposal to that end lately published."

Printmaking in the colonies slowly ground on. A jolt was felt in 1770 when Henry Pelham of Boston put out his line engraving *The Fruits of Arbitrary Power, or the Bloody Massacre.* This print, of which only two copies are known, is regarded as a major piece of pre-Revolutionary propaganda, responsible for focusing the wrath of many Colonials on

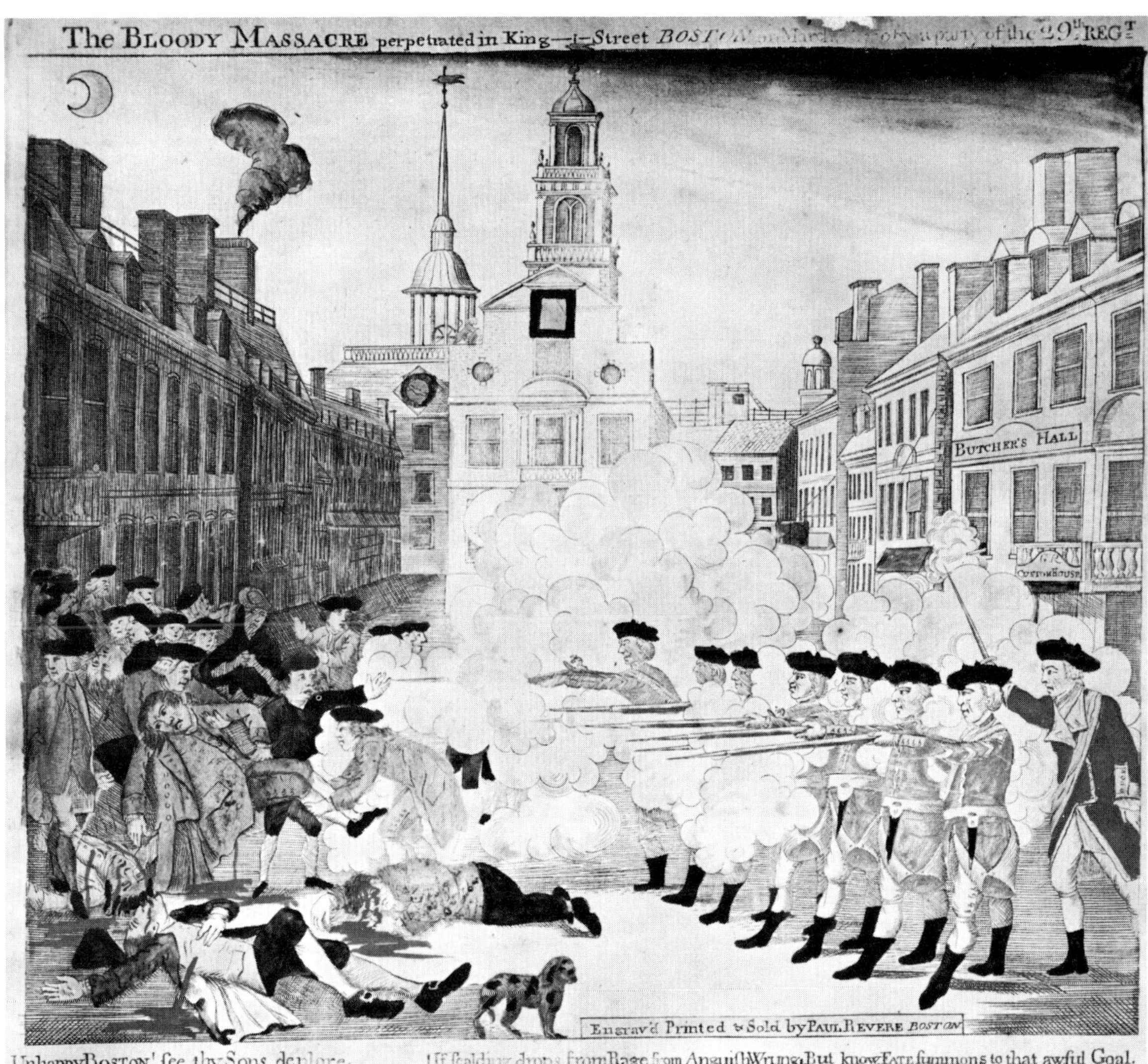

The Bloody Massacre . . ., engraved by Paul Revere, 1770, paper size, $10\frac{3}{4}$ x $9\frac{1}{4}$ inches. Revere's most famous print (*The Henry Francis du Pont Winterthur Museum*)

the British. Interestingly, Henry Pelham, the perpetrator of the print and half-brother of John Singleton Copley, was a Loyalist and left America in 1776 to join Copley in London. He remained in Great Britain and died in Ireland in 1806.

Paul Revere was probably shown a copy of the Pelham drawing for the print and quickly made his own engraving of *The Bloody Massacre . . .* which was on sale only three weeks after the event and a full week before Pelham's. The illustrations in the Pelham and Revere prints are almost identical, which lead the irate Pelham to write to Revere, "When I heard you was cutting a plate of the late Murder, I thought it impossible as I knew you was not capable of doing it unless you copied it from mine."

Three weeks later Revere published another print, *A View of Part of the Town of Boston in New England and British Ships of War Landing their Troops, 1768.* The event had taken place eighteen months earlier. It is difficult to know whether Revere put it out because he was an astute businessman or an ardent patriot. Four years later in 1774 he engraved another patriotic picture, a cartoon-like composition, *The Able Doctor, or America Swallowing the Bitter Draught.* This comment on the Boston Port Bill shows the British Prime Minister, Lord North, forcing tea down America's throat. The print is an exact copy of a pro-colonial cartoon in an English periodical of 1774.

A View of Part of the Town of Boston in New England and British Ships of War Landing Their Troops! 1768, engraving by Paul Revere, 1770, plate size, 10⅛ x 15⅞ inches (*The Henry Francis du Pont Winterthur Museum*)

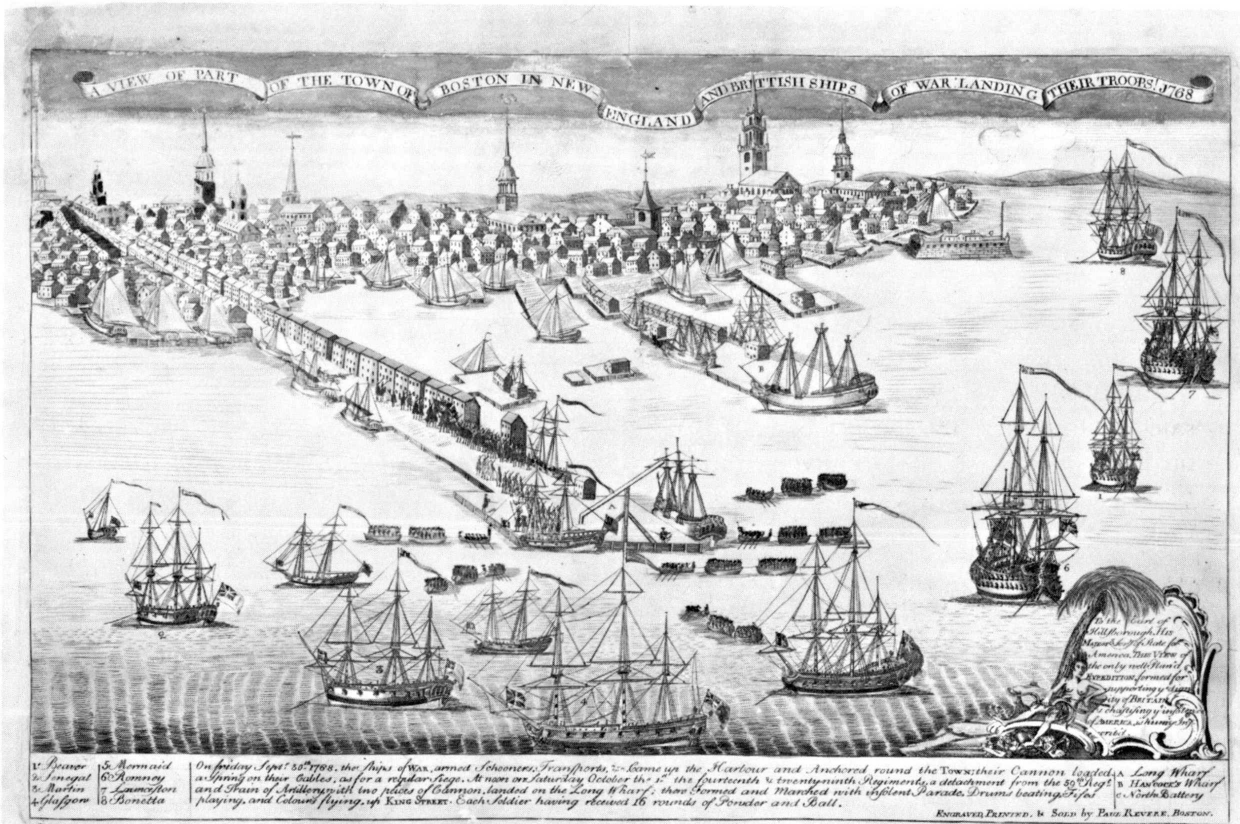

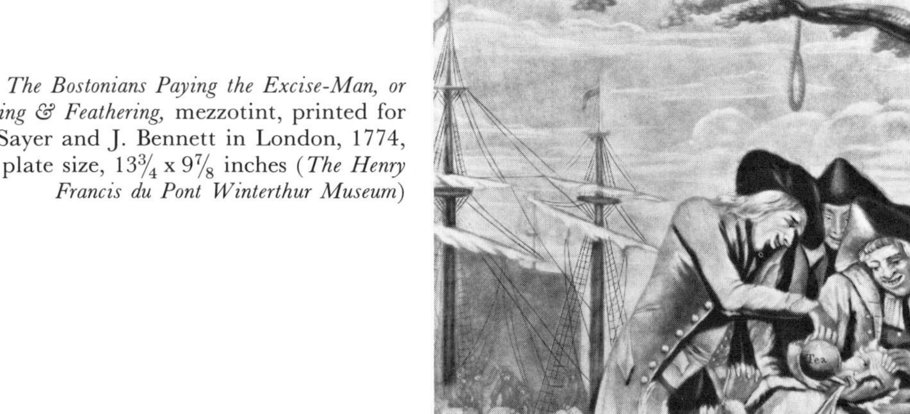

The Bostonians Paying the Excise-Man, or Tarring & Feathering, mezzotint, printed for R. Sayer and J. Bennett in London, 1774, plate size, 13¾ x 9⅞ inches (*The Henry Francis du Pont Winterthur Museum*)

Some interesting pre-revolutionary political cartoons were published by others but the next major print occurs when Amos Doolittle made a set of four engravings of the battles at Lexington and Concord, April 19, 1775. The scenes from which the engravings were made were painted by Ralph Earl soon after the battles with Doolittle acting as his model. Doolittle, who later became one of the most prolific engravers in Connecticut, and Ralph Earl, a principal American portrait painter, were both members of the Governor's Guard at the time of the battles. That fall Doolittle engraved and published the prints, offering them for sale at the store of Mr. James Lockwood, near the College in New Haven, on December 13, 1775. An advertisement two months later in the *Connecticut Gazette* of February 23, 1776 reads:

"Just Published in New Haven And to be Sold by the Printer hereof, Four different Views of the Battles of Lexington, Concord, etc. on the nineteenth of April 1775.

Plate I The Battle of Lexington

Plate II A View of the Town of Concord with the Ministerial Troops destroying the Stores

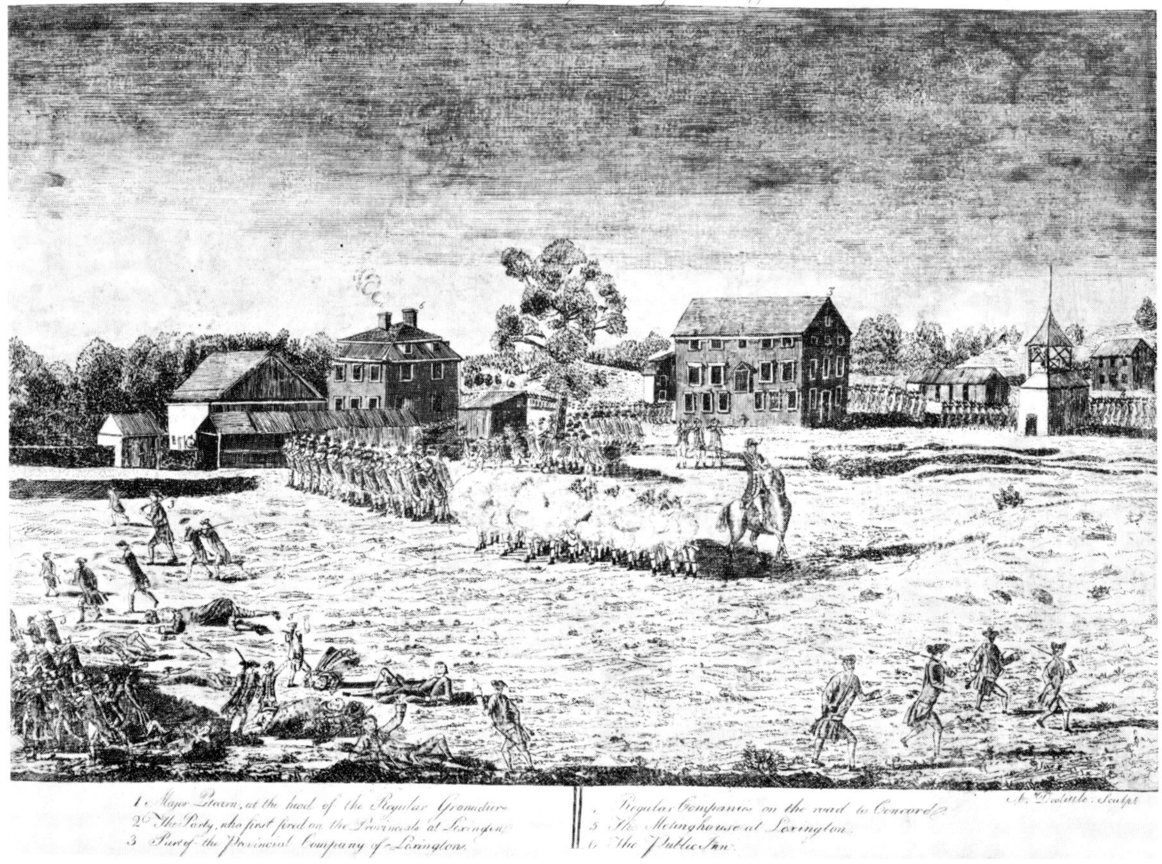

The Battle of Lexington, April 19, 1775, engraving by Amos Doolittle after a painting by Ralph Earl. Printed in New Haven, Connecticut, 1775, 13¾ x 19 inches. One of a series of four depicting the first battles of the American Revolution (*The Henry Francis du Pont Winterthur Museum*)

Plate III The Battle at the North Bridge in Concord
Plate IV The South Part of Lexington where the first Detachment were join'd by Lord Piercy.

The above Four Plates are neatly graven on Copper, from original Paintings taken on the Spot. Price Six Shillings per Set for the plain ones, or Eight Shillings coloured."

Portraits of American patriots were put out in line engravings, mezzotint and etchings both during and after the war. Most were in keeping with the relatively crude character of the pre-revolutionary prints. The prints of Edward Savage are more professional than most but they too display the primitive feeling characteristic of American prints of the seventeenth and eighteenth centuries.

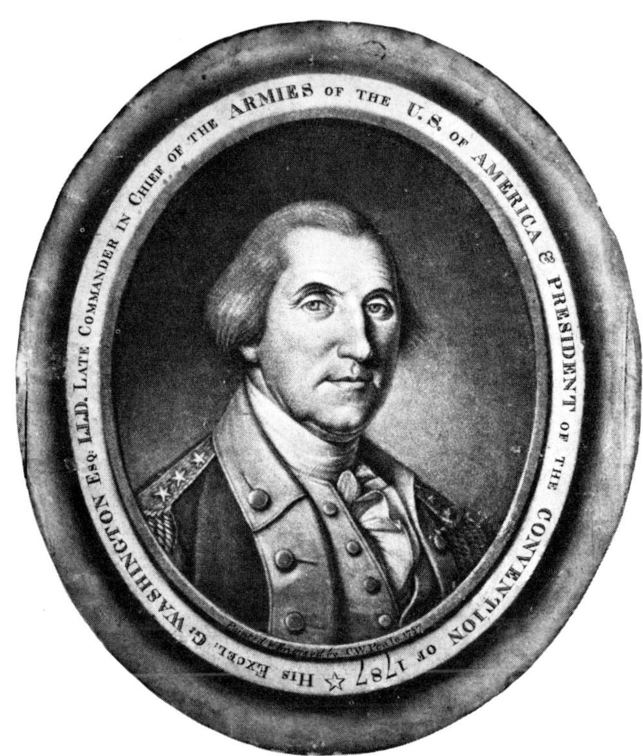

His Excel. G. Washington Esq. . . ., mezzotint by *Charles Wilson Peale, Philadelphia, 1787,* 7¼ x 6 inches (*The Henry Francis du Pont Winterthur Museum*)

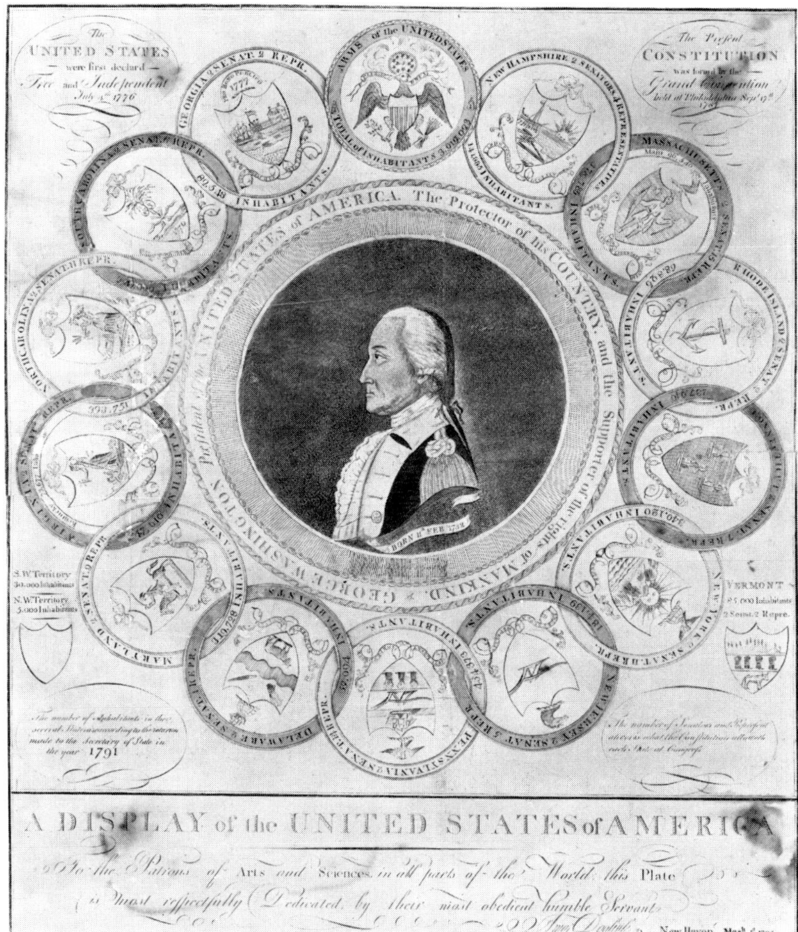

A Display of the United States of America, stipple and line engraving by Amos Doolittle in New Haven, 20⅝ x 17¼ inches. This print was issued in 1794—one of many put out by Doolittle as the statistics of the United States changed. He issued "A New Display" when John Adams became president

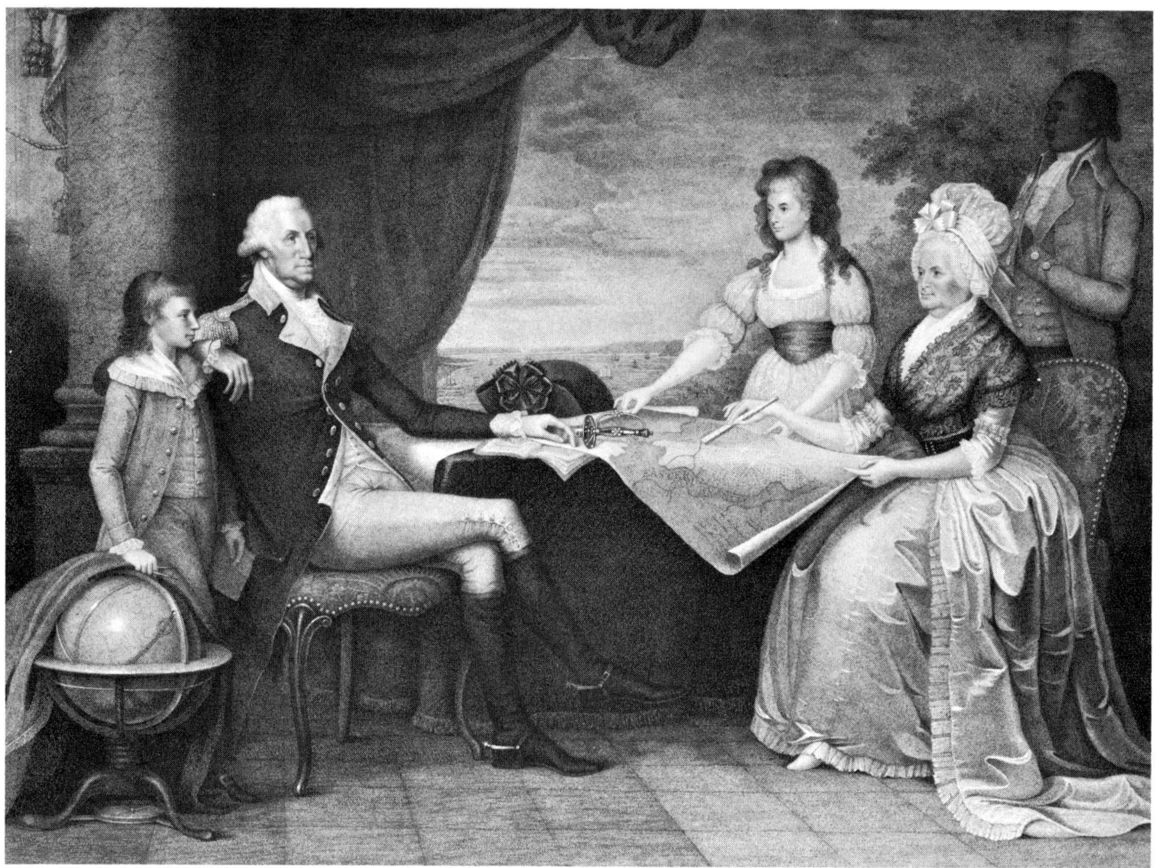

The Washington Family, stipple engraving, printed and engraved by Edward Savage, *c.* 1790 (*The Metropolitan Museum of Art, Gift of W. H. Huntington,* 1883)

Nineteenth-Century Prints

The primitive feeling of American prints did not end abruptly in 1800, but there was a gradual improvement in rendition, as trained artists came from England and the Continent and as equipment and training improved in America. The primitiveness of the early prints have devotees in today's collecting community. On the other hand there are few who support the cold results of many of the later nineteenth-century steel engravings which were done by narrow professionals with little artistic talent.

William Birch and his son Thomas Birch are in the group of trained engravers and etchers to come to America. They emigrated to the United States in 1794 after the elder Birch had a career in England, exhibiting frequently in London from 1775 to 1794. The activities of this talented pair were not limited to engraving. The father also established a reputation in America for his miniature and enamel portraits. The son Thomas was only fifteen when he came to America, but by 1812 he too had won a reputation for himself as a painter of winter scenes and naval battles of the War of 1812. From 1798 to 1800, the two worked together as

William Birch and Son, drawing, engraving and publishing twenty-eight colored plates for a book showing *The City of Philadelphia in the State of Pennsylvania North America as it Appeared in the Year 1800.* A print of a view of New York was put out in 1802 and one of Mt. Vernon in 1803. Both the New York and Mount Vernon prints were drawn by the older Birch and engraved by Samuel Seymour. The Philadelphia prints, of high quality, represent the earliest large set published in America.

Alexander Wilson, artist of the widely collected "Wilson birds," also came from abroad. He was born in Scotland and came to America in 1794. Shortly after 1800 he started collecting material and sketches on American birds and in 1808 put out the first of nine volumes of *American Ornithology.* The seventy-six bird plates, showing 264 species, were engraved and etched by Alexander Lawson, John Warnicke and others and the books were published in Philadelphia between 1808 and 1814. Wilson died in 1813 before publication was complete. This was the first book published in America on American birds and the first important American scholarly book with hand-colored plates. John James Audubon

View of Philadelphia, Second Street from Market Street with Christ's Church, engraving, Designed & Published by W. Birch, Enamel Painter, 1800 (*Museum of Fine Arts, Boston, Gift of Sylvester Rosa Koehler*)

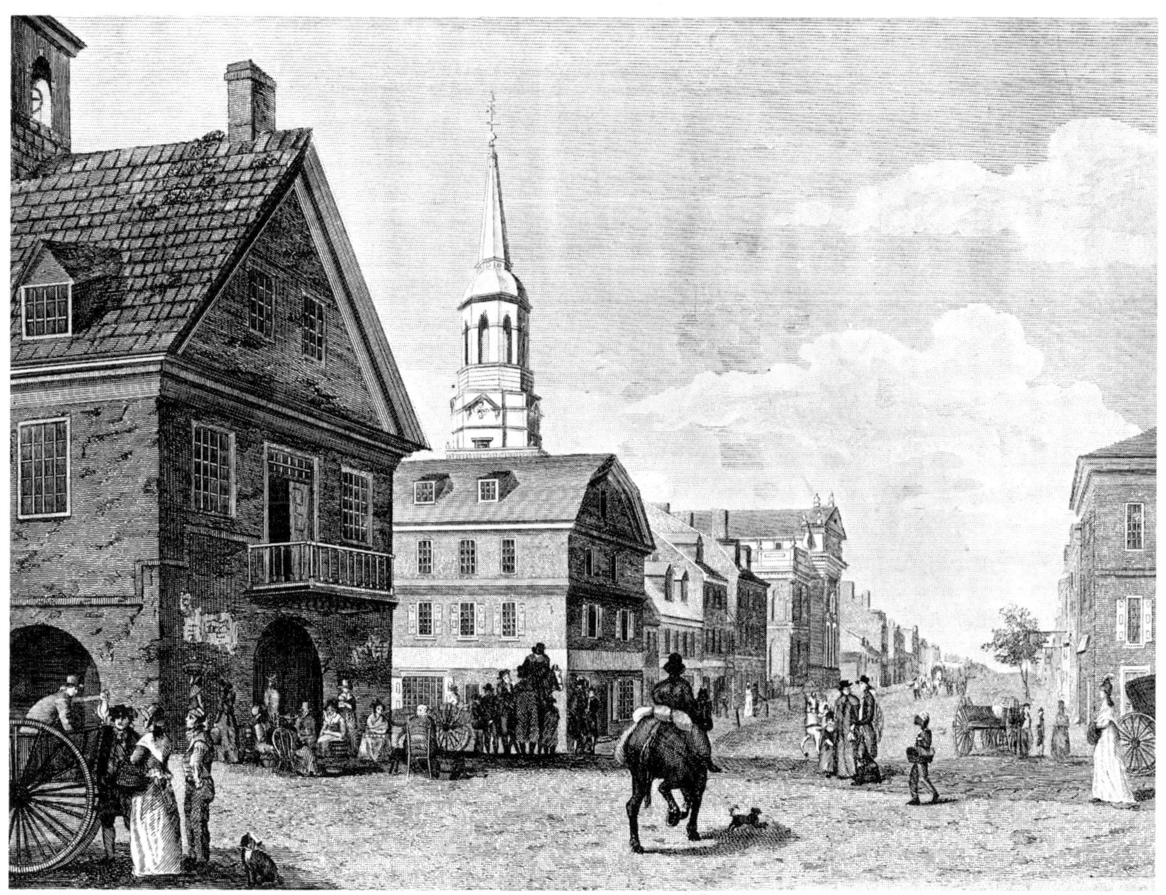

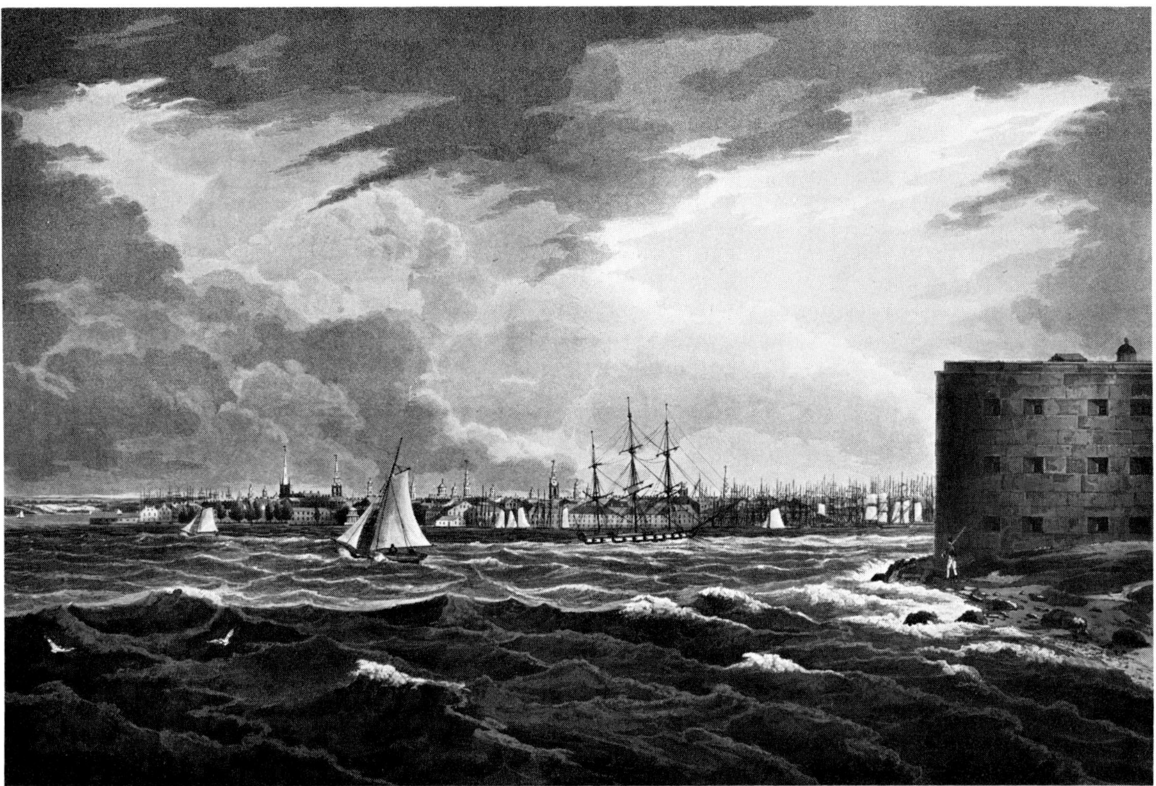

New York, from Governors Island, No. 20 of the *Hudson River Portfolio,* aquatint, from a painting by W. G. Wall, engraved by J. Hill, *c.* 1825, $14\frac{1}{2}$ x $21\frac{3}{8}$ inches (*Museum of Fine Arts, Boston, M. and M. Karolik Collection*)

published his masterpiece with far more artistic and dramatic plates some twenty years later so that Wilson is often forgotten.

The next important group of prints, also in book form, was *Picturesque Views of American Scenery,* including eighteen colored aquatint views of towns and scenery, published in Philadelphia from 1819 to 1820. These prints from scenes painted by Joshua Shaw were engraved by John Hill. Shaw came to this country from England in 1817 after achieving recognition as a painter by exhibiting at the Royal Academy and other London galleries. He continued his painting career in this country and today some of his paintings are in the collections of several important museums. John Hill also emigrated from England where he had established a reputation as an engraver before coming to the United States in 1816. *Picturesque Views of American Scenery* was his first important commission in America. In 1822 he moved from Philadelphia to New York City where he worked on William Guy Wall's *Hudson River Portfolio.*

William Guy Wall was born in Dublin, Ireland in 1792. He, too, received his training before coming to America in 1818 and settling in New York City. Twenty of his well-received Hudson River watercolor paintings were engraved and published in book form in the popular *Hudson River Portfolio.* The first four were engraved by J. R. Smith and the rest by John Hill. These attractive aquatint views, in color, are approximately $14\frac{1}{2} \times 21\frac{1}{2}$ inches. They were published between 1820 and 1828.

Next in point of time is Asher B. Durand whom James Flexner calls the "only American who can be ranked among major nineteenth century engravers." Durand was born in what is now Maplewood, New Jersey in 1796. From 1812 to 1817 he was apprenticed to Peter Maverick, a well-known engraver working in Newark, New Jersey. After completing his apprenticeship, he worked as a partner of Maverick until 1820, copying prints from English books and working on plates for banknotes. At that time John Trumbull was looking for a competent engraver who would not charge much to make the plate for prints of his painting, the *Declaration of Independence.* Trumbull's subscription scheme was in financial trouble so he persuaded Durand to make the plate for three thousand dollars as compared to the seven thousand dollars for the same work demanded by James Heath, an English engraver in London. The work took three years before the $29\frac{11}{16}$ inch $\times$ $30\frac{1}{4}$ inch plate was finished but the effort firmly established the young Durand as a major engraver. He continued as an engraver until 1835, in business for himself and in various partnerships. His work includes plates for banknotes, book illustrations and portraits from paintings by Thomas Sully, John Vanderlyn and Charles Ingham. Perhaps his most important works were six plates produced for a projected but never achieved serial publication called *The American Landscape,* and his final major work, *Ariadne,* the reclining nude that had been painted by John Vanderlyn. In 1835, Durand's interest shifted to painting and he soon became a leading member of the new Hudson River School of landscape artists. From 1845 to 1861 he served as president of the National Academy of Design which he had helped create in 1826.

The next important set of decorative prints after the *Hudson River Portfolio* were nineteen large folio views of American cities painted and engraved by W. J. Bennett, some published by H. I. Magarey and some by Parker & Clover. These 16 inch $\times$ 23 inch aquatint views in color are considered by many to be the finest large prints of American cities in existence. Bennett was born in England and had a long artistic career there before coming to America in 1826 at the age of thirty-nine. This was his most important American work. The colored prints sold for four dollars and five dollars each which was comparable to the more popular Currier and Ives large folio lithographs put out ten or fifteen years later.

By 1840 Cole and Durand had firmly established the Hudson River School of painting and interest in American art ran high. In 1839 the

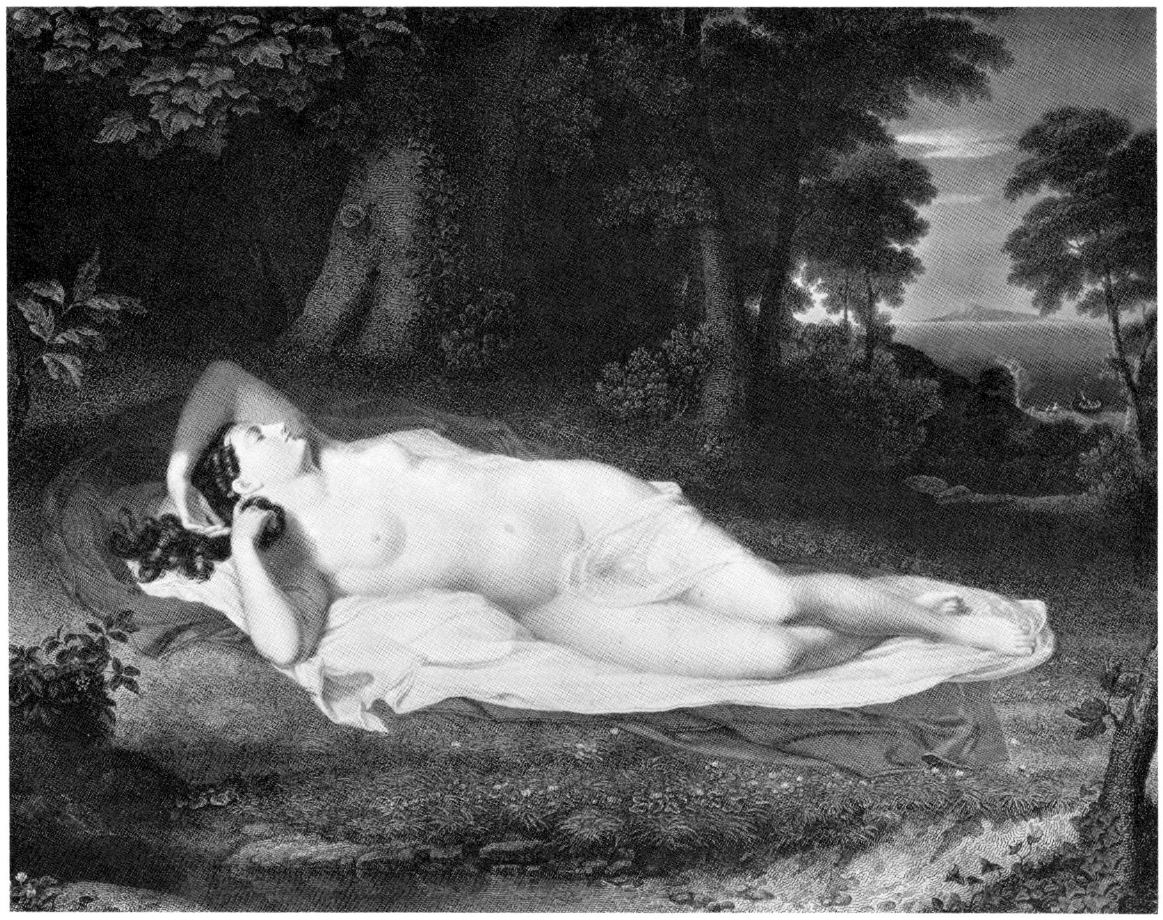

Ariadne, engraving by Asher B. Durand after a painting by Vanderlyn, 1835, $14\frac{3}{16}$ x $17\frac{3}{4}$ inches (*The Metropolitan Museum of Art, the Harris Brisbane Dick Fund,* 1927)

Apollo Association for the Advancement of the Fine Arts in the United States was formed. The name was changed in 1844 to the American Art Union. The purpose of the Art Union was to encourage the growth of fine arts in the United States and to this end it established an annual lottery of art work which had been bought from American artists during the year. Funds for these purchases came from a five-dollar annual subscription fee. Each member had a chance of winning a painting during the drawing of the lottery, but win or lose, he received a print which was given each year starting in 1840 to all subscribers.

In 1840 there were only 686 members and they all received a mezzotint of *General Marion in His Swamp Encampment Inviting a British Officer to Dinner,* by John Blake White, engraved by John Sartain, and printed by J. Dalton. A second mezzotint was given to the 937 members in 1841. In 1849 a steel engraving of each of the four pictures in the *Voyage of Life* series by Thomas Cole was given to the almost 19,000 members. The membership roles had grown to a point where it was necessary to use steel engravings. This was the peak membership year and in 1852 the American Art Union suspended operations when the lottery system was declared illegal.

Other late offerings included:

The Capture of Major André after a painting by A. B. Durand, offered 1845 to'46

Old '76 and Young '48 after a painting by Richard C. Woodville, offered 1851 to '53

Bargaining for a Horse after a painting by William Sidney Mount, offered 1851 to '53

The Art Union prints are identified by the seal on the bottom margins.

At the time of the demise of the Art Union the French print publishers Goupil, Vibert & Co. began offering prints based on American paintings. Goupil had operated a New York branch starting in 1846 but originally sold only French prints. One of their first American prints, copyrighted in 1853, was a steel engraving of *Washington Crossing the Delaware* after a painting by Emanuel Leutze. Over the years the printing machinery had been improved making possible this enormous print, 22⅜

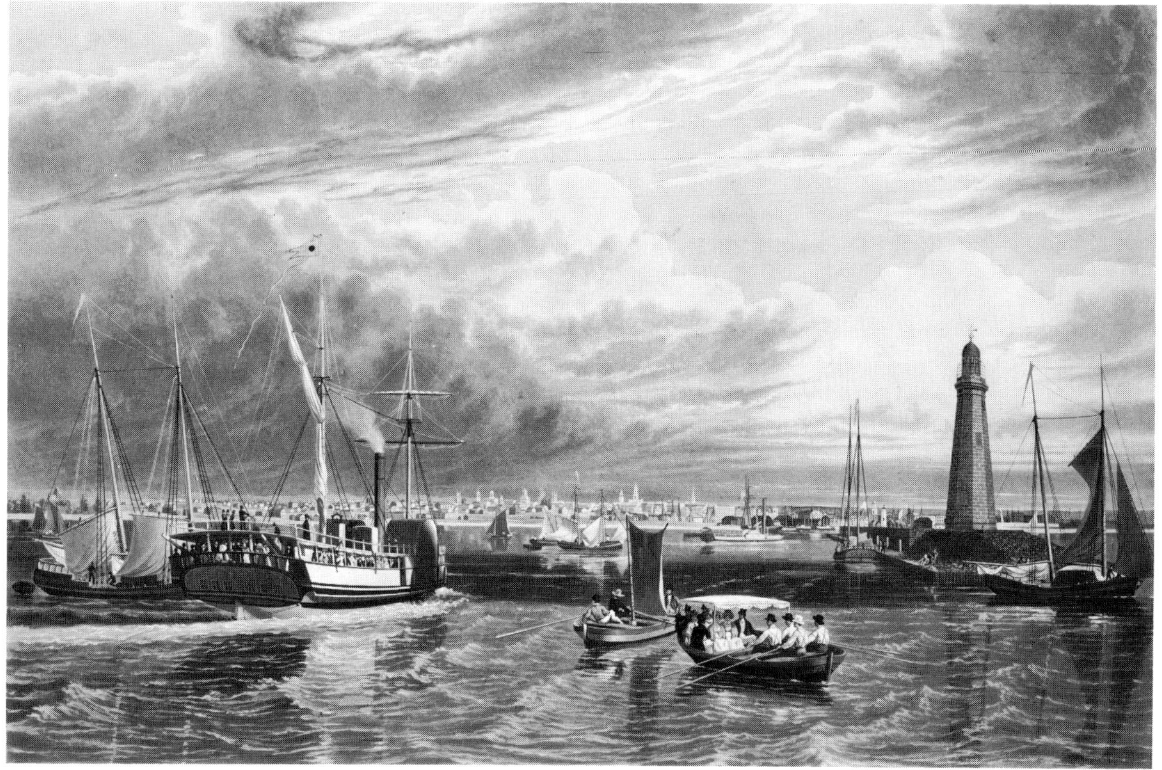

Buffalo, from Lake Erie, aquatint by W. J. Bennett based on a sketch by J. W. Hill, published by H. J. Megarey, N.Y., 1835 (*Museum of Fine Arts, Boston, M. and M. Karolik Collection*)

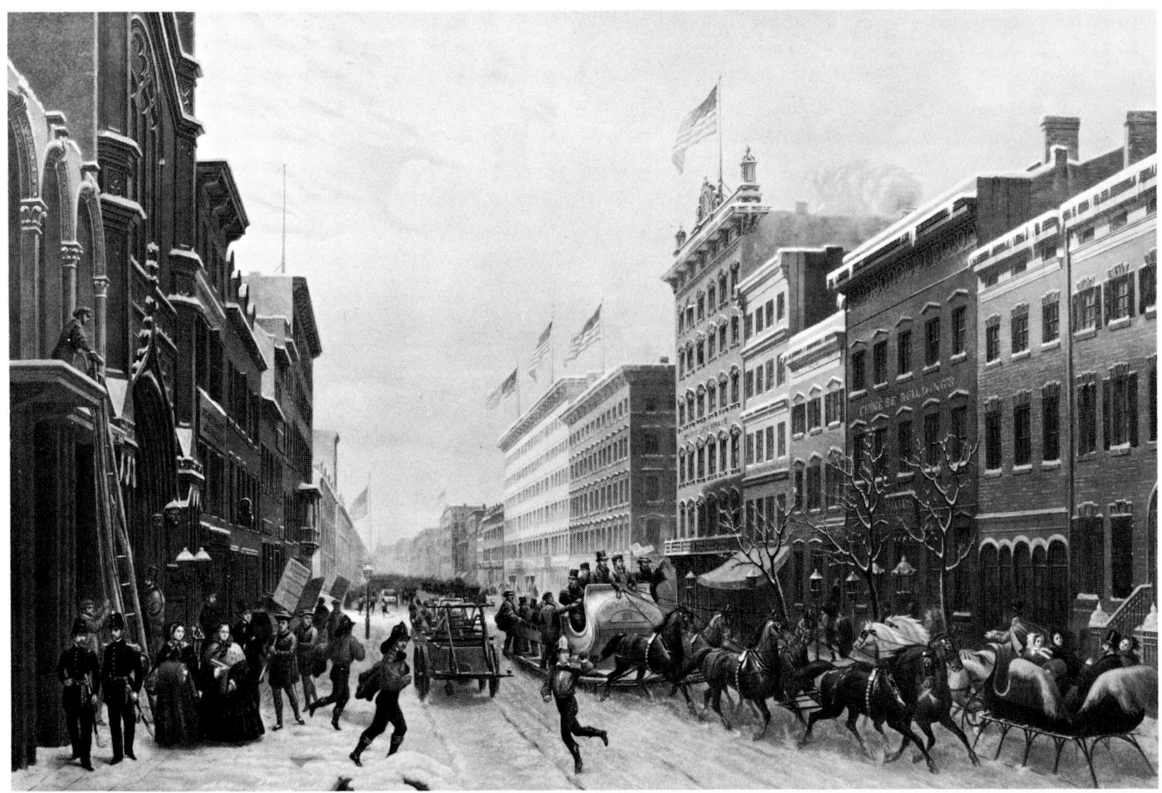

New York, Winter Scene in Broadway, aquatint by Giradet after a painting by Sebron, published by M. Knoedler in 1857, printed and distributed by Goupil & Co., plate size, 27¾ x 38⅞ inches

inch × 38½ inches. Unfortunately, it embodies the mechanical qualities that many connoisseurs today find objectionable in nineteenth-century engravings. Goupil did distribute some desirable prints, however, including a hand-colored aquatint *New York, Winter Scene in Broadway.*

For about thirty years, between 1850 and 1880, great numbers of very large, inexpensive steel engravings were printed, framed and hung in the living room of American homes. Part of the popularity can be traced to the mark-of-culture factor of the Art Union prints. Most of the uncolored editions by artists and engravers such as A. H. Ritchie can now be found in the corners of second-hand furniture shops. A few, however, are recognized as important American prints. An outstanding example of American genre, published in 1854, is *The County Election,* engraved by John Sartain after a painting by G. C. Bingham. Little sorting has been attempted with these engravings and from time to time other gems are recognized.

After about 1870, the commercial exploitation of engraved prints was gradually dampened by the chromolithograph. This new print form was particularly well-suited to landscapes and many of the "Hudson

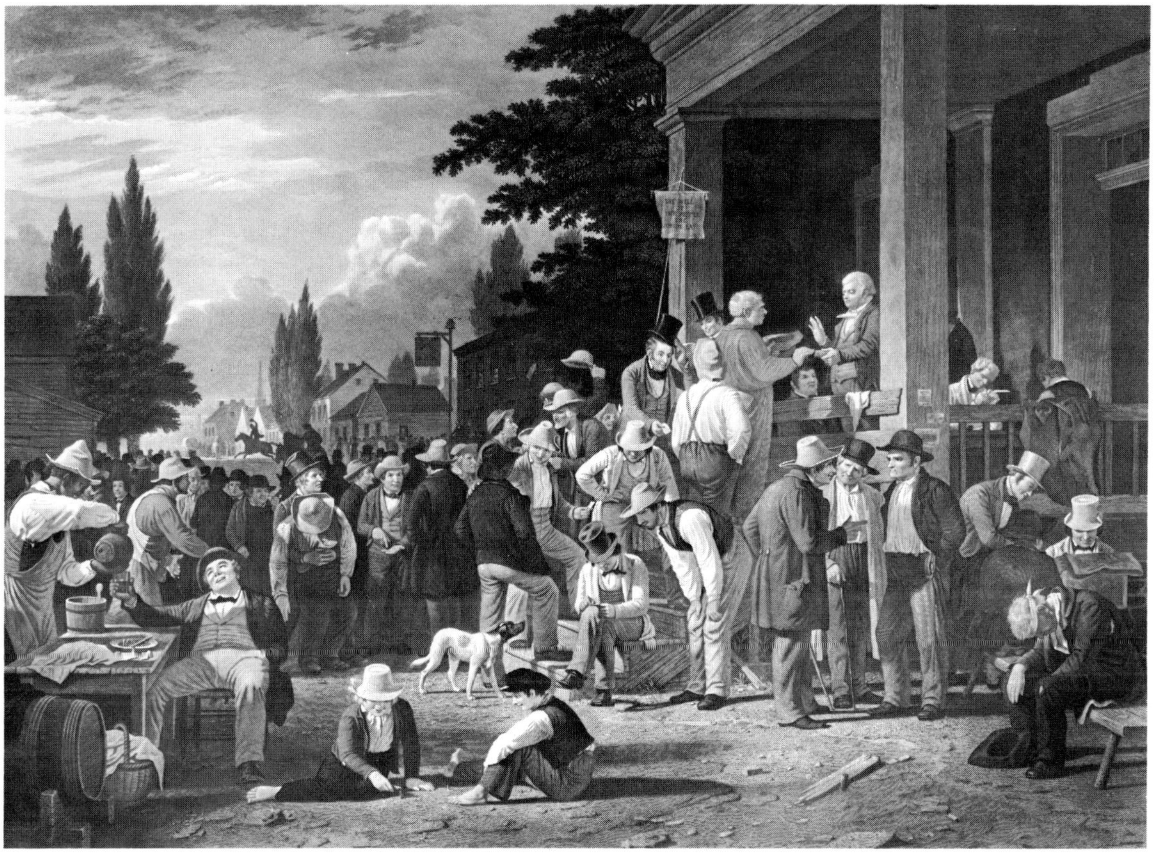

The County Election, engraving by John Sartain after a painting by George Caleb Bingham, N.Y., 1854, 22 x 30 inches (*Museum of Fine Arts, Boston, M. and M. Karolik Collection*)

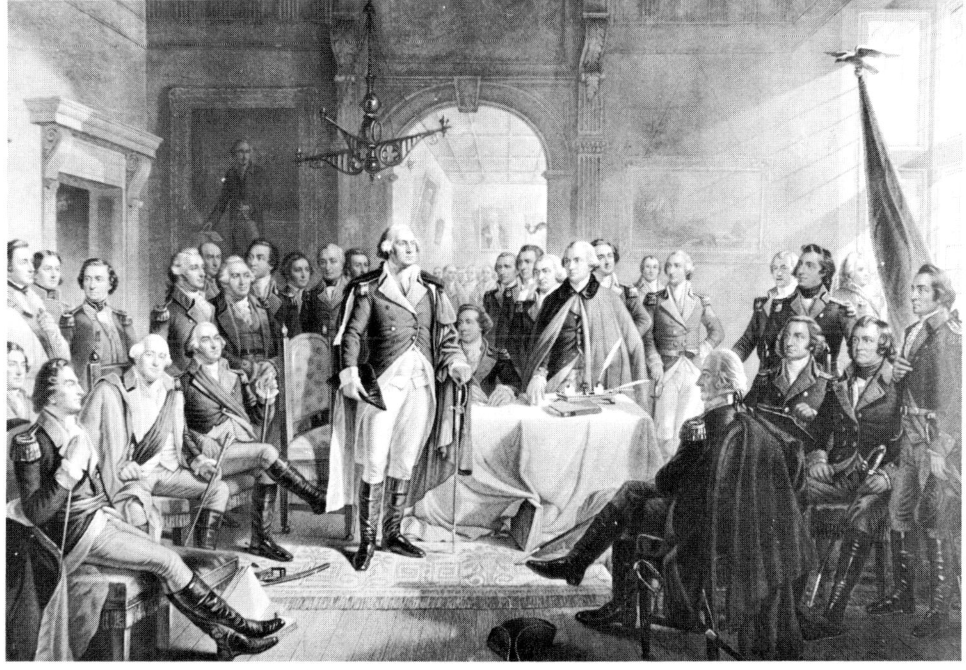

Washington and his Generals, engraving, drawn and engraved by A. H. Ritchie, N.A., 1870, plate size, 22 x 27½ inches

River" paintings were reproduced in this way. Engraving and etching gradually acquired new stature as art forms toward the end of the century.

This relatively brief review of American engravings naturally does not include comments on every work. Some other specialized prints are discussed, however, in the chapters on Miscellaneous Prints and Nature Prints.

CHAPTER FOUR American Lithography other than Currier & Ives

Versatility

The versatility of lithography made it a prolific graphic medium during the nineteenth century. Lithography was used to reproduce maps, books and periodical illustrations, architectural building plans, fashion illustrations, political campaign material, cartoons, diplomas, certificates, posters, handbills, letterheads, labels, trade cards, keepsakes, puzzles and decorative prints. Before music could be produced by the push of a button or the turn of a dial, sheet music was a highly important commodity in the printing trades. The production of illustrated covers to enticingly package the sheet music was a major source of income for many lithographic firms. In New England the hand-drawn family records were replaced by lithographs with blanks to be filled in with names and dates. The embroidered or water-color memorial pictures whose conventionalized symbols included weeping willows, churchyards, tombstones and grieving figures and which were carefully executed by girls and women to commemorate the death of a family member, or sometimes a public figure, also appeared in lithograph form ready to be filled in.

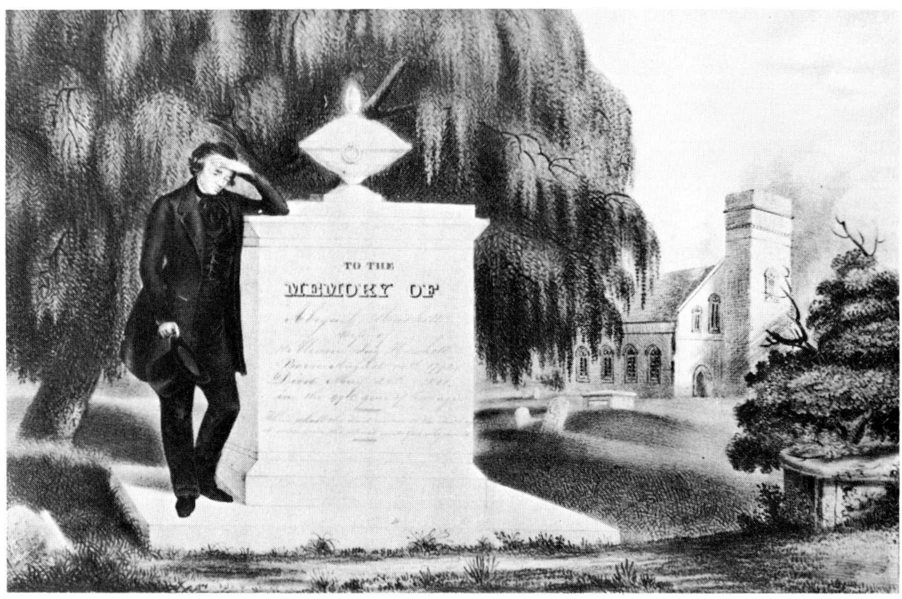

To the Memory of, N. Currier, 2 Spruce Street, N.Y., J. L. McGee, del., $8\frac{3}{4}$ x $12\frac{3}{4}$ inches. Hand colored lithograph.

As an Art Medium

As an artist's medium the lithograph is superb. No intermediary is necessary to transpose the artist's design onto a metal plate or wood block for he can sketch directly on the stone with the fluid ease and freedom of a drawing. Various textures and techniques can be imitated or reproduced. Deep velvety blacks can be printed, as well as frosty whites. Tone can be produced without resorting to crosshatching, lines or stippling for creating atmospheric landscape effects or body contours.

In America the lithograph was not exploited to its full potential as it was in France by Géricault, Delacroix and others early in the nineteenth century. At the end of the century the great renaissance of black and white and color lithography took place mostly in France. In England the process was impeded in every way possible by British engravers and aquatinters who felt threatened by it and pressured Parliament to exclude the German lithographic stone with a prohibitive import duty. Artists in England and America were further hampered by the prevailing attitude toward lithography which viewed it as a cheap inferior short-cut method of reproduction. In 1857 the influential critic Ruskin said, "Let no lithographic work come into your house if you can help it." Even the firm of Currier and Ives, which made no social pretensions, felt it necessary to advertise its lithographs as "Cheap Engravings for the People." Books with lithographed plates frequently bear the credit "engraved by." Engraving was the reproductive medium with class and the only one considered suitable for the reproduction of fine paintings. Some early lithographers even tried to make their work look like engraving by using lines and stipple techniques on stone.

The Popular Image

But Ruskin notwithstanding, lithography gained wide public acceptance in the form of the popular image. The early settlers had not brought with them the tradition of the popular religious image, nor was there a strong tradition of religious themes in our painting during the seventeenth, eighteenth or nineteenth centuries. In its place the secular print was everywhere and influenced how Americans saw their country, their leaders, their society and their institutions.

Lithography was hailed as the truly democratic art, art for the people. It provided a cheap means for the people to see what their leaders looked like. Vast quantities of portraits both of the now obscure and of those of enduring reputation were published. George Washington must have been a folk hero without parallel in our own time. There are portraits of him with and without horse, with and without Martha, as

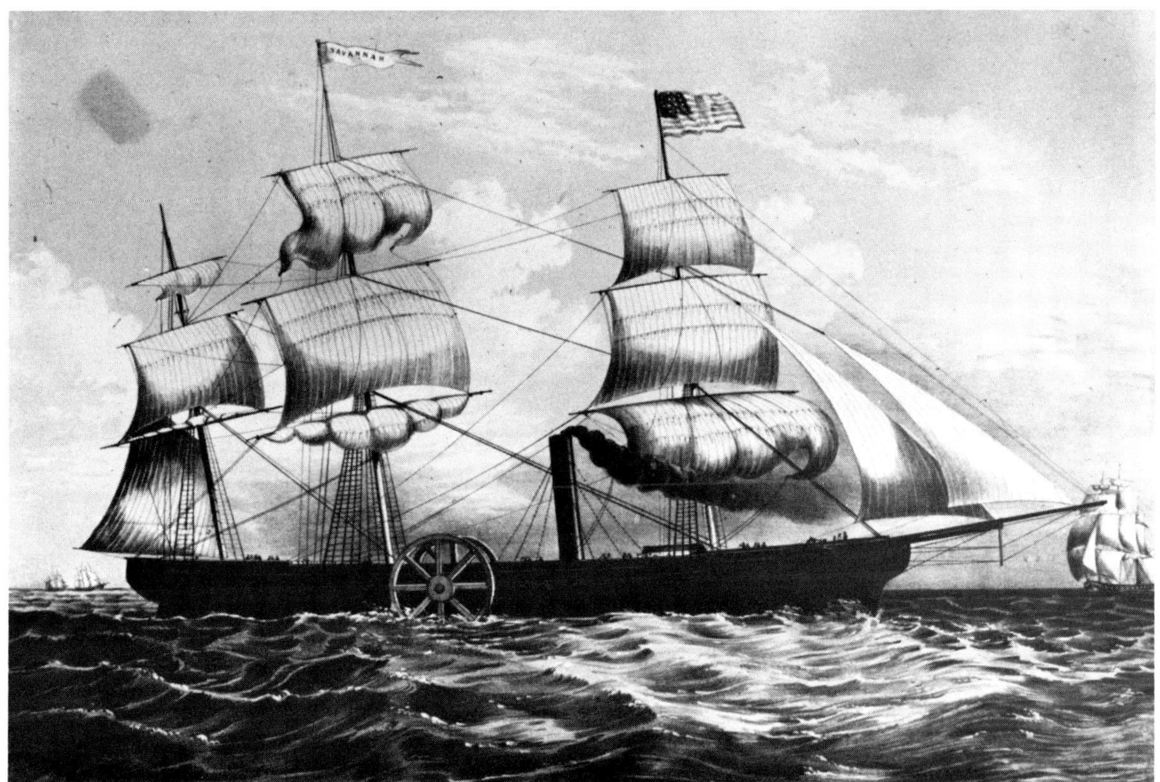

Steam Ship "Savannah" Capt. Moses Rodgers/ The First Steamship That Crossed the Atlantic Ocean, lithographed by G. Hayward, N.Y., 14 x 21 inches (*The Harry T. Peters "America on Stone" Lithography Collection, Smithsonian Institution*)

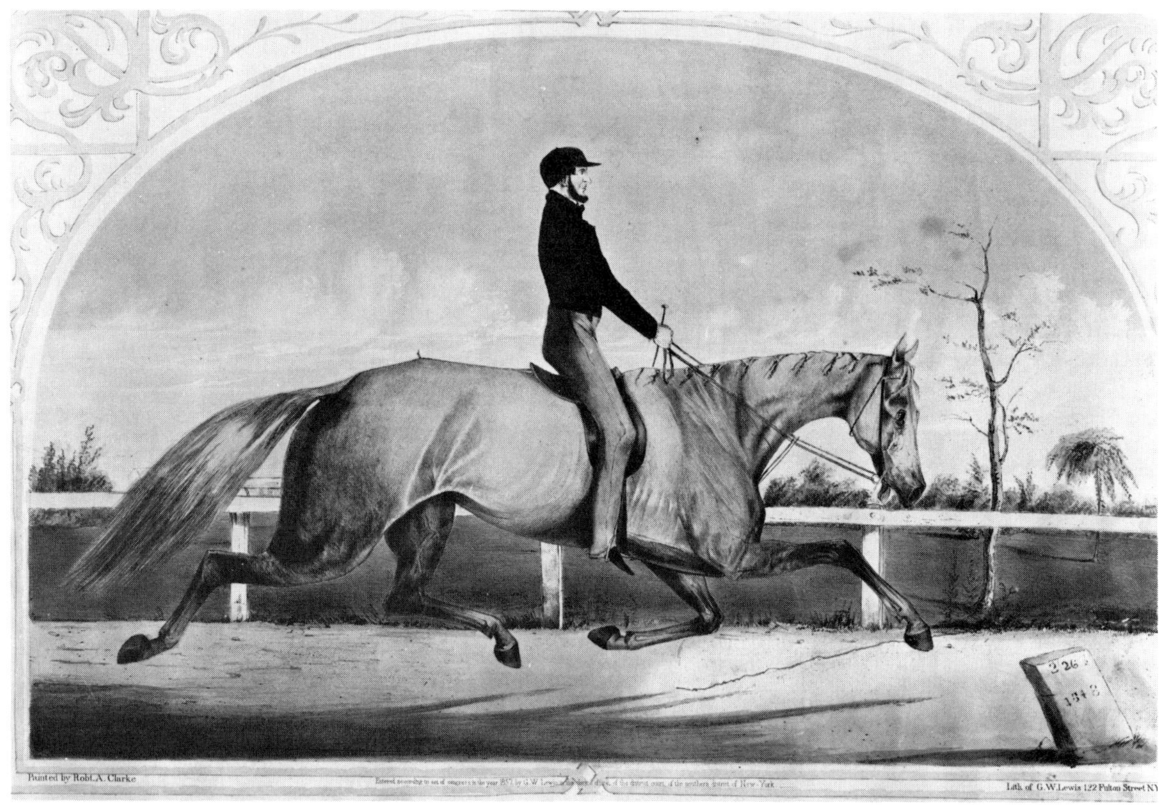

Lady Suffolk / The Celebrated Trotting Mare, lithographed by G. W. Lewis, New York. From original painting by Robert A. Clarke, 1844, 14 x $20\frac{1}{2}$ inches (*The Harry T. Peters "America on Stone" Lithography Collection, Smithsonian Institution*)

soldier, civilian, Freemason and even as a ghost visiting his tomb. Mount Vernon and Washington's tomb shared in the adulation. Many of these prints served as models for folk artists such as William Prior and for needlework pictures.

Some of the lithographic firms were quick to exploit the news possibilities of the lithograph. The visual presentation was especially appreciated by the illiterate and non-English speaking sections of the population. The drama of disasters of all kinds such as ships lost at sea with frail humans clinging to the wreckage and raging fires engulfing whole cities were favorite subjects. The pride of the burgeoning country in its progress was pictured in its sleek clipper ships, steamboats, railroads, suspension bridges and public buildings. The opening of the frontier, of the West and California provided scenes full of the promise of adventure. When the Civil War broke out, every aspect of the war was rushed into print, the battles, the officers, the deathbed scenes, the encampments.

As the country developed prosperous classes with time and money

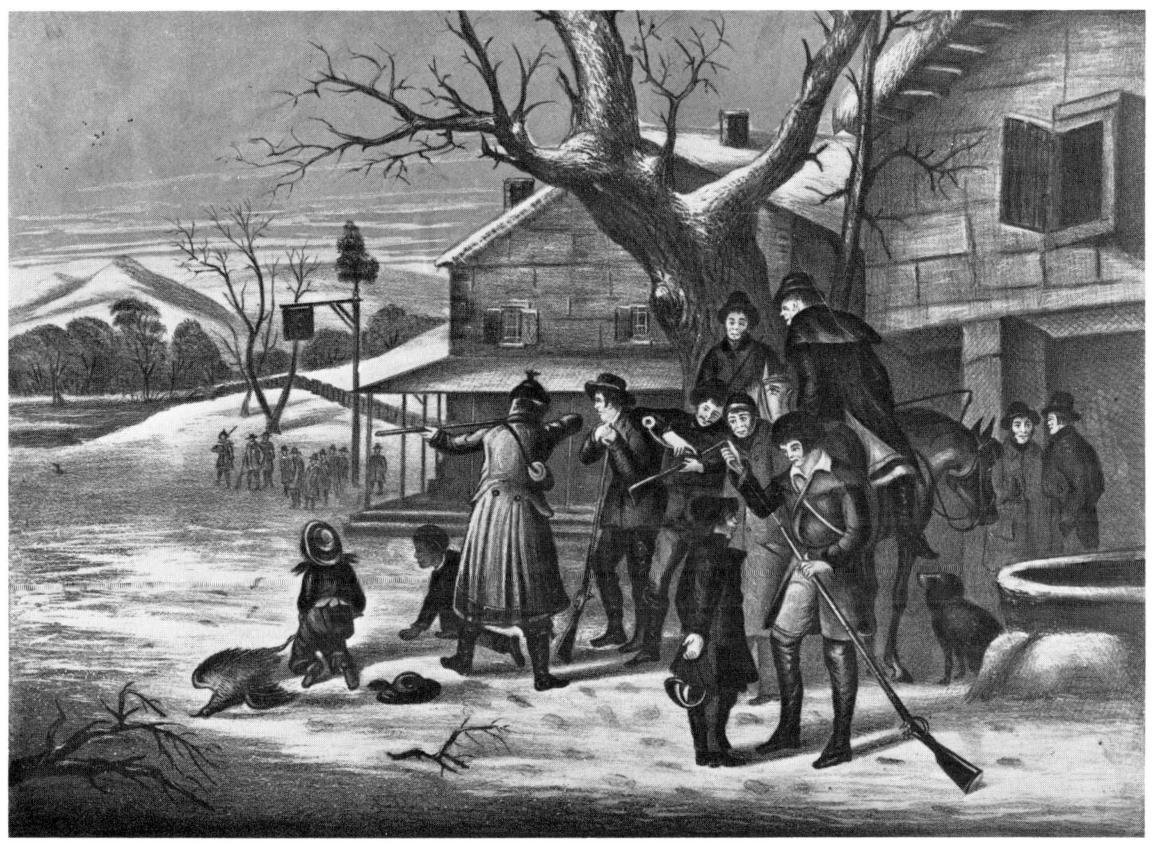

Shooting Turkeys for Thanksgiving-Day, published by J. Childs, Philadelphia, $10\frac{3}{8}$ x $14\frac{1}{2}$ inches (*The Harry T. Peters "America on Stone" Lithography Collection, Smithsonian Institution*)

for leisure, their activities such as yachting, hunting, fishing, racing and the breeding of horses are shown. In general, the view of life is cheerful and optimistic. There is little indication of the effect of the growing factory system on the lives of women and children. Even so, these prints abound in social and political commentary. Temperance prints indicate the concern with the drinking problem. Marriage had its share of proponents and detractors in "before" and "after" versions. Occasionally, slavery and the Indians are dealt with. Political stances were lampooned and political personages caricatured.

There is a large group of fancy or sentimental prints, generally of children, pets, girls, young women or dandies. The women are presented as sweet, pretty, somewhat plump with ample bosoms and wasp waists, embodying modesty and purity without character, intelligence or significant occupation other than motherhood. The children are neat, clean and pleasant cherubs who spend their days riding ponies and playing with pets. Occasionally some of the comics show mischievous boys who are insulting, coarsely crude and troublemaking.

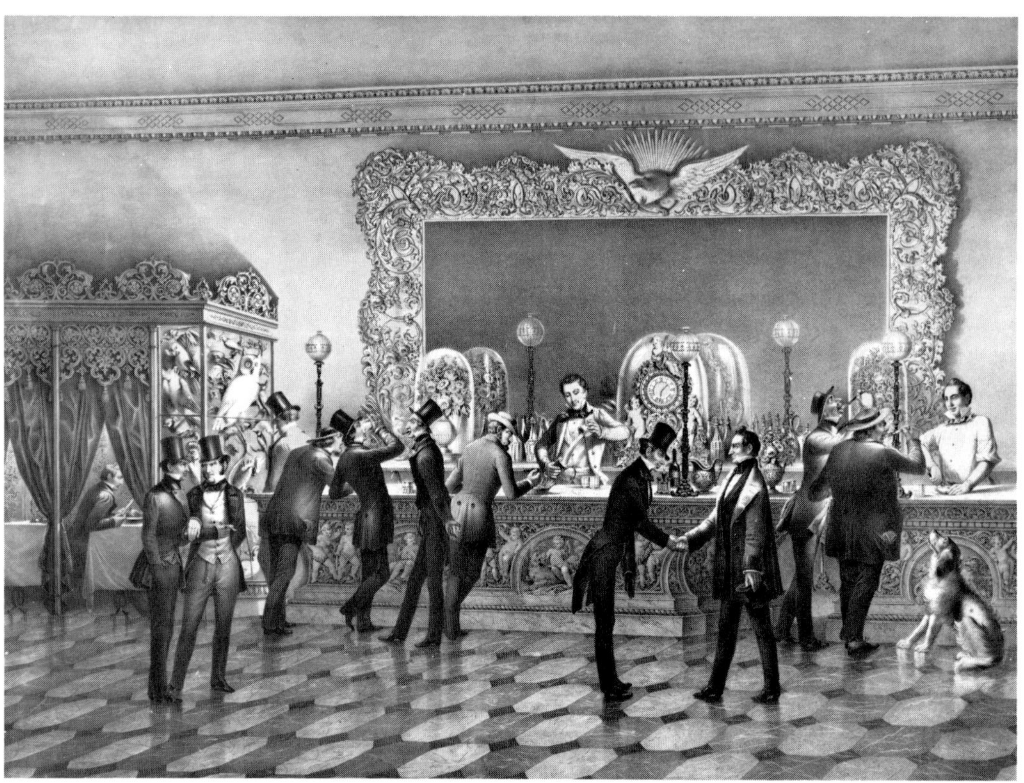

Temperance, but No Maine-Law, composed and drawn on Stone by A. Fay, printed and published by A. Fay, Hoboken, N.J., 1854, 19 x 25¼ inches

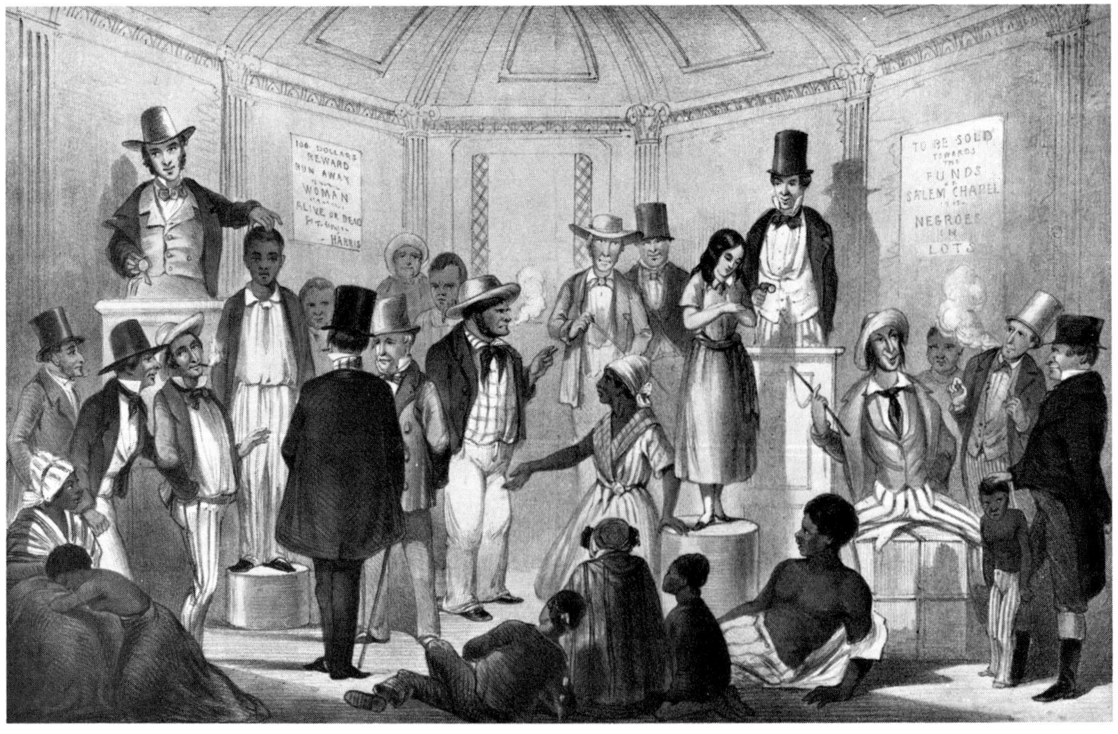

The Slave Sale./ The Hammer Falls . . . "he has got the girl body & soul unless god help her," Anonymous, 7⅝ x 12 inches (*The Harry T. Peters "America on Stone" Lithography Collection, Smithsonian Institution*)

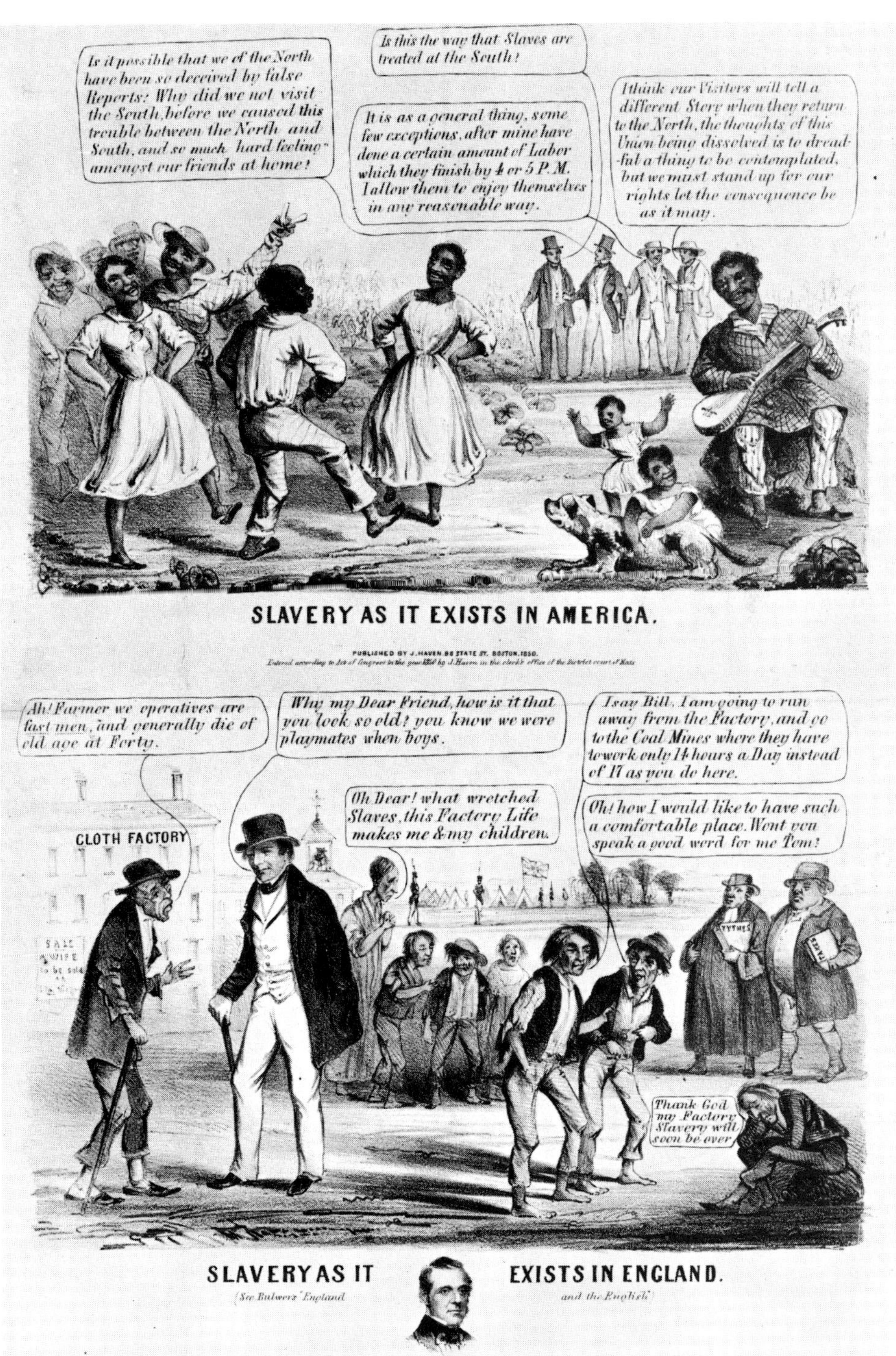

Slavery as it Exists in America. Slavery as it Exists in England,
published by J. Haven, Boston, 1850, medium folio vignettes
(*The Harry T. Peters "America on Stone" Lithography Collection, Smithsonian Institution*)

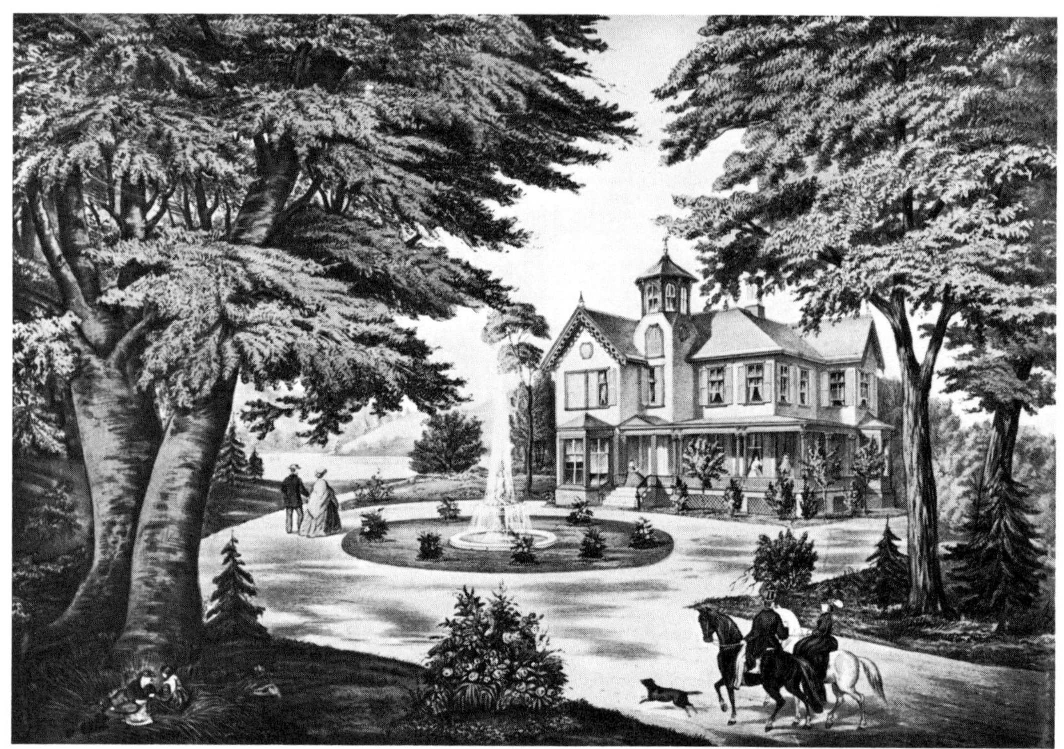

Summer Scene in the Country, J. Kelly & Sons, Philadelphia, 1866, 17½ x 25 inches

Views

Brightly hand-colored views made to fit stock frames were immensely popular as substitutes for paintings. Favorite subjects were scenic spots along the Hudson River, Niagara Falls, Lake George in New York, and Yosemite Falls. Prints were bought as souvenirs of a visit to a vacation spot or natural wonder. Bird's-eye views of cities and towns were done by itinerant artists for sale to the residents to keep or to send to friends to show them their home towns. The nostalgic rural view, the home in the country, the farm, the simpler life untouched by industrialization were other subjects which appealed to many.

Many of the views were published as a part of a series in an album or portfolio. About 1826-28 Anthony Imbert issued a series of sixteen *Views of the Public Buildings in the City of New York,* before the destructive fire of 1835. A much later New York series was done in 1850 by Henry Hoff. *Panorama and Views of Philadelphia and its Vicinity* from drawings by J. C. Wild was lithographed by J. T. Bowen in 1838 and again in a larger size in 1848. Wild also drew and lithographed *The Valley of the Mississippi Illustrated in a Series of Views.* Six *Views of Trenton Falls* near Utica, New York were lithographed by John Pendleton; *Pacific Views*

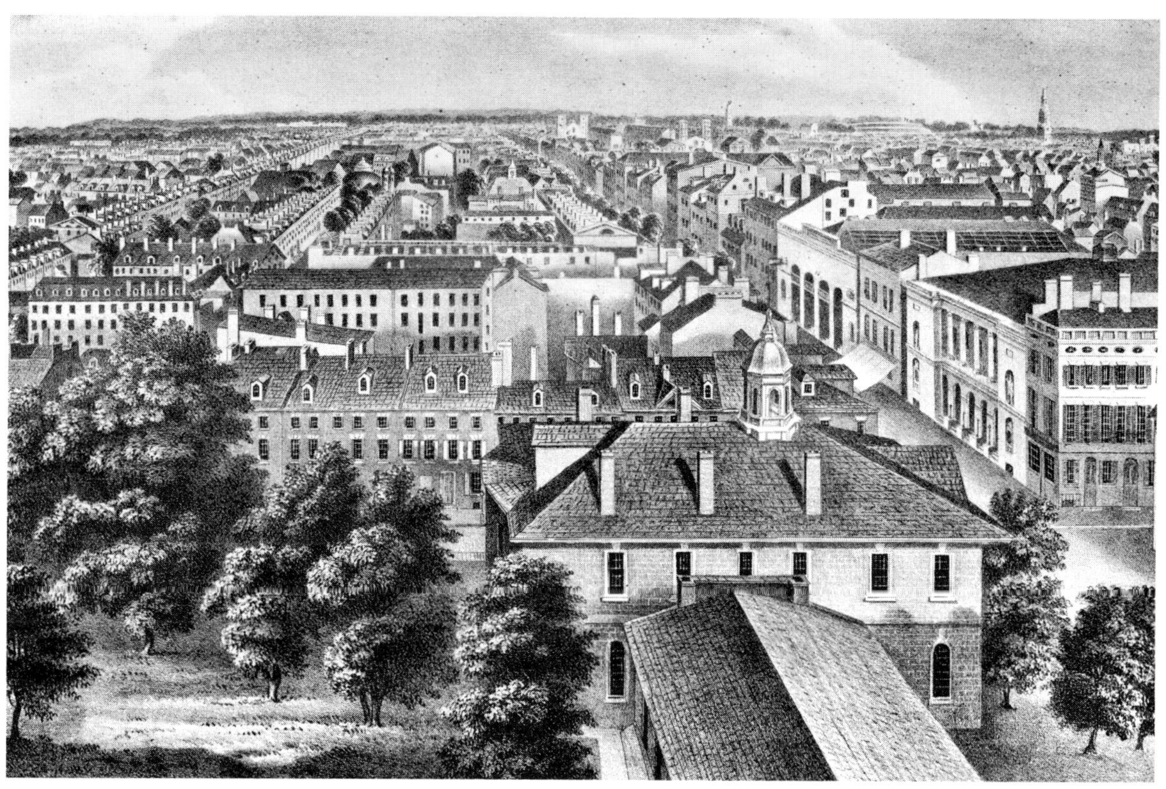

Panorama of Philadelphia, from *Panorama and Views of Philadelphia and its Vicinity,* a 4to book of views by J. C. Wild, 1838, lithographed by J. T. Bowen

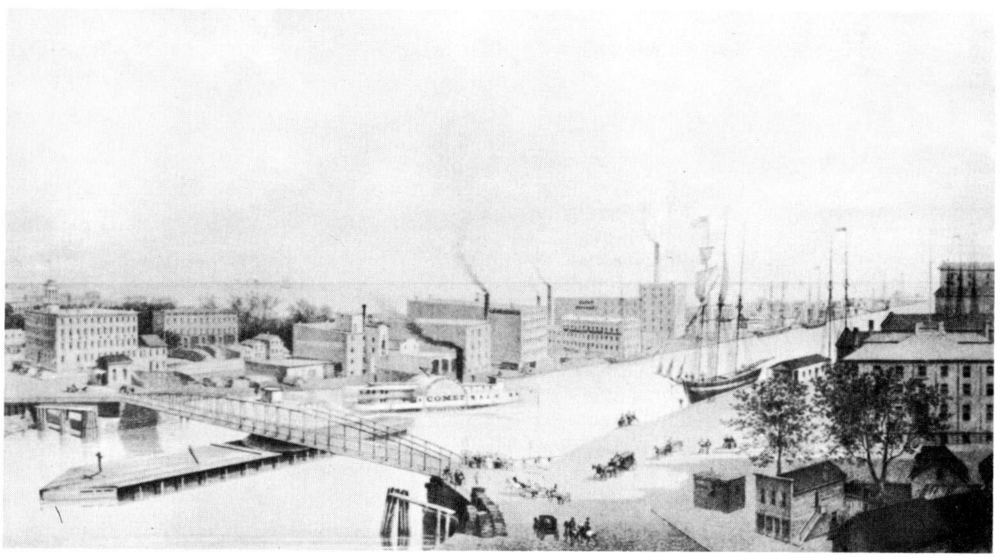

View of Rush St. Bridge &c/ From Nortons Block River St., (from *Nature* by E. Whitefield, lithographed and printed by Carl Shober, Chicago, 1861, small folio

by Kuchel and Dresel of San Francisco, 1855–56; and *Pencil Sketches of Colorado* drawn by Alfred E. Mathews and lithographed by J. Bien in 1866. Mathews followed this with another series of western states. In 1857 Endicott issued the *Album of New England Scenery* which consists of twelve medium folio views of New England cities. A series showing Chicago in the 1830's was issued by Jevne and Almini in 1866. The most important series is Edwin Whitefield's *Original Views of North American Cities* which gives us an extensive record of many parts of the country starting with Albany and Troy around 1845 and continuing on through Ohio, New York, Massachusetts, Illinois and Minnesota. Various firms lithographed his views, among them Endicott, Lewis and Brown, and F. Michelin.

Many more subjects were covered by our nineteenth-century lithographers, and there are unquestionably exceptions to the generalizations that have been made here. Some of the prints have been carefully preserved and some have been long since destroyed as of trivial value, but those remaining are worth rooting out and tracking down.

Development of lithography in America

Lithography was discovered by Alois Senefelder about 1798 in Germany but it took some twenty years before there was much more than occasional experimentation with the new medium here. A notice in the *National Intelligencer and Washington Advisor* in 1808 states that "Dr. Mitchell of New York received a lithographic stone and inks from Paris and made some experiments in this new art." Others experimented with Vermont marble, Indiana limestone and Kentucky limestone but none were as satisfactory as the expensive imported Solenhofen stone. An early experimenter was Bass Otis who is generally credited with the first recorded American lithographs in 1818 and 1819. Technically, his initial attempts are a combination of stone etching and lithography. Stone etching is a process in which some of the stone surface is eaten away by acid and is actually a relief method. Otis' portrait of the Reverend Abner Kneeland appeared as a frontispiece to a book of his sermons published in 1818, and in 1819 the *Bath House* appeared in the *Analectic Magazine.*

Alois Senefelder had developed his *Complete Course of Lithography* by 1818 and it was translated into English in 1819. This spread the technology and helped to standardize the techniques. However, the existing presses were unsuitable for printing lithographs. Senefelder had invented a new press which he patented in 1801. In this press the pressure was applied by a scraper blade which was swept across a leather tympan covering the stone. A variation of this was to pass the stone beneath a fixed scraper blade. Printing was still a more or less haphazard process in 1818 when Senefelder wrote:

> "I am only too well aware . . . of a grave defect in lithography, which is that the beauty and even the number of impressions depend mainly on the skill and industry of the printers. A good press is necessary, to be sure; but even with the best a poor workman will produce nothing but trash, because in this respect lithography is far more difficult than any other printing process."

Despite various improvements, the hand press dominated until 1860 and made the printing of lithographs a relatively slow and cumbersome process.

The period from 1820 to 1855 saw the rapid spread of lithography aided by the arrival of artists and pressmen from Europe with the latest techniques. The business was unstable and artists and lithographers switched from firm to firm, from city to city, or broke away and established their own firms. Firms prospered and went bankrupt; partnerships were made and dissolved sometimes after only a year. Most of the firms did special jobs commissioned for specific purposes. A few like Currier and Ives, the Kelloggs, Baillie, Haskell and Allen, Sarony and Major, and Endicott made prints for general distribution but music covers, maps, book and magazine illustrations, advertisements, real estate plans and commissioned portraits formed the bulk of the output. As wood engraving became cheaper and quicker, it became an important competitor in many of these areas.

One of the first lithographic houses was Barnett and Doolittle of New York. Isaac Doolittle was born in New Haven in 1784 but spent many years in France where he met William Armand Barnet, the son of the American Consul in Paris. They learned lithography in Paris and were in partnership in New York in 1821–1822. In 1822 J. V. Seaman published *A Grammar of Botany* which contained twenty-one plates lithographed by Barnet and Doolittle and is the first American book illustrated with lithographs. The second is *The Timber Merchant's Guide* published in Baltimore in 1823 with thirty lithographs by Henry Stone, a Washington, D.C. lithographer.

By 1824 Chanou and Desobry and Peter Maverick were working in New York as lithographers. Previously, Maverick had been an engraver in New York and in Newark, New Jersey where he was a partner of Asher B. Durand in 1817. By 1825 Anthony Imbert was also at work in New York. Imbert was a former French Naval officer who studied painting and drawing while a prisoner in England during one of Europe's wars. He was chosen to do the lithographs for Colden's *Canal Book,* a *Memoir* of the first passage through the Erie Canal. An extrava-

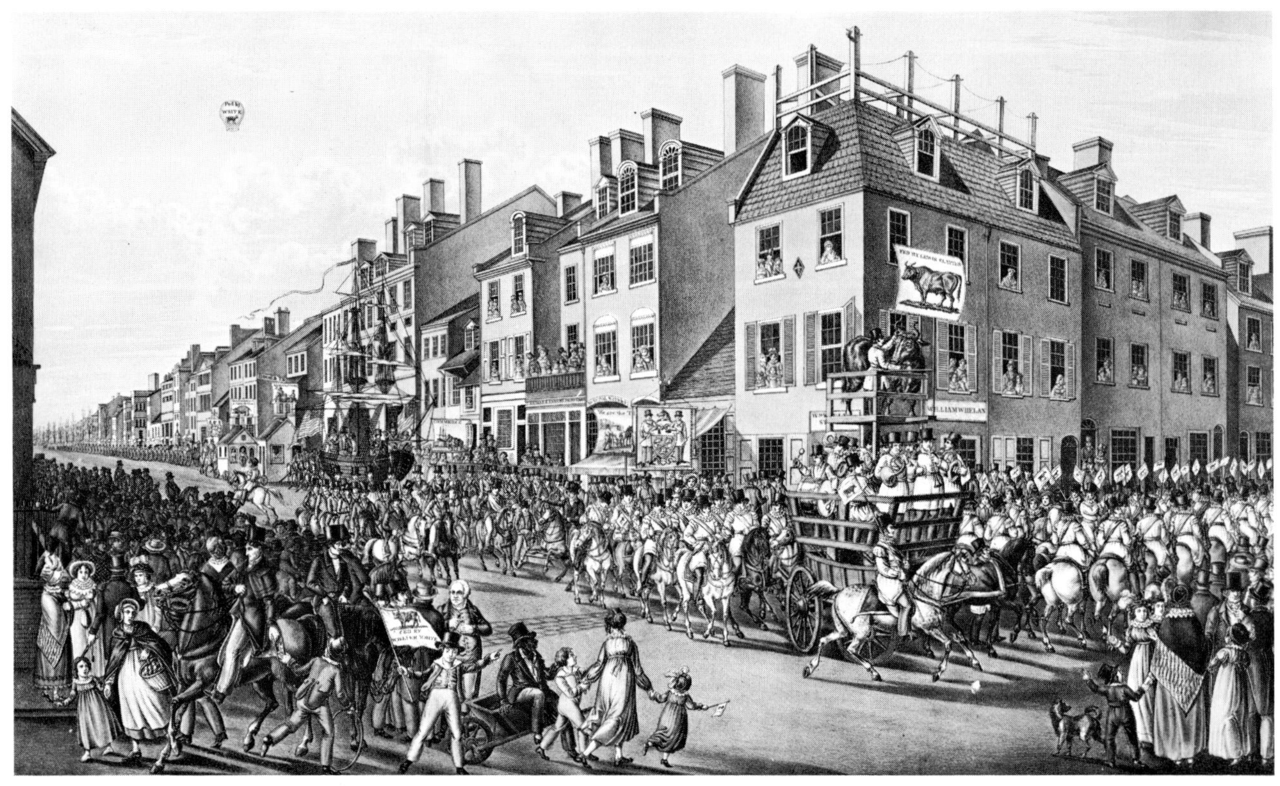

Procession of Victuallers/ of Philadelphia on the 15th of March, 1821, Conducted under the Direction of Mr. William White. "The occasion that gave rise to this Splendid Procession was the conveying of the meat of the stock of exhibition Cattle to Market which for number quality beauty and variety has never been slaughtered at any one time in this or probably any other country, etc." Drawn by J. L. Krimmel, Dubois lithograph, $23\frac{3}{8}$ x $14\frac{1}{8}$ inches (*The Harry T. Peters "America on Stone" Lithography Collection, Smithsonian Institution*)

ganza of festivities marked the event and were illustrated in the *Memoir.*

In 1826 the first major lithographic house in the United States, that of the Pendletons, began in Boston. The Pendletons were the fountainhead from which artists, lithographers and other skilled workers spread out to Philadelphia and New York to work for others or to start their own businesses. William S. Pendleton was a partner of the engraver Abel Bowen in 1825, but joined his brother John the next year to go into lithography. John went to Europe and brought back about a ton of lithographic stone, transfer paper, ink and crayons, as well as a pressman. The silver medal of the Franklin Institute of Philadelphia was awarded the Pendletons in 1826 "for the best specimen of lithography executed in the United States," and the next year Rembrandt Peale received the same award for his portrait of Washington for the firm.

Nathaniel Currier was an apprentice to the Pendletons but left in 1833. John Pendleton left his brother and had a business in New York in 1829 which he sold in 1834 to Stodart, a music publisher, and

Nathaniel Currier. This was the beginning of the firm of Currier and Ives which came to dominate the lithography industry. John Pendleton was also associated with Francis Kearney and Cephas Childs in Philadelphia as Pendleton, Kearney and Childs. In 1831 this became Childs and Inman who were responsible for bringing Peter S. Duval from France. But Duval left them to form a partnership with Lehman and then went on to found a major firm which became a pioneer in color printing.

The artists associated with the Pendletons also fanned out among the fledgling firms. A partial list includes Rembrandt Peale, M. E. D. Brown, J. L. Krimmel, Bass Otis, Henry Inman, Moses Swett, D. C. Johnson, Thomas Badger, Belknap, H. Reinagle, James Kidder, Harding, S. S. Osgood, H. Walton, L. R. Streeter, T. Campbell, T. Wageman, A. H. Hoffy, Wm. R. Browne, S. F. B. Morse, J. V. N. Throop and A. J. Davis.

During the 1830's other firms that began were the Mesiers, Henry R. Robinson, the Endicotts and Bufford in New York, M. E. D. Brown in Philadelphia and the Kelloggs in Hartford. William S. Pendleton sold out to Thomas Moore in 1836 who sold out to Benjamin W. Thayer in 1840. John H. Bufford, who started as an apprentice for Pendleton, worked for Endicott and N. Currier in New York before establishing a business of his own in 1835. He returned to Boston in 1841 to join Thayer in a continuation of the Pendleton firm.

In the forties lithography gained great momentum and many new firms sprang up. Some of those that had started in the thirties, such as Currier, Duval, Robinson, the Kelloggs and Bufford, continued on, while the new entrants included D'Avignon, the Ensigns, Hall & Mooney, Herline, Hoffy, Jones, Ketterlinus, Klauprecht & Menzel, Lane

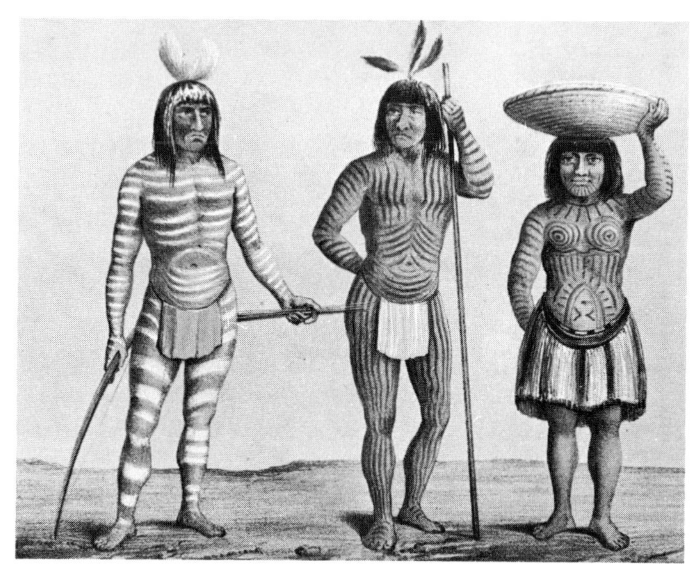

Mojave Indians, illustration by H. B. Mollhausen for Volume III of *Explorations and Surveys for a Railroad Route from the Mississippi River to the Pacific Ocean,* Washington, 1856, lithographed by T. Sinclair, 6 x 9 inches

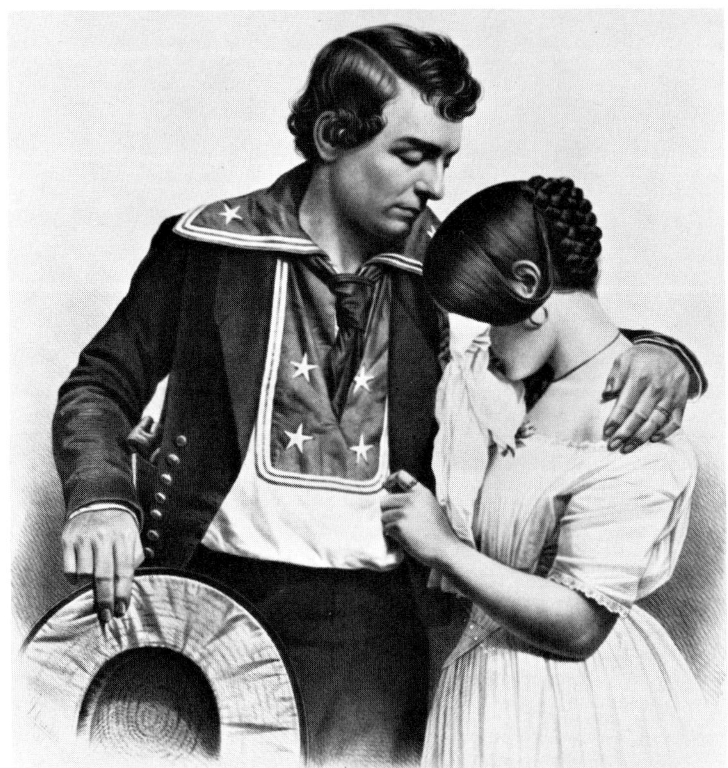

The Sailor's Farewell, from a daguerreotype by Ives, drawn on stone by L. Grozelier, printed by S. W. Chandler & Bro., Boston, 1865, $23\frac{1}{4}$ x $19\frac{1}{2}$ inches (*The Harry T. Peters "America on Stone" Lithography Collection, Smithsonian Institution*)

& Scott, Lewis, Magee, Mayer, Michelin, Nagel & Weingartner, the Palmers, Rease, Sarony, the Sharps, Sinclair, Strong, Thayer, Wagner & McGuigan and Weber. In California where the gold rush lured lithographers as well as prospectors, Britton & Rey and Butler were there to print the action.

Even as the industry was blossoming, developments were taking place which were sowing the seeds of its destruction. The daguerreotype was invented in 1839 and in 1843 Matthew B. Brady opened his studio in New York. A daguerreotype is a one-of-a-kind likeness so that it was not a rival in the sense of being a reproductive medium. Actually, it was a rich source for lithographs since the daguerreotype was used as a model from which large numbers of lithographic portraits were reproduced. Francis D'Avignon lithographed many of Brady's portraits. Eventually, true photographs reproducible from a negative were made practical and raised many questions about the function of lithography and other print media. Brady opened a photography studio in 1855. Napoleon Sarony became interested in photography while still a lithographer and set up a studio in 1867 or 1868. The invention of the half-tone plate in the 1880's with the great commercial advantage of

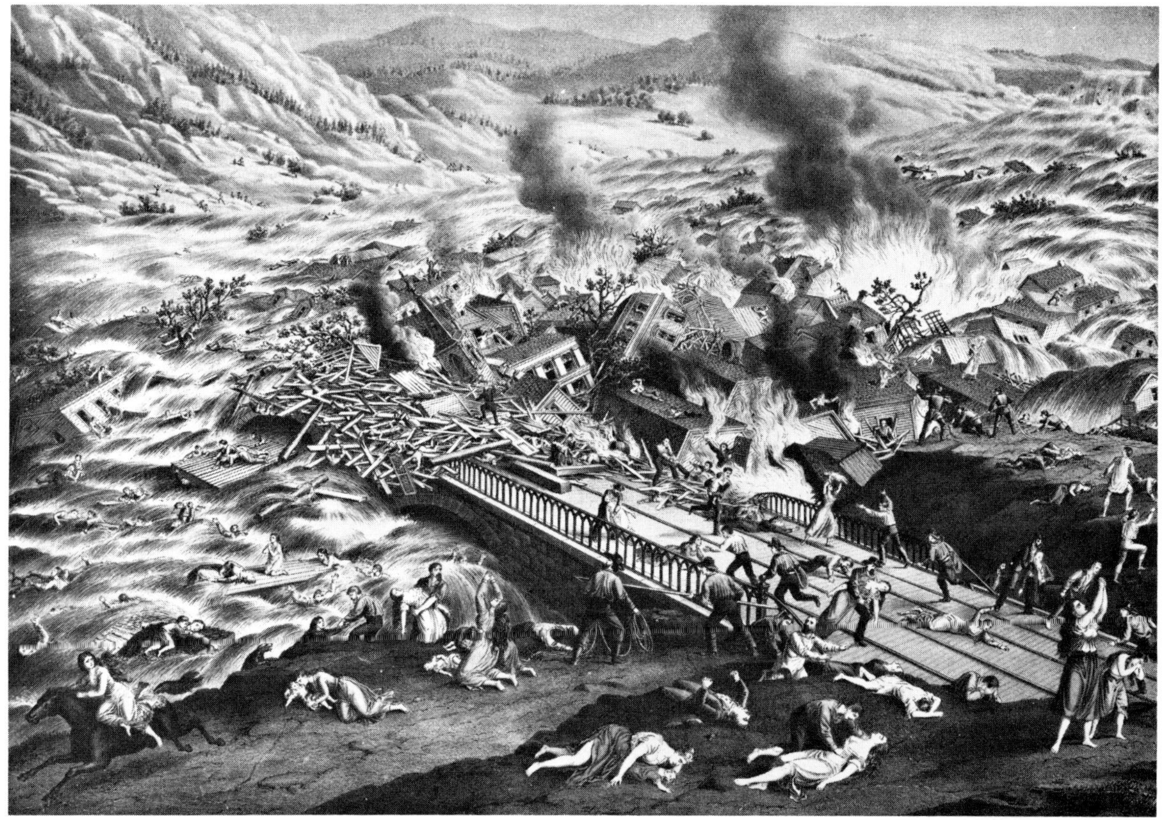

The Great Conemaugh Valley Disaster, Flood & Fire at Johnstown, Pa., chromolithograph by Kurz and Allison, 1890, $17\frac{1}{2}$ x 25 inches (*The Harry T. Peters "America on Stone" Lithography Collection, Smithsonian Institution*)

printing in the same press as type was a mortal blow to stone lithography.

As soon as the basics of black and white were mastered, the search was on for color lithography. William Sharp experimented with color printing in the 1840's. Peter S. Duval was working on the same problem and in 1850 and 1851 was awarded prizes by the Franklin Institute. Louis Rosenthal, also in Philadelphia, produced the first set of chromolithographed book illustrations receiving the Franklin Institute prize in 1851 for chromolithography. Louis Prang, in Boston, was an early worker with printed colors. It was a slow and tedious process. A different stone was used for each color which resulted in the intractable problem of lining up the stones so as to put each color in its proper place on the picture. One way was to put the stone in a wooden frame with brass pins which would puncture the paper at the corners of the picture. These pinholes then served as guides for subsequent stones. In time, these chromolithographs became wildly colorful and were widely used for advertising. Together with the steam press which took over in the '70's and '80's, the character and thrust of lithography was changed.

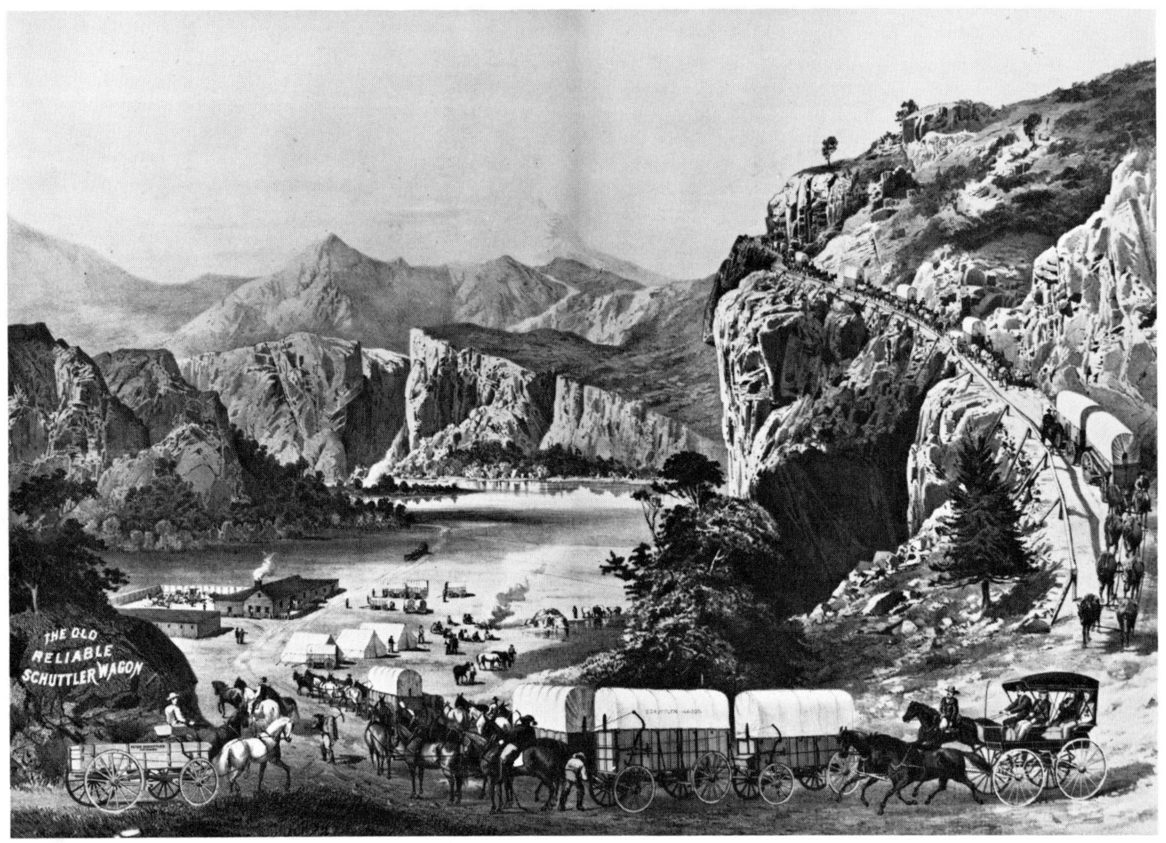

The Old Reliable Schuttler Wagon, chromolithograph. Advertisement of Peter Schuttler, wagon maker of Chicago, Clay & Co., Chicago, $17\frac{1}{4}$ x $24\frac{1}{4}$ inches (*The Harry T. Peters "America on Stone" Lithography Collection, Smithsonian Institution*)

The Artists

William Dunlap wrote in 1837 in his *History of the Arts of Design:*

> "The first lithographic establishment of which I have any knowledge was made amidst many difficulties by Mr. Imbert of New York. They are now almost innumerable throughout the United States. But however beautiful or perfect the plates are, the credit is transferred to the master of the establishment, and the artist is sunk. This must change. The artist must be announced and must be master.

Mr. Dunlap's indignation was justified. The artists worked anonymously for the most part. The industry served artists somewhat in the same way as vaudeville served stage performers. It was a place where beginners could be trained and find employment. Some of these rose to stardom and left the industry, some achieved enough status to be given credit on the plates and some spent their lives working without any recognition. Some of our major artists who worked with or for lithographic firms at some time include Rembrandt Peale, William Rimmer, Thomas Birch, Fitz Hugh Lane, Winslow Homer, Thomas Doughty, Henry Inman and George Catlin.

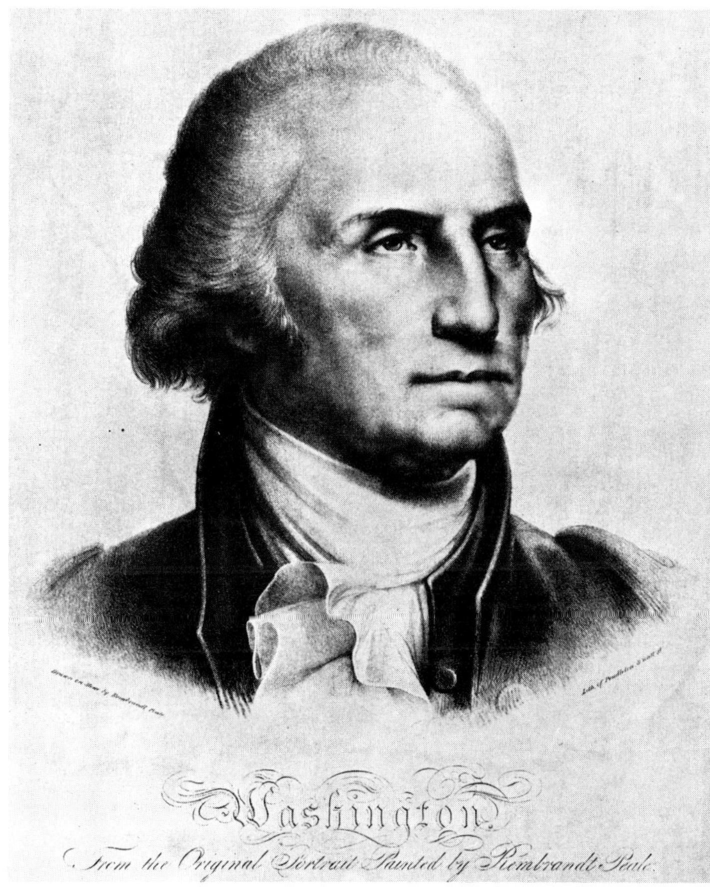

Washington/ From the Original Portrait Painted by Rembrandt Peale, drawn on stone by Rembrandt Peale, lithographed by Pendleton, 16¾ x 12⅝ inches (*The Harry T. Peters "America on Stone" Lithography Collection, Smithsonian Institution*)

Rembrandt Peale was one of the first American artists to study lithography seriously. His first published lithograph is the *Head of Lord Byron* but he is best known for his portraits of Washington. Thomas Doughty did illustrations for the *Cabinet of Natural History and Rural Sports,* first issued in monthly parts and later in three volumes. M. E. D. Brown also supplied illustrations. The animal prints in these volumes became source material for Currier and Ives and other firms.

Fitz Hugh Lane was apprenticed to the Pendleton Brothers where he worked on trade cards and music sheet covers. His later development as one of our major marine painters is evidenced in his lithographic views of Gloucester and New Bedford and portraits of steam packets. Winslow Homer was apprenticed to Bufford in 1855 at age nineteen. He was assigned the usual apprentice tasks, working on music sheet covers and the then-popular album or trade cards. Upon the completion of his apprenticeship, he left, vowing never again to be chained to a desk. In 1863 Homer's *Campaign Sketches* of the Civil War were put on stone in his New York studio, and then printed by Louis Prang. Prang also issued as chromolithographs a series of twenty-four album cards by Homer,

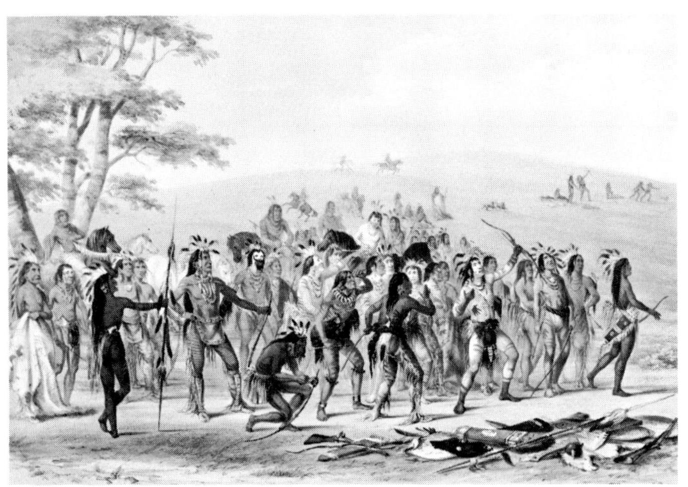

Archery of the Mandans, by George Catlin, lithographed by Day & Haghe, London, 1845 (*Courtesy Kenneth Nebenzahl, Inc.*)

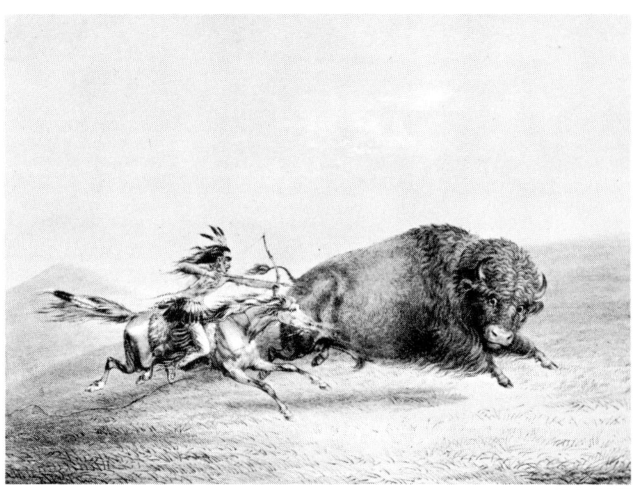

Buffalo Hunt Chase, by George Catlin, lithographed by Day & Haghe, London, 1845. From the *North American Indian Portfolio* (*Courtesy Kenneth Nebenzahl, Inc.*)

all on the same subject of camp life except for a cartoon and a sentimental. These are signed only with the initials "W. H."

George Catlin had some experience with lithography as early as 1825 when six of his prints were included in the famous Colden *Canal Book* commemorating the completion of the Erie Canal. After years of painting and studying Indian customs, his *North American Portfolio* was published in 1844. The twenty-five lithographs from Catlin's sketches were made in London by Day and Haghe, "Lithographers to the Queen." The New York firm of J. A. Ackerman (not to be confused with the English Rudolph Ackerman) reissued the *Portfolio* with additional plates in 1845. Catlin's paintings and lithographs became the convention for the representation of the West and many copied him.

But for each artist who achieved his reputation outside of lithography, many more remained essentially lithographic artists. Portraiture was an important area in which some artists specialized. Charles Fenderich used the medium to realize textures and surfaces as well as character. In 1837 he embarked upon an ambitious project to portray living American statesmen. Albert Newsam, a deaf-mute artist, was known for producing exact likenesses from life and copying daguerreotypes with great precision. The *Portrait Gallery of Distinguished American Citizens* contains silhouettes by William H. Brown and was lithographed by E. B. and E. C. Kellogg in 1845. Francis D'Avignon, the leading portrait lithographer of New York City, did *The Gallery of Illustrious Americans* from daguerreotypes by Brady. Others were Joseph E. Baker, who did theatrical portraits for Bufford and Edward W. Clay, who did brilliant satirical portraits for numerous lithographers.

Other artists developed specialties in other areas. Charles Parsons was responsible for many of the ship, boat and railroad subjects for Endicott and Currier and Ives. Theodore Marsden turned out sporting and horse subjects for Goupil and Bufford. Hugh Reinagle, a New York theatre-scene painter, was the artist for a number of important early views. Farm and Indian scenes are credited to F. O. C. Darley. John B. Bachelder was important for Civil War prints. Edwin Whitefield produced a large series of views of American cities executed with great attention to detail. The list could be extended greatly, but little is known about some of those except for a name which appears here and there on a print.

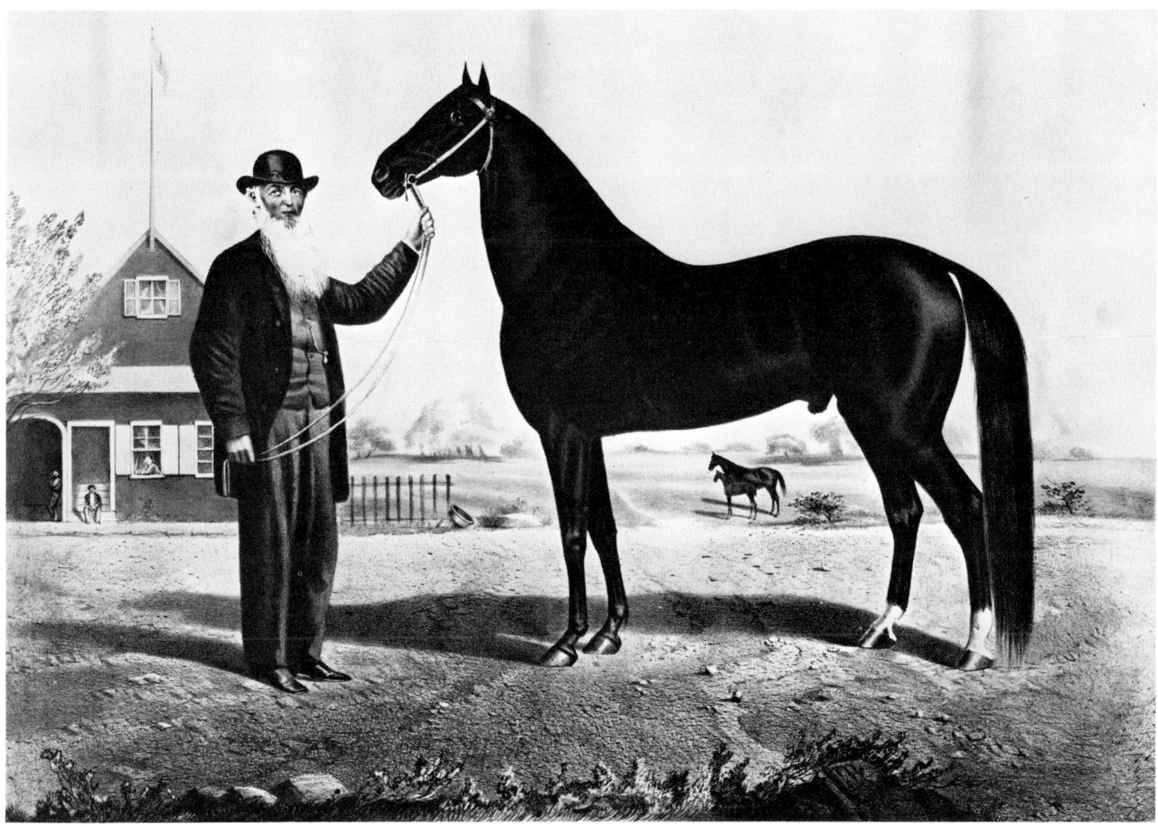

Hambletonian, painted by Theodore Marsden, drawn on stone by Henry A. Thomas, lithographed and published by Henry C. Eno, New York, 1866, 19 x 25 inches (*The Harry T. Peters "America on Stone" Lithography Collection, Smithsonian Institution*)

The Lithographers

Lithographer is an imprecise term which is variously used to indicate the artist who made the design, the artist who put the design on stone, the person who pulled the impression or the firm that published the lithograph. In fact, the roles were often interchangeable. There were, however, individuals whose speciality was putting the work on stone and who occasionally merited the credit "On stone by." In lithographs that were later to be hand-colored, the designs and outlines had to be simplified so as to lend themselves readily to coloring.

The easiest way to classify lithographs is by the firm that lithographed them. Although many old lithographs are found without identification as to maker, when there is a credit line, it is most often that of the firm. Accordingly, a list follows with a brief summary of the business careers of some nineteenth-century lithographic firms of greatest interest to the collector. The prints mentioned are under no circumstances a complete or even representative listing. They are a scattering of the rare, attractive, historically important or just typical in order to give some indication of the range or thrust of the firm's output. Most issued so many that a complete listing would be impossible.

List of Lithographic Firms

James S. Baillie 1847–1855 New York City

James S. Baillie was selling picture frames in New York in 1838, was an artist in 1841, and from 1843–1847 a colorer for N. Currier. His own lithographs were modeled after those of Currier in aiming at a wide popular market and use many of the same subjects. Comics and sentimentals were put out in large numbers, such as *Life and Age of Man, Life and Age of Woman* and *Son of Temperance.* Some other categories include the historical with *Surrender of Cornwallis, The Landing of Columbus,* and *Perry's Victory on Lake Erie;* the political with *Grand National Whig Banner, Z. Taylor, M. Fillmore;* the sporting with *The Great Fight between Tom Hyer & Yankee Sullivan, for $10,000* and the marine with *South Sea Whale Fishery* and *North Sea Whale Fishery,* There are also many views and portraits. In general, the subjects are not so well done as Currier's but appear to have been issued in large numbers.

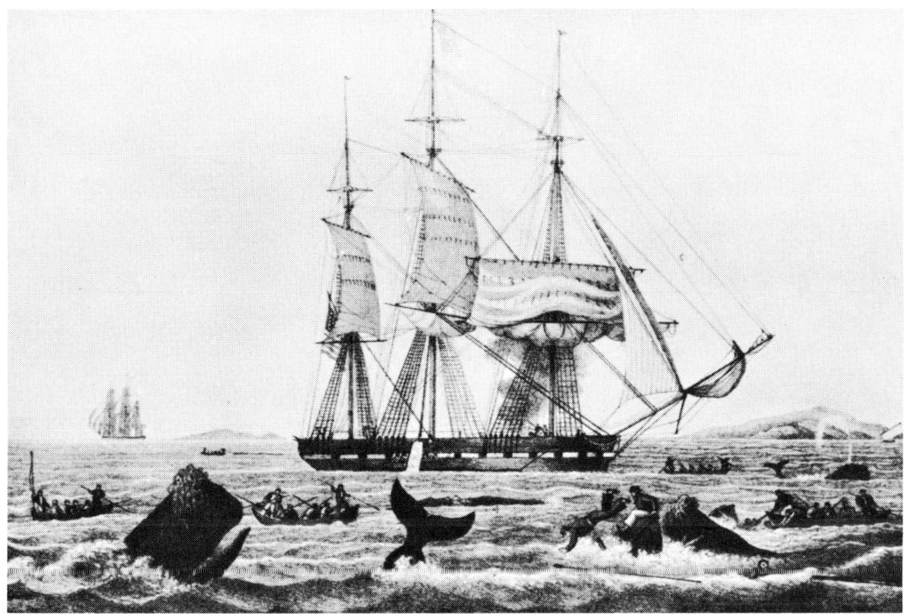

James Baillie, lithographer and publisher, New York, *South Sea Whale Fishery,* small folio

Julius Bien 1850–1868 New York City

Bien was born in Germany in 1826 and was one of the large number of people who emigrated as a result of the revolution of 1848. He set himself up in business in New York with one lithographic hand press, producing book illustrations including some technical work on locomotive boilers. In 1860 he began work on the reissue of Audubon's *Birds of America,* making chromolithographs by transfer from the copper plates. This project was interrupted by the Civil War and never completed. Bien also made some New York City views, a view of Denver, and a print of a ten-wheel freight locomotive. His interest in cartography led to the production of large numbers of maps of the new surveys in the West for the Federal government. He gained the reputation of being the finest American cartographer of the nineteenth century. He died in 1909.

John T. Bowen 1834–1838 New York City, 1839–1856 Philadelphia

Bowen was born in England around 1801 and died in Philadelphia in 1856, or thereabouts. Bowen was a print colorer before going into business with C. Bowen in 1835, a short-lived partnership, since by 1836 he was in business by himself. *The Great Fire of the City of New-York, 16 December, 1835* was published in 1836. His series of twenty views, *The Panorama and Views of Philadelphia and Its Vicinity*

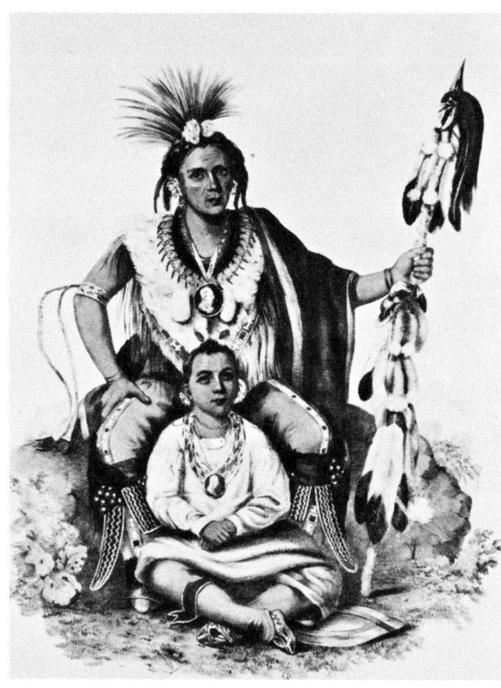

J. T. Bowen, *Keokuk/ Chief of the Sacs,* drawn, printed and colored at J. T. Bowen's, published by F. W. Greenough, Philadelphia, 1836, medium folio. From McKenney and Hall's *History of the Indian Tribes of North America.*

after J. C. Wild was first issued in 1838 and reissued in a larger size in 1848. Other noteworthy prints are his view of the Great Falls of the Missouri and *Log Cabin Politicians,* about the 1840 presidential campaign of W. H. Harrison. Bowen did the plates for McKenney & Hall's *History of the Indian Tribes of North America,* 1838–1844. The plates of this book frequently appear as free prints. He also did cartoons, portraits and book illustrations. *John T. Bowen's United States Drawing Book* contains thirty-seven views among which are those of Harvard, Yale, Albany and Philadelphia. Bowen lithographed the plates for the octavo edition of Audubon's *Birds of America* 1840–1844; the *Viviparous Quadrupeds of North America,* large folio 1942–1848 and some of the octavo edition in 1849.

Britton & Rey et al

Joseph Britton 1847 New York City;
Pollard & Britton 1852, *Britton & Rey* 1852–1858, *Britton & Co.* 1859–1866 all in San Francisco

Joseph Britton was born in England in 1825 and died in San Francisco in 1901. He was a lithographer in New York before going to California at the time of the gold rush. After a partnership with J. C. Pollard he entered in an association with his brother-in-law,

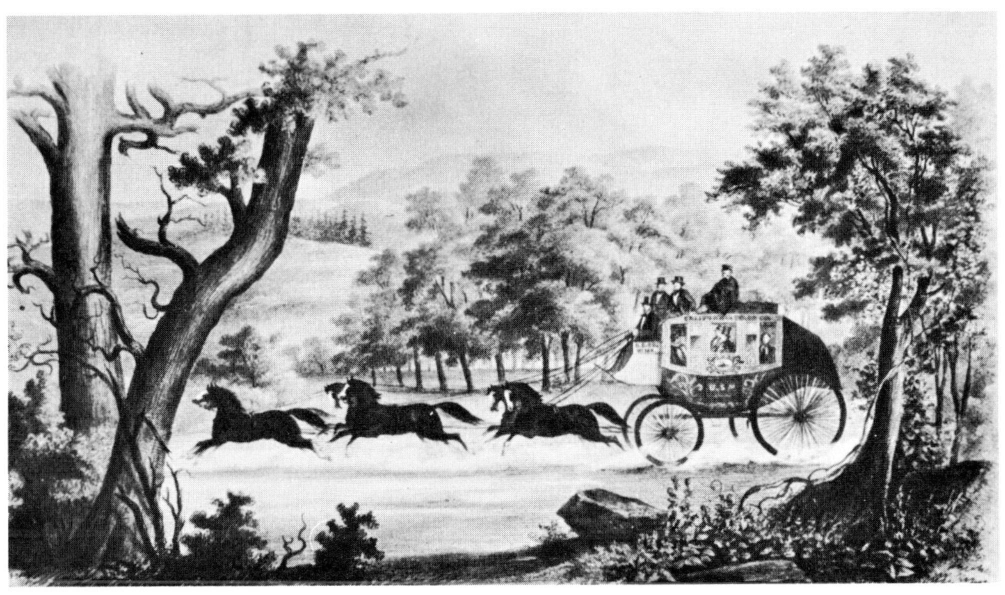

Britton & Co., *California Stage Company/ Incorporated December 1853,* Lithographed by Britton & Co., San Francisco, large folio

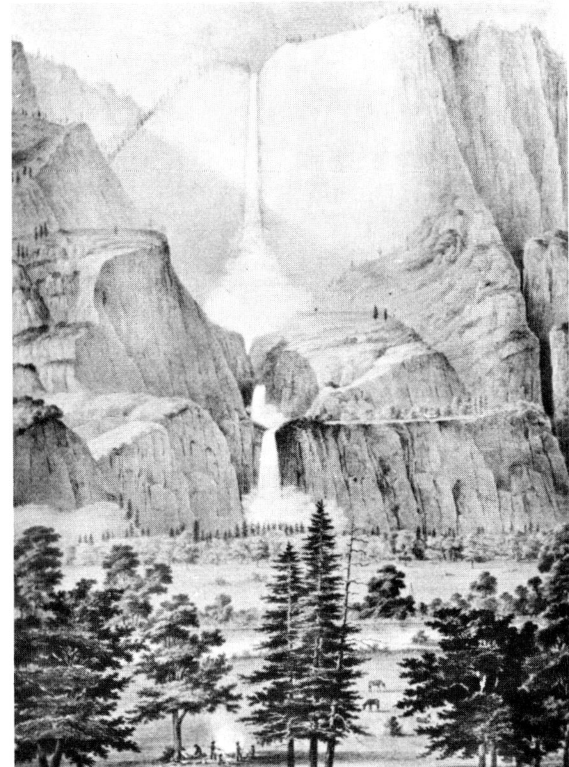

Britton & Rey, *The Yo-Semite Falls,* sketched from nature by T. A. Ayres, printed by Britton & Rey. On stone by Kuchel & Dresel, San Francisco, published by Hutchings & Rosenfield, 1855, large folio

Jacques J. Rey, a former Alsatian. They then went into the plumbing business with a man named O'Brien. The following year Britton returned to lithography with Britton & Co. Britton and Rey are notable as the lithographers of the gold rush and California which they illustrated with a long series of views. Some titles documenting this colorful period are *California Stage Company, Incorporated December, 1853; Certificate of Membership. Committee of Vigilance of San Francisco,* 1856; *View of Chinese, Tuolumne County,* an 1852 view of a camp of Chinese laborers; *View of the Golden Gate, Entrance to the Bay of San Francisco,* an 1852 view of the notorious mining and gambling town.

John H. Bufford et al 1835–1839 New York City, 1840-c. 1871 Boston
B. W. Thayer and J. E. Moody 1841–1842
B. W. Thayer 1843–1844
A. G. Dawes 1845
B. W. Thayer 1851

John Bufford began his career as an apprentice under William S. Pendleton in Boston and then went to New York where he worked for Endicott and Nathaniel Currier. After his return to Boston, he started the firm of J. H. Bufford & Co.

The business grew to be one of the major ones of the period with a vast output, both in kind and number. The *Boston Evening Traveler* of March 18, 1864 states that "the firm has general agencies

J. H. Bufford, *On the Prairie,* Chas. Wimar, Pinxit. On stone by L. Grozelier, printed at J. H. Bufford's, published by J. E. Tilton & Co., Boston, 1860

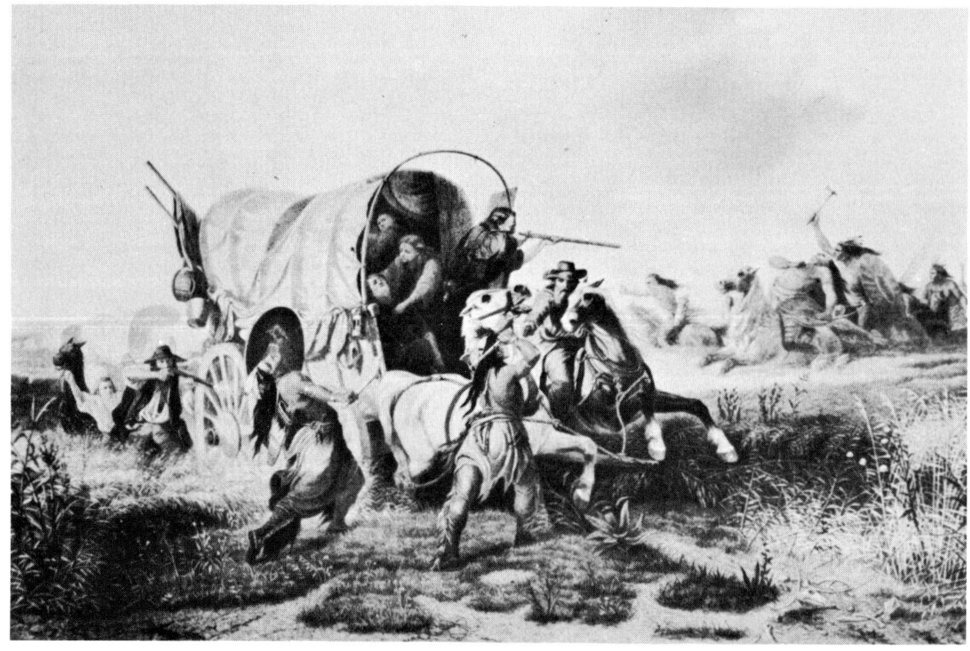

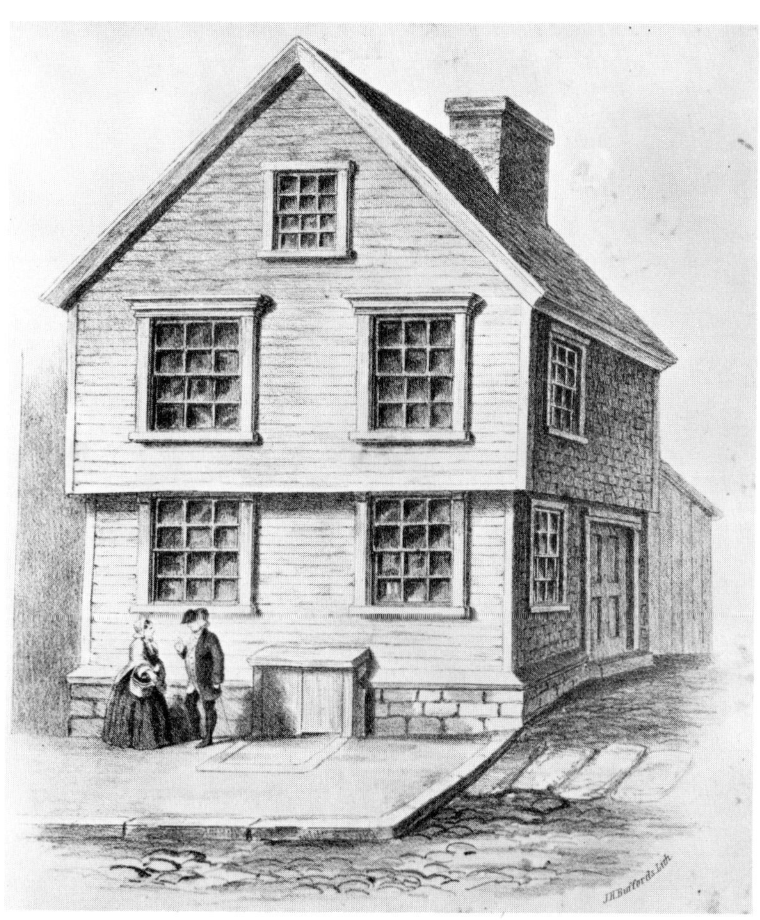

J. H. Bufford, *Birthplace of Franklin in Milk Street* (*The Metropolitan Museum of Art, Gift of William H. Huntington, 1883*)

in all the large cities and subordinate salesrooms in myriads of towns" and that the house has more than a hundred employees and that it stands at "the very head of the business."

Among the artists who worked for Bufford are F. D'Avignon, L. Grozelier, Alexander J. Davis, John B. Bachelder, Theodore Marsden, J. P. Newell, Benjamin Russell and Charles Wimar. While an apprentice from 1855–1857, Winslow Homer drew *Massachusetts Senate, 1856,* which includes forty-two excellent portraits and a small view of Boston.

There are such a large number of prints that only a random sample can be given. The large folio *Skating in Central Park, New York,* 1861, portrays many colorful skating costumes and is as desirable as the Currier of the same subject. Other New York City views include the large folios *Merchant's Exchange, New York; Fifth Avenue Hotel, New York;* the medium folio *St. Mark's Church, New York;* and the small folio *Hanover Buildings, Hanover Square, N.Y.* Boston subjects include *Hancock House, Beacon St. Boston, Mass.; Boston Massacre* and a set of five views of Beacon Hill. There is a rare 1836 view of

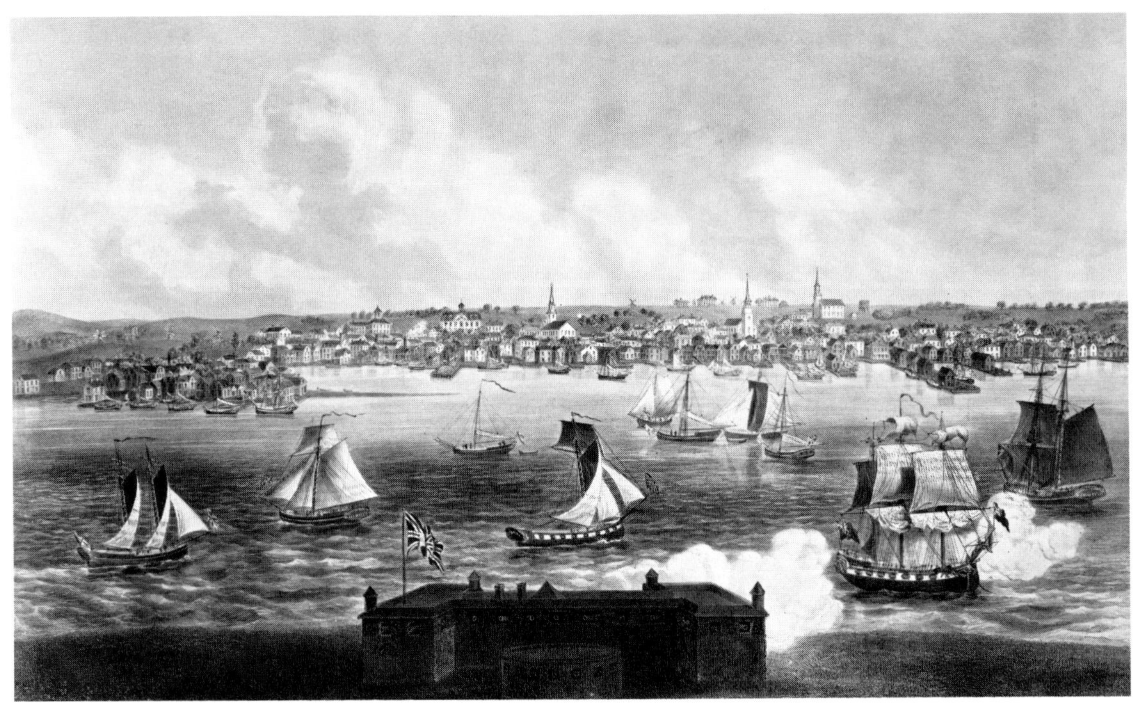

J. H. Bufford, lithographers, *Newport, R.I. in 1730,* From the painting and on stone by J. P. Newell, 1864, $17\frac{5}{8}$ x $27\frac{1}{2}$ inches

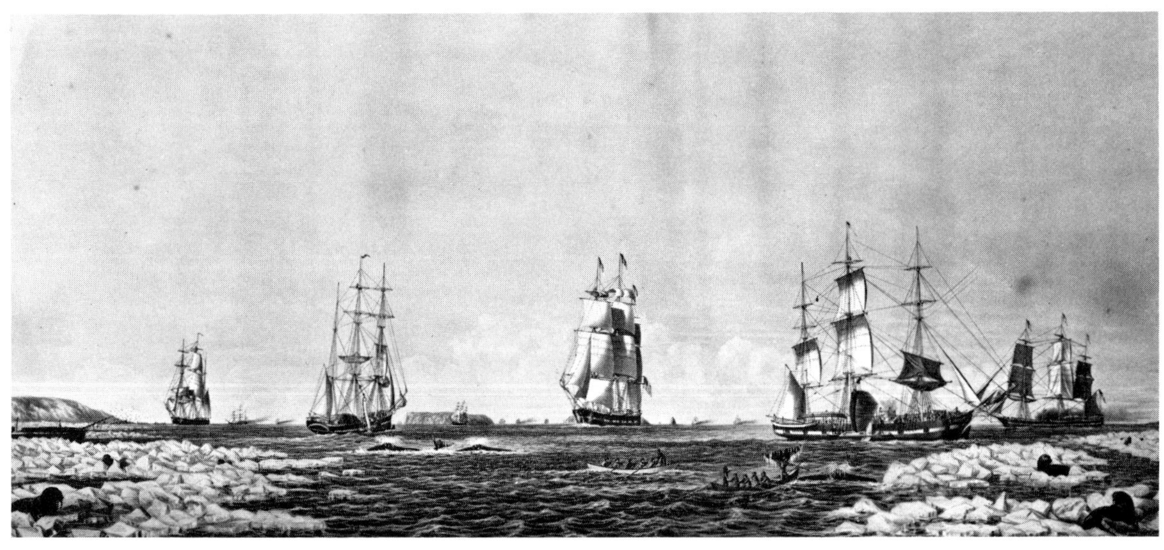

J. H. Bufford, *Right Whaling in Behering Straits and Artic Ocean with its Varieties,* from drawing by Benjamin Russell, 1871, $16\frac{1}{2}$ x $32\frac{7}{8}$ inches (*The Harry T. Peters "America on Stone" Lithography Collection, Smithsonian Institution*)

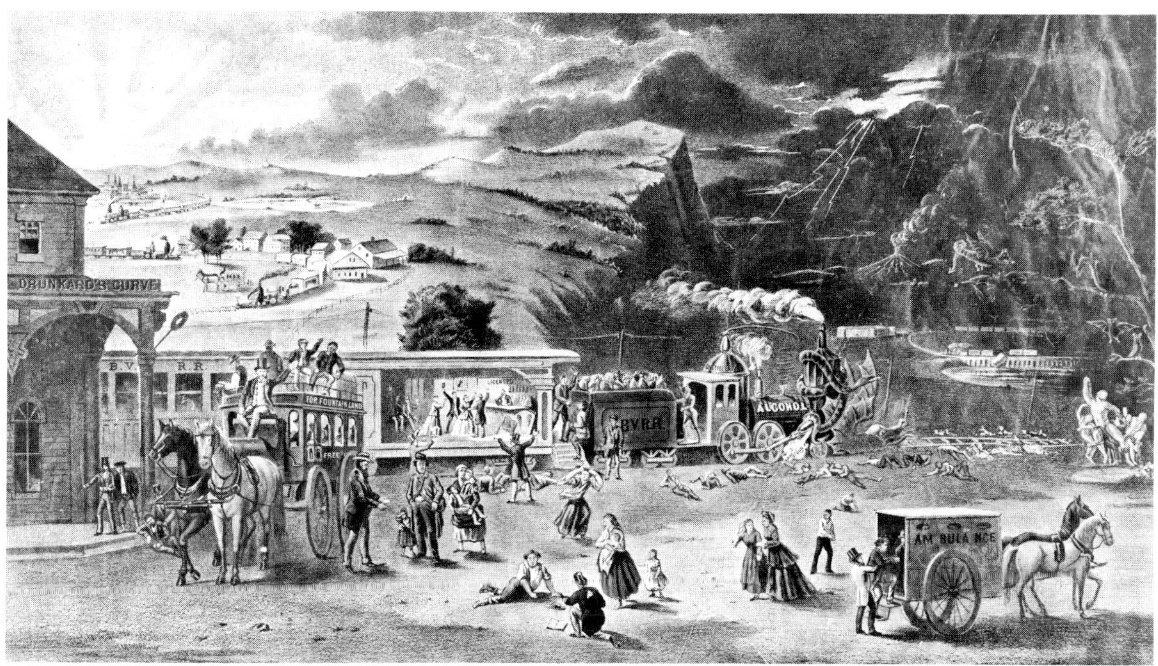

J. H. Bufford's Sons, *Black Valley Railroad*, temperance print showing express from Drunkard's Curve pulled by "Alcohol," 12 x 19 inches (*The Harry T. Peters "America on Stone" Lithography Collection, Smithsonian Institution*)

Princeton University. Another skating print in small folio is *Jamaica Pond, 1858* (Massachusetts). Bufford issued a number of sets of views among which are views of the Adirondack Mountains and *Scenery of the White Mountains*, 1848, with sixteen large folio plates. Alexander J. Davis drew a set of architectural views which were lithographed in 1837 in large folio with the title *Rural Residences.*

An outstanding western was painted by Charles Wimar, *On the Prairie,* and ranks with any of the other western prints. Some of the best whaling lithographs are the Bufford large folio *Right Whaling in Behering Straits & Arctic Ocean with its Varieties* and *Sperm Whaling with its Varieties,* both from drawings by Benjamin Russell. There is also a set of five medium folios of whaling subjects which includes *Abandonment of the Whalers in the Arctic Ocean, Sept. 1871.*

Bufford also produced Civil War, naval and marine prints. The large folio *Missionary Packet "Morning Star" Passing Boston Light* is from a painting by C. Drew; *Moonlight View of the Action off Anton Lizardo, March 6th, 1860* after Thompson and the *Bombardment of Fort Hatteras & Clark by the U.S. Fleet* is from a drawing by seaman Francis Garland of the U.S. Ship Cumberland.

The famous horses of the period were represented by *Black Hawk—Lady Suffolk* from the painting by Theodore Marsden;

Sherman Black Hawk from a painting by Charles Humphreys and the *Famous Roan Horse Capt. McGowan.* In addition, Bufford turned out the usual types of sentimental, temperance, advertising, music sheet cover, book and magazine illustrations. Bufford prints are a favorite of collectors with many fine subjects executed with distinction.

Cephas G. Childs et al 1829–1845 Philadelphia
Pendleton, Kearney & Childs c. 1829 or 1830
Childs & Inman 1831–1833
Childs & Lehman 1835–1836

Childs was born in Bucks County, Pennsylvania in 1793 and died in 1871. His father was a farmer. Both parents died when he was young. In 1812 he was apprenticed to an engraver, Gideon Fairman, but the next year enlisted with the Washington Guards of Philadelphia. After serving in the war, he returned to Philadelphia and became an engraver. He exhibited in the Pennsylvania Academy in 1824 and from 1827–1830 engraved and published his views of Philadelphia. He joined John Pendleton and Francis Kearney, a banknote engraver, to form the firm of Pendleton, Kearney, & Childs in 1829 or 1830. Childs went to Europe in 1831 to study lithography and upon his return joined the painter, Henry Inman, in the firm of Childs & Inman. They brought P. S. Duval from France who also became an important lithographer. Others associated with Childs were G. H. Lehman, Albert Newsam and T. & H. Doughty. Injuries sustained on board ship during his 1831 voyage caused him to give up much of his lithographic work and he later engaged in various aspects of commercial publishing.

His views and portraits are of greatest interest, with Philadelphia represented by *Fairmount Waterworks from the Forebay,* 1833 and *Skating. Scene on the River Delaware at Philadelphia, Feb. 12th, 1831.* Washington views include *Mount Vernon,* T. Doughty, del., from a drawing by H. Reinagle, 1832; *Northeast View of the Capitol; Southwest View of the President's House* after Lehman and *Tomb of Washington,* J. R. Smith, del., on stone by Howard Doughty. Among the portraits are *Mrs. Inman,* by Inman after T. Sully, 1831; *DeWitt Clinton,* 1830; *Henry Clay* by Newsam after J. Wood; *David Crockett* 1834 and the celebrated actress *Fanny Kemble* after Sully.

The Childs output covered a wide range of subjects including historicals, naval views, animal studies, sentimentals, caricatures, theatricals and advertisements. Their work for *The Cabinet of Natural History and American Rural Sports,* 1830–1831 and other pioneering publications was an important contribution.

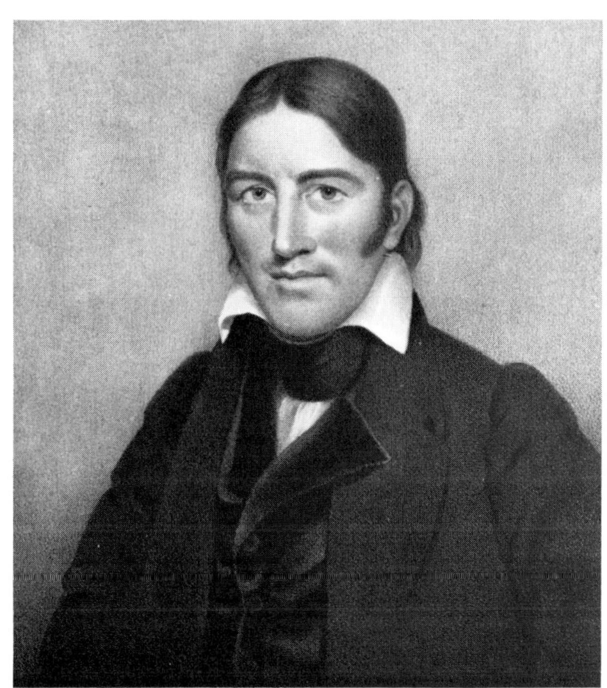

Childs & Lehman, *David Crockett,* Painted by S. S. Osgood, Childs & Lehman, lithographers, Philadelphia, 1834, $9\frac{1}{4}$ x $7\frac{1}{2}$ inches (*The Harry T. Peters "America on Stone" lithography Collection, Smithsonian Institution*)

Nathaniel Currier and Currier and Ives

This, by far the most prolific and successful firm, is covered in a separate chapter.

Peter S. Duval et al, 1835–1860, Philadelphia;
Lehman & Duval 1835–1837
Huddy & Duval 1839–1843
Peter S. Duval 1843–1855
Rosenthal, Duval & Prang 1856
P. S. Duval & Son 1858–1879

Childs & Inman brought Peter S. Duval from France in 1831 to superintend their lithography. Duval was an early experimenter with color printing and in 1850 and 1851 was awarded prizes by the Franklin Institute for his contributions. In 1850, he printed in oil a huge chromolithograph, *Washington's Triumphal Entry into New York, November 25th, 1783.*

Aside from his achievements in color printing, Duval issued many fine lithographs. Some of the artists who worked with him are Albert Newsam, Charles Fenderich, W. J. Hubbard, A. Kollner, and Francis D'Avignon. The views include a very large *Bird's Eye View of Philadelphia,* J. Bachman, del.; *View of the Wire Bridge at Fairmount; Southwest View of Lancaster in Pennsylvania; Baltimore in 1752*

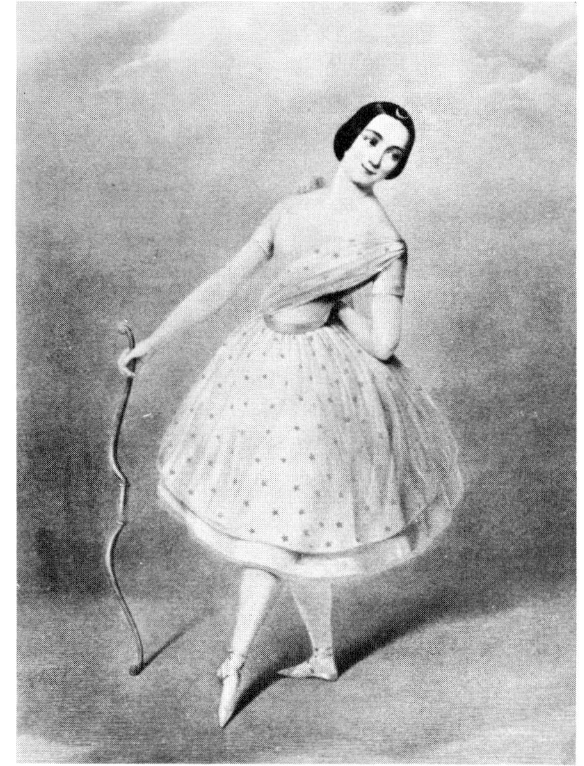

P. S. Duval, *Miss Mary Ann Lee, as Beatrix in la Jolie fille de Gande,* painted from life and on stone by F. D'Avignon, P. S. Duval Lithograph, Philadelphia. Mary Ann Lee was a dancer who made her debut in 1839 and continued as a performer through the 1840's

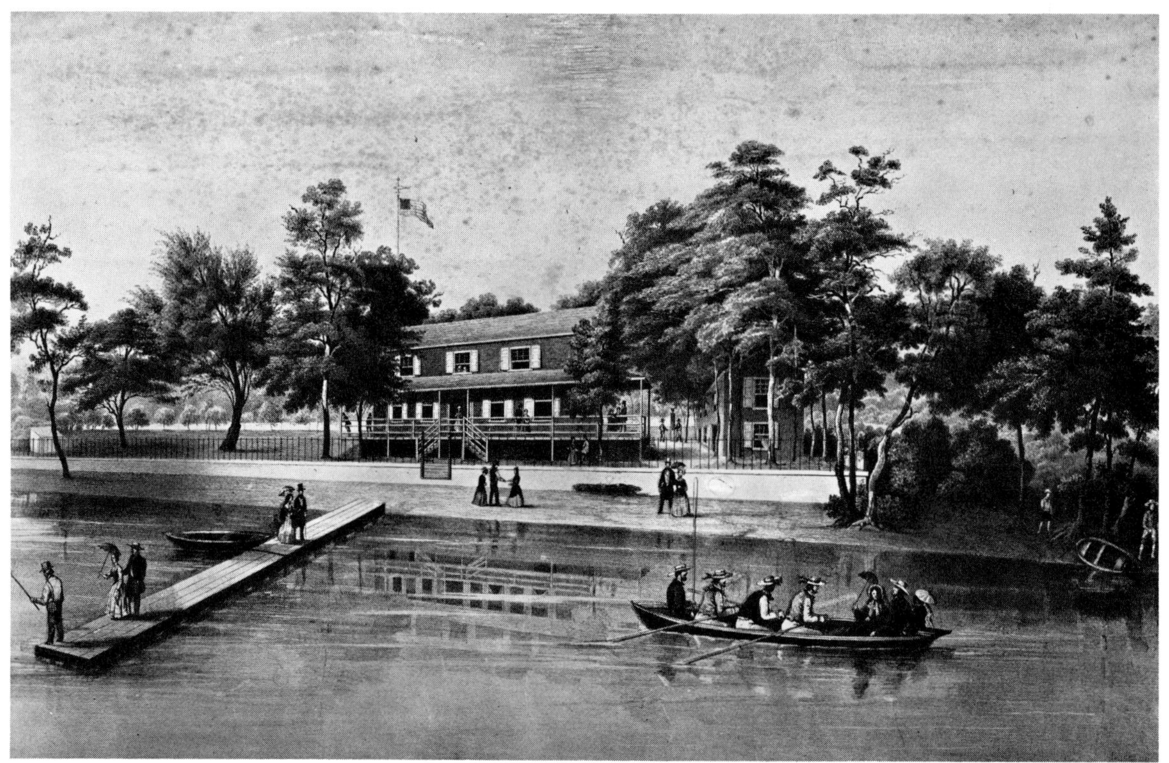

P. S. Duval, *Tammany Fish House on the Pea Shore, R. Delaware,* drawn from nature by Thomas S. Scott, P. S. Duval's Steam Lithograph Press, Philadelphia, $17\frac{1}{2}$ x $25\frac{1}{4}$ inches (*The Harry T. Peters "America on Stone" Lithography Collection, Smithsonian Institution*)

and *Louisville, Ky.* Among the large number of portraits are the first eleven presidents by Albert Newsam; *Miss Mary Anne Lee as Beatrix in La Jolie Fille de Gande,* a portrait of the dancer by D'Avignon, 1839 and four plates by August Kollner for a *Life of Washington* published in 1842.

There are also military and naval prints of the Mexican and Civil Wars; *Meeting of Generals Grant and Lee Preparatory to the Surrender of General Lee; The Artillery Corps of Philadelphia Greys* and *U.S. Ship North Carolina off Cape Horn, April 22, 1837.* Often mentioned as one of the best fishing lithographs is the large folio *Tammany Fish House on the Pea Shore, R. Delaware,* drawn from nature by Thos. S. Scott. A small fishing print is *Shad Fishing (Taking up the Net) On the Delaware, opposite Philadelphia. Scene at the U.S. Agricultural Society Fair, Philadelphia, 1856* is a lively and colorful print. Duval also produced many miscellaneous prints, separately and to be included as illustrations in scientific and general publications.

The Endicotts et al

George Endicott 1828–1829, Baltimore
Endicott & Swett 1830–1831 Baltimore
Endicott & Swett 1832–1834 New York City
George Endicott 1834–1844 New York City
G & W Endicott 1845–1848
Sarah L. Endicott, widow of George 1849
William Endicott & Co. 1849–1851
Endicott & Co. 1852–1886 (Francis Endicott 1853–1886)
George Endicott, II 1887–1891

The mid-century advertisements of the Endicotts claim that the company was founded in 1828. In this year George Endicott was a lithographer in Baltimore. Around 1830, he was joined by Moses Swett who had previously worked for the Pendletons. In December of 1831 the pair moved to New York City. After Swett's departure from the firm in 1834, it became mainly a family affair. George was joined by his brother William in 1845 to form G & W Endicott. After George's death in 1848, William continued until his own death in 1851. Then Sarah, George's widow, organized Endicott & Co. with their son, Francis, taking her place in 1853. After Francis' death in 1886, George II took over for a few years but abdicated to go into the insurance business.

The longevity of the firm is mirrored in the vast quantities of lithographs issued by them. Endicott & Swett's output includes *Battle of North Point, near Baltimore, Sept. 12, 1814; Columbus & Sally Miller . . . Centreville Track, May 9th, 1830;* and the extraordinary

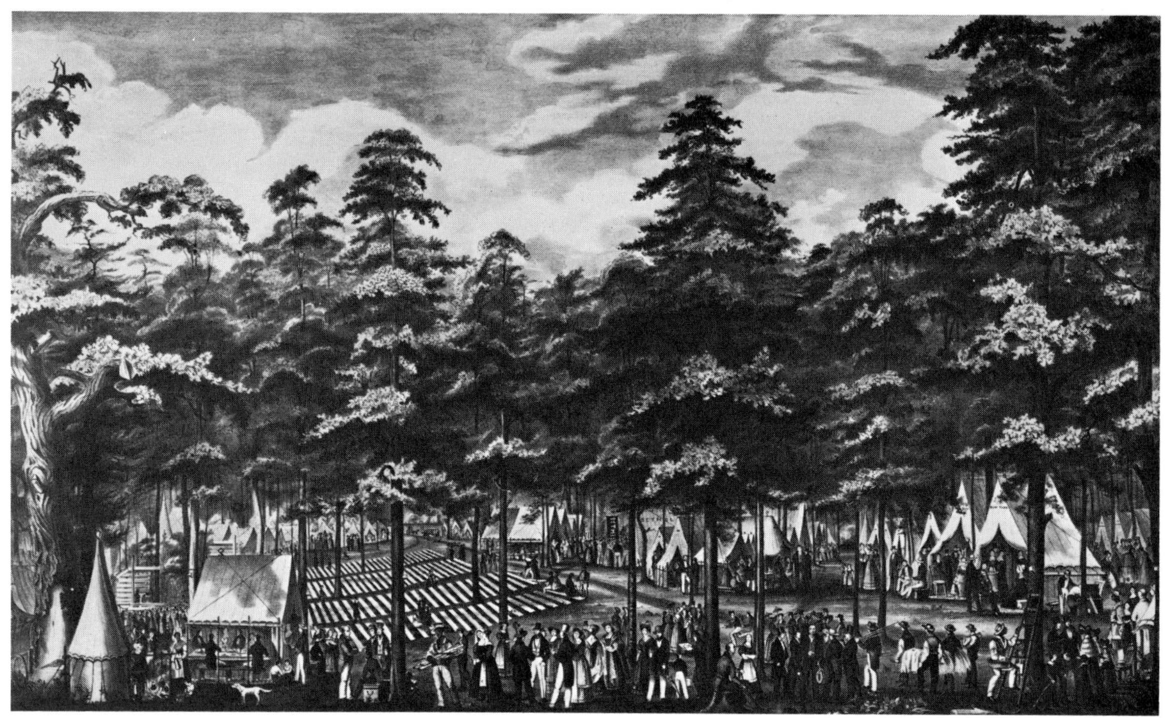

George Endicott, *Sing-Sing Camp Meeting, 1838. . .*, painted by Joseph B. Smith, Lithographics, of Endicott, New York, 1839, $19\frac{1}{4}$ x $31\frac{5}{8}$ inches (*The Harry T. Peters "America on Stone" Lithography Collection, Smithsonian Institution*)

Baptising Scene. Near the White Fort Hudson River, New-York, 1834 showing an adult baptism near the Battery. Among George Endicott's views is a group by J. W. Hill: *Manhattanville, New York; Patterson, N.J.: Hackett's Town* and *Rockland Lake.* The large folio *Sing-Sing Camp Meeting, 1838* is an important record of a uniquely American social and religious happening. *The Attempted Assassination of the President of the United States, Jan 30, 1835 Drawn from a sketch by an eye witness,* depicts a tragically recurring American episode. G. & W. Endicott views include *Front View of the New York Post Office,* 1845; *Camp at Corpus Christi* and *Design of the National Monument by Robt. Mills of S.C. archt.,* 1849. The artist, Charles Parsons, put the latter on stone as he did many others for the Endicotts.

Parsons was born in England and came to this country at the age of nine. At the age of twelve he was apprenticed to George Endicott and lived in his home. He became an important contributor to the firm and drew many of the ships and boats which became such an important part of the Endicott output. The partnership of William and Francis as Endicott & Co., issued many of the steamships and steamboats all done in the same cool, clean style. A trade list offers.

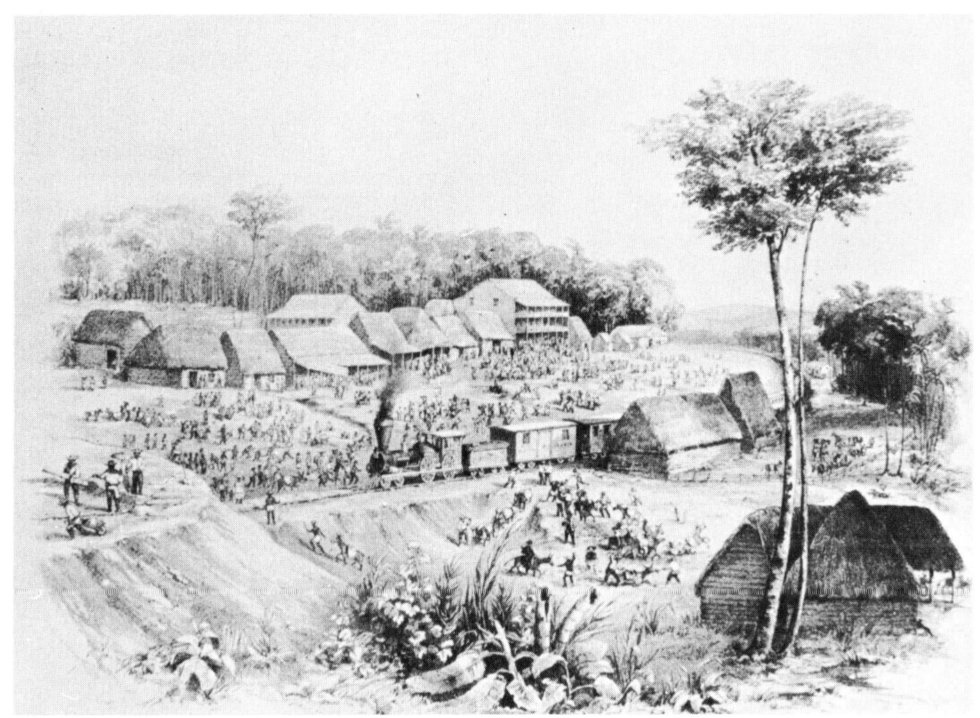

Endicott & Co., *View of Culebra or the Summit/ the Terminus of the Panama Railroad in Dec. 1854,* C. Parsons Lithograph, sketched from nature by F. N. Otis, M.D., Endicott & Co., New York, 1854

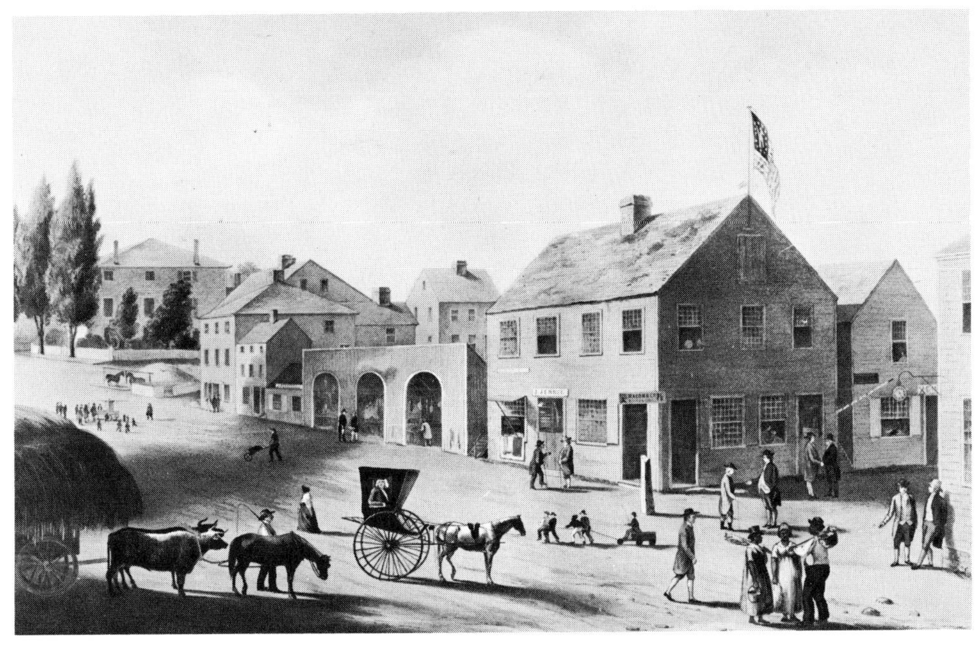

Endicott & Co., *New Bedford Fifty Years Ago,* from the painting by William A. Wall, Endicott & Co., 1858, $15\frac{1}{2} \times 23\frac{1}{2}$ inches

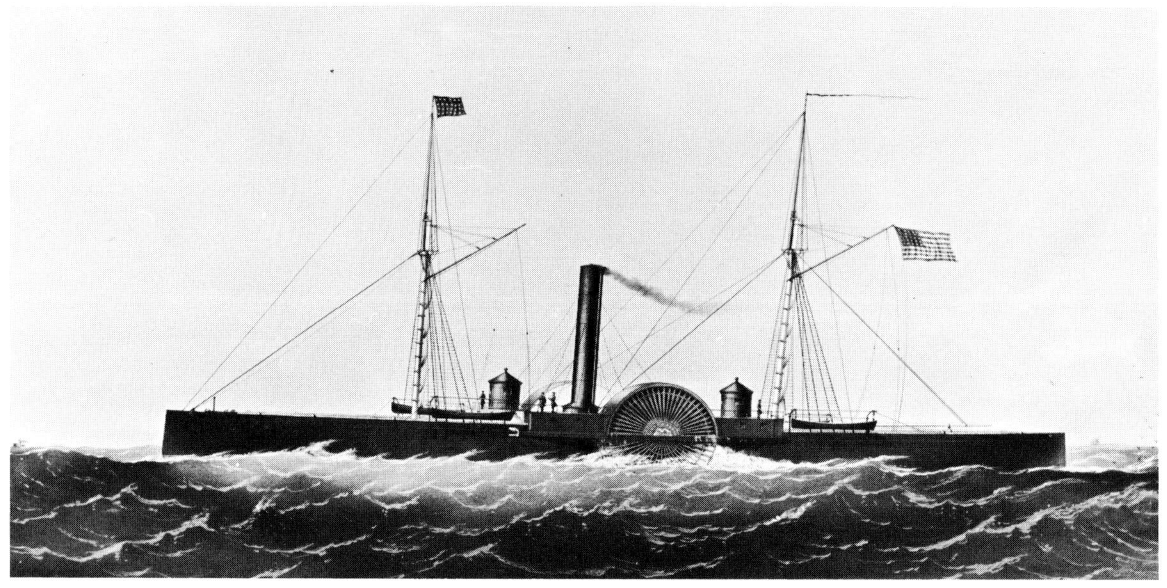

Endicott & Co., *U.S. Gunboat "Chicopee,"* by C. Parsons, 1863, 15¾ x 30 inches

FINE COLORED PRINTS PUBLISHED AND FOR SALE BY ENDICOTT & CO

Lithographers in every branch of the art

This offering lists by name some thirty-eight "U.S. MONITORS, at $1.50 EACH size of paper 19 × 30 inches;" "U.S. IRON CLADS, AT $2.00 EACH;" twenty-nine U.S. GUN-BOATS, AT $1.00 EACH. Extra Colored, AT $2.00, size, 24 × 36 inches;" eight "U.S. SCREW SLOOPS, AT $2.00 EACH. 24 × 36 inches;" nine "U.S. MONITORS, in Storm, at $2.00 each. Size, 20 × 33 inches" and in addition over two dozen miscellaneous vessels. Some of the well-known steamers are *Sarah Sands, 1850; Mary Powell;* the *Baltic* and the *Albany, 1880* with West Point in the background. Some of these steamships are hand-colored and some are chromolithographed.

Two excellent large folio whaling prints, *Sperm Whaling, No. 1—The Chase,* 1859 and *Sperm Whaling, No. 2—The Captive,* 1862 are from drawings by A. Van Beest and R. S. Gifford, corrected by Benj. Russell. Some in the ever-important category of views are a number of New York City: *An Interior View of the Crystal Palace,* 1853; *The First Methodist Church and Parsonage in America* and *City Residence of Mr. Daniel Parish, New York.* Other views are *Poughkeepsie From Opposite Side of the Hudson River. Whitefield's Views of North*

American Cities No. 27, 1852; *New Bedford, Fifty Years Ago* from a painting by Wm. A. Wall, 1858 and *Post Office, San Francisco, California. Fireman's Muster, Merrimack Square, Manchester, N.H. September 15th, 1859* was praised by Harry T. Peters as one of the largest and best lithographs he had ever seen. Endicott & Co. also issued portraits, horse prints, war prints, sentimentals, caricatures and many unusually high quality advertising lithographs. Music sheet covers were done by all the Endicotts.

Haskell & Allen 1871– *c.* 1875, thereafter Boston

A relatively late entry into the lithographic arena, Haskell & Allen produced a large number of prints during their brief existence. Many of their subjects are the same as Currier and Ives with closely similar titles, but their quality is seldom as good. The drawing, the lithography and even the paper are in general inferior to Bufford, Endicott, and Currier and Ives. However, some of the

Haskell and Allen, *Winter,* 17¼ x 24⅛ inches (*The Harry T. Peters "America on Stone" Lithography Collection, Smithsonian Institution*)

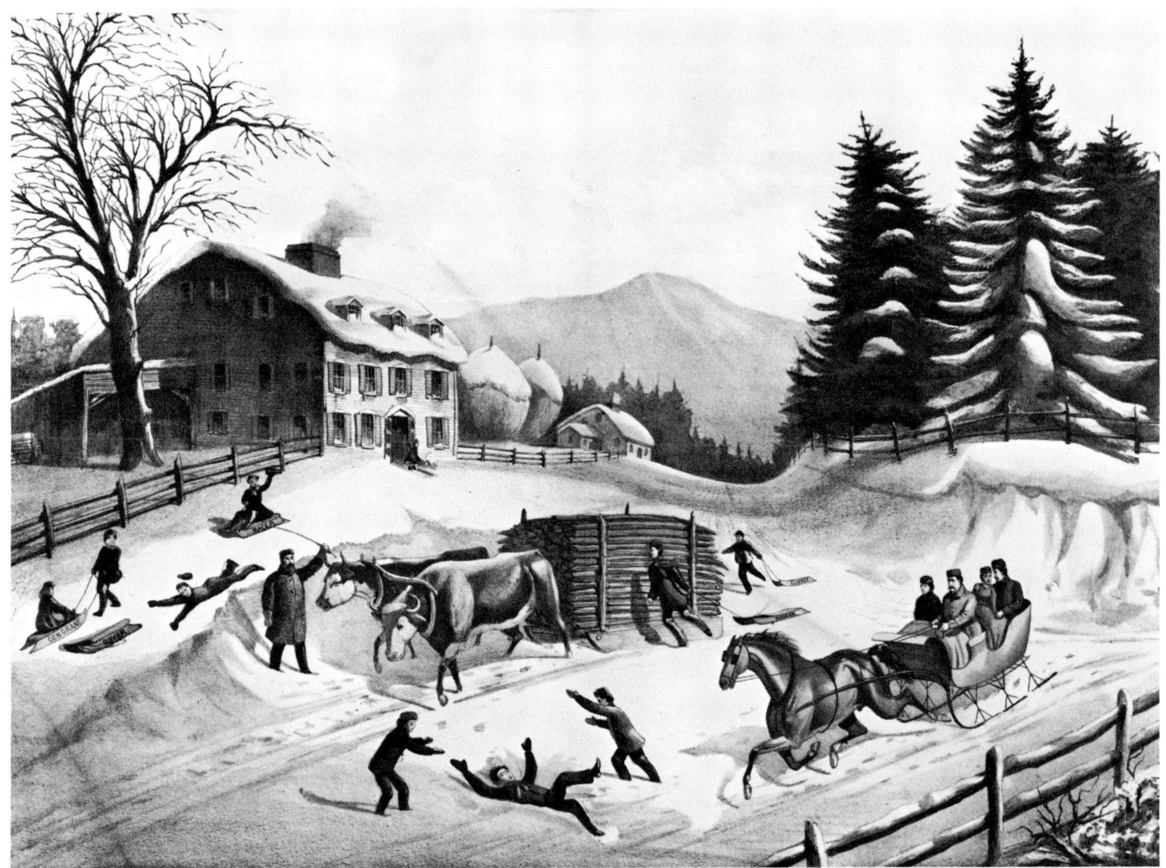

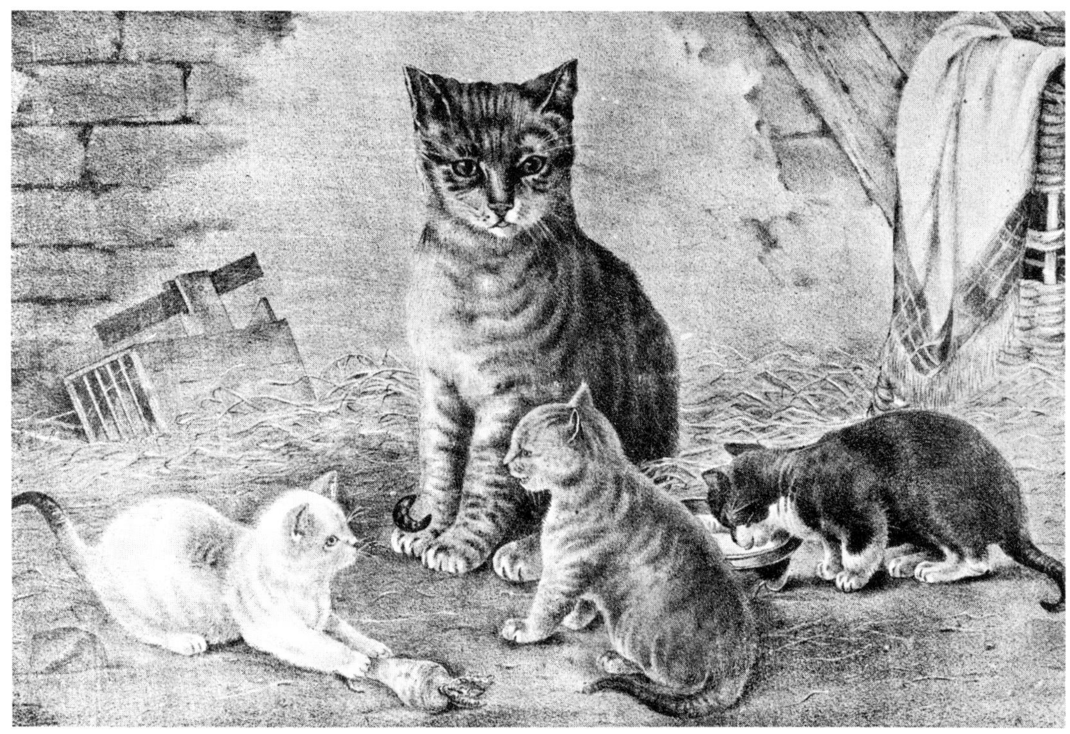

Haskell and Allen, *Pussy's Family,* $8\frac{1}{4}$ x $12\frac{1}{2}$ inches (*The Harry T. Peters "America on Stone" Lithography Collection, Smithsonian Institution*)

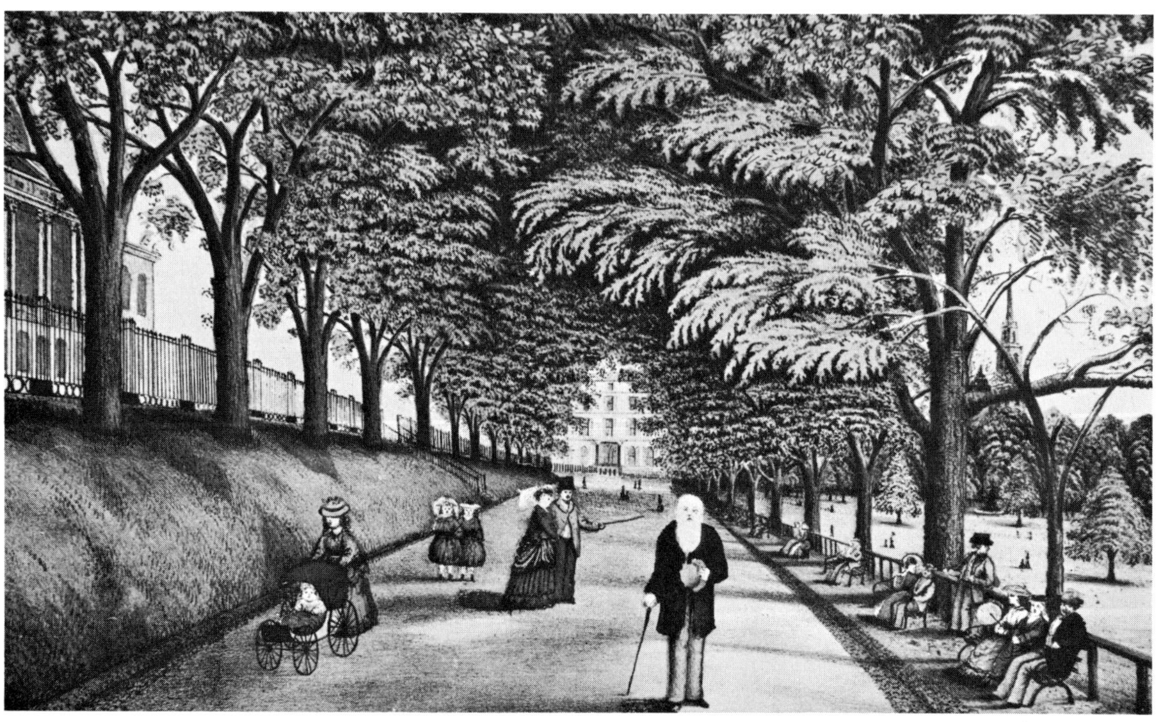

Haskell and Allen, *Boston Common/ Beacon St. Mall Looking towards Park St,* $8\frac{1}{4}$ x 13 inches prints have considerable merit and are worthy of a collector's attention. The horses are their best-known group, the best one being *Dexter, Ethan Allen & Mate.* Others are *Trotting Cracks on the Brighton Road* and *Fearnaught Stallions.* There are four large folios of the seasons and a marine of four schooners, *A Breezy Day Outside.* The *Union Pacific Rail Road* and *Midnight Race on the Mississippi* are western subjects. The view of *Boston Common* is one of their charming small folios.

Anthony Imbert 1825–1835 New York City

Imbert was an important pioneer lithographer in New York City. He was a former French Naval Officer who had studied drawing and painting while in England as prisoner of the British. By 1825 he was listed as a painter in New York City. Shortly after his arrival

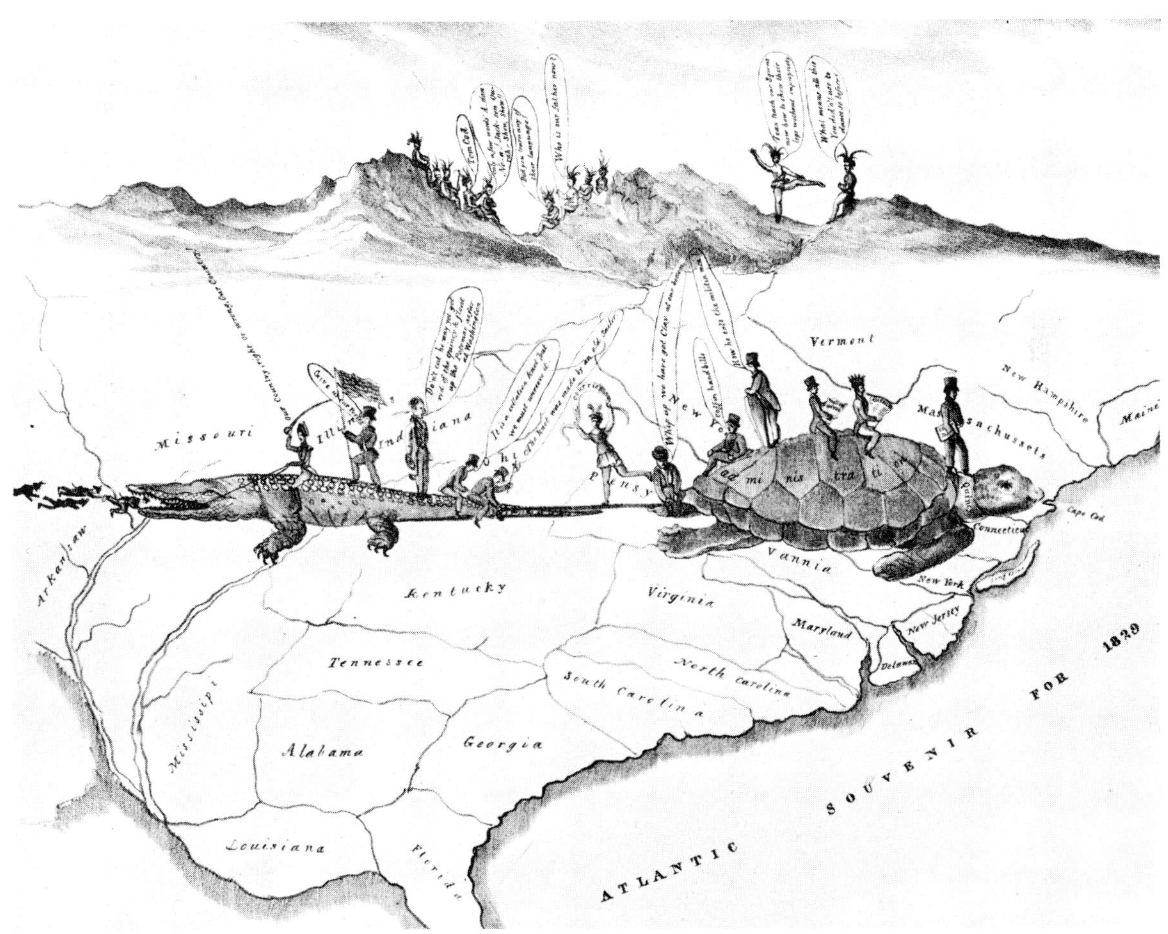

Imbert, *A New Map of the United States with the Additional Territories,* a cartoon of the presidential campaign of 1828 with Jackson as the alligator and John Quincy Adams and the administration as the turtle, $10\frac{1}{8}$ x $12\frac{7}{8}$ inches (*The Harry T. Peters "America on Stone" Lithography Collection, Smithsonian Institution*)

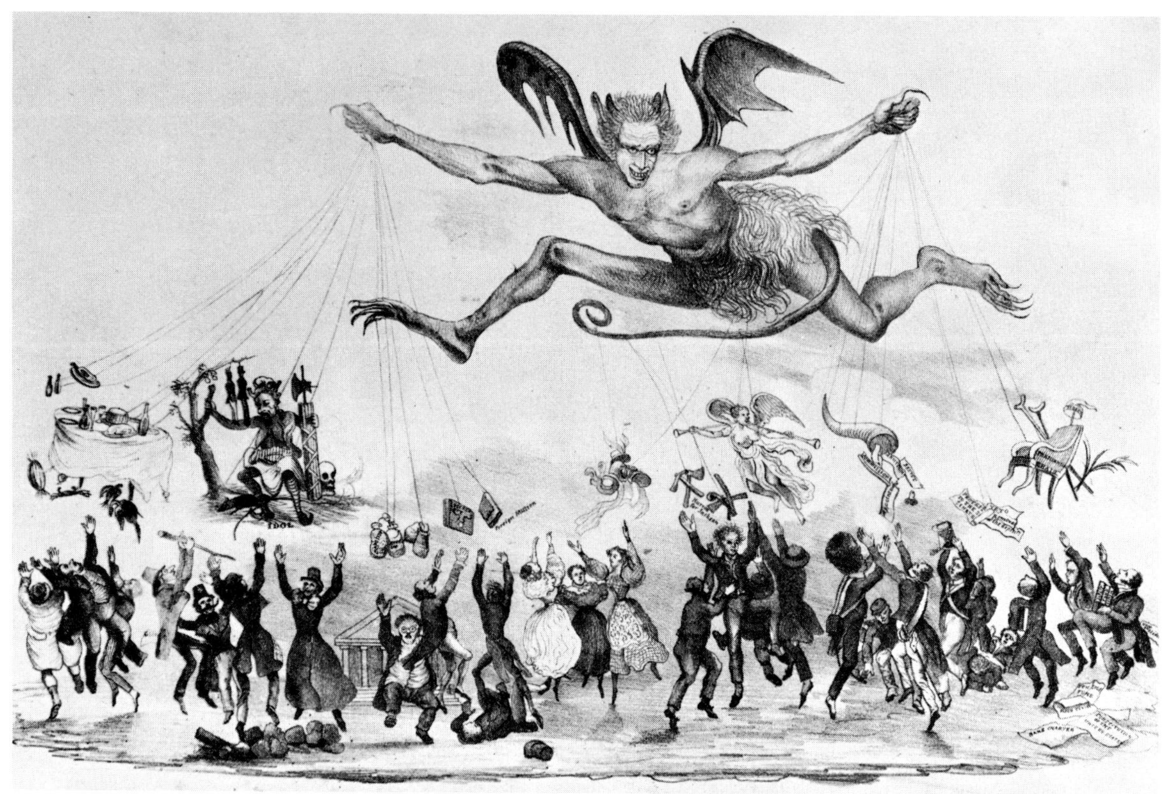

Imbert, *Office Hunters for the Year 1834,* a cartoon attacking Jackson and the spoils system, $9\frac{3}{8}$ x $15\frac{1}{8}$ inches (*The Harry T. Peters "America on Stone" Lithography Collection, Smithsonian Institution*)

there he was selected by the Committee of Arrangements to prepare the lithographs for the *Memoir prepared at the request of the Common Council of the City of New York, and presented to the Mayor of the city, at the celebration of the completion of the New York canals* by Cadwallader D. Colden, 1825. The complete book ($8\frac{1}{8} \times 10\frac{1}{8}$ inches) with Appendix contains 410 pages, seventeen engravings, and thirty-seven lithographs. These thirty-seven lithographs by Imbert are of considerable historic interest. They cover various aspects of the Canal Celebration showing the fleet; fire departments and organizations in the procession; maps; views, mostly by Catlin and facsimile letters from surviving signers of the Declaration of Independence and Gen. Lafayette written in reply to letters from the Committee.

Another major project by Imbert was the lithographing of a series of New York City views drawn by Alexander J. Davis, 1826–1829. Imbert issued a number of early comics and some outstanding early political cartoons. *A New Map of the United States with the Additional Territories on an improved Plan, Exhibiting a View of the Rocky Mountains Surveyed by a Company of Winebago Indians in 1828* represents Jackson as the alligator eating militiamen and pulling in the opposite direction from that of the turtle representing John Quincy Adams and the administration. This cartoon of the presidential campaign of 1828 is one of the earliest made. *Office Hunters for the Year 1834* is a fierce attack on the introduction of the spoils system by Jackson showing deposits, revenue, foreign missions, commissions, appointments, army commissions and other rewards dangling on strings above greedy hands.

Imbert's work also included portraits, book and magazine illustrations, caricatures, music sheet covers and views. He died sometime between 1835 and 1838. A pathetic New York City Directory entry for 1838–39 lists "Mary Imbert, widow of Anthony, boys' clothing, 186 Canal Street."

The Kelloggs et al

D. W. Kellogg & Co. 1830–1842 Hartford (Daniel Wright Kellogg)
E. B. & E. C. Kellogg 1842–1848 Hartford (Edmund Burke Kellogg 1855–1867 and Elijah Chapman Kellogg)
Kelloggs & Thayer 1846–1847 New York (E. B. & E. C. Kellogg, Horace Thayer)
Kelloggs & Comstock 1848–1850 Hartford & New York (E. B. & E. C. Kellogg, John C. Comstock)
E. B. Kellogg 1850–1855 Hartford
E. C. Kellogg 1850–1855 Hartford
J. G. Kellogg 1844–1862 Hartford (Jarvis G. Kellogg)
Kellogg & Hanmer 1845 Harford (J. G. Kellogg, Samuel Hanmer, Jr.)
Kellogg & Co. 1848 Hartford (J. G. Kellogg, George G. Gratacap)
Kellogg & Bulkely 1867 and after Hartford

Daniel Kellogg and his wife, the former Susanna Griggs, had twelve children all born in Hartford, four of whom became lithographers: Jarvis Griggs (*b.*1805–*d.*1873), Daniel Wright (*b.*1807–*d.*1874), Edmund Burke (*b.*1809–*d.*1873), and Elijah Chapman (*b.*1811–*d.*1881). Daniel W. was the first lithographer and was joined by his three brothers, all engravers, around 1830. The firm had varying and additional partners and associates, most of whom were relatives. Starting from their base in Hartford, the brothers also opened a New York office and one in Buffalo.

This company turned out an enormous number of lithographs aimed at the same market as Currier and Ives, inexpensive prints to be sold directly to the public. Most of the small folio Currier and Ives subjects are represented but hardly rival them in execu-

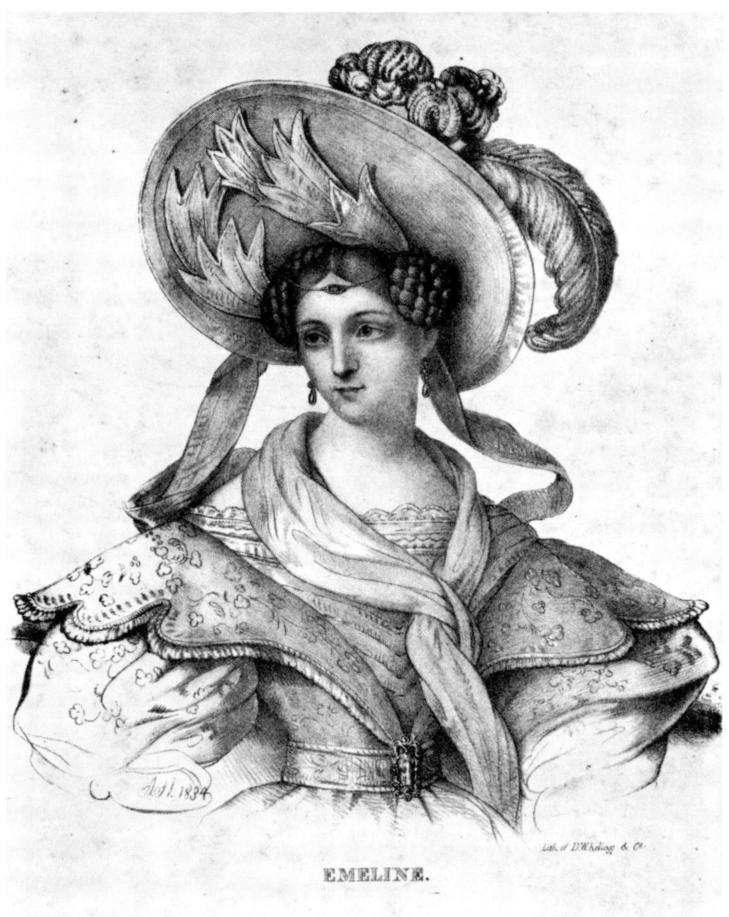

D. W. Kellogg & Co., *Emeline,* 1834, 11 x 9½ inches (*The Harry T. Peters "America on Stone" Lithography Collection, Smithsonian Institution*)

tion. Although their quality is above average, it is not outstanding. Proportionately fewer of their lithographs are signed by artists than is the case for most houses and it may be that artists of established reputation were not employed by the Kelloggs. Their total output of small folios was probably second only to Currier and Ives in quantity.

Best known is the *Portrait Gallery* by W. H. Brown which was lithographed by E. B. & E. C. Kellogg in 1845. The subjects include Washington, John Quincy Adams, John Caldwell Calhoun, Martin Van Buren and Henry Clay, whose silhouettes appear against an appropriate background. These were illustrations for a book but some free prints exist. Most of the edition was destroyed in a fire and as a result these prints are very rare. The book was reissued in 1931 with virtually full-size facsimiles of the plates.

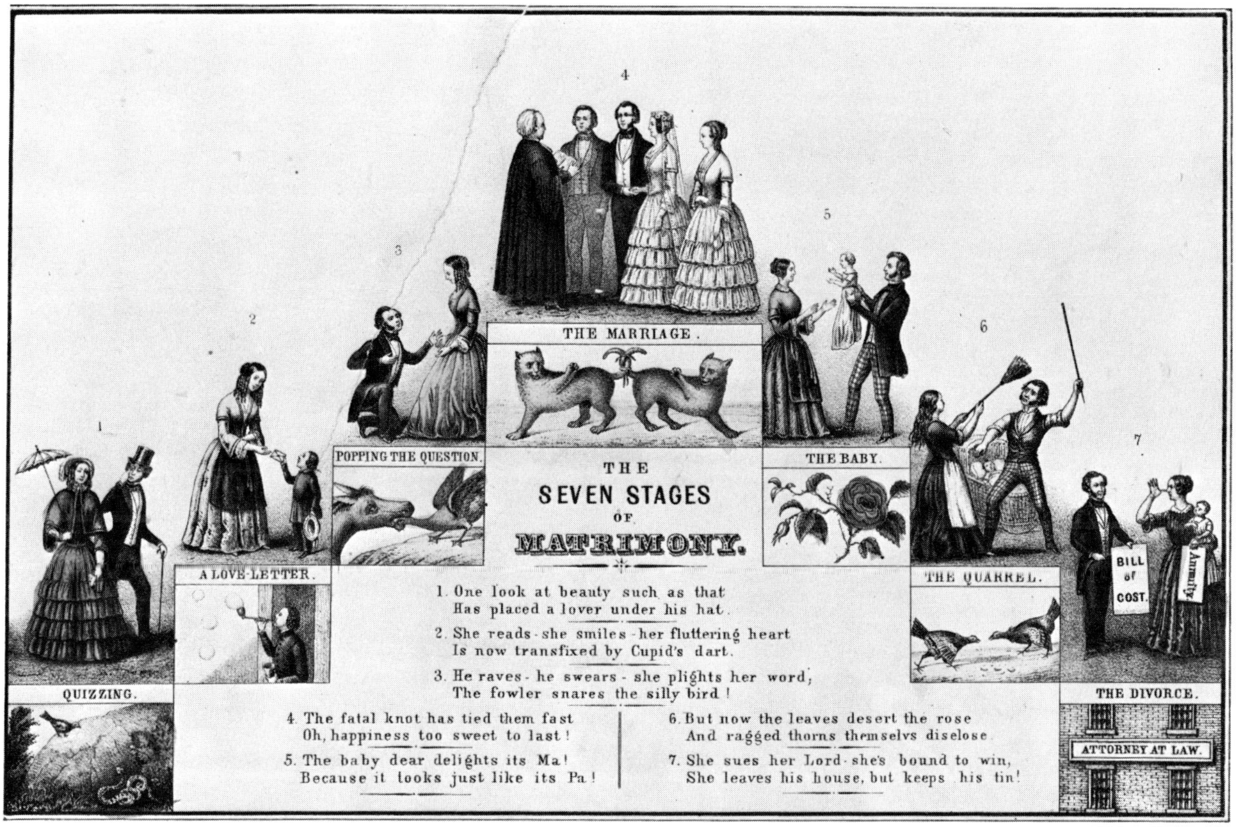

THE SEVEN STAGES OF MATRIMONY.

1 QUIZZING.

2 A LOVE-LETTER.

3 POPPING THE QUESTION.

4 THE MARRIAGE.

5 THE BABY.

6 THE QUARREL.

7 THE DIVORCE.

BILL of COST.

Annuity

ATTORNEY AT LAW.

1. One look at beauty such as that
Has placed a lover under his hat.

2. She reads - she smiles - her fluttering heart
Is now transfixed by Cupid's dart.

3. He raves - he swears - she plights her word;
The fowler snares the silly bird!

4. The fatal knot has tied them fast
Oh, happiness too sweet to last!

5. The baby dear delights its Ma!
Because it looks just like its Pa!

6. But now the leaves desert the rose
And ragged thorns themselvs disclose.

7. She sues her Lord - she's bound to win,
She leaves his house, but keeps his tin!

E. C. Kellogg & Co., N.Y.C. and Hartford; Horace Thayer & Co., Buffalo, *The Seven Stages of Matrimony,* 8½ x 13 inches (*The Harry T. Peters "America on Stone" Lithography Collection, Smithsonian Institution*)

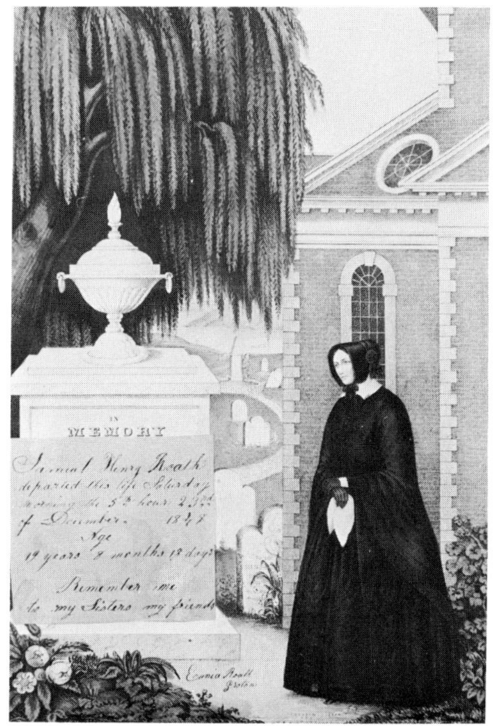

Kellogg & Comstock, N.Y.C. and Hartford; D. Needham, Buffalo, *In Memory,* 12½ x 8½ inches

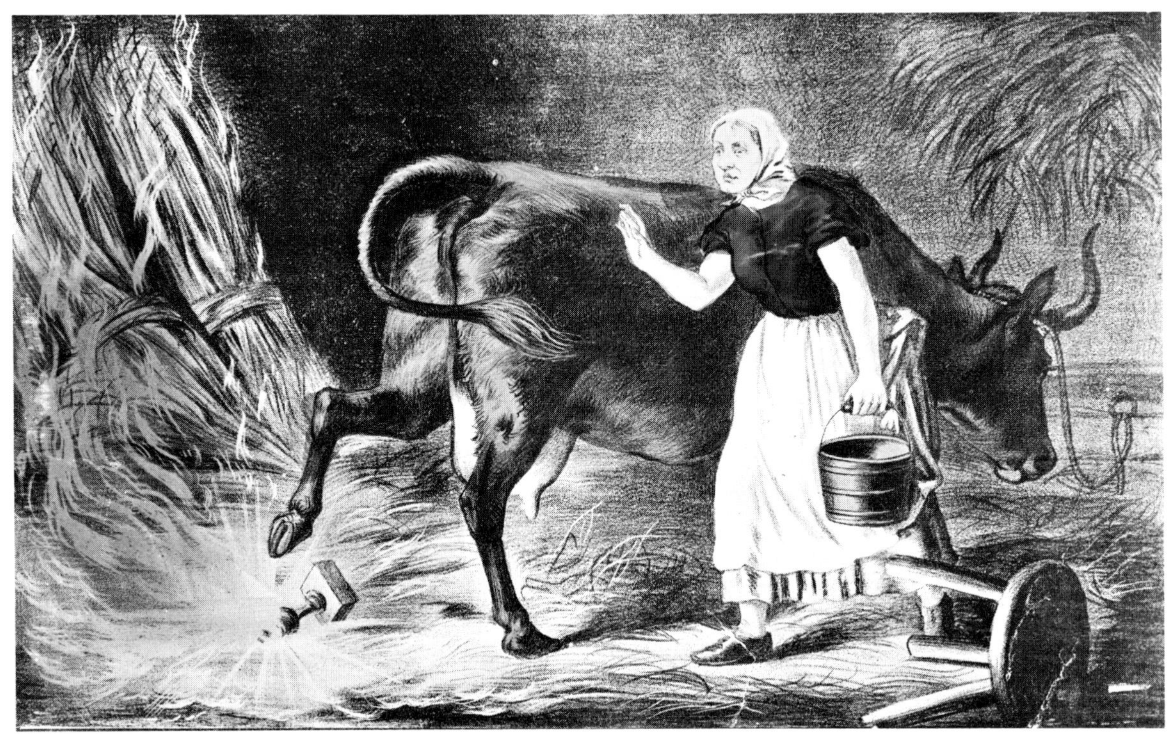

Kellogg & Bulkeley Co., *The Cause of the Great Chicago Fire Oct. 9th 1871/ A Warning to all Who Use Kerosene Lamps/ Never forget that more lives have been lost, and more comfortable homes burned up by a Careless Use of this light than any other ever introduced into common use.* $8\frac{1}{2}$ x $13\frac{3}{4}$ inches (*The Harry T. Peters "America on Stone" Lithography Collection, Smithsonian Institution*)

The Kelloggs made the usual portraits, historicals and views: *Pocahontas Saving the Life of Captain John Smith; Atlanta, Georgia* and a set of *Chicago in Flames.* The westerns are among their better prints; *California Gold Diggers, Indian Buffalo Hunt* and *Independent Gold Hunter on his Way to California.* Their best efforts seem to have been channeled into their sentimentals, which must have been made in enormous numbers, judging by their prevalence. The drawing is well above the usual quality for the type and they have a distinctive style about them which Peters calls "a special languor." They include girls' names; *Map of the Fortified Country of Man's Heart; The Seven Stages of Matrimony; Son of Temperance; Daughter of Temperance* and *The Life and Age of Man.*

Nagel, Weinga(e)rtner, et al

Louis Nagel 1844–1845 New York City
Nagel and Mayer 1846 New York City
Louis Nagel 1847–1848 New York City
Nagel & Weingartner 1849–1856 New York City

Nagel & Lewis c. 1857 New York City
Nagel, Fishbourne & Kuchel 1862–1863 San Francisco

Louis Nagel was born in Germany about 1817 and was working in New York City as a lithographer by 1844. He worked alone and in association with a number of partners of which Nagel and Weingartner is the most important. Their portraits include one of Daguerre drawn by D'Avignon, President Tyler and his Cabinet and President Taylor and his Cabinet. They printed *The Night Watch,* an exciting western scene from a painting by J. W. Audubon, as well as some of the plates for the second edition, the upright octavo, 1849, of the *viviparous Quadrupeds of North America.* In 1852–1854 they printed the *United States Militia Album* showing all the various uniforms and equipment. After 1857 Nagel was in San Francisco where he issued a five-section panoramic view of the city. The San Francisco group also did an 1862 view of San Francisco, a view of the Mission Dolores and a set of sixteen views of *The Mammoth Tree Grove, Calaveras Co., California, and its Avenues.*

Nagel & Lewis, *Sleighing in New York,* composed and lithographed by Th. Benecke, Printed by Nagel & Lewis, New York, 1855, $21\frac{1}{2}$ x $30\frac{1}{2}$ inches

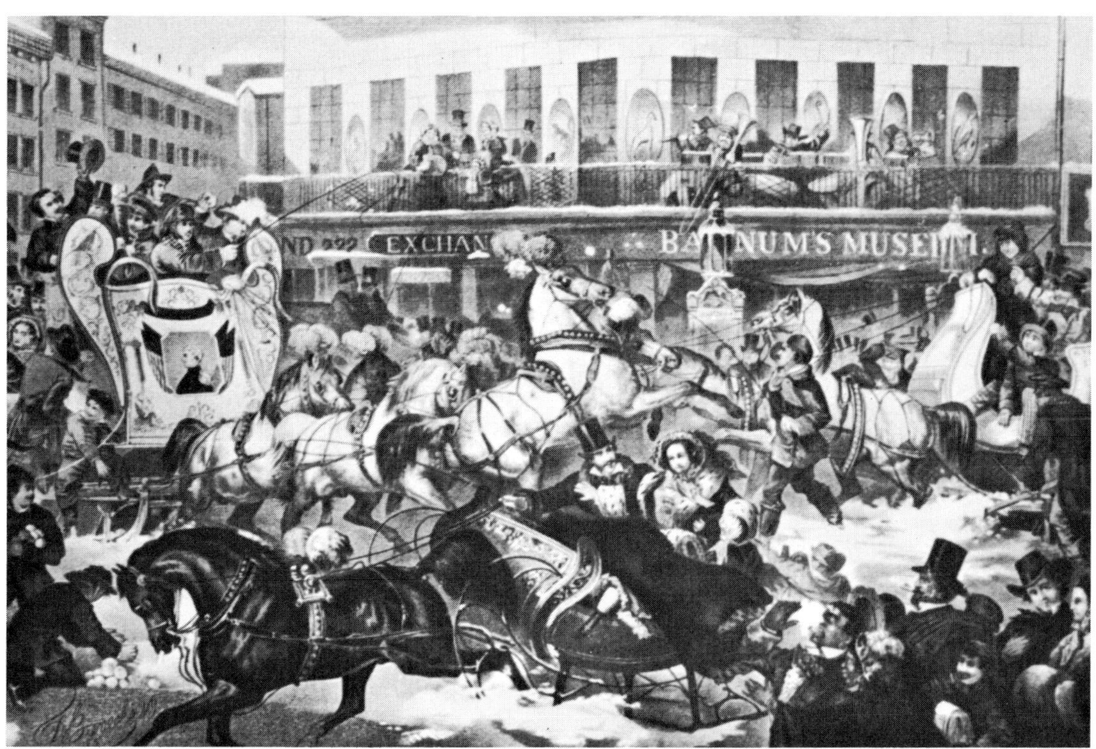

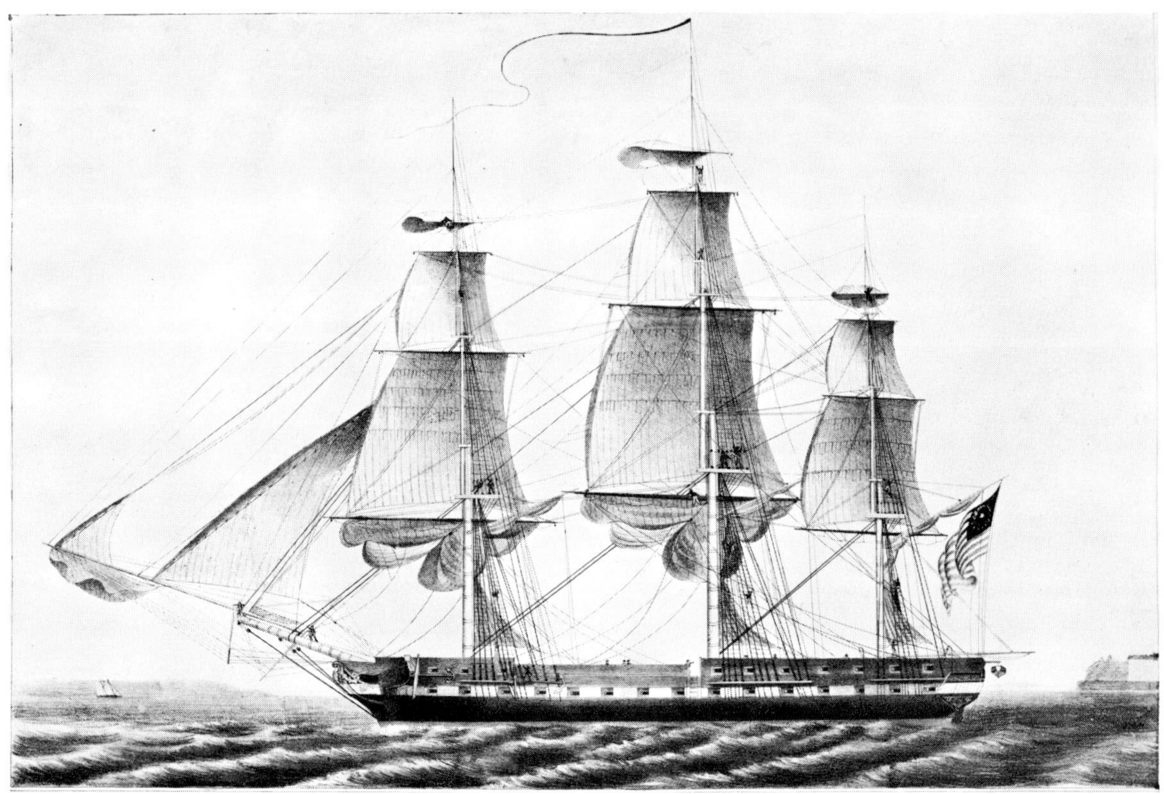

Pendleton, *U.S. Frigate Constitution,* drawn by William Marsh, Jr., Pendleton's Lithograph, 14 x 20⅝ inches

The Pendletons

W. S. and J. B. Pendleton 1826–1829 Boston
W. S. Pendleton 1830–1836 Boston
Pendleton (J. B.), Kearney & Childs c. 1829 Philadelphia
J. B. Pendleton 1829–1834 New York City

William S. Pendleton was born in 1795 and John B. in 1798, both sons of an English sea captain who had settled in New York. The brothers worked for the Peale Museum in Philadelphia installing gas lighting fixtures and taking charge of traveling exhibits. By 1825, William was an engraver in Boston with Abel Bowen. About 1825, William bought some lithographic supplies from a merchant who had brought them back from Europe. Since John happened to be in Europe at this time, his brother wrote to him about buying additional lithographic materials. In response, John brought back about a ton of prepared lithographic stone, transfer paper and transfer ink and crayons, and further arranged for two trained workers to come along. Thus began the first commercially successful lithographic firm in this country.

John B. Pendleton soon separated from his brother. In 1829 he was working in New York and in 1829 or 1830 was associated with the firm of Pendleton, Kearney and Childs in Philadelphia. In 1830 he became established in New York City and continued in business until 1834 when he sold out to Nathaniel Currier and a music publisher named Stodart. After this he was a bookseller, publisher, carpenter and proprietor of a planing mill. He died in 1866.

W. S. Pendleton continued on after his brother left and in 1831 had four lithographic presses and four copper plate presses when he absorbed the Annin & Smith Lithographic Company which had been in existence for three years. In 1836 W. S. Pendleton sold out to Thomas Moore, his bookkeeper, and went into bank-note engraving. Later he entered the hardware business in Philadelphia, retiring at the start of the Civil War. He died in 1879.

The Pendletons were a prime influence in the establishment of lithography in this country. They encouraged and trained many artists and lithographers who fanned out into other firms. Nathaniel Currier, for one, was a Pendleton apprentice in Boston before going to New York. Most of the Pendleton lithography was special work done to order, rather than popular prints to be sold directly to the people. The General Court of Massachusetts passed a law in 1830 which required all the cities and towns to provide maps made from accurate surveys. The Pendletons made many of these, as well as certificates, scientific illustrations, book and magazine illustrations and music sheet covers.

However, there are many fine collectable prints of all kinds. Harry T. Peters calls the portrait of Washington, on stone by Rembrandt Peale and printed by the Pendletons, the greatest American lithograph. *View of the Town of Gloucester, Mass.* by F. H. Lane; *View of Yale College; J. Fenimore Cooper. The Author of the Spy* and *Quincy Rail-Way* showing horses drawing carts along rails are prints of interest. Two New York views by John Pendleton, *View of St. Paul's Church and the Broadway Stages* and *Columbia College* are well known. Most of the prints by the Pendletons were not colored.

Louis Prang et al

Rosenthal, Duval & Prang c. 1856 Philadelphia
Prang & Mayer (Julius) 1856–1860 Boston
Louis Prang & Co. 1860 until 1890's Boston

Prang was born in 1824, the son of a calico printer in Breslau, Germany. As the president of a democratic club, he fled when the Revolution of 1848 broke out, arriving in New York in 1850.

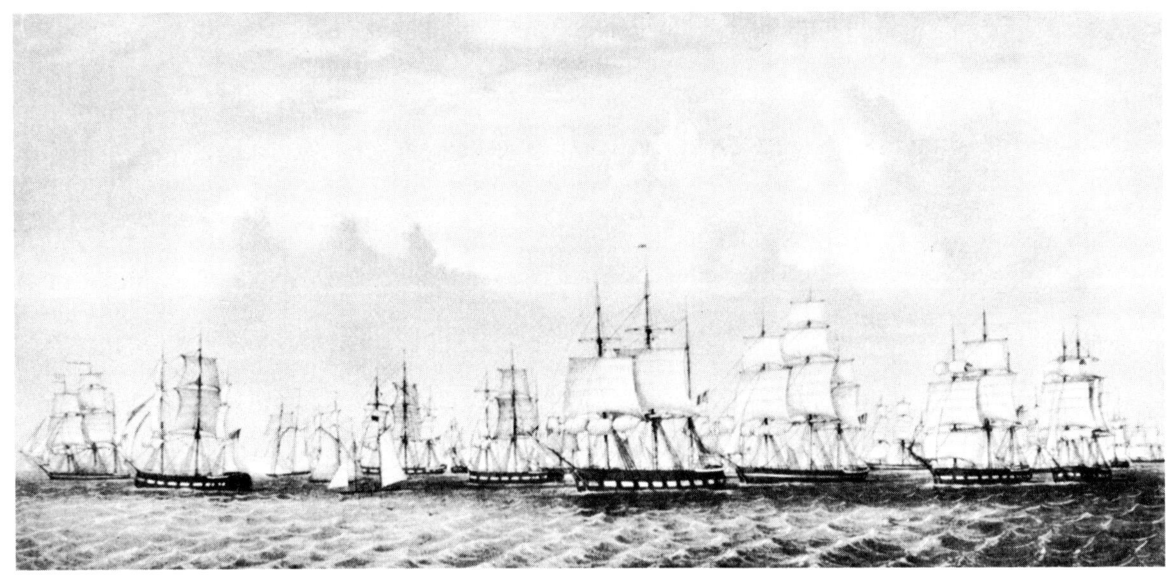

L. Prang & Co., *View of the Stone Fleet which Sailed from New Bedford Nov. 16, 1861,* copyrighted by Benjamin Russell 1862, L. Prang & Co., Boston, large folio

Around 1856 he was associated with Rosenthal and Duval in Philadelphia, sharing their interest in color printing. He went to Boston where he was in partnership with Julius Mayer from 1857 to 1860, when his business became Louis Prang & Co. Sometime after 1864 he moved into a four-story building on Roxbury Street which accommodated one hundred and fifty to three hundred and fifty workers. With many skilled printers recruited in Europe, Prang perfected the art of color printing and was successful in using as many as thirty-two colors in a single picture. He went further by reproducing water colors and oil paintings by simulating the texture of the paper or canvas. In his early period he produced many fine hand-colored lithographs. Later, he concentrated on chromolithography in Christmas cards, advertisements, and book plates. He died in 1909.

The years with Mayer produced the beautiful large view, *New Bedford, Mass.,* the large *Bird's Eye View of Harvard College and Old Cambridge* and one of the best whaling prints, *Sperm Whaling- The Conflict,* 1859. Louis Prang & Co. lithographed the large folio, *The View of the Stone Fleet which Sailed from New Bedford Nov. 16th, 1861,* which shows the old whalers bought by the Federal Government to be filled with stones and sunk in southern harbors as a blockade. There are portraits of Martha and George Washington after Stuart, Civil War officers and political cartoons. Prang published the set of six *Campaign Sketches* of Winslow Homer, as well as a series of 24 album cards, *Life in Camp.*

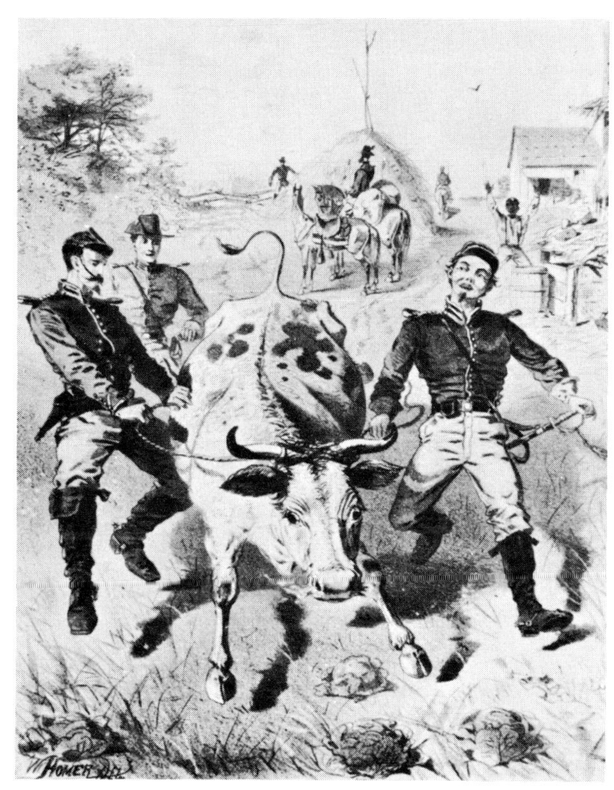

L. Prang & Co., *Foraging* from *Campaign Sketches* by Winslow Homer, Lithographed and Published by L. Prang & Co., Boston. Paper size about 11 x 14 inches.

Sarony, Major, Knapp

Napoleon Sarony, Sarony & Co. 1840–1845 New York City
Sarony & Major 1846–1857
Sarony, Major & Knapp 1857–1867
Major & Knapp 1867 into the 1870's

Napoleon Sarony was handsome, gregarious, vivacious and loved giving and going to parties. His wide circle of friends included many actors and actresses of whom he made portraits. He was born in Quebec in 1821 and came to New York around 1836 where he studied under Archibald Robertson, drew cartoons and marines for Henry R. Robinson and then worked for Nathaniel Currier. It was his print of the steamboat *Lexington* that launched them both into prominence in the field. In 1846, Henry B. Major, also a former Currier employee, joined Sarony to form the firm of Sarony & Major. Sometime around 1855 Henry B. Major was replaced by Richard Major, forming Sarony, Major & Knapp. In 1860 they occupied four large lofts and had forty presses. Sarony's interest in portraiture involved him in photography and he set up a studio around 1867 which became highly successful. He left this for foreign travel and began doing lithographic portraits again when he needed money. On a second trip to Europe he opened a photographic studio in England which achieved an international reputation. Back in New York, he made another fortune by selling photographic devices which he invented. He died in 1896.

Sarony is noted for his many fine portraits, especially of entertainers. A famous early view is *The Burning of the Old National Theatre, corner of Leonard and Church, The Church of Saint Esprit, Corner of Church and Franklin and the Dutch Reformed Church on Franklin Street, September 23rd, 1839.* The work that solidified his reputation was the series of four large folios of the expedition to Japan by Commodore Perry in 1853–1854. The best known print by Sarony & Major is *The Storming of Chapultepec. Sept. 13th, 1847* from a painting by Walker printed in colors and with the curious credit "N. Currier as sole agent." Another Mexican War record is the portfolio of eight naval views, *Naval Scenes in the Mexican War,* after drawings

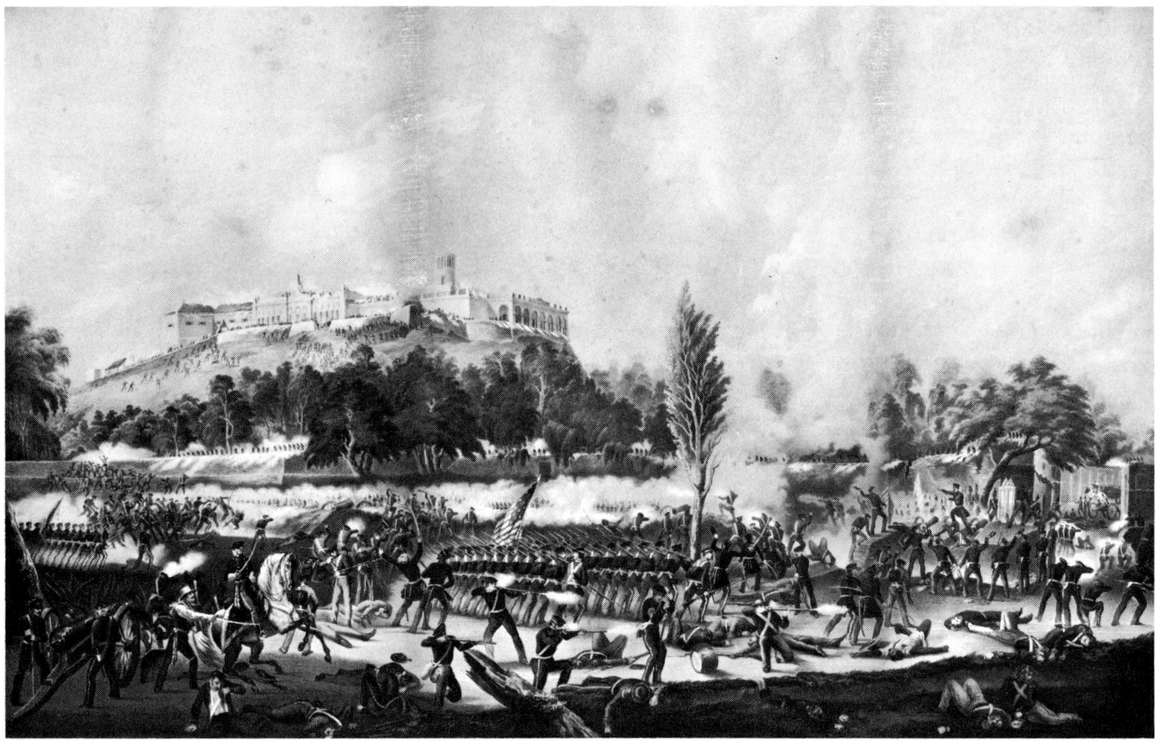

Sarony & Major, *The Storming of Chapultepec, Sept. 13, 1847,* drawn on stone, printed in colors, and published by Sarony & Major, from a painting by Walker, N. Currier Sole Agent, 1848, 23$\frac{5}{8}$ x 35$\frac{7}{8}$ inches (*The Harry T. Peters "America on Stone" Lithography Collection, Smithsonian Institution*)

by H. Walke, a naval lieutenant who was on the bomb brig *Vesuvius* during Commodore M. C. Perry's expedition up the Tuxpan River. There are many other views of this war with bombardments, capitulations, victories and repulsions of charges. Historicals of earlier periods such as *Destruction of the Tea in Boston Harbor* and *The Declaration of Independence* were also issued.

Among the views are the dramatic and important *View of Sutter's Mill & Culloma Valley,* some New York City views and *View of Norwich, From the West side of the River* by F. H. Lane, "Lith & Printed in colors by Sarony & Major" in 1849. Sarony & Major were responsible for a large number of sentimentals which are sparkling and dashing in their portrayal of male and female beauty. The men have an almost feminine prettiness with their pinched waists and large soulful eyes. Many other prints could be listed: *The Funeral Car Used at the Obsequies to the Hon. Henry Clay . . . , Wreck of the Steamer Atlantic,* and prints in books, portfolios and music sheet covers. Sarony, Major & Knapp supplied large numbers of illustrations for medical and scientific reports, government survey and exploration reports and other book illustrations. They did maps, music sheet titles and portraits, as well as views, a Civil War prison camp scene, a circus parade and a very early baseball print. Major & Knapp made a series of the steamships of the Inman Line and large Civil War scenes as well as the usual types of prints.

CHAPTER FIVE Currier and Ives

History

Boston, "hub of the universe," has an unacknowledged claim to fame as the birthplace of Nathaniel Currier in 1813 in the satellite town of Roxbury. To repeat an oft-told tale, Currier began his career as an apprentice at the age of fifteen with the firm of William S. and John Pendleton of Boston in 1828. Pendleton was the first American firm to make a commercial success of lithography and this training was a cornerstone in Currier's later progress. After further experience in Philadelphia under M. E. D. Brown, a master lithographer, he settled in New York City where he and a man named Stodart bought out the business of John Pendleton. This partnership lasted only one year and in 1835, at the age of twenty-two he established his own business at One Wall Street. A year later he moved to Nassau Street and two years later in 1838 he obtained space for his plant at Two Spruce Street. His early efforts are described in the city directories as "Publishers," "Print Publishers," "Publishers of Prints and Engravings" and "Lithographers." His output was mostly letterheads and commercial forms, music, maps and a few prints.

A pivotal episode occurred in January of 1840 when the wooden steamboat "Lexington" burned and sank in Long Island Sound with a

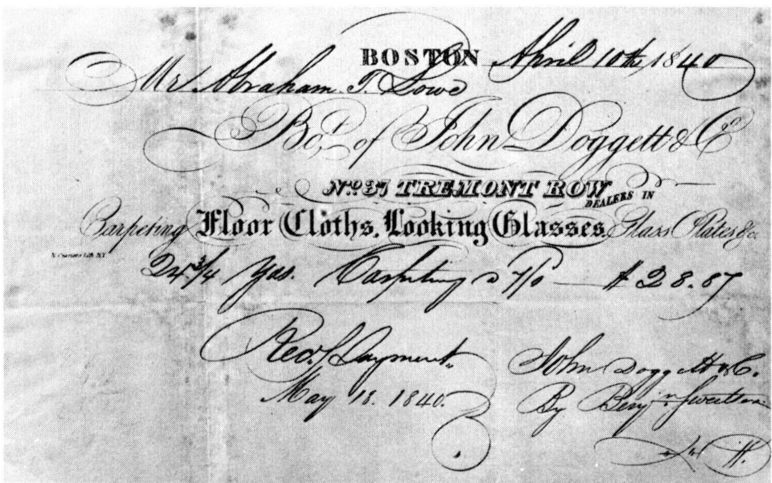
BOSTON April 10th 1840

Mr Abraham T. Lowe

Bot of John Doggett & Co

No 35 TREMONT ROW DEALERS IN

Carpeting Floor Cloths, Looking Glasses, Glass Plates &c.

24 3/4 yds. Carpeting @ 7/6 — $28.87

Recd Payment
May 11. 1840

John Doggett & Co.
By Benj [illegible]

Letterhead of a Boston firm, lithographed by N. Currier in New York prior to April, 1840

loss of over one hundred lives. The New York newspaper, *The Sun,* quickly commissioned Currier to produce a print of the disaster which was included in an extra edition on the street only one week after the tragedy. Thus began pictorial journalism. The impact of this "instant" news picture was electrifying and Currier continued to sell colored versions of this print for months after the sinking. In this era before modern news photography and television, the *Awful Conflagration of the Steam Boat Lexington in Long Island Sound* established a base for the entrepreneurial efforts of Currier, enabling him to build a nationwide business. His target was success and his aim included only those items he thought would sell well in the romantically based Victorian America. As his advertisements stated, he concentrated on making "Colored Engravings for the People." The seven thousand five hundred or so prints put out by his firm in its seventy-two years include almost every subject acceptable to the average American. There are prints showing modern industrial progress, but only in a romantic vein, such as gleaming steamboats and streaking trains. The list does not include factories and the industrial based slums in the cities. Gallant courtship was depicted without a hint of sex. His output mirrored to a remarkable degree the thinking and attitudes of his time.

Long before modern advertising and public relations, Currier understood the impact of a few well-chosen words for a title. His favorites included key words like "awful," "dreadful," "great," "famous," "American," "champion," "celebrated" and "home." Themes were assigned to pictures with only meager substance to support them, such as *Home to Thanksgiving,* an attractive winter scene which could just as

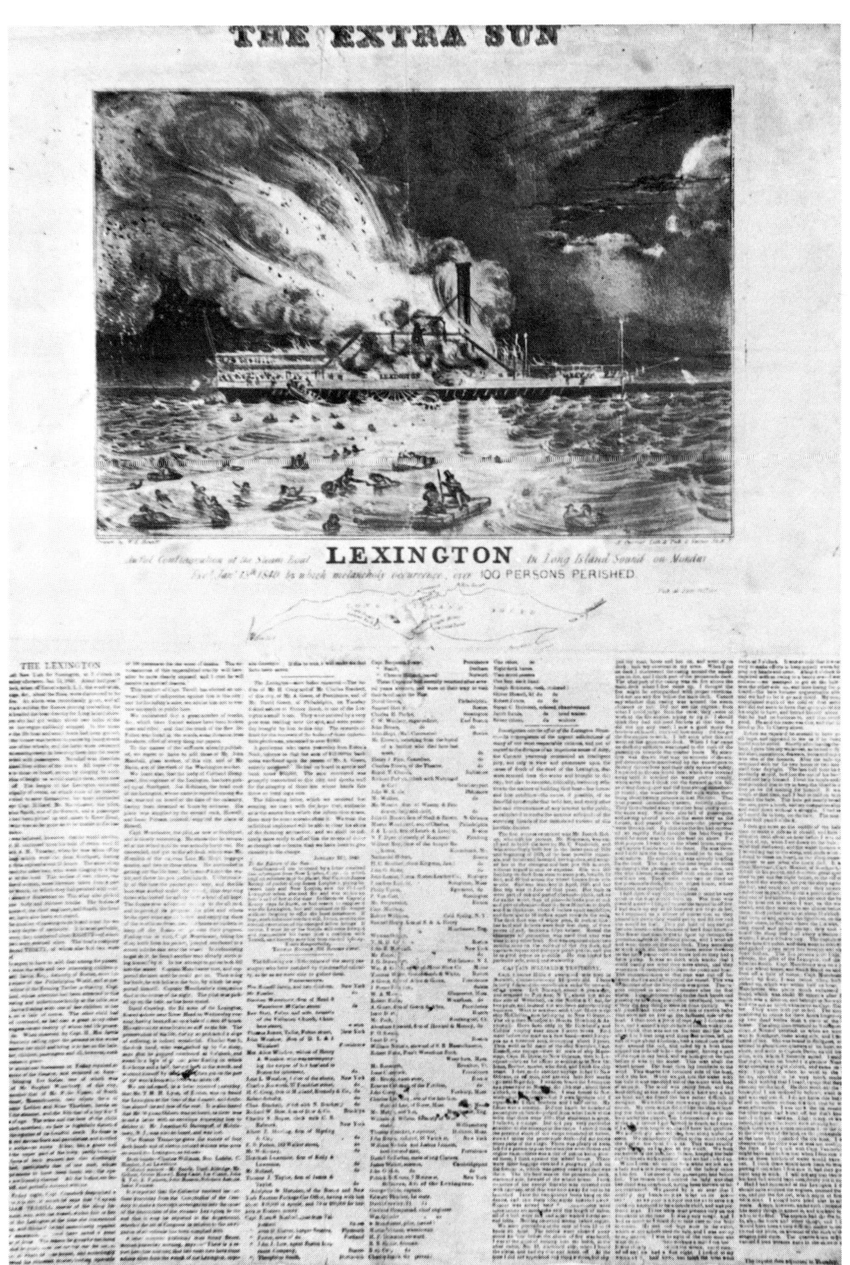

THE EXTRA SUN

LEXINGTON

Awful Conflagration of the Steam Boat LEXINGTON in Long Island Sound on Monday Eve'g Jan. 13th 1840 by which melancholy occurrence, over 100 PERSONS PERISHED.

THE LEXINGTON

Awful Conflagration of the Steam Boat Lexington in Long Island Sound on Monday/ Eve'g Jan. 13, 1840 etc., *The Sun Extra,* lithographed picture, $8\frac{1}{2}$ x 12 inches, drawn by W. K. Hewitt and published and lithographed by N. Currier. The newspaper text is typeset (*Collection of Ladd MacMillan*)

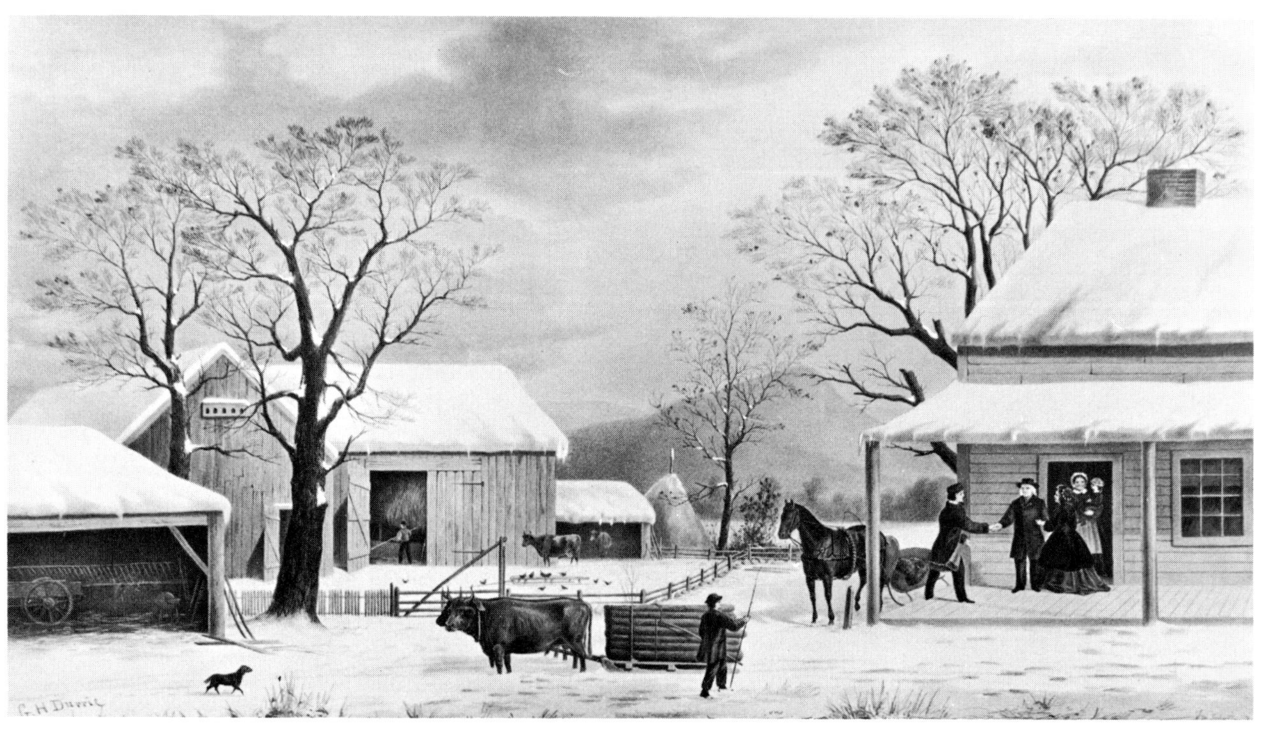

Home to Thanksgiving, after a painting by G. H. Durrie, published by Currier and Ives in 1867. Hand-colored lithograph, $14\frac{3}{4}$ x 25 inches (*Collection of Ladd MacMillan*)

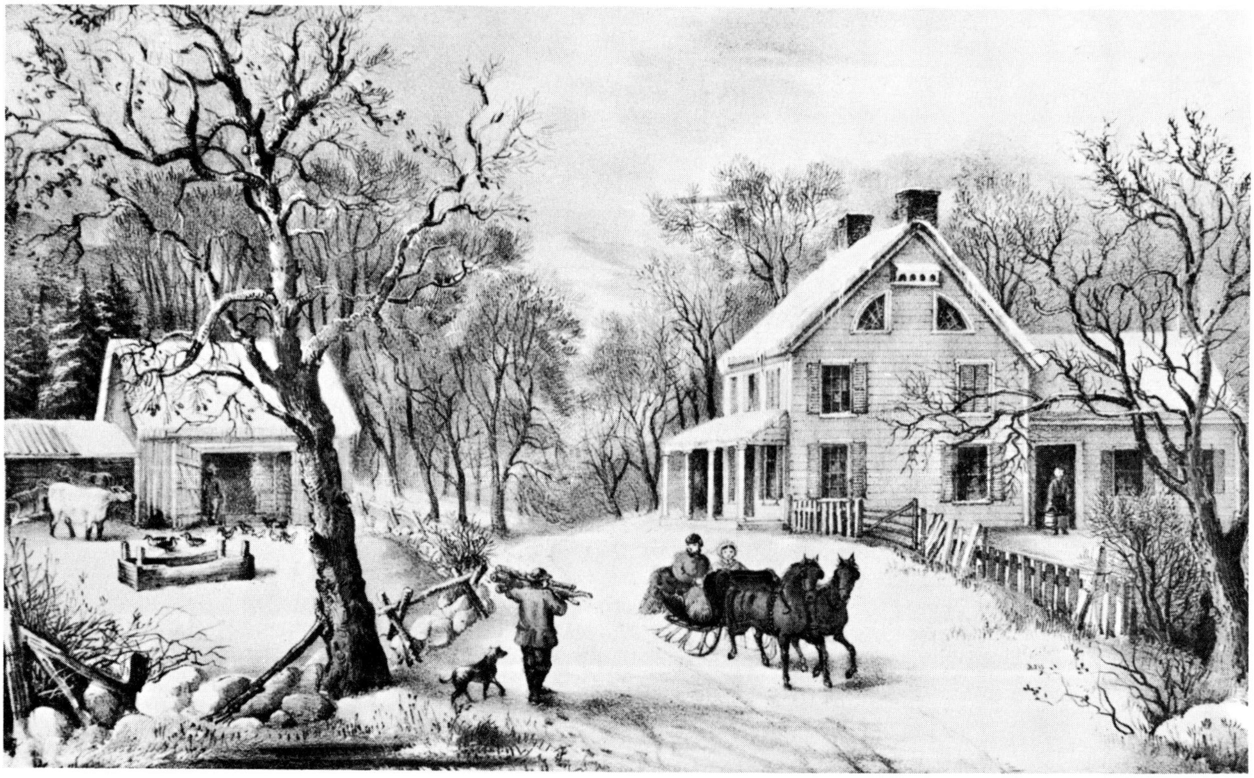

American Homestead/ Winter, published by Currier and Ives, 1868. Hand-colored lithograph, 8 x $12\frac{1}{2}$ inches well have been called *Thanks for the Ride.* Often a series of two to six or more prints were made with the obvious hope that the customer would eventually buy the whole group. Today his most popular series is *American Homestead/Summer/Autumn/Winter/Spring.* Currier was also concerned with composition and quality, hiring good artists and taking a personal hand in supervision.

A remarkably broad and successful sales and distribution system was set up. Prints were sold in the New York store and also by mail order for twenty cents each or six for one dollar for the small folio size, about 8 by 12 inches; and one dollar and fifty cents to four dollars for the large folio prints, 14 by 20 inches and over. In addition, they were sold at wholesale prices to local peddlers and to agents in cities throughout the country. The local agents in turn sold to peddlers in their area. The wholesale price for the small prints was six dollars per hundred. The peddlers sold them for twenty or twenty-five cents each, a handsome mark-up. Since the prints sold easily, the peddlers were very active and reasonably prosperous. The firm also had an office in London, presumably operating on the same principles. A significant number of prints were sold in England, France and Germany. The small folio, *View of New York from Weehawken,* also carries the title in French and German.

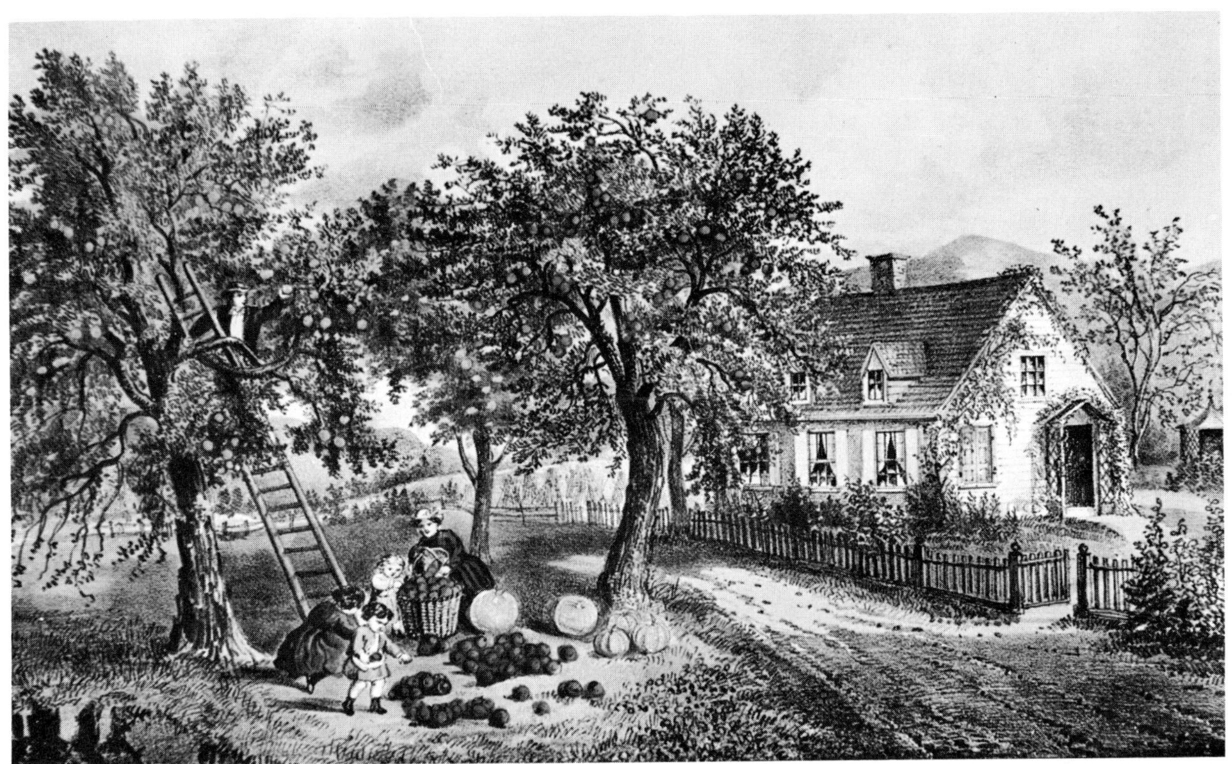

American Homestead/ Autumn, published by Currier and Ives, 1868. Hand-colored lithograph, $7\frac{15}{16}$ x $12\frac{1}{2}$ inches

At various times from the founding of the firm in 1835 to its closing in 1907 there was competition from others with similar prints and distribution systems. The earlier competitors never achieved comparable success mainly because their prints failed to have the same popular appeal. Toward the end, the chromolithographers overtook Currier and Ives but during the period when their product was the high style they had no serious competitor. During their prime some who tried to compete were:

James S. Baillie, New York active 1847–1855
John H. Bufford, New York 1835–1839, Boston 1840–1871
Endicott et al, Baltimore 1828–1831, New York 1831–1886
Haskell and Allen, Boston 1871– *c.* 1875
The Kelloggs et al, 1830–1867 and after, Hartford, New York City
Thomas Kelly, New York, ca. 1870
Sarony and Major, New York, 1846–1857
Sarony, Major, and Knapp, New York, 1857–1867

In 1852 Nathaniel Currier hired James Ives, husband of Currier's brother's wife's sister, as a clerk, bookkeeper, artist and lithographer. Ives' talents were great and many of the management decisions that led to success were made in consultation with him. He was made a partner in 1857 and the name of the firm was changed to Currier and Ives. Today, prints bearing the name of N. Currier or Currier and Ives are considered the same and both are popularly called Currier and Ives.

When framed, many of the prints were used in homes as decoration and provided the person of average income a substitute for the prohibitively expensive oil paintings. Scenes of various cities or sections of the country were often bought as souvenirs of a trip. Small prints were used as merit awards and given as prizes for the best speller in school. Currier and Ives fully describe the uses for their racing and horse prints on the bottom of a mail order sheet put out about 1893.

> "These Pictures are the Cheapest Ornaments in the World. They form most interesting and attractive features for Libraries, Smoking Rooms, Hotels, Bar and Billiard Rooms, Stable Offices or Private Stable Parlors. Also for display by dealers in Harness, Carriages and Horse Furniture of all descriptions.
> Remember the low price: 20 cents each, or six pictures for one dollar which enables Horsemen to possess the whole series at a nominal cost.
> They will be sent by Mail, post paid, promptly on Receipt of Price."

Credit was not extended. The prints were sent after receipt of the money. The booklet for fire prints, which is illustrated, suggests that these prints would be of interest to firemen, insurance companies and agents and all who are interested in the fire department.

Front page of an advertising booklet for fire pictures issued by Currier and Ives in 1884. Eight pages, each 8 x $5\frac{1}{2}$ inches

CURRIER & IVES'

Illustrated and Descriptive List

—OF—

Celebrated Fire Pictures,

COMPRISING THE SERIES OF SIX PLATES ENTITLED

THE LIFE OF A FIREMAN,

THE FOUR PLATES ENTITLED

THE AMERICAN FIREMAN,

And Others,

ALL ELEGANTLY COLORED.

WE desire to call the attention of Firemen, Insurance Companies and Agents, and all interested in the Fire Department, to the prints illustrated and described in the following pages. They depict scenes familiar to firemen, and will awaken the memory of many a hard fight with the fiery element.

They are very elaborate and correct in every particular, the apparatus and figures being carefully sketched from actual scenes coming under the artist's observation in his attendance at many metropolitan conflagrations, and are exceedingly attractive and appropriate ornaments for firemen's parlors and meeting rooms, as well as for Insurance Offices and Hotels. Any of the prints will be promptly forwarded by mail to any part of the United States on receipt of price.

ADDRESS,

CURRIER & IVES,

Publishers,

115 NASSAU STREET, NEW YORK.

(Copyright, 1884, by Currier & Ives, N. Y.)

CURRIER & IVES' Series of Splendid Colored Pictures

—OF—

THE LIFE OF A FIREMAN.

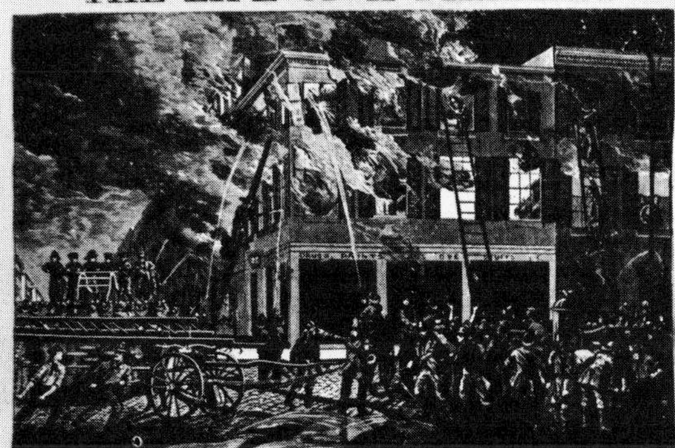

PLATE 3.—THE FIRE.

"NOW, THEN, WITH A WILL." "SHAKE HER UP, BOYS."

A thrilling representation of an extensive conflagration. On the left of of the picture stands a truck from which the members are taking the ladders. Some are already raised, and from an upper window of the burning building emerges a fireman rescuing a little child from the flames, which seem to pursue their prey. Conspicuous in the foreground the Chief Engineer appears, giving his orders. Men are seen upon the ladders with axe in hand, hose upon the roofs of neighboring houses, and all the details incident to the occurrence of a fire in the city.

Size sheet, 26x36 inches. Price, $3.

Sheldon's New York Volunteer Fire Department.

Story of the Volunteer Fire Deparment of New York City. By GEORGE W. SHELDON. With Characteristic Illustrations. 8vo, Cloth, $4.50.

No old "institution" of New York offers so many picturesque contrasts and romantic incidents in the course of its eventful history as the Volunteer Fire Department of New York. Its record of heroic acts and notable sacrifices is long and glorious.

CURRIER & IVES' Series of Splendid Colored Pictures

—OF—

THE LIFE OF A FIREMAN.

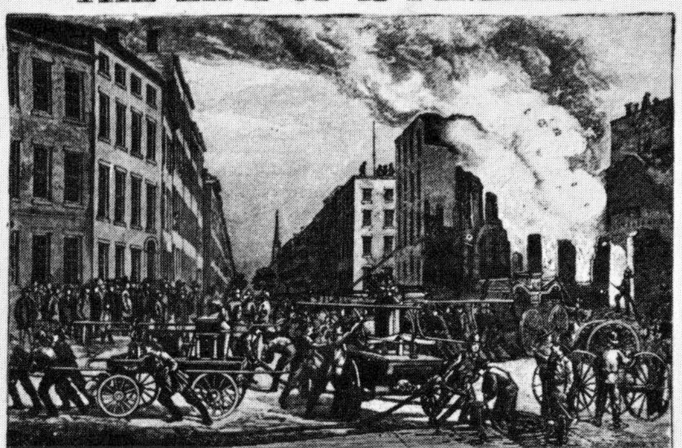

PLATE 4.—THE RUINS.

"TAKE UP." "MAN YO R ROPE."

On the right are the ruins, in which the flames still appear, and a heavy smoke rises up; but the enemy is conquered, and the firemen are "limbering up," and starting for home. The position and details of the engines are beautifully represented, and the scene is very pleasing and impressive.

Size sheet, 26x36 inches. Price, $3.

Sheldon's New York Volunteer Fire Department.

Story of the Volunteer Fire Department of New York City. By GEORGE W. SHELDON. With Characteristic Illustrations. 8vo, Cloth, $4.50.

No old "institution" of New York offers so many picturesque contrasts and romantic incidents in the course of its eventful history as the Volunteer Fire Department of New York. Its record of heroic acts and notable sacrifices is long and glorious.

Centerfold from the same booklet. Illustrations are wood engravings

Currier retired in 1880 and died in 1888. Ives died in 1895. Although the business was carried on by their sons it lost the drive that made it successful. Competition from news pictures in papers and from the chromolithographers such as Prang with their more natural color effects was too much and in 1907 the business ended. The assets, including some stones, were sold at auction. Later, a few of these stones, notably from the *Darktown* series and the large folio clipper ships were used by others to make restrikes.

The Artists

Credit for good management and the ability to hire the right people to execute their plans is rightfully due to Nathaniel Currier and James Ives. The artists who actually created the images deserve equal credit for the success of the firm and even more from us today for picturing the essence of America in the countless interesting details of their work. Currier and Ives used three different types of artists. One type was the artist who drew or painted for the express purpose of having his output put on stone. Some of these were house artists who worked for the firm, some were free-lancers, and some worked for other firms but carried out certain work under contract. A second type was the lithographer who translated an existing painting or drawing to the stone, simplifying it so that it could be successfully produced and colored. The third group included "fine art" artists, some of the best names in the country, whose paintings were used in this commercial way.

In the group of staff artists the most versatile and prolific was Frances (Fanny) Flora Bond Palmer. In addition to being an artist, she was also the foremost woman lithographer of her day and is credited with putting over two hundred pictures on stone, including such classics as *A Midnight Race on the Mississippi* and *The American Express Train.* F. F. Palmer was born in England and came to America in 1844 with her husband Edmund (or Edward) Seymour Palmer and their two children. They settled in New York City and in 1846 formed a lithographic and publishing business called F & S Palmer. Among other works, they lithographed some of the flower prints for A. B. Strong's book, *The American Flora.* In 1849 they apparently had financial problems, and it is reported that N. Currier bought the business and hired Fanny to work for him. Her husband's fondness for drink made her the family breadwinner, working for Currier until her death in 1876 at the age of sixty-four. She contributed to the artistic aspects of an enormous number of Currier and Ives prints and her name is on many medium and large size folios. She covered a remarkable range with Mississippi steam boats,

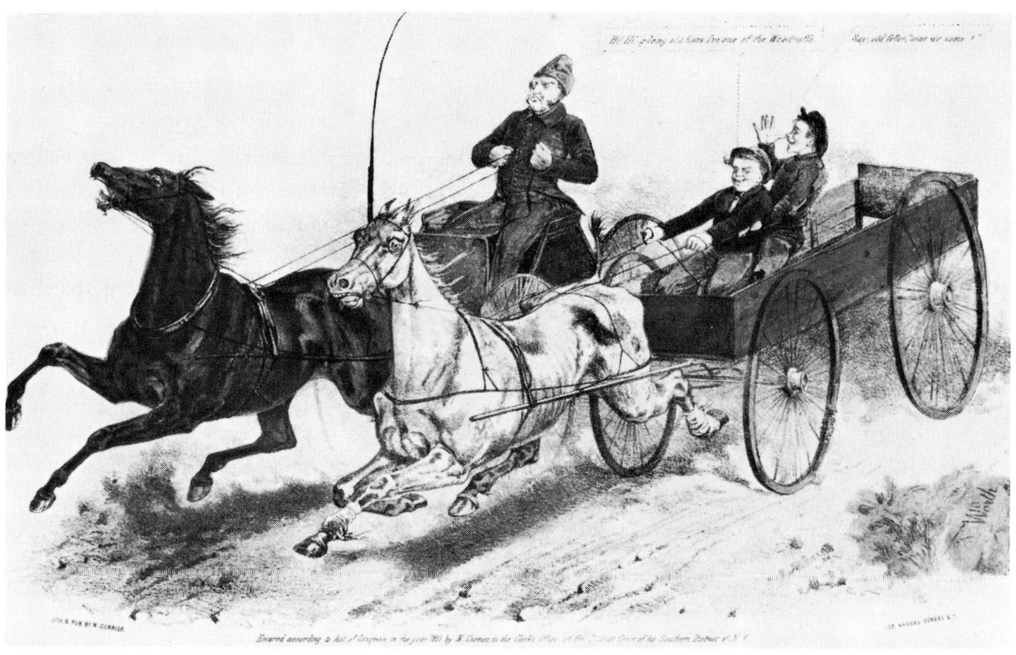

A Brush on the Road, Mile Heats, Best Two in Three, the first comic by Thomas Worth, published by N. Currier, 1855. Hand-colored lithograph, small folio vignette

hunting and fishing scenes, scenic views, portraits of game and fish, still lifes, clipper ships and steamboats; almost the full gamut of the firm's production.

Louis Maurer, also an artist-lithographer, was a German immigrant working for Currier and Ives from 1852 to 1860 and for years after that on special commissions. Although his work covered a wide spectrum, he is known particularly for horse and fire-fighting prints. Thomas Worth, a native New Yorker, was the most prolific of the outside free-lance contributors. Comics were his specialty and his first, *A Brush on the Road, Mile Heats, Best Two in Three,* is illustrated. He is the creator of the famous and popular *Darktown* series and some of the trotter prints including *Trotting Cracks at the Forge.* Charles Parsons came to this country from England in 1830 and soon after became an apprentice in the lithographic firm of Endicott & Co. Throughout most of his career until his retirement in 1892 he did work for Currier and Ives either free-lance or through other companies: Endicott & Co. and Harper and Brothers. He is best known for his marine work, both as artist and lithographer. His versatility is shown by other types of subjects such as the lithographing of *The American Fields Sports* series painted by A. F. Tait.

On stone by C. Parsons, L. Maurer, lith. or even *F. F. Palmer, Del.* were credit lines or signatures permitted to prominent lithographers. Palmer, Parsons and Maurer were all artists as well as skilled lithographers, as were some others in the field. The task of the lithographer was to translate the artist's painting onto stone. Since Currier and Ives was a commercial enterprise rather than an artistic one, this translation consisted of simplifying the forms and details to allow easy and uncomplicated hand-coloring and reducing to a minimum subtle shading and fine details. All of this required skill and artistic sense. A fast, experienced worker could do the stone for a small folio in about a week. Like the commercial artists, some of the lithographers were employed full time by the firm, some freelanced, and some worked for other firms that contracted to do work for Currier and Ives. The principal lithographers at one time or another during the life of the firm were John Cameron, Otto Knirsch, L. Maurer, C. Parsons, Napoleon Sarony, C. Severin, J. Schutz and Franz Venino. Some like J. Schutz, who did most of the lettering on Currier and Ives prints, had specialties, but most worked on the entire composition.

The third category of artists were the professionals who had one or more of their paintings reproduced as lithographs. The principal "fine art" artists used by the firm together with their special areas follow:

J. E. Butterworth—Clipper ships and marine subjects, including *Clipper Ship Flying Cloud*

George Catlin—Indians and western subjects

George H. Durrie—Winter scenes including *Home to Thanksgiving.* He was nicknamed *the snowman.*

Eastman Johnson—One print, *"Husking,"* but it is number one of the *Best Fifty*

A. F. Tait—Sporting, nature, western and outdoor life subjects. Ten of the *Best Fifty* large folios are by Tait

William Walker-Southern scenes including *The Levee-New Orleans*

Production

There are no records of the total number of prints produced nor of the total number made of any particular print. One clue, however, is that Thomas Worth demanded and got a raise when the production for one of his prints of the *Darktown* comic series reached the seventy-three thousand level. Another clue is that some of the popular "disaster" prints had to be produced using several stones in order to keep up with demand. From these fragments of information we can only conclude that vast numbers were made.

Stones for popular prints were kept in storage and new runs were made when the supply ran low. Some, such as the *American Homestead* series, although first made in 1869, were still offered for sale thirty-five years later. It is estimated that in the 1870's fully fifty per cent of the total number of titles of the firm from its beginning were still being offered for sale. Over the years the stones were sometimes modified by changing titles, backgrounds, etc. and N. Currier to Currier and Ives after 1857. Besides changes in state, the different runs often had changes in coloring and type of paper.

Most of the prints were colored by hand using water colors, but some were sold uncolored. Many of the later ones, in the 1880's and 1890's, were printed in oil colors. The early small and medium hand-colored prints were generally colored in the plant on a production line basis with each woman on the line applying a particular color and the entire group following a sample print often colored by Mrs. Palmer or one of the other artists. Some, however, were jobbed out to other firms and to home colorists. The large folios were usually executed with more care and skill and were farmed out to young artists and colorists to be done at home.

Sparkle and life were added to many of the prints by painting the dark areas with a water solution of gum arabic. When dry, this vegetable gum left a shiny area on the surface of the paper which can still be seen on many of the prints. Gum arabic was also used on some prints as a binding agent for opaque colored powders, forming a gouache.

History of Collecting

Currier and Ives are the most widely collected American prints. Even before the firm closed its doors for the last time in 1907 there were a few collectors who selected prints from the thousands stored in boxes and bins in their small plain retail outlet. With these people as a collecting nucleus some of the desirable categories were sold at auction and traded within the group. Clipper ships were popular enough so that Max Williams, a New York dealer in ship models, relics and prints, made what now seems to be an infinite number of restrikes from six of the original stones. Although not colored so well as the original and on somewhat different paper, the passage of time since they were put out in 1915 makes them difficult for today's collector to detect and they are frequently furiously bid up at auction in the mistaken belief that they are a product of Currier and Ives. These restrikes all in large folio size are:

Clipper Ship Dreadnought off Tuskar Light
Clipper Ship Dreadnought off Sandy Hook
Clipper Ship Flying Cloud

Clipper Ship Ocean Express
Clipper Ship Sweepstakes
Clipper Ship Three Brothers

Soon after World War I, interest in American antiques built up rapidly with Currier and Ives lithographs prominent in the trend. Interest broadened to include most of the collecting categories including some sentimentals and the prices reflected this. Typical of the meteoric price rise is the auction record of the print, *American Country Life—Pleasures of Winter:*

YEAR	AUCTION PRICE
1917	$ 0.75
1920	7.50
1922	20.00
1923	57.50
1924	50.00
1925	40.00
. . . .	
1930	90.00

Harry T. Peters, Fred J. Peters, Jane Cooper Bland, and Harry Shaw Newman, the owner of the Old Print Shop in New York, must be included among the leading organizers of the collecting community. Harry Peters, in his two-volume book *Currier and Ives—Printmakers to the American People,* traced the history of the firm and included a check list of about five thousand prints. In *Currier and Ives, A Manual for Collectors* by Jane Cooper Bland, auction and retail prices are given for most of the prints. Fred Peters wrote three books on special areas: clipper ships, railroad and Western, and sporting. Harry Shaw Newman promoted the prints and in 1932 organized a "jury" to select the fifty best large folio prints, followed in 1933 by the fifty best small and medium folio prints. The lists printed below represent a selection which is still pleasing to collectors today although perhaps ten times this number could be included as equally desirable:

Fifty Best Large Folio

1. *Husking*
2. *American Forest Scene—Maple Sugaring*
3. *Central Park, Winter—The Skating Pond*
4. *Home to Thanksgiving*
5. *Life of a Hunter—A Tight Fix*
6. *Life on the Prairie—The Buffalo Hunt*

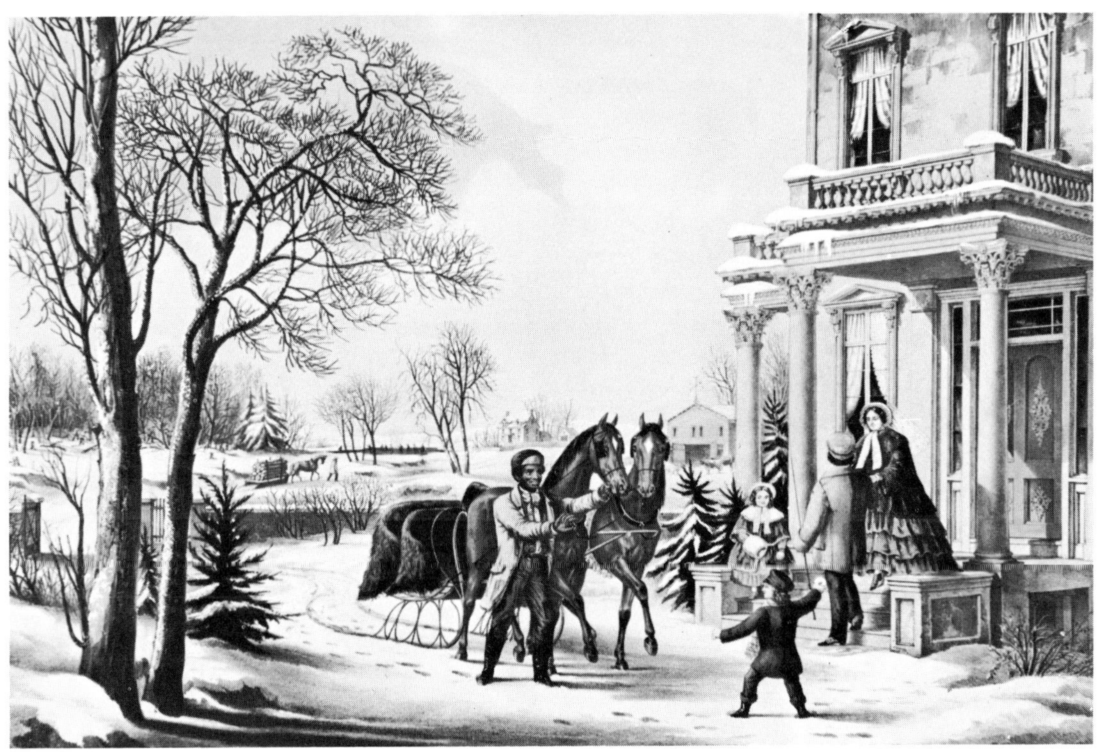

American Country Life/ Pleasures of Winter, by F. F. Palmer, published by N. Currier in 1855. Hand-colored lithograph, $16\frac{7}{8}$ x 24 inches

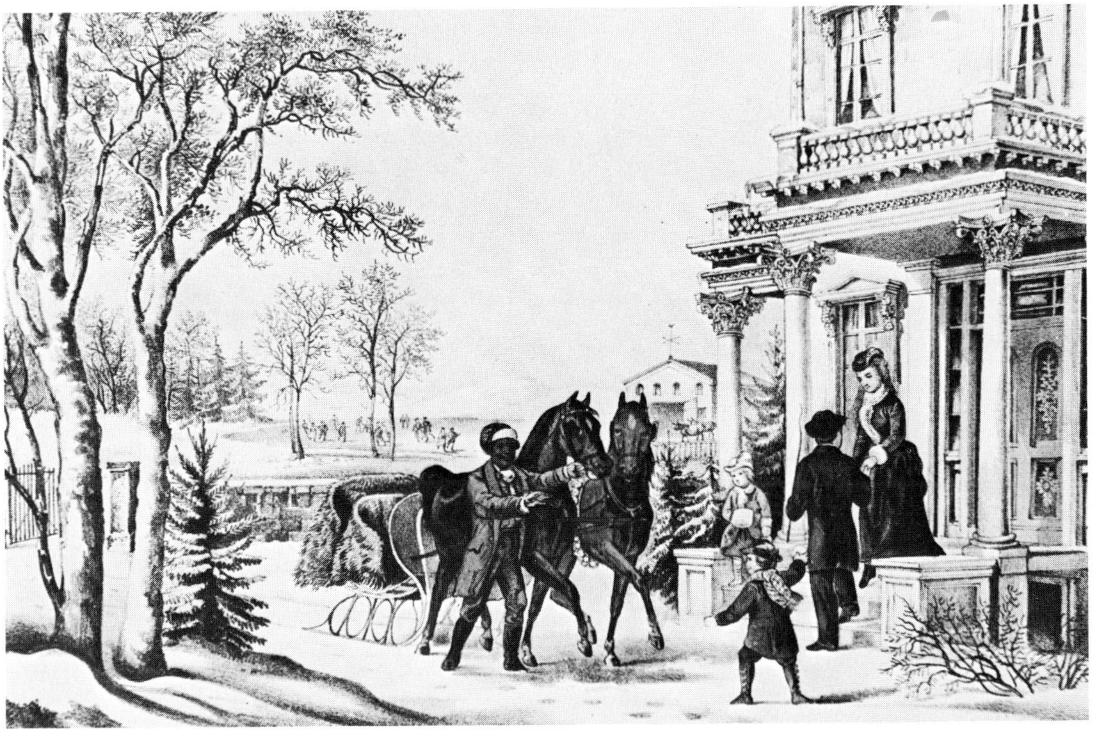

Pleasures of the Country/ Winter, published by Currier and Ives, undated. One of a dozen or so examples of a small folio print with a design similar to a large folio

7. *The Lightning Express Trains Leaving the Junction*
8. *Peytona and Fashion*
9. *The Rocky Mountains—Emigrants Crossing the Plains*
10. *Trolling for Blue Fish*
11. *Whale Fishery—The Sperm Whale in a Flurry*
12. *Winter in the Country—The Old Grist Mill*
13. *American Farm Scenes, No. 4 (Winter)*
14. *American National Game of Baseball*
15. *American Winter Sports—Trout Fishing on Chateaugay Lake*
16. *Mink Trapping—Prime*
17. *Preparing for Market*
18. *Winter in the Country—Getting Ice*
19. *Across the Continent—Westward the Course of Empire Takes Its Way*
20. *Life on the Prairie—The Trapper's Defense*
21. *The Midnight Race on the Mississippi*
22. *The Road—Winter*
23. *Summer Scenes in New York Harbor*
24. *Trotting Cracks at the Forge*
25. *View of San Francisco*
26. *Wreck of the Steamship "San Francisco"*
27. *Taking the Back Track*
28. *American Field Sports—Flush'd*
29. *American Hunting Scenes—A Good Chance*
30. *American Winter Scenes—Morning*
31. *Autumn in New England—Cider Making*
32. *Catching a Trout*
33. *Clipper Ship "Nightingale"*
34. *The Life of a Fireman—The Race*
35. *Mac and Zachary Taylor*
36. *New England Winter Scene*
37. *Rail Shooting on the Delaware*
38. *Snowed Up—Ruffed Grouse—Winter*
39. *Surrender of General Burgoyne at Saratoga*
40. *Surrender of Cornwallis at Yorktown*
41. *Clipper Ship "Red Jacket"*
42. *American Winter Sports—Deer Shooting on the Shattagee*
43. *The Bark "Theoxena"*
44. *The Cares of a Family*
45. *The Celebrated Horse Lexington*

46. *Grand Drive—Central Park*
47. *The Great Fire at Chicago*
48. *Landscape, Fruit and Flowers*
49. *The Life of a Fireman—The Metropolitan System*
50. *The Splendid Naval Triumph on the Mississippi*

Fifty Best Small and Medium Folio

1. *The Express Train* (N. Currier, undated, by J. Schutz)
2. *American Railroad Scene—Snowbound* (Currier and Ives, 1871)
3. *Beach Snipe Shooting*
4. *Ice-Boat Race on the Hudson*
5. *Central Park in Winter*
6. *The Star of the Road*
7. *The High Bridge at Harlem, N.Y.* (N. Currier, 1849, horse and buggy in foreground)
8. *Maple Sugaring, Early Spring in the Northern Woods*
9. *Shakers Near Lebanon*
10. *Winter Sports—Pickerel Fishing*
11. *The American Clipper Ship Witch of the Wave*
12. *Gold Mining in California*
13. *The Great International Boat Race*
14. *Wild Turkey Shooting*
15. *Perry's Victory on Lake Erie*
16. *Washington at Mount Vernon, 1797*
17. *The Whale Fishery. "Laying on"*
18. *Chatham Square, New York*
19. *Water Rail Shooting*
20. *The Sleigh Race* (N. Currier, 1848)
21. *Franklin's Experiment*
22. *Washington Crossing the Delaware* (Currier and Ives, undated, Washington and soldiers in boat)
23. *American Homestead—Winter*
24. *Washington Taking Leave of the Officers of his Army* (N. Currier, 1848)
25. *Steamboat Knickerbocker*
26. *Kiss Me Quick!/Children this is the third time . . . etc.*
27. *On the Mississippi Loading Cotton*
28. *Bound Down the River*
29. *American Whalers Crushed in the Ice*
30. *Dartmouth College*

31. *Terrific Combat Between the Monitor, 2 Guns, and the Merrimac, 10 Guns* (Monitor on left, gunboats in rear, firing)
32. *General Francis Marion*
33. *Art of Making Money Plenty*
34. *Hon. Abraham Lincoln* (bust to right, beardless, oval)
35. *Gen. George Washington* (three-quarters figure, uniform, with cape)
36. *Black Bass Spearing*
37. *Early Winter*
38. *Woodcock Shooting* (N. Currier, 1855)
39. *"Dutchman" and "Hiram Woodruff"*
40. *Great Conflagration at Pittsburgh, Pa.*
41. *Bear Hunting, Close Quarters* (winter scene)
42. *The Destruction of Tea at Boston Harbor*
43. *Cornwallis is Taken*
44. *Landing of the Pilgrims at Plymouth, 11th Dec., 1620* (Currier and Ives, 1876)
45. *The Great Fight for the Championship*
46. *Benjamin Franklin* (N. Currier, 1847)
47. *Noah's Ark* (gnarled tree on right, serpent entwined around one of two palm trees on left, no human figures in foreground)
48. *Black Eyed Susan* (N. Currier, 1848)
49. *The Bloomer Costume* (N. Currier, 1851)
50. *The Clipper Yacht "America"* (N. Currier, undated, small folio)

Each of the "best fifty" large folio prints was illustrated in the *New York Sun,* one each day, starting in January 1933. The pictures were enthusiastically received by the reading public and the editions of the paper were quickly sold out. This exposure contributed enormously to making Currier and Ives a household word. Before long reproductions of the prints were used on calendars, Christmas cards and prints to be used as decorative accessories. The popularization of the name increased the number and awareness of collectors, creating a demand that virtually exhausted the supply from attics and barns.

A special note of caution is in order at this point. Many of the most popular large folio prints were photomechanically reproduced at various times since the 1930's. Some are so expertly done that a novice is easily misled, and they are regularly bought at auctions where thousands of dollars are paid for a twenty-five dollar reproduction. These reproductions are often very close to the size of the original and are partly hand-colored to add to the problem of identification. Furthermore, those made twenty or thirty years ago are beginning to show some signs of age. The inexperienced become foolhardy if they fail to seek the advice of a reputable and competent dealer or collector before spending a large amount for a print.

Collecting Categories

Although some collections are eclectic and unbounded, most have a well-defined domain. Some may include only the "best fifty;" others, prints by particular artists such as Durrie. Usually, a collector chooses a subject from one or more of the following collecting categories:

- Winter scenes
- Hunting, fishing, and game
- Ships and yachts
- Fire scenes
- Farm, rural, and genre
- Railroad, pioneer, and Indian
- Horses and racing
- Views, historicals, politicals, sentimentals, fruits, and flowers

Some of the key prints in these categories are discussed in the following:

Winter Scenes

For most people, the winter scenes are the embodiment of Currier and Ives nostalgia. Their whiteness and absence of large areas of strong color make them easy to use with modern decor, and with their quiet themes of home and wholesome outdoor fun they have become one of the highest priced and most sought after of Currier and Ives print categories. The nine large folio prints from paintings by George Durrie form the backbone of this group. The most popular is *Home to Thanksgiving* but the more available *The Farmer's Home—Winter* and *Farm Yard in Winter* are just as appealing. Fanny Palmer created a good number of the "Christmas Card" prints including *American Winter Scenes/ Morning,* and its mate *Evening; Winter Morning* and its mate *Winter Evening. The Road/ Winter* and *Central Park, Winter—The Skating Pond* are two other choice winter scenes. Small folios include *American Homestead—Winter,* one of the "best fifty;" *Central Park, Winter—The Skating Carnival,* a simplified version of the large folio; *Frozen Up* and *Maple Sugaring, Early Spring in the Northern Woods.* Small folio prints are not generally credited to the artist but there are strong indications that Mrs. Palmer and George Durrie had a hand with some of these.

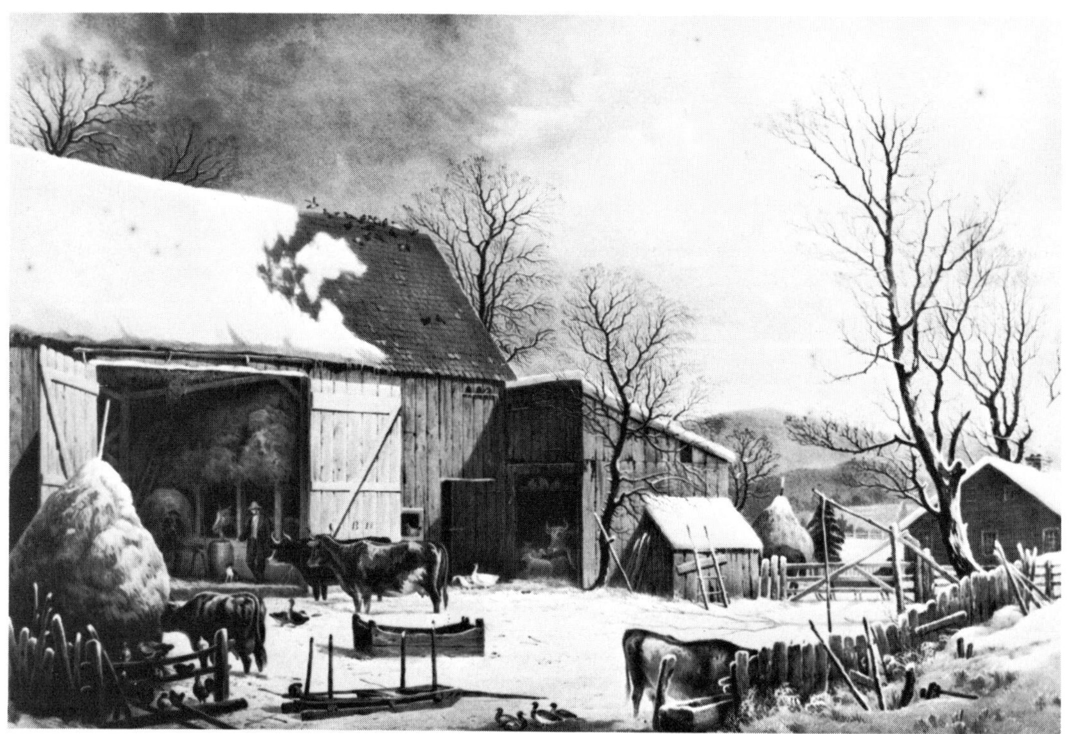

The Farm-Yard in Winter, after a painting by G. H. Durrie, published by Currier and Ives, 1861. Hand-colored lithograph, 16¼ x 23$\frac{9}{16}$ inches

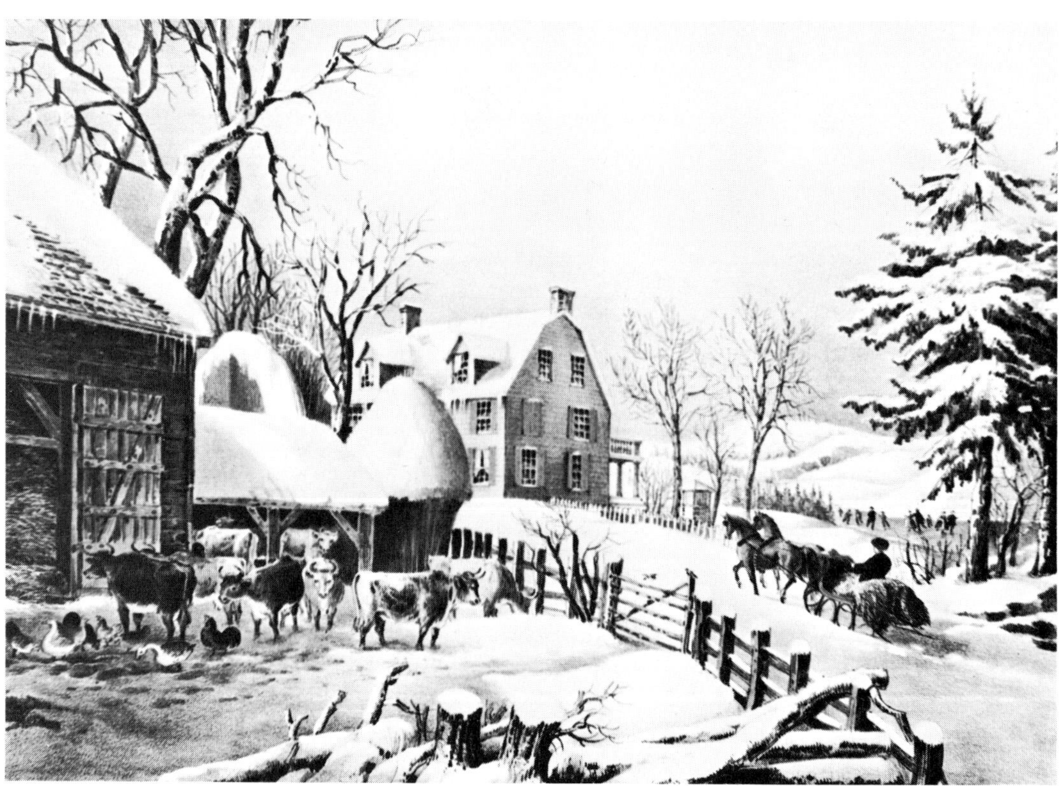

Winter Morning, by F. F. Palmer, published by Currier and Ives, 1861. Hand-colored lithograph, 11⅚ x 15⅚ inches

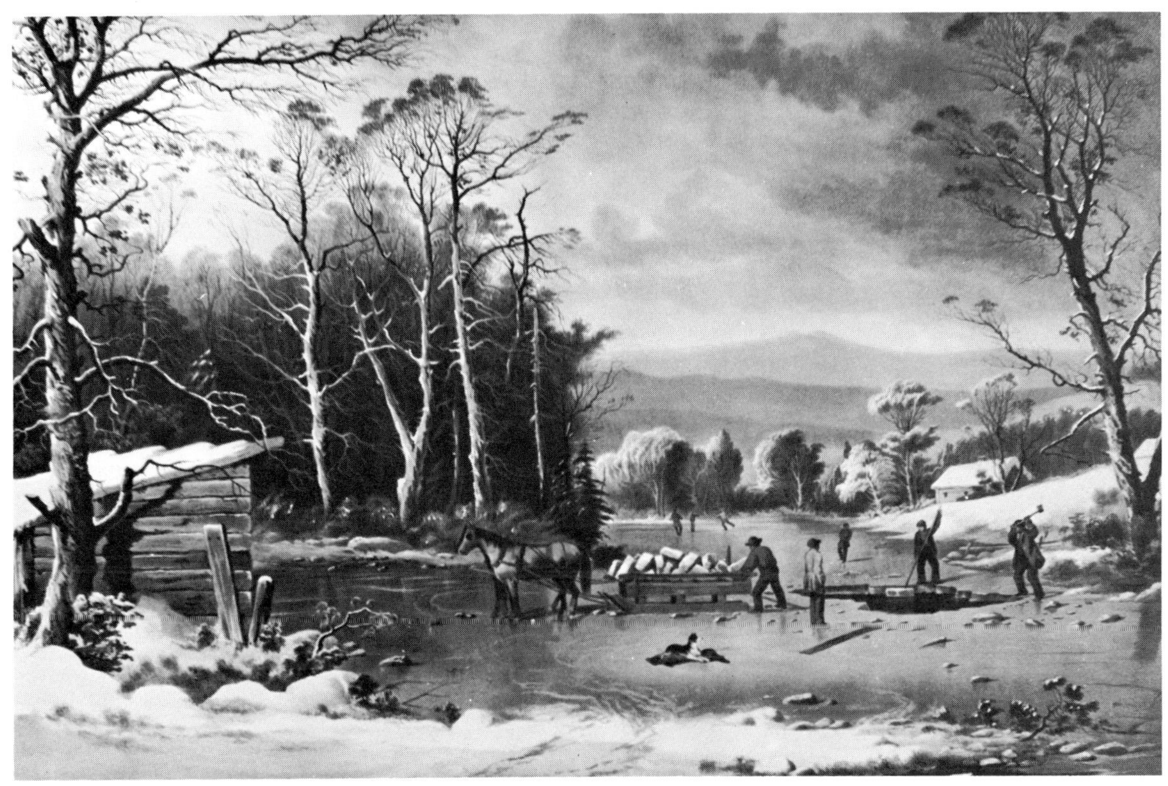

Winter in the Country/ Getting Ice, after a painting by G. H. Durrie, published by Currier and Ives, 1864. Hand-colored lithograph, 18½ x 27¹⁄₁₆ inches (*Collection of Ladd MacMillan*)

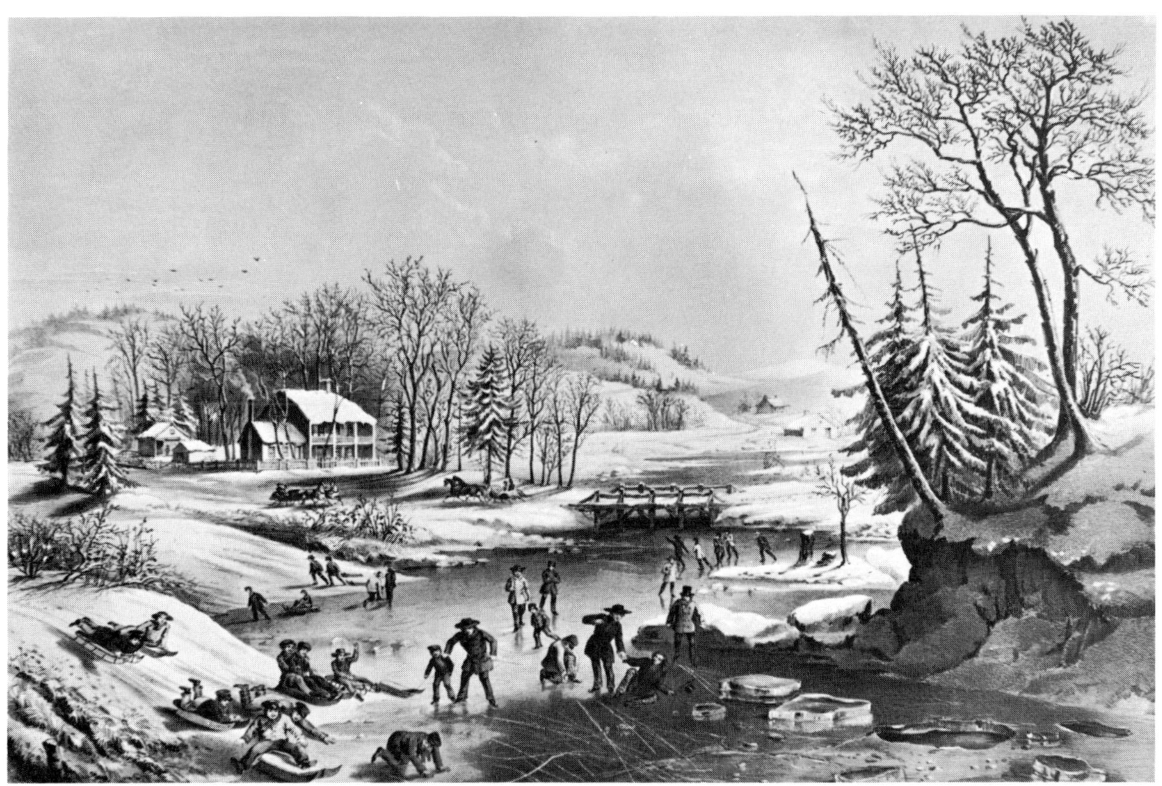

American Winter Scenes/ Morning, by F. F. Palmer, published by Currier and Ives, 1854. Tint stone and hand-colored lithograph, 16½ x 24¹⁄₁₆ inches

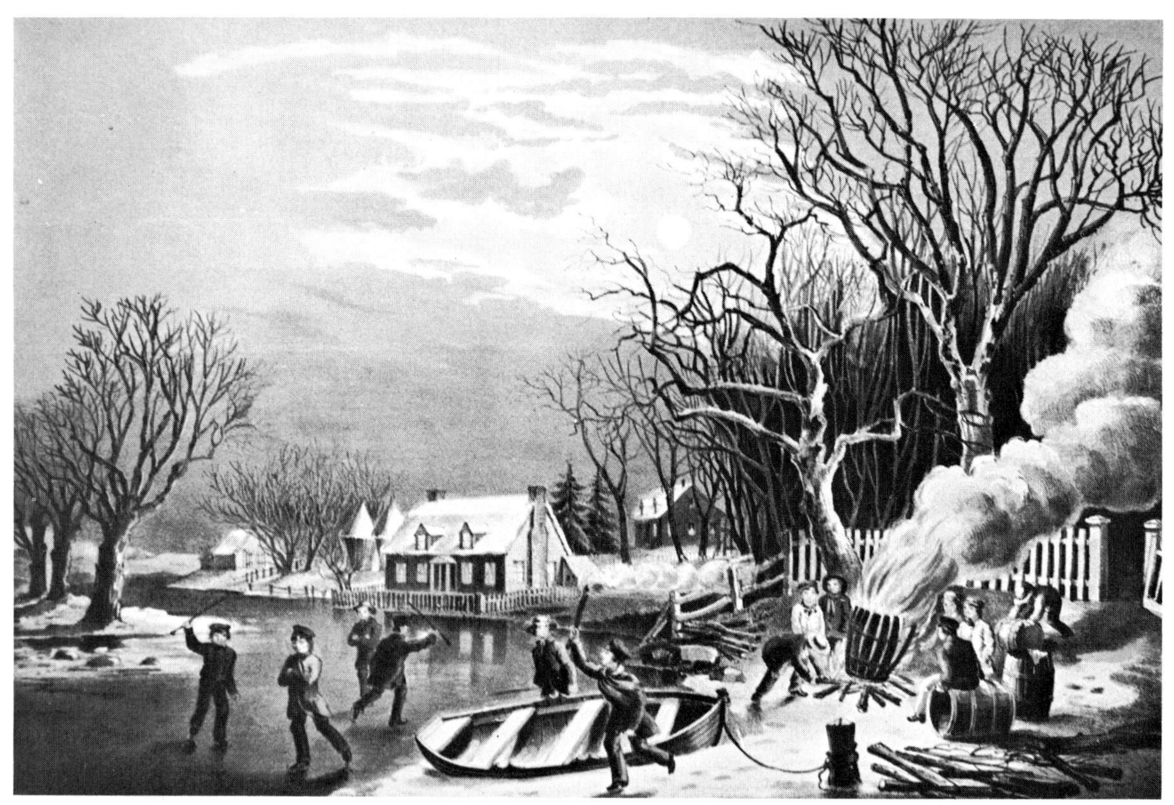

Winter Evening, published by N. Currier, 1854. Hand-colored lithograph, $10\frac{3}{8}$ x 15 inches

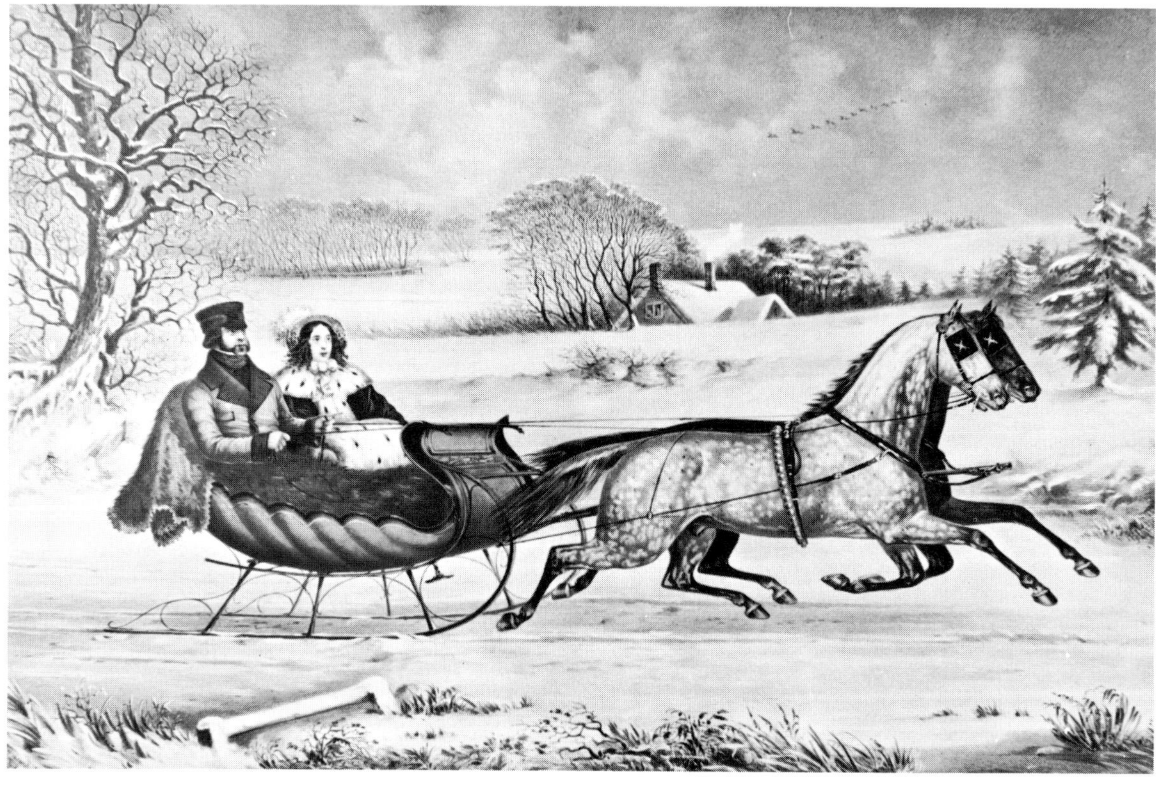

The Road—Winter, published by N. Currier, 1853. Hand-colored lithograph, $17\frac{11}{16}$ x $26\frac{1}{2}$ inches (*Collection of Ladd MacMillan*)

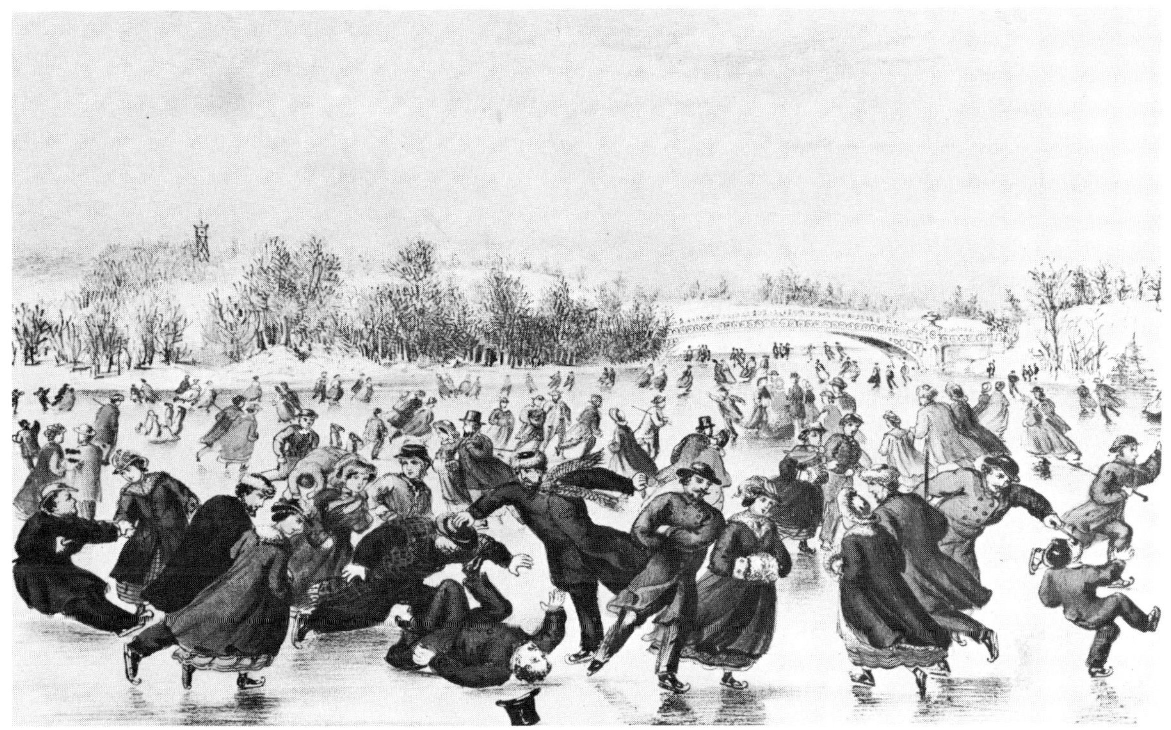

Central Park Winter/ The Skating Carnival, published by Currier and Ives. Hand-colored lithograph, $8\frac{1}{16}$ x $12\frac{3}{4}$ inches

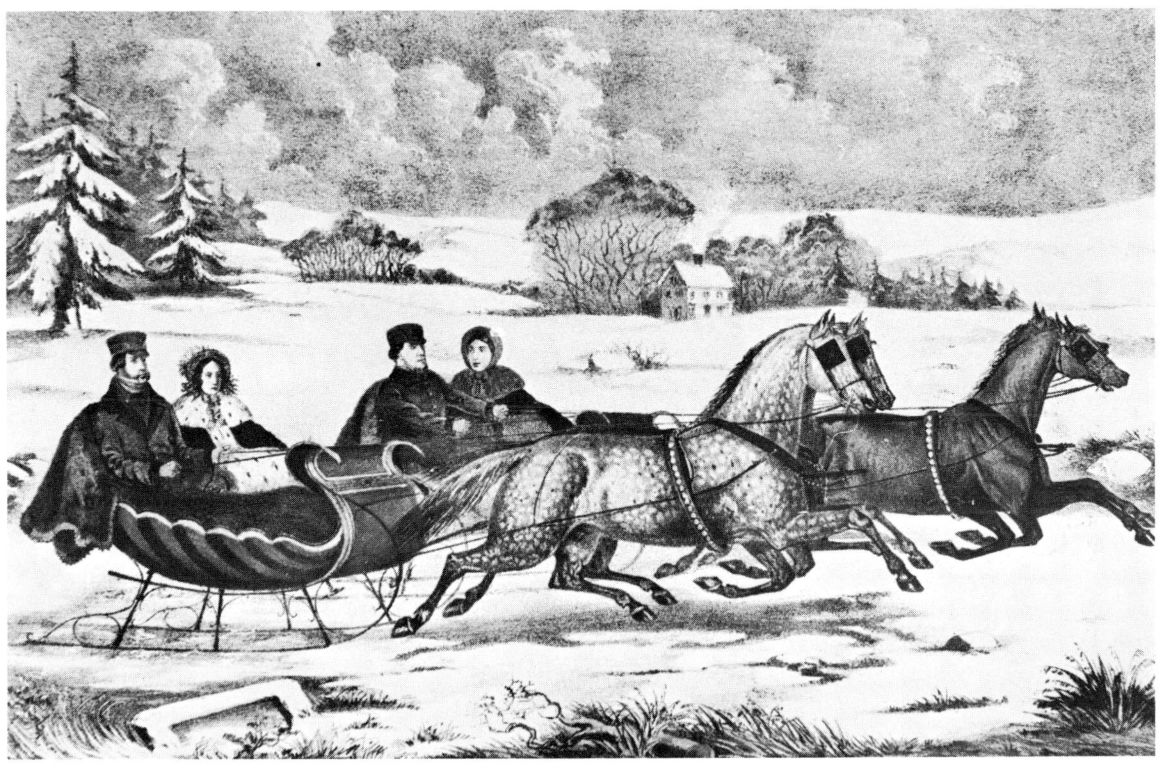

The Sleigh Race, published by Currier and Ives. A small folio print with elements of design similar to *The Road—Winter*

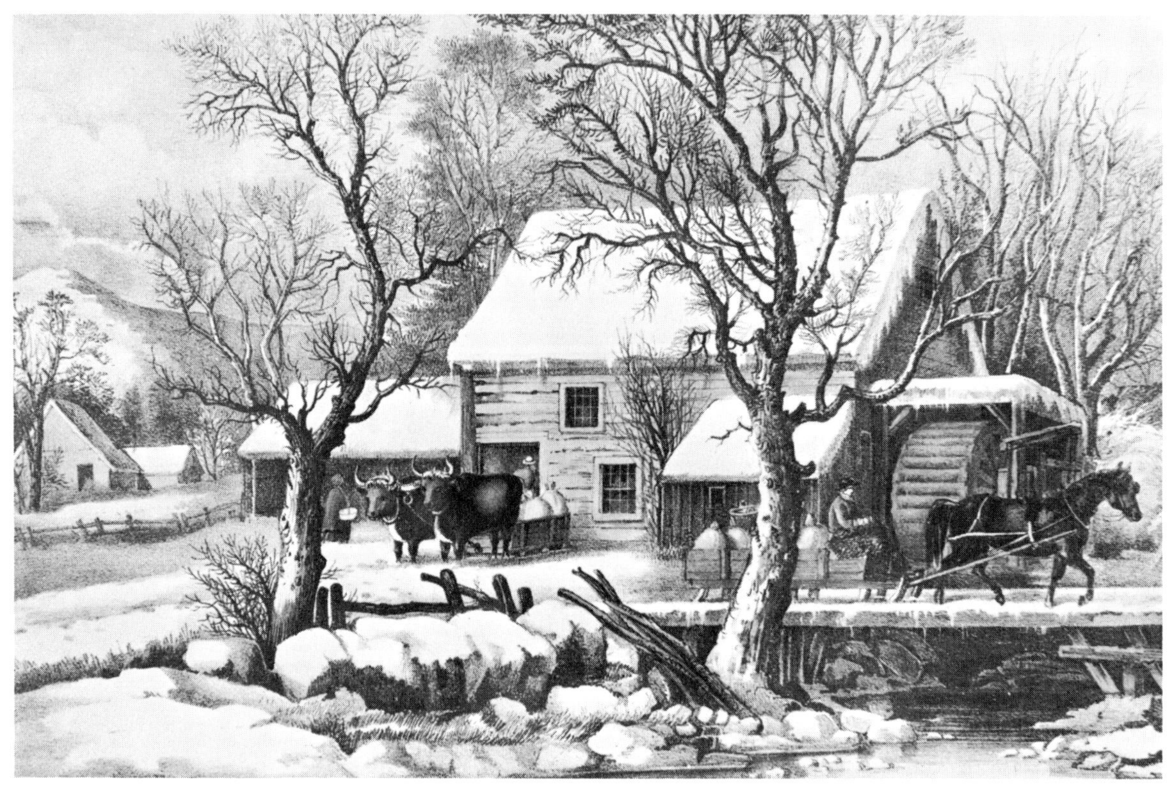

Frozen-Up, published by Currier and Ives, 1872. Hand-colored lithograph, $8\frac{1}{2}$ x $12\frac{1}{2}$ inches

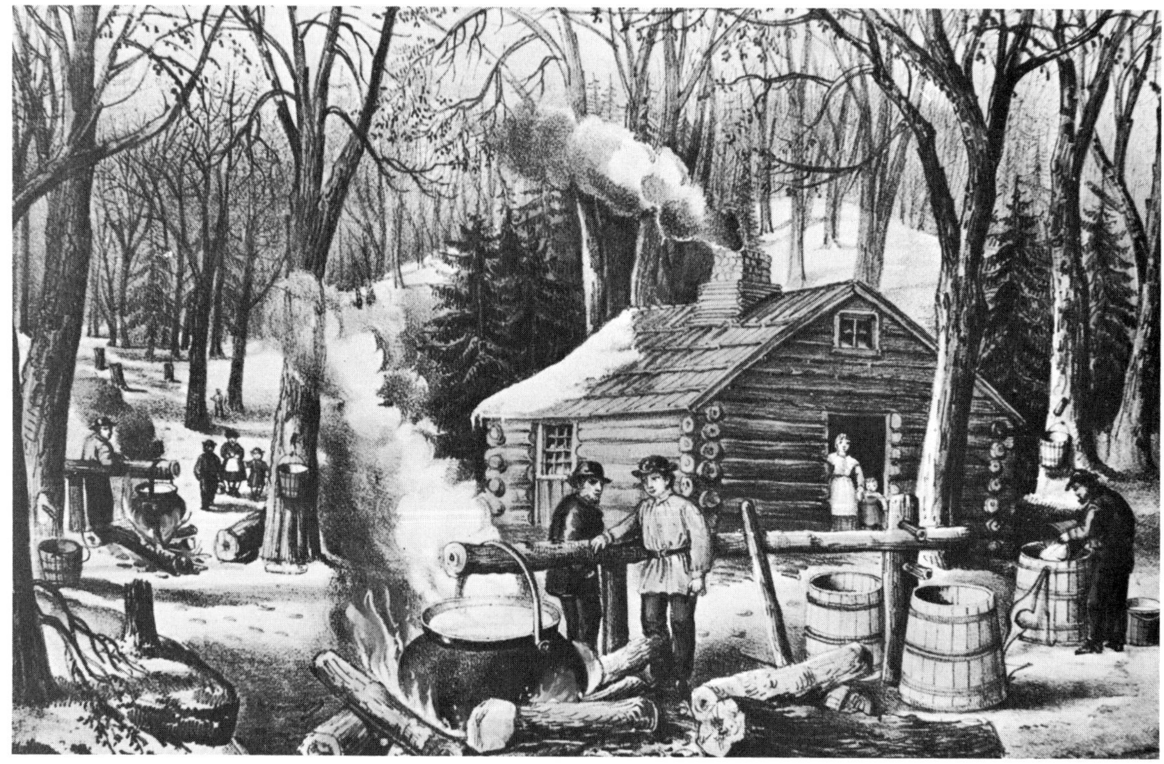

Maple Sugaring/ Early Spring in the Northern Woods, published by Currier and Ives, 1872. Hand-colored lithograph, $8\frac{7}{16}$ x $12\frac{1}{2}$ inches (*Collection of Ladd MacMillan*)

Hunting, Fishing and Game

In his book, *Sporting Prints by Currier and Ives,* Fred Peters catalogues and illustrates a total of one hundred ninety-two prints in this group. This large number reflects the pre-ecology interest in hunting and fishing in a less populated nineteenth-century America. *The Life of a Hunter—A Tight Fix,* which set a series of auction records, is one of the rarest and most expensive of all Currier and Ives prints.

Mrs. Palmer made heavy contributions to this class with her "Long Island Series" of bird hunting scenes, all of which were painted on Long Island (N.Y.) except for *Rail Shooting on the Delaware. Rail Shooting* is number thirty-seven of the "best fifty" and the rarest of the set. The six prints in the series reputedly show her husband and son as hunters. *Trolling for Bluefish* by Mrs. Palmer, with some assistance from Thomas Worth, is a striking picture and one of the best fishing prints. The hunter's bag and the fisherman's catch were also subjects that were carefully pictured. Typical of these is *Brook Trout—Just Caught.*

Some of the bird, wildlife, and hunting paintings by A. F. Tait were used for Currier and Ives prints. His *Cares of a Family* and *A Rising Family* are considered to be among the best American nature prints. The four prints of *American Field Sports* form an attractive and popular group.

Although the large folios are more impressive, the small folio prints in this group are also desirable and widely collected. Among them are *Beach Snipe Shooting, Woodcock Shooting* and *Wild Turkey Shooting.*

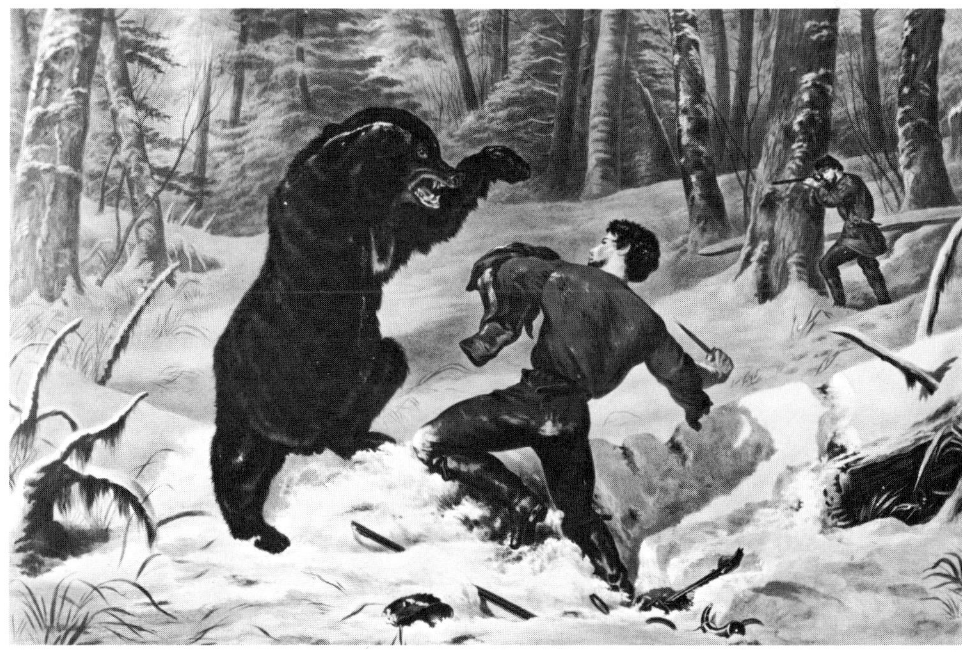

The Life of a Hunter/ A Tight Fix, after a painting by A. F. Tait, published by Currier and Ives, 1861. Hand-colored lithograph, $18\frac{3}{4}$ x $27\frac{1}{16}$ inches (*Collection of Ladd MacMillan*)

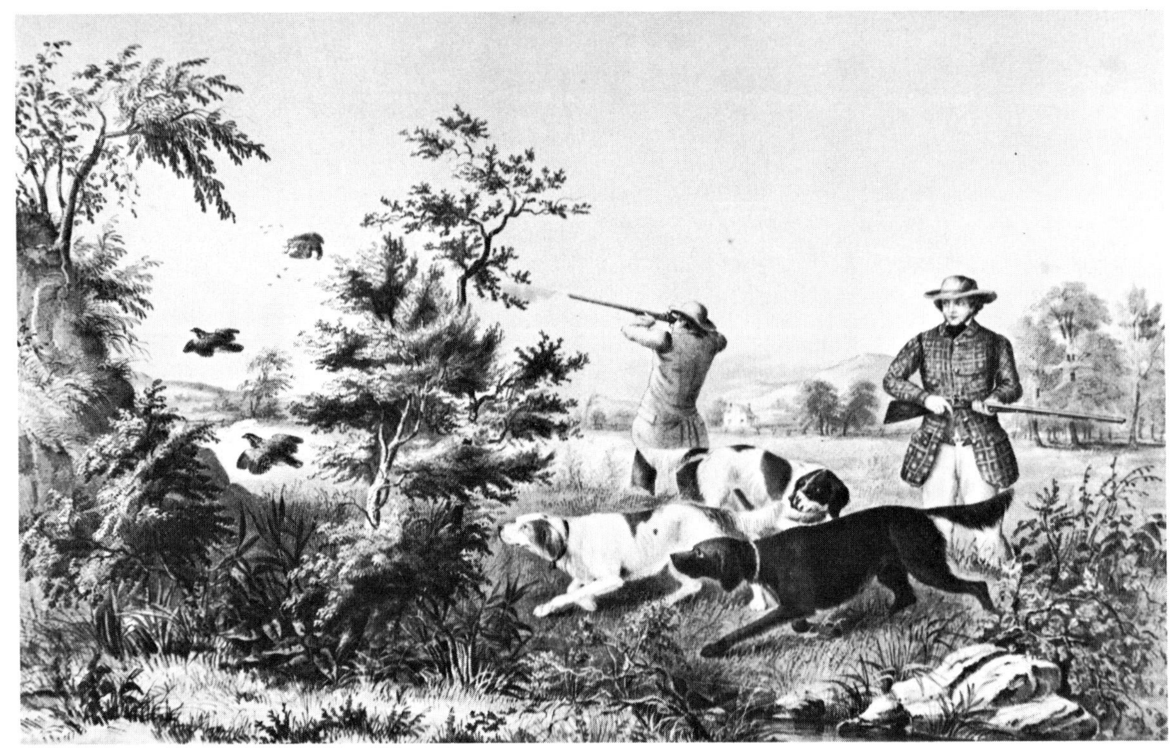

Quail Shooting, by F. F. Palmer, published by N. Currier, 1852. One of the "Long Island" series. Hand-colored lithograph, 13 x 20⅜ inches

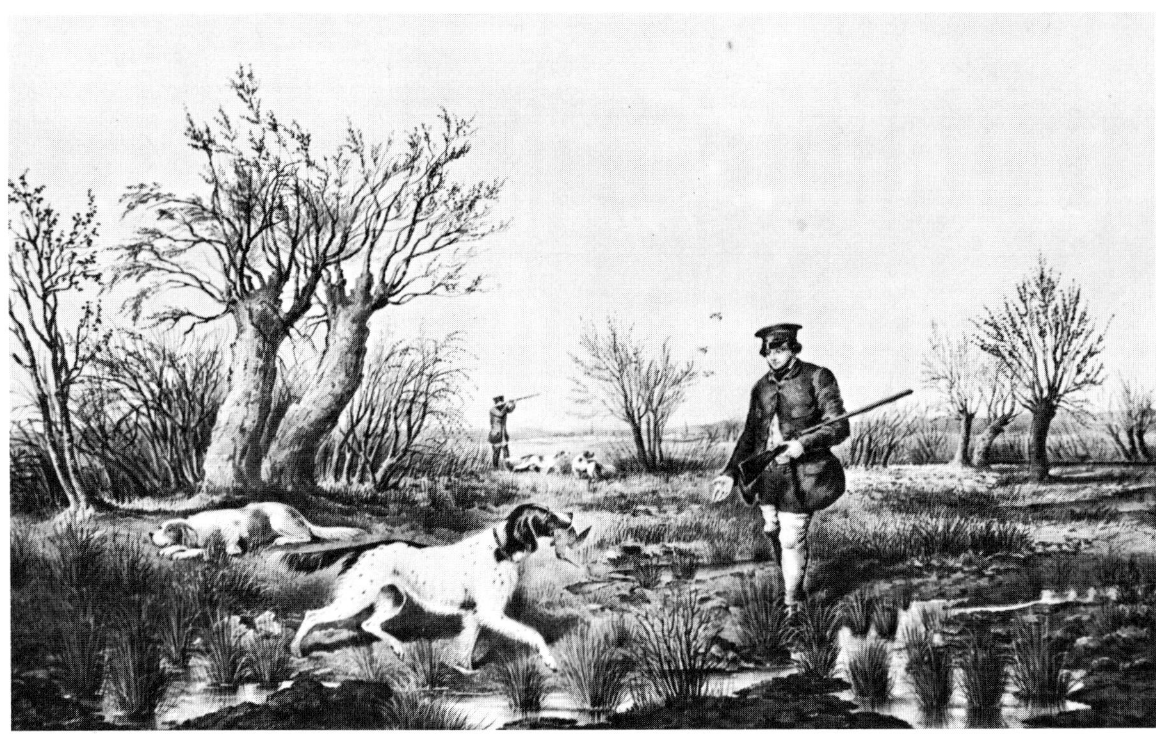

Snipe Shooting, by F. F. Palmer, published by N. Currier, 1852. One of the "Long Island" series. Hand-colored lithograph, 12⁹⁄₁₆ x 20⁵⁄₁₆ inches

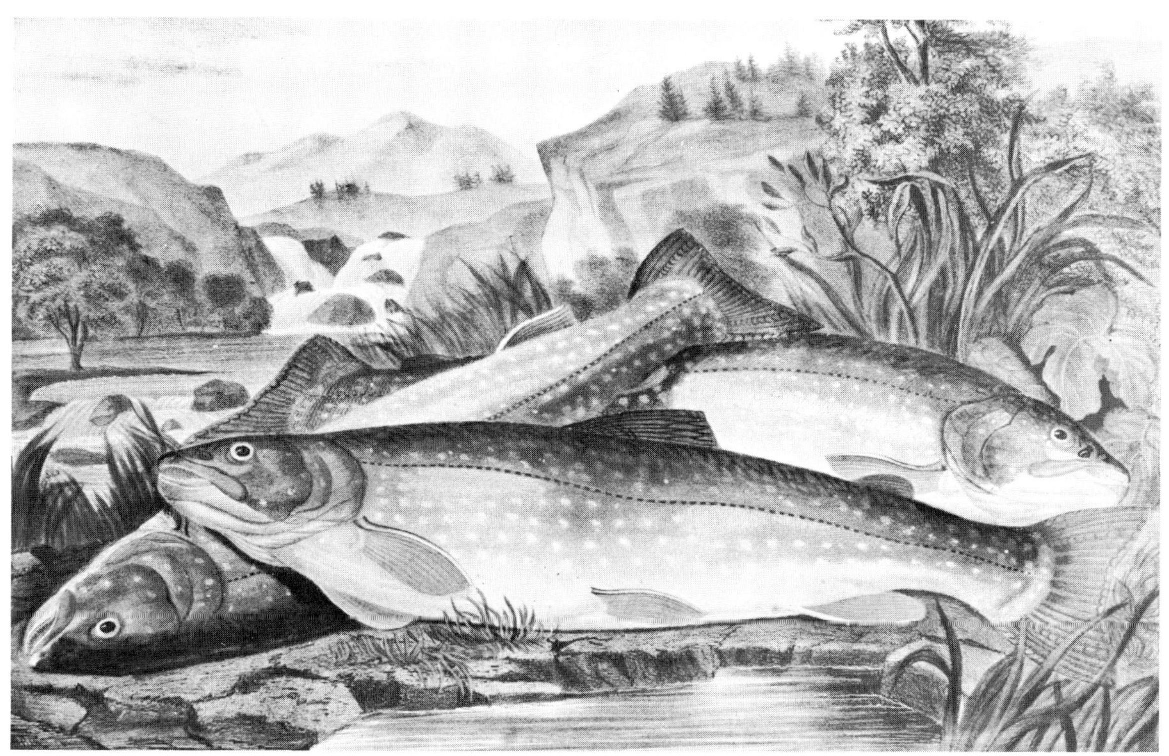

Brook Trout/ Just Caught, published by Currier and Ives. Hand-colored lighograph, 11 x $16\frac{7}{8}$ inches

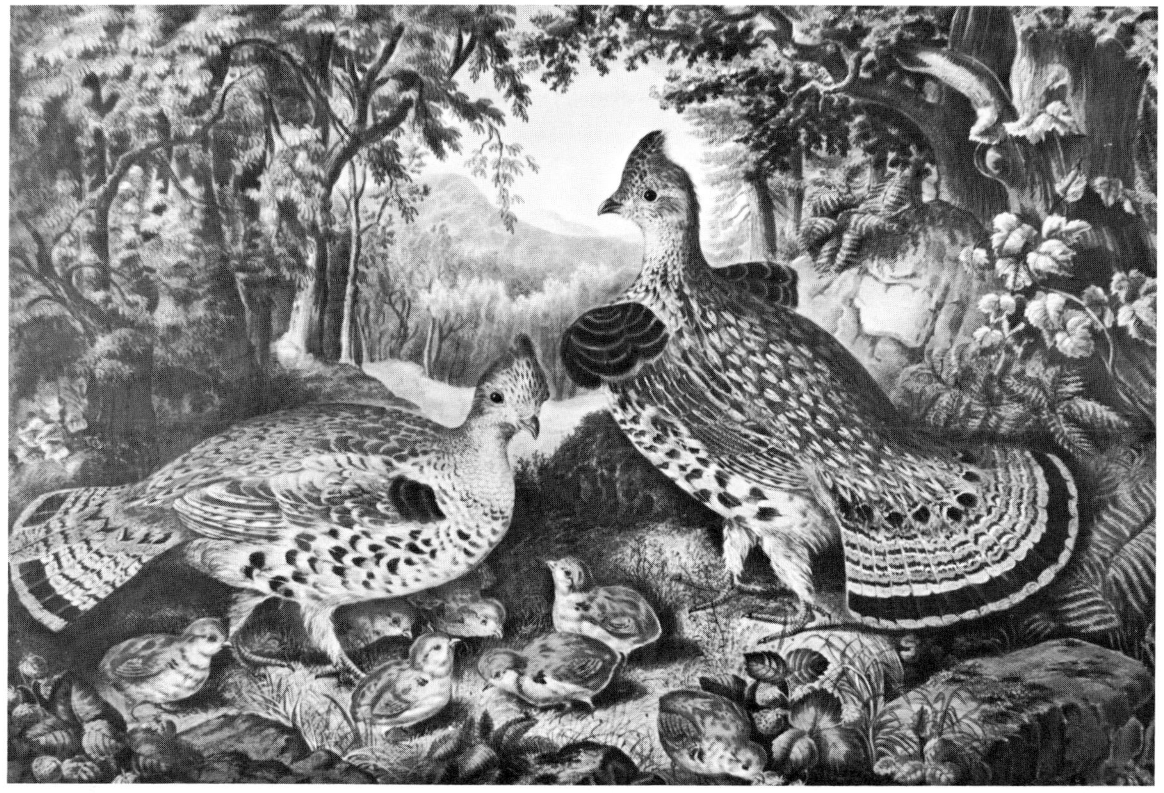

The Happy Family/ Ruffed Grouse and Young, by F. F. Palmer, published by Currier and Ives, 1866. One of the most attractive game prints. Hand-colored lithograph, $19\frac{13}{16}$ x $27\frac{13}{16}$ inches

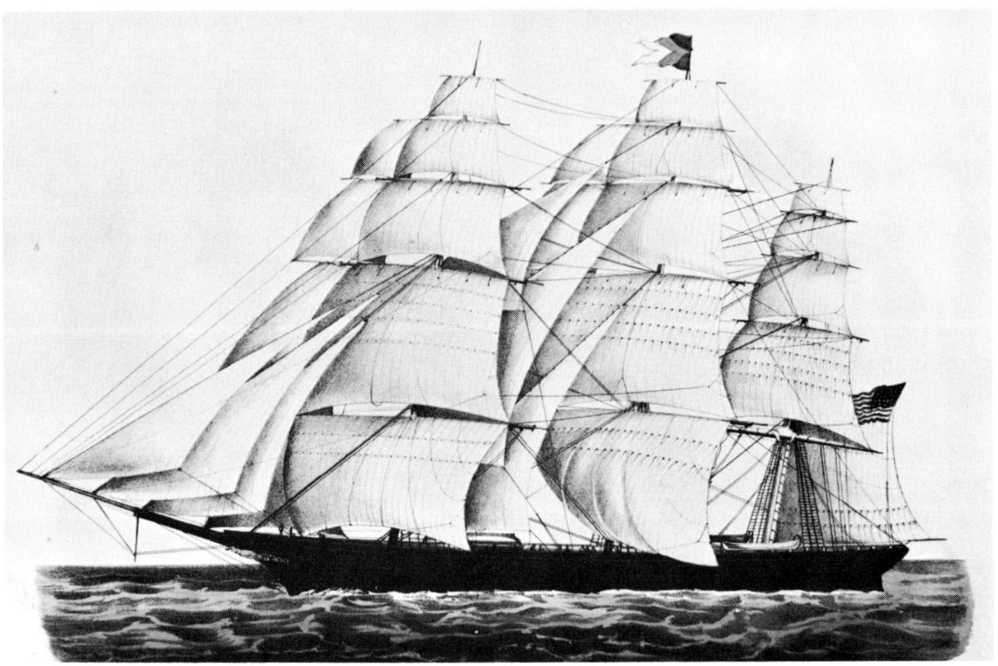

Homeward Bound, published by Currier and Ives, small folio.

Ships and Yachts

America's romance with the sea has made and kept the twenty large folio and thirty-four small folio clipper ship prints popular. As far back as 1915 Max Williams found demand for the clipper ship prints sufficient to warrant making the restrikes. Some of the small folio clipper ships such as *Outward Bound* and *Homeward Bound* are even admired by land-lubbers.

Whaling scenes are a class in themselves with a total of fifteen, most rather rare, including *The American Whaler, The Whale Fishery/ The Sperm Whale in a Flurry* and *The Whale Fishery/ Attacking a "Right" Whale- "Cutting In."*

The transition from sail to steam which took place during the life of the firm is portrayed in many of the prints, since the firm was always interested in the newest and latest in every field. Starting with early steamships like the *U.S. Mail Steamship Adriatic,* they continued to feature them as late as 1898 in *The White Squadron. Our Victorious Fleet in Cuban Waters,* one of Currier and Ives' last prints.

The wealth and affluence of some Americans which came about as a result of our industrial development enabled some to indulge in the sport of building and racing yachts. These events caught the public fancy so that a long series of prints was issued, showing individual yachts such as *The Yacht Dauntless of N.Y., 268 Tons; The Clipper Yacht America,* number fifty of the "best fifty;" as well as races like *The Great International Boat Race, Aug. 27th, 1869.*

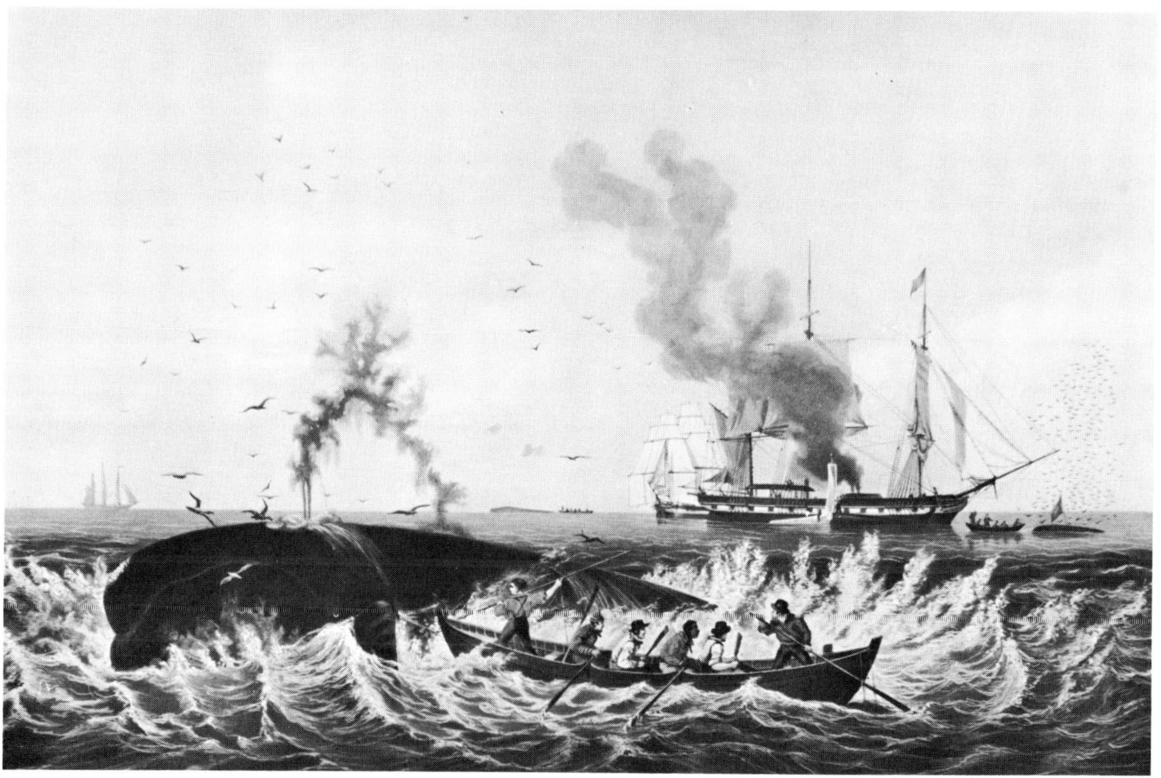

The Whale Fishery/ Attacking a "Right" Whale, and "Cutting In," published by Currier and Ives, undated. Hand-colored lithograph, $16\frac{3}{16}$ x $23\frac{3}{4}$ inches (*Collection of Ladd MacMillan*)

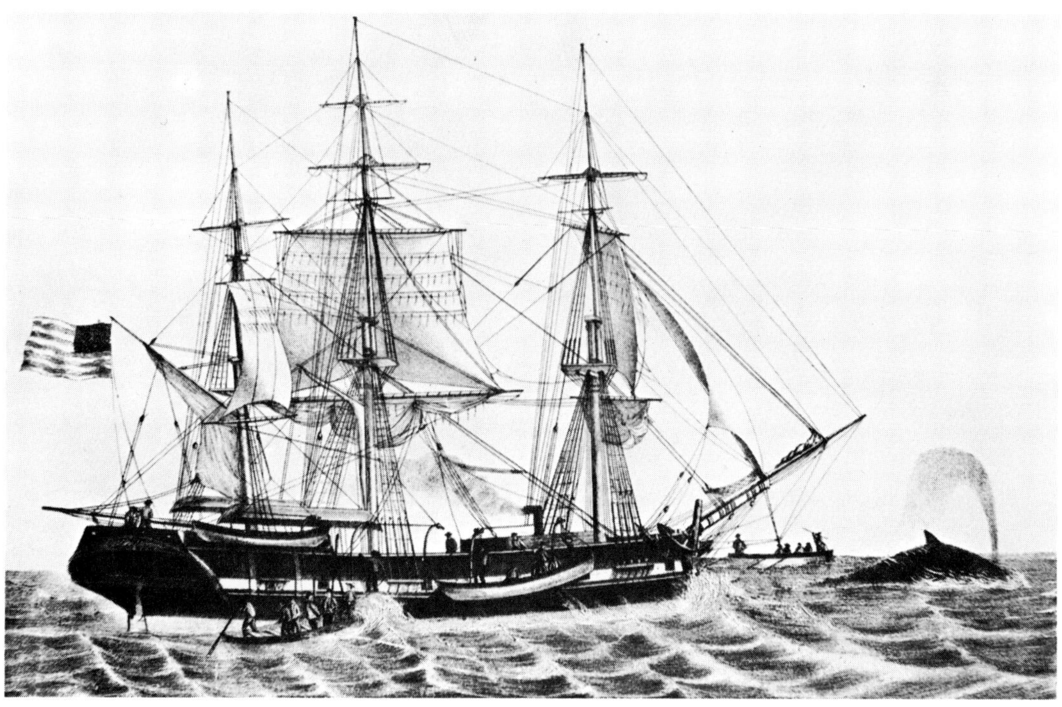

American Whaler, published by N. Currier. Hand-colored lithograph, $8\frac{9}{16}$ x $12\frac{13}{16}$ inches

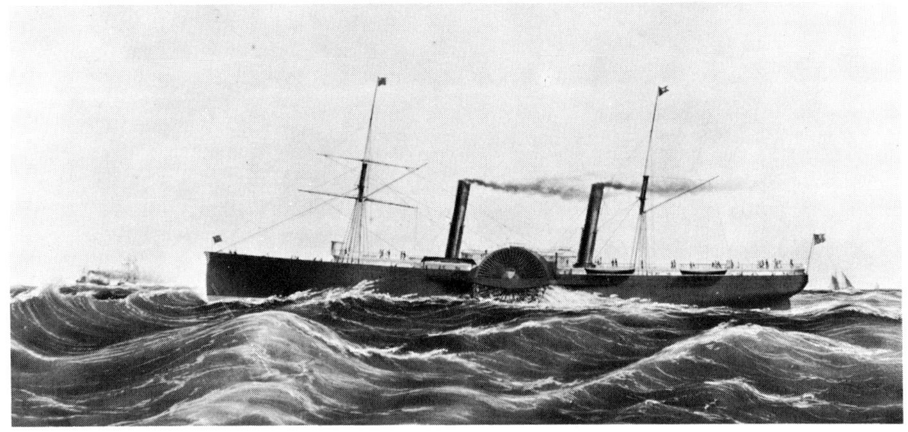

U.S. Mail Steamship Adriatic, C. Parsons, Del., published by N. Currier, 1856. Hand-colored lithograph, 16⅛ x 24½ inches

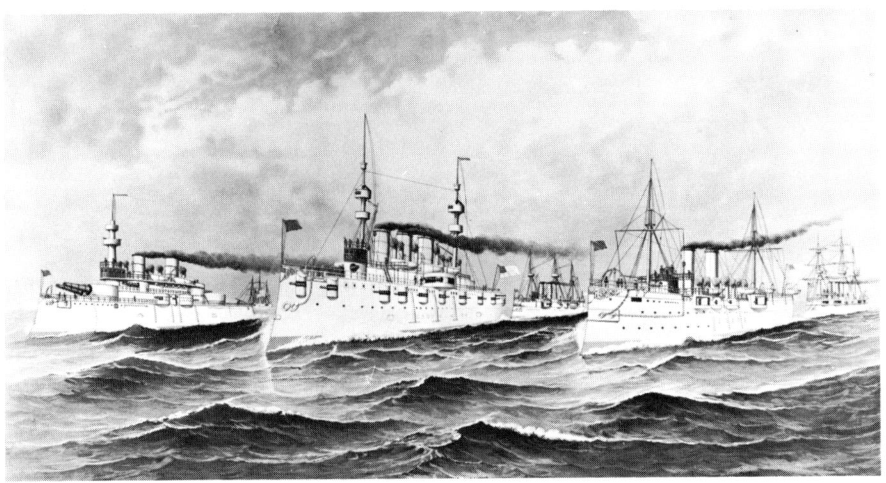

"The White Squadron," U.S. Navy, published by Currier and Ives, 1893, printed in oils, 19 x 34½ inches

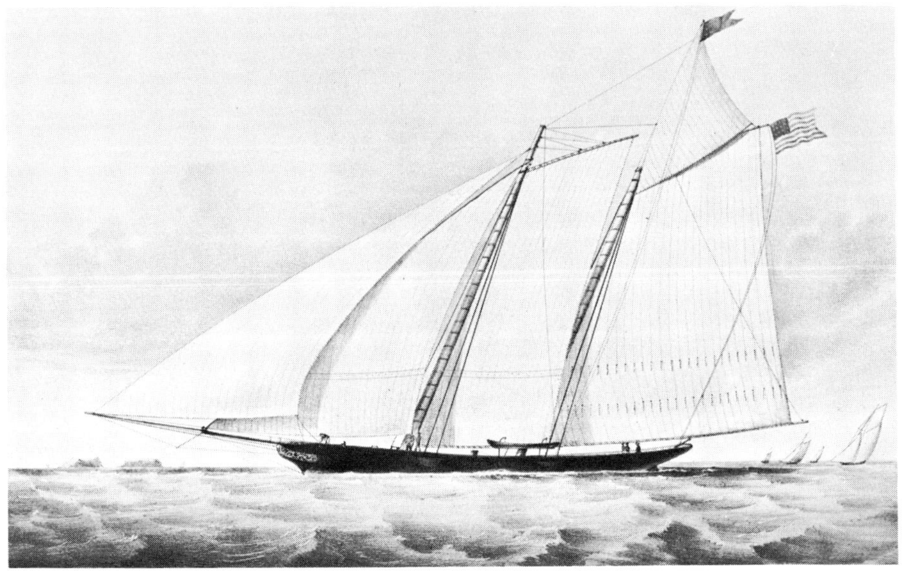

The Clipper Yacht "America," published by N. Currier, undated. Hand-colored lithograph, 8 x 12$^{5}/_{16}$ inches

Fire Scenes

A Currier and Ives *Illustrated and Descriptive List of Celebrated Fire Pictures, Comprising the series of six plates entitled THE LIFE OF A FIREMAN, the four plates entitled THE AMERICAN FIREMAN, and others All Elegantly Colored* was issued in 1884, thirty years after the first set of four *Life of a Fireman* prints was issued by N. Currier. As the booklet describes them, "They are very elaborate and correct in every particular, the apparatus and figures being carefully sketched from actual scenes coming under the artist's observation in his attendance at many metropolitan conflagrations . . ." The first four of the *Life of of a Fireman: The Fire, The Night Alarm, The Race* (number thirty-four of the "best fifty") and *The Ruins,* all issued in 1854, were done by L. Maurer. *The New Era, Steam and Muscle* by C. Parsons was issued in 1861 and *The Metropolitan System* by J. Cameron in 1866, number forty-nine of the "best fifty," making a total of six in this dramatic series. The set of four medium folios, *The American Fireman/ Always Ready, Facing the Enemy, Prompt to the Rescue, Rushing to the Conflict* were also by Maurer. Currier is said to be the man pictured in *The American Fireman/ Always Ready* and was, in fact, a member of a volunteer New York fire company. Large numbers of other fire prints were made showing specific fires such as *The Great Fire at Boston, November 9th and 10th, 1872,* and *The Great Fire at Chicago, Oct. 8th, 1871.* From their first print of the "Lexington" disaster, burning ships were often included in their output.

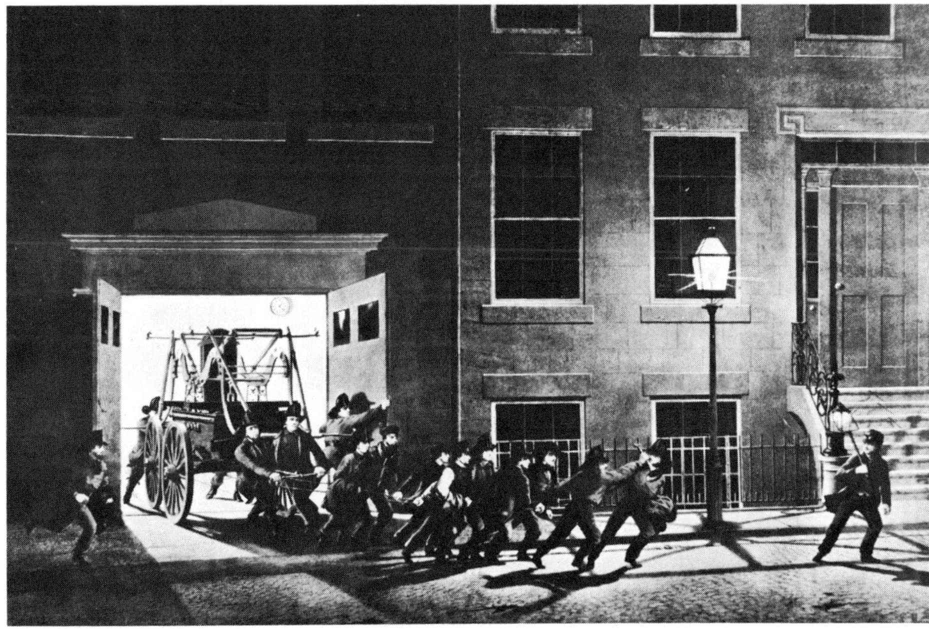

The Life of a Fireman/ The Night Alarm, L. Maurer, Del., published by N. Currier, 1854. Hand-colored lithograph, $16\frac{7}{8}$ x $25\frac{7}{8}$ inches

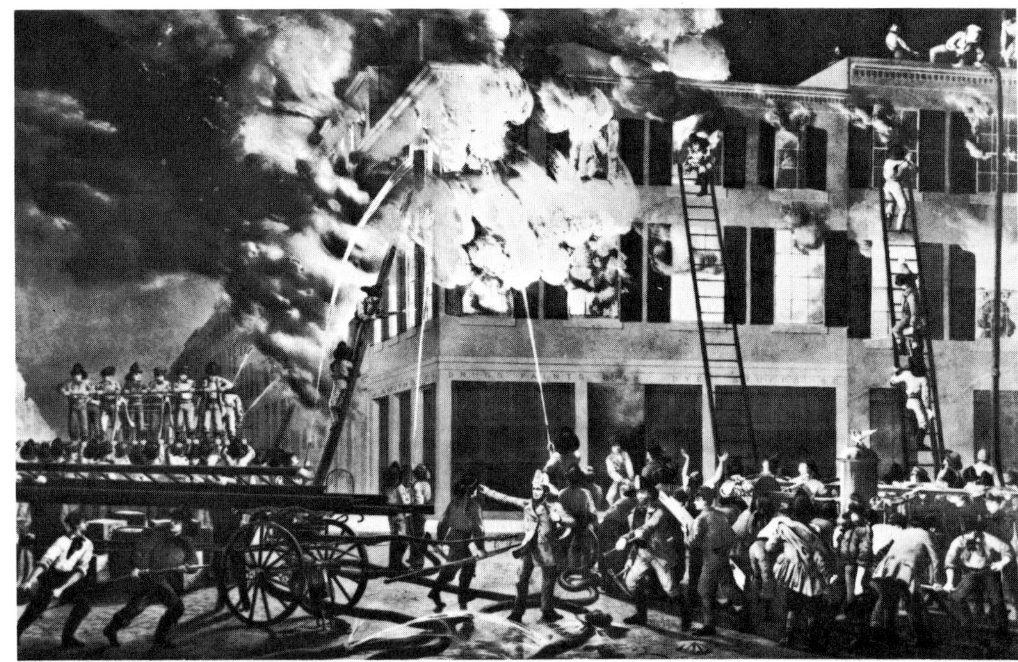

The Life of a Fireman/ The Fire, L. Maurer. Del., published by N. Currier, 1854. Hand-colored lithograph, $17\frac{1}{8}$ x $25\frac{7}{8}$ inches

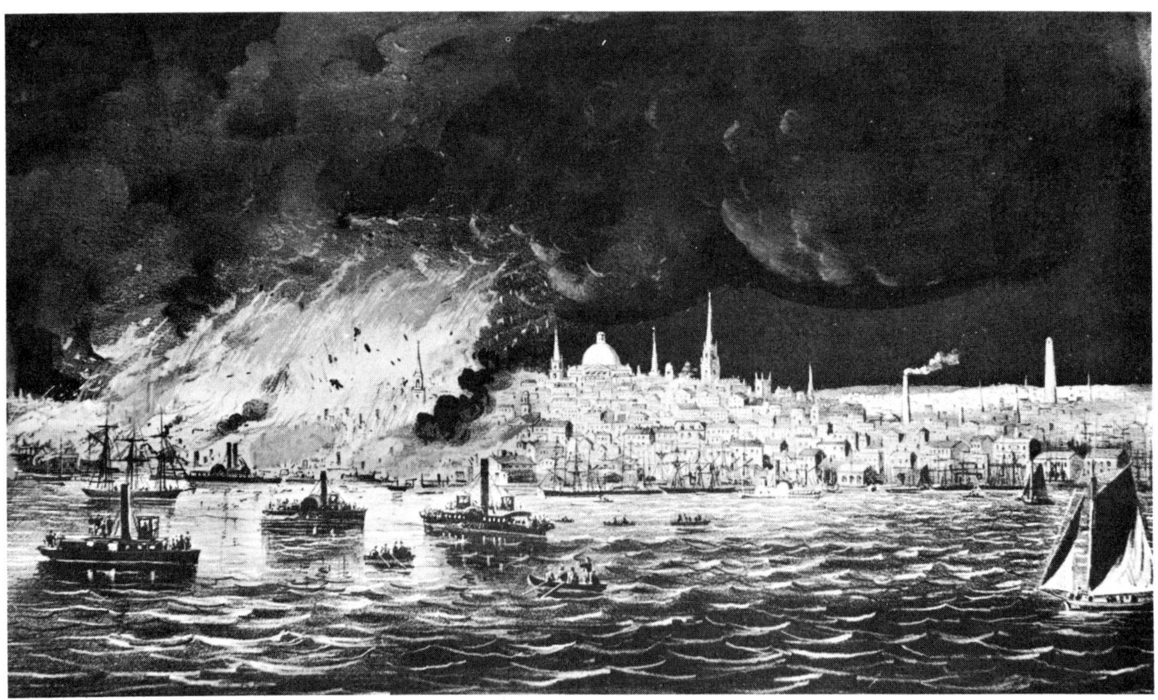

The Great Fire at Boston, November 9 & 10, 1872, published by Currier and Ives, 1872. Hand-colored lithograph, 8 x $12\frac{11}{16}$ inches

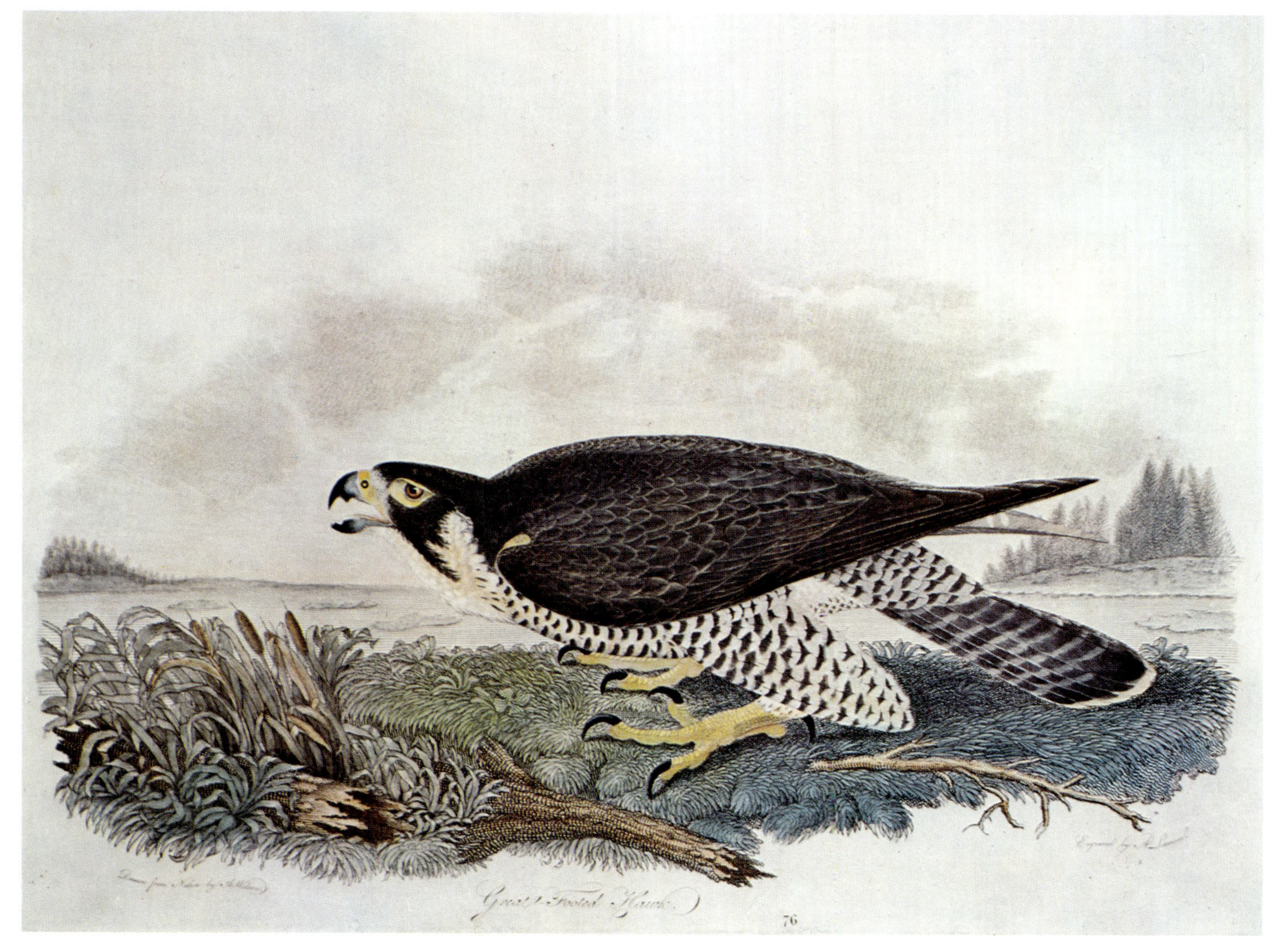

Great-Footed Hawk drawn by A. Wilson and engraved by A. Lawson. Plate 76 from *American Ornithology* by Alexander Wilson. Hand-colored vignette engraved and etched *ca.* 1814. Plate size 10½ x 13¼ inches. See Chapters II and VI.

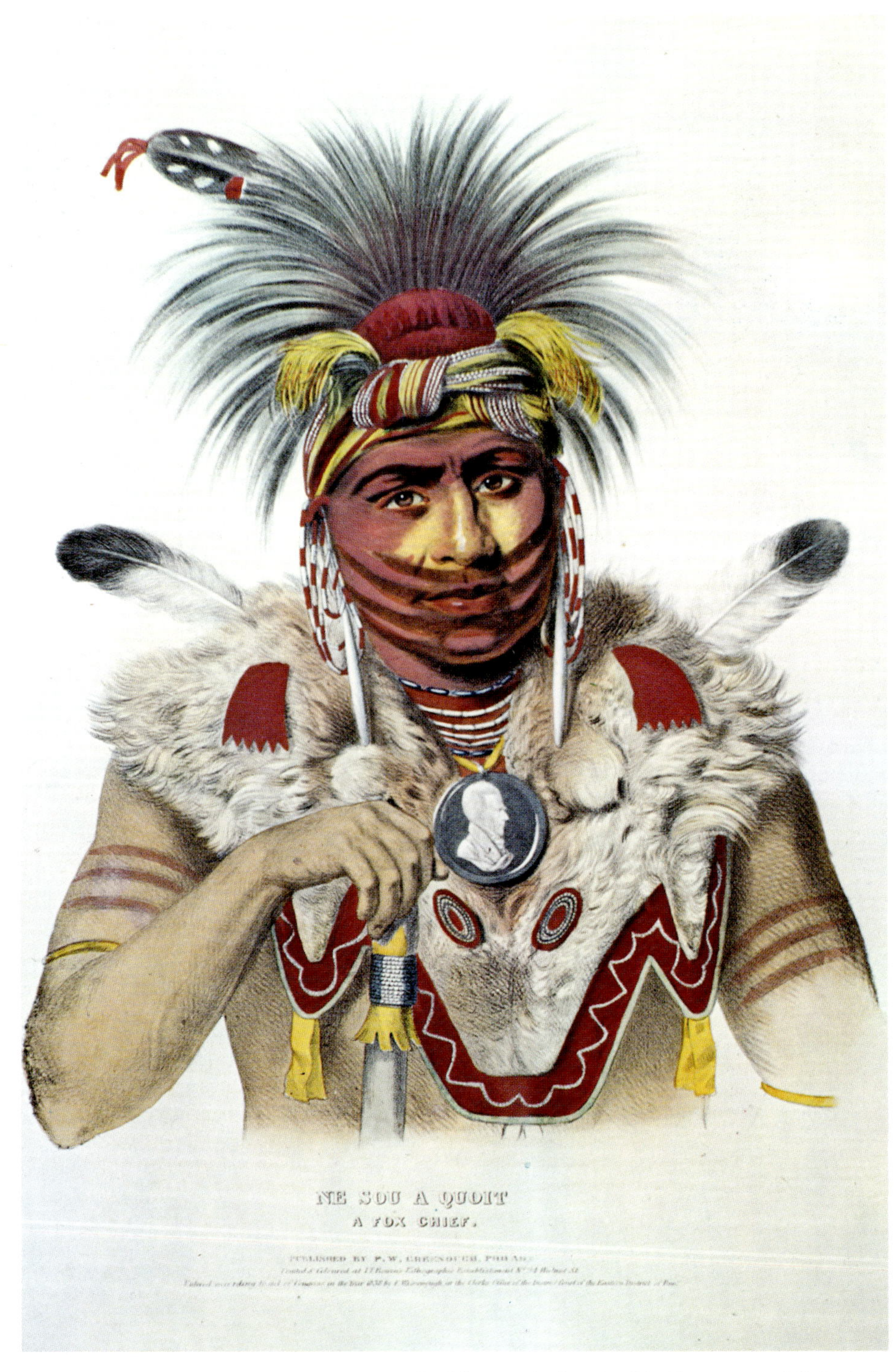

Ne Sou A Quoit/A Fox Chief, hand-colored lithograph by J. T. Bowen, published by F. W. Greenough, 1836. Plate from Volume II of *History of the Indian Tribes of North America* by T. L. M'Kenney and J. Hall. Vignette on paper 19⅞ x 14 inches. See Chapter IV.

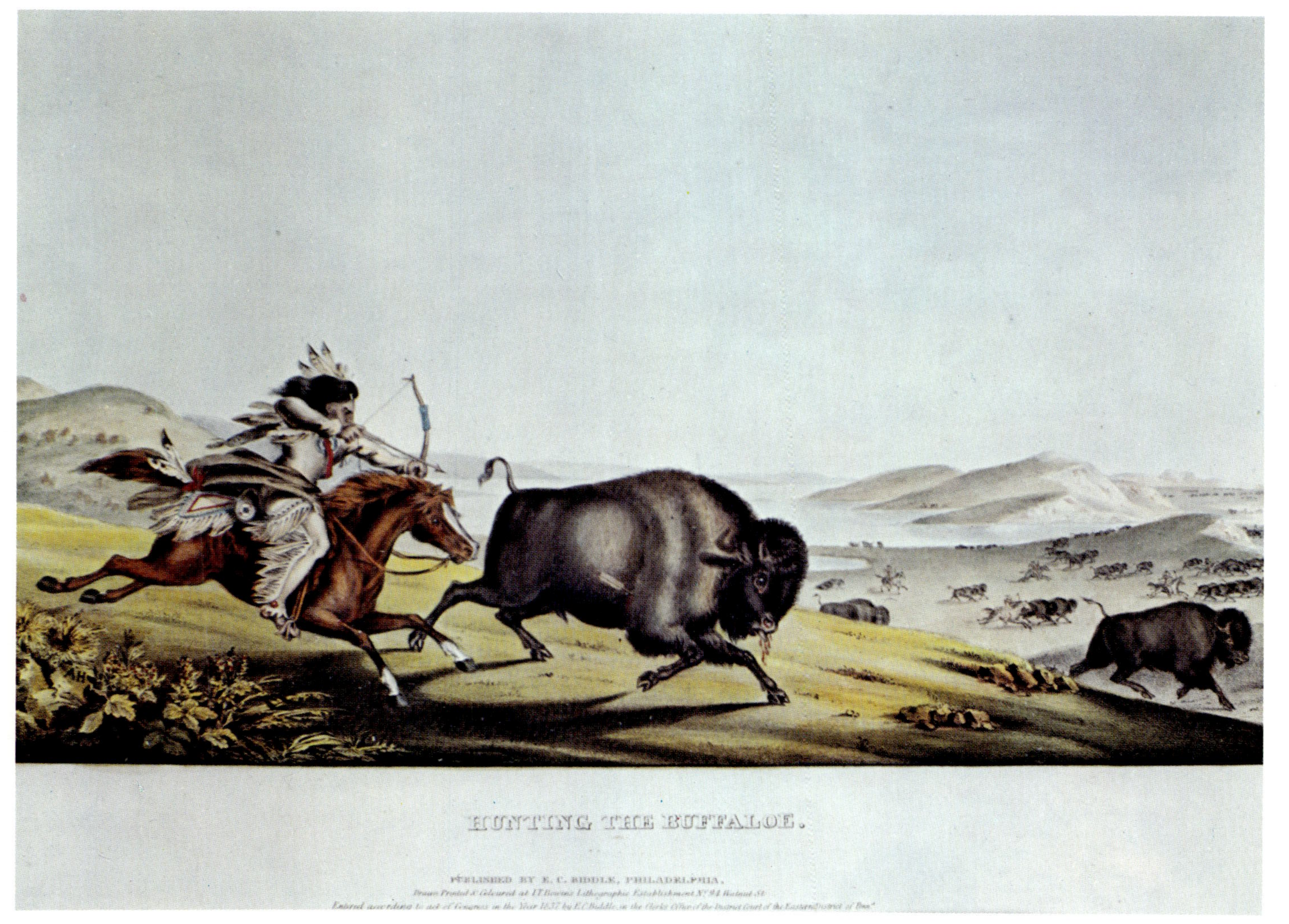

Hunting the Buffalo, hand-colored lithograph by J. T. Bowen, published by E. C. Biddle, 1837. Frontispiece to Volume II of *History of the Indian Tribes of North America* by T. L. M'Kenney and J. Hall. 9 x 15¼ inches. See Chapter IV.

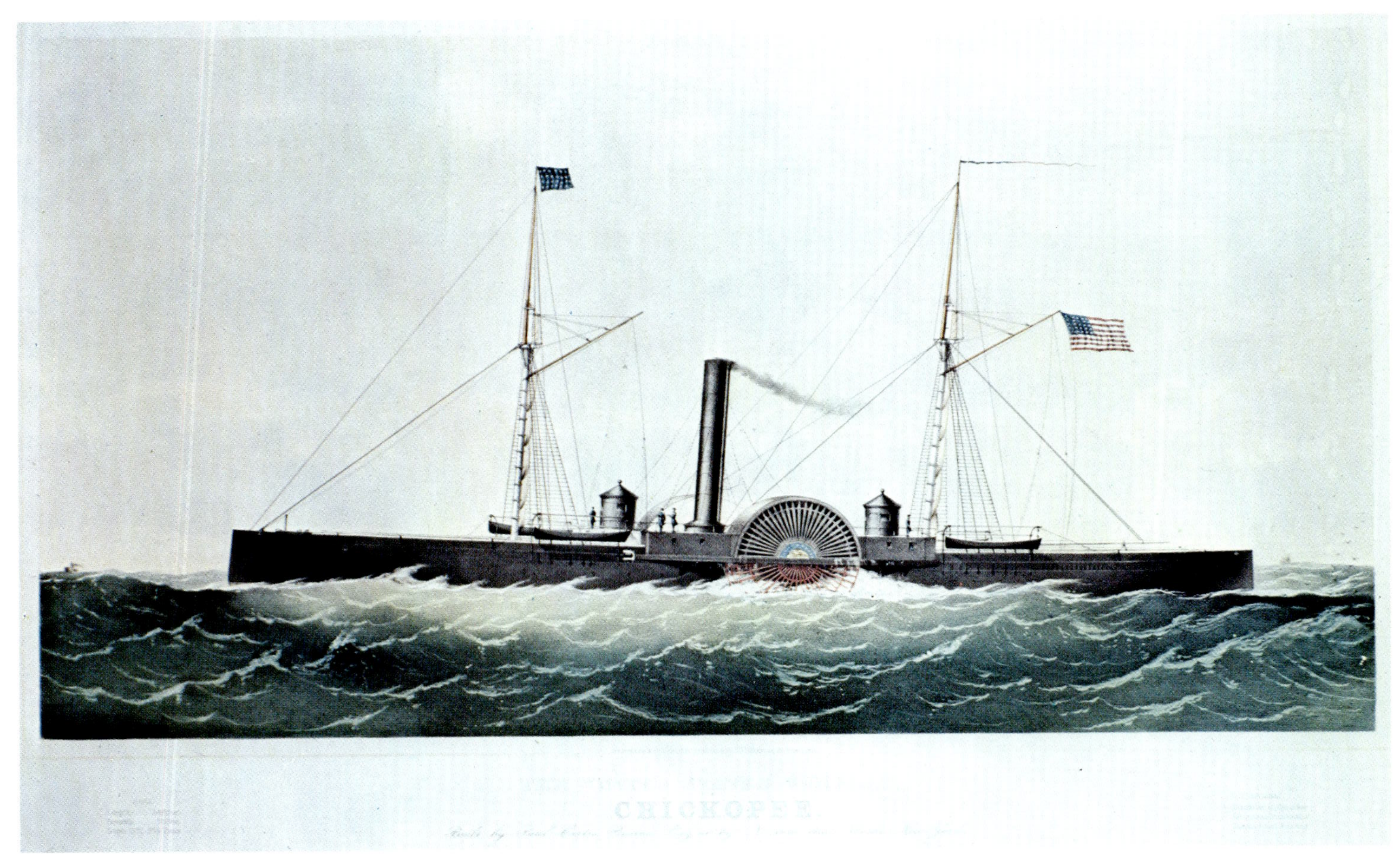

The United States Gunboat Chicopee etc., by C. Parsons, published by Endicott and Co. 1863. One of a large group of war related prints published during the Civil War. Colored lithograph $15\frac{1}{2} \times 29\frac{3}{4}$ inches. See Chapter IV.

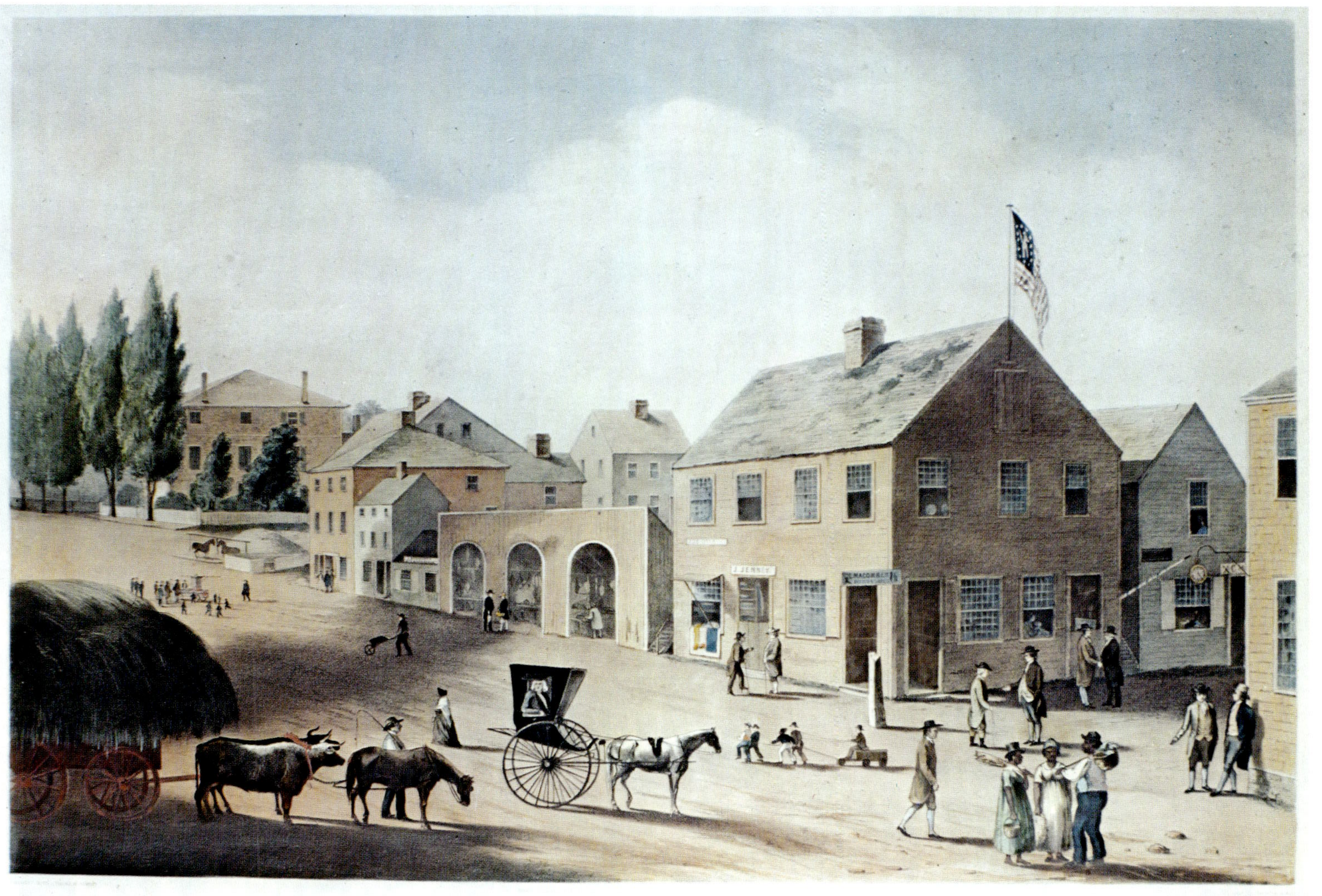

New Bedford Fifty Years Ago after a painting by William A. Wall. Published by Endicott & Co. in 1858. Hand-colored lithograph 15½ x 23½ inches. See Chapter IV.

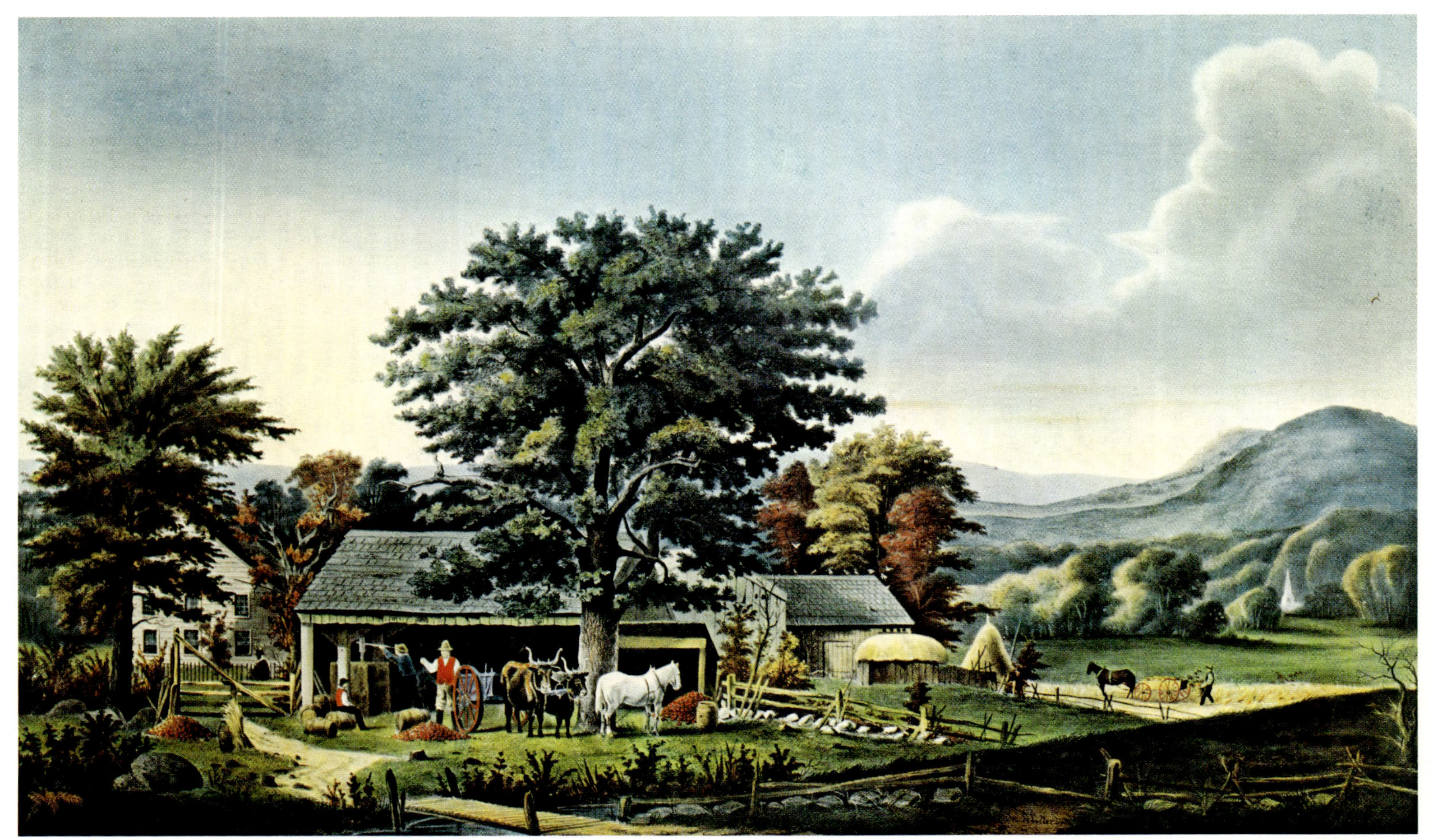

Autumn in New England/Cider Making after a painting by G. H. Durrie and published by Currier and Ives in 1866. Hand-colored lithograph $14\frac{13}{16}$ x $25\frac{1}{4}$ inches. Number 31 of the "best fifty." See Chapter V. Collection of Ladd MacMillan, photograph courtesy Heritage Plantation of Sandwich.

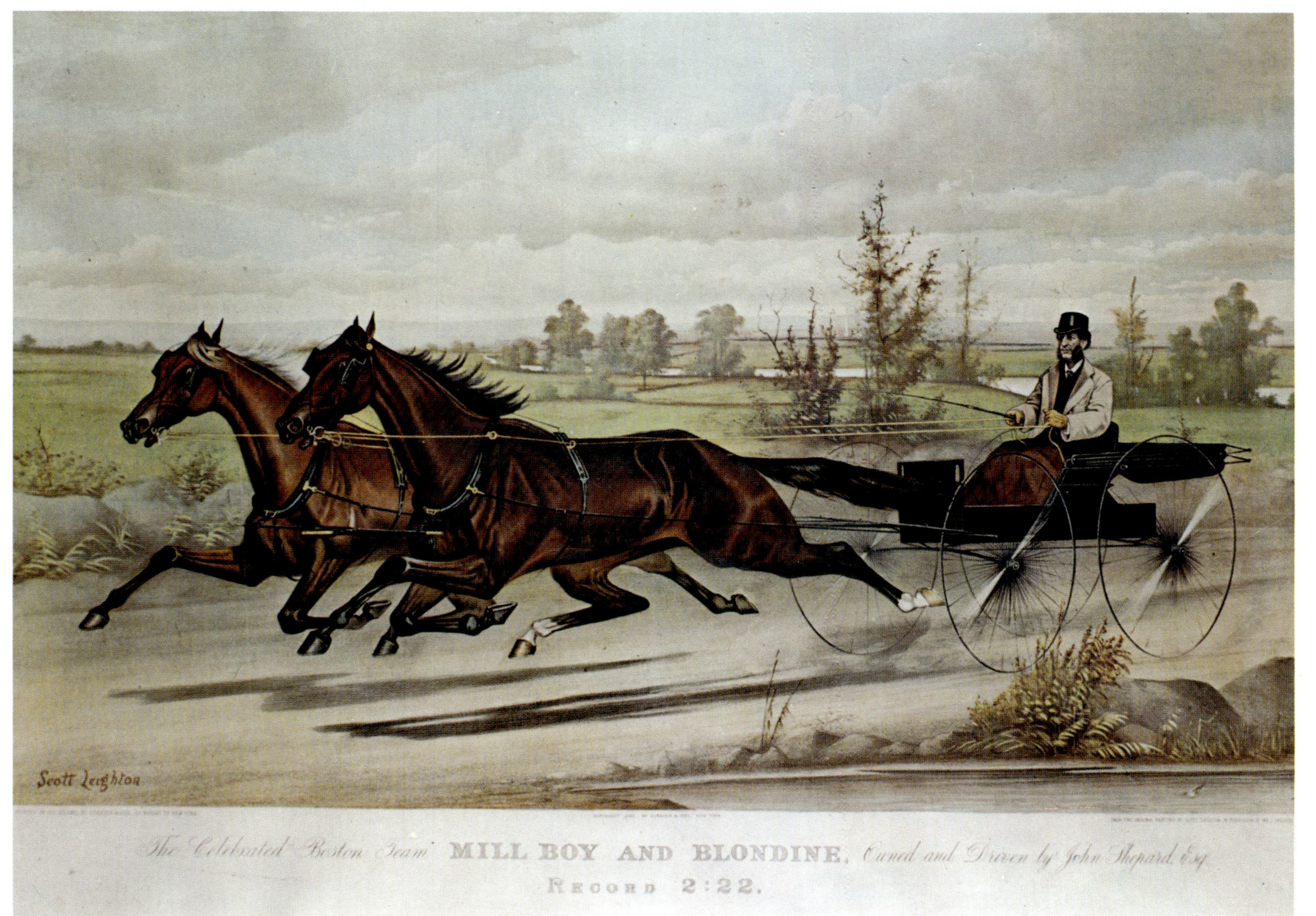

Celebrated Boston Team Mill-Boy and Blondine etc., after a painting by Scott Leighton. Published by Currier and Ives in 1882. Lithograph printed in oil colors, 20½ x 33 inches. See Chapter V.

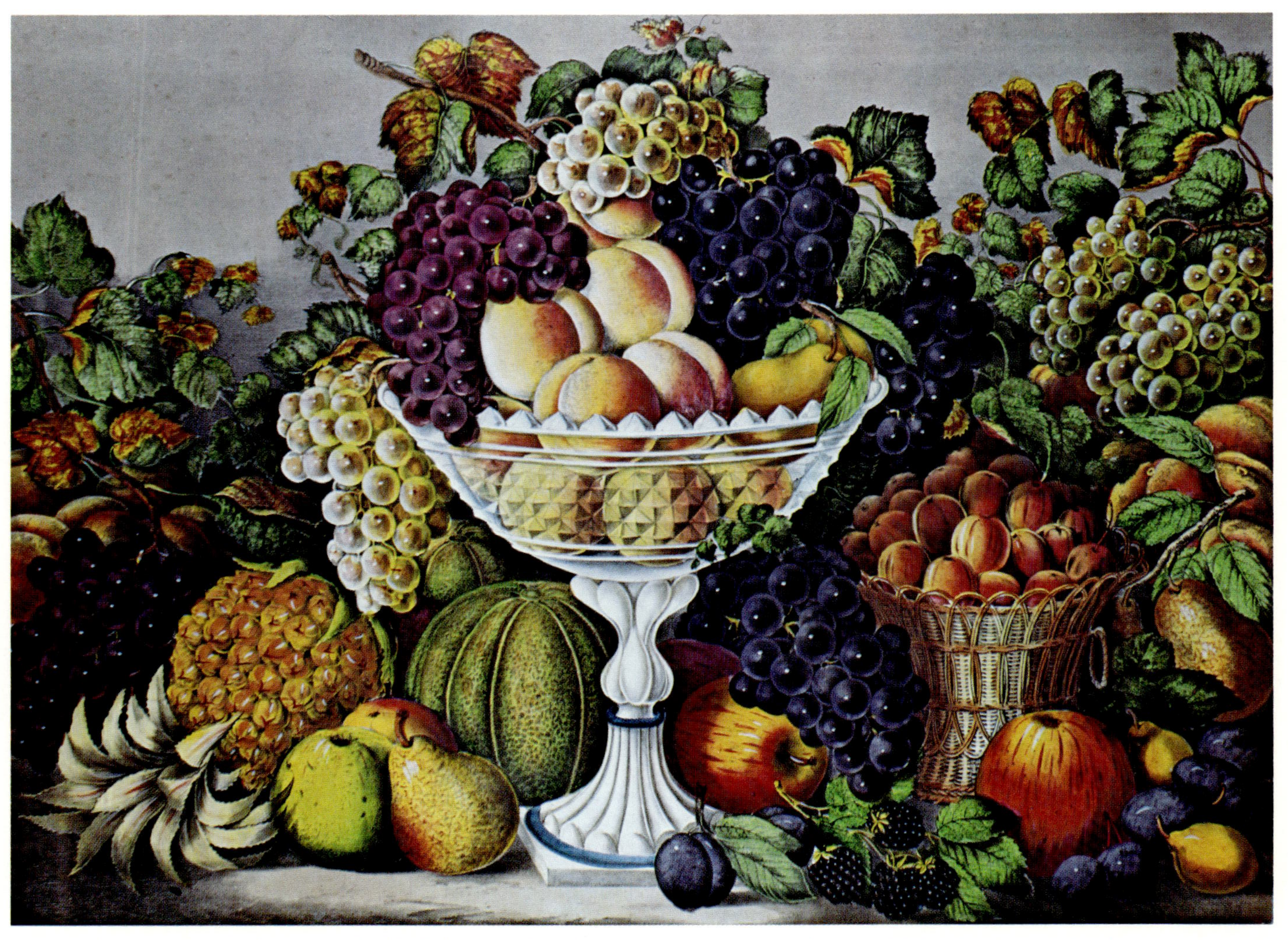

American Autumn Fruits drawn by F. F. Palmer and published by Currier and Ives in 1865. Hand-colored lithograph 20 x 27⅞ inches. See Chapter V.

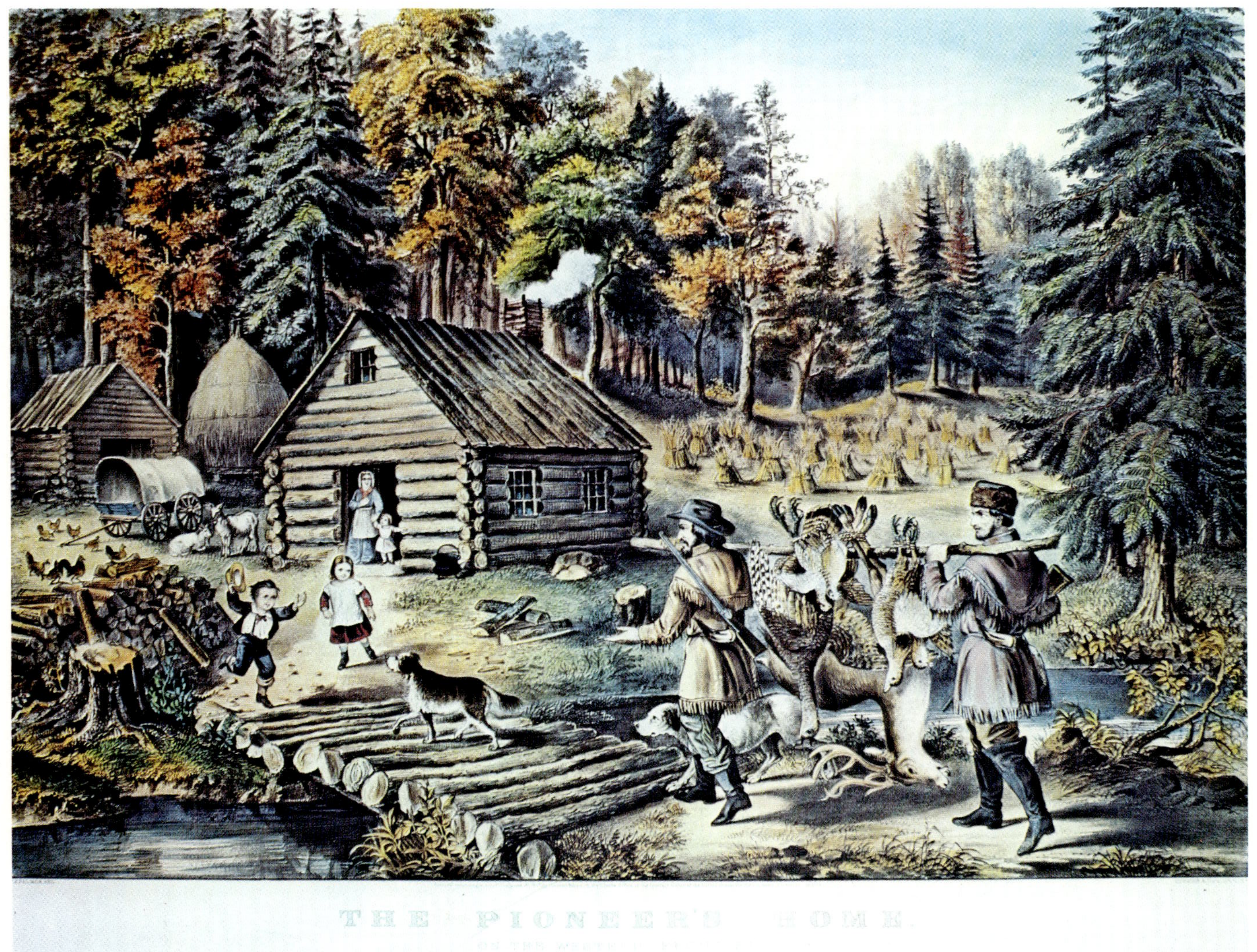

The Pioneer's Home/On the Western Frontier drawn by F. F. Palmer and published by Currier and Ives in 1867. Hand-colored lithograph $18\frac{3}{4} \times 26\frac{7}{8}$ inches. See Chapter V.

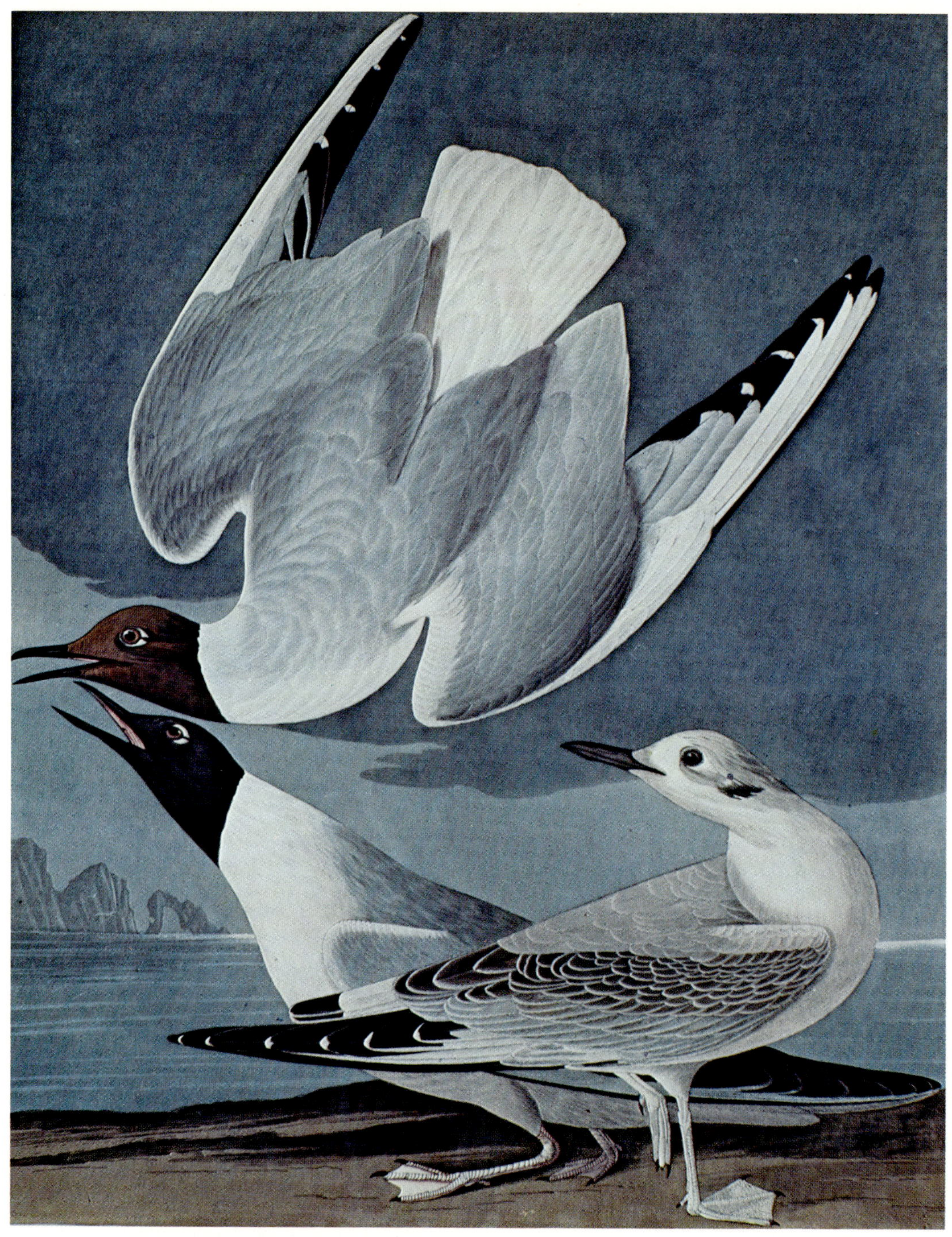

Bonapartian Gull after a painting by J. J. Audubon. Hand-colored engraving and aquatint by R. Havell, London, 1836. Plate 324 from the *Birds of America*. Plate size 21 x 16¾ inches. A striking composition made by cutting out the birds and pasting them upon a painted background. See Chapter VI.

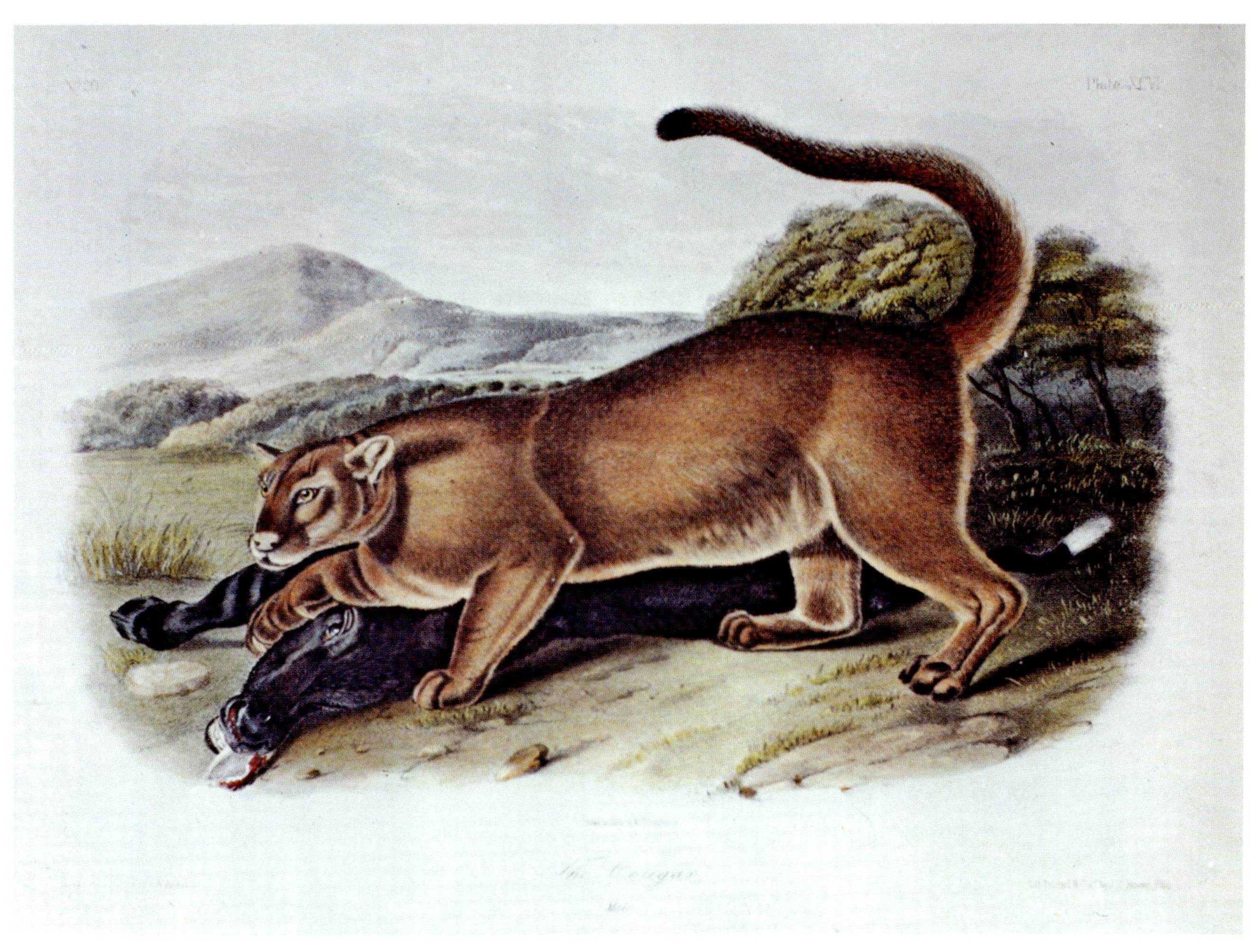

The Cougar/Male after a drawing by J. W. Audubon. Plate 96 from the *Quadrupeds of North America*, octavo edition, by John James Audubon and John Bachman. Lithograph with printed and hand-coloring by J. T. Bowen *ca.* 1851. Vignette on paper 6¾ x 10¼ inches. See Chapter VI.

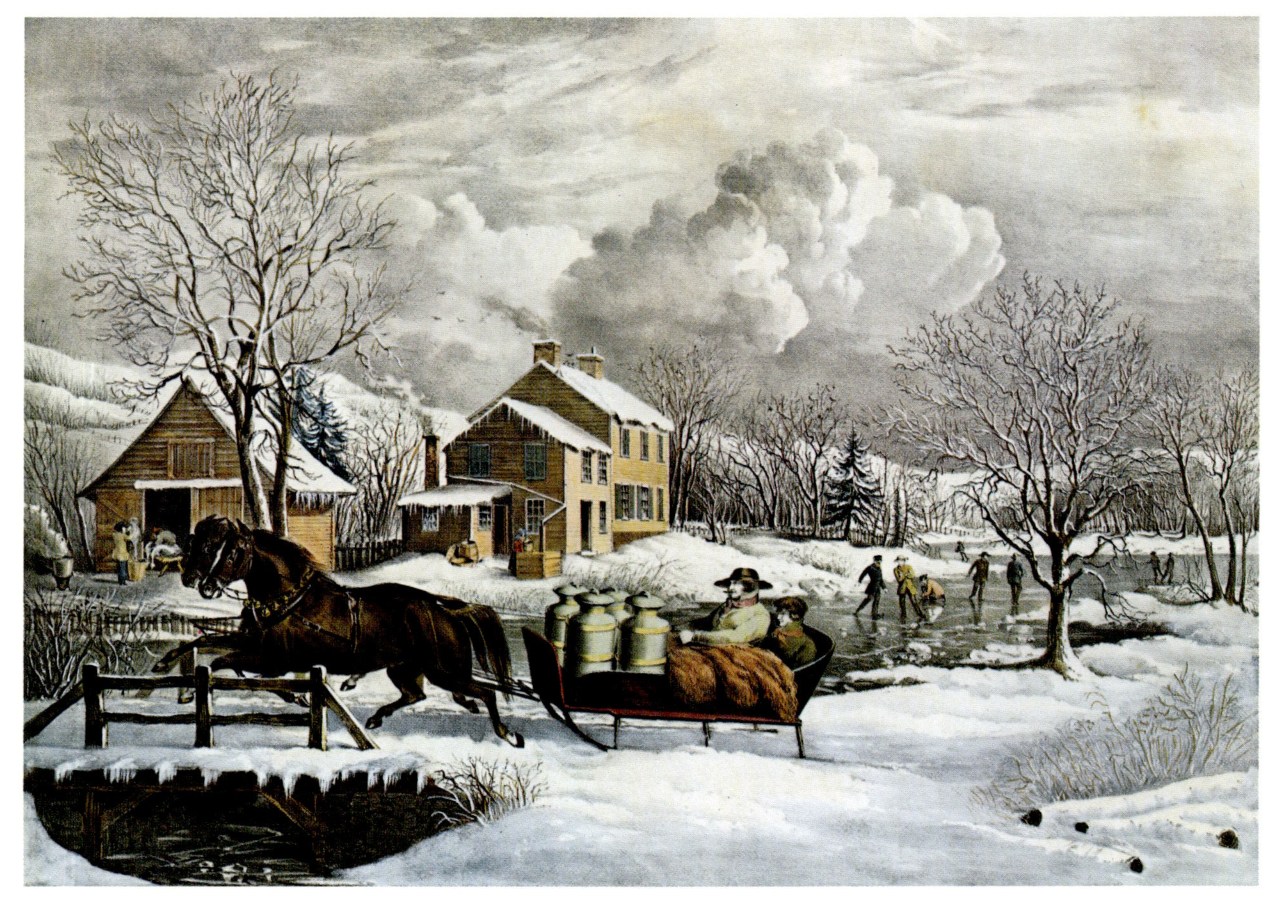

American Farm Scenes/No. 4 (winter) drawn by F. F. Palmer and published by N. Currier in 1853. Hand-colored lithograph 16¾ x 24 inches. See Chapter V.

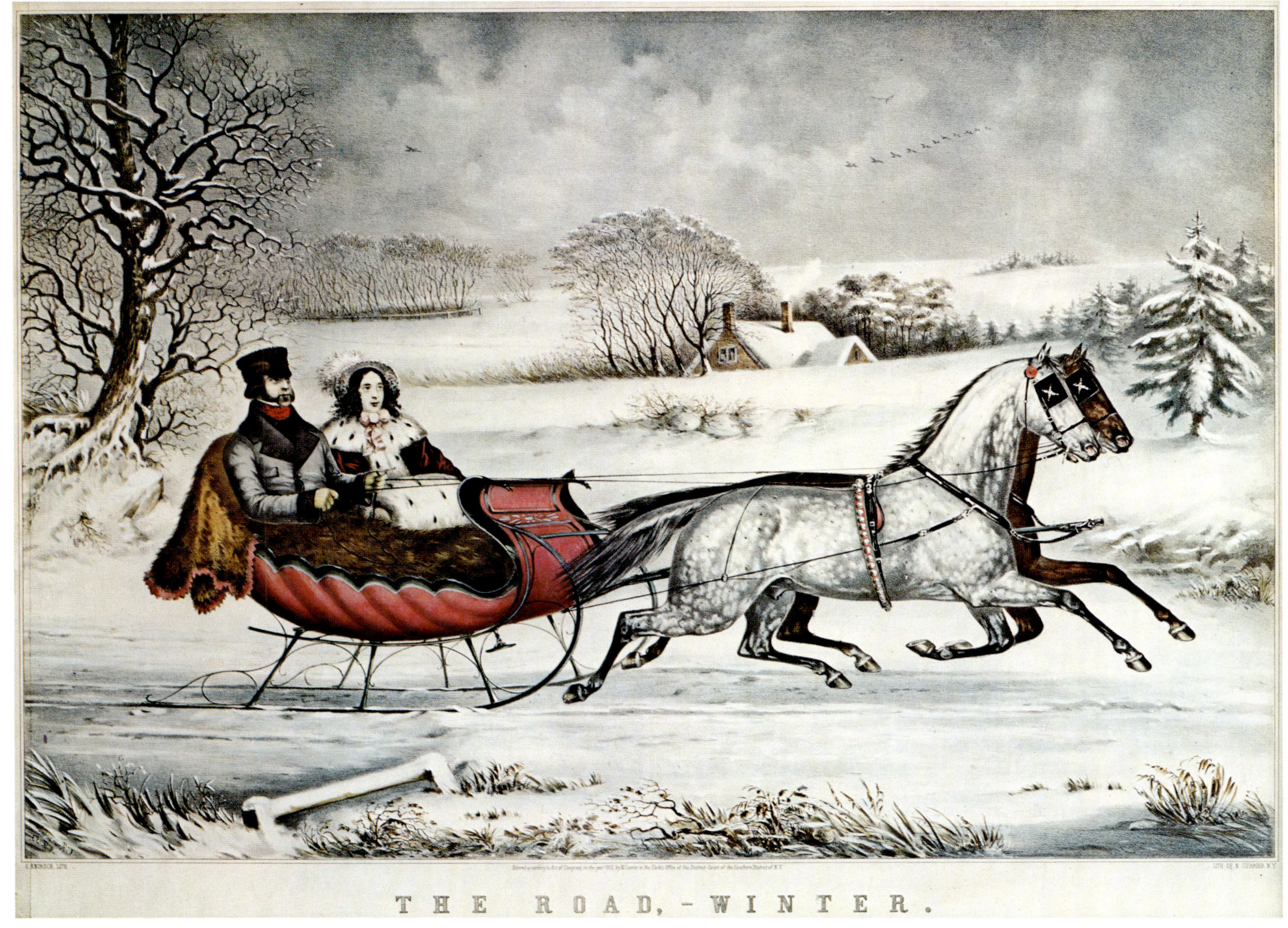

The Road,-Winter, O. Knirsch lithographer, published by N. Currier in 1853. Number 22 of the "best fifty." Hand-colored lithograph 17¾ x 26½ inches. See Chapter V. Collection of Ladd MacMillan, photograph courtesy Heritage Plantation of Sandwich.

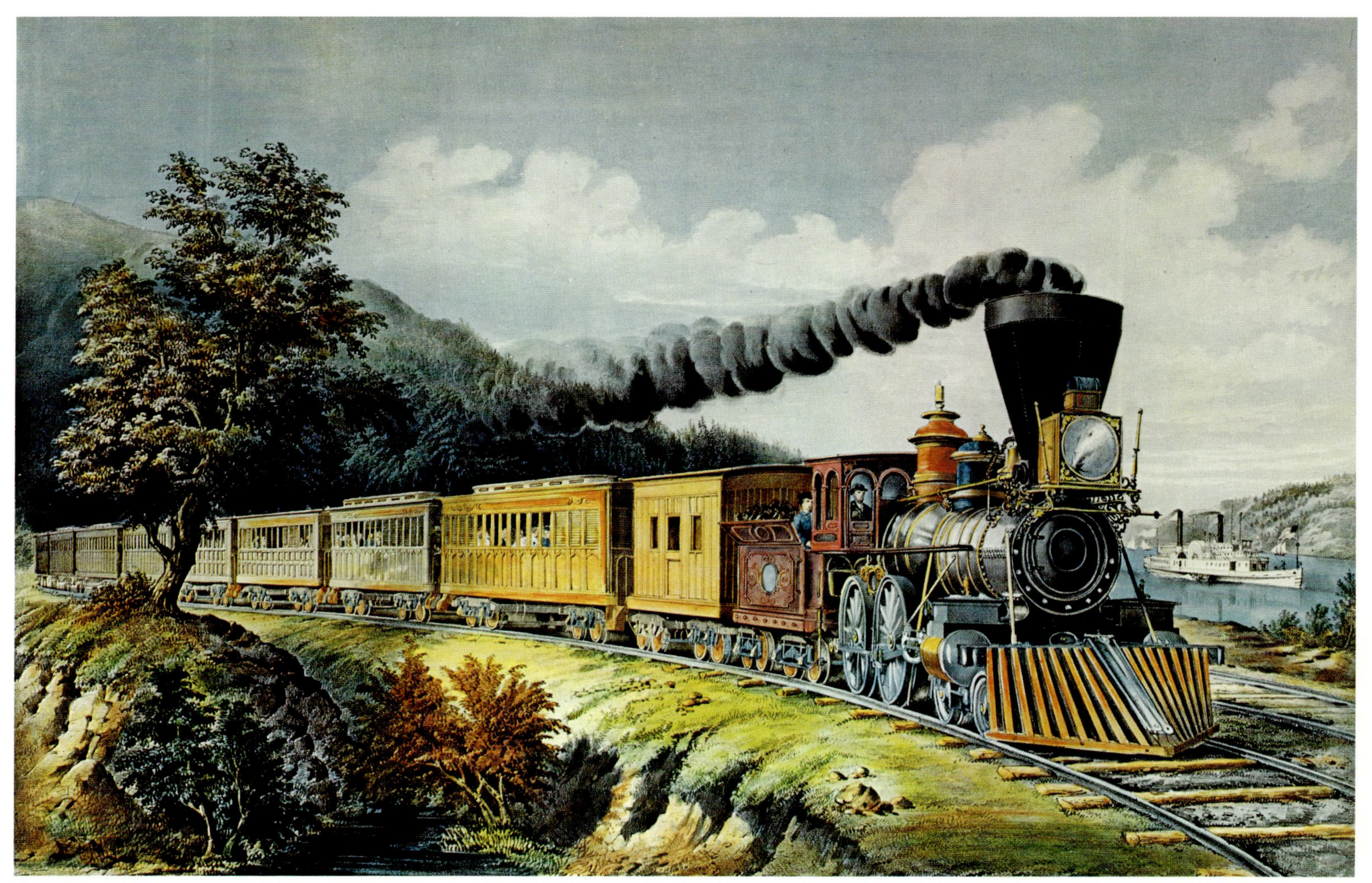

American Express Train drawn by F. F. Palmer and published by Currier and Ives in 1864. Hand-colored lithograph 18 x 31 inches. See Chapter V. Collection of Ladd MacMillan, photograph courtesy fo Heritage Plantation of Sandwich.

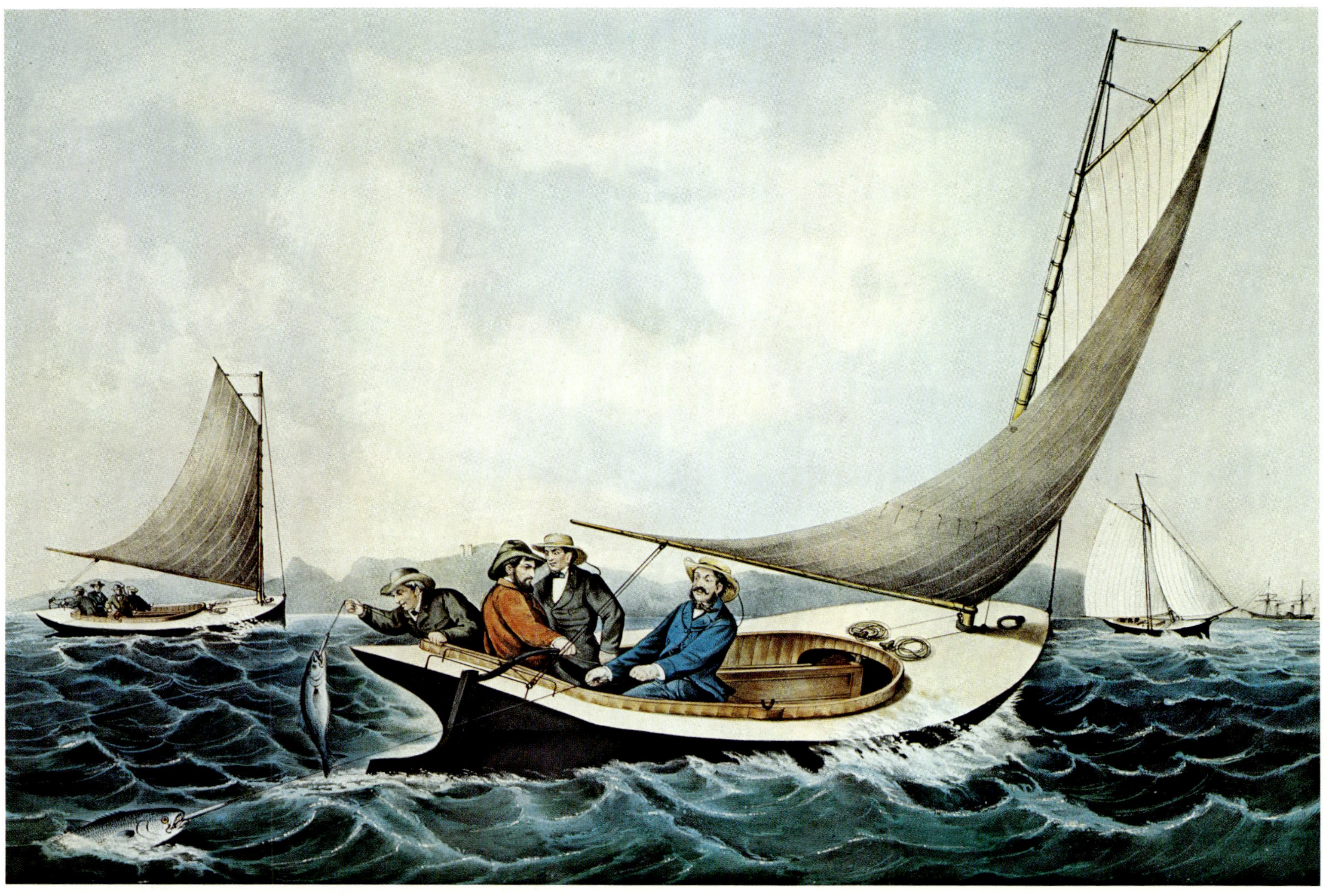

Trolling for Blue Fish drawn by F. F. Palmer and published by Currier and Ives in 1866. Hand-colored lithograph $18\frac{1}{2}$ x $27\frac{7}{8}$ inches. Number 10 of the "best fifty." See Chapter V. Collection of Heritage Plantation of Sandwich.

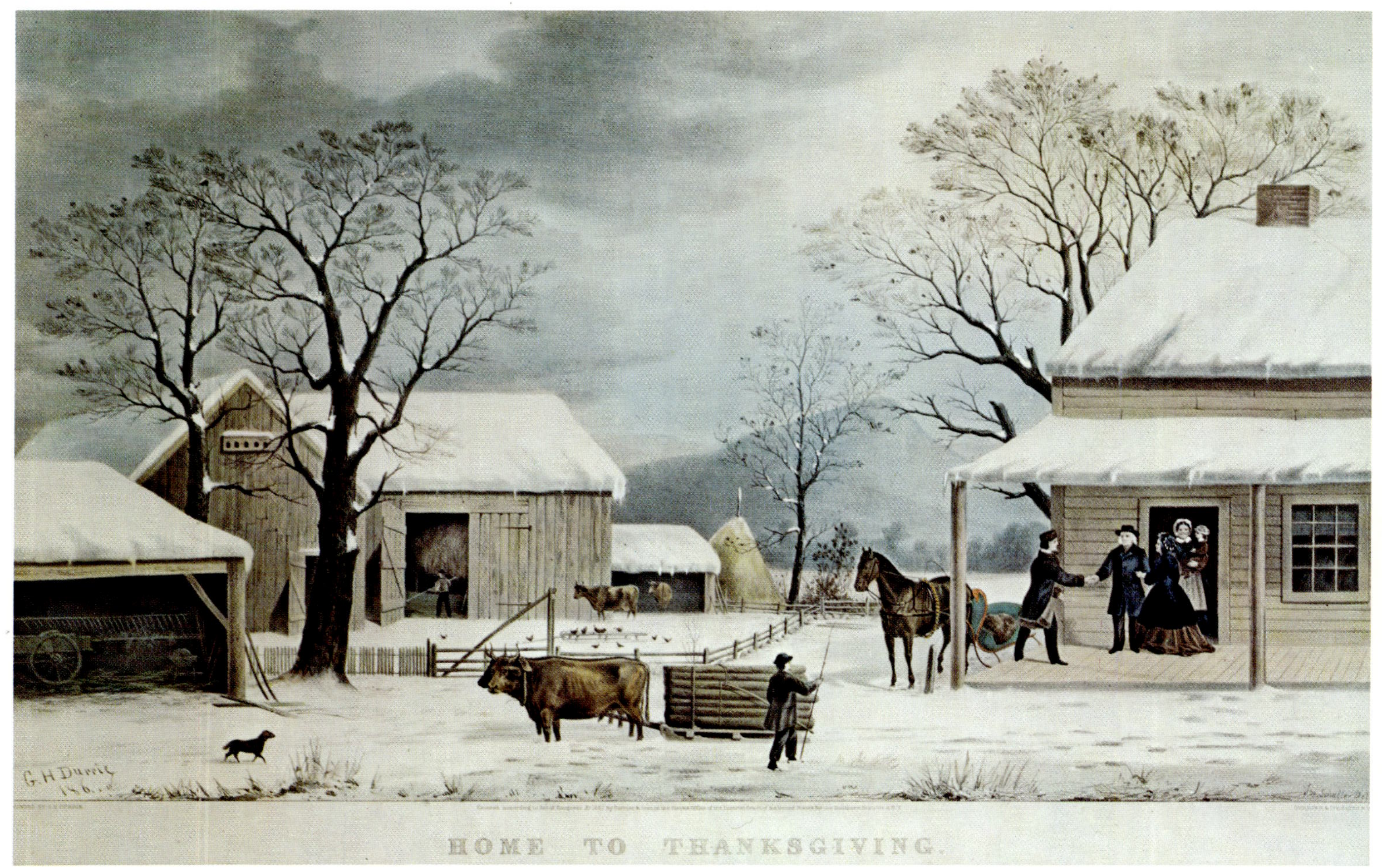

Home to Thanksgiving after a painting by G. H. Durrie and published by Currier and Ives in 1867. Hand-colored lithograph 14¾ x 25 inches. Number 4 of the "best fifty." See Chapter V. Collection of Ladd MacMillan, photograph courtesy of Heritage Plantation of Sandwich.

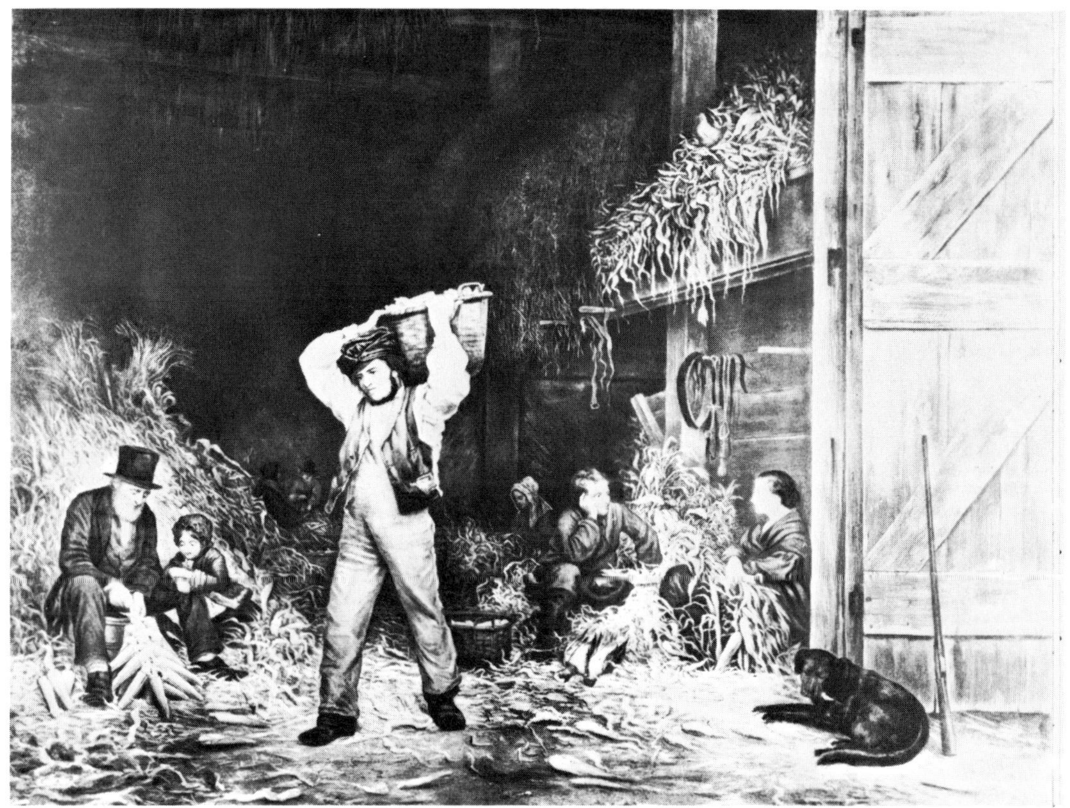

"Husking," after a painting by Eastman Johnson, published by Currier and Ives, 1861. Hand-colored lithograph, 21$\frac{1}{16}$ x 27$\frac{3}{8}$ inches. Number one of the "Best Fifty" large folio

Farm, Rural and Genre

Heading the list in this very large category is *"Husking"* after the painting by Eastman Johnson, selected by nine out of ten judges as number one of the "best fifty." It is considered one of the best American lithographs, portraying subtleties of shadows from which the luminous figures emerge. Other important prints include *Autumn in New England—Cider Making* from the painting by G. H. Durrie and the pair, *Haying-Time. The First Load* and *Haying-Time. The Last Load* by F. F. Palmer and J. Cameron. The ubiquitous Mrs. Palmer contributed two series of four each with the changes of season as the theme: *American Farm Scenes* (spring, summer, fall, winter) and *American Country Life/ May Morning, October Afternoon, Summer's Evening, Pleasures of Winter.* The small folio series *American Homestead* (spring, summer, fall, winter) are the most popular and most often photomechanically reproduced. There are hundreds of single prints such as *The Roadside Mill* and *Life in the Country—Morning* which are charming, attractive and often available.

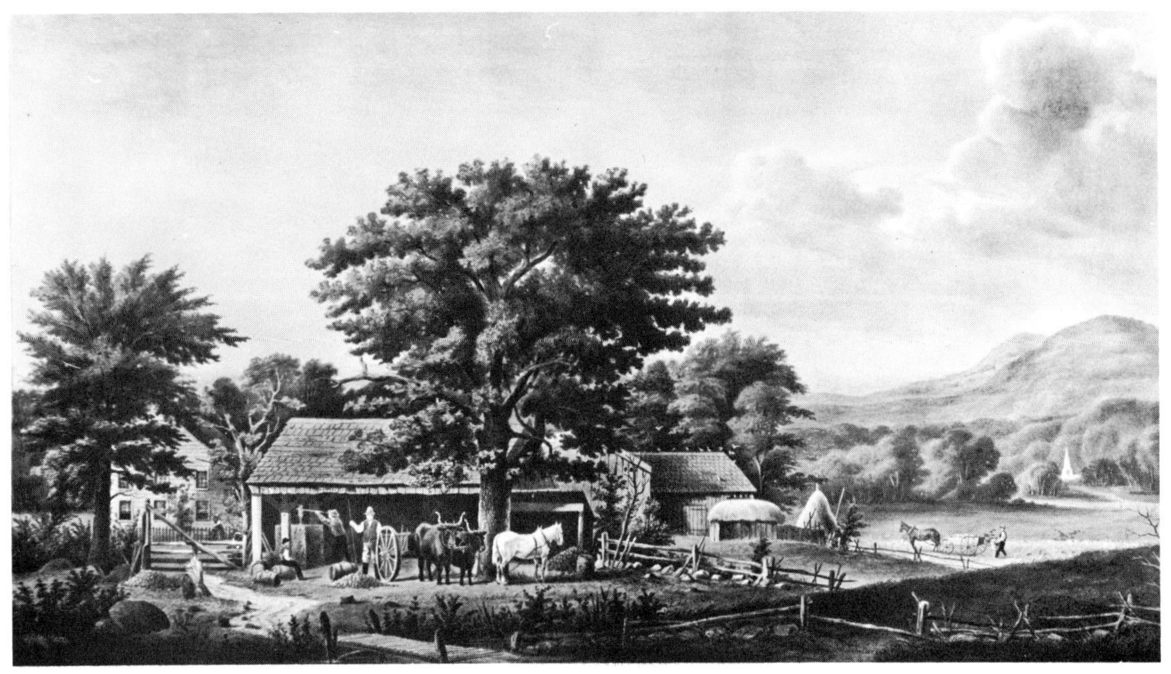

Autumn in New England/ Cider Making, after a painting by G. H. Durrie, published by Currier and Ives, 1866. Hand-colored lithograph, $14^{13}/_{16}$ x $25^{1}/_{4}$ inches

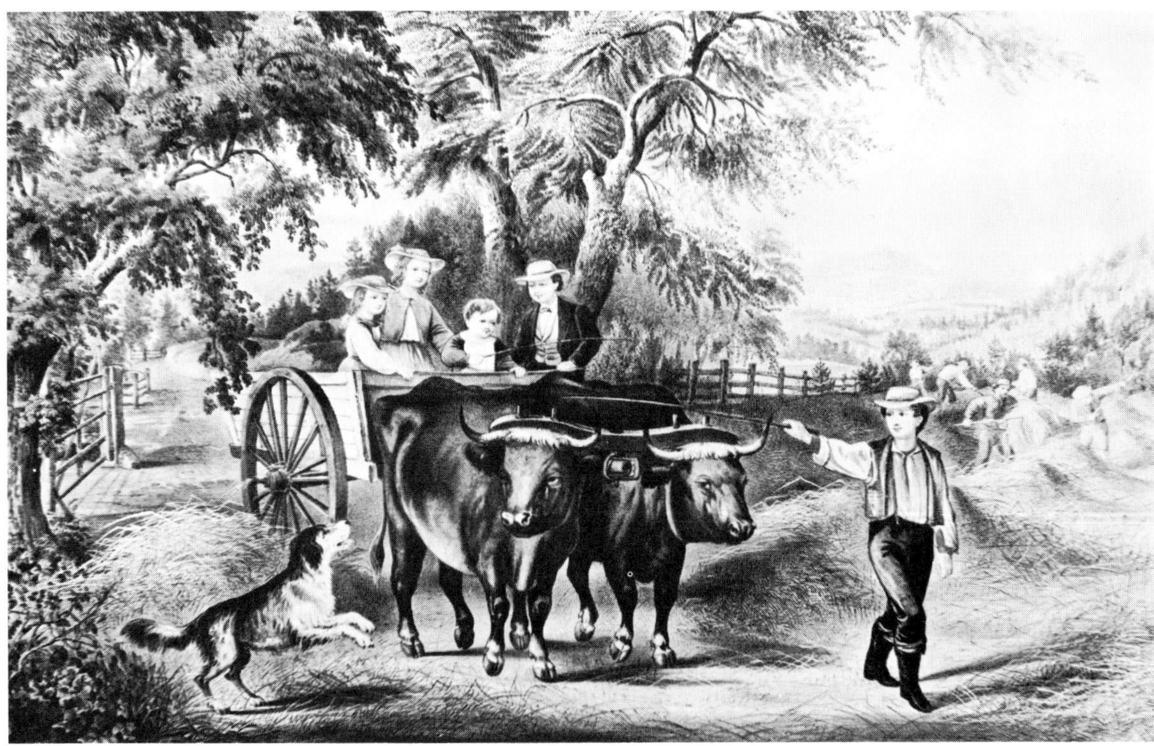

Haying-Time. The First Load, J. M. Ives, Del., drawn by F. F. Palmer and published by Currier and Ives, 1868. Hand-colored lithograph, $15^{7}/_{8}$ x $23^{7}/_{8}$ inches

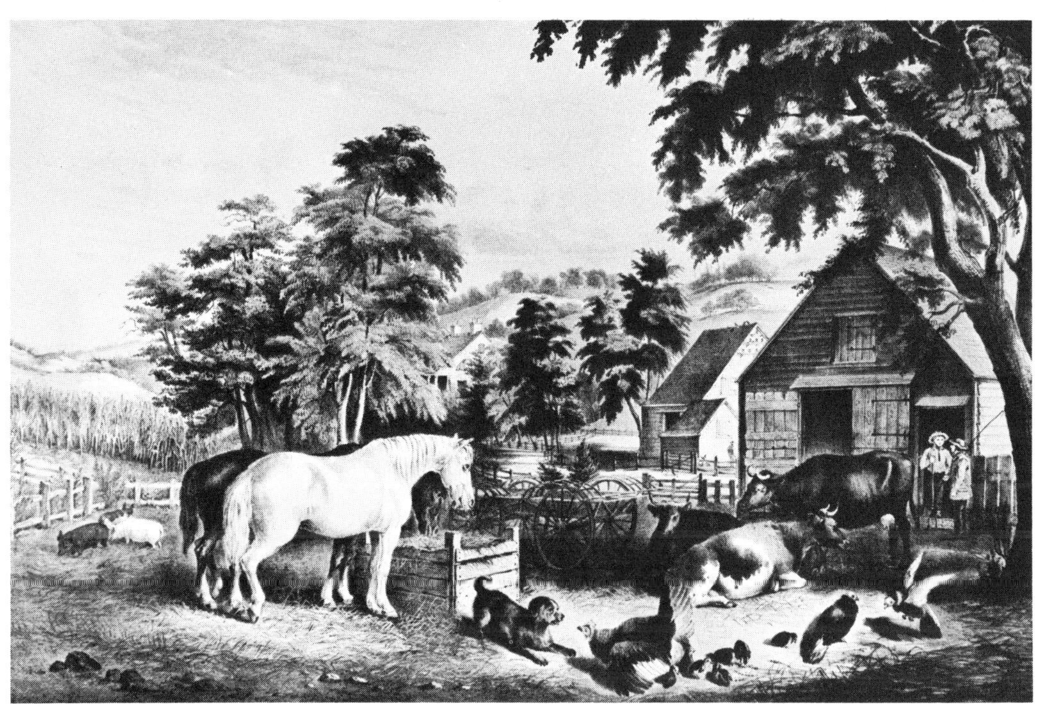

American Farm Scenes/ No. 3 (Autumn), by F. F. Palmer and published by N. Currier, 1853. Hand-colored lithograph, $16^{15}/_{16}$ x $24^{1}/_{16}$ inches

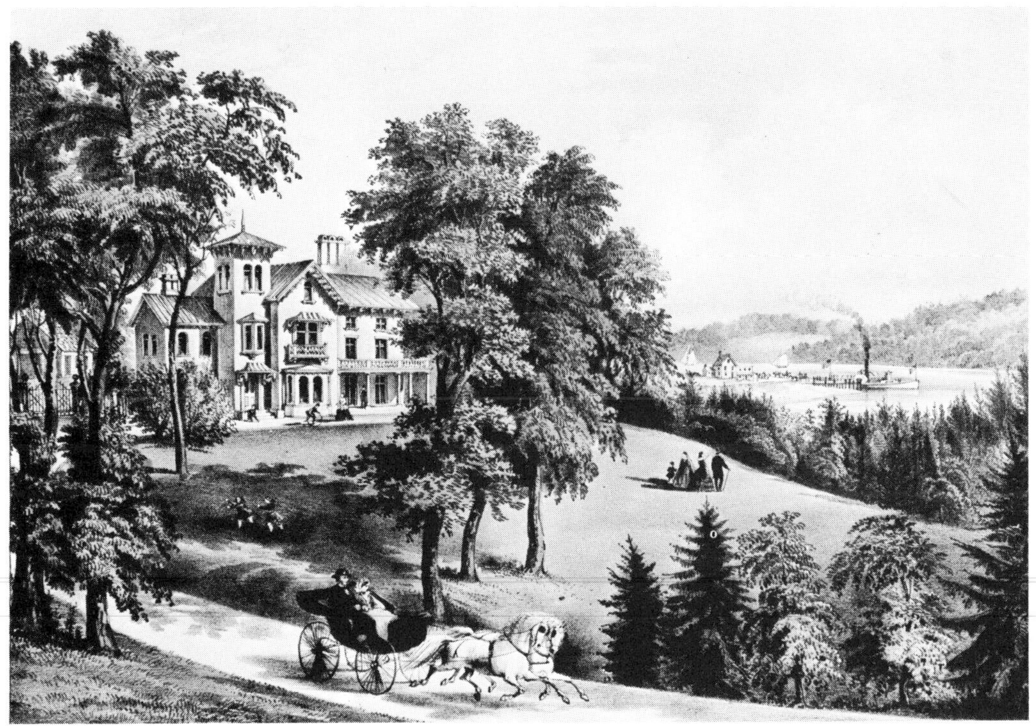

Life in the Country—Morning, by F. F. Palmer and published by Currier and Ives, 1862. Hand-colored lithograph, $11^{3}/_{16}$ x $15^{7}/_{16}$ inches

Railroad, Pioneer and Indian

This group of strange bedfellows is related through its connections with the nostalgia of the Old West. The railroad prints have a large following among railroad buffs who are not necessarily also interested in the West. As a group the railroad prints are few in number, rare and expensive. *The Express Train* is the title of five different prints, one of which is a large folio. The earliest, an undated N. Currier published sometime between 1838 and 1856 when the firm was at 152 Nassau Street and which was drawn on stone by J. Schutz, was selected unanimously as number one of the "best fifty" small folio prints. *Prairie Fires of the Great West* is a railroad, fire and Western print and collected by all three groups of collectors.

A very scarce and beautiful pioneer print is *The Rocky Mountains/ Emigrants Crossing the Plains* by, once again, F. F. Palmer. A series of prairie prints by A. F. Tait often picture Indians and have exciting titles like *A Check—Keep Your Distance* and *The Last War-Whoop.* Among the desirable small folio prints are *Gold Mining in California* and the winter scene *Home in the Wilderness.* Prints of the paintings by Catlin are the heart of the Indian group with *Buffalo Hunt Under the White Wolf Skin* and the *Indian Bear Dance.*

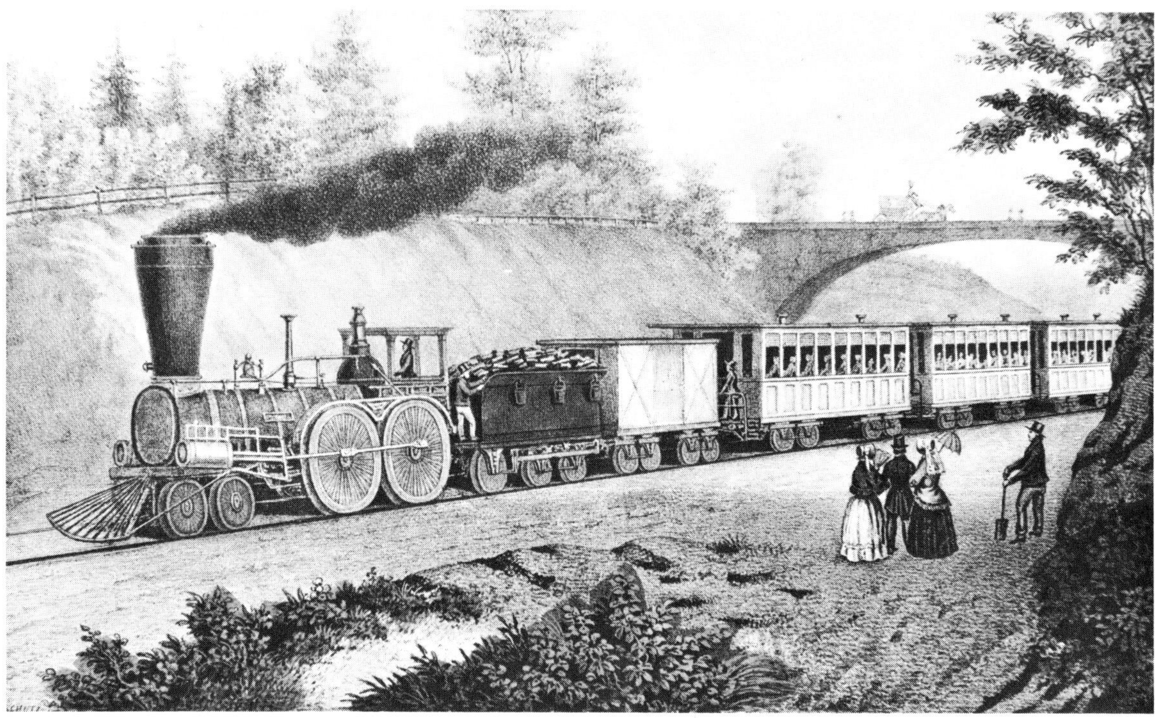

The Express Train, J. Schutz, Del., published by Currier and Ives, undated. Number one of the "best fifty" small folio. Hand-colored lithograph. $7\frac{3}{4}$ x $12\frac{1}{2}$ inches. (*Collection of Ladd MacMillan*)

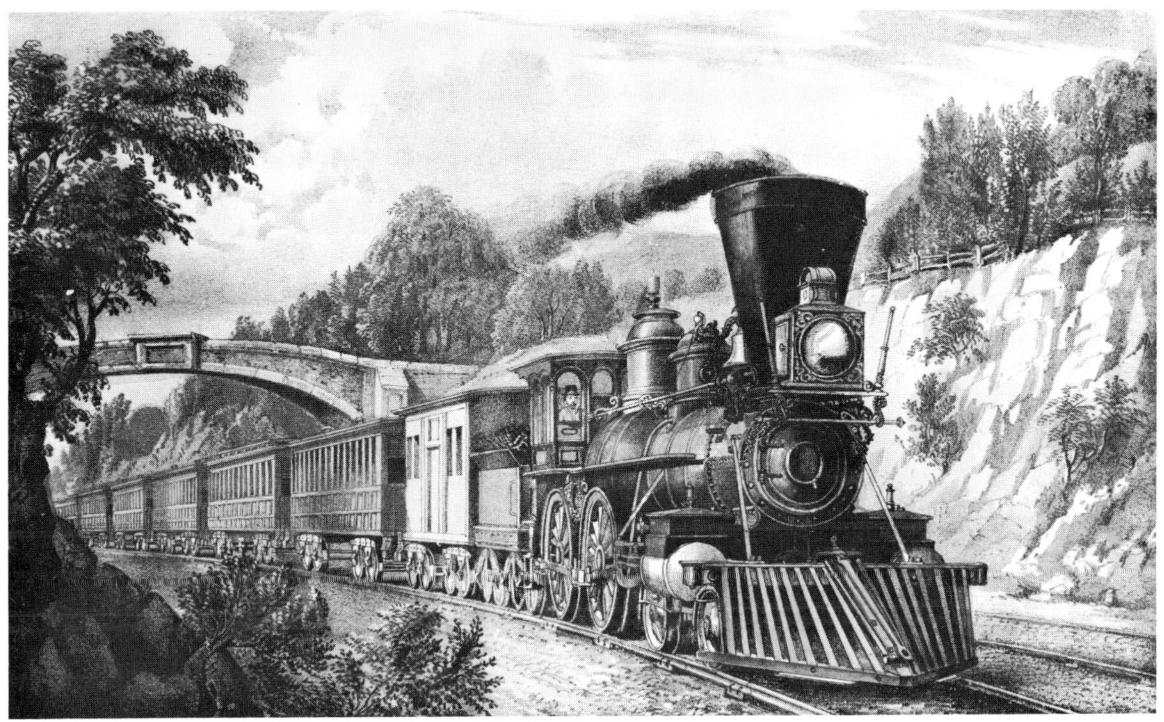

The Express Train, published by Currier and Ives, 1870. Hand-colored lithograph, 8 x 12½ inches.

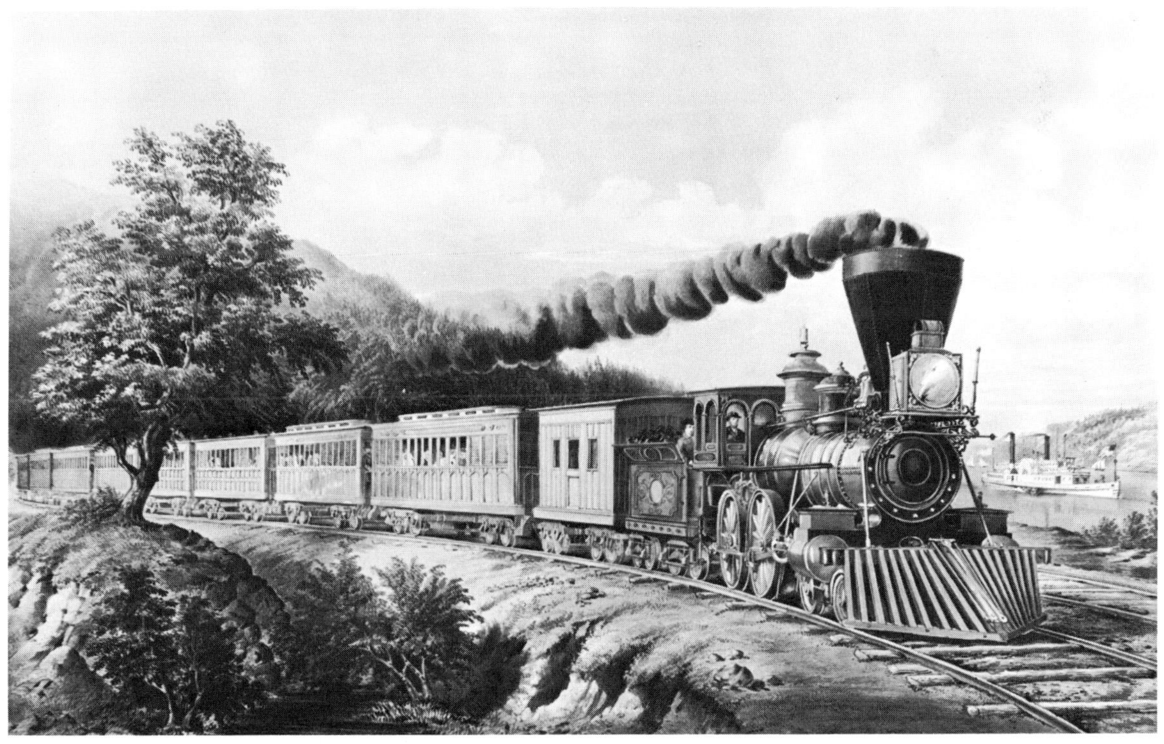

The American Express Train, F. F. Palmer, Del., published by Currier and Ives, 1864. Hand-colored lithograph, 18 x 31 inches (*Collection of Ladd MacMillan*)

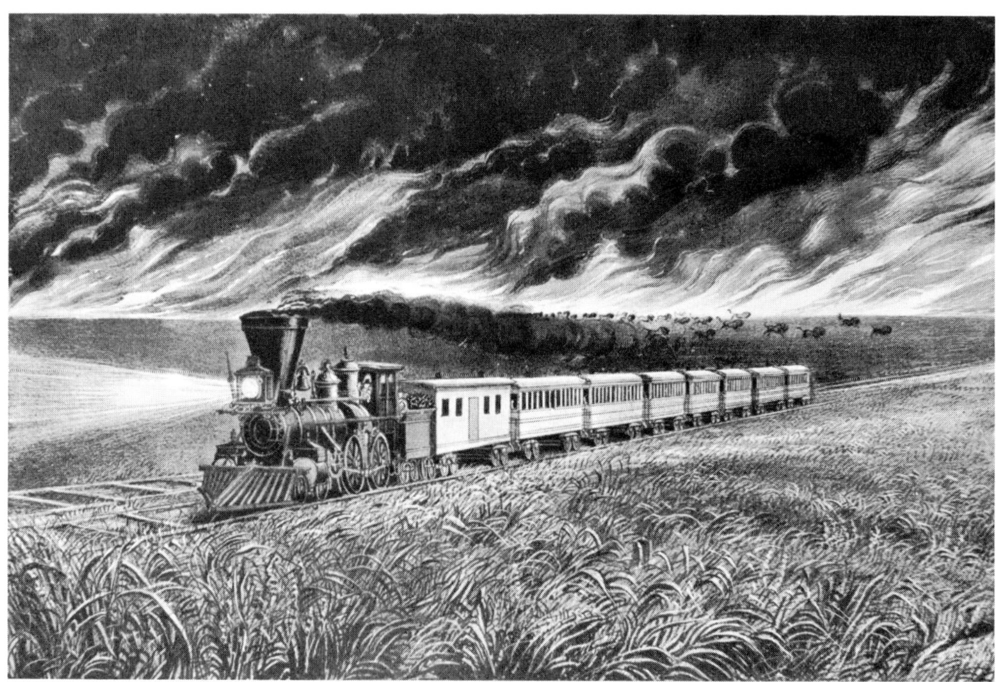

Prairie Fires of the Great West, published by Currier and Ives, 1871. Hand-colored lithograph, $8\frac{7}{16}$ x $12\frac{1}{2}$ inches (*Collection of Ladd MacMillan*)

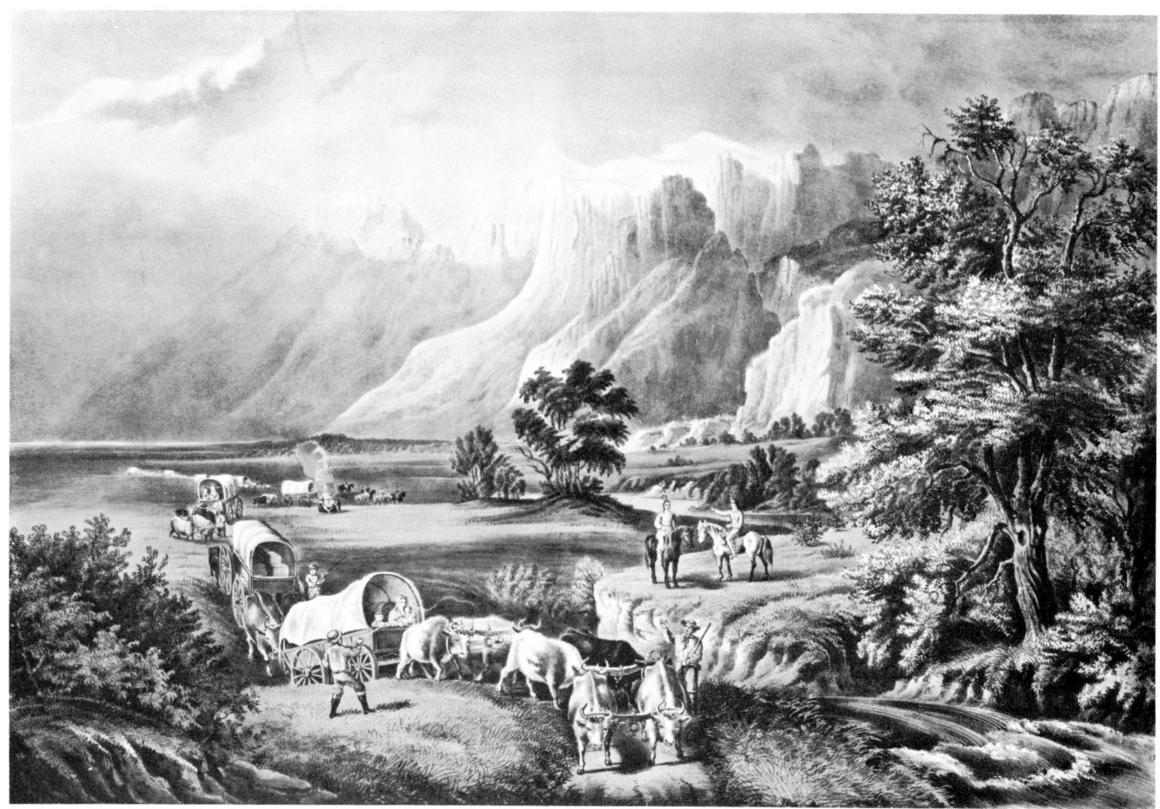

The Rocky Mountains/ Emigrants Crossing the Plains, by F. F. Palmer, published by Currier and Ives, 1866. Hand-colored lithograph, $17\frac{7}{16}$ x $25\frac{13}{16}$ inches

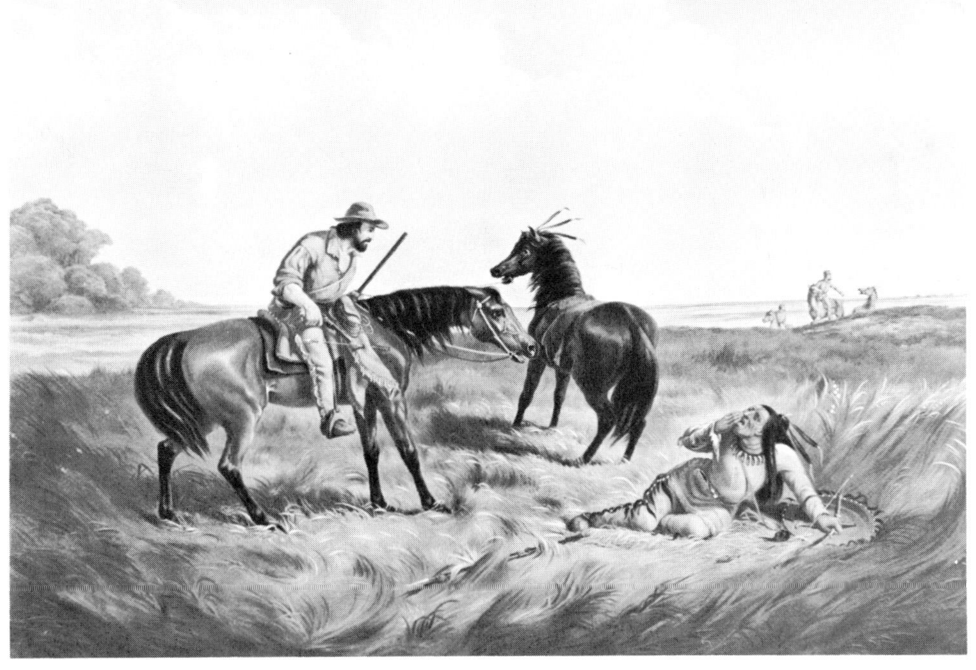

The Last War-Whoop, after a painting by A. F. Tait, published by Currier and Ives, 1856. Hand-colored lithograph, $18\frac{3}{16}$ x $25\frac{9}{16}$ inches

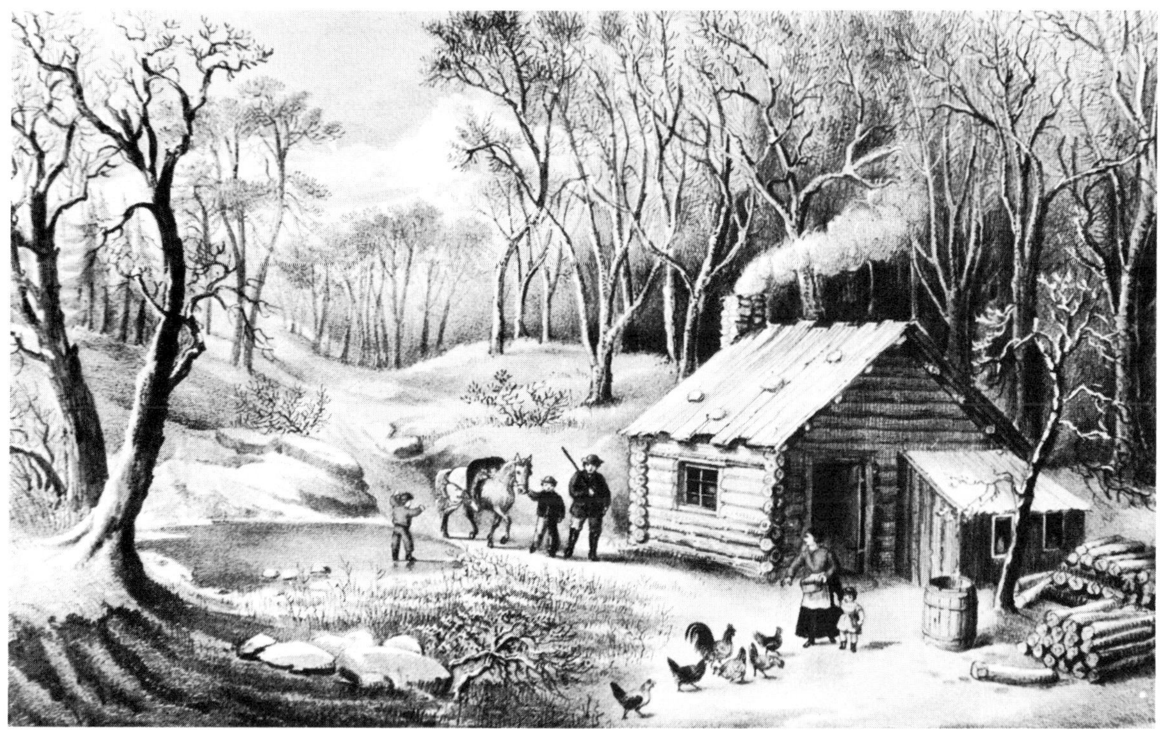

A Home in the Wilderness, published by Currier and Ives, 1870. Hand-colored lithograph, 8 x $12\frac{1}{2}$ inches

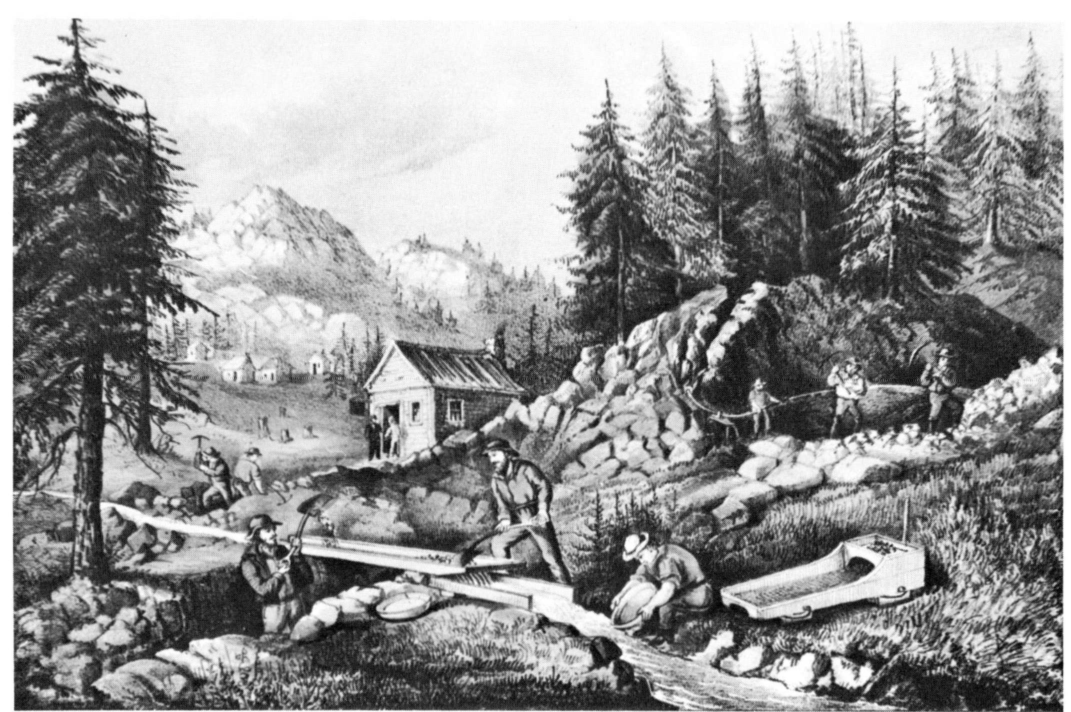

Gold Mining in California, published by Currier and Ives, 1871. Hand-colored lithograph, $8\frac{1}{2}$ x $12\frac{1}{2}$ inches (*Collection of Ladd MacMillan*)

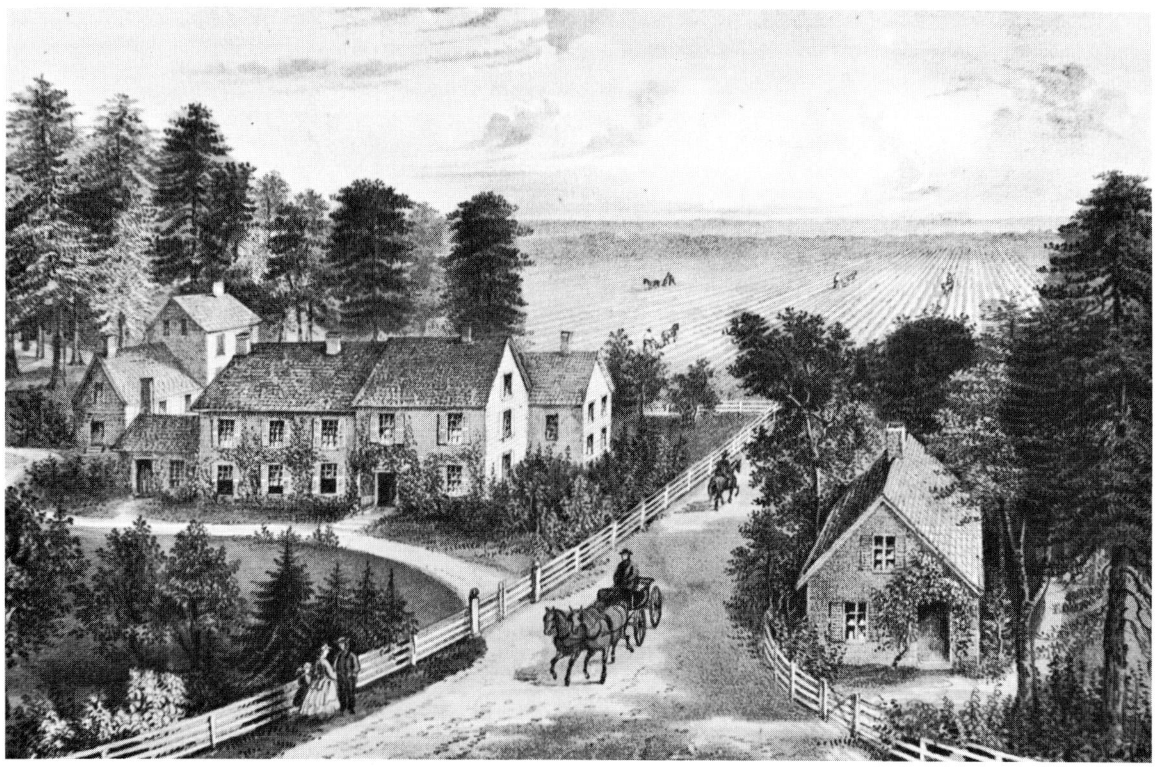

The Western Farmer's Home, published by Currier and Ives, 1871. Hand-colored lithograph, $8\frac{1}{2}$ x $12\frac{1}{2}$ inches

Horses and Horse Racing

Horses, including trotting and racing prints, with well over five hundred titles to choose from, form one of the major collecting categories. The large number came about as a result of the news value of the prints. Bars and stables needed new prints when a record race was run or a new champion emerged. Today, many collect horse prints because of the excellent decorative value of the Currier and Ives horse prints. They have a sleek and linear quality in a simple uncrowded composition which projects well. Some collect special blood lines such as Morgan horses, while others just like horses in general.

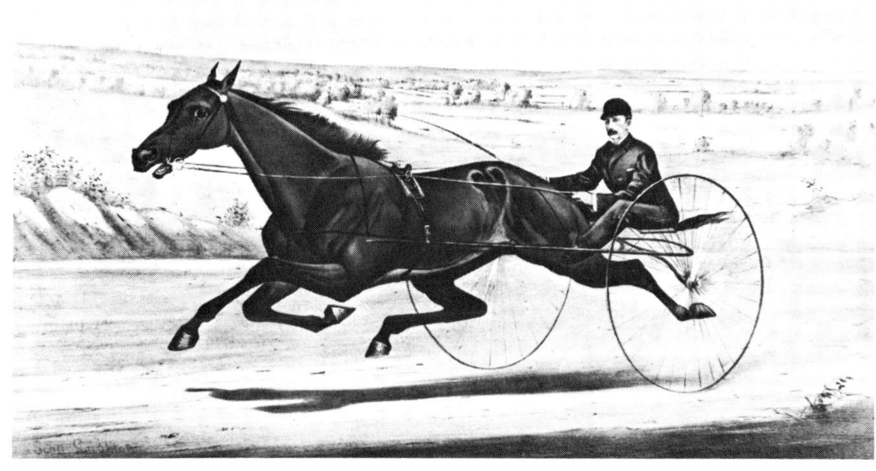

Queen of the Turf "Maud S", etc., on stone by Scott Leighton, published by Currier and Ives, 1880. Printed in oil colors, 18¼ x 28 inches

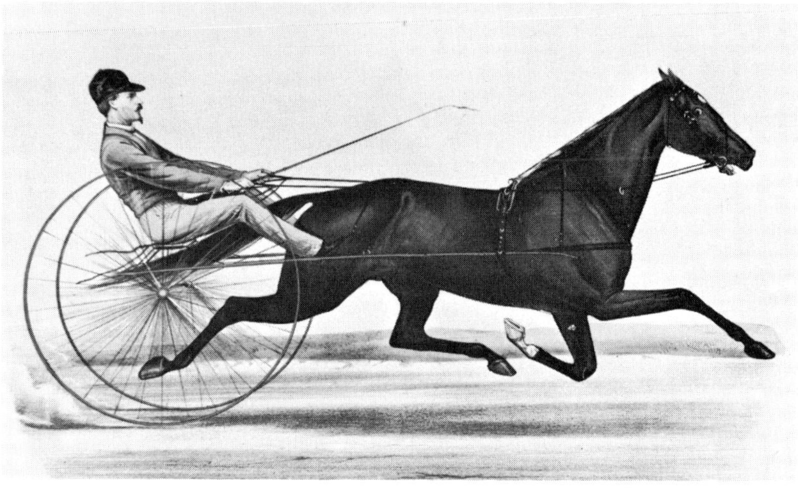

Edwin Forrest, etc., published by Currier and Ives, 1878. Printed in oil colors with additional hand-coloring, small folio vignette

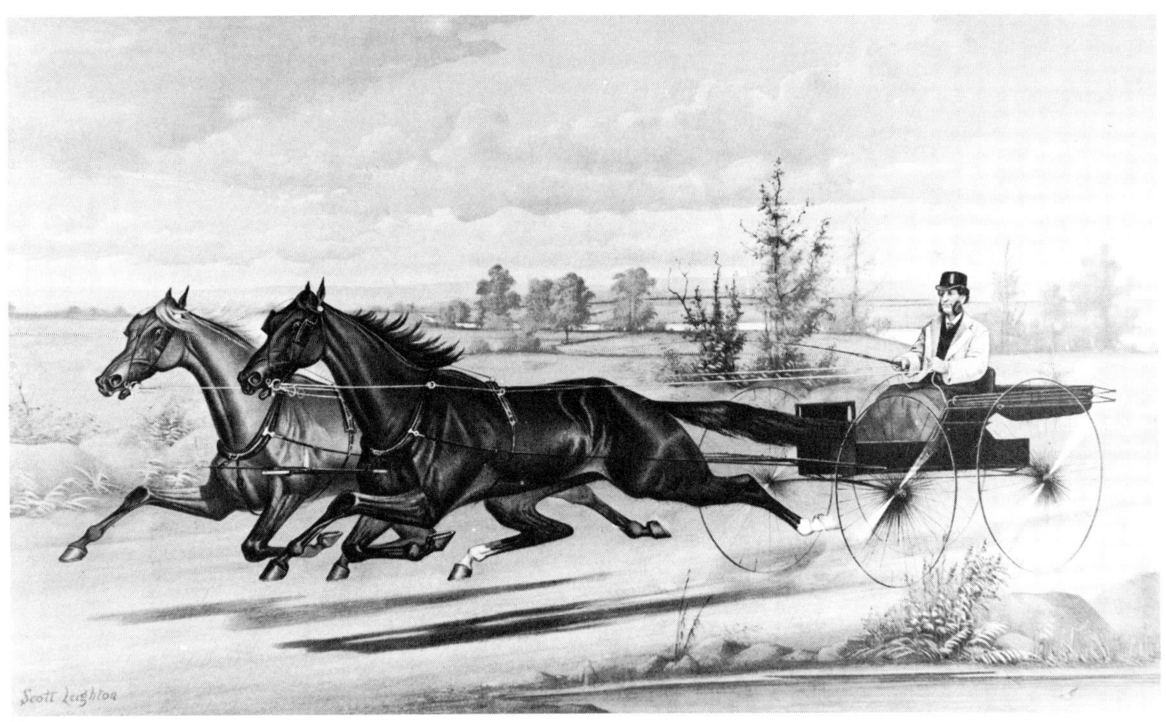

Celebrated Boston Team Mill-Boy and Blondine, etc., after a painting by Scott Leighton, published by Currier and Ives, 1882. Printed in oil colors, $20\frac{1}{2}$ x 33 inches

Other Categories

An examination of the "best fifty" will show some important prints which do not fall into any of the foregoing groups. Representative examples of some of these additional categories are illustrated:

Sports
Views
Fruits and Flowers
Comics
Mississippi River
Patriotic
Sentimentals
Advertising

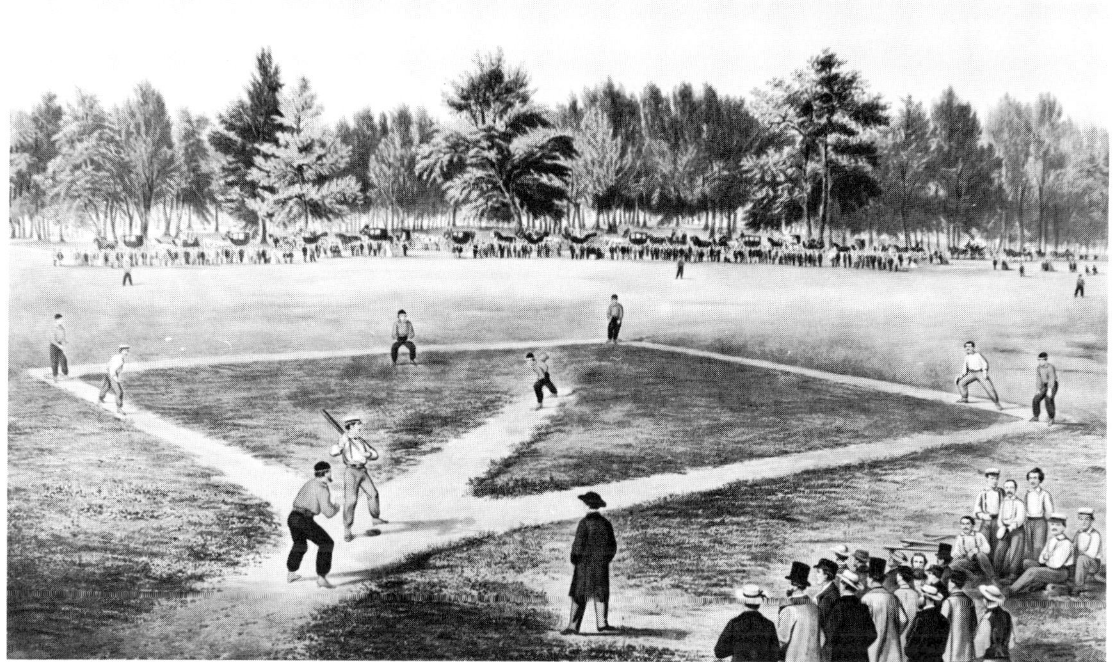

The American National Game of Baseball, etc., published by Currier and Ives, 1866. The only baseball print published by Currier and Ives. Hand-colored lithograph, 19⅞ x 29⅞ inches (*Collection of Ladd MacMillan*)

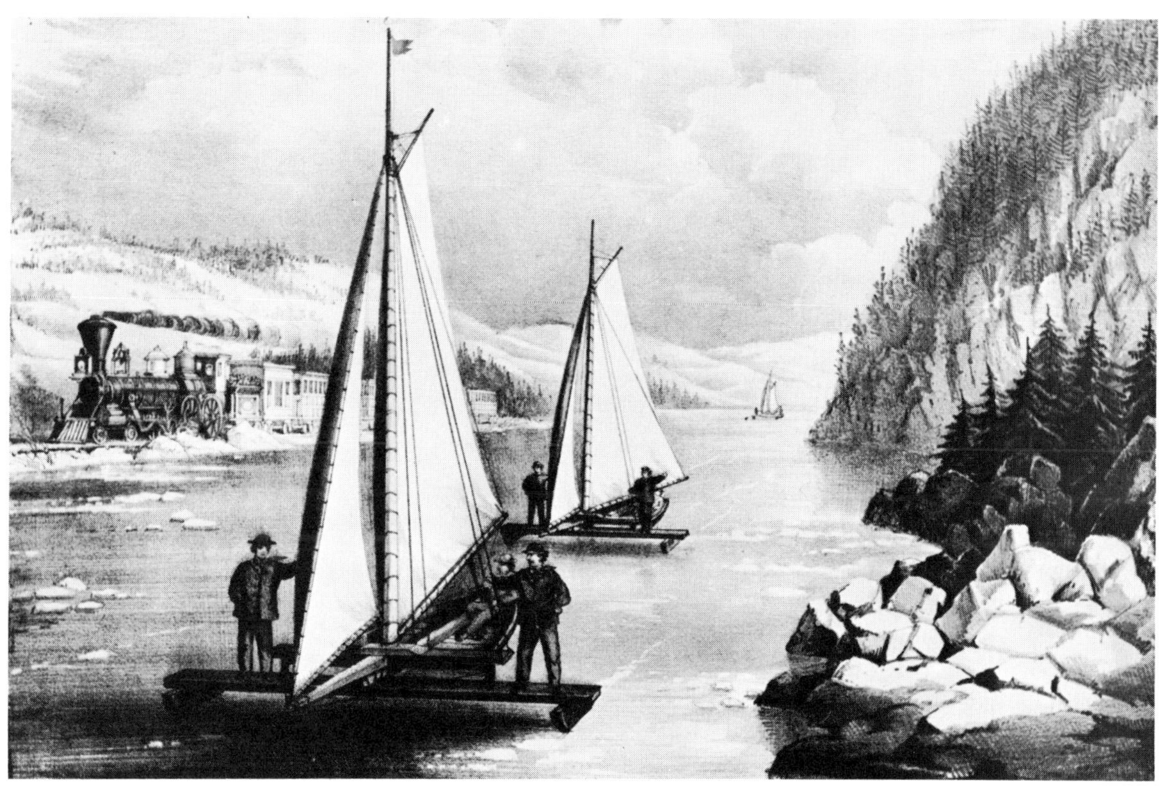

Ice-Boat Race on the Hudson, published by Currier and Ives, undated. Hand-colored lithograph, 8½ x 12½ inches

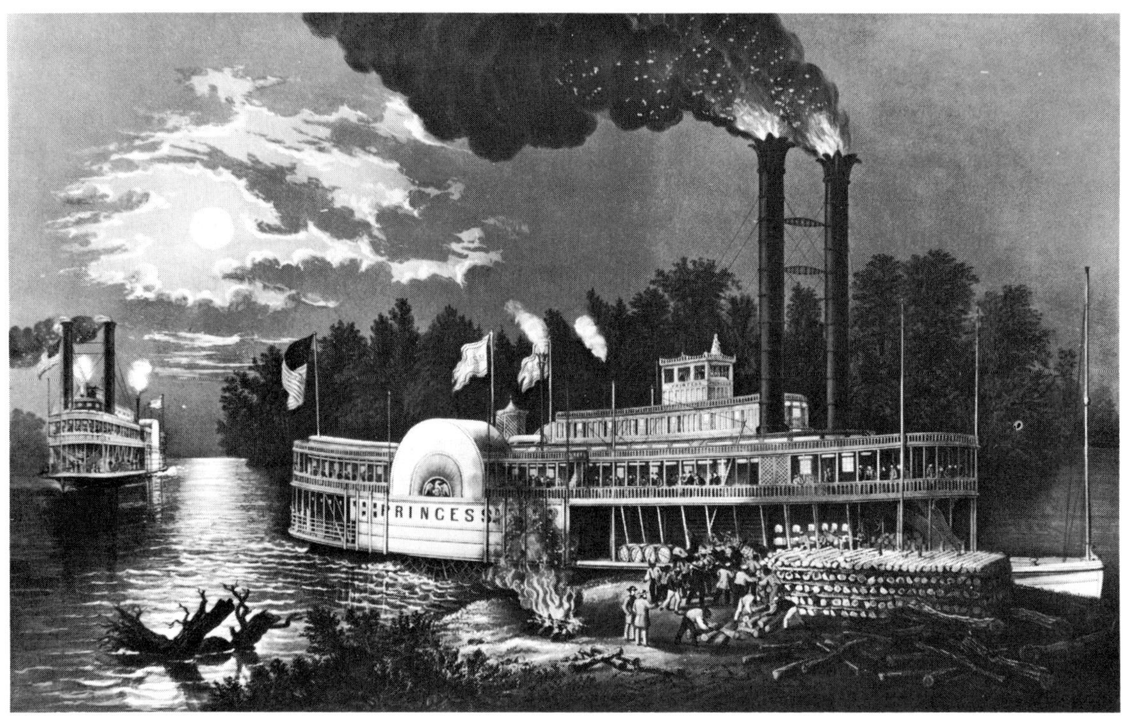

"Wooding Up" on the Mississippi, by F. F. Palmer, published by Currier and Ives, 1863. Hand-colored lithograph, $18\frac{1}{4}$ x $27\frac{13}{16}$ inches (*Collection of Ladd MacMillan*)

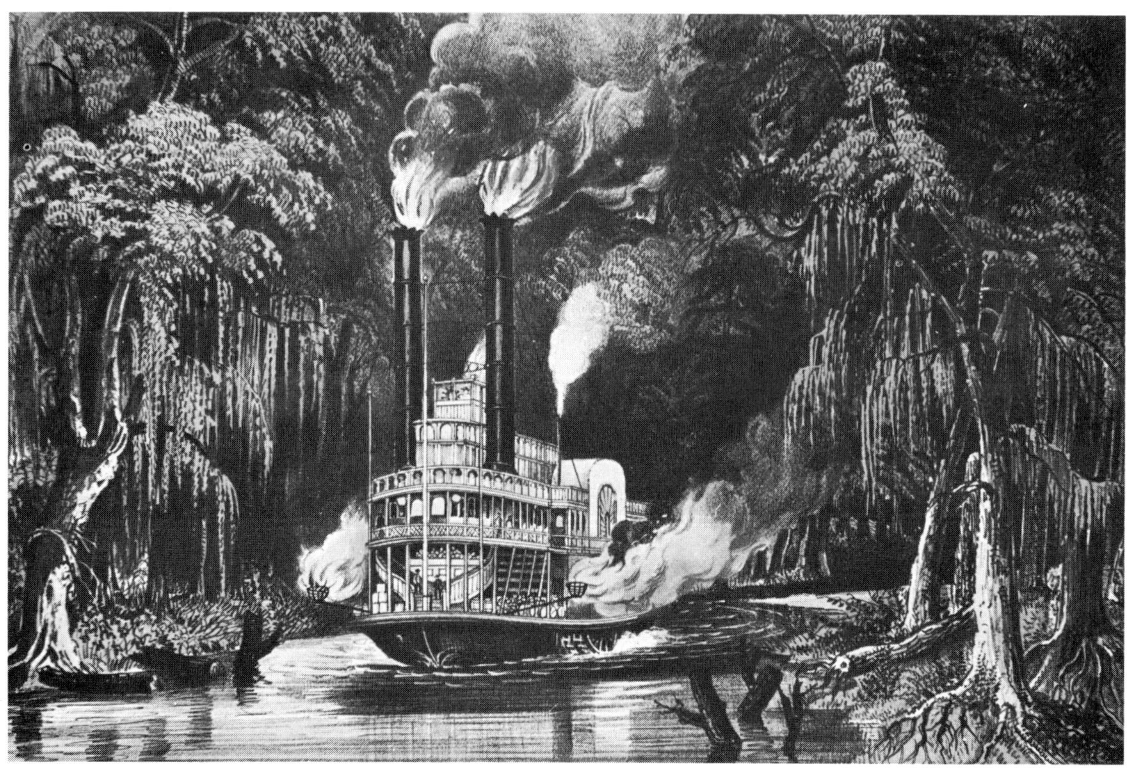

Through the Bayou by Torchlight, published by Currier and Ives, undated. Hand-colored lithograph, small folio (*Collection of Ladd MacMillan*)

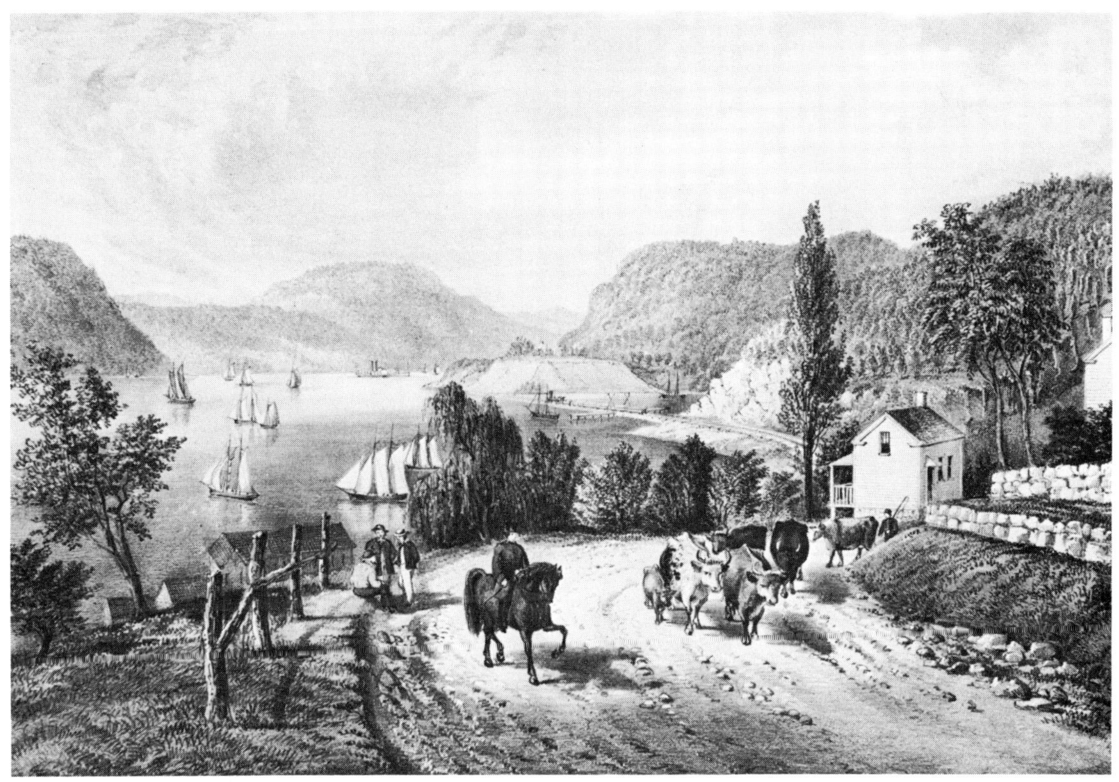

View From Peekskill/ Hudson River, N.Y., by F. F. Palmer, published by Currier and Ives, 1862. Hand-colored lithograph, $10\frac{7}{8}$ x $15\frac{3}{8}$ inches

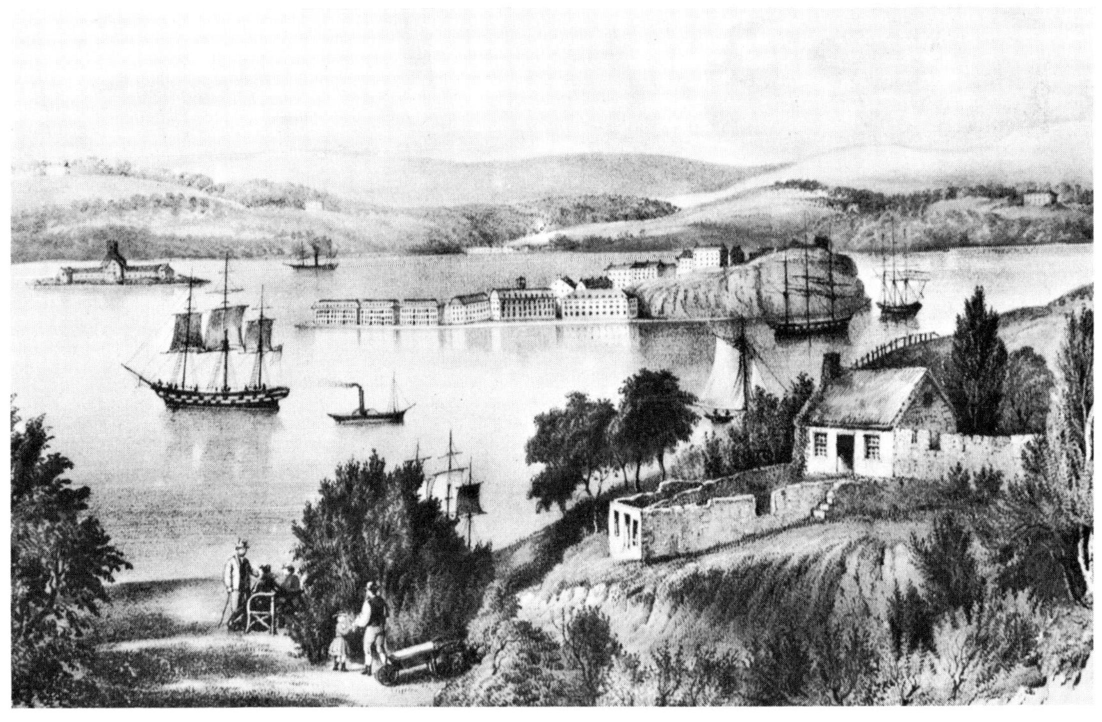

The Cove of Cork, published by Currier and Ives, undated. One of Currier and Ives foreign views. Hand-colored lithograph, 8 x $12\frac{1}{2}$ inches

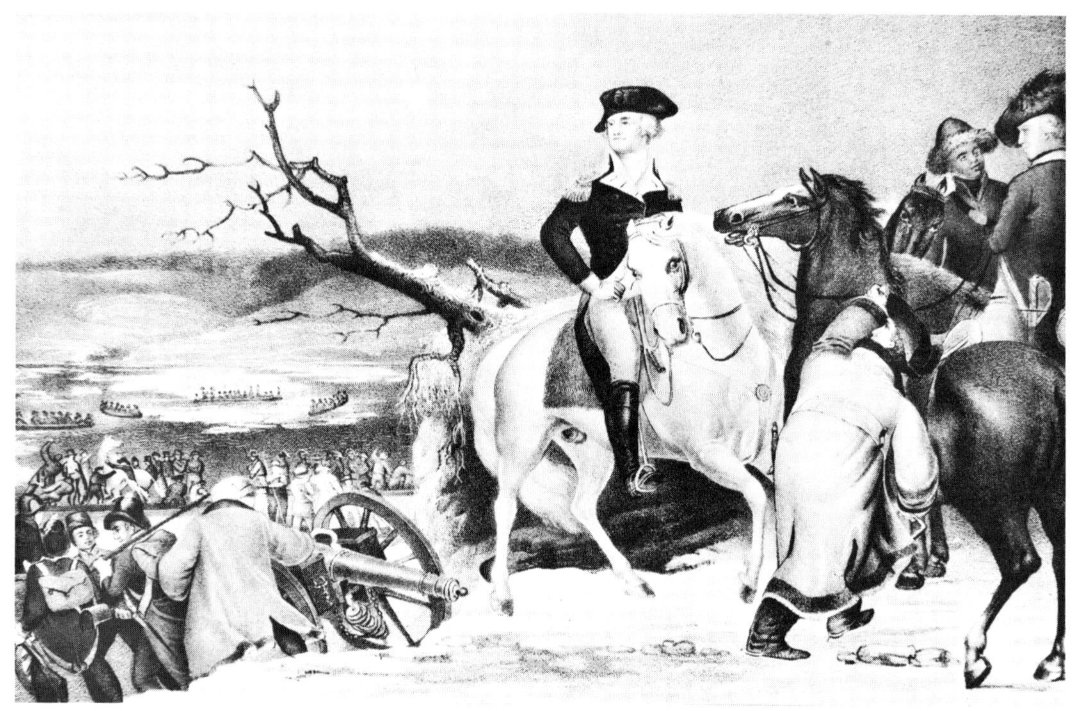

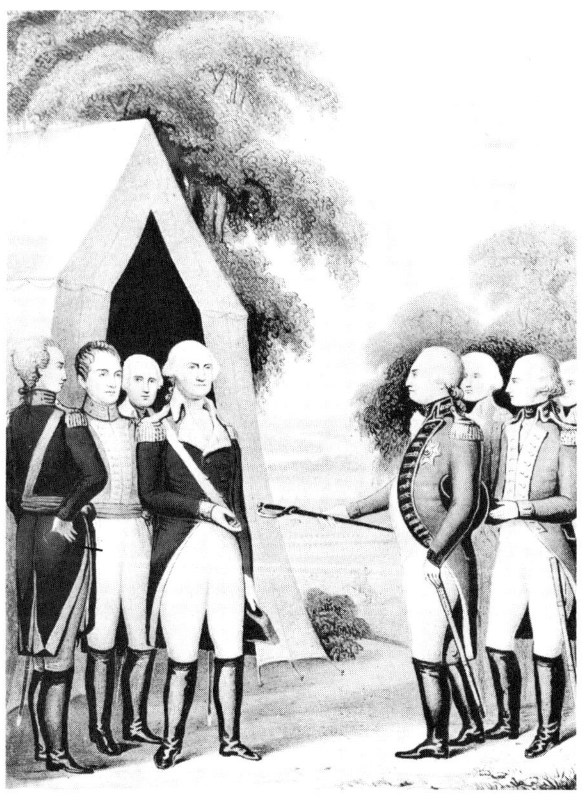

ABOVE *Washington Crossing the Delaware,* etc., published by N. Currier, undated. After the painting, *The Passage of the Delaware,* by T. Sully now in the Museum of Fine Arts, Boston. Hand-colored lithograph, $8\frac{1}{8}$ x $12\frac{1}{2}$ inches. LEFT *Surrender of Cornwallis at Yorktown, Va. October 1781,* published by N. Currier, 1845. Hand-colored lithograph, $11\frac{7}{8}$ x $8\frac{9}{16}$ inches

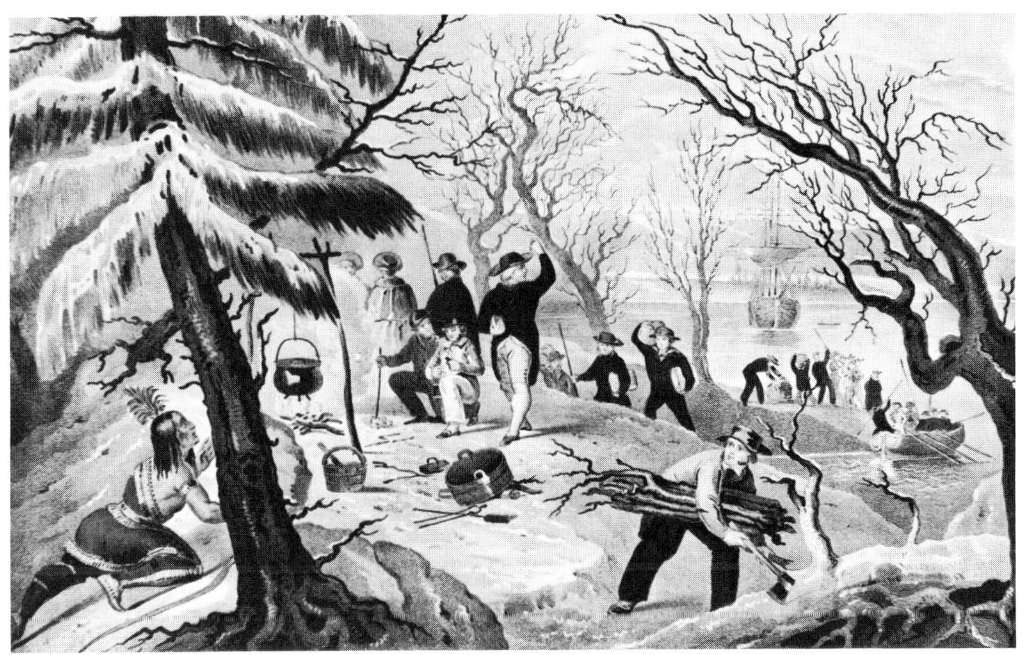

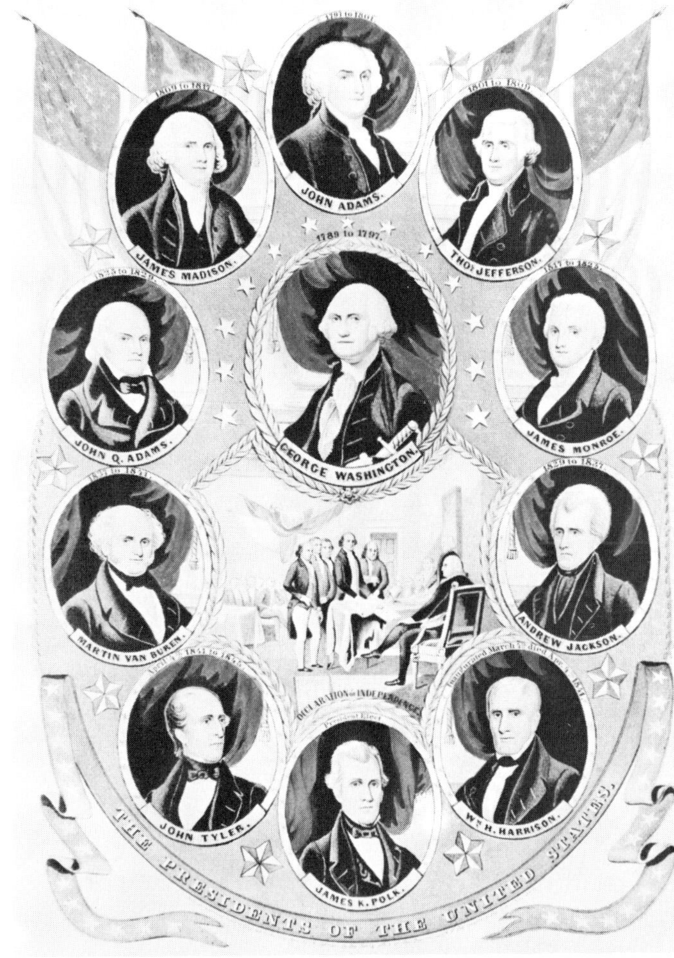

ABOVE *Landing of the Pilgrims at Plymouth,* etc., published by N. Currier, undated. Hand-colored lithograph, $8\frac{1}{4}$ x $12\frac{11}{16}$ inches. RIGHT *The Presidents of the U.S.,* published by N. Currier, 1844. A new updated version was put out every few years from 1842 to 1869. Hand-colored lithograph, small folio vignette

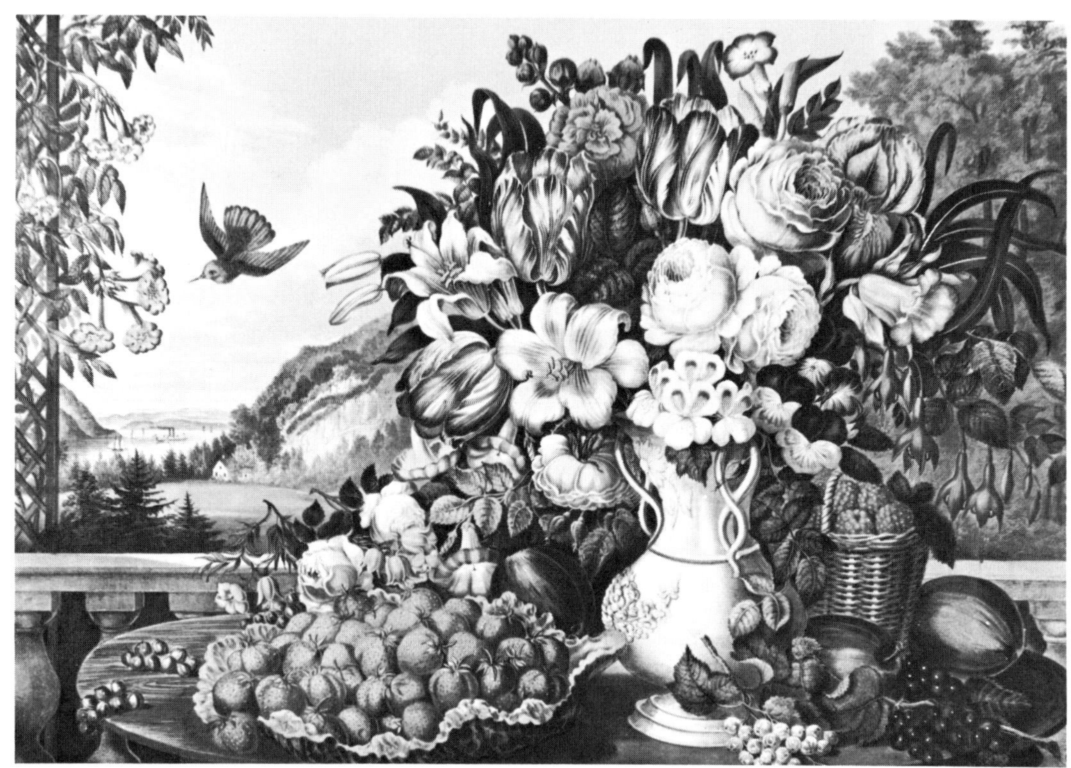

Landscape, Fruit and Flowers, by F. F. Palmer, published by Currier and Ives, 1862. Hand-colored lithograph, 19¾ x 27½ inches (*Collection of Ladd MacMillan*)

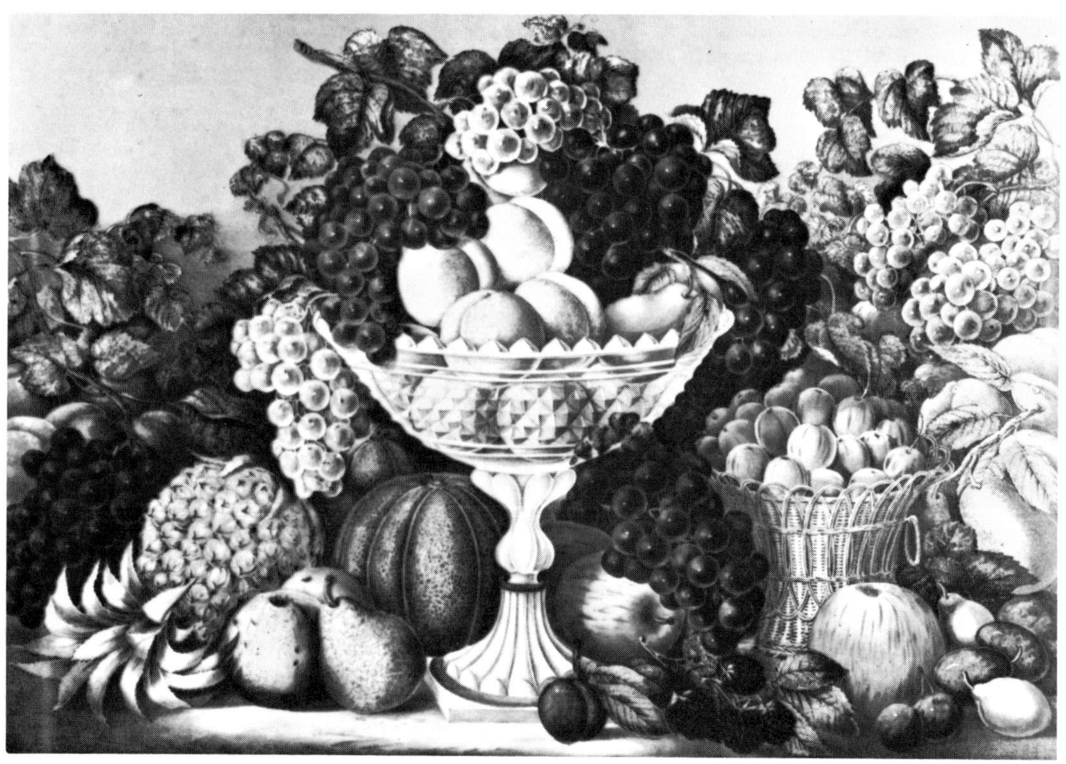

American Autumn Fruits, by F. F. Palmer, published by Currier and Ives, 1865. Hand-colored lithograph, 20 x 27⅞ inches

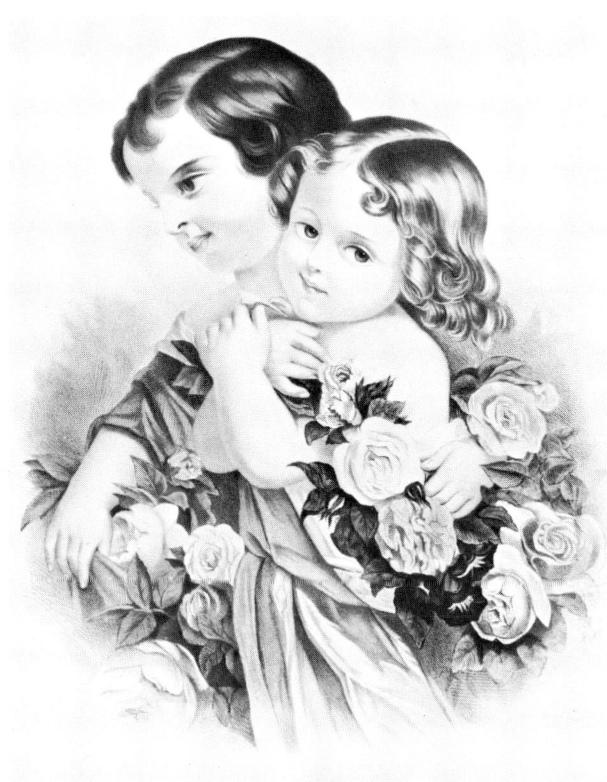

The Sunny Hour, published by Currier and Ives, undated. Hand-colored lithograph, medium folio vignette

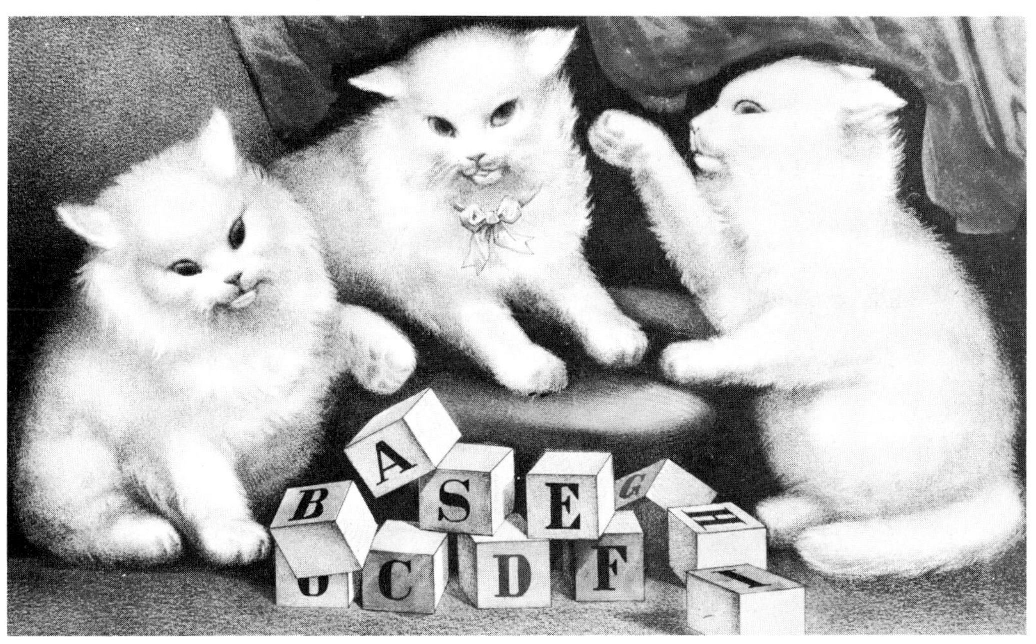

My Little White Kitties/ Learning Their ABC's, published by Currier and Ives, undated. Hand-colored lithograph, 8 x 12½ inches.

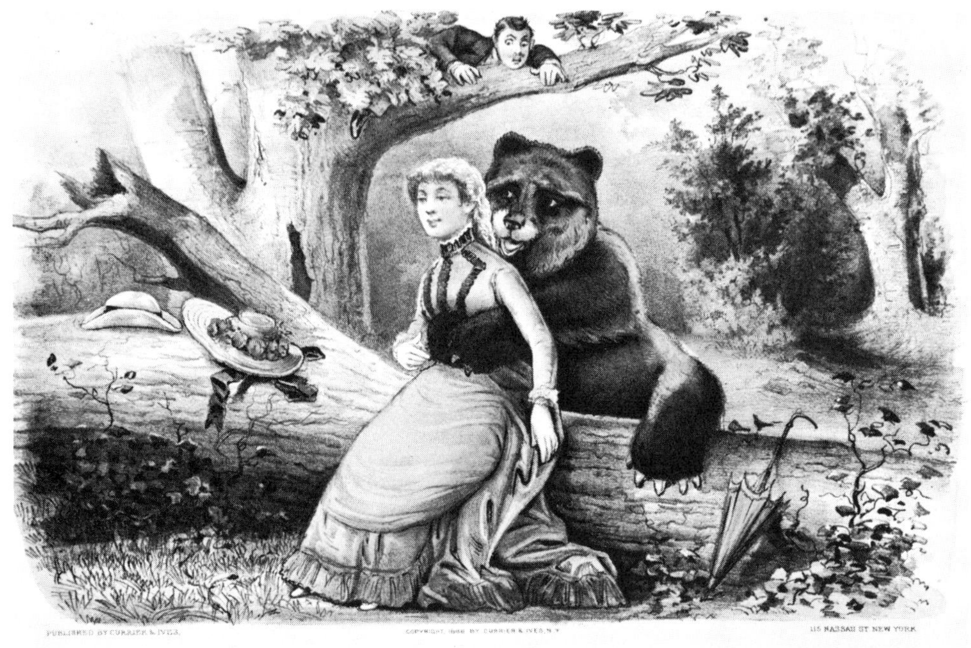

HUG ME CLOSER GEORGE!

Hug Me Closer George!, published by Currier and Ives, 1886. Small folio vignette (*Collection of Ladd MacMillan*)

FINE FAMILY CARRIAGES

OF EVERY DESCRIPTION

ALWAYS IN STOCK.

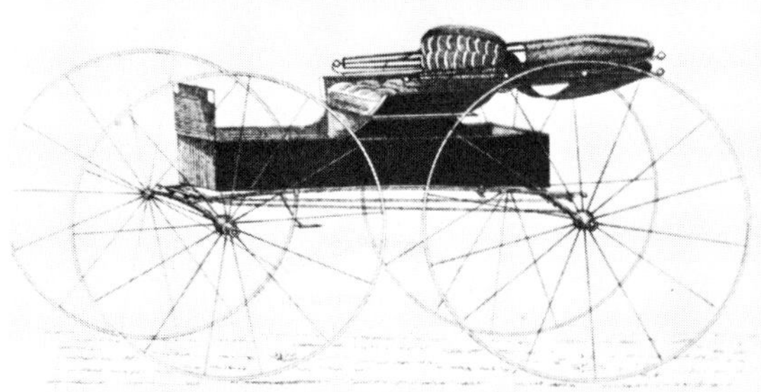

LIGHT ROAD AND SPEEDING

WAGONS,

SKELETONS AND SULKIES,

BEST QUALITY AT MODERATE PRICES.

J. N. Mansuy, *President.* N. Brigham Hall, *Sec'y and Treas.*

ESTABLISHED 1841.

THE

MANSUY CARRIAGE MANUFACTURING CO.

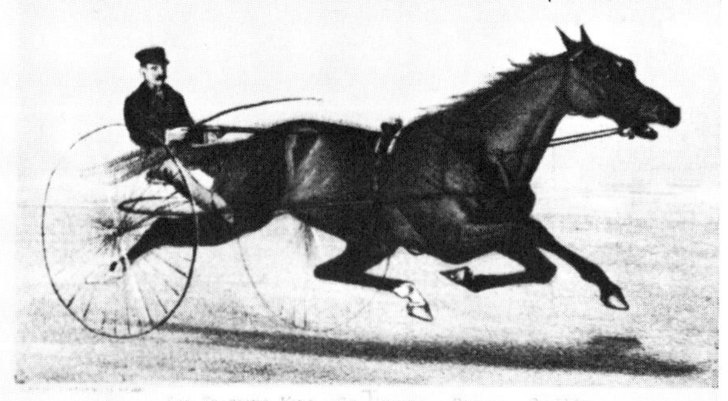

MANUFACTURERS OF

FASHIONABLE CARRIAGES

OF THE HIGHEST GRADE.

Nos. 17, 19 and 21 ELM STREET,

HARTFORD, CONN.

Advertising sheets by Currier and Ives, 1881 (*Collection of Ladd MacMillan*)

CHAPTER SIX Nature Prints

During the eighteenth and nineteenth centuries, the first serious efforts were made to scientifically classify American natural history. From the time of the discovery of America, Europeans were fascinated with the animals and plants as well as with the Indians and the scenery of this wild territory. This interest led to a series of books with scientific orientation, some with color plates, by European naturalists who visited this country. In the nineteenth century American nature lovers, such as J. J. Audubon, continued this work and issued new and revised descriptions in books often illustrated with beautiful color plates. Many of these books have been cut apart and the plates framed or put into print collections. This group of book plates is augmented by single non-scientific prints lithographed by Currier and Ives and others later in the nineteenth century.

Mark Catesby and Other European Ornithologists

One of the earliest and best known illustrated works on American nature is the two volume set *The Natural History of Carolina, Florida, and the Bahama Islands* published in London in 1727–43, written and illustrated by Mark Catesby. The first volume includes one hundred plates, etched and colored personally by Catesby and his wife representing what he considered to be the one hundred two species of American birds. Volume

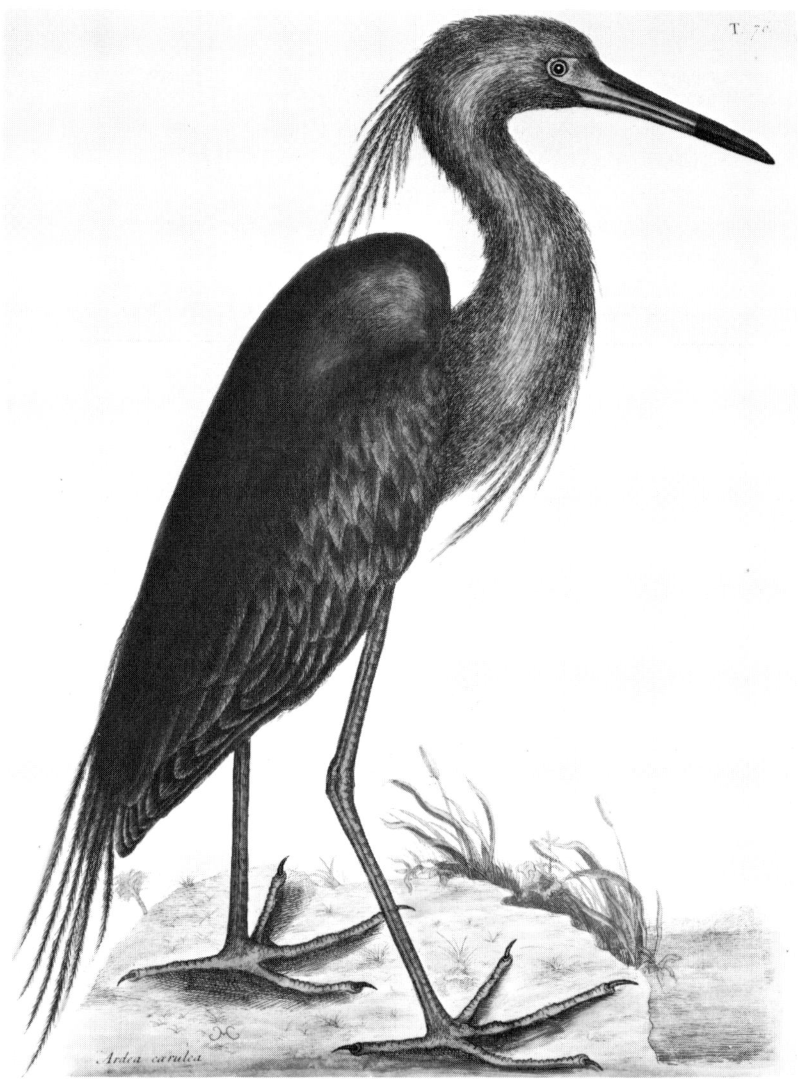

The Blue Heron, etching by Mark Catesby, *The Natural History of Carolina, Florida, and the Bahama Islands,* Volume I, plate 76, 1727–31. Plate size $13^3/_4$ x 10 inches (*National Gallery of Art, Washington, D.C., Gift of Dr. and Mrs. George B. Green*)

II contains one hundred twenty plates of fish, reptiles, insects, plants and animals. Only one hundred fifty sets were completed of the first edition but later editions were published in 1754 and 1771, after Catesby's death in 1749. Both the second and third editions use the original plates but there are changes in the text and George Edwards made minor changes in the plates. Editions were also published in German.

Catesby made two trips to America with his book, the result of the second trip made between 1722 and 1726. These trips were sponsored by a group of Englishmen including Sir Hans Sloane, physician to King George III and head of the Royal Society. The purpose of the trips was the cataloguing and collecting of specimens of the "beneficial and beautiful Productions" of the English dominions. In the preface to his first volume Catesby describes how he captured the color and vitality of the subjects:

> In designing the Plants, I always did them while fresh and just gather'd: And the Animals, particularly the Birds, I painted them while alive (except a very few) and gave them their gestures particular to every kind of Bird, and where it would admit of, I have adapted the Birds to those Plants on which they fed, or have any Relation to. Fish which do not retain their Colours when out of their Element, I painted at different Times, having a succession of them procur'd while the former lost their Colours . . . . Reptiles will live many months without Sustenance, so that I had no difficulty in Painting them while living

"Colonial Audubon" and "Father of American Ornithology" are titles sometimes given to Catesby. His artistically strong prints are beautiful and decorative. With the plants and animals in natural positions rather than in stiff profile, he set a new standard for scientific illustration. His style was later adopted by Wilson, Audubon and others.

George Edwards, who revised some of Catesby's plates, won the title "Father of British Ornithology" with his own book. Edwards, like Catesby, was patronized by Sir Hans Sloane. Edwards was made librarian of the Royal College of Physicians in 1733 and while in that capacity produced four volumes of *Natural History of Uncommon Birds* between 1743 and 1751. About two hundred fifty plates are included in these volumes, about one quarter of them North American birds. His print output of North American birds from this and later publications is almost equal in number to Catesby's but unlike Catesby, Edwards receives scant recognition today for his work.

In the last years of the eighteenth century Louis Jean Pierre Vieillot collaborated with the artist Jean Baptiste Audebert in producing a book on American birds. The book, *Naturelle des oiseaux de l'Amérique septentrionale* was published in sections in Paris starting in 1807, seven years after the death of Audebert. Although the work contains one hundred thirty-one professionally executed plates and Vieillot was a competent ornithologist, the book met with a poor reception when published.

In the nearly nineteenth century, P. John Selby published *Birds of Britain* with plates engraved by W. H. Lizars of Edinburgh, who later did the first ten plates of J. J. Audubon's work. Some of the birds shown by Selby are common to both America and Britain. John Gould (1804–1881), also an Englishman, is best known for his *Birds of Great Britain* but he also published books on birds in Australia and elsewhere. In

1844–50 a monograph on *Partridge of America* included thirty-two hand-colored lithographs. Other minor works appeared but by the beginning of the nineteenth century American naturalists were at work producing their own books and prints.

Alexander Wilson and his Birds

Alexander Wilson (*b.* 1766 Scotland; *d.* 1813 United States), author and artist of *American Ornithology: Or the Natural History of the Birds of the United States* (Philadelphia: Bradford and Inskeep, 1808–1814, nine volumes) is the first important ornithologist to write and publish in the United States. His book includes seventy-six hand-colored plates, the first hand-colored plates in a major work published in the United States. They were engraved and etched by five engravers, but principally by Alexander Lawson and John G. Warnicke. Volume 9 was published after Wilson's death and includes a biography written by George Ord. The paper size of the prints is 15¼ inches by 12 inches with the impression typically 13½ inches by 10 inches.

Wilson was a self-taught artist and naturalist who spent his early years in Scotland as a weaver, peddler and poet. In 1794 at the age of twenty-eight he migrated to the United States, departing from Belfast and arriving in New Castle, Delaware. He walked to Philadelphia, a distance of thirty-five miles, and during this walk had his first sighting of an American bird, a red-headed woodpecker. He thought the bird the most beautiful he had ever seen.

After arriving in Philadelphia he eventually found a job as a teacher in Gray's Ferry, now a part of West Philadelphia. This was close to Bartram's Botanical Gardens and through his great interest in ornithology he became friends with William Bartram, one of the prominent naturalists in the United States. Using Bartram's library he became acquainted with the works of Catesby and Edwards, and through the teaching of Alexander Lawson, a fellow countryman, soon learned to draw. Wilson had the opportunity to talk to the nature scholars of the era who visited Bartram's home. With this background he spent the early years of the 1800's working on his book. After 1806, as an assistant editor, he revised the natural history sections of *Rees's New Cyclopedia.*

Wilson persuaded Samuel Bradford, the publisher of *Rees's,* to also publish his own work and in September, 1808, the first volume was ready. He then spent the remaining five years of his life soliciting sales and traveling the country gathering information for successive volumes. During the spring of 1810, while on a trip down the Ohio River, he met John J. Audubon in his frontier store in Louisville. He solicited Audubon to subscribe to his book and showed him the two finished

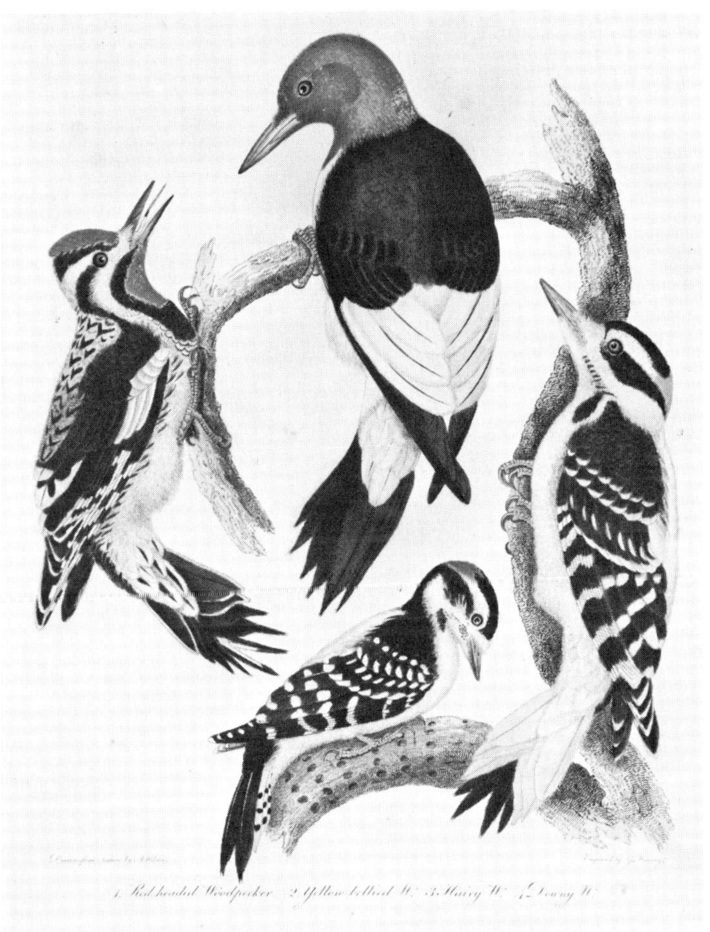

Red-headed Woodpecker . . . , hand-colored engraving and etching by G. Murray, after a drawing by Alexander Wilson, c. 1810, plate size, 13 x 10 inches. This bird is said to be the first one sighted by Wilson after landing in America.

volumes. Instead of subscribing, Audubon showed Wilson examples of his watercolors and told him that he, too, was interested in publishing. This meeting was a disappointment to Wilson, who had considered his project unique and had expected that it would be many years before another attempt was made.

Wilson spent the next two and one half years working on Volumes Three through Seven. Volumes Eight and Nine were published after his death in 1813. A supplement was published in Philadelphia by an admirer and fellow naturalist, Prince Charles Lucien Bonaparte. Artists Titian Peale and A. Rider assisted in this addition to Wilson's original seventy-six plates with much of the engraving being done by Alexander Lawson. Wilson's original work together with Bonaparte's supplement was soon overshadowed by Audubon's great work, whose publication began in 1827.

John J. Audubon and His Works

John James Audubon (*b.* 1785 Haiti; *d.* 1851 United States) had a deep passion for the wilderness and the study of nature which often won out over the needs of his family. He is believed to have been born in Haiti, the illegitimate son of a French admiral and a native Creole. During an uprising his mother was killed but he escaped to France with his father. He lived in Nantes before being sent to his father's estate in Mill Grove near Philadelphia in 1803. There the eighteen-year-old Audubon became interested in American birds and in a neighbor, Lucy Bakewell, whom he later married.

The young Audubon tried many ways to make a living including working as a taxidermist, portrait painter, French teacher and proprietor of the frontier store in Louisville where he met Alexander Wilson in 1810. This meeting undoubtedly spurred him on to publish his own work, so he spent the next fifteen years wandering in search of birds. He captured the birds, killed them, and wired them into position. He drew and colored the birds himself but backgrounds and plants were often put in by others.

In 1826 he took his bird paintings to be exhibited in England and while there made arrangements for prints to be made for a book, *The Birds of America.* He wrote in his diary that the pictures "will be brought up and finished in such a superb style as to eclipse all of the kind in existence." The prediction proved to be true.

The book was sold through subscription by Audubon at two guineas the part or £ 182/14s the set ($1,000). It is believed that fewer than two hundred bound sets were made up. The prints are beautifully hand-colored aquatints and etchings, each printed on double elephant folio paper (approximately 39½ inches by 26½ inches) made by Whatman in England. A total of four hundred thirty-five plates were issued in eighty-seven parts of five plates each, all showing the birds life size. The parts are generally found bound in four volumes, and a descriptive text, *Ornithological Biography,* partly written by William McGilivray, was issued separately. The first ten plates were engraved by William H. Lizars of Edinburgh but they were retouched later by Robert Havell and his son, Robert Havell, Jr. in London, who also did the remaining plates. The work went on over the years from 1827 to 1838. Almost half of the two hundred seventy-nine subscribers dropped out before all plates were complete. It is not known how many of each print were made but it is believed that there may have been as many as three hundred impressions of the earlier ones. Prints were made at different times during the eleven years the work went on and some of the earlier prints are known in different states.

Today these stunning plates of the Havell Edition have achieved the status of fine art and are often exhibited in the leading art museums

RIGHT *Great American Cock Male (Wild Turkey)*, hand-colored engraving, etching, and aquatint by W. H. Lizars, retouched by R. Havell, Jr., London, 1829, after a painting by John James Audubon, *The Birds of America,* Plate 1, paper size, 38½ x 26 inches. Audubon's most sought-after print

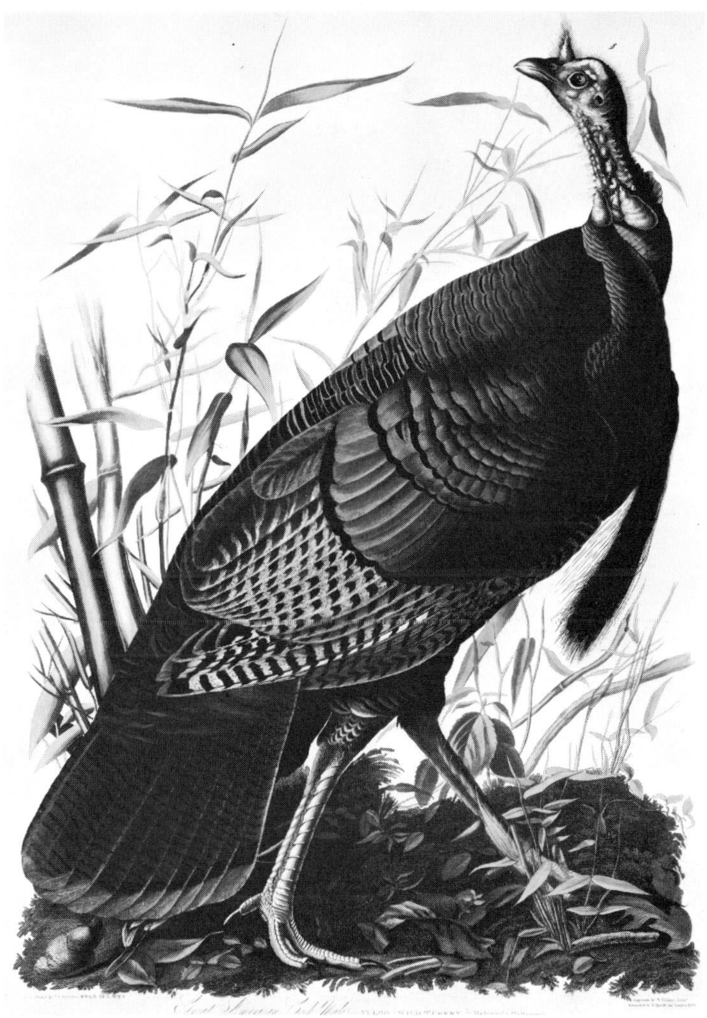

BELOW *White-headed Eagle,* hand-colored engraving, etching, and aquatint by R. Havell, London, 1836, after a painting by John James Audubon, *The Birds of America,* Plate 31, paper size, 26 x 38½ inches. Our national symbol

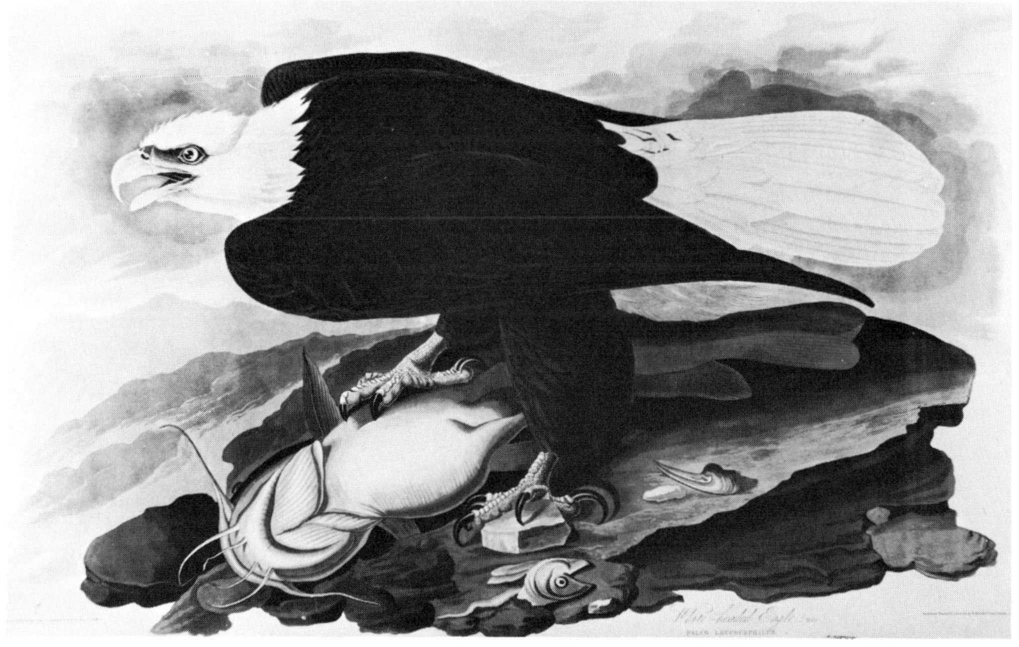

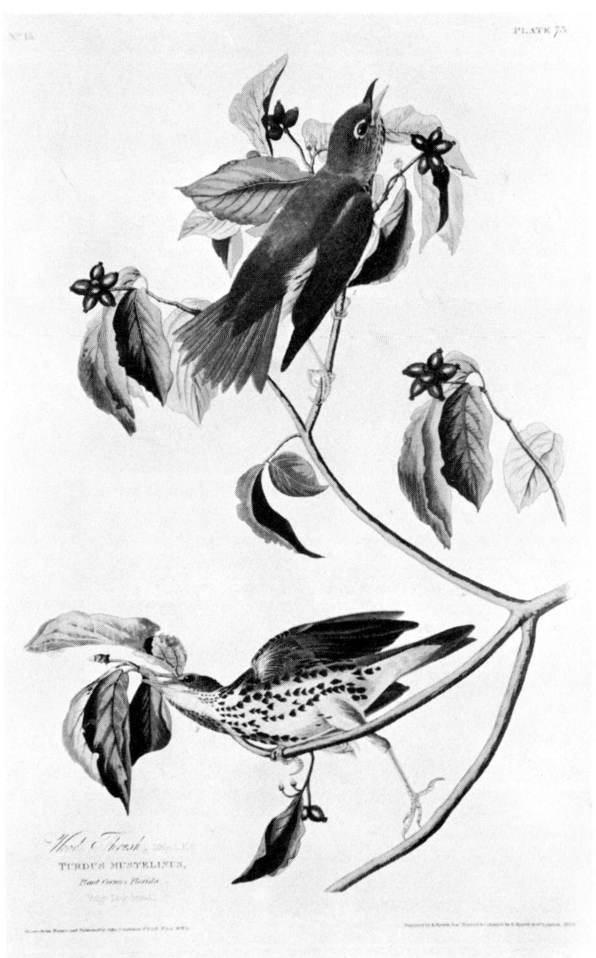

Wood-Thrush, hand-colored engraving, etching, and aquatint by R. Havell, London, 1836, after a painting by John James Audubon, *The Birds of America,* Plate 75, plate size, $19\frac{1}{4}$ x $12\frac{1}{8}$ inches. This is said to have been Audubon's favorite bird

of the country. Audubon subordinated nature to art by sometimes posing the birds in unnatural or even impossible attitudes for artistic reasons. The improbable positions of the Bonapartian Gulls shown in the illustration creates a striking pattern, achieved in this case by cutting the shapes of the bird or birds out and pasting them on the painting. By treating the bird shapes as abstract patterns he created bold designs particularly pleasing to the modern eye. The smaller songbirds are placed in graceful and delicate settings appropriate to their size. In the *Wood Thrush,* Audubon's favorite because of its dependably cheerful song, the bodies of the birds follow the lines of the branch of the dogwood tree on which they sit. All but two of the original four hundred thirty-five water color paintings for the *Birds of America* are now owned by the New York Historical Society of New York City.

The only reissue of these prints in the double elephant size was

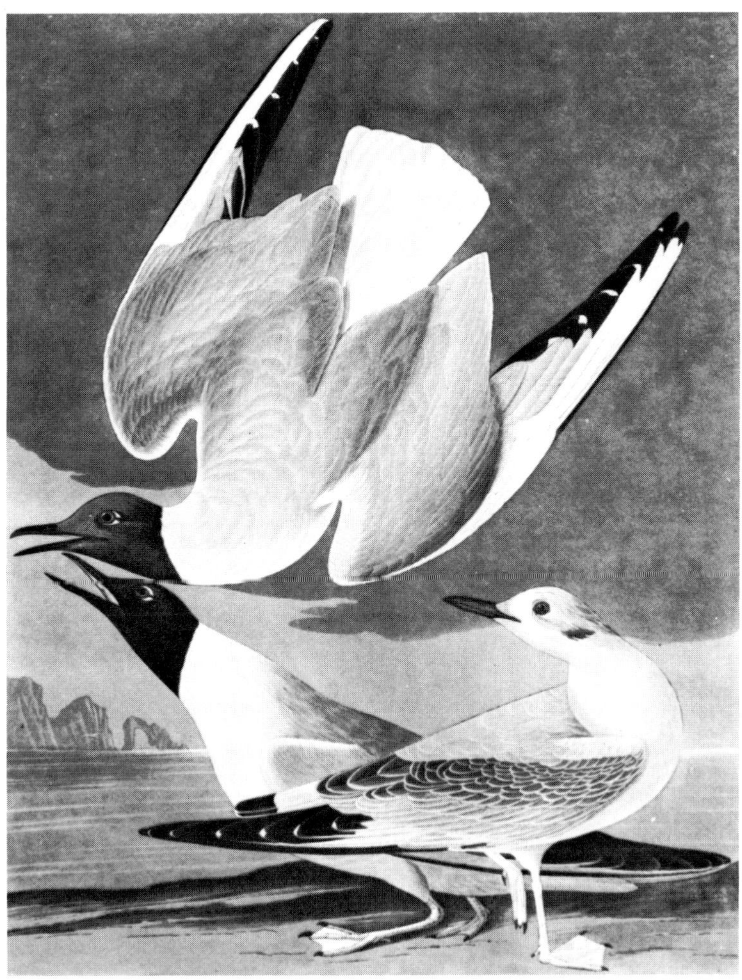

Bonapartian Gull, hand-colored engraving, etching, and aquatint by R. Havell, London, 1836, after a painting by John James Audubon, *The Birds of America,* Plate 324, plate size, 21 x 16¾ inches. A striking composition made by cutting out the birds and pasting them on a painted background

made by Julius Bien, a German immigrant lithographer working in New York between 1850 and 1868. His *Birds* are chromolithographs made by a transfer process from the original copper plates. He reproduced one hundred six plates with many of the small ones printed two on a page. The work was interrupted in 1860 by the Civil War and never completed. These prints differ in important respects from the Havell Edition. The coloring is not hand-done, the image is not as crisp, and the paper is not so good a quality.

Audubon recognized that there was a market for a cheaper and smaller version so in 1840–44 the first of the octavo editions was issued. These editions of the *Birds of America* appeared in seven volumes with text and included a total of five hundred hand-colored lithographed plates. J. T. Bowen of Philadelphia carried out most of the lithography. Unlike the large English Havell Edition the prints in the octavo edition are convenient book size on paper 10 inches by 6½ inches. Many of

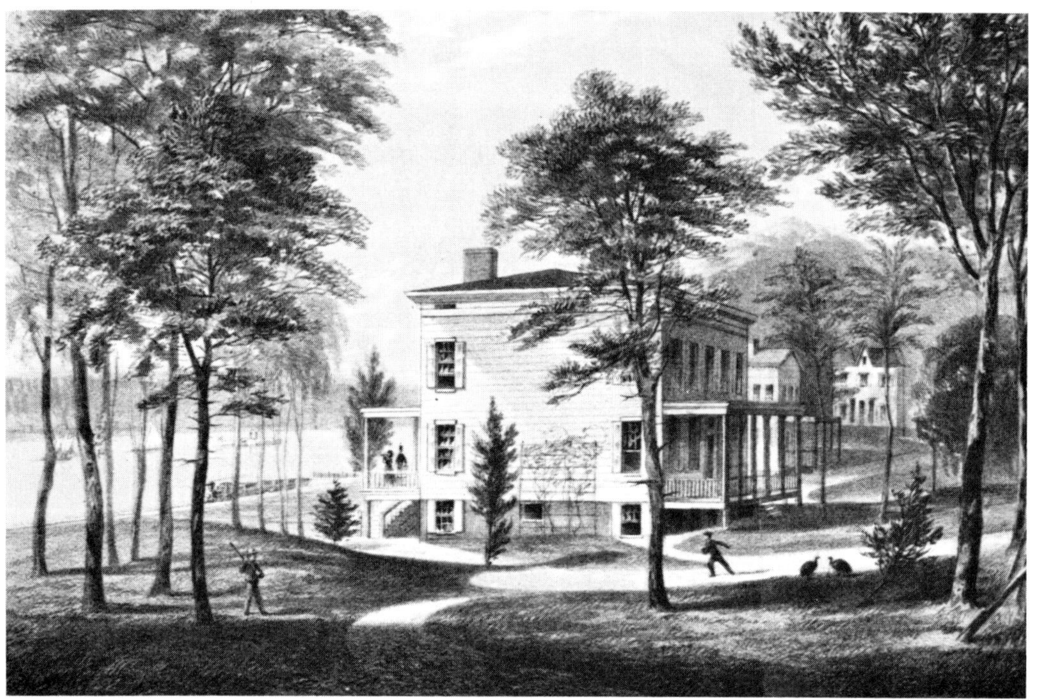

The Audubon Estate on the Banks of the Hudson, Foot of 156th St. at Carmansville, colored lithograph by Major and Knapp, N.Y., published in *Manual of the Corporation of the City of New York,* by D. T. Valentine, 1865, $5\frac{3}{4}$ x $8\frac{1}{2}$ inches

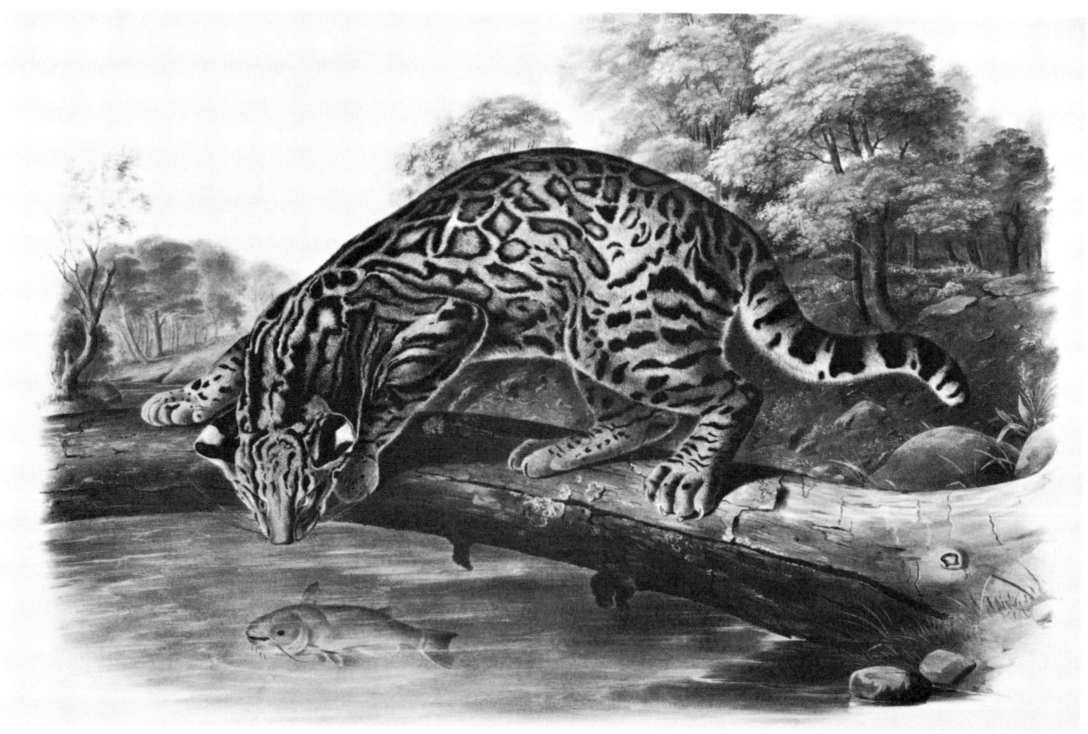

Ocelot or Leopard-Cat, hand-colored lithograph by J. T. Bowen, Philadelphia, 1846, after a drawing by J. W. Audubon, *Viviparous Quadrupeds of North America,* Plate 86. Vignette on paper, $21\frac{1}{2}$ x 27 inches

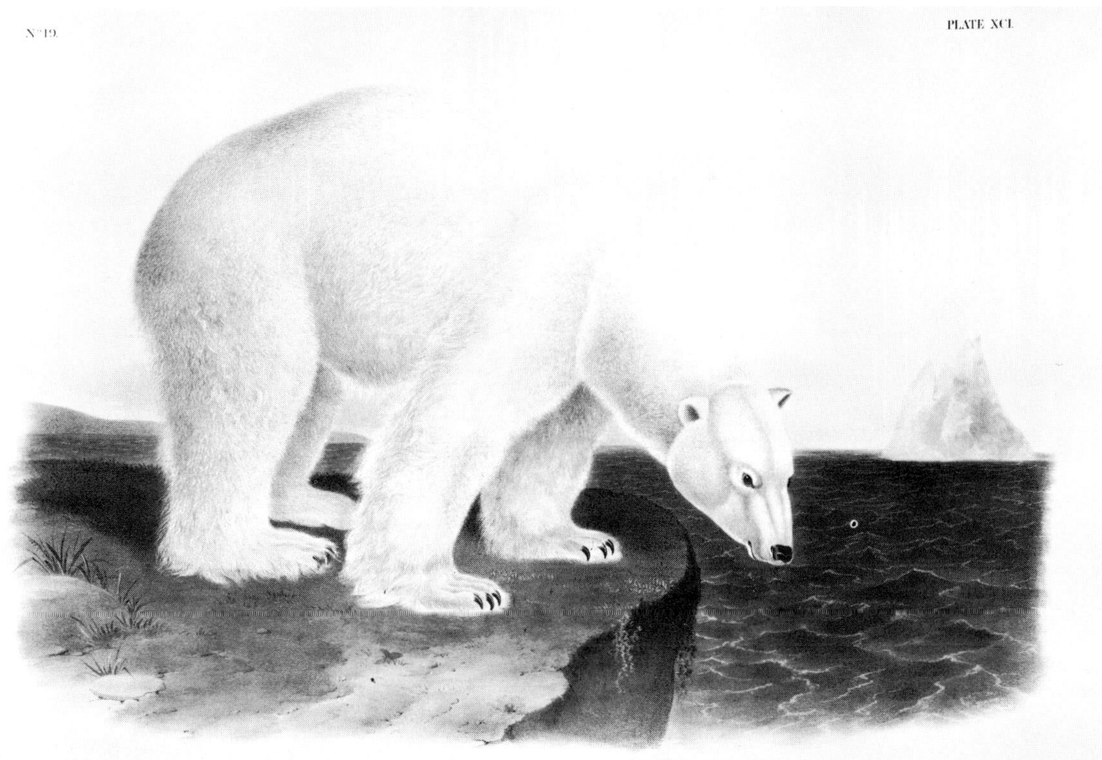

Polar Bear, hand-colored lithograph by J. T. Bowen, Philadelphia, 1846, after a drawing by J. W. Audubon, *Viviparous Quadrupeds of North America,* Plate 91. Vignette on paper, 21½ x 27 inches

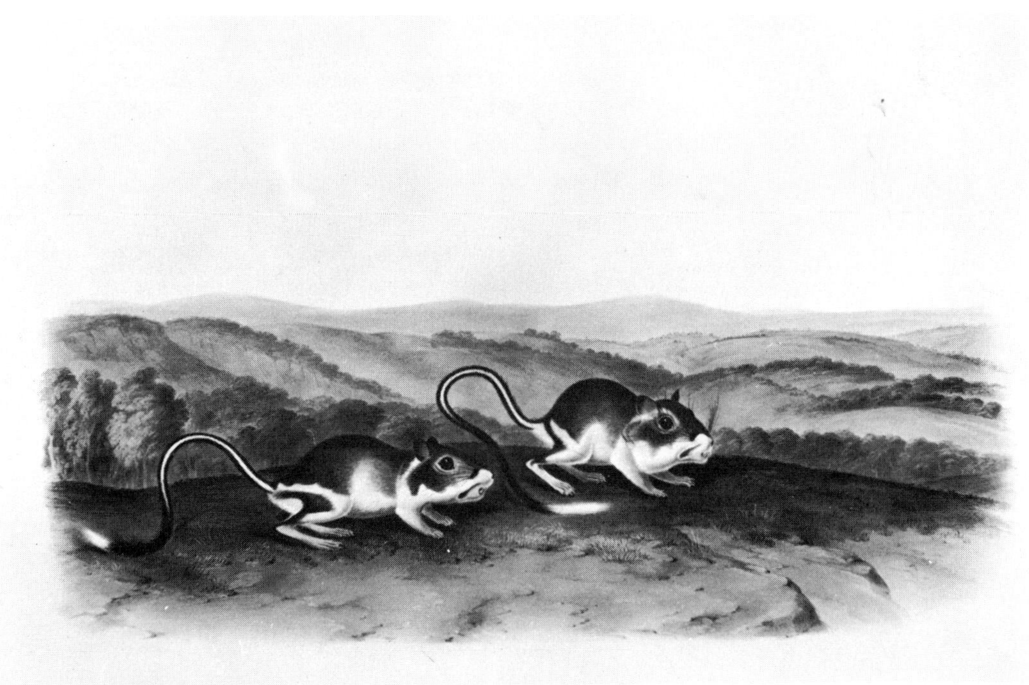

Pouched Jerboa Mouse, hand-colored lithograph by J. T. Bowen, Philadelphia, 1847, after a drawing by J. W. Audubon, *Viviparous Quadrupeds of North America,* Plate 130. Vignette on paper, 21½ x 27 inches

the plates are almost exact copies of the larger ones in composition and color. Sixty-five plates, mostly of species found in the western part of the country, were added to this edition.

Throughout most of the production of the *Birds of America* Audubon was helped by his two sons, Victor Gifford, and the younger, John Woodhouse. Both were artists in their own right. John W. painted nearly half of the plates for the *Quadrupeds of America* and reduced all of the pictures for the small editions of both the *Birds* and the *Quadrupeds*.

The *Viviparous Quadrupeds of North America*, its full title, has hand-colored lithographs after watercolors by J. J. Audubon and J. W. Audubon most of which were printed and colored by J. T. Bowen. It was published in New York between 1845 and 1848 with an accompanying text written by Dr. John Bachman. These superb animal illustrations are printed on elephant folio size paper, approximately 21½ inches by 27 inches. Unlike the birds which were portrayed life-size, Audubon was forced to compromise when it came to the bison and other large quadrupeds. A total of one hundred fifty plates were included in the original issue and a supplement of 1854 added six to these. An octavo edition in three volumes with 155 plates was published in 1849, 1851 and 1854. This was the last of the works by J. J. Audubon.

Other Nineteenth-Century American Books

In addition to the giants of American nature publications there are a number of lesser but still significant works using illustrative plates which range from the tolerable to the superior—ones by artists like Thomas Doughty and Daniel Elliot. Some mention should be made of these books but the choices are mainly subjective. This list is composed of those which mark some milestone such as the first use of a particular print process, and those which are widely collected. Ten such books are discussed below with additional titles given in the Appendix. They are given in chronological order.

1. *Travels Through North and South Carolina* by William Bartram, Philadelphia, 1791.
   This is a record of a field trip made by the noted naturalist with engraved plates that are attributed to the skill of James Trenchard. The original drawings were made by Bartram and include such creatures as the great soft-shelled tortoise of East Florida.
2. *Vegetable Materia Medica* by William P. C. Barton, Philadelphia, 1817–1819.
   Hand-colored intaglio plates are used to "present true imitations of the plants" as Barton put it. He had to hire

six people to color for him although he had initially planned to do it himself. This is the earliest botanical book using colored engravings produced in America.

3. *American Medical Botany* by Dr. Jacob Bigelow, Boston, 1817, 1818, 1820, in three volumes.
   The engraved plates of plants in Volume I were printed in black and then hand-colored. These are very attractive but the method was too time-consuming for the one thousand or so books planned. In Volumes II and III Bigelow succeeded in printing directly in color from aquatint plates. The individual colors were applied selectively to the plate, the excess wiped off and then printed. Small areas were then hand-touched. This is the first book in the United States which was printed with color using an intaglio process.
4. *The Grammar of Botany* by Sir James Edward Smith, published by J. V. Seaman, New York, 1822.
   This is the first book published in America to use lithographed plates. Twenty-one plates, hand-colored, were drawn by A. J. Stansburg and lithographed by Barnet and Doolittle. Each plate is on paper 9 inches by $5\frac{1}{2}$ inches.
5. *Cabinet of Natural History and American Rural Sports* by J. and Thos. Doughty, Philadelphia, 1830 or 1832, in two volumes and an unfinished third. Fifty-seven plates.
   Thomas Doughty, an important early American painter sometimes called the "father of the Hudson River school of painting," drew many of the plates for the first volume. These are handsome well-colored lithographs "on stone" by Doughty and produced by M. E. D. Brown. Brown was an early lithographer working in Philadelphia and an early employer of Nathaniel Currier. The most noteworthy plates are the "Wild Turkey" and "American Buffalo."
6. *North American Herpetology* by John Edward Holbrook, Philadelphia, 1836–1838, in four volume volumes.
   Rattlesnakes, turtles and similar creatures are depicted in the one hundred eleven prints in this book which used a lithotint process finished with colors applied by hand. The tint stone was a forerunner of lithotint. In this early process the entire surface was colored with a transparent tint, often tan, applied over the original impression. The effect was to soften the contrast with the white paper and to give the print a mellow look. In this book the technique is carried one step further in that tints are applied selectively to different areas of the tint stone.

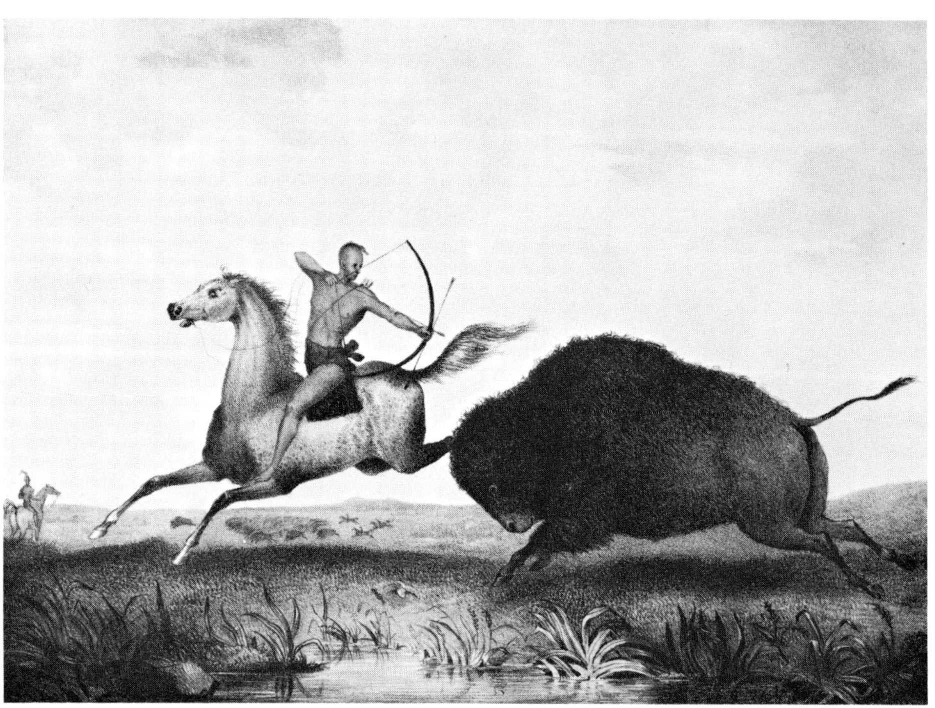

American Buffaloes, hand-colored lithograph by M. E. D. Brown, Philadelphia, 1830–32, from a sketch by Thomas Doughty, *Cabinet of Natural History and American Rural Sports,* Plate 15, Volume II. Thomas Doughty was one of the founders of the Hudson River School of painting

7. *American Vegetable Practice* by Morris Mattson, Boston, 1841. One of the first, if not the first, book in America which contains prints made using the chromolithographic process. In this process a series of stones is used, each one applying a different color. The lithography was done by William Sharp, a pioneer color lithographer from London who came to this country in 1838 or 1839. Plates include "White Pond Lily," "Purple Lady Slipper" and "Bittersweet."
8. *American Wild Flowers in their Native Haunts* by Emma C. Embury, New York and Philadelphia, 1845.
   Illustrations in this book are hand-colored lithographs from original paintings by Edwin Whitefield, the English landscape and flower painter who came to America about 1840. The book includes twenty plates with colored plants against black and white landscape views.
9. *The American Flora or History of Plants and Wildflowers* by A. B. Strong, M.D., Green and Spencer, New York, 1848–1850, four volumes with one hundred ninety-five lithographs.

This book contains beautifully drawn and hand-colored flower prints, lithographed by F. & S. Palmer, New York City.

10. *The New and Heretofore Unfigured Species of the Birds of North America* by Daniel Geraud Elliot, New York, 1866–1869, seventy-two color plates.
The color plates lithographed by Bowen and Co. of Philadelphia are highly decorative and collectible. The size of a typical plate is 18 inches by 23 inches.

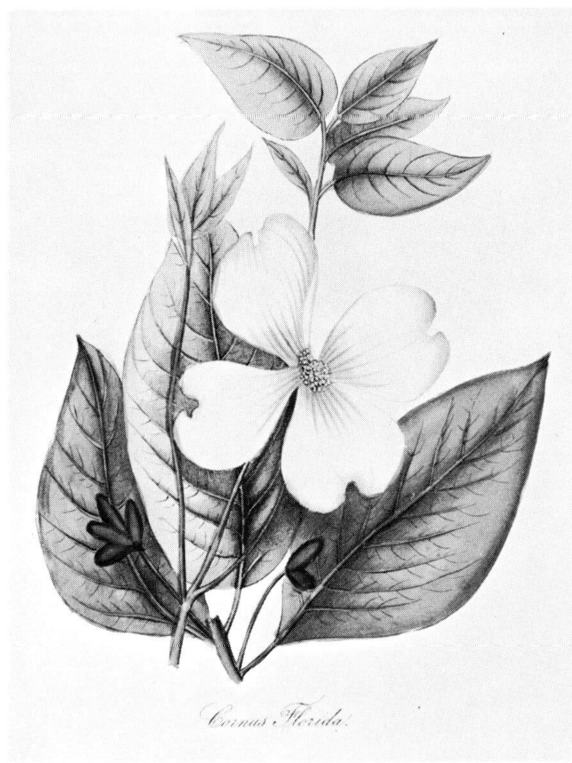

Dogwood, hand-colored lithograph by F. & S. Palmer, N.Y., 1848–50, plate from *The American Flora or History of Plants and Wildflowers* by A. B. Strong, M.D.

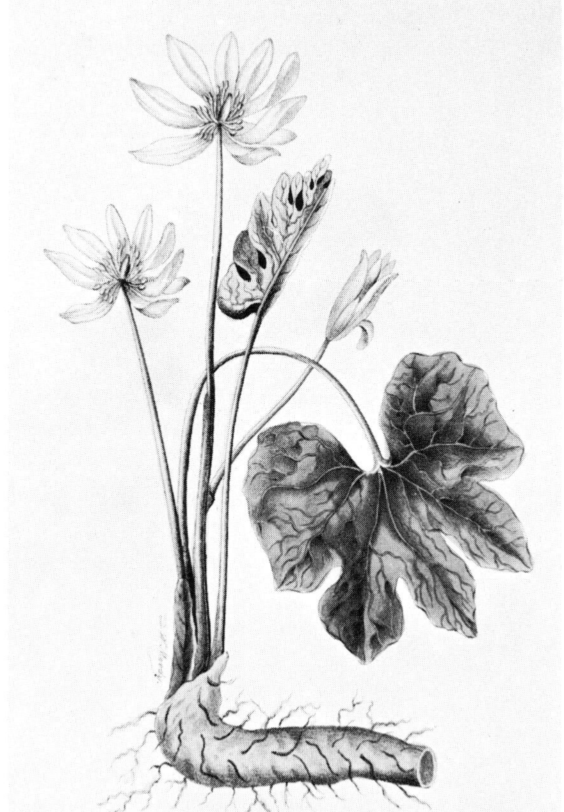

Bloodroot, hand-colored lithograph by F. & S. Palmer, N.Y., 1848–50, plate from *The American Flora or History of Plants and Wildflowers* by A. B. Strong, M.D.

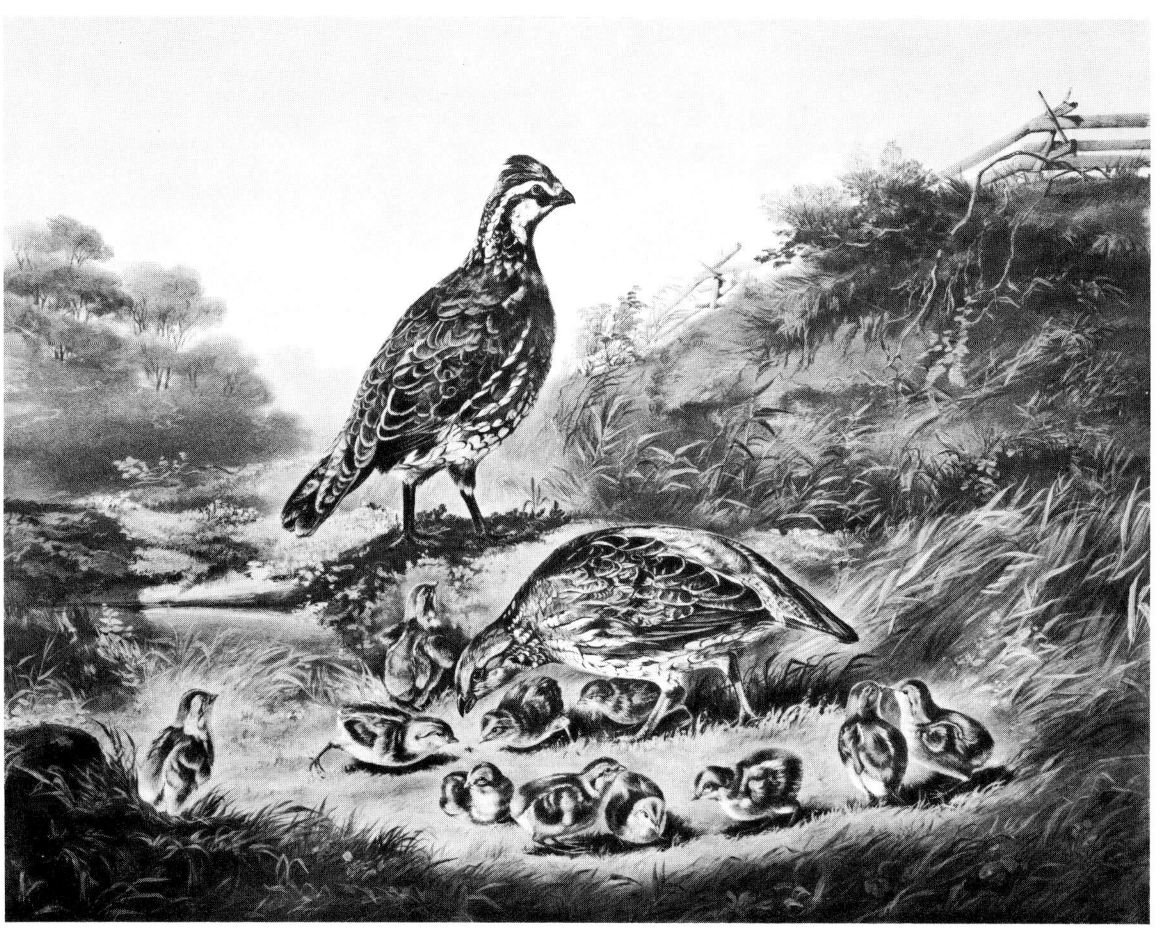

The Cares of A Family, hand-colored lithograph by N. Currier, N.Y., 1856, from a painting by A. F. Tait, 18¾ x 22¾ inches. Number 44 of "best fifty"

Decorative Nature Prints

All of the nature prints discussed so far are plates from books, each of which tries in its own way to be scientific and objective. Nathaniel Currier and the other commercial "decorative print lithographers" were not blind to the demand for such prints and they met this demand. These prints are decorative rather than anatomical, emotionally appealing rather than objective.

Currier and Ives, the bellwether of the group, produced over thirty game bird prints by artists like A. F. Tait and F. F. Palmer. These include some of the finest bird prints produced. With their inimitable flair, Currier and Ives added titles with dramatic and emotional overtones. The best examples are *Snowed up/ Ruffed Grouse in Winter, The Cares of a Family, The Happy Family/ Ruffed Grouse and Young, A Rising Family* and *The Haunts of the Wild Swan.* About twenty game animal prints were published by them. Perhaps the best known is *The Home of the Deer/*

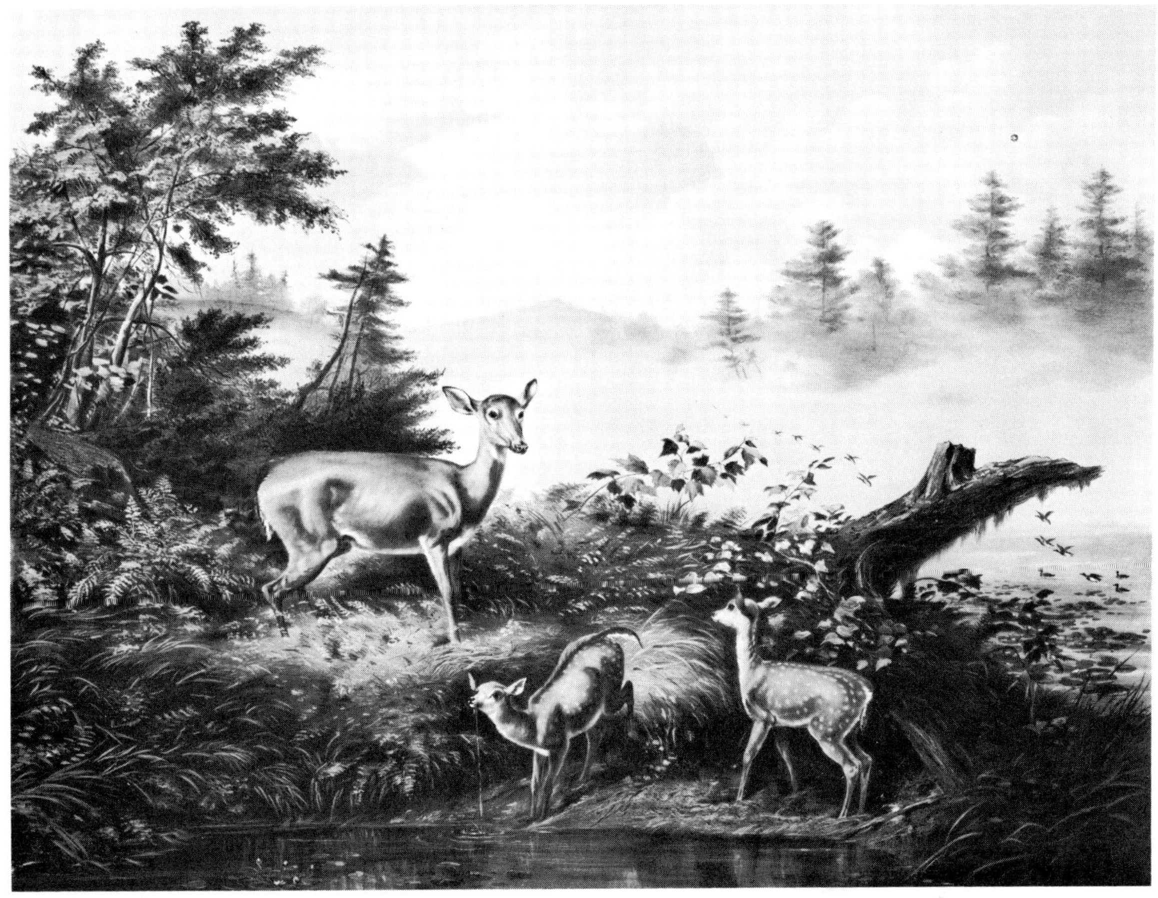

The Home of the Deer/ Morning in the Adirondacks, hand-colored lithograph by Currier and Ives, N.Y., 1862, from a painting by A. F. Tait, on stone by C. Parsons, $18\frac{7}{16}$ x $23\frac{13}{16}$ inches

Morning in the Adirondacks from the painting by A. F. Tait. Others include *The Happy Mother, Deer and Faun, Moose and Wolves* and the *Stag at Bay.* The importance of fishing as a nineteenth-century sport was acknowledged by prints such as F. F. Palmer's detailed portraits in *American Game Fish.*

Currier and Ives also issued more than one hundred flower prints and an almost equal number of fruit titles. Other lithographers such as Sarony, Major and Knapp produced nature prints but in fewer numbers. *A Bevy of Quails* by Sarony, Major and Knapp published in 1862 after a painting by J. S. Hill, compares favorably with the work of Currier and Ives.

Even if not strictly in this category, two groups of prints merit attention. Although taken from books, these prints are used for decorative purposes because of their size and attractiveness. One of these books is *Upland Game Birds and Water Fowl of the United States* by Alexander Pope, Jr. Twenty chromolithographed prints were included in a portfolio with some description which was put out by Charles Scribner's Sons, New York, in 1877. The second and similar work, also with twenty chromolithographs, *Game Fishes of the United States* by S. A. Kilbourne with text by G. Goode, was published in 1879, also by Scribners.

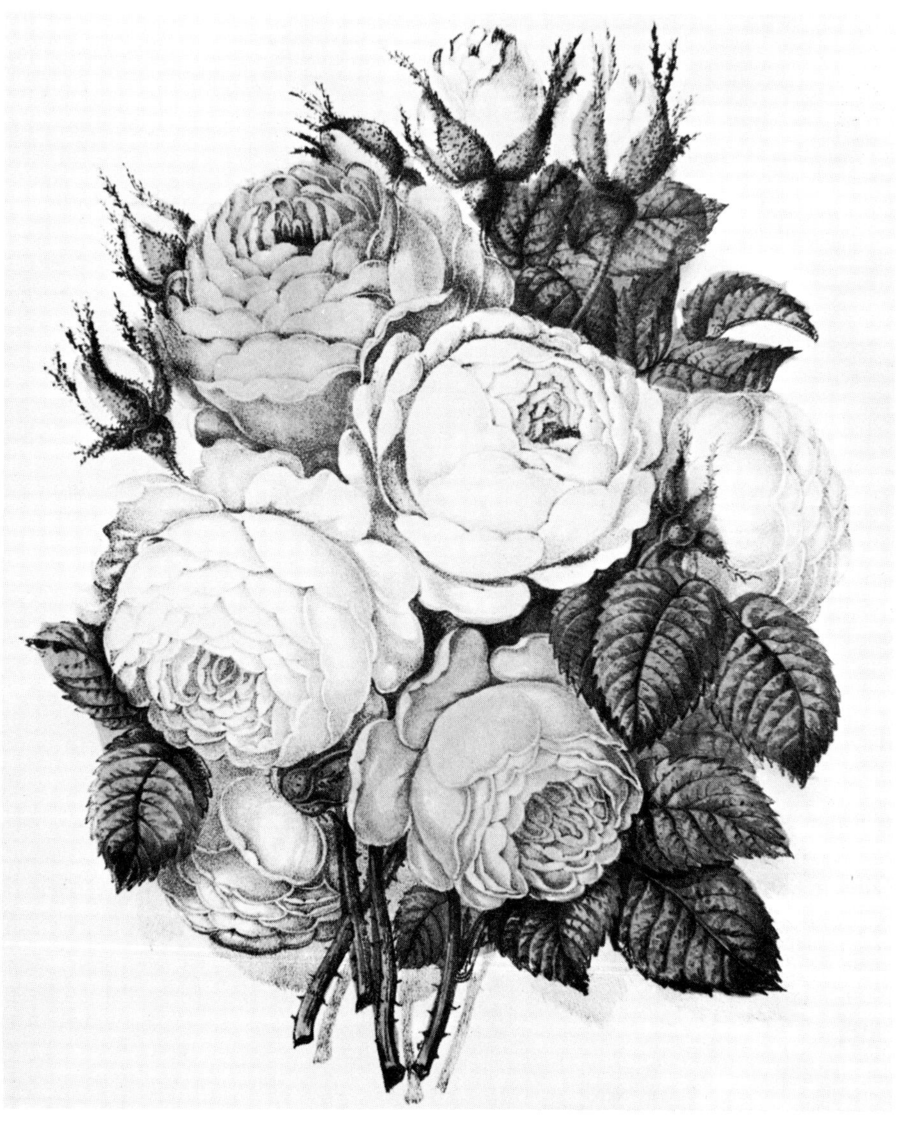

The Hundred Leaf Rose, hand-colored lithograph by Currier and Ives, N.Y., 1870. Small folio vignette

CHAPTER SEVEN Miscellaneous Prints

There are literally hundreds of categories of prints, from labels on jars of preserves to fine art prints. Some of the more important not included in other chapters are discussed below. Maps, paper money, greeting cards and most of the other topics are important collector categories and are themselves the subject of full length books.

Maps

It does not take a fertile imagination to see the need for maps in an unexplored land. The first maps were hand-drawn for use by the explorer who made them. The earliest known printed map to include America is one of the world by Matteo Giovanni Contarini, printed in 1506. The only known copy is in the British Museum. It is difficult to recognize America as we know it to be from this map. In the 1530's, however, enough pieces were put together so that world maps showed North and South America emerging from the mists and by the end of the sixteenth century the land masses are easily recognizable. Many of these early maps are in color with engraved figures and views and are extremely attractive. These "fancies" were produced as decorative hangings or for

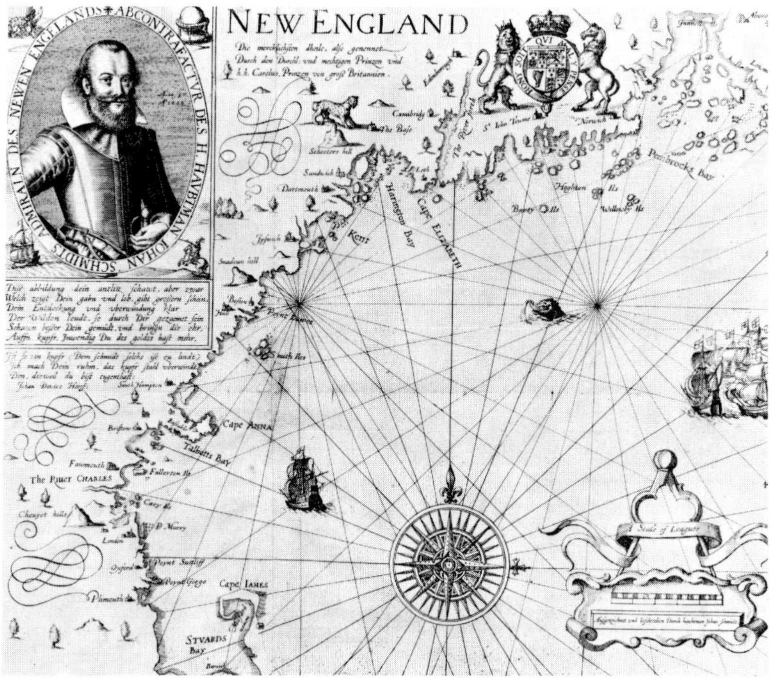

New England, by Capt. John Smith, first published in London in 1614. This, the first separate map of New England, was based on Smith's own expedition to the region. The copy shown is a German version published in 1617, engraving, $11\frac{1}{2}$ x $13\frac{1}{2}$ inches (*Kenneth Nebenzahl, Inc.*)

use in elaborate atlases. They were made in most of the European countries, particularly those with some stake in the exploration of the new world.

Early in the seventeenth century detailed maps of specific areas of America were published. An interesting one is a map of New England by Captain John Smith which was first printed in 1614, with later editions being published until 1634. This is the first separate map of New England and is based on Smith's own expedition to that region. Sometimes referred to as the foundation map of New England cartography, it shows Massachusetts Bay from Cape Cod to Penobscot Bay with an engraved portrait of Captain Smith in one corner with the caption, "The Portraictuer of Captayne John Smith—Admirall of New England." Copies were distributed personally in western England by Smith in order to promote colonization. Later copies were published in Germany, perhaps for the same purpose.

Since printing did not start in America until the late seventeenth century, and was of very limited output until late in the eighteenth century, it was necessary for the colonists to import engraved maps.

Advertisements for imported maps appeared in the *Boston News Letter* as early as 1713. A more definitive offering, however, appeared in the *New England Courant,* July 24-31, 1725:

> Prints and Maps To be sold by Mr. William Price, Print and Map-Seller over against the Town-House, a new chart of the British Empire in North America, with the distinct Colonies granted by Letters Patent, from Cape Canso to St. Matthia's River; Also a new and correct Prospect of the Town of Boston, curiously engrav'd, and an exact Plan of the Town, shewing its Streets, Lanes, and Public Buildings; likewise a great Variety of other Prints and Maps, in Frames or without, and great Variety of fine Looking-Glasses, Tea-Tables and Sconces, Toys and small Pictures for Children. At the same Place may be had all Sorts of Picture-Frames made, and the best Sort of London Crown Glass to put over Prints.

As was discussed in an earlier chapter, John Foster of Boston, America's first print maker, printed America's first map, a woodcut of New England called the *White Hills Map.* It appeared as an illustration in the book, *A Narrative of the Troubles with the Indians in New-England,* by William Hubbard, published in 1677. Woodcut maps are unusual as late as the eighteenth century and one of the few made was issued by Benjamin Franklin in 1733 showing the Maryland-Pennsylvania boundaries as agreed upon by Lord Baltimore and the Penns.

Almost all of the maps produced in America in the eighteenth century were line engravings made by the few engravers then working in America. Some of these extremely rare museum pieces include: *A New Chart of the English Empire in North America,* engraved by Francis Dewing, Boston, 1717; *The Town of Boston,* engraved by Francis Dewing, Boston, 1722; *Map of New York,* printed by William Bradford, New York, 1735; *A Plan of the City and Fortress of Louisbourg with a small Plan of the Harbour,* engraved by Peter Pelham in 1745 and *A Map of Pennsylvania, New Jersey, New York, and the Three Delaware Counties,* engraved by Lawrence Hebert, Philadelphia, 1749.

About 1770, in the immediate pre-war period, even this small output slowed and continued at a very low rate until after the Revolution. Maps of the American Revolution showing specific battle areas were produced in England, however, and these are now eagerly sought by American collectors. After the Revolution engravers were quick to start producing the working, rather than decorative, maps demanded by a population eager to explore and open new territories. One of these is Amos Doolittle, who worked from 1775 to 1832 in the small city of New Haven. He is represented in the Connecticut Historical Society by at least fourteen different maps which almost certainly does not represent

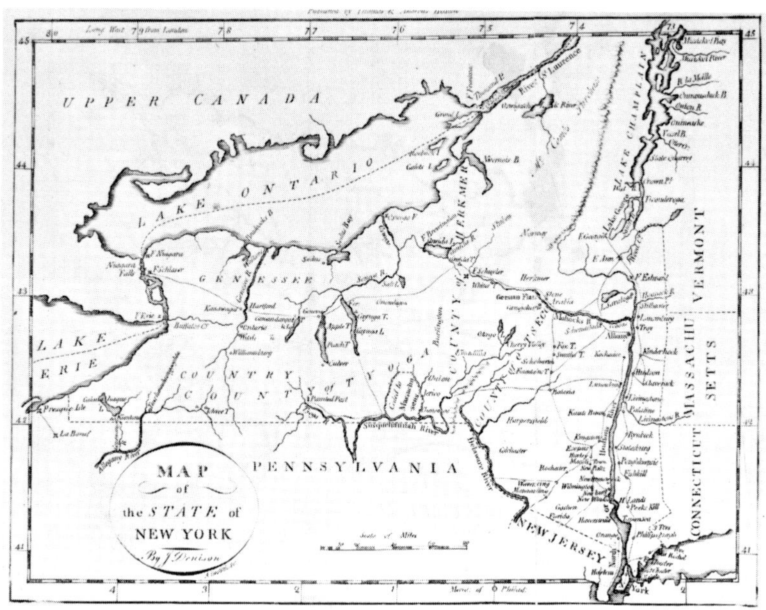

Map of the State of New York, by J. Denison, Boston, engraved by A. Doolittle, 1796, $7\frac{1}{2}$ x $9\frac{1}{2}$ inches (*Kenneth Nebenzahl, Inc.*)

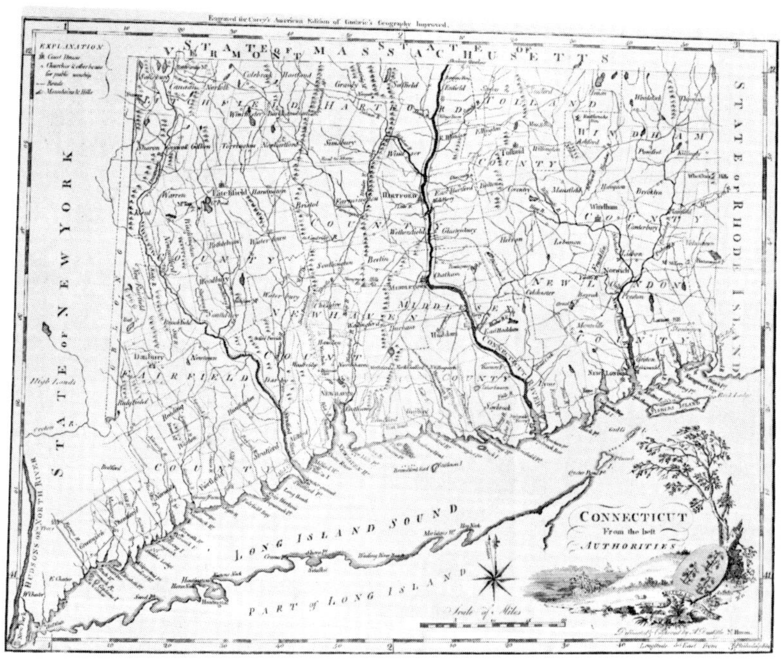

Connecticut from the best Authorities, drawn and engraved by Amos Doolittle of New Haven for Carey's American edition of Guthrie's improved geography, Philadelphia, 1795. One of the few eighteenth-century maps of Connecticut, 12 x 15 inches (*Kenneth Nebenzahl, Inc.*) *Nebenzahl, Inc.*)

his full output. The years 1820 to 1840 are sometimes called the golden age of American cartography as a result of the vast outpouring of atlases and other maps. Some of the later ones were lithographed but many were still engraved.

From the 1820's on government requirements further enlarged the production of maps. In 1830, for example, the legislature of Massachusetts passed a law requiring all cities, towns and districts to make and file maps with the state. These were made to a specified scale so that there would be uniformity. This legislation provided Pendleton, America's first successful commercial lithographer, with a major source of income, producing scores and scores of local maps. A later lithographer in the 1850's, Julius Bien, was called "our first great scientific cartographer" by Harry T. Peters. In addition to turning out chromolithographs of Audubon's *Birds of America,* he also produced thousands of maps related to the surveys in the West as well as of other sections of the country.

Collectors of maps, in common with collectors of other material, favor the colored and decorated over the plain, and the historic over the mundane.

Paper Money and Security Prints

Paper money, bank notes, lottery tickets, etc. are called security prints because they represent money and offer profit to the good counterfeiter. Our first paper money, made from copper plates engraved by John Coney, the silversmith, was issued December 10, 1690 by the Massachusetts Bay Colony. These were the first engravings made and printed in America but unfortunately were counterfeited soon after they were issued. Counterfeiting was a continuing problem so long as the genuine bill was produced by copper engraving, since any competent engraver could forge copies. To add to the complication the copper plates for the genuine bills lasted poorly so that the old ones were retouched after a few thousand copies were printed and new ones were constantly being made. With so many small variations in printing to contend with it was impossible for the user of the bills to tell the real from the counterfeit.

Nevertheless, paper money continued to be made throughout the eighteenth and early nineteenth century using copperplate engraving, and, in some cases, even woodcuts. To cut down on counterfeiting the early bills were individually signed by leaders in the state and many were also printed in two colors. Some eighteenth-century bills are ominously marked, "To Counterfeit is Death." Benjamin Franklin printed many of the notes issued by Pennsylvania and Delaware. Paul Revere engraved and printed the Massachusetts Bay Colony notes in 1775 and

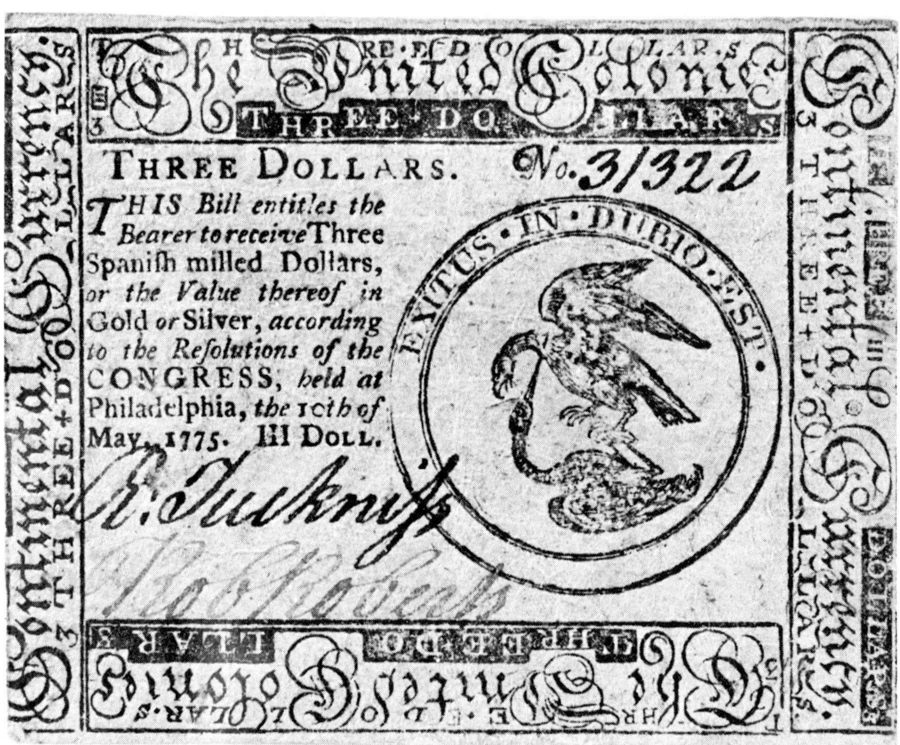

Continental Currency, three Spanish milled dollar notes issued by the United Colonies, May 10, 1775, in Philadelphia. Vignette of heron and eagle engaged in combat has motto "Exitus in dubio est"—and the end is in doubt. Typeset, probably with woodcut for borders and vignette, $2\frac{3}{4}$ x $3\frac{1}{2}$ inches

1776. Colonial and Continental currencies represent one of the few types of eighteenth-century prints that are still obtainable at reasonable prices and as a bonus have enormous historic significance and interest.

The United States was one of the leaders in developing security printing, one of the few areas where America made important contributions in the development of a printing technique. Jacob Perkins, an engineer from Massachusetts, did much of the original work and in this he was encouraged by the Commonwealth of Massachusetts. He developed and modified techniques from about 1795 to 1810, at which time he patented his siderography process in England and tried to get the Bank of England to use it. To make life even more difficult for the counterfeiter, Perkins also used engraving machines and engine lathes to make complicated patterns. The final result was that an intricate pattern of lines, figures and curves, as used in a bank note, could be successfully printed in identical form by many machines each with a printing plate produced from the same master.

The siderography process itself used an engraved original made on a thick block of soft steel. The steel was heated in a furnace until the surface became hot, whereupon it was quenched in water or oil thus casehardening the once hot surface. A small cylinder of soft steel was then rolled repeatedly over this die plate until the design was transferred to the cylinder. The cylinder with a relief design was then heat-hardened and used as a master. It was rolled over as many soft steel printing plates as needed, transferring the relief design on the roller to an intaglio design on the printing plate. Before use these intaglio plates were also heat-hardened. Obviously, this process could be repeated many times and each printing plate would produce bank notes or other security prints that were identical to the prints produced by sister plates or the master plate.

National currency was not issued until 1861. From 1793 until 1861 the country was blanketed by issues of State Bank Notes. Each of these notes had a different design and during that period many of the major engravers in America had commissions to design such currency.

Trade Cards

Only the cards remain today together with a somewhat vague idea about how they were used. Trade cards, usually on heavy paper or cardboard, included the tradesman's name, something about what he sold or the service he rendered, and usually some form of decoration. Some were used in the same ways as modern business cards are used. Others were given out in shops, especially during the latter part of the nineteenth century when many children collected and kept albums of the cards. For this reason they are sometimes called album cards. Other trade cards were so large that they probably were used as advertising posters or delivered by small boys to every house on the block as reminders of the tradesman's services or merchandise.

In size they vary from about the dimensions of a modern business card, 2 inches × $3\frac{1}{2}$ inches, up to the size of small advertising posters. Most of them, however, are 4 inches × 6 inches or smaller. The earliest American ones to survive, *c.* 1730, were printed with metal type, often with printer's flowers or some other decorative border. Later in the eighteenth century and also into the nineteenth century, the engravers of the day lent their talents to the design and production of trade cards. Luminaries such as Paul Revere and professional engravers like Alexander Lawson took such assignments. The finished product ranged from simple cards to elaborate works of art.

About 1850 lithographers entered the field and made special small colored cards that sometimes were simplified versions of their larger prints. These were often pre-printed and stocked awaiting only an order to print in the name, address and sales message of the merchant who ordered them. Currier and Ives published a single page list of their cards

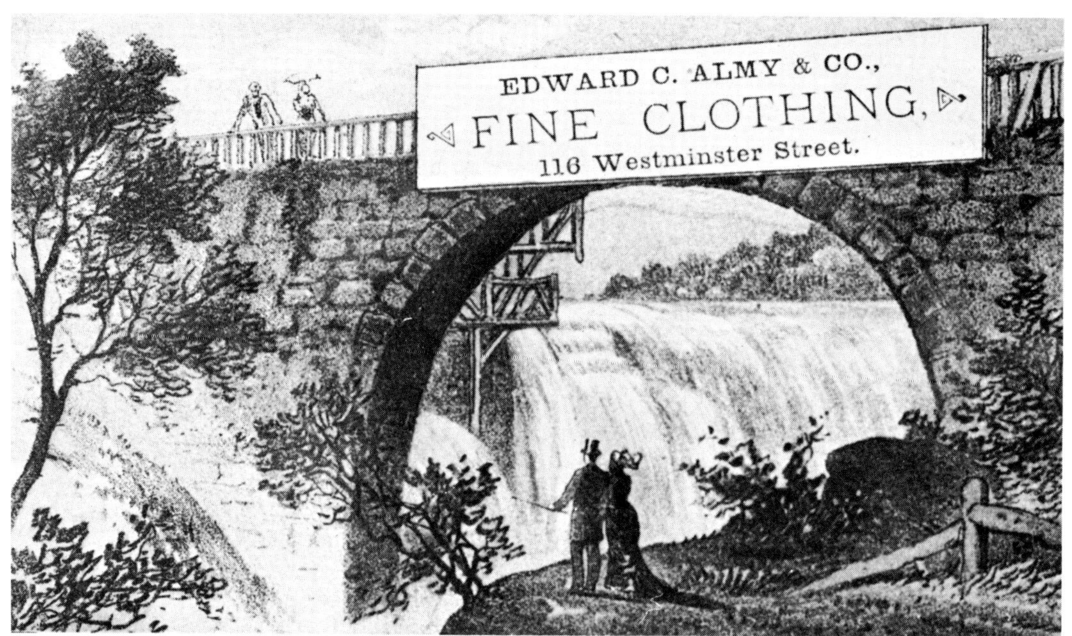

Trade card, chromolithograph by Frank G. Bufford, card size, 3¼ x 5½ inches

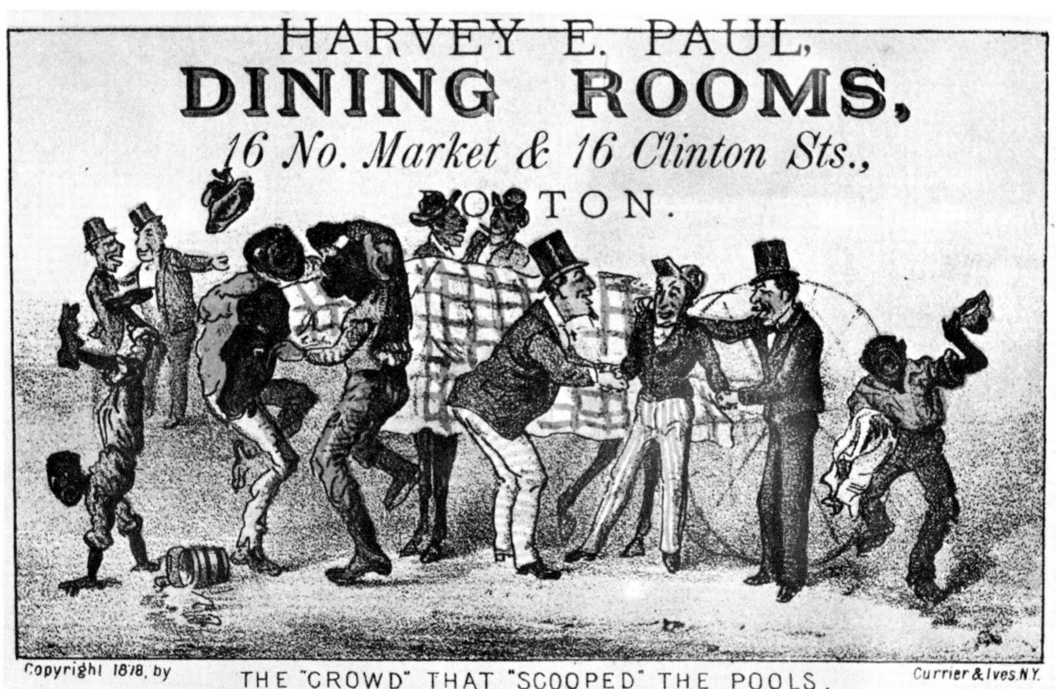

Trade card, chromolithograph by Currier and Ives, 1878, card size, 3¼ x 5⅛ inches (*Collection of Ladd MacMillan*)

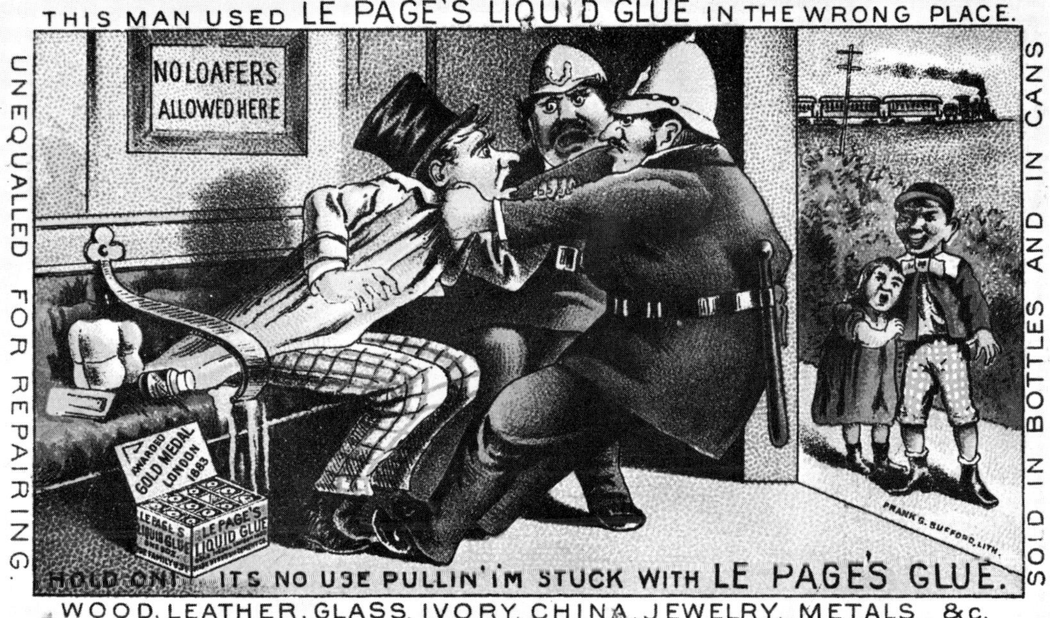

Trade card, chromolithograph by Frank G. Bufford, card size $3\frac{1}{4}$ x $5\frac{1}{2}$ inches

about 1880. Currier and Ives, however, were not as active in this field as some of the other lithographers such as Major and Knapp. Most of these late cards were chromolithographed.

Late in the century, after manufacturing companies began regional or national distribution, they sometimes used the trade card as an advertising vehicle. Le Page glue, for example, would have its message in comic form on the face of the card and the back would include the name of the merchant from whom the glue could be bought. Such advertising cards were probably supplied free of charge to the merchant by the company.

The pictures on the late cards were made to appeal both to the adult who took them and the children who collected them. Comics were popular, so were Gilbert and Sullivan motifs, Punch and Judy, Jumbo and the Statue of Liberty.

Broadsides, Handbills, Playbills and Posters

This group of large or relatively large printed sheets, often with illustrations, has overlapping definitions so that the names do not precisely define the item. For example, some handbills were given out as advertisements in the street before a theatre performance and then served as playbills and programs. Another question is when does a broadside become a poster?

Except for playbills which were kept as momentos, most of these large single prints received as much contemporary consideration as we give to last month's candy bar wrapper. They were considered temporary so that the paper was usually only as strong and permanent as the use required. As a group they present an interesting illustrated story of American sales promotion. These posters, often flamboyant, are not the works of art of the aesthetic level of the Moulin Rouge posters designed by Henri de Toulouse-Lautrec in the 1890's.

The earliest sheets were printed and had no illustrations. A playbill of the Nassau Street Theatre in New York for the March 26, 1750 performance, part of the Harvard College Theatre Collection, is the earliest surviving playbill known. After the Revolution some of the sheets were illustrated using woodblocks and engravings. Peter R. Maverick, the first of the engraving Mavericks, engraved a relatively large illustration of a racing and stud horse named "Sourkrout" in 1797. This was included at the top of a broadside used for advertising the service. Circus posters in the early nineteenth century were sometimes lavishly illustrated with woodcuts.

When lithography became available for commercial use about 1830, the character of these display sheets changed. The illustration, rather than the printing, often became the dominant feature on the print. Commercial lithographers such as Currier and Ives sometimes overprinted the sales message on their regular prints. An insurance advertisement by the United States Accident Association used the Currier and Ives print *The Danger Signal* which shows two trains approaching one another on a single track line. The Adams Express Company used the N. Currier print *American "Express" Train.* The practice was widely used by steamship and other commercial ventures. Many of the prints, however, were also custom-made for the particular poster, particularly later in the nineteenth century. Chromolithography added to the potential of display posters and some of these, especially the gay and bright Barnum and Bailey circus posters of the early twentieth century, are now being actively collected.

Sheet Music Covers

What a generation does for entertainment depends upon the options that are available. Without modern electronics, the camera, and the automobile, singing and dancing naturally assumed a major role. Home music was an important form of home entertainment from Colonial times up until World War I and the thousands of pieces of sheet music available, particularly from about 1800 on, are testimony to this fact.

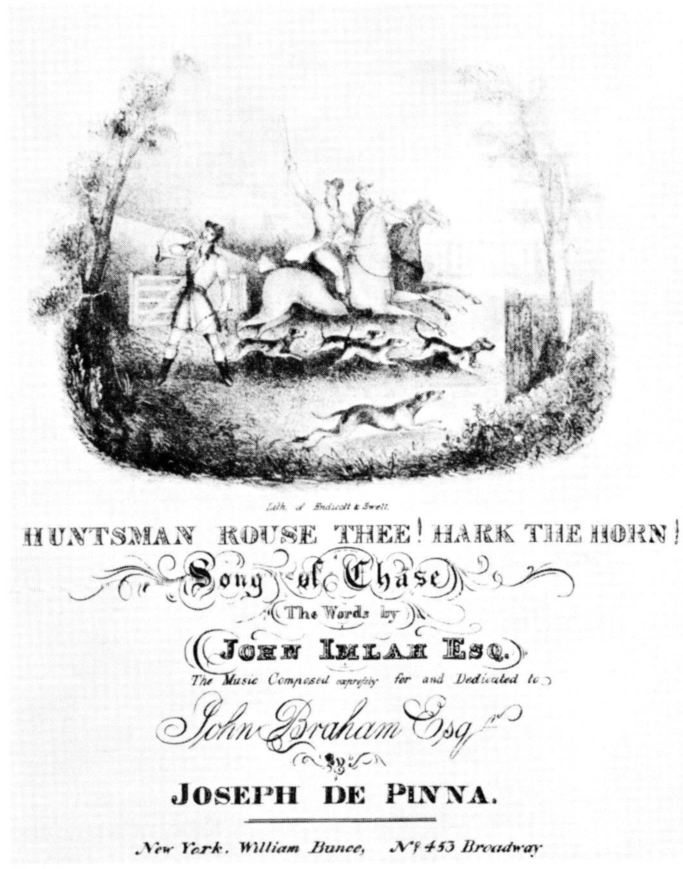

Early sheet music cover, *Song of the Chase,* lithographed by Endicott and Swett, N.Y.C., 1831–34

Very few of the early music sheets had engraved or other forms of illustrations. The music itself was usually printed from engraved plates, a practice continued until the 1850's. In 1826, the Pendleton brothers of Boston started a trend when they made a lithograph to illustrate the cover of "The Log House," a song composed by Anton Philip Heinrich:

> Far in the West an endless wood
> Sighs to the rushing Cat . . . aracts flood!
> 'Twas there an humble log-house stood . . .
> etc.

Heinrich never became a great American composer but the American marketing mania had started and most of the sheet music was thereafter packaged within a lithographed cover. Some of the illustrations were in black and white, some were tinted using tint stones and some were hand-colored.

David Claypool Johnson was the artist for the first of Pendleton's and America's illustrated music sheets. Starting in 1832, Fitz Hugh Lane and Benjamin Champney also worked for Pendleton as apprentices. Lane designed and drew some of the sheets put out by Pendleton and he continued this work with Thomas Moore, Pendleton's successor in Boston. The *Salem Mechanic Light Infantry Quick Step* was drawn by Lane, lithographed by Moore's Lithography and the entire music sheet was published by Ives and Putnam in Salem about 1837. The scene shows the volunteer militia mustered on the Salem Common with the McIntire Arch and some tents in the background.

Another famous American artist, Winslow Homer, also started his career working on sheet music covers while he was a lithographer's apprentice for John H. Bufford about 1855. Although the work is not usually signed, ten covers have been attributed to him including *Minnie Clyde, The Wheelbarrow Polka* and *Rogers Quick Step.*

Music cover prints followed the same pattern as other prints taking on each innovation and invention of printing. The music publishing companies themselves were as unstable as companies in the lithography business with partnerships and locations changing frequently. The sheets were usually sold in bookstores, and, in the eighteenth century, sometimes by subscription.

American Views Published Abroad

From the time of Columbus, Europeans were curious to see what things looked like in the new exotic territory. About 1590, Theodore de Bry, a Flemish engraver and publisher who lived in Frankfurt, Germany produced some of the earliest prints of America. These were based on paintings by the artist Jacques Le Moyne de Morgue who went to Florida in 1564 with the Laudonnière expedition and John White, the artist in the 1585 expedition of Sir Walter Raleigh to Virginia.

In 1719 and 1722 London engravers made the prints for William Burgis' views of New York and Boston which were paid for by subscribers in America. These and other similar views of Charleston in 1739 and Philadelphia in 1754 were copied and reissued in Europe. John Carwitham engraved a smaller version of the Burgis view of Boston which was published about 1760. In 1768 *Scenographia Americana* was published in London containing twenty-eight to seventy-four (depending on the issue) engravings made by British officials and army and navy officers. A collection of over two hundred fifty maps, charts and views is contained in *Atlantic Neptune* published between 1763 and 1784 for the British Admiralty by J. F. W. DesBarres.

The *Vues d'Optique* which are often available have an amusing character that warrants explanation. These hand-colored etchings were printed in the second half of the eighteenth century in both Augsburg and Paris. They were used by itinerant showmen in Europe who went

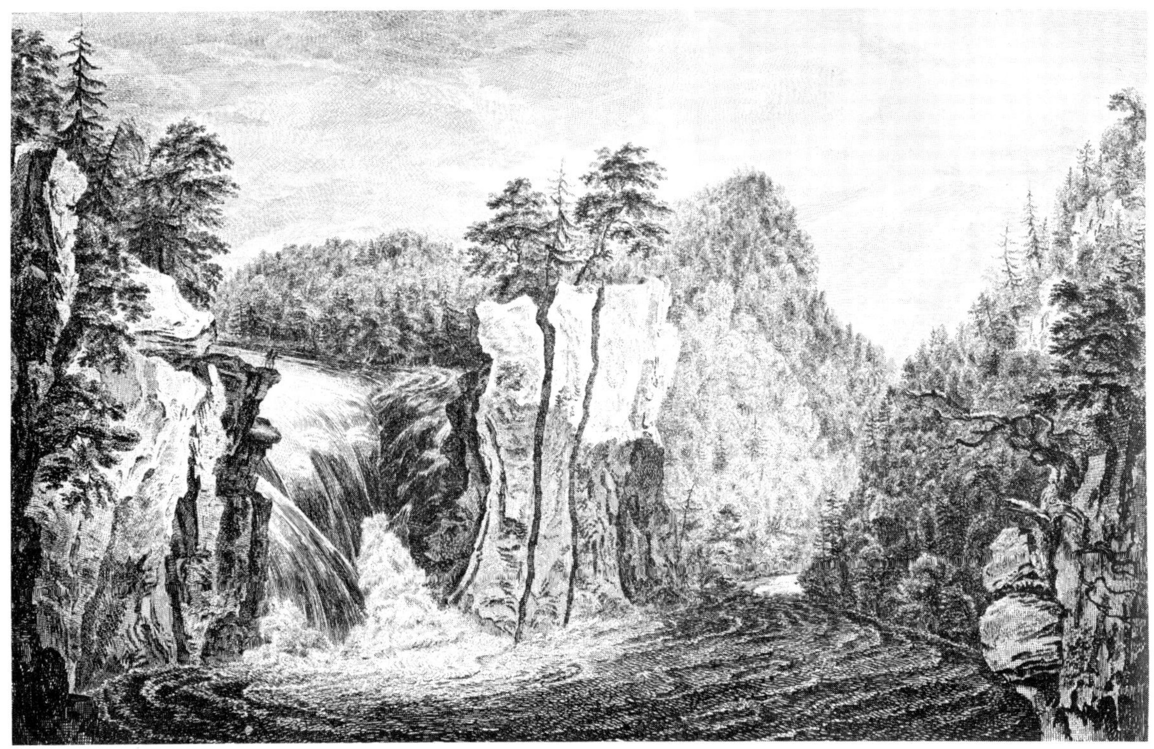

A View of the Falls on the Passaick from *Scenographia Americana,* London, 1768, sketched by his Excellency Governor Pownal, engraving by Sandby, plate size, $14\frac{1}{8}$ x $20\frac{7}{8}$ inches

from village to village showing pictures of Versailles and other splendors with their mirrored optical boxes. The pictures, with captions usually in French and German, were intended to show the curious villager authentic views of cities in Europe and America. A reverse caption at the top of the print enabled the operator to read the title right side up. The etched view of the city hall in Boston which is illustrated is amusing in that all of the buildings are in baroque style and the Indians, dressed in European clothes, are walking in the street carrying bows, arrows and spears. The artist merely appropriated an Italian street scene and sprinkled some "natives" on it.

There were many books of prints and single prints published in Europe in the nineteenth century including:

J. Milbert, *Itinéraire Pittoresque du Fleuve Hudson,* lithographed by Deroy etc., Paris, 1828–29.
Picturesque Views in North America, lithographed in Paris, 1825.

Englemann, *Vues de L'Amérique du Nord,* lithographed in Paris, 1825–1830.

Henry Lewis, *Das Illustrierte Mississippithal,* lithographed in Düsseldorf in 1854.

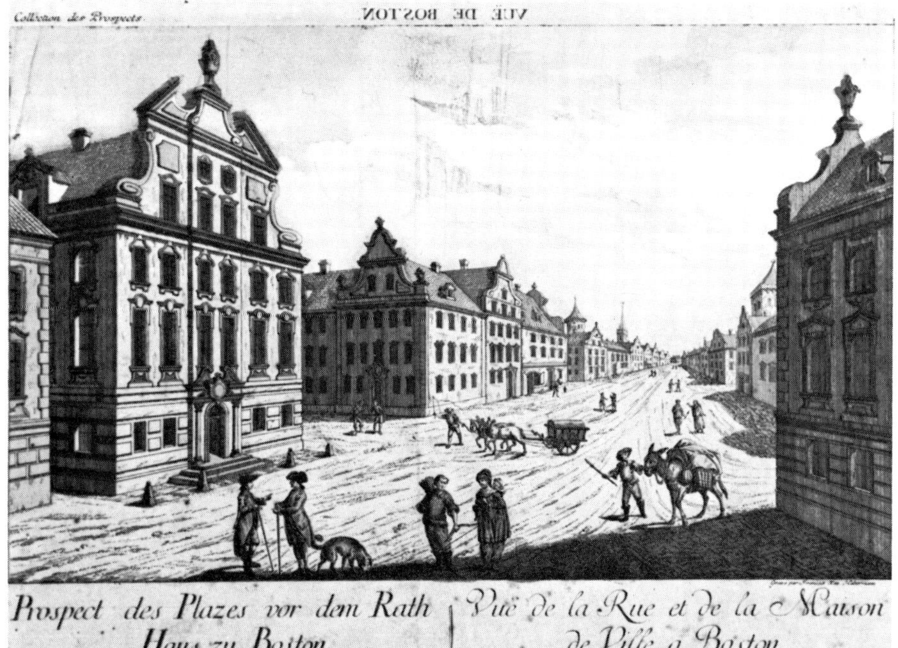

One of the Vues d'Optique, the *View of the Street and Boston City Hall,* hand-colored etching by Francois Habermann, Augsburg, c. 1780, plate size approximately $12\frac{1}{2}$ x 16 inches

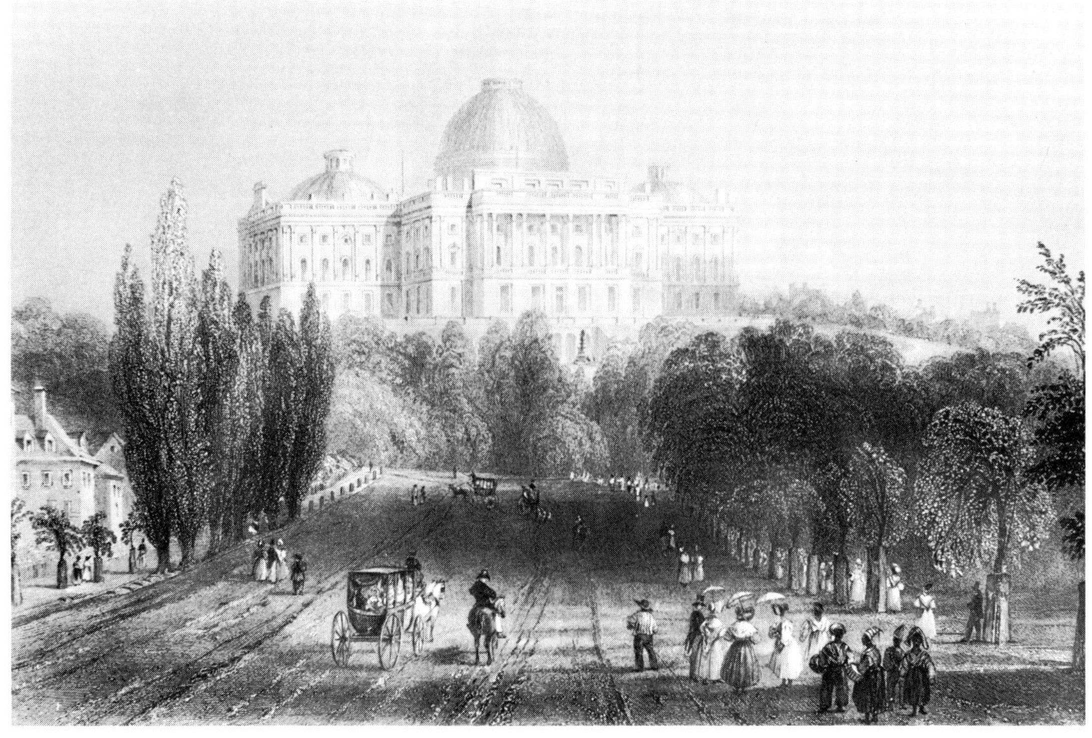

View of the Capitol at Washington, drawn by W. H. Bartlett and engraved by R. Wallis, London, 1839, picture size, $4\frac{3}{4}$ x $7\frac{1}{8}$ inches

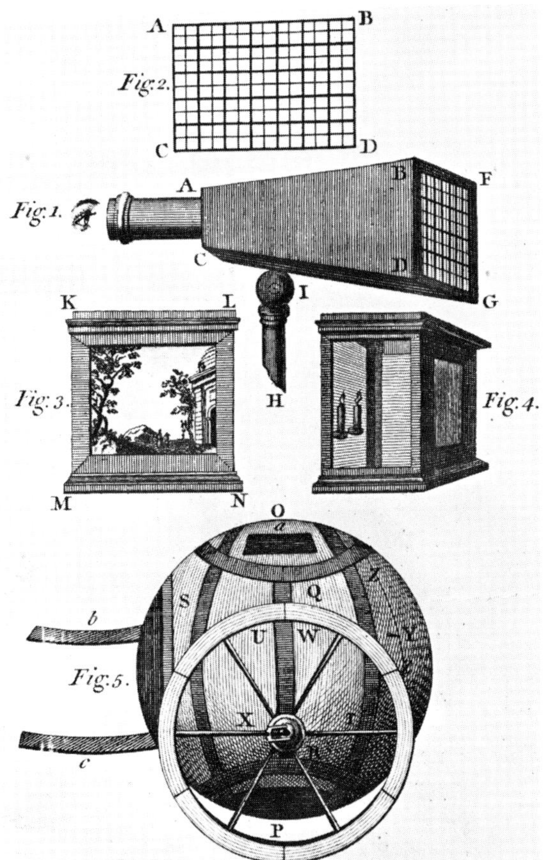

Instructions for making an optical box for home use. In this device, Figures 3 and 4, the prints are viewed by having candlelight shine through the thin paper. From *The Universal Magazine,* London, April, 1778, etching, plate size, 7 x 4½ inches

But by far the most available and widely collected are the Bartlett prints. These steel engravings of the landscape and cities in the north-eastern part of the United States are based on the sketches made by William Henry Bartlett during his visit to America in 1836. They were engraved by thirty or so engravers and the one hundred nineteen plates were issued in monthly installments from 1837 to 1839 by George Virtue in London. Each part had four steel engravings together with a text by Nathaniel P. Willis, a well-known American poet and journalist, who had accompanied Bartlett on his travels. In 1840 the first bound edition was published by Virtue with the title *American Scenery; or Land, Lake, and River* with illustrations of a "transatlantic nature." Later editions were published, some in French and German.

Each engraving measures approximately 7¼ inches by 4¾ inches but they are not all exactly the same size. All of the prints were issued uncolored so that the color on the ones seen today is a later embellishment. Two of the prints, *The Silver Cascade in the Notch of the White*

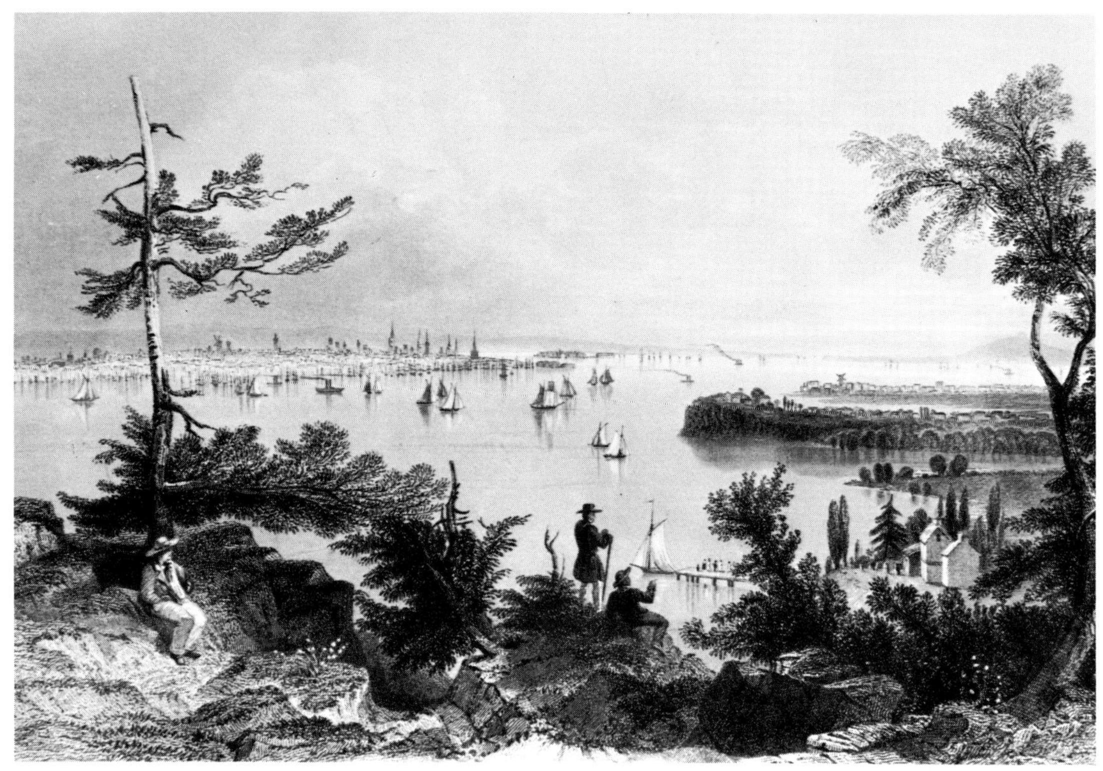

View of New York, From Weehawken, drawn by W. H. Bartlett and engraved by R. Wallis, London, 1839, picture size, $4\frac{3}{4}$ x $7\frac{1}{8}$ inches

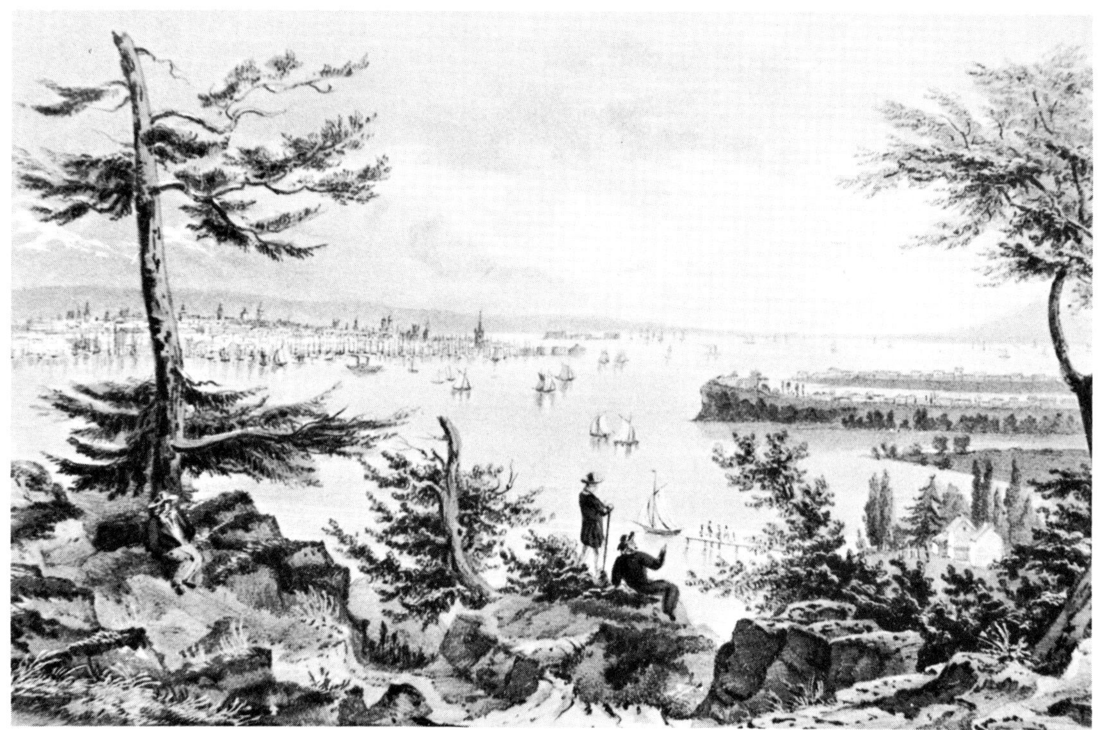

View of New York/ From Weehawken, published by N. Currier, N.Y., 1848. Hand-colored lithograph, $8\frac{3}{16}$ x 12 inches. Obviously a copy of the Bartlett print

Mountains and *Desert Rock Light House* (Maine) are after paintings by Thomas Doughty, but the rest are by Bartlett and are so marked on each engraving. Most of the Bartlett views are done in the idealized romantic style popular at the time. These prints were widely used in Europe and America as source material for views of American scenery. Artists, both academy trained and primitive, American and European, copied parts or the entire print in their own paintings. China and pottery manufacturers and lithographers were just as quick to make use of the Bartlett prints.

Wood Engravings

A high percentage of the books and periodicals published during the nineteenth century used wood engravings for illustrations. The design on the wood is in relief so that the blocks can be set and printed in the same frame with the metal type used for letters. Thomas Bewick, an Englishman, won an award for developing this technique in 1775. By 1793 Alexander Anderson had introduced the technique in America. During his lifetime, Anderson alone is estimated to have made nearly ten thousand wood engravings. The total number made by all the wood engravers working in this country is beyond estimation.

Due to the limited trunk size of the box tree which was found best for this use, a large picture is usually made of many blocks fastened together. White lines caused by the joins can often be seen in the finished print. Sometimes different engravers worked on separate blocks in order to speed completion. The blocks were then fastened together and the lines connecting the blocks were worked over by a finishing engraver. Sometimes the block carried the signature of the wood engraver, sometimes that of the artist, sometimes both, but more often neither. In order to make large runs for which the wood block would not stand up, a metal casting called an electrotype was made using the wood block as a model. The actual printing was then made from the metal plates.

The most popular wood engravings are the illustrations by Winslow Homer which appeared in *Harper's Weekly, Ballou's Pictorial Drawing Room Companion, Every Saturday, Our Young Folks* and other periodicals. As a young man Homer spent twenty years as an illustrator for popular weeklies. About three hundred wood engravings can be identified as being drawn by him although many are unsigned. These weekly journals had become popular about 1855, and Homer contributed to them until 1875 when he switched to water color and oil painting. Many of his drawings and the wood engravings printed from them are works of art and rank among the best wood engravings ever produced.

Homer was born in Boston in 1836 and spent most of his childhood

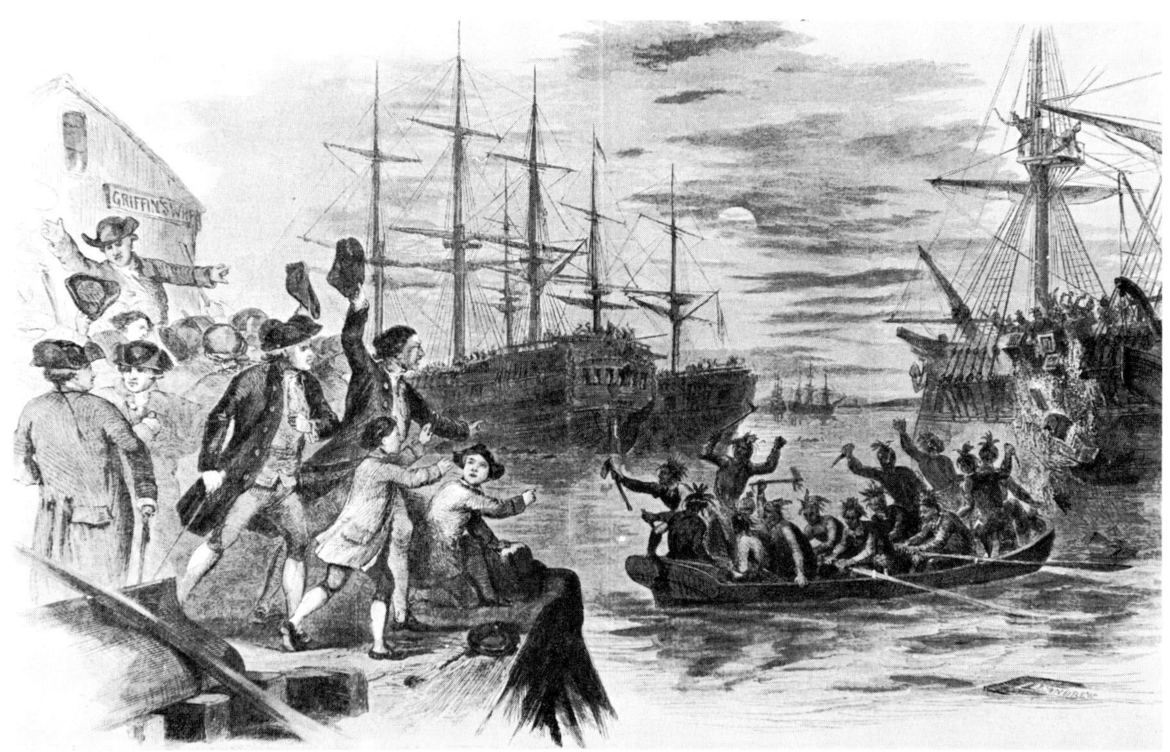

The Boston Tea Party, published in *Ballou's Pictorial Drawing Room Companion,* Boston, c. 1873, wood engraving by J. Andrew. Vignette approximately 13½ x 21 inches

and teen years in Cambridge. At the age of nineteen he became an apprentice to Bufford Lithographers leaving in 1857 when his two years were up. He became a free lance illustrator making drawings which were engraved in wood by professional wood engravers for *Ballou's Pictorial Drawing Room Companion,* and later New York's *Harper's Weekly.* During the Civil War he took a permanent job as a picture correspondent for *Harper's,* returning to free-lancing after the war. The subjects of his illustrations reflect the events of his life. The early pictures from 1857–1860 are of Boston scenes. From approximately 1860–1865 he was involved with portraying the Civil War. For the next ten years after the Civil War his work included some of the most charming genre produced during this time. From this period come *Snap-the-Whip, Fire-Works on the Night of the Fourth of July,* and *On the Bluff at Long Branch at the Bathing Hour.* From the war years there is the dramatic *Sharpshooter on Picket Duty* and *Thanksgiving in Camp.* Homer later used a few of his wood engravings as the basis for paintings.

The pictorial weeklies engaged artists to travel with various expeditions and with troops during wars. Some of these excursions resulted in authentic pictorial records by contemporary observers which are not otherwise available. *Harper's Weekly* featured illustrations by "our special

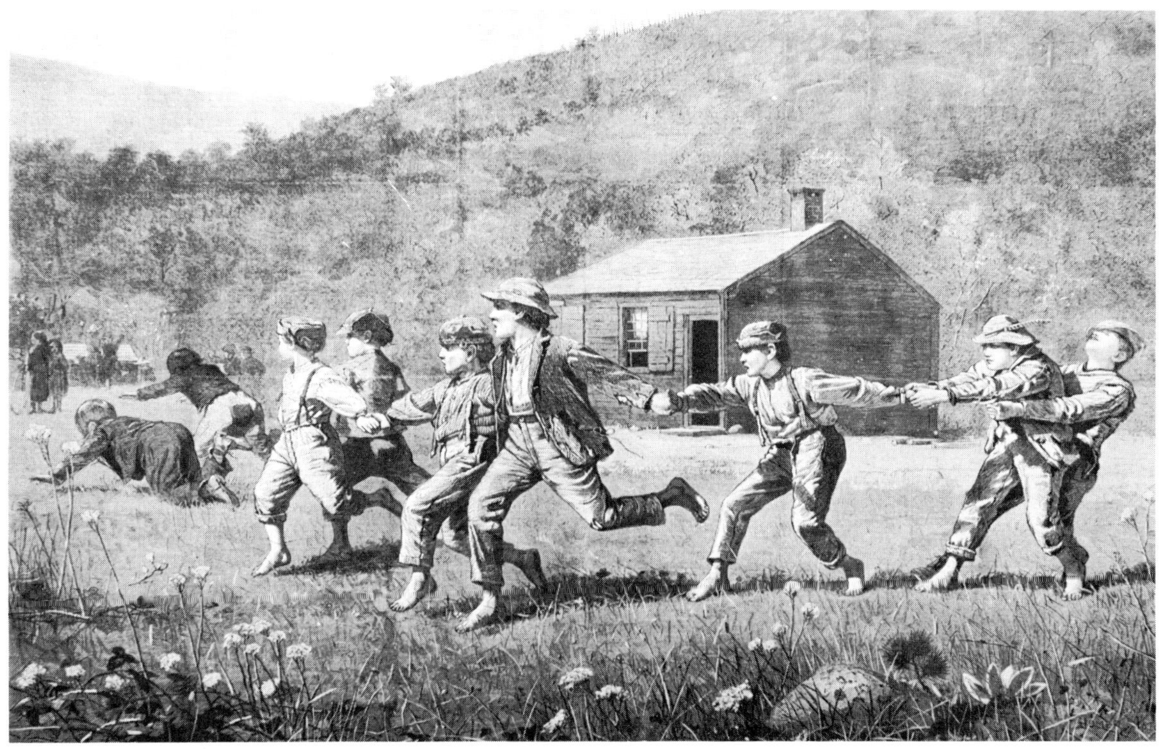

Snap-the-Whip, drawn by Winslow Homer and published in *Harper's Weekly,* September 20, 1873, wood engraving, $8\frac{3}{8}$ x $12\frac{3}{4}$ inches

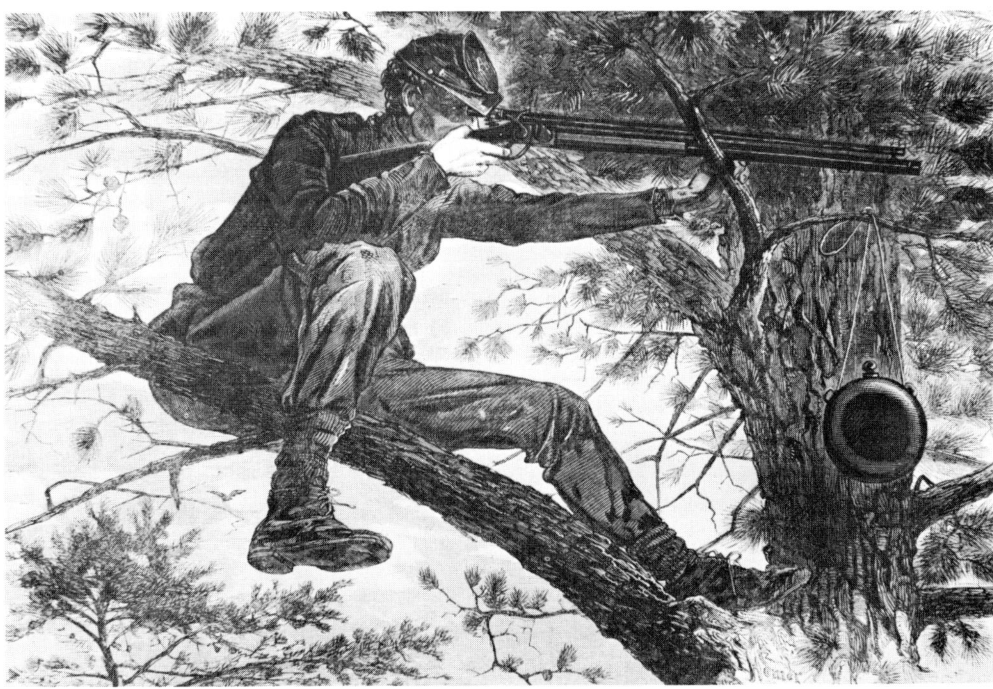

The Army of the Potomac—A Sharp-Shooter on Picket Duty, drawn by Winslow Homer and published in *Harper's Weekly,* November 15, 1862, wood engraving, $9\frac{1}{8}$ x $13\frac{3}{4}$ inches. This print was used by Homer as the basis for his first painting to be publicly exhibited

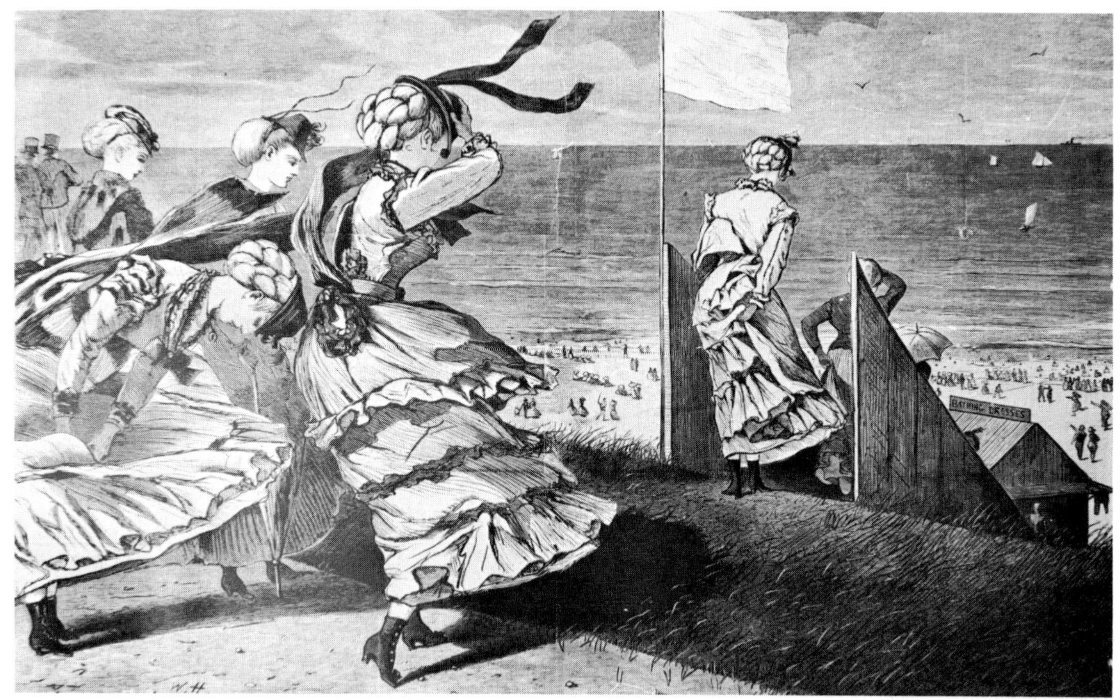

On the Bluff at Long Branch, At the Bathing Hour, drawn by Winslow Homer and published in *Harper's Weekly,* August 6, 1870, wood engraving, 8⅞ x 13⅝ inches

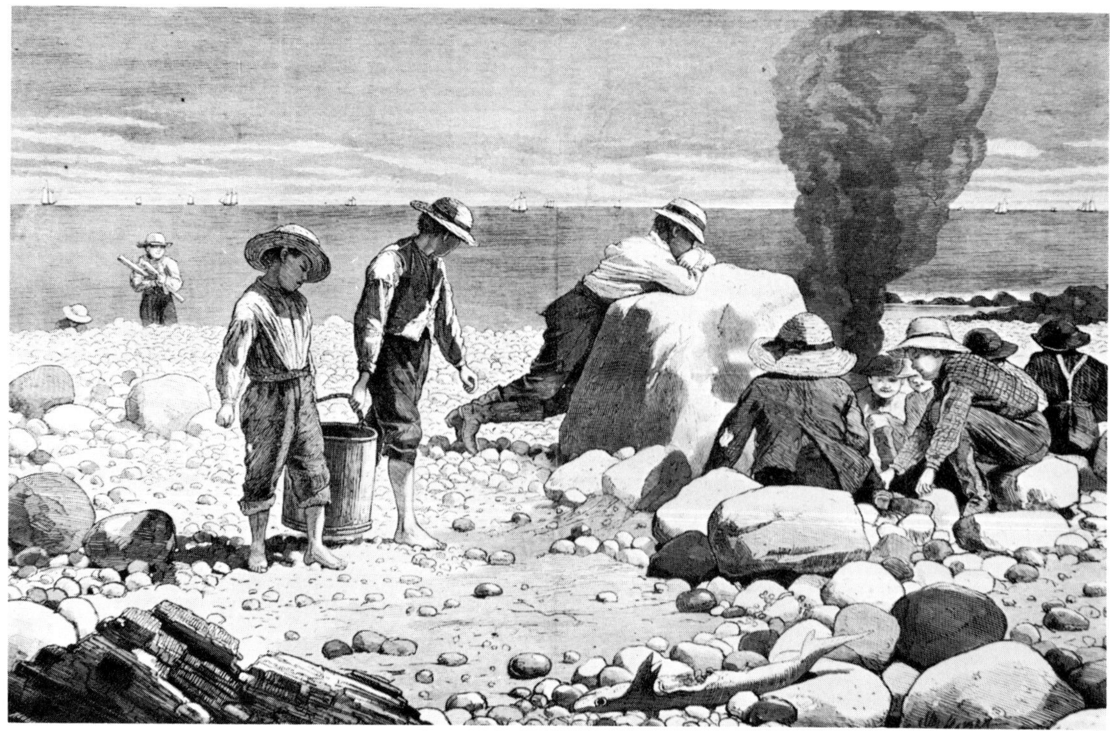

Sea Side Sketches—A Clam-Bake, drawn by Winslow Homer and published in *Harper's Weekly,* August 23, 1873, wood engraving, 9¼ x 14 inches

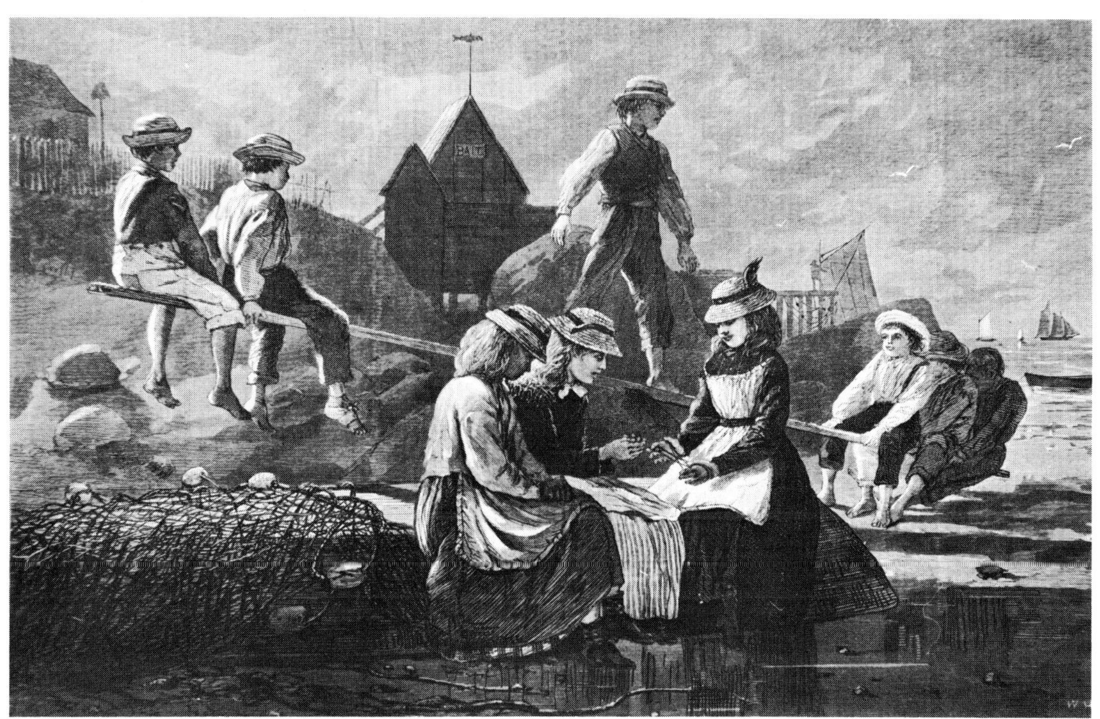

See Saw—Gloucester Massachusetts, drawn by Winslow Homer and published in *Harper's Weekly,* September 12, 1874, wood engraving, $9\frac{1}{8}$ x $13\frac{3}{4}$ inches

artist". During the Civil War this role was filled by Alfred R. Waud, and Theodore R. Davis as well as Winslow Homer and others. In 1873 the artists Paul Frenzeny and Jules Tavernier were commissioned by *Harper's Weekly* to make a series of sketches on an expedition from New York City to San Francisco. Their direct observations of the living conditions of the West as they found them appeared in *Harper's* over the next several years. Many of these works are signed jointly as Frenzeny-Tavernier. Both Tavernier and Frenzeny were beguiled by the bohemian life of San Francisco. Tavernier became an alcoholic but Frenzeny continued sketching life in California and Nevada including a number of observations of the Chinese.

Frenzeny contributed sketches to the weeklies and other periodicals through most of the 1880's. Other artists who contributed western subjects were Henry F. Farny, William A. Rogers, Charles Graham, Rufus F. Zogbaum and, of course, Frederick Remington. Remington's first illustrations were published as wood engravings by *Harper's Weekly* in the early 1880's. He continued as an illustrator in *Harper's* and other publications for twenty-five years spanning the transition from wood engravings to photomechanical reproduction methods. In 1888 and 1889 a few photomechanical reproductions appear in *Harper's Weekly* but by 1890 the transition is largely accomplished. Remington is outstanding

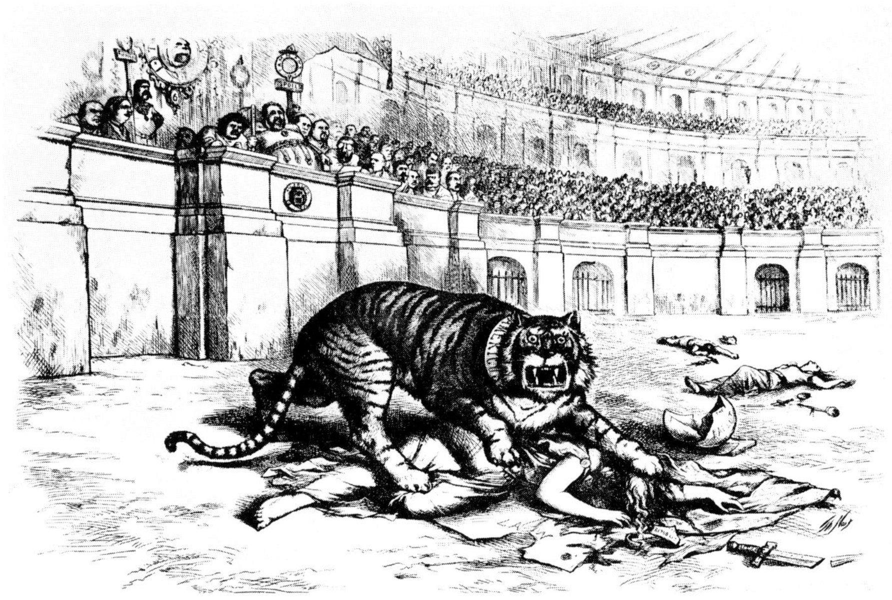

The Tammany Tiger Loose, drawn by Thomas Nast and published in *Harper's Weekly,* November 11, 1871, wood engraving, vignette

in his portrayal of vigorous action such as cowboys on rearing horses.

Although Thomas Nast drew for *Harper's* during the Civil War, mainly on themes relating to the war but not of actual battle, he only hit his stride with his political cartoons of the 1870's and after. The simple linear drawings he used for his cartoons translated effectively into wood engravings. His most famous cartoon is one in his campaign against the corruption of Tammany Hall. The large double-page illustration appeared November 11, 1871, two days before election and is credited with turning the tide against Tweed. The caption states, "The Tammany Tiger Loose—What are you going to do about it?". Boss Tweed is quoted as saying, "I don't care what they print about me, most of my constituents can't read anyway—but them damn pictures!" Nast also made the elephant the accepted symbol for the Republican party. In contrast to his jugular political cartoons, he created the cherubic, jovial image of Santa Claus accepted by all today.

Other artists specialized in various social and cultural subjects. The sporting prints of Arthur B. Frost are highly regarded for their accuracy and sympathetic portrayal of hunting and fishing. In addition to prints by recognized artists and illustrators, there is a wide range of those whose subject matter is of special interest: old views of cities and towns, sports, yachts and yachting, political events, railroads, fires, natural catastrophes, and new inventions. Early protest against despoiling the environment, wanton killing of birds and animals, industrial pollution, and miserable living conditions in the inner cities is to be found among these.

Greeting Cards

The sending of printed cards for every occasion is a modern custom that has its roots in the early handmade St. Valentine cards. In America, handmade valentine cards, some of them very beautifully executed, were used in the mid-eighteenth century and possibly earlier. The valentine tradition goes back much further in England where even earlier cards are known. Some of the earliest American ones are those put out by Elton & Co. of New York City in the 1830's. Turner & Fisher, a wood engraver and stationer in Philadelphia, sold cards in the 1840's as did T. W. Strong of New York. Between 1842 and 1851, Strong made a specialty of valentines. One of his advertisements reads:

> Valentines! Valentines! All varieties of Valentines, imported and domestic, humorous, witty, comic . . . got up in the most superb manner, without regard to expense. Also envelopes and Valentine Writers, and everything connected with Valentines, to suit all customers, prices varying from six cents to ten dollars; for sale wholesale and retail at Thomas W. Strong's Great Depot of Valentines, 98 Nassau St.

Later entries include P. J. Cozzens in N.Y.; Esther Howland in Worcester, Massachusetts, a specialist in valentines; G. C. Whitney & Co., successor to Howland about 1880 and Louis Prang in Boston.

Esther Howland is an unusual personality and one of the makers whose cards are sought by collectors. She graduated from Mount Holyoke College in 1847 and by 1849 she had an established business making valentines. Through energy, artistic ability and good business sense she built the sales volume to about one hundred thousand dollars annually. Later she made Christmas cards before selling out to George C. Whitney and Co. about 1880. Her cards are often stamped with a red "H" on the back or have an "H" in the center of a heart. These early cards are rare.

Louis Prang, sometimes referred to as the Father of American Christmas Cards, published his first yuletide greetings in 1874. Earlier, personal letters of Christmas greetings to friends were used. In England a hand-colored lithographed card was put out in 1842 or 1843 designed by John Horsely on commission from Henry Cole. Kate Greenaway, in some respects a later English version of America's Esther Howland, designed chromolithographed cards in the era of Louis Prang. Her work is widely collected.

Prang's first cards, expertly designed and printed, were of flowers, birds and kittens. Realizing their limitations, he announced an open competition for the best Christmas card design in the spring of 1880. Noted artists including Samuel Colman and John LaFarge were judges for the exhibit held at New York's American Artists' Galleries. First prize of one thousand dollars was awarded to Elihu Vedder, a prominent artist.

The combination of good designs with his color printing skill won Prang a major share of the market both in this country and in England and caused several English competitors to give up making Christmas cards. In the 1890's, however, inexpensive quality cards from Germany flooded the market so that Prang sold his business and retired. New Year greetings, then Easter greetings, which were followed by cards for Mother's Day after the official proclamation in 1915, have extended the kinds and numbers of cards sent.

Fashion Plates

Fashion periodicals with the accompanying fashion plates were started in France in the late eighteenth century. They were an outgrowth of coiffure design publications issued in Paris every two weeks beginning about 1775. The *Gallery of Fashions* put out in London between 1793 and 1802 was started by a German familiar with the Parisian publications. The English periodical included colored etchings and aquatints.

The first American woman's magazine, *Godey's Lady's Book,* was started in 1830 by Louis Antoine Godey. Similar magazines, *Peterson's Ladies National Magazine* and *Graham's Magazine of Literature and Art,* were begun soon after, also in Philadelphia. *The Columbian Magazine,* first published as a miscellany in 1786, moved to New York from Philadelphia in the 1840's and then also began issuing fashion plates. These publications appeared monthly and contained stories and articles of interest to women, uncolored engravings of paintings, and a fashion plate showing the latest styles in dresses, cloaks, hats and children's clothing. The early prints were nearly always hand-colored and were usually steel engravings, although some wood engravings and an occasional lithograph were used. Many of the print designs were pirated from French and English publications and some such as the *Columbian Magazine* and *Graham's* even imported the printed sheets from Europe. The fastidious ladies of the period saved the monthly issues and often had them bound into a book at the end of the year. The plates are printed on paper approximately 6 inches × 9½ inches in size, but frequently the later ones of the 1860's and 1870's are fold-outs almost double this size. Some of them have interior backgrounds showing the furnishings of the period. In the 1850's, *Harper's Weekly* also entered the fashion plate business with a few uncolored wood engravings in each issue. Another late entry into the field was *Frank Leslie's Ladies Journal,* published from about 1854 to 1876.

The most interesting of these fashion publications is *Godey's Lady's Book.* Godey's parents fled from France during the Revolution and settled in New York where Louis Antoine was born in 1804. The boy had little education but was fond of books and reading. He operated a news stand and bookshop in New York City before going to Philadelphia in the 1820's, where he worked for a time as a clerk on a newspaper before starting his magazine in 1830. It was edited for almost fifty years by Sarah Josepha Hale. She was one of the early female professional writers, a career somewhat forced on her in order to support five children after her husband's death. In addition to editing *Godey's,* she wrote *Women's Record, or Sketches of Distinguished Women* and *Poems for our Children.* One of her poems is the familiar *Mary Had a Little Lamb.* She was also active in the woman's rights movement, seeking the removal of some of the restrictions against them, and wrote many editorials urging the establishment of women's colleges. In another direction, her efforts caused President Lincoln to declare Thanksgiving Day a national holiday. *Godey's Lady's Book* influenced decisions beyond the choice of a bonnet. Early in the history of the magazine it used material from other publications, but the keen interest shown in the publication by American women led to the publishing of original material by American women writers. The plates were done by some of the best metal and wood engravers in Philadelphia and New York, including A. L. Dick, Alfred Jones, and B. F. Waitt.

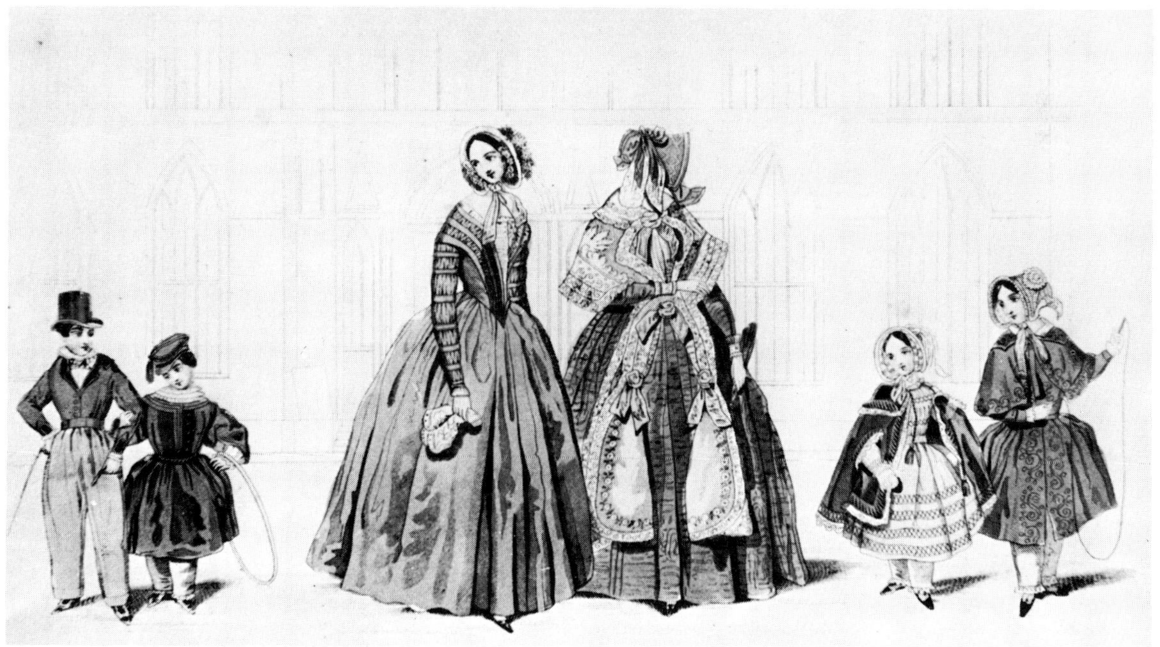

Fashion plate from *Godey's Lady's Book* for March, 1843. Hand-colored engraving, vignette on paper, 6⅛ x 9¾ inches

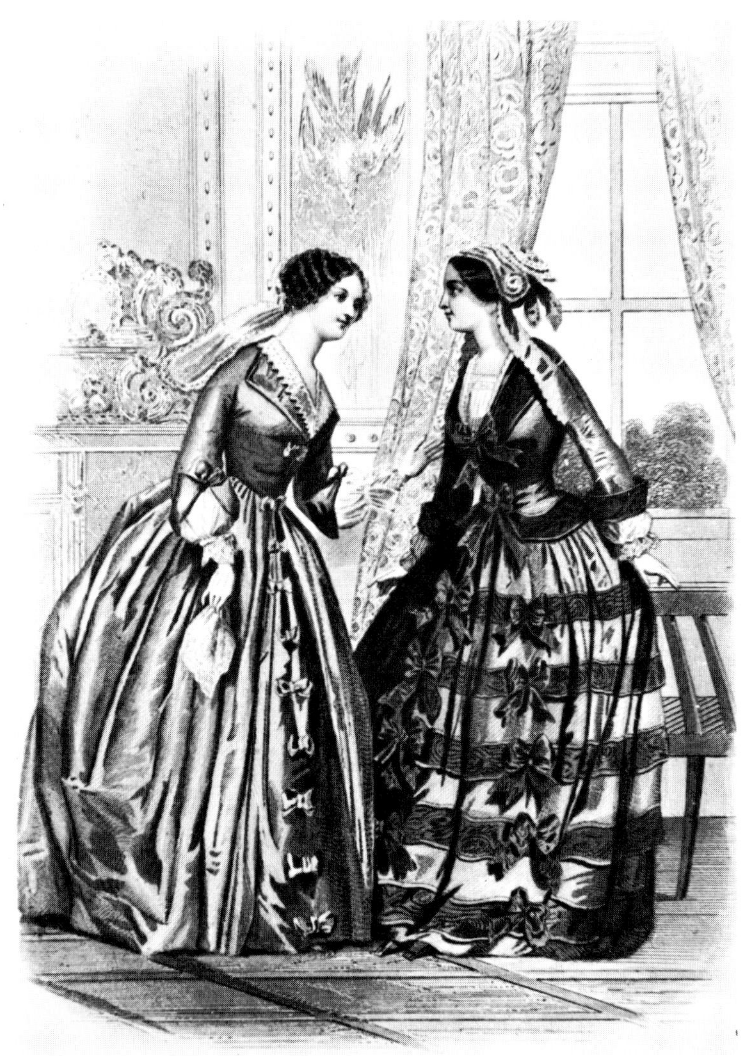

Fashion plate from *Godey's Lady's Book,* 1853. Hand-colored engraving by B. F. Waitt, vignette on paper $9\frac{1}{2} \times 5\frac{3}{4}$ inches

CHAPTER EIGHT Care, Preservation and Buying of Prints

Avid collectors spend enormous amounts of time, energy and thought as well as money on their collections. Therefore, it is only prudent that a reasonable effort be made for the care and preservation of the prints after they are bought. Too often this is not the case, and details such as matting and framing are left to the "expert" neighborhood framing shop, Usually this is disastrous although it is not the intention of the proprietor that it be so. The current commercial practice that he follows treats prints as decorative objects intended to be replaced in a few years, an objective that is usually achieved. The intent of this chapter is to supply the background information that will be useful for the intelligent care of a collection of prints.

Nature of Paper

This book deals only with prints on paper although in unusual cases other materials have been used. The paper may be thick, thin, old handmade or modern machine-made but since the foundation is paper the life of a print is no longer than the life of the paper on which it is printed. The weaknesses of paper are many but with proper treatment and care most prints can be preserved for centuries.

Paper is a felted sheet of vegetable fibers which for centuries was made from cotton or linen cloth which was macerated by soaking and beating and made into a mash by mixing with water. A screen was dipped into this slurry to scoop up a layer of these matted fibers which when dried became a sheet of paper. This crude paper has blotter-like properties which requires further finishing for most uses. For writing and printing the sheet is usually sized with a solution which until modern times was made with animal gelatin. The size both stiffens the paper and keeps the ink from blurring. As a further step many papers are also hammered or rolled in order to harden and smooth the surface.

As the typesetting and printing process improved and as the demand for books and printed matter grew, the demand for paper naturally expanded apace. From about 1500 on a great effort went into improving all aspects of paper making from the raw material to paper-making machines. Although these improvements reduced the cost and improved the surface of the paper, the innovations often left impurities which were the seeds of self-destruction. As examples, in the mid-seventeenth century alum (potassium aluminum sulfate) was added to the gelatin size as a preservative and hardener. Then about 1790 chlorine was used as a bleach so that off-white and colored rags could be used to make the much sought after white paper. About 1850 an alum and rosin size was substituted for the earlier gelatin size. In the 1860's the use of wood pulp was introduced and the permanence of such paper is still being studied. These and other changes in the paper making process added impurities which in time reacted and created sulfuric acid as well as other harmful by-products not normally created in the earlier and purer papers. This acid destruction is especially severe for the nineteenth and early twentieth-century papers but fortunately, in some cases, such recognition is the first necessary step to preservation.

Damage to Prints

It is possible to list at least seven major causes of damage to paper and prints.

1. Chemical deterioration
2. Mildew and foxing
3. Water and other stains
4. Insect damage
5. Fading of colors
6. Tears and folds
7. Dust and dirt

Some of the causes for chemical deterioration have already been discussed. A nineteenth-century print that is very yellow and brittle is almost surely suffering from some chemical deterioration, usually a paper that is excessively acid. A competent paper restorer can extend the life of the print by neutralizing the paper. Short of this the best practice is to keep the print dry and protected from further chemical damage.

Mildew and attack by other microorganisms can be a serious problem, especially in damp environments with the sizing acting as a nutrient to encourage such growth. Damaged areas often turn brown as a result of the mold reacting with previously colorless iron impurities in the paper. These spots are called foxing and can be very disfiguring.

Very few old prints are found that are free of serious staining. Some of these are clearly seen in the as-found nineteenth-century Haskell & Allen print illustrated. Typically such prints were framed flat against the glass with pine back-boards used to hold the glass and print in place. Resins from this wood backing add to the overall yellowing of the paper which probably would have yellowed anyway from the action of acids left by the paper-making process. A knot in the backboard is a particularly resinous area which produces a dark stain very difficult to remove. Two dark vertical stripes can be seen which correspond in position to the narrow open spaces between three wooden backboards. These stripes are the result of sulfur dioxide in the air acting on the exposed paper. Sulfur dioxide when combined with water or water vapor quickly forms damaging sulfuric acid. The sulfur dioxide itself was probably created by the burning of coal or oil for heating or by illuminating gas during the gas light era. Water stains can also be seen along the edge which are the result of condensation of moist air between the print and the glass. An air space as provided by a mat would have avoided this damage. Small foxing marks are also present but they cannot be seen in the photograph. Also unclear in the illustration is the dirt along the bottom quarter of the print carried there by a convection stream of dirty air. This air stream flowed between cracks in the unsealed backboard and then into the space between the print and the glass as the print hung on the wall. All of these pitfalls are avoided by proper framing. Fortunately most of the damage to this print could be corrected by restoration as seen in the "after" illustration.

Insect damage to prints can be severe. The sizing is especially appetizing to silverfish and it is not unusual for them to skim the surface devouring the print along with the sizing. At times insects also bore holes to go to the other side of the paper. Woodworms, cockroaches and termites are troublesome in special situations. Prints considered safely stored in attics, barns or warehouses are often damaged this way.

Both the color of the paper and the water or oil colors used in coloring the print can be altered by exposure to light, by gasses in the air or by chemical reaction with the paper. Light is by far the most common cause of fading and the preventive is obvious. Prints should never be hung in direct sunlight or in very bright light. If the collection is large enough it is a good idea to rotate displays and to keep choice pieces in dark storage areas when not on exhibit.

Although tears and folds can be repaired by an expert restorer, once torn or folded a print drastically loses value. It is important, therefore, to mount and store prints properly in order to minimize chances of such damage.

Dust and dirt can be the most serious cause of damage to prints because it is often impossible to clean the surface without disfiguring the print. Proper handling and protection reduces this hazard to a low level.

Matting and Framing

Good prints are expensive and their resale value can be drastically reduced by damage caused by improper handling. With few exceptions all prints should be matted even if they are not going to be framed. It is a small expense that can pay high dividends.

The quality of the materials used in matting is so important that it deserves to be discussed first. Most mat boards and backboards available in local art stores are made of poor quality wood pulp paperboard but usually with a good quality paper on the outside. When cut for a mat, however, the inner paper board is exposed and as the paperboard deteriorates it stains the print along this edge. In most cases it takes only a few years for this stain to become noticeable and after five years it is disfiguring. The solution is to use only acid-free mat board both as the backboard and mat. This is sold as "museum board," rag mat, conservation board, or sometimes simply acid-free mat board. Although not easily located, its use is essential if the print is not to be damaged. Often a local art museum or art gallery knows local sources of supply.

Modern matting consists of attaching the print to acid-free paperboard backing with a second acid-free cutout mat on the face as illustrated. These two mounting boards should be hinged together using cloth tape so that the resulting housing is strong and rigid. The print itself should be hinged to the backboard using gummed linen tape or acid-free paper hinges. If such hinging material is not easily available a satisfactory substitute can be made from gummed flaps of white envelopes of high quality rag paper. The pendant type hinge shown is usually more satisfactory than the hidden hinge for large prints. Proportion the size of the hinge to the size of the picture. *Never* use "Scotch" type tapes

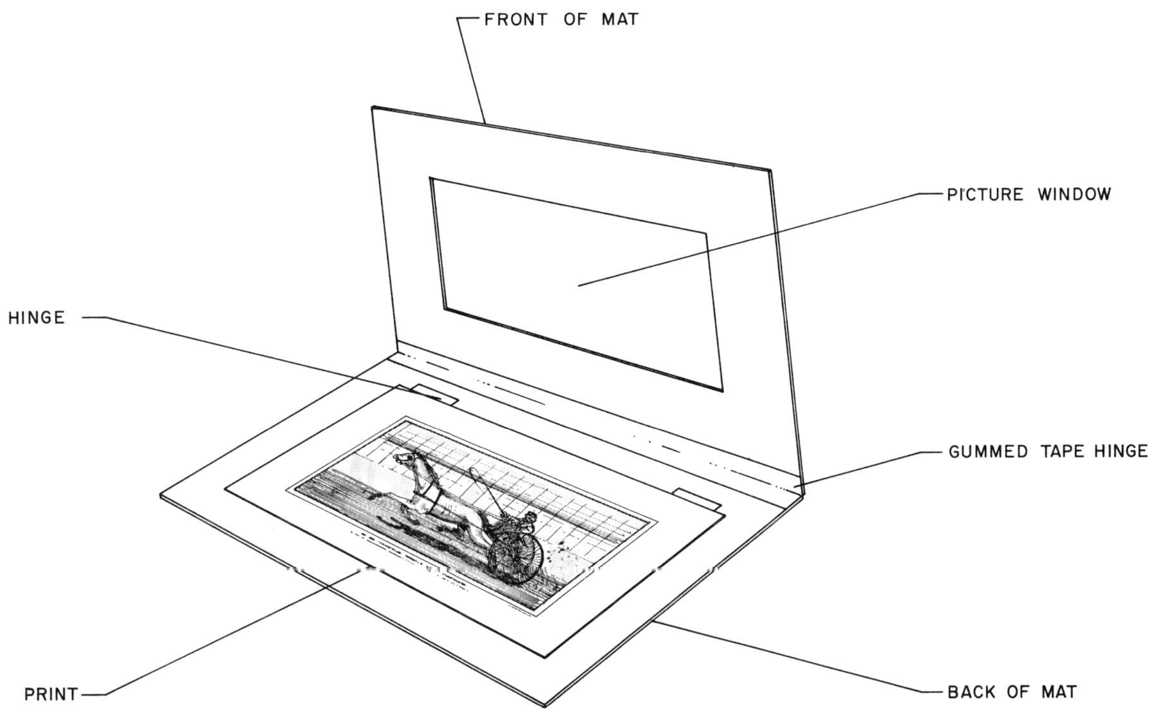

Print Mat

A common construction for the print mat, suitable for storage or framing (*Drawn by Sheridan P. Barnard*)

for they cause permanent damage. Use only glues that can be easily removed by slightly dampening the back of the hinge. Remember, the first rule is that anything you do should be reversible without damage to the print.

It is usually a very bad move to glue the print to the backboard. Generally this is advisable only when the print is torn or weak and needs added support. Most collectors avoid buying glued down (called mounted or laid down) prints because it is more difficult to determine authenticity and to examine them for repairs. For example, some Currier and Ives clipper ships were restruck from the original stones. One of the telling factors is the thickness and feel of the paper, a quality smothered by the mounting. Mounting prevents the examination of prints for expertly-mended tears that, while not visible from the front, can be detected when held up to the light. If a collector or dealer cannot clear these points he must assume the worst in his estimate of value. The neighborhood framer customarily mounts prints using the cheapest pulp

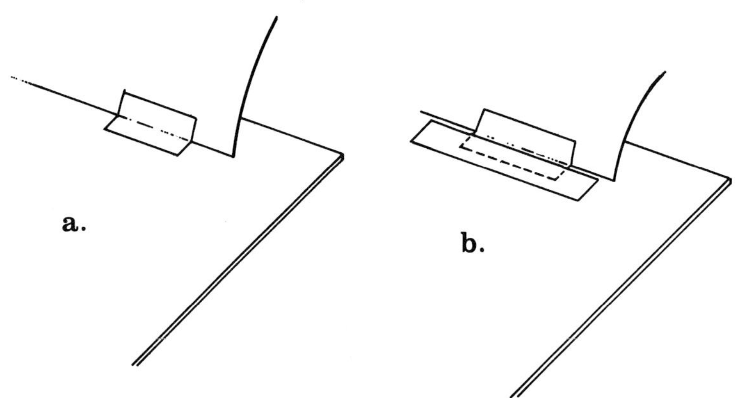

Folded Hinges

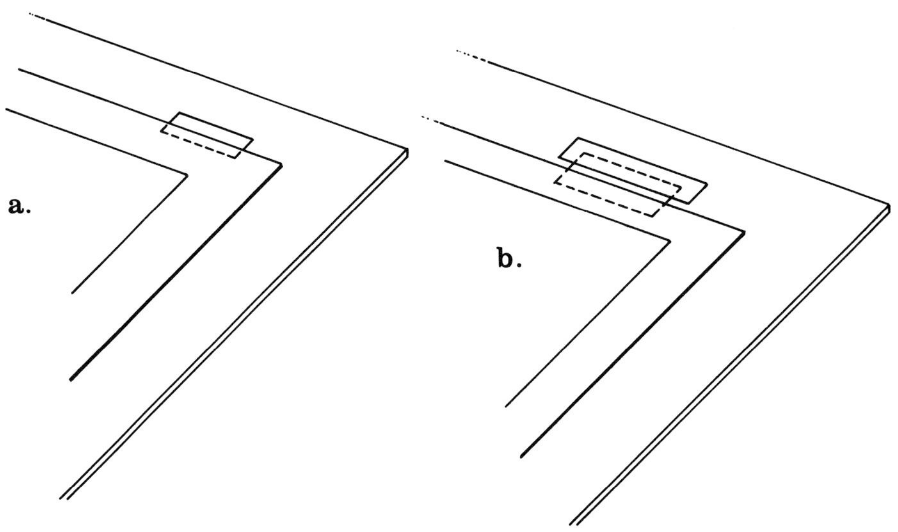

Pendant Hinges

Types of hinges for holding the print in the mat. Pendant hinges are best for large pictures. Folded hinges must be used when the hinge cannot be covered by the mat. The "b" illustrations show hinges reinforced with an added strip of tape or paper

paper backboard in order to keep them flat and free of waves. Never let him do it. This pulp paperboard will ruin the print. A print so glued down must be unmounted if it is to be preserved. If this type of mounting is required for strength, have it done by a professional paper restorer who will use the correct adhesive and mount the print on conservation quality acid-free paper.

For almost all except the very largest prints, the four ply matting

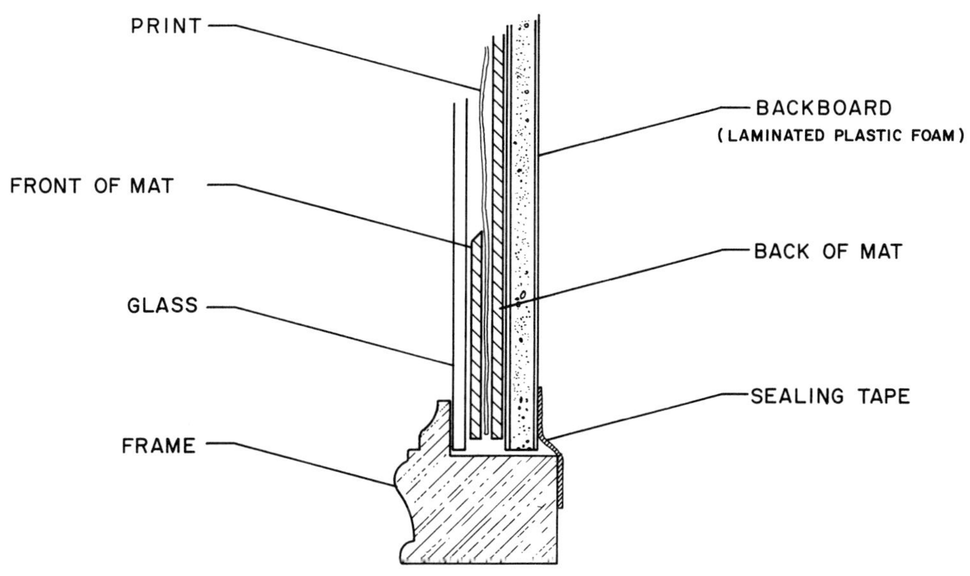

Cross Section of a Framed Print

board—approximately 1/16 inch thick—is stiff enough and provides adequate glass-to-print spacing when framed. Thicker board or a double layer of four ply boards should be used on prints over 30 inches long in the longer dimension. The matted print is easily framed as illustrated. The choice of frame molding is a matter of individual taste and will be left that way. Make sure that the print is not pushed against the glass as a result of any warp in the backboard. The purpose of the air space is to keep the print from being stained if there is moisture condensation on the inside of the glass caused by rapidly changing climatic conditions. Obviously a warped backboard can abort this goal. A second purpose is to keep prints with gum arabic highlights or gouache from sticking to the glass.

Rubbing a small amount of some long-lived insecticide along the back edge of the mat will discourage silverfish from eating what has been so carefully put together. A glued paper backing or tape along the edge between the backboard and the frame is also prudent in order to keep out dust and other foreign matter.

Non-glare glass is sometimes used on commercially-framed reproduction prints but is not recommended for original prints. Such glass is frosted on the outside and so does not provide a polished surface for reflections. To see anything at all, however, the print must be as close as possible to the glass. The use of a mat moves the print too far away and thoroughly distorts the colors and sharpness of outline.

Storage

An ideal print storage area is one that provides protection from physical damage, chemical deterioration, dust and dirt, light damage, moisture, fungus, insects and possibly fire and theft. This is a tall order and can be only partially achieved in the home. A dry closet that can be locked and does not get exhaust gases from the furnace or garage is a good starting point. The floor and baseboard should be treated with a long-lasting insecticide in order to discourage silverfish. A built-in electric light is a big convenience.

A simple wooden rack with vertical partitions can be built on the floor to hold framed prints. Unframed but matted prints can be kept in the proper size Solander boxes and stored on shelves. The Solander box is a cardboard box made of acid-free paper and arranged with snaps and hinges so that it can be easily opened. The contents of the box can be listed on paper labels attached to the outside. Alternately, such "loose" prints can be kept in steel files available in drafting supply houses. The matted prints should have a translucent acid-free paper sheet between the print and the mat. This is a good precaution in order to minimize chances of abrasion to the face of the print when it is taken out for examination. Although many households cannot afford the loss of an entire closet, perhaps some aspects of the full closet storage area can be incorporated in modified form elsewhere.

Cleaning and Restoration

Like surgery, the cleaning and restoration of prints is simple in concept but is more likely to be successful after personal instruction and practice. Also like surgery, if properly done it is beneficial and can extend the life of the print but if poorly done it can be fatal. Some of the general procedures used and an evaluation of correctable faults are discussed in this section but specifics on how to implement these is left to the books on restoration listed in the bibliography.

Restoration has two components, sometimes divergent, a cosmetic and a conservation vector. The cosmetic direction is concerned with the attractiveness of the print while the conservation is concerned with longevity and maintaining all original qualities. How these are played off against one another is a matter of choice. In general the following steps are considered in restoration although usually only a few are applied to any particular print.

1. Removal of loose dust and dirt
2. Bleaching the paper
3. Neutralizing the acid in the paper
4. Removing spots and stains
5. Repairing tears and creases
6. Resizing
7. Touchup
8. Mounting, applying borders, filling holes, etc.

Old prints still in the original frames are almost always covered with dust and loose dirt and must be cleaned before anything can be done. Dirt rubbed into the paper is about the most difficult disfigurement to remove. If the print was cleaned at one time and properly framed the chances are that it does not need further cleaning. A good rule in general is to do only what is necessary. Dust and dirt are best removed using the specially prepared powder used in drafting rooms or with a kneadable eraser that is pushed down and then pulled off. Never wipe the eraser or a dust cloth across the print.

Even the brownest paper can usually be bleached back to a cream or white color using chlorine gas or one of the chlorine-based bleaches. If not properly neutralized this step can leave a very destructive residue. Bleaching should not be attempted by the untrained. The bleaching brightens the picture, removes most water and backboard stains, but it also removes or changes some colors in colored prints. Most prints that require bleaching also require neutralization of the acids in the paper. This is an important step in preservation and is usually accomplished by spraying the back of the paper with a suitable alkaline solution or in some cases by soaking the print in a tray of cold water.

Spots and stains not removed by the bleaching operation can often be removed by using the proper solvent or chemical. If the nature of a particular stain is known, be sure to tell the restorer so that he can decide on the best treatment.

Tears and folds can usually be repaired so that they are almost invisible. The degree of perfection is first dependent on the skill and experience of the operator and after that it is proportional to the time and effort he spends on the repair. Even the most perfectly repaired tear, however, can usually be detected by examining the print carefully when held up to a strong light.

There can be an amazing improvement in the appearance of a print

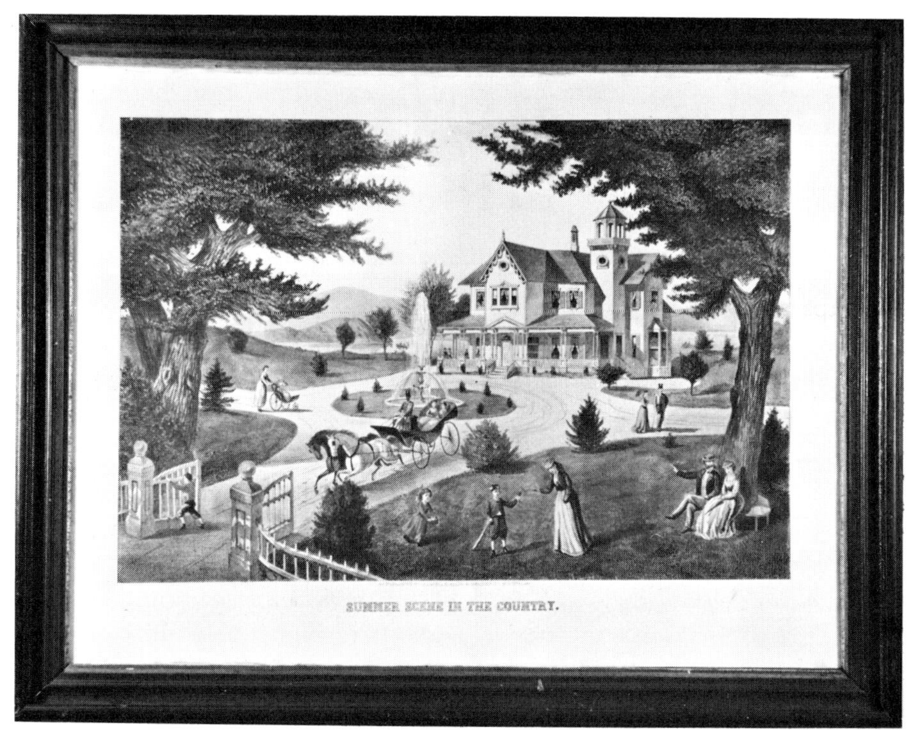

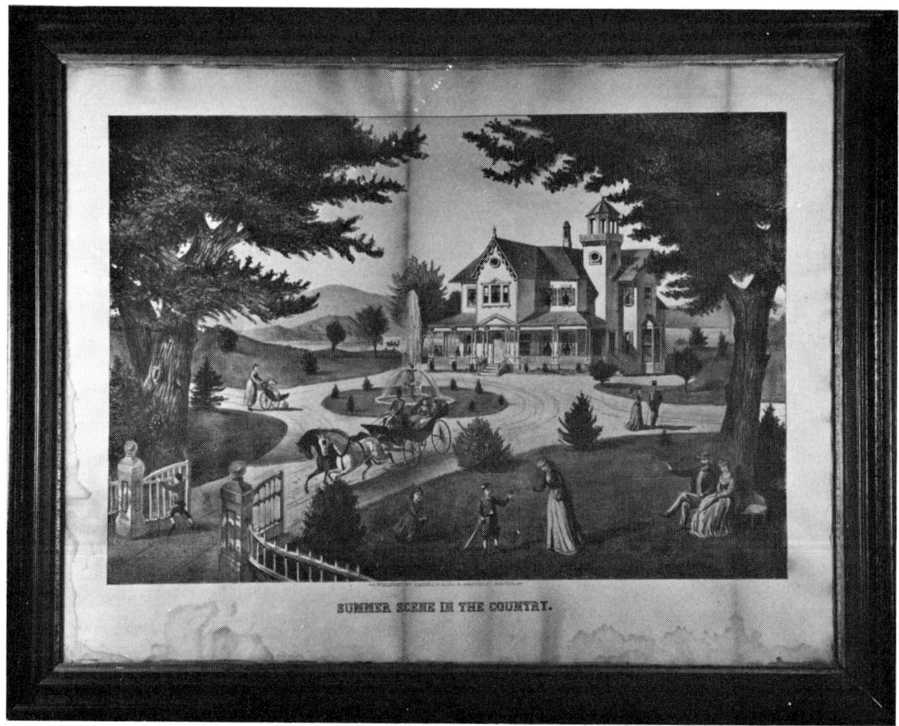

The "before" and "after" photographs demonstrate the effectiveness of professional cleaning in whitening paper browned by age and in removing board and water stains as well as dirt. *Summer Scene in the Country,* large folio lithograph by Haskell and Allen after restoration. Although a good rule in any restoration is to do only what is necessary there are certain steps such as neutralizing acid-paper that are highly beneficial and add to the ultimate life of the print.

Random Comments about Buying Prints

Perhaps the greatest mistakes made by the novice collector are caused by his failure to understand the importance of condition and the drastic effect that it has on the value of a print. Unlike a painting, a print is not a unique item (except for great rarities). Nevertheless, all impressions of a particular print are not necessarily alike. Differences may occur at the time the impression was pulled or may occur during the life history of the print. The variations originating at the time of printing are called "quality of impression." For example, as a copper plate is used wear occurs which obscures fine details, breaks may appear in the lettering and border lines and there is a loss of depth and richness. Quality of impression is of greatest importance in methods that show rapid deterioration such as drypoint, mezzotint and copperplate line engraving.

Events during the life history of the print which have affected its physical condition lessen its value according to the extent of the damage. Tears into the picture are major flaws. Also important are creases, insect damage, foxing, stains, scratches, fading and holes. Cutting the margins was often done to fit the print into a frame and the loss of value depends on the extent of the surgery. Clipping which still leaves a satisfactory margin is acceptable but if the main body of the picture has been even slightly trimmed or the title margin cut off, the print is no longer in a collector's category. Since few prints have survived the years unscathed, the search for prime condition must be tempered with reality.

Reputable dealers price their prints according to condition as well as rarity and demand. A poor example is priced less than a choice one. The condition also muddies the waters of auctions where the unwary can pay high prices for torn or damaged prints with the misconception that a good bargain has been made. A dealer usually presents his prints in mats so that the purchaser can examine them front and back, the best way to see what he is buying.

APPENDIX I Glossary of Print Terms

ad vivum Sometimes used on engraved portraits to indicate that the work was done from life and not from a painting.

after A print which is engraved or lithographed *after* a painting means that the painting was the source from which the print was copied.

applied margins When original margins have been cut off, replacements are sometimes added. Sometimes called remargined.

aquatint A tonal engraving process in which the plate is covered with small islands of rosin before treatment with acid. Also used to describe a print made by this process which leaves a characteristic grainy effect. See Chapter II.

artist's proofs The first prints pulled from the finished plates which are considered satisfactory by both the artist and the engraver or lithographer. Often signed by both. Also, first prints reserved for the artist's personal use. In modern print making these would be outside of the regular edition.

board marks Stain on paper from resins and contaminants in the wood boards formerly used as backing when framing prints. Brown stripes on prints in spaces between boards were usually caused by paper deterioration due to the action of the sulphur dioxide in the air.

broadside A single printed sheet of paper, sometimes illustrated, to be posted for all to read. It was used for proclamations, announcements and advertising.

burin Engraver's tool made of hard steel and with a sharp cutting edge. Also called a graver.

burr Ridge thrown up in making a line engraving, particularly with the drypoint technique. The burr causes the printed line to be somewhat fuzzy and soft. The burr wears rapidly and is one means of judging whether a print is an early or a late impression.

chromolithograph, "chromo" A color lithographic technique using different stones or plates for each color. See Chapter II.

collector's mark A stamped mark on the front or back of a print to show that it was or is part of a particular collection. Used mainly in Europe.

cross hatching An engraving technique used to produce tone. Two systems of parallel lines are cut at an angle to one another. The depth of the tone depends on the spacing between the lines and their thickness.

del. (delineavit) Literally, "he drew it," in Latin. Del. after an artist's name on an engraving usually indicates that the print was done from a drawing rather than a painting. On a lithograph it can also mean "drawn on stone by," the lithographer, or the artist who drew or painted the original design.

double elephant folio A paper stock, size 26¾ inches by 40 inches. A term used chiefly in Great Britain. Audubon's *Birds* were printed on this size paper and then trimmed slightly.

drypoint Engravings made using a sharp point to scratch the surface of the copperplate rather than the burin which is used for conventional line engravings. Also used to describe the technique. See Chapter II.

elephant folio A paper stock, size 23 inches by 28 inches. A term used chiefly in Great Britain.

engraver's proof Prints pulled by the engraver to permit him to check the progress of his work.

engraving An intaglio print-making process with many variations. Also a print made by one of these processes. See Chapter II.

etching An engraving process in which the plate is first coated with wax which is then scratched away to produce the design. The plate is then treated with acid which etches the unprotected lines into the plate. Prints are made by inking the plate and wiping so that only the etched lines print. Also used to describe prints made by this process. See Chapter II.

exc., excud., excudit Published by, also printed by.

f., fec., fecit Made, etched, or engraved by.

folio Paper size of books and prints between 8 inches by 13 inches and 15 by 22 inches, approximately, but usually in the 11 by 17 inch range.

foxed, foxing Brownish spots on the print caused by a combination of dampness, fungus and impurities in the paper.

gouache An opaque water paint made by mixing the pigment with a binder such as gum arabic. Also, the painting made using such paint.

graver See burin.

ground "Laying the ground" means to prepare a metal plate for etching or aquatint by coating with an acid-resistant coating.

gum arabic A water soluble vegetable gum sometimes used as a binder for gouache. Also used in water solution without pigment as a coating over selected areas of a colored print. Frequently used on hand-colored lithographs to add sparkle and life to dark areas.

half-tone A photographic tone-printing technique characterized by a matrix or grid of dots. Depending on the half-tone screen used, these dots can be easily seen or can require considerable magnification to detect. Halftone printing is a common method of making modern reproductions. See Chapter II.

imp., imprimavit Printed, printer.

impression A print made from a metal plate, wood block or stone.

inc., incid., incidit Engraved.

India paper Sometimes called rice paper. A tough, thin paper with a dull surface. Proof impressions of engravings are sometimes made on India paper.

intaglio The engraving printing process or prints made by these techniques are classified as intaglio methods or intaglio prints. See Chapter II.

inv., invenit designed or invented.

laid down Print is pasted to a supporting piece of paper or cardboard. Also called mounted.

laid paper Early type of handmade paper usually before 1800. When held to a bright light the laid lines can be seen, a pattern of fine equally spaced parallel lines intersecting at right angles fewer, thicker, more widely spaced lines. Sometimes a watermark pattern is included, also formed by the way in which the wires are laid. Genuine handmade laid paper can be distinguished from imitations by the way in which the fibers congregate along the more widely spaced wires with a thickening of the paper along them.

large folio An inexact term used to describe print size. For Currier and Ives and similar lithographs, it usually means print size over 14 by 20 inches. See *print size.*

letterpress Printed material below the illustration including title, lithographer, publisher and similar information.

line engraving One of two basic categories of engraving which includes etching and drypoint, in which shading is accomplished by various linear patterns. See Chapter II.

lithograph A print made using the lithographic process. See Chapter II.

lith., lith. by After a name indicates that the individual was the lithographer who drew the picture on stone either from his own design or after another person's work. It can also mean that the print was made by the lithographic process.

margin The blank paper which borders the printed area of a print. Also sometimes the paper outside of the platemark of an engraving.

medium folio An inexact term used to describe print size. For Currier and Ives and similar lithographs it usually means a size between 9 by 14 inches and 14 by 20 inches. See *print size.*

mezzotint A tonal engraving made by first roughening the surface of the plate and then producing the picture by flattening and burnishing selected areas, which print as highlights. Portraits were often made using the mezzotint process.

mounted See *laid down.*

octavo Size of book, or print from an octavo size book, about $5\frac{1}{2}$ by $8\frac{1}{2}$ inches.

photo-engraving, photo-lithography Printing processes in which the image is transferred to the printing plate by photographic means. See Chapter II.

pinx., pinxt., pinxit Painted, painter.

planographic A printing process such as lithography which uses a flat printing surface. See Chapter II.

plate mark On engraved prints, the ridge in the paper made by the edges of the printing plate digging into the paper during printing, causing distortion in the paper.

print size For lithographs, it is most often the size of the picture area exclusive of margins and printed titles. Sometimes the printed titles are included in the size but this is not a common practice. The dimensions are usually given in inches and fractions thereof, but some references use the older standard of inches and sixteenths of an inch written in decimal form with the decimal representing sixteenths of an inch rather than hundredths. Thus, 12.10 inches designates $12^{10}/_{16}$ inches or $12^{5}/_{8}$ inches.

proof before letters A print, before the title and other printed matter have been added in the margin below the print. See also *artists's proof* and *engraver's proof.*

publisher The business organization or person responsible for issuing the print. The publisher may or may not also be the printer, lithographer or other party to its production.

register Refers to the correct placement, relative to each other, of successive imprints such as the application of different colors. In order to assure good register, lithographs made using more than one stone have two pin holes at opposite edges of the print, to aid in alignment.

relief printing Printing technique using a raised design on a plate or block. The rubber stamp is an example of relief printing.

reproduction A copy of a print made from other than the original stone, plate or block.

reproductive print A print reproducing a work in another medium, usually a painting.

restrike A print made from the original plate, stone or block but at some later date, usually long after the original publication.

ruling machine A mechanical aid used for creating tones in engravings by ruling in parallel lines in the sky and other large areas. This and similar mechanical aids contribute to the cold, stiff appearance of many steel engravings.

sc., sculp., sculpsit Engraved, indicates the engraver.

serigraph A print made by the serigraph or silk screen process.

size See *print size.*

small folio An inexact term used to describe print size. For Currier and Ives and similar lithographs, it usually means a print size about $8\frac{1}{2}$ by $12\frac{1}{2}$ inches. See *print size.*

state A term applied to different stages in the development of a print each time there is an alteration in the plate, stone or block. May be applied to any change whatever, even lettering.

steel engraving Either an engraved print or the technique which uses an engraved steel plate for printing. Steel wears better during printing than a copper plate but the difficulty encountered in working the harder metal produces a stiffer, dryer looking print.

steel facing A technique for using a copper plate for engraving but electroplating a steel surface on it which increases its printing life.

stipple A tonal engraving technique using small dots to create the design. Also a print made using this process. See Chapter II.

time-toned Refers to the change in paper color turning it tannish or light brown as a result of time and chemical action.

tinted, tint stone, tint plate Often a neutral color such as tan is applied over all or part of a print. This reduces the contrast with the white paper and changes the effect. In lithographs the tint is applied with a tint stone. In engravings it is sometimes applied with an aquatint plate.

tone process Engraving process such as aquatint, stipple and mezzotint, where tone is achieved without resorting to lines and linear structures. See Chapter II.

vignette A print without a definite boundary line, gradually fading into the unprinted area. Also a small decorative design or illustration. Sometimes the main picture is surrounded by vignettes or small illustrations relating to it.

watermark A design put in during the manufacture of the paper which is made by varying the density of the paper. It can be seen by holding the paper up to light. Important for the identification or confirmation of the authenticity of certain prints.

woodcut A print made using a relief process in which the design is cut into the side of a block of wood. See Chapter II.

wood engraving A print process where the design is cut into the end grain of a block of wood. Also a print made from such a block. See Chapter II.

wove paper An improved paper made so as to eliminate the ridges and hollows of the earlier laid paper. Modern paper is wove paper.

APPENDIX II Names in American Printmaking 1670 to 1880

Tens of thousands of men and women worked on making prints in America in the period from 1670 to 1880. First in importance, perhaps, are the artists and illustrators, but unfortunately their names were usually omitted from the letterpress or any other part of the print. Next come the engravers, wood engravers and lithographers who prepared the plate, and after that the printers and publishers whose names are most often on the print. Competition, personality and economic conditions forced most of these people to operate in a whirlpool of changes with only a few partnerships, businesses or associations lasting for an extended period. Many individuals worked only part time at printmaking while others changed their trade or profession during difficult periods. Some produced only a few prints while others, such as Currier and Ives, produced over seven thousand different ones.

This list of names most prominent in American printmaking is a selection of a small percentage of those recorded as having worked in the field. It aims to focus on those names that today's collector is most likely to encounter in books, articles and especially the market place. No particular significance should be attached to any name that has been omitted. It may have been overlooked or may not have fallen within the guidelines used in preparing the list. In that case other more complete references should be checked.

ABERNETHIE, THOMAS. Engraver, native of Scotland, but working Charleston, S.C. from 1785–96.

ACKERMAN, EMIL (1840–?). Lithographer, born in Dresden, Germany, settled in America in 1848 and was apprenticed to Max Rosenthal in Philadelphia *c.* 1856. Later went to Boston. *Black Valley Rail Road,* signed "E. Ackerman, Lith. 134 Washington St., Boston," is one of the best temperance prints.

ACKERMAN, JAMES (*c.* 1813–?). Lithographer worked in N.Y.C. *c.* 1838–1865. Established a sign- and banner-painting firm with Edward A. Miller. Did hand-colored lithographs of flowers and birds for nature books and illustrations for government reports.

AITKEN, ROBERT (1734–1802). Engraver, printer and publisher who was born in Scotland but worked for many years (1769–1802) in Philadelphia. He probably re-engraved *A Correct View of the Late Battle at Charlestown,* depicting the Battle of Bunker Hill as seen by Bernard Romans (June 17, 1775). From 1775 to 1776 he issued the *Pennsylvania Magazine,* for which he engraved various illustrations.

AKIN, JAMES (*c.* 1773–1846). Engraver and lithographer, born in South Carolina but active primarily in Philadelphia *c.* 1808–1846. Drayton's *View of South Carolina,* Charleston S.C., 1802, contained his earliest engravings. He worked for a short period *c.* 1804 in Salem, Mass. In Philadelphia he engraved book plates, drew caricatures on stone and published prints with William Harrison, Jr.

ALEXANDER, FRANCIS (1800–1880). Lithographer and artist in Boston from *c.* 1827 to 1853. Studied with Alexander Robertson (in N.Y.C.) and with Gilbert Stuart. Was a leading Boston portrait painter, and produced some of the earliest portraits on stone. Was associated with W. S. Pendleton.

ALLARDICE, SAMUEL (?–1798). Engraver working in Philadelphia in the 1790's.

ALLEN, LUTHER (1780–1821). Engraver and portrait painter, born in Connecticut, moved to Ithaca, N.Y. in 1802. His only noted engravings are a bookplate, an engraving based on S. King's *A South West View of Newport, R.I.,* and a quarto mezzotint portrait of Rev. Stephen Williams, D. D.

ALLERDICE, see ALLARDICE.

ANDERSON, ALEXANDER (1775–1870). Wood engraver and miniaturist, born and lived most of his life in N.Y.C. Although trained as a physician, he started wood engraving around 1793 and became the first wood engraver in the U.S. Contributed as many as 10,000 cuts to books, periodicals, etc. and was the first in this country to use Thomas Bewick's "white-line" technique.

ANDREW, JOHN (1815–1875). Wood engraver, born in England, worked in Boston *c.* 1851–1875. Partner in Baker and Andrew, 1853–54; and Andrew and Filmer. 1858–60.

ANDREWS, JOSEPH (1805–1873). Engraver of the mid-1800's. taught by Abel Bowen, a wood engraver, and by William Hoagland. His best known works include *Plymouth Rock, 1620,* based on Rothermel's painting (engraved from 1855–1869) and a plate of Washington after Stuart. He is considered one of the best American line-engravers.

ANNIN, PHINEAS F. Wood engraver in N.Y.C., 1852–58, partner in Whitney and Annin, 1852; Whitney, Jocelyn and Annin, 1853–55 and Loomis and Annin, 1858.

ANNIN and SMITH-SENEFELDER LITHOGRAPHIC COMPANY. William B. Annin, engraver, worked in Boston from about 1813 to 1839. In the 1820's, he and George G. Smith started the engraving firm, Annin and Smith. Then, *c.* 1828, the Senefelder Lithographic Co. was established by G. G. Smith, W. B. Annin, Hazen Morse, John Chorley and Thomas Edwards. In 1831, William S. Pendleton took over the business and sometimes used the Senefelder name.

ANTHONY, ANDREW VARICK STOUT (1835–1906). Wood engraver in California *c.* 1853 as partner of Anthony and Baker. In N.Y.C., 1855–58, and in Boston, 1878–1906.

ARMSTRONG, CHARLES. Lithographer working in both Boston and New York, 1872–76. Some of his works are *Live Sports on Boston Common,* 1875, *The March of Miles Standish,* 1875 and portraits.

ARMSTRONG, THOMAS. Wood engraver in San

Francisco from *c.* 1849–1857. He engraved the *View of the City and Harbor of San Francisco, California, 1849.*

ARMSTRONG, WILLIAM G. (1823–1890). Engraver and artist working in Philadelphia.

ATWILL, JOSEPH F. Music publisher in New York, 1833–49, published *The Flower Dance of the Viennoise Children,* printed by Sarony and Major, and *Croton Water Celebration, 1842.*

AUDUBON, JOHN JAMES (1785–1851). One of the foremost American naturalists, born in Haiti, was sent to America in 1806 by his father, a French naval officer. He spent most of his life searching out and painting American birds and animals. These paintings formed the basis for the *Birds of America* published in England and *Viviparous Quadrupeds of North America* published in the U.S. See chapter on Nature Prints for additional details.

AUDUBON, JOHN WOODHOUSE (1812–1862). Wildlife and portrait painter, son of John James Audubon. Worked primarily around N.Y.C from *c.* 1839 to 1862. He was trained by his father and assisted him with his work as early as 1833. He painted about half of the plates for *Viviparous Quadrupeds of North America* and prepared the smaller plates for the octavo editions of the *Birds* and the *Quadrupeds.*

AUDUBON, VICTOR GIFFORD (1809–1860). Wildlife painter, elder son of John James Audubon. Went to England in 1832 to help with the publication of his father's, *Birds of America.* Worked in N.Y.C. from 1840 to his death.

AUTENRIETH (AUTENREITH), CHARLES. Artist in New York known for his drawings of New York University, City Hall, etc., which were incorporated as lithographs into the *Views of New York,* published by Hoff.

AYRES, THOMAS A. Painter, worked for many years in San Francisco, *c.* 1850's. Known for his views of California, especially Yosemite Valley.

BACHELDER, JOHN B. (1825–1894). Artist, designer and publisher of Civil War and other prints, in Boston, *c.* 1860's. He painted views of Salem, Worchester (Mass.) and Providence (R.I.) and the *Firemen's Muster, Merrimac Square, Manchester, N.H.* issued by Endicott in 1859.

BACHMANN, JOHN. Lithographer, artist and publisher in New York, Brooklyn and Jersey City. Helped produce numerous views of N.Y.C. from 1849 to 1879.

BAILLIE, JAMES S. Artist, colorer and lithographer in New York, *c.* 1840 to 1855. He colored prints for N. Currier, later issued many prints in competition with Currier including *North Sea Whale Fishery, Life and Age of Man* and *Surrender of Cornwallis.*

BAKER, et al. Engravers in wood and metal in Boston. Baker and Andrew, 1854; (W. J. Baker and J. Andrew). Baker and Smith, 1852. W. J. Baker and D. T. Smith and Baker, Smith and Andrew, 1853–54.

BAKER, GEORGE H. (1827–1906). Lithographer, artist and publisher, worked in Sacramento, 1852–62, and San Francisco, 1862–1906. Dealt with mining camp subjects and scenes of California.

BAKER, JOSEPH E. Artist and lithographer in Boston, *c.* 1850's, and in N.Y. in the 60's. Apprenticed by Bufford along with Winslow Homer. Did *The March of Miles Standish* for Armstrong.

BAKER, SAMUEL F. Wood engraver, N.Y.C., 1846–56.

BAKEWELL, THOMAS. London publisher. He published what is known as the "Bakewell Re-issue of 1746" of the Burgis view of New York.

BALCH, VISTUS (1799–1884). Engraver in Utica, Albany and New York from the 1820's to 40's. Headed various engraving establishments such as Balch, Stiles & Co., 1828–30 Balch, Stiles, Wright & Co., 1831–32 and Balch & Co., 1833.

BALL, W. Lithographer in N.Y.C., *c.* 1830, did noted series of presidential portraits.

BANCROFT, MONSON. Lithographer, publisher and store owner in N.Y.C., *c.* 1830's and 40's.

BANNISTER, JAMES (1821–1901). Engraver, born in England, immigrated to the U.S. *c.* 1845, and worked in N.Y.C.

BARBER, JOHN WARNER (1798–1885). Engraver, historian and publisher, he began his career in East Windsor, Conn. where he was apprenticed to the engraver, Abner Reed. His travels over eastern U.S. provided him with the material for his historical books, which he illustrated with engravings, and published. They are *History and Antiquities of New Haven,* 1831, *Connecticut Historical Collections,* 1836 and *Views in New Haven and Vicinity,* 1825. He is particularly known for his engraving of New Haven Green with Buildings of Yale College.

BARNET and DOOLITTLE. William A. Barnet and Isaac Doolittle established the first lithographic company in America in N.Y.C., *c.* 1821. Made plates for *A Grammar of Botany* by Sir J. E. Smith, the first book in America to use lithographed plates.

BARRALET, JOHN JAMES (*c.* 1747–1815). Engraver and painter. He was a successful painter and book illustrator in Dublin, where he was born, and in London. In 1795 he came to America and continued working as a book illustrator with the engraver, Alexander Lawson. He also invented a ruling machine for engravers and improved inks.

BARTHOLOMEW, W. N. (1822–1898). Landscape painter and publisher of lithographed drawing books and cards. Was drawing teacher in Boston, 1852–1871.

BARTLETT, WILLIAM HENRY (1809–1854). Landscape artist, born in London. He visited the U.S. four times from 1836 to 1852 during which periods he produced sepia drawings which were then made into engravings in *American Scenery* by Nathaniel P. Willis, published in 1840. Other drawings served as the basis of engravings in his *History of the United States of North America,* completed by B. B. Woodward, and published posthumously in 1856.

BEARD, JAMES HENRY (1812–1893). Portrait and animal painter, primarily in Cincinnati, 1834–1870, and N.Y.C., 1870 on.

BEAUGUREAU. Philadelphia lithographer, worked for P. S. Duval, 1845.

BECK, GEORGE (*c.* 1750–1812). Landscape painter, born in England, worked primarily in Baltimore, *c.* 1795–97 and Phila., 1798–1807. Some of his scenes were published around 1801–09 by Atkins and Nightingale, London.

BELLEW, FRANK HENRY TEMPLE (1828–88). Comic illustrator, born in India, worked in America in N.Y.C., 1850–88.

BENCKE and SCOTT. Lithographers in New York from about 1875–80. Did views of New York, portraits and advertising for the stage.

BENECKE, THOMAS D. Lithographer in N.Y.C., 1855-56. *Sleighing in New York,* a colorful print showing Barnum's Museum, is the most important recorded work.

BENNETT, WILLIAM JAMES (1787–1844). Aquatint engraver and landscape painter, he left his native England and settled in America in 1816, primarily in N.Y.C., *c.* 1826–43. During his trips to such cities as Baltimore, Boston, Buffalo and Detroit, he produced a fine series of aquatints called *Views of American Cities.*

BEYER, EDWARD (1820–1865). German painter, lived in the U.S., largely in Virginia, from 1848–57. Painted a collection of views of Virginia which were lithographed in Berlin and published as the *Album of Virginia.*

BICKNELL, ALBION HARRIS (1837–1915). Painter, engraver and etcher. Studied in Turner (Me.) and Boston and worked in Boston *c.* 1857–60.

BIEN, JULIUS (1826–1909). Lithographer and map maker, active in N.Y.C. from about 1850 to 1868. Issued chromolithographs of *Birds of America* by Audubon. This is the only issue other than the first Havell prints in the full double elephant size. First great American map maker.

BINGHAM & DODD. John H. Bingham and William Henry Dodd, lithographers in Hartford, Conn. from 1860–83. Produced some views of the Civil War.

BINGHAM, GEORGE CALEB (1811–1879). Genre and portrait painter, born in Virginia, but resided for most of his life in Missouri. His scenes were made into engravings by Thomas Doney, John Sartain and Gautier.

BIRCH FAMILY OF NEW YORK. Thomas, and later his son Thomas A., were music publishers and printers working in N.Y.C. from 1820–90.

BIRCH, THOMAS (1779–1851). Landscape, portrait and marine artist, and son of William Russell Birch. Born in England but spent his active working years in Philadelphia, *c.* 1794–1851. He is known particularly for his naval scenes from the War of 1812, which were engraved by Tiebout, Tanner and Lawson.

BIRCH, WILLIAM RUSSELL (1755–1834). Philadelphia engraver, enamel painter, etcher and print publisher. He left England in 1794 and lived in Pennsylvania for the rest of his life. In 1800 he and his son, Thomas Birch, published a series of *Views of Philadelphia,* and later, views of country seats.

BISBEE, EZRA. Lithographer and portrait painter in N.Y.C. and Brooklyn from 1820–56.

BISBEE, JOHN. Lithographer, publisher and portrait painter in N.Y.C. from 1821–40. Worked for Endicott and Swett for a time.

BLELOCK & CO. Lithographers and publishers in New Orleans. William Blelock, C. S. Titcomb and A. Eyrich were associated with the firm.

BLODGET, SAMUEL. Artist, worked in America *c.* 1755. He witnessed and drew a scene from the *Battle of Lake George,* engraved by Thomas Johnston. This is the first historical print engraved in the U.S.

BLOOD & EVANS. Boston lithographic printers, 1857–58. Partners, were John H. Blood and Charles A. Evans.

BLUMNER, FREDERICK. Lithographer and painter in N.Y.C., 1856–59, and Brooklyn, 1859.

BOBBETT, ALBERT or ALFRED (*c.* 1824-*c.* 1888). Wood engraver born in England and worked in N.Y.C., 1848–88. Partner in Bobbett & Edmonds, 1848–54 and Bobbett and Hooper, 1856–70.

BOELL, WILLIAM. Lithographer in N.Y.C., 1854–57, and Philadelphia 1859–60 and after. In N.Y.C. was partner with George W. Lewis, 1855, and with Francis Michelin, 1856–58. Did views of New York and Philadelphia.

BOETTICHER (or BOTTICHER) OTTO (*c.* 1816–?). Military artist and lithographer, active in N.Y.C. from 1851–58, where he worked with Charles Gildemeister. In the 1850's and 60's he produced some lithographs of military scenes.

BOGERT, J. AUGUSTUS. Wood engraver, 1850–81. In N.Y.C., 1850.

BONAR & CUMMINGS. N.Y. lithographers, *c.* 1847, produced views and portraits. Thomas Bonar continued in business alone from 1848–67.

BOOKHOUT, EDWARD. Wood engraver in N.Y.C., 1842–60.

BOQUETA DE WOISERI, J. L. Painter and engraver. Views of New Orleans, 1803, Boston, 1810. In N.Y.C., 1807–11.

BORNET, J. Artist and lithographer in N.Y.C. from 1850–55, produced 18 small views of N.Y.C., 1850.

BOSQUI, EDWARD (1832–1917). Printer and amateur landscape painter, born in Canada but spent most of his life after 1850 in San Francisco. Founded Bosqui's Engraving and Printing Co., San Francisco's largest.

BOURNE, GEORGE M. Publisher around the 1830's. *Views of New York City,* drawn and engraved primarily by Charles Burton and James

Smillie, respectively, was published by Bourne in 1831.

BOURQUIN, FREDERICK. Lithographer in both N.Y. and Philadelphia, *c.* 1843 to the 1860's. Established the firm, F. Bourquin & Co.

BOUVÉ & SHARP. Ephraim W. Bouvé and William Sharp, Boston engravers and lithographers from 1843–45. Bouvé continued on by himself after 1845. He died in 1897.

BOWEN, ABEL (1790–1850). Publisher, wood and copper engraver who worked in Boston in the 1810's and 20's, becoming the topmost engraver in that city. His noted works include *The Naval Monument,* containing many of his engravings depicting the War of 1812, and a woodcut called the *View of Colonel Johnson's Engagement with the Savages near the Moravian Town,* 1812.

BOWEN, JOHN T. (*c.* 1801–*c.* 1856). Lithographer in N.Y.C., 1834–38, and Philadelphia, 1839–56, produced twenty views of Philadelphia after J. C. Wild, 1838–40. Best known as lithographer for Audubon's octavo issue of *Birds of America,* the large plates for the *Quadrupeds* and some plates for the octavo issue, and plates for McKenney & Hall's book, *History of the Indian Tribes of North America.*

BOWER, JOHN, Book illustrator and engraver who worked from 1809–19 in Philadelphia. His noted engravings are two scenes from the War of 1812: *The Battle of Patapsco Neck, Sept. 12, 1814* and *The Bombardment of Fort McHenry near Baltimore, Sept. 13, 1814.*

BOWES, JOSEPH. Engraver and architect working in Philadelphia, 1794–98.

BOYD, JOHN. Engraver working in Philadelphia, 1810–25.

BRADFORD, L. H. & CO. Boston lithographic and engraving firm, 1854–59, established by Lodowick H. Bradford.

BRADY, MATHEW B. (*c.* 1823–96). Lithographer, photographer and artist in N.Y. in the second half of the 1800's. Many lithographic portraits were made from daguerreotypes and photographs taken by this early master.

BRAINARD, C. H. Lithographer working in N.Y.C. in the late 1850's.

BRETON, W. L. Philadelphia painter *c.* 1830–39, known for his views of ships.

BRETT, ALPHONSE. Lithographer working in Philadelphia, 1848–59 and in N.Y.C. from 1860 to at least 1864.

BREUKER & KESSLER. Lithographers working in Philadelphia from about 1867 to at least 1876.

BREWSTER, EDMUND. Painter and engraver, active *c.* 1818 to 1839 in both Philadelphia and New Orleans.

BRIDPORT, HUGH (*c.* 1794–1868). Artist, born in London, worked and lived in Philadelphia. Did work for Pendleton; Kennedy and Lucas, etc., *c.* 1816 to *c.* 1850.

BRIEM, JOHN. Lithographer and printer working in N.Y.C., 1875–80.

BRIGGS, JOHN. Lithographer working in N.Y.C. at least from 1834–37.

BRIGHTLY, JOSEPH H. (*c.* 1818–?). Wood engraver, born in England, active in Philadelphia and N.Y.C., 1841–58.

BRITTON & REY. Lithographers in San Francisco, 1852–58. Partners were Jos. Britton and J. J. Rey, succeeded by Britton & Co. from 1859–66. Did California views and scenes. Britton was also a partner in firm of Pollard & Britton in 1852.

BROMLEY & CO. Publishers and lithographers in N.Y.C., *c.* 1864.

BROOKS, VINCENT, DAY & SON. English lithographers, (London) did a series of prints on the pioneer West *c.* 1868.

BROWN, ARTHUR. Lithographer in N.Y.C. from 1854 to at least 1868 as A. Brown or Brown & Co.

BROWN, ELIPHALET (1816–1886). Artist and lithographer working in N.Y.C. *c.* 1839–52, in partnership as E. & J. Brown, 1846–48, and Brown & Severyn, 1851–53. He went to Japan with Perry, 1852–54, and on his return did a series of views of the expedition in association with Sarony & Co.

BROWN, GEORGE LORING (1814–1889). Painter, lithographer and etcher who worked primarily in Boston and N.Y.C. from *c.* 1834–39 and 1859 to *c.* 1870. (He was in Europe from about 1839 to 1859.)

BROWN, M. E. D. An early and expert lithographer working in Philadelphia 1832–34. N. Currier worked for him for a short time. Was active as a painter until 1896.

BROWN, WILLIAM H. (1808–83). Silhouettist noted for his *Portrait Gallery of Distinguished Americans,* a collection of full length silhouettes published by E. B. and E. C. Kellogg in 1846. Fire destroyed most of the original issue. Reproductions were issued *c.* 1930.

BROWNE, WILLIAM R. Lithographer in N.Y.C., *c.* 1837.

BROWNSON, WILLIAM M. & CO. Lithographers in N.Y.C., 1840–51 or 56.

BRY, THEODORE DE (1528–1598). Flemish engraver and printer, *c.* 1580–90, who published the earliest prints of the North American Indians. His *Great Voyages* was published in 1590 and 1591.

BUCK, JAMES. Publisher in Boston, *c.* 1750. In 1749, he published the view of Yale College drawn and engraved by John Greenwood and Thomas Johnston, respectively.

BUELL, CHARLES. Lithographer in Buffalo, 1852–57, partner in Mooney & Buell, 1852, and Warren & Buell, 1856.

BUFFORD, JOHN H. A leading American lithographer working in N.Y.C., 1835–39, and Boston, 1840–1871 on. From 1841–51 he also worked with B. W. Thayer, and after about 1865, used name of J. H. Bufford & Son. He was a major lithographer with a large output covering almost every subject and aspect of lithography. Peters says he made "among the very best of whaling lithographs," and "his sense of the essential in the general field seems to have been second only to that of Currier and Ives."

BURGIS, WILLIAM. English-born artist and publisher of views and maps, active from 1716–31. Some of his most famous views are of Boston Harbor, *c.* 1720, New York Harbor, *c.* 1718 and Harvard College, *c.* 1726.

BURRILL, EDWARD. Lithographer in Boston, *c.* 1860.

BURT, CHARLES (1823–92). Engraver, born in Edinburgh, Scotland and active in N.Y.C., *c.* 1850. He engraved book illustrations and after 1850 he worked mainly in banknote engraving.

BURTON, CHARLES W. Artist and lithographer working in N.Y.C. *c.* 1849. Did views of N.Y.C. and Providence as well as other work for Sarony & Major, Pendleton, etc.

BUTLER, BENJAMIN F. Lithographer in New Orleans, 1841, N.Y.C., 1846–48 and San Francisco, 1852–59.

BUTTERSWORTH, JAMES E. (1817–1894). Marine, portrait and landscape painter. Known for his ship paintings which were lithographed by Currier and Ives.

BUTTRE, JOHN CHESTER (1821–1893). Publisher, wood engraver and painter in N.Y.C. in the mid- and late-1800's. Was a partner in the engraving firm, Rice & Buttre, in N.Y.C. from 1848–50. Published *The American Portrait Gallery,* N.Y.C., 1880–81.

CALLENDER, BENJAMIN (1773–1856). Engraver of maps in Boston until 1798 and then in Northfield, Mass. until 1856.

CALYO, NICOLINO V. (1798–1884). Painter, a native of Naples, came to the U.S. in the 1830's, worked in Baltimore up to 1835 and in N.Y.C. until about 1850. Some of his better known scenes are the aquatint views of New York's Great Fire, the views from the Mexican War and an overlook of the Connecticut River.

CAMERON, JOHN. Expert lithographer working in N.Y.C., 1848–62. Did many of the horses and comics for Currier and Ives. In business for himself between 1852–62. In

1859–60, was part of two short partnerships, Lawrence & Cameron and Cameron & Walsh. Even though he had his own business there are few prints issued by him. Most of his work was for Currier and Ives. Was especially known for horse prints.

CAMP, J. HENRY (1822–81). Lithographer, born in Prussia, came to America *c.* 1840 and settled in Philadelphia. Was partner in Brechemin & Camp, 1848, Camp & Koeler, 1848 and J. Henry Camp, 1849–59.

CAMPBELL, THOMAS (1790–1858). Artist and lithographer in Baltimore, 1833–35, in Cincinnati, 1840–44 and in Louisville, 1845.

CANOVA, DOMINICO. Artist and lithographer working in N.Y.C., *c.* 1825, partner in Canova & Farby, 1831–32.

CARTER, FRANKLIN N. Lithographer working in Boston, 1858–67.

CARTWRIGHT, T. English engraver, who engraved many of George Beck's American paintings, *c.* 1801–09.

CARWITHAM, JOHN. English engraver, active 1723–64. Noted views of Boston, New York and Philadelphia.

CARY, WILLIAM M. (1840–1922). Painter and illustrator of Indians and the West. Many of his illustrations were published in *Harper's Weekly* and other illustrated newspapers in the late 1860's and 70's.

CASILEAR, JOHN W. (1811–1893). Engraver and landscape painter who worked primarily in N.Y.C. He studied with Peter Maverick and A. B. Durand.

CASTLEMAN, FRANCIS. French lithographer, published *Vues de l'Amérique du Nord,* (Paris, 1842), after his visit to America, *c.* 1838–40.

CATESBY, MARK (*c.* 1679–1749). English naturalist, artist and etcher who was in America on two trips. The first, from 1712–19, was spent mostly in Virginia, and the second, from 1722–25, in Florida, the Carolinas, Georgia and the Bahamas. A result of these trips was the important books, *Natural History of Carolina, Florida, and the Bahama Islands,* (1731–43 in London), with over 100 plates etched by Catesby. See chapter on Nature Prints for additional details.

CATHERWOOD, FREDERICK (1799–1854). English painter who spent a good part of his time from 1836 to 1845 in N.Y.C., and travelled widely. He is particularly known for his illustrations of the Mayan ruins in Central America and for his view, *New York from Governor's Island,* 1846.

CATLIN, GEORGE (1796–1872). American artist best known for his paintings of the American Indian. Many are included in *North American Indian Portfolio,* first published in England in 1844 and then in N.Y.C. in 1845. Some plates were copied by Currier and Ives.

CHANDLER & CO. Lithographers in Boston, *c.* 1854–56. Partners were brothers Samuel W. and John G. Chandler. Did mainly illustrations for books.

CHARLES, WILLIAM (1776–1820). Etcher and engraver, born in Edinburgh. From 1806–14 he was in N.Y.C. and from 1814–20 he worked in Philadelphia. He illustrated novels and produced cartoons of the War of 1812.

CHENARD, ANTHONY F. Lithographer, *c.* 1831–*c.* 1839.

CHENEY, JOHN (1801–1885). Lithographer, engraver and painter from about 1820–57 in Hartford, N.Y.C., Philadelphia and Boston. Trained by Asaph Willard (Hartford, *c.* 1820) and in Pendleton's firm (Boston, 1826).

CHILDS, CEPHAS G. (1793–1871). Lithographer, engraver and publisher in Philadelphia between 1829 and 1845. Partnerships included Pendleton, Kearney & Childs, 1829 or '30, Childs & Inman, 1831–33 and Childs & Lehman, 1835–36. An expert lithographer who did many views, portraits and plates for J. & T. Doughty's *Cabinet of Natural History and American Rural Sports.*

CHILDS, JOHN. Artist and lithographer in N.Y.C., 1830–44 and Philadelphia, 1848–1862 on. Produced a large number of prints on many subjects.

CHILLAS, DAVID. Philadelphia lithographer from 1852–59.

CLARKE, THOMAS. Engraver in Philadelphia, 1798, and N.Y.C., 1799–1800.

CLAY, EDWARD W. (1799–1857). Lithographer, engraver and artist working in Philadelphia and N.Y.C., *c.* 1829–40. Did work for Baillie, Pendleton and others.

CLAY, H. M. Artist and publisher working in Buffalo, *c.* 1860.

CLAY & COMPANY, et al. Other lithographic firms include Clay & Richmond and Clay, Cosack & Co., working in Buffalo and Chicago, *c.* 1865–80.

CLEVELAND, J. A. (1811–after 1859). Artist, working mostly in N.Y.C. *c.* 1840–50, did marine paintings, lithographed by Weingartner's, among other things.

CLOVER, LEWIS P. Publisher of aquatints by William J. Bennett, 1834–38.

COLE, J. F. (1837–1892). Artist in Boston who did some work for Prang.

COLEN, J. H. Lithographer in N.Y.C., *c.* 1840–50.

COLLINS, JOHN. Lithographer and artist in Philadelphia, 1833–69.

COMBE, VOLTAIRE. Lithographer working in N.Y.C. for Currier and Ives, Major & Knapp and Sarony.

COMPTON, R. J. Lithographer and engraver working in Buffalo (1851–56), and St. Louis (1859–*c.* 1865).

CONY (CONEY), JOHN. (1655–1722). Silversmith and engraver working in Boston.

COOK, CHARLES. Lithographer and engraver working in Boston, 1843–54.

COOKE, ROBERT. Lithographer, in Boston in the 1830's, was chief draftsman for T. Moore.

COOKE, W. B. & CO. Publisher in San Francisco, *c.* 1850.

COOKE & LE COUNT. Lithographers in San Francisco, *c.* 1850.

COPLEY, JOHN SINGLETON (1738–1815). One of America's great painters (primarily Boston, Philadelphia and N.Y.C.) from 1753–74. In 1774 he moved to England and spent the remainder of his life in London. His stepfather and half-brother were Peter Pelham and Henry Pelham, respectively. Although primarily a painter, he made one mezzotint in 1753 in Boston, (a portrait of the Rev. William Welsteed).

CORAM, THOMAS (1757–1811). Engraver and artist born in England and working in Charleston, S.C., 1769–1811.

COX, THOMAS, JR. (*c.* 1831–?). Wood engraver in N.Y.C., 1850–60, partner in Richardson & Cox, who illustrated many books.

CREHEN, C. G. (1829–1891 on). Lithographer and artist born in Paris, worked in N.Y.C. 1848–60, and other cities. Worked for Nagel & Weingartner and others.

CREHEN, E. Lithographer working in Richmond, *c.* 1860.

CROOME, WILLIAM (1790–1860). Engraver, both wood and metal, helped organize Boston Bewick Co. in 1834. In Philadelphia in 1840's and 1850's. Partner, in 1841–42, of Croome, Meignelle & Minot, and also Croome & Minot.

CROSBY, CHARLES H. (1819–1896). Boston engraver, lithographer and printer from about 1847 to after 1860. Partner with Emery N. Moore in the engraving and lithographic firm, Moore and Crosby. 1852–56.

CULVER, PAGE & HOYNE. Lithographers in Chicago, *c.* 1862

CURRIER AND IVES. Lithographic firm in N.Y.C., called N. Currier, was started by Nathaniel Currier in 1833. In 1857, James M. Ives joined him, and the firm, which existed until 1907, was renamed Currier and Ives. Among the artists and lithographers they employed were James Buttersworth,

George Henry Durrie, Louis Maurer and Napoleon Sarony. See chapter on Currier and Ives.

CURRIER, CHARLES (1818–1887). Lithographer in N.Y.C., for many years associated with his brother Nathaniel Currier and his brother-in-law James Ives, partners in Currier & Ives. Also published prints in his own name. He developed an improved lithographic crayon.

CUSHMAN, GEORGE HEWITT (1814–1876). Artist and engraver working early in Hartford and Boston, and then in Philadelphia, *c.* 1842–*c.* 1862.

DACRE, HENRY (*c.* 1820–?). English-born lithographer, working in Philadelphia with P.S. Duval, 1847–50.

DANFORTH, MOSELEY ISAAC (1800–1862). Engraver and artist working in Hartford, *c.* 1818, New Haven, *c.* 1821, N.Y.C., 1825–27, London, 1827–39 and N.Y.C., 1839–62. Partner in Danforth, Underwood & Co., 1839–43, Danforth, Bald, Spencer & Hufty, 1843, Danforth, Spencer & Hufty, 1844–46, etc.

DARLEY, FELIX OCTAVIUS CARR (1822–1888). Artist and illustrator working in Philadelphia, 1842–48, N.Y.C., 1848–59, and Claymont, Del., 1859–88. Worked for Sarony, Major & Knapp, T. Sinclair, Knoedler and others.

D'AVIGNON, FRANCIS. Lithographer and artist, born in Russia of French parents, worked in N.Y.C., 1844–59 and Boston, 1859–60. Worker for C. Currier, P. S. Duval and others. Was in business for himself and in partnerships, D'Avignon & Hoffman, 1849, Brady, D'Avignon & Co., 1850 and D'Avignon & Brainerd, 1859–60. Did *Gallery of Illustrious Americans* in 1850 from daguerreotypes by Brady.

DAVIS, ALEXANDER J. (1803–1892). Architect and lithographer working in N.Y.C. in 1820's, started in lithography by W. S. Pendleton of Boston.

DAVIS, THEODORE RUSSELL (1840–94). Illustrator and artist-correspondent for *Harper's Weekly* c. 1861–84. After the war he traveled through the South and West illustrating those regions.

DAWKINS, HENRY. Engraver in N.Y.C. and Philadelphia, *c.* 1750's through '80's. For a short time he assisted James Turner. He engraved caricatures, bills of credit and book illustrations, and was particularly recognized for his *View of Nassau Hall* at Princeton College.

DELEVAN & COMPANY. Lithographers in N.Y.C., *c.* 1868.

DESOBRY, PROSPER. Lithographer, active in N.Y.C. from 1824–44, involved with Chanou and Desobry, 1824.

DEVEREUX, GEORGE T. (*c.* 1812–?). Wood engraver and artist in Boston 1837–44, and Philadelphia 1847–50, 1855–60. Partner in Boston firm of Devereux & Brown.

DEWING, FRANCIS. English copperplate engraver and printer, worked in Boston, 1716–23 before returning to England. Engraved and printed the *Bonner Map* of 1722, delineating Boston.

DODSON, RICHARD W. (1812–1867). Engraver and artist working in Philadelphia.

DONEY, THOMAS. French-born engraver of mezzotints, active in N.Y.C., 1844-49, and associated with the American Art Union. Did Bingham's *Jolly Flatboatmen.*

DOOLITTLE, AMOS (1754–1832). New Haven engraver in the late 1700's and early 1800's. In 1775 he engraved and published four scenes of the Battles of Lexington and Concord by Ralph Earl. He is also known for his engraving of Peter Lacour's drawing of Federal Hall in N.Y., during Washington's first inauguration.

DOOLITTLE, ISAAC. Lithographer in N.Y.C., partner in Barnet & Doolittle, *c.* 1821–22.

DORIVAL, JOHN. N.Y.C. lithographer, 1826–38.

DOUGHTY, J. &. T. Brothers John and Thomas Doughty, best known for 57 plates in *Cabinet of Natural History and American Rural Sports* published in Philadelphia in 1830, '32, '33, in association with Childs & Inman. T. Doughty (1793–1856), an important American artist and one of the founders of the *Hudson River School* of painting, did the lithographic plates for Vol. I of the three volume set.

DRAYTON, JOSEPH. Engraver and artist working in Philadelphia *c.* 1819–*c.* 1838. Joined the Wilkes expedition as an artist in 1838, and on conclusion in 1842, it is believed he went to Washington to work on the reports.

DREW, CLEMENT (1807 or 1810–*c.* 1889). Marine artist working in Boston 1841–60, and later in Gloucester, Mass. Did work for Bufford, also published lithographs.

DROUAILLET, GUSTAV. Lithographer in San Francisco in 1860 and after.

DUBOIS, GEORGE. German-born lithographer, active in Philadelphia *c.* 1850.

DUMCKE & KEIL. N.Y.C. lithographers, 1856–57, the partners were John D. Dumcke and Valentine Keil.

DUPRÉ, E. C. Lithographer born in France, working in St. Louis, 1837–40.

DURAND, ASHER BROWN (1796–1886). Engraver and later an important American painter. He was an apprentice of the engraver Peter Maverick (1812–17), and in 1823 completed the plate of Trumbull's *Declaration of Independence.* Among his students were Lewis P. Clover, Jr. and John W. Casilear. Around 1835 he switched from engraving to painting and was an early artist of the *Hudson River School* of landscape painting.

DURAND, CYRUS (1787–1868). Banknote engraver and inventor, brother of A. B. Durand, worked in N.Y.C., 1826–58. Established Cyrus Durand & Co., 1839–42 and Durand, Baldwin & Co., 1849–50.

DURRIE, GEORGE HENRY (1820–1863). Painter who worked primarily in New Haven *c.* 1840–63, known for his winter scenes, some of which were lithographed and published by Currier and Ives.

DUVAL, P. S. (et al.). One of America's leading lithographers, born in France, worked in Philadelphia, and worked for Childs & Inman, *c.* 1831–35. Then various partnerships included Lehman & Duval, 1835–37, Huddy & Duval, 1839–43, Rosenthal, Duval & Prang, 1856 and P. S. Duval & Son, 1858–79. After his retirement in 1879, firm became Duval & Hunter, until dissolved in 1893. His firm issued a large number of prints in almost all categories.

EARL, RALPH (1751–1801). Important American painter, active in Connecticut during the late 1700's, except during the Revolution, when he fled to England (1778–1785). His drawings of the Battles of Lexington and Concord were engraved by A. Doolittle.

EDDY, ISAAC (1777–1847). Engraver in Weathersfield, Vt. until 1826 and from 1826–47 in Troy, N.Y. where he manufactured ink.

EDMONDS, CHARLES (*c.* 1823–?). English wood engraver and artist, in N.Y.C., 1848–60. Partner in Bobbett & Edmonds, 1848–54.

EDWARDS, THOMAS. Lithographer, miniature and portrait painter, and silhouettist in Boston, 1822–56. Worked for the Senefelder Lithographic Co. in 1830.

EDWIN, DAVID (1776–1841). Stipple engraver, came to Philadelphia from England in 1797 and worked with Edward Savage until 1801. He engraved a few Gilbert Stuart portraits.

EHRGOTT, P. E. German lithographer worked in Cincinnati, 1850–70. Partnerships included Ehrgott & Forbriger, 1857–69 and Ehrgott & Krebs, 1870.

ELTON, ROBERT H. Active as a N.Y.C. engraver and lithographer, *c.* 1840–50.

EMMES, THOMAS. Engraver in Boston in late seventeenth and early eighteenth centuries. Did portrait of Increase Mather, *c.* 1701, the earliest known engraving on copper by an American.

ENDICOTT (et al.). One of the leading names in nineteenth-century American lithography, founded by George Endicott in Baltimore in 1828. In 1830, Endicott & Swett was formed and in 1831 moved to N.Y.C. Thereafter, they remained in N.Y.C., but with the following changes in name: Endicott & Swett, 1830–44; George Endicott, 1834–44; G & W Endicott (for William), 1845–48; William Endicott & Co., 1849–51; Endicott & Co. (William & Francis), 1852–86 and George (II) Endicott, 1887–92. Their output was very large in almost all categories. Today they are especially well known for their steamship prints.

ENSIGN, EDWARD. Labeled a lithographer by Peters and a map and book publisher by the N.Y.C. directories, 1841–60. Worked with Timothy Ensign, 1841–48, Ensign & Thayer, 1849–51 and Ensign, Bridgman & Fanning, from 1854.

EYTINGE, CLARENCE. Lithographer in N.Y.C., 1853–58.

EYTINGE, ROBERT. Lithographer in N.Y.C., 1853–56.

EYTINGE, SOLOMON (1833–1905). Artist and illustrator on staff of *Harper's Weekly* for many years.

FABRONIOUS, DOMINIQUE C. Lithographer and artist, born in Belgium, worked in Philadelphia *c.* 1855, Cincinnati, *c.* 1859, Boston, 1861–64 and N.Y.C., 1865–72.

FAIRMAN, GIDEON (1774–1827). Banknote engraver and artist in Albany and then Philadelphia after 1810.

FARNY, HENRY F. (1847–1916). Artist and illustrator especially of Indians and the West. Supplied many illustrations for *Harper's Weekly, Leslie's Weekly,* and in the late 1870's, for McGuffey's readers.

FAY, AUGUSTUS. Wood engraver and lithographer in N.YC., 1848–60, partner of Alfred Swinton, 1852–53.

FENDERICH, CHARLES. Artist and lithographer, born in Germany, worked in Philadelphia, 1833–34 with John C. Wild as Fenderich & Wild. Did work for Lehman & Duval, 1835–37, went to Washington, D.C. and opened Lithographic Repository, 1837–43, where he did many political portraits. He was in San Francisco, *c.* 1850–70.

FIELD, ROBERT (*c.* 1769–1819). Engraver and artist, born in England, worked in Philadelphia, 1794–1800, Washington, D.C., 1800–05, Boston, 1805–08, then Halifax, N.S. until 1816 and the island of Jamaica, 1816–19.

FILMER, JOHN. Wood engraver in Boston, *c.* 1860, partner in Andrew & Filmer.

FIRKS, HENRY. Artist, in San Francisco in 1849, painted view of San Francisco published by Endicott.

FLEETWOOD, ANTHONY, Lithographer, born in England, *c.* 1800, worked in N.Y.C., 1827–47 and Cincinnati, 1847–60.

FORBES, WILLIAM H. & CO. Lithographer working in Boston, *c.* 1867.

FORBRIGER, ADOLF. Lithographer, in Cincinnati, 1858–60 and partner in Ehrgott & Forbriger.

FOREMAN, EDGAR W. Lithographer, in N.Y.C., 1846–48, put out view of N.Y.C. in 1848 with Eliphalet M. Brown, Jr.

FORSYTH, JOHN. Architect and lithographic draftsman in N.Y.C. from 1845–49.

FOSTER, JOHN (1648–1681). Boston printer and maker of woodcuts, active in the 1670's. His signed woodcut print of the Rev. Richard Mather is considered the first print made in America.

FRANCIS, JOHN F. (1808–1886). Portrait and important still-life painter in Philadelphia. In 1838, P. S. Duval issued print, *Joseph Ritner,* after painting by Francis.

FREDERICKS, ALFRED. Artist and illustrator active in N.Y.C., 1853–81.

FRENZENY, PAUL. French-born illustrator for *Harper's Weekly* beginning in 1868. Commissioned by them in 1873 to make sketches on an expedition from N.Y.C. to San Francisco with fellow artist Jules Tavernier.

FRITSCH, F. J. Lithographer in N.Y.C., 1843–44, known for his military prints.

FUCHS, F. & THEO. Lithographers in Philadelphia, 1856–59.

GALLAUDET, ELISHA (*c.* 1730–1805). Engraver working in N.Y.C.

GIBSON & CO. Engravers and lithographers in Cincinnati, 1851–60. Firm included George, John, Robert and Stephen Gibson.

GIFFORD, CHARLES B. Artist and lithographer working in San Francisco in the 1860's and 70's.

GIFFORD, ROBERT SWAIN (1840–1905). Painter of landscapes and etcher working Boston, New Bedford, Mass. and N.Y.C. Artist for two whaling lithographs for Endicott.

GIHON, WILLIAM B. Wood engraver in Philadelphia, 1845–60, partner in Gilbert & Gihon, 1846–50's.

GILBERT, REUBEN S. Wood engraver in Philadelphia, *c.* 1830–50, partner in Gilbert & Gihon, 1846–1850's.

GILDEMEISTER, CHARLES (1820–69). German-born artist and lithographer, worked in N.Y.C., 1850-58.

GILES, J. L. Lithographer in N.Y.C., *c.* 1860–70.

GIMBREDE, THOMAS (1781–1832). Engraver and artist, born in France, worked in N.Y.C., 1802–19, except for brief stay in Baltimore in 1810. Was drawing master at West Point, 1819–32.

GOBRECHT, CHRISTIAN (1785–1844). Engraver, die-sinker and medallist, worked in Lancaster, Pa. *c.* 1800 Baltimore, to 1811 and Philadelphia, 1811–44. Was engraver at U.S. Mint, 1834–44.

GOODMAN, CHARLES (1796–1835). Engraver in Philadelphia, *c.* 1816–22, when he became a lawyer. Partner in Goodman & Piggot, 1817–22.

GOUPIL & CO. New York branch of famous French publishers associated with M. Knoedler. Published engravings and lithographs in N.Y.C., 1852–57.

GRAHAM, CHARLES (1852–1911). Staff-artist for Harper Bros. *c.* 1877–92, then free-lance artist. Supplied many city views and western subjects to *Harper's Weekly.*

GRAHAM, CURTIS B. (1814–90). Lithographer in N.Y.C., 1835–36 with brother John R. Graham, as Graham & Price, 1836 and as Curtis B. Graham, 1836–41 in N.Y.C. and 1842 in Washington, D.C.

GRAHAM, GEORGE. Engraver in Philadelphia, *c.* 1797, N.Y.C., *c.* 1804, Boston, *c.* 1812 and Philadelphia, *c.* 1813.

GRATACAP, GEORGE G. Lithographer in N.Y.C., 1845–46 and with Kellogg & Co. in Hartford, 1848.

GREEN (or GREENE), WILLIAM. Lithographer in N.Y.C., New Orleans, Albany, N.Y. and Hartford, 1836–56. Probably partner in Greene & Fishbourne, N.Y.C., 1836, Greene & McGowran, N.Y.C., 1837, Green & Fishbourne, New Orleans, 1838–41 and Case & Green, Hartford, 1849–52.

GREENOUGH, FREDERICK W. A publisher of part of McKenney & Hall's *History of the Indian Tribes of North America,* with plates lithographed by J. T. Bowen.

GRIDLEY, ENOCH G. Engraver, worked in N.Y.C., 1803–04 and Philadelphia, *c.* 1804–18.

GROZELIER, LEOPOLD (1830–1865). Artist and lithographer, born in France, worked in N.Y.C., 1852 and Boston, 1854–65.

HAAS, P. Lithographer and publisher in Washington, D.C., 1837–45.

HAINES, WILLIAM (1778–1848). Engraver and artist, born in England, worked in Philadelphia, 1802–09, then returned to England.

HALL, JOHN H. Lithographer and wood engraver, worked mostly in Albany, 1826–48. Did some work in Lancaster, Mass., 1830 and in Boston, 1834.

HALL & MOONEY. Lithographers and engravers in Buffalo, 1839–50, as John P. Hall and Lawrence Mooney. After 1850, became Mooney & Buell and from 1853–63, Lawrence Mooney.

HALPIN, FREDERICK W. (1805–1880). Engraver, born in England, worked in N.Y.C., *c.* 1842–60 and after.

HAMLIN, WILLIAM (1772–1869). Engraver in Providence, R.I., *c.* 1795–1809, when he changed professions.

HARRIS, JOHN. English engraver of the New York (1719) and Boston (1722) views by William Burgis.

HART, CHARLES. Lithographer in N.Y.C., *c.* 1862–*c.* 1868.

HART, JOHN. Lithographer in Philadelphia, 1854–57.

HARTWELL, ALONZO (1805–1873). Artist and engraver, active in Boston and other areas of Mass. as an engraver, *c.* 1826–51. After 1851, he became a portrait artist and seems to have given up engraving.

HARVEY, GEORGE (*c.* 1800–*c.* 1878). Painter, native of England, worked in America (primarily the West, N.Y.C., and Boston), from *c.* 1820–42. Four of his watercolor scenes, *Atmospheric Views of North America,* were engraved in aquatint by William J. Bennett and published in London in 1841 as the *Primitive Forest in America, at the Four Seasons of the Year.*

HASKELL & ALLEN. An important lithographic house in Boston, 1871–*c.* 75, that produced prints in competition with Currier and Ives. A reasonably large number of titles were produced, but quality is uneven. Known for their horse prints.

HATCH & CO. Lithographers in N.Y.C., 1855–73, then N.Y.C. and Boston, 1875, George W. Hatch, Jr. Also partner in Hatch and Severin, 1853, in N.Y.C.

HATCH, GEORGE W. (1805–1867). Engraver and artist, pupil of A. B. Durand, worked in Albany and N.Y.C. A founder of the American Bank Note Co.

HAUGG, LOUIS. Lithographer in Philadelphia, 1856–94.

HAVELL, ROBERT JR. (1793–1878). English-born engraver and painter. From 1827–38, he engraved all but ten of the plates for the *Birds of America* by Audubon. Came to America in 1839 and settled in New York, where he painted landscapes and engraved aquatint scenes of Boston, New York and other cities.

HAYWOOD, GEORGE. English lithographer, in N.Y.C., 1834–72.

HEAP, GEORGE. Surveyor, known for his drawing of Philadelphia (the "Scull-Heap" view) which was engraved and published in London, 1754.

HENNESSY, WILLIAM JOHN (1839–1917). Artist and illustrator, born in Ireland, worked in N.Y.C. and, after 1870, in Europe.

HEPPENHEIMER, FREDERICK. Lithographer in N.Y.C., 1851–76. Partnerships were Hartman & Heppenheimer, 1851 and Heppenheimer & Maurer (Louis Maurer), 1872–84.

HERLINE, EDWARD. German lithographer, in Philadelphia 1850–60 and '70. Partner in Herline & Hensel.

HERRICK, HENRY W. (1824–?). Wood engraver and artist, worked in Concord and Hopkinton, N.H., *c.* 1848, and then N.Y.C., 1848–65. Returned to New Hampshire in 1865 and died there after 1904.

HILL, JAMES. Engraver in Charlestown, Mass., *c.* 1803.

HILL, JOHN (1770–1850). English engraver and artist, active in New York, 1819–50. Engraved the plates for the *Picturesque Views of American Scenery* by Joshua Shaw (Phila. *c.* 1820) and those for William Guy Wall's *Hudson River Portfolio* (N.Y., 1820–25). Seventeen aquatints by Hill appeared in Lucas' *Progressive Drawing Book* (Baltimore, *c.* 1827).

HILL, JOHN WILLIAM (1812–79). Son of John Hill, the engraver, primarily a painter, active in

New York in mid 1800's. He led the "naturalism" trend of painting in America. Many of his views became the basis of engravings and lithographs executed by others.

HILL, SAMUEL. Boston engraver and copperplate printer, active from 1789–1803. Did engravings for the *Massachusetts Magazine,* 1789–96.

HILLER, JOSEPH SR. (1748–1814). Engraver and silversmith working in Salem and Lancaster, Mass. Engraved portraits of John Hancock and George and Martha Washington.

HINSHELWOOD, ROBERT (*c.* 1812–*c.* 1875). Engraver and artist, born in Scotland, worked in N.Y.C., *c.* 1835-*c.* 1875.

HITCHCOCK, DEWITT C. Wood engraver and illustrator, active 1845–79. In Boston, 1847–50, and '52, Cincinnati, 1850–51 and N.Y.C., 1858–79.

HOEN, AUGUST. German lithographer who settled in Baltimore. Worked for Edward Weber, an uncle, as lithographer in 1835. Became A. Hoen & Co. about 1850, after he took over business. Continued on into the twentieth century with plants in Baltimore and Richmond.

HOFF, HENRY. Lithographer working in N.Y.C., 1850–53.

HOFFY, ALFRED M. Lithographer, artist and publisher, active in N.Y.C., 1835–38 and worked in Philadelphia, *c.* 1840–*c.* 1860. Illustrated for Huddy & Duval's *U.S. Military Magazine.* In 1860, published his *North American Pomologist.*

HOLLAND, THOMAS R. (*c.* 1816–?). Boston engraver, 1839–60 and after. Started the firms T. R. Holland & Co. in 1855 and Holland & Stinson in 1856.

HOMER, WINSLOW (1836–1910). One of the greatest American artists. Started as lithographer's apprentice for J. H. Bufford in Boston in 1855, designing sheet music covers. From 1857–73, he was illustrator for *Ballou's Pictorial* in Boston and later *Harper's Weekly* in N.Y.C. Many wood engravings after Homer appear in these and other publications. He also did a small amount of lithographic work for Prang about 1863. After 1873 he devoted himself to painting.

HOOGLAND, WILLIAM (*c.* 1795–1832). Line and stipple engraver, active in N.Y.C., 1814–21, *c.* 1828–32 and in Boston, 1821-*c.* 1828. Instructed John Cheney and Joseph Andrews. Engraved many scenes for *The Naval Monument,* published by Abel Bowen in Boston, 1816.

HOPPIN, AUGUSTUS (1828–1896). Illustrator for magazine and book publishers.

HORNOR, THOMAS. English engraver, etcher and watercolor artist, who worked in N.Y.C. *c.* 1830's. Around 1834, he drew and etched *Broadway, New York,* which was aquatinted by John Hill.

HUDDY & DUVAL. William M. Huddy and Peter S. Duval, lithographers in Philadelphia, 1839–1841. Published *The United States Military Magazine* with plates of military costume.

HUMPHREYS, WILLIAM (1794–1865). Engraver, Born in Ireland, worked in Philadelphia, *c.* 1814-27, England, 1827–43 and Philadelphia 1843–45.

HURD, NATHANIEL (1729–1777). Silversmith and engraver, worked in Boston.

IMBERT, ANTHONY. Marine painter and pioneer lithographer in N.Y.C., *c.* 1825–35. Made plates for the illustrations of Colden's *Erie Canal Memoir.* Later did prints of scenes of N.Y.C. after A. J. Davis, *c.* 1827.

INGER, CHRISTIAN. Lithographer in Philadelphia, *c.* 1858.

INMAN, HENRY (1801–46). Important American painter who also did portraits on stone. Partner in lithographic firm of Childs & Inman.

JENKINS & COLBURN. Daniel S. Jenkins and Luke

Colburn, lithographers in Boston, 1836–40.

JENNYS, RICHARD. Engraver and artist working in Boston, *c.* 1766–*c.* 1771, Charleston, S.C., 1783–84 and New Milford, Conn., *c.* 1792–99.

JEVNE & ALMINI. Major Chicago lithographic firm, started *c.* 1866. Published *Chicago Illustrated, 1830.*

JOHNSON, EASTMAN (1824–1906). Major American painter. Did some work reproduced by lithography, the most notable being *Husking,* produced by Currier and Ives.

JOHNSTON, DAVID CLAYPOOL (1799–1865). Illustrator, lithographer and engraver working in Philadelphia and Boston. Known for his caricatures.

JOHNSTON, THOMAS (1708–1767). Painter and engraver, worked in Boston, *c.* 1727 to his death. Engraved the *Prospect of Yale College,* 1749, drawn by John Greenwood, a student of Johnston, and published by James Buck. Other engravings include *A View of Quebec* (1759), *The Battle Fought near Lake George* (1755), drawn by S. Blodget, published by T. Jefferys and *Plan of Boston,* drawn by W. Burgis.

JONES, ALFRED (1819–1900). English-born engraver, worked in N.Y.C. Engraved *Farmers Nooning* in 1836.

JONES, EDWARD. Lithographer in N.Y.C., 1844–49. Partnerships include Jones & Palmer, 1844 and Jones & Newman, 1847–48.

JUSTH, QUIROT & CO. Lithographers in San Francisco, *c.* 1851. Published views of California.

KARST, JOHN (1836–1922). Wood engraver, born in Germany, came to America as an infant. Book illustrator as early as 1855.

KEARNEY, FRANCIS (1785–1837). Engraver and lithographer, worked in N.Y.C. *c.* 1800–10 Philadelphia 1810–33. Studied under Peter Maverick and was a member of Tanner. Kearney & Tiebout, Tanner, Vallance, Kearney & Co and Pendleton, Kearney & Childs, 1829–30.

KEENAN, WILLIAM (*c.* 1810–?). Engraver and lithographer in Charleston, S.C., *c.* 1828, 1835–55, and Philadelphia 1830-33.

KELLOGGS. The Kellogg family had a very large lithographic business centered in Hartford but with offices or an agent in N.Y.C. and Buffalo. They came closest to rivaling Currier and Ives in the quantity and character of their work. In various partnerships and with various members of the family participating, they sold prints from *c.* 1830–75. The main partnerships and associations were: D. W. Kellogg & Co., Hartford, 1830–42; E. B. & E. C. Kellogg, Hartford, and N.Y.C., 1842–48; Kelloggs & Comstock, Hartford and N.Y.C., 1848–50; E. B. & E. C. Kellogg, worked independently, 1850–55; E. B. & E. C. Kellogg, Hartford and N.Y.C., 1855–67; Kellogg & Bulkeley, Hartford, 1867–75 on and Kellogg & Thayer, N.Y.C. agent, 1846-47.

KELLY, JOHN & SONS. Publishers in Philadelphia and N.Y.C., *c.* 1866.

KELLY, THOMAS (*c.* 1795-*c.* 1841). Engraver, born in Ireland, worked in Boston, Philadelphia and N.Y.C. in 1830's.

KELLY, THOMAS. Publisher and printer of lithographs and engravings in N.Y.C., *c.* 1870. Many of his prints are available but little is known of T. Kelly.

KENNEDY & LUCAS. Philadelphia lithographers, 1829–35, partners were David Kennedy and William B. Lucas.

KETTERLINUS, EUGENE. Philadelphia lithographer active from 1843–76. The firm he established still existed in 1931.

KIDDER, JAMES. Boston engraver, artist and aquatintist, *c.* 1813–*c.* 1840. Worked for Abel Bowen, *c.* 1823. Produced views of Boston, White Mountains, etc.

KILBOURNE, SAMUEL A. (1836–1881). Fish and landscape painter known for his fish prints in *Game Fishes of the United States,* published in 1879.

KILBURN, SAMUEL S. JR. Wood engraver in Boston, studied under Abel Bowen in 1830's. Partner in Kilburn & Mallory, 1852–65.

KIMMEL, CHRISTOPHER. German-born lithographer, engraver and printer, worked in N.Y.C., 1850–76. Partner in the firms of Capewell & Kimmel, 1853–60, Kimmel & Forster and Kimmel & Voight.

KINNERSLEY, AUGUSTUS F. Wood engraver working in N.Y.C., 1845–51.

KLAUPRECH & MENZEL. Cincinnati lithographic firm, active from 1840–59. Partners were Emil Klauprech and Adolphus Menzel. Known especially for Ohio scenes.

KNAPP, JOSEPH F. Artist and lithographer in N.Y.C. before joining Sarony & Major in 1856 which then became Sarony, Major & Knapp until 1867. After Sarony's retirement in 1867, firm continued as Major & Knapp until 1871.

KNEASS, WILLIAM (1780–1840). Engraver in Philadelphia, 1804–40, partner in Kneass & Delleher and Kneass, Young & Co. Engraver and die sinker at the U.S. Mint, 1824–40.

KNIRSCH, OTTO. German-born lithographer, one of Currier and Ives' most talented employees. After 1858, worked in Philadelphia.

KOELLNER, AUGUST (1813–*c.* 1878). Lithographer and painter, mainly in Philadelphia, *c.* 1840–70. Worked on the *U.S. Military Magazine* for Huddy & Duval. Later, made 54 watercolors of American cities which were lithographed by Deroy, (Paris) and published as *Views of American Cities,* by Goupil, Vibert in 1848–51. Partner in Koellner, Camp & Co., 1851.

KRAMER, PETER (1823–1907). Bavarian-born lithographer and painter, active in Philadelphia, 1848–58. Worked for P. S. Duval and the Rosenthals. Returned to Germany and later came to N.Y.C., where he stayed until his death.

KRAMP, WILLIAM C. Lithographer, worked in N.Y.C., 1836–42.

KRIMMEL, JOHN LEWIS (1789–1821). Artist, native of Germany, came to Philadelphia in 1810. Many of his paintings were lithographed, including *Procession of Victuallers of Philadelphia.*

KUCHEL & DRESEL. Lithographers in San Francisco. 1853–65. Partners were Charles C. Kuchel and Emil Dresel. Known for the *Pacific Views.* 1855–60, of California and Oregon towns.

KURZ & ALLISON. Louis Kurz (1833–1921), an Austrian, and Alexander Allison started partnerships in Chicago in 1880 and continued at least until 1899. Known for chromolithographic Civil War battle scenes. Kurz did earlier work in Milwaukee in 1850's with Henry Seifert. He also founded Chicago Lithographic Co., 1863–71, and in the 1870's headed the American Oleograph Co. in Milwaukee.

LANE & SCOTT. Lithographers in Boston, *c.* 1840–47. Partners were Fitz Hugh Lane, later prominent American marine painter, and John W. A. Scott.

LANGRIDGE, JAMES L. (*c.* 1837–?). Wood engraver, born in England, worked in N.Y.C., 1850–*c.* 1880.

LAWSON, ALEXANDER (1773–1846). Engraver, born in Scotland, worked in Philadelphia 1794–1846. Worked on plates for Alexander Wilson's *American Ornithology* and its supplement by C. L. Bonaparte.

LEEFE, GEORGE E. B. Lithographer in N.Y.C., 1849–58, partner in Risso & Leefe, 1849–50, and Michelin & Leefe, 1852–53.

LEHMAN, GEORGE (*c.* 1800–1870). Artist, lithographer and engraver, worked in Philadelphia. Started lithography in 1831. Partner with C. G. Childs, 1835, Lehman & Duval, 1835–37 and Lehman & Baldwin.

LEIGHTON, SCOTT. Painted horses for Currier and Ives.

LENEY, WILLIAM S. (1769–1831). English-born engraver, worked in N.Y.C., 1805–20, when he retired to a farm in Montreal.

LEONHARDT, THEODORE (1818–1877). Lithographer and engraver, born in Saxony, active primarily in Philadelphia, 1850–77.

Worked for Traubel, Schnabel & Finkeldy, then started his own business.

LEWIS, GEORGE W. N.Y.C. lithographer, 1841–60, and a partner of the firm Lewis & Brown from 1844–48.

LEWIS, HENRY. (1819–1904) European-born artist who in (1846–48) traveled up and down the Mississippi sketching. He returned to Europe in 1850 where he published *Das Illustrierte Mississippithal* Düsseldorf, 1854.

LEWIS, JAMES OTTO (1799–1858). Painter, engraver. Painted many portraits of Indians while attending treaty conferences in Wisconsin and Indiana during the 1820's which were published in Philadelphia in 1835 in *The Aboriginal Port-Folio.* This publication was overshadowed by the more successful ones of Catlin and McKenney and Hall.

LONGACRE, JAMES B. (1794–1869). Line and stipple engraver and artist working in Philadelphia *c.* 1819–1844, in his own business and in 1844–69 as chief engraver at the U.S. Mint. Noted for portrait of Andrew Jackson after Sully, engravings for Sanderson's *Biography of the Signers of the Declaration of Independence,* 1820 and in 1834–39 published the *National Portrait Gallery of Distinguished Americans.*

LOSSING, BENSON JOHN (1813–1891). Wood engraver in N.Y.C., 1839–69 and after. Partner in Lossing & Barritt, 1847–69. Noted for work on books of American history and biography.

MCENTEE, JERVIS (1828–1891). Landscape artist in New York from 1858. Member of "Hudson River School."

MCFARLANE, D. Painter of ships, active during 1850's and 60's. Currier and Ives made lithographs of some of his paintings. Little is known of this important marine artist. Some authorities list him as American and others as English.

MCLELLAN, DAVID and JAMES. Lithographers, born in Scotland, worked in N.Y.C., 1851–67.

MCLENAN, JOHN (1827–1866). Illustrator, worked in N.Y.C., 1850–66, mainly on book illustrations.

MAGEE, JOHN L. Lithographer in N.Y.C., 1844–47 and in Philadelphia, 1850–67. Did cartoons and also what Peters calls the best baseball print.

MAGNUS, CHARLES. Lithographer in N.Y.C. and Washington, D.C., *c.* 1854–*c.* 1877.

MAJOR, HENRY B. Lithographer in N.Y.C. 1844–54 of Sarony & Major.

MANOUVRIER, JULES. New Orleans lithographer, 1841–70. Partner of P. Snell (Manouvrier & Snell) 1841–53 and Dionis (or Dennis) Simon, after 1860.

MARSDEN, THEODORE. Artist in N.Y.C., *c.* 1857–67. Did sporting pictures for Goupil, Bufford and others.

MARSH, HENRY. Wood engraver in Boston, 1848–after 1860. Partner in Hitchcock & Marsh, 1848.

MASON, ABRAHAM JOHN (1794–?). Wood engraver, born in London, worked in N.Y.C., 1829–39. Published treatise on wood engraving and was Professor of Wood Engraving at the National Academy.

MATHEWS, ALFRED E. (1831–1874). Painter, topographical artist and lithographer, born in England, active in mid-1800's. Produced Civil War sketches and later lithographs of Colorado, Montana, Rocky Mountains and other Western scenes.

MAURER, LOUIS (1832–1932). German-born lithographer and artist, came to N.Y.C., where he became one of Currier and Ives' principal lithographers, 1851–*c.* 1860. Worked for Major & Knapp, *c.* 1860–61. Also did freelance work and from 1872–84 was a partner in Maurer & Heppenheimer.

THE MAVERICKS. A family of engravers and later lithographers and engravers in and about N.Y.C. with over a dozen active members. Peter Rushton Maverick (1755–1811) was an engraver and silversmith. He taught engraving to his sons Peter, Andrew and

Samuel. Peter (1780–1831) was the partner in an engraving business with A. B. Durand 1817–20. He, his son Peter Jr., and his four daughters were also lithographers who worked in N.Y.C., 1820–46.

MAYER, FERDINAND. German-born lithographer, worked in N.Y.C., *c.* 1845–*c.* 1877. Partner in Nagel & Mayer, 1846 and Mayer & Korff, 1849–51. Firm later called Ferdinand Mayer & Sons, 1854–*c.* 1877.

MAYER, JULIUS. Lithographer in Boston, 1857–72. Partner in Prang & Mayer, 1857–60, Mayer & Stetfield, 1861–62 and J. Mayer & Co., 1863–72.

MAYER, MERKEL & OTTOMAN. Lithographers in N.Y.C., *c.* 1869.

MEADOWS, CHRISTIAN. English-born engraver, immigrated to America *c.* 1830 and worked in Boston *c.* 1839–49. While employed by the printer and engraver W. W. Wilson, in Boston, he was arrested and convicted of counterfeiting. While in prison he engraved his most noted work, a view of Dartmouth College, 1851. After his release, he worked at least until 1859.

MEGAREY, HENRY J. Publisher in N.Y.C. Works include W. G. Wall's *Hudson River Portfolio,* 1821–25 and a series of three views by W. J. Bennett, *c.* 1834.

MESIER, EDWARD S. Lithographer in N.Y.C., 1832–51.

MICHELIN, FRANCIS. Lithographer in Boston, 1840–41, as partner of Sharp, Michelin & Co. In N.Y.C. from 1844–58. Other partnerships include Michelin & Creifield, 1844, Michelin & Cuipers, 1844–45, Michelin & Leefe, 1852–53, Michelin & Shattuck, 1853–54 and Boell & Michelin, 1856–58.

MIDDLETON, ELIJAH C. Partner in various Cincinnati engraving, lithographic and printing houses, including Middleton, Wallace & Co., 1855–58 and Middleton, Strobridge & Co., 1859–64.

MILBERT, JACQUES G. (1766–1840). French artist. In America 1815–23 to make drawings for *A Series of Picturesque Views in North America,* 1825, and *Itinéraire Pittoresque du Fleuve Hudson et des Parties Laterales,* 1828–29. Both were lithographed in Paris.

MÖLLHAUSEN, HEINRICH BALDUIN (1825–1905). German artist and writer. During second of his three trips to this country, he accompanied the government railroad survey expedition along the 35th parallel and was the principal illustrator for the report.

MOORE, THOMAS. English lithographer, worked in Boston, 1835–41. Successor to Pendleton.

MORSE, NATHANIEL (1688–1748). Silversmith and engraver in Boston.

MORSE, W. H. Wood engraver, active *c.* 1851–1879.

MOUNT, WILLIAM SIDNEY (1807–1868). One of America's important painters. Known especially for his genre paintings, many of which were made into lithographs and engravings.

MULLIKEN, JONATHAN (1746–1782). Engraver and clockmaker in Boston area. Made facsimile of Paul Revere's Boston Massacre print in 1782.

NAGEL, WEINGA(E)RTNER, et al. Lithographers in N.Y.C. and San Francisco. Partnerships included Louis Nagel (alone), 1844–45; Nagel & Mayer, 1846; Nagel & Weingartner, 1849–56; Nagel & Lewis, *c.* 1857, all in N.Y.C. Then, Louis Nagel (alone), *c.* 1857–62 and Nagel, Fishbourne & Kuchel, *c.* 1863, in San Francisco.

NAGLE, JAMES (*c.* 1769–1822). Engraver in Philadelphia, *c.* 1819–22.

NAHL BROTHERS. H. W. A. Nahl and Charles C. Nahl, German-born half-brothers, artists and lithographers, worked in San Francisco, *c.* 1855–70 and after.

NAST, THOMAS (1840–1902). Cartoonist and illustrator, born in Germany, came to America as a child. Worked in N.Y.C. for *Frank Leslie's Illustrated Newspaper, c.* 1855, and

New York Illustrated News, 1859. Joined *Harper's Weekly* in 1862 and remained with them almost twenty-five years during which time he turned to political cartoons and exposed the Tweed Ring. After leaving Harper's he published his own paper, *Nast's Weekly,* 1892–93.

NEAGLE, JOHN B. (*c.* 1796–1866). English-born engraver, worked in Philadelphia, *c.* 1815–66.

NEBEL, CARL. Artist for D. Appleton's battle scenes of the Mexican War, 1851.

NEW ENGLAND LITHOGRAPHIC STEAM PRINTING CO. Boston company from 1867–72 on, associated with Bufford.

NEWSAM, ALBERT (1809–1864). Artist, lithographer and engraver in Philadelphia, 1827–59. Worked for Childs and Duval.

NORMAN, JOHN (*c.* 1748–1817). English-born engraver, worked first in Philadelphia, *c.* 1774–80, then in Boston. Engraved portraits, landscapes and buildings for various publishers, including portraits of the heroes of the Revolution. Did engraving of George Washington in 1779.

OKEY, SAMUEL. London-born mezzotint engraver, worked in Newport, R.I., 1773–80. First engraver in America to reproduce old master paintings.

ONKEN, OTTO. German-born lithographer, worked in Cincinnati, *c.* 1848–60.

ORR, JOHN WILLIAM (1815–87). Wood engraver, born in Ireland, came to America as an infant. Worked in Buffalo and Albany, *c.* 1840–44 and in N.Y.C., 1844–*c.* 1880. Worked with Nathaniel Orr, probably his brother, as J. W. and N. Orr, 1844–46.

OTIS, BASS (1784–1861). Artist and lithographer. Lived and worked at various times in Boston, N.Y.C. and Philadelphia. Credited with producing the first lithograph in America in 1818, and in 1819 made a lithograph for the *Analectic Magazine,* of a mill scene. The latter is often called America's first lithograph.

PALMER, F. and S. Fanny and Seymour Palmer, lithographers and artists in N.Y.C., 1846–49. The same F. Palmer who later worked for Currier and Ives.

PALMER, FANNY (FRANCES FLORA BOND), (*c.* 1812–1876). Leading artist working for Currier and Ives. See chapter on Currier and Ives.

PAPPRILL, HENRY. Aquatint engraver of two views of N.Y.C., 1846 and 1848.

PARADISE, JOHN W. (1809–1862). Engraver and artist, student of A. B. Durand, worked in N.Y.C., 1828–62.

PARKYNS, GEORGE ISHAM (*c.* 1750-*c.* 1820). English-born artist and aquatint engraver who completed four of a projected series of twenty views of America, *c.* 1797, including Mt. Vernon, Annapolis and two views of Washington.

PARSONS, CHARLES (1821–1910). English-born artist and lithographer, worked in N.Y.C. for Endicott & Co., *c.* 1833-*c.* 1861. During this period he also did many lithographs for Currier and Ives. After 1863 he became head of art department of Harper Bros.

PEALE, CHARLES WILLSON (1741–1827). One of America's important artists, who also did a few mezzotint portraits, including one of *His Excellency George Washington.*

PEALE, REMBRANDT (1778–1860). One of America's great painters. Did some lithographic work *c.* 1826–*c.* 1833.

PEALE, TITIAN RAMSAY (1799–1885) Illustrator of works on natural history. Served as artist-naturalist on several western expeditions. He drew some of the birds for C. L. Bonaparte's supplement to Wilson's *Ornithology.*

PEASE, JOSEPH I. (1809–1883). Engraver and artist, worked in New Haven, *c.* 1832, Albany, 1834 and Philadelphia, 1835–50. Later lived in Stockbridge, Mass. and Salisbury, Conn.

PELHAM, HENRY (1749–1806). Artist and engraver, youngest son of Peter Pelham. Did prototype of *Boston Massacre* and accused Paul Revere of copying the design. A Loyalist, he left America in 1776 and never returned.

PELHAM, PETER (*c.* 1697–1751). Mezzotint engraver, born in London, migrated to America in 1727 and settled in Boston, where he did a portrait of Cotton Mather the same year. Worked in Newport, 1734–37 and again in Boston, 1737–51. He was the earliest mezzotint engraver in America.

PENDLETONS. In 1825, John B. Pendleton (1798–1866) started the first commercially successful lithographic business in America. Working in Boston, he was joined in 1826 by his brother, William S. (1795–1879). The two worked together until 1828 or '29 when John went to Philadelphia as a partner of Pendleton, Kearney & Childs. After about a year, John moved to N.Y.C. and was in business there from 1829–34. William continued the business in Boston until 1836. N. Currier was an apprentice to the Pendletons in Boston and subsequently bought out John's business in N.Y.C. Much of the Pendletons' work was special commissions, such as the maps they lithographed for many Massachusetts communities.

PILLINER, FREDERICK J. Lithographer and wood engraver in Boston 1853–54 as partner in Schenck & Pilliner, and then in Philadelphia, 1856–61.

POPE, ALEXANDER, JR. Known for prints in *Celebrated Dogs of America,* published by Cassino in Boston, 1880 and *Upland Game Birds and Water Fowl of the United States,* published by Scribner's in New York, 1877.

POUPARD, JAMES. Engraver, artist and goldsmith, from Martinique, worked in Philadelphia, 1769–1807, and N.Y.C., *c.* 1814.

PRANG, LOUIS (1824–1909). Born in Germany, came to America in 1850, settled in Boston. Taught himself wood engraving and worked as an engraver until 1856. From 1856–60 he was in the lithographic business with Julius Mayer, as Prang & Mayer. Continued in the business alone, and after the Civil War started making chromolithographs. He was very successful and is known for his Christmas cards and chromos of paintings. Retired in 1899.

PRUD'HOMME, JOHN FRANCIS EUGENE (1800–1892). Born in St. Thomas, West Indies, came to N.Y.C. in 1807. Became an engraver apprentice to T. Gimbrede in 1814. From 1821–52, was an engraver of portraits and bookplates. Engraver for N.Y.C. banknote firm 1852–69, and in the same capacity for the Bureau of Engraving & Printing, Washington, D.C., 1869–85.

QUIROT. Lithographer in San Francisco as partner in Justh, Quirot & Co. in 1851. Had his own business, 1851–53.

RAWDON, FREEMAN (*c.* 1801–1859). Engraver in N.Y.C., 1833–59. Associated with firm of Rawdon, Wright & Hatch (& Edson after 1847). Brother of Ralph Rawdon.

RAWDON, RALPH. Engraver in Cheshire, Conn., *c.* 1813, in Albany, N.Y., 1816–34 and in N.Y.C., 1835–77.

REASE, WILLIAM H. Lithographer, worked in Philadelphia, 1844–60 and after.

REED, ABNER (1771–1866). Engraver, printer and artist, worked in N.Y.C. and Hartford.

REINAGLE, HUGH (*c.* 1788–1834). Artist, worked in N.Y.C., Philadelphia, New Orleans and Albany. Maverick, Pendleton, Childs & Inman and others, made prints after his work.

REMINGTON, FREDERICK (1861–1909) Painter, sculptor, etcher and illustrator, especially of Western scenes. His early illustrations appeared in *Harper's Weekly* as wood engravings.

REVERE, PAUL (1735–1818). American patriot, silversmith and engraver. Issued engravings just prior to the Revolution, including *Landing of the British Troops in Boston,* 1770, *Boston Massacre,* 1770, *View of Harvard College,* 1768 and engraved plates for the Massachusetts paper currency, 1775–76.

RICHARDSON, JAMES H. Wood engraver, worked in N.Y.C., 1848–80. Partner in Orr & Richardson, 1848, and Richardson & Cox, 1853–59.

RIDER, A. Book illustrator and lithographer *c.* 1830. Possibly same as Alexander Rider.

RISSO, CHARLES. Lithographer in N.Y.C. and New Orleans, 1832–50 and after. Partner in Risso & Browne, 1832–38 and Risso & Leefe, 1846–*c.* 1850.

ROBERTS, BISHOP (?–1739). Artist and engraver, worked in Charleston, S.C., 1735–39. Did view of Charleston, *c.* 1737.

ROBERTS, WILLIAM (*c.* 1829–?). Wood engraver in N.Y.C., 1846–76 and partner in Butler & Roberts, 1846.

ROBERTSON, ALEXANDER. Lithographer in N.Y.C., 1852–60, partner in Robertson & Seibert, 1854–57 and Robertson, Seibert & Shearman, 1859–60.

ROBINSON, HENRY R. Lithographer, printer and publisher in N.Y.C., 1836–51.

ROGERS, WILLIAM ALLEN (1854–1931). Illustrator, cartoonist and Western artist. Joined Harper Brothers in 1877 and supplied many Western illustrations to *Harper's Weekly.*

ROLLINSON, WILLIAM (1762–1842). English-born engraver, arrived in N.Y.C. in 1788. Worked on book illustrations, banknotes and did stipple portraits, including one of Alexander Hamilton in 1804. Did an aquatint view of N.Y.C. in 1801.

ROMANS, BERNARD (1720–1784). Dutch-born engraver, educated in England, came to America in 1755 to work as a botanist and engineer. Worked in Florida for a time and published work on natural history of the region in 1775. Was present at the Battle of Bunker Hill and published an *Exact View of the Late Battle at Charlestown,* in Philadelphia in 1775.

ROSENTHALS. Four Rosenthal brothers from Russian Poland worked in Philadelphia as lithographers, printers and publishers. Louis did early work on the development of chromolithography and received an award for the work from the Franklin Institute in 1851. Approximate active dates are Louis, *c.* 1850–75, Max, *c.* 1850–84, Morris, *c.* 1860 and Simon, *c.* 1860.

RUSSELL, BENJAMIN (1804–1885). Artist and publisher in New Bedford, Mass., known for his whaling scenes.

SACHSE, EDWARD (1804–1873). Lithographer and printer, native of Germany, worked in Baltimore, *c.* 1850–*c.* 1870.

SAGE & SONS. Lithographers in Buffalo, 1856–60.

SAINT-MÉMIN, CHARLES BALTHAZAR JULIEN FEVRET DE (1770–1852). Artist and engraver born in France, came to America with his parents *c.* 1793. Worked in America *c.* 1793–1810; 1812–14 in N.Y.C., Philadelphia, Baltimore, Washington, etc. Known for his profiles made with the aid of a physionotrace and also two views of New York. Made about 800 engraved miniature profiles of distinguished Americans.

SARONY, NAPOLEON (1821–1896) et al. Born in Quebec, Sarony was a major lithographer in N.Y.C. from *c.* 1836–67. Worked for N. Currier and from 1846-57 with Henry B. Major as Sarony & Major. This was expanded from 1857-67 with the addition of Joseph F. Knapp to become Sarony, Major & Knapp. Sarony left the business in 1867 and it continued until 1871 as Major & Knapp. The series of firms produced a large number of prints in almost all categories

SARTAIN, JOHN (1808–1897). English-born engraver and artist, came to America in 1830 and settled in Philadelphia. Very prolific engraver. Works include Bingham's *County Election* and *Martial Law.* Also published magazines, including his own *Union Magazine of Literature and Art,* 1849–52. Four of his children also became artists or engravers.

SAVAGE, EDWARD (1761–1817). Artist and engraver, worked in Boston, N.Y.C. and Philadelphia, Credited with making first aquatint in America, *Action between the Constellation and L'Insurgent,* in 1798.

SCHAUS, W. Publisher in N.Y.C., *c.* 1850-*c.* 1860.

SCHILE, H. Publisher of lithographs in N.Y.C., *c.* 1870.

SCHOFF, STEPHEN A. (1818–1904). Engraver, worked in Boston, *c.* 1834 and 1850's and 1860's, also Washington, N.Y.C., Newtonville, Mass., Brandon, Vt. and Norfolk, Conn.

SCOLES, JOHN. Engraver in N.Y.C., 1793–1844.

SCULL, NICHOLAS (?–1762). Cartographer and surveyor in Penna., *c.* 1848. Directed preparation of *East Prospect of the City of Philadelphia,* 1754.

SCHUTZ, J. Lithographer, worked for Currier and Ives and specialized in lettering.

SEVERIN, CHARLES. Lithographer, born in Poland, active in N.Y.C., *c.* 1845–*c.* 1865. Worked for Currier and Ives and was for a time a partner with E. Brown, 1851–53 and G. E. Hatch, 1853–54.

SEYMOUR, JOSEPH H. Engraver in Worcester, Mass., 1791–95 and in Philadelphia, 1796–1822.

SEYMOUR, SAMUEL. Engraver, artist on S. H. Long's Rocky Mountain expedition, 1819–20 and second expedition to the upper reaches of the Mississippi, 1823. Listed in Philadelphia, 1796–1823. Probably brother of Joseph H.

SHARP, WILLIAM (*c.* 1802–?) Lithographer born in England, settled in Boston in 1838 or '39. Pioneered in the use of color lithography. Did mostly book illustrations. Sharp family had many members in the lithographic business.

SHAW, JOSHUA (1776–1860). English-born artist who drew originals for *Picturesque Views of America,* engraved by John Hill in Philadelphia, 1819–20.

SHOBER, CHARLES. Lithographer in Philadelphia, 1856–57 and in Chicago, 1858–83. Partner of C. Reen, 1857–58. Founder, *c.* 1860, of the Chicago Lithographic Co.

SINCLAIR, THOMAS S. (*c.* 1805–1881). Lithographer, born in the Orkney Islands north of Scotland, came to America *c.* 1830, first in N.Y.C., then *c.* 1835 in Philadelphia. Started his own business *c.* 1839 and was joined by his sons, Thomas, Jr. and William, *c.* 1850. Firm continued until 1889. Did many types of work including decorative prints, fashion plates and illustrations for books.

SMILLIE, JAMES (1807–1885). Scotland-born engraver and artist, Worked in N.Y.C. after 1829. Did landscape engravings and is noted for *Voyage of Life* series painted by T. Cole. After 1861 worked almost exclusively on banknote engraving.

SMITH, JOHN RUBENS (1775–1849). English-born artist, engraver and lithographer, worked in Boston, 1809–14 and in N.Y.C., 1814–49. In the 1830's he was also in Philadelphia. Engraved portraits and did some of the aquatints for the *Hudson River Portfolio.*

SMITHER, JAMES. Engraver in Philadelphia, 1768–1778.

SNYDER, HENRY. Early stipple engraver, *c.* 1800–*c.* 1830, in N.Y.C. Boston and Albany.

SPARROW, THOMAS (*c.* 1746–?). Engraver and silversmith, worked in Annapolis, *c.* 1759, Philadelphia, *c.* 1759–*c.* 1764 and Annapolis, *c.* 1764–*c.* 1784.

STONE, HENRY. Pioneer lithographer, born in England, worked in Washington, D.C., *c.* 1822–*c.* 1846.

STRICKLAND, WILLIAM (1788–1854). Artist, architect and engraver, worked in N.Y.C., *c.* 1808, Philadelphia, 1809–45 and Nashville, 1845–54. Mainly an architect but did engraving as well, including views, portraits and book plates.

STRONG, THOMAS W. Wood engraver, lithographer and publisher, worked in N.Y.C., 1842–51. Dealer in valentines as well as other items and prints.

SWETT, MOSES. Lithographer in Boston, 1826–29, N.Y.C., 1830–36 and Washington, D.C., 1837. Associated with Pendleton; Annin & Smith; and Senefelder Lithographic Co. in Boston. Worked with Endicott in N.Y.C.

TAIT, ARTHUR FITZWILLIAM (1819–1905). Important American artist, specialized in animals and sporting scenes. Born in England, came to America in 1850 and settled in N.Y.C. Many of his paintings were made into lithographs by Currier and Ives.

TANNER, BENJAMIN (1775–1848). Engraver in N.Y.C., *c.* 1790–1799 and in Philadelphia, 1799–*c.* 1845. Partner in Tanner, Kearney & Tiebout, 1817–24 and Tanner, Vallance, Kearney & Co., 1818–20. Did banknote engraving, also portraits and naval prints including *Perry's Victory on Lake Erie,* 1815.

TAPPAN & BRADFORD. Lithographers and engravers in Boston, 1849–54.

TAVERNIER, JULES (1844–1889) Began working as an illustrator when he came to this country from France in 1871. In 1873, he and Paul Frenzeny were commissioned by *Harper's Weekly* to make sketches of an expedition from N.Y.C. to San Francisco.

TENNANT, WILLIAM. Drew view of Nassau Hall, Princeton, in 1763 which was engraved by Henry Dawkins.

THACKARA, JAMES (1767–1848). Engraver and stationer in Philadelphia and partner in Thackara & Vallance, 1791–97.

THAYER, BENJAMIN W. Lithographer and engraver in Boston, 1841–53.

THOMAS, HENRY A. (1834–1904). Artist and lithographer in N.Y.C.

TIEBOUT, CORNELIUS (*c.* 1773–1832). American-born engraver, worked in N.Y.C., 1789–93 and 1796–99, Philadelphia, 1799–*c.* 1825 and New Harmony, Indiana, 1825–32. Partner in Tanner, Kearney & Tiebout. Did banknote engraving, good stipple portraits and plates for T. Say's books on shells and insects.

TOMS, WILLIAM HENRY (*c.* 1700–*c.* 1750). Engraver in London of Roberts' view of Charleston, S.C., 1739.

TRENCHARD, JAMES (1747–?). Engraver in Philadelphia, *c.* 1780. Works include portraits, view of State House in Philadelphia after C. W. Peale, 1778 and illustrations for *Columbian Magazine* of which he was a founder and, for a time, editor.

TRUMBULL, JOHN (1756–1843). Important American painter of historical subjects. Some of his paintings were used as the basis for engravings, including the *Declaration of Independence,* engraved by A. B. Durand in 1820.

TURNER, JAMES (?–1759). Engraver, worked in Boston, 1744–48 and in Philadelphia, *c.* 1758. Did woodcut view of Boston for the cover of The *American Magazine,* 1744–45, map of the Middle Colonies, 1755 and map of Philadelphia, *c.* 1758.

VALENTINE, DAVID THOMAS (1801–1870). Deputy Clerk of the Common Council in N.Y.C. in which position he published the *Manuals of the Corporation of the City of New York,* 1841–70. These books contain many illustrations of scenes in N.Y.C.

VALLANCE, JOHN (*c.* 1770–1823). Engraver, native of Scotland, worked in Philadelphia 1791–1823. Partner in Thackara and Vallance, 1791–97, and Tanner, Vallance, Kearney & Co., 1817-19.

VAN BEEST, ALFRED (1820–1860). Dutch-born marine and landscape painter. Working New Bedford, Mass. and N.Y.C. Artist for two of Endicott's whaling lithographs.

VENINO, FRANCIS (FRANZ). Artist and lithographer in N.Y.C. during the 1850's. In 1852, made lithograph of Trumbull's *Surrender of Cornwallis* for N. Currier.

WAGNER, THOMAS S. Lithographer in Philadelphia *c.* 1840–*c.* 1865, partner in Pinkerton, Wagner & McGuigan, 1844–45 and Wagner & McGuigan, 1846–58.

WAIT (or WAITE), BENJAMIN FRANKLIN (1817–?). Wood engraver active in Philadelphia, *c.* 1845–84.

WALKER, WILLIAM AIKEN (*c.* 1838–1921). Important American painter of southern genre scenes. Spent most of his life in Charleston. Currier and Ives lithographed some of his paintings.

WALL, WILLIAM GUY (1792–after 1864). Irish-born artist, worked in N.Y.C., 1818–*c.* 1836 and 1856. Painted many views of the Hudson River and N.Y.C. Twenty of these watercolors were published in the *Hudson River Portfolio,* 1820–28. Other views by him were also engraved, including *New York from Weehawken, New York from Brooklyn Heights,* 1823 and *City Hall,* 1826.

WALTON, HENRY. English artist of views of towns in upper New York State issued by Bufford and others. In Ithaca 1830–46.

WAUD, ALFRED (1828–91) Illustrator and artist-correspondent for *Harper's Weekly* from 1858 when he immigrated to this country from England. Supplied many Civil War illustrations which appeared in *Harper's* as wood engravings. After the war he toured the South and the West for the same publication.

WAUD, WILLIAM (?–1878). Civil War illustrator for *Leslie's Illustrated Weekly* and *Harper's Weekly.* Brother of Alfred and came from England with him.

WEBER, EDWARD. Lithographer in Baltimore, *c.* 1835–51.

WHITEFIELD, EDWIN. English-born artist known for his *Original Views of North American Cities.* Worked from about 1845–92

WHITNEY, ELIAS JAMES (1827–?). Wood engraver in N.Y.C. Partner in Whitney & Annin, Whitney, Jocelyn & Annin and Whitney & Jocelyn, all in the period 1852–57.

WILD, JOHN C. (*c.* 1804–1846). Artist and lithographer, native of Switzerland, worked in Philadelphia, Cincinnati and St. Louis, *c.* 1830–46.

WILSON, ALEXANDER (1766–1813). Scotland-born artist and ornithologist, author and artist of *American Ornithology,* 1808–14. See chapter on Nature Prints.

WOLLEY, WILLIAM. English-born engraver and artist, worked in N.Y.C. and Philadelphia, *c.* 1800. Did portraits of George and Martha Washington.

WORTH, THOMAS (1834–1917). Comic, genre and racing horse artist whose work was lithographed by Currier and Ives.

YEAGER, JOSEPH (*c.* 1792–1859). Engraver, worked in Philadelphia, *c.* 1809–*c.* 1849. Works include *Procession of the Victuallers of Philadelphia,* 1821, and the *Battle of New Orleans and Death of Major General Packenham,* 1815. Also publisher of children's books.

ZAKRESKI (also ZABRESKI and ZACHRESKY), ALEXANDER. Lithographer in San Francisco, 1850–58.

ZOGBAUM, RUFUS F. (1849–1925) Illustrator for *Harper's Weekly* in the 1880's. Set pattern for portrayal of cowboys followed later by Remington and others. Later, military and naval artist.

APPENDIX III Selected List of Nineteenth-Century Color Plate Books

This selected list of nineteenth-century color plate books includes most of the books that are of interest to collectors of American prints. Since no color plate books of any importance were produced in America in the eighteenth century, only nineteenth-century works are listed. Beginning with Birch's views of Philadelphia in 1800, the number of books with color plates increased throughout the nineteenth century at an accelerating pace until the number reached unmanageable numbers for listing after 1900. Most of the prints made late in the century were done mechanically (color-printed) rather than individually hand colored and lack the freshness and vitality of the earlier works.

Prints to about 1830 are usually hand-colored engravings, the term being loosely used here to include intaglio prints such as etchings, aquatints, etc. After 1830 hand-colored or hand-touched lithographs were widely used. Later plates, after 1870, are mostly chromolithographs.

For the sake of brevity the listings contain only the most necessary information. The date given is the date of the publication of the edition with the largest number of color plates, which is frequently the first edition. Other editions, if any, are generally omitted. Most of the books were published in Boston, New York or Philadelphia, the centers of the publishing trade. A notable exception is the series of United States Government survey and exploration reports which were usually published in Washington, D.C. The bracket following the date gives the size of the book, usually in publishing terms, followed by a slash which gives the number of color plates. In some cases the number of color plates cannot be sharply defined and for these books the number is an estimate.

The approximate book sizes and notations are:
F. — folio, 11″ × 17″ average (from $8\frac{1}{2}$″ × 13″ to 15″ × 22″)
4to. — quarto, $8\frac{1}{2}$″ × 11″ average
8vo. — octavo, $5\frac{1}{2}$″ × $8\frac{1}{2}$″ average
12mo. and 16mo. are very small books.

Abert, Lt. J. W.
Expedition Report (Arkansas and Comanche Indians). 1846, (8vo./12 lithographs)

Album
United States Album (portraits of presidents, etc.), 1844–5, (4to./6)

Allen, J. F.
Victoria Regia; or The Great Water Lilly of America, 1854, (28″ × 22″/6)

Almanach
Charles Stokes & Co's *Illustrated Almanach of Fashion,* 1864, (8vo./12)

Armed Forces
Army & Navy of the U.S. (uniforms), by Barrie of Philadelphia, 1890–6, (small F./44)

Arnold and Samuels
The Living World (birds, animals, etc.), 1868, (4to./40), 2 vols.

Astronomy
Illustrated Astronomy 1844, (8vo./63)

Audsley, G. A.
The Ornamental Arts of Japan, 1883–4, (4to./69), 2 vols.

Audubon, J. J.
The Birds of America, 1841–4, (8vo./500), 7 vols. First edition has hand-colored lithographs. Changes in coloring techniques in later editions.

Audubon, J. J. (In collaboration with John Bachman)
The Viviparous Quadrupeds of North America, 1845–8, (elephant F./150 lithographed plates), 3 vols. 1854 supplement-6 additional plates

Audubon, J. J.
Quadrupeds of North America, 1849, '51, '54, (8vo./155), 3 vols.

Audubon, J. W.
Illustrated Notes on an Expedition through Mexico and California in 1849–50, 1852, (F./4)

Badger, Mrs. C. M.
Floral Belles from the Greenhouse and Garden, 1867, (F./16)

Badger, Mrs. C. M.
Wild Flowers Drawn and Colored from Nature, 1859, (small F./22)

Baird, S. F.; Brewer, T. M.; Ridgeway, R.
A History of North American Birds, 1875, (4to./64 chromolithographs), 3 vols.

Baird, S. F.; Cassin, J.; Lawrence, G. N.
The Birds of North America, 1860, (4to./100), 2 vols. (Reissue of vol. 9 of 1858 Pacific Railroad Reports)

Baird, S. F.
Report on the U.S. and Mexican Boundary Survey Vol. II (Zoology and Birds of the Boundary), 1859, (4to./25)

Ball, E. C.
Christian Armour, 1866, (4to./litho. by Major & Knapp Co.)

Barton, Wm. P. C.
A Flora of North America, 1821,'22,'23 (4to./136), 3 vols.

Barton, Wm. P. C.
Vegetable Material Medica of the United States (medical plants), 1817–18, 4to./50), 2 vols.

Bendire, Capt. C.
Life Histories of North American Birds (Prints of bird eggs), 1892–5, (4to./19), 2 vols.

Beyer, E.
Album of Virginia (scenes), 1858, (F./40)

Bible
The Holy Bible, E. H. Butler, 1850, Philadelphia, (4to./19)

Bigelow, J.
American Medical Botany (botanical plates), 1817–20, (7 × 10½″/60) 3 vols.

Bigland, J.
Natural History of Animals, 1828, (12mo./12)

Bigland, J.
Natural History of Birds, Fishes, Reptiles and Insects, 1828, (12mo./12)

Billings, J. D.
Hard Tack and Coffee (army life), 1887, (8vo./6)

Binney, A.
The Terrestrial Air-Breathing Molluscs of the United States, 1851–78, (8vo./80 approx.), 5 vols.

Birch, Wm. R.

The City of Philadelphia in the State of Pennsylvania North America as it Appeared in the Year 1800, 1800, (15″ × 19″/26 or 28)

Birch, Wm. R.
The Country Seats of the United States of North America (scenes), 1808, (8vo./20)

Blanchan, N.
Birds that Hunt and are Hunted, 1898, (10″ × 10″/48)

Bonaparte, C. L. J. L.
American Ornithology (Supplement to Wilson), 1825,'28,'33, (4to./27), 4 vols.

Bourke, J. G.
The Snake-Dance of the Moquis of Arizona, 1884, (8vo./17)

Boys' Sports
The American Boy's Book of Sports and Games, 1864, (12mo./4)

Bradford, D.
The Wonders of the Heavens (astronomy), 1837, (4to./4)

Brewer, T. M.
Smithsonian Contributions to Knowledge, North American Oology, (4to./5)

Bridges, F.
Birds and Blossoms, 1887, (4to./8)

Brinkley, Capt. H.
Japan, Described and Illustrated by the Japanese, 1897–8, (12″ × 15″/60)

Brooklyn
History of the Brooklyn and Long Island Fair, Feb. 22, 1864, 1864, (4to./5)

Brownell, C.
The Indian Races of North and South America, 1856, (8vo./34)

Buel, J. W.
The Border Outlaws and Border Bandits (Jesse James, etc.), 1881, (12mo./12)

Buel, J. W.
Heroes of the Dark Continent, 1890, (8″ × 11″/4)

Buel, J. W.
Heroes of the Plains, 1881, (8vo./16)

Bulfinch, T.
The Age of Chivalry, 1859, (12mo./6)

Burroughs, J.
Squirrels and Other Fur Bearers, 1900, (12mo./15)

Capen, E. A.
Oology of New England (Bird eggs), 1886, (4to./25)

Carolina
A Wreath from the Woods of Carolina (wild flowers), 1859, (8vo./11)

Carson, J., M.D.
Illustrations of Medical Botany, 1847, (4to./100), 5 vols.

Cassin, J.
Illustrations of the Birds of California, Texas, Oregon, British and Russian America, 1853–5, (8vo./50)

Cassin, J.
United States Exploring Expedition during the Years 1838–1842 (birds and animals), 1858, (4 to./53), 2 vols.

Catlin, G.
North American Indian Portfolio, 1845, (large F./25), (Slightly earlier edition with original plates was published in London)

Catlin, G.
A Religious Ceremony and Other Customs of the Mandans, 1867, (8vo./13)

Catlin, G.
Views of Niagara, 1831, (4to./8)

Challamel, M. A.
The History of Fashion in France, 1882, (8vo./20)

Chapman, F. M.
Bird Life, 1898, (8vo./75)

Child, G. W.
Specimens of Theatrical Cuts, 1869, (9½″ × 12″)

Clark, E. L.
Daleth or the Homestead of the Nations (Prints of Egypt), 1864, (8vo./8)

Clarkson, L.
The Gathering of the Lilies, 1877, (4to./4)

Clarkson, L.
Indian Summer; Autumn Poems and Sketches (flowers), 1881, (4to./12)

Cleaveland, N.
The Flowers Personified, 1849, (8vo./25)

Clouds
Illustrative Cloud Forms for the Guidance of Observers in the Classification of Clouds, 1897,

(12mo./16), (by C. G. Sigsbee/plates by Croneau)
Combe, W.
The Tour of Dr. Syntax in Search of the Picturesque, 1820, (8vo./81)
Comstock, J. L. and Comstock, J. C.
The Illustrated Botany, 1850, (8vo./50)
Conrad, T. A.
Monography of the Family Unionidae (fresh water shells), 1836, (8vo./65)
Conrad, T. A.
New Fresh Water Shells of the United States, 1834, (12mo./9)
Cook, Clarence
What Shall We Do with Our Walls? (Victorian wall treatment), 1881, (8vo./5)
Cook, Clarence
Costumes of the Time of the French Revolution 1790–93, Together with English Costumes during the Years 1795–1806, 1889, (F./69)
Cooper, J. G. and Suckley, G.
The Natural History of Washington Territory (animals, plants), 1859, (4to./55)
Cooper, S. F.
Rural Hours by a Lady (birds, flowers), 1851, (8vo./20)
Cory, C. B.
The Beautiful and Curious Birds of the World, 1883, (F./20)
Costume
Mirror of the Graces (fashions), 1813, (16mo./4)
Cozzens, F. S. and Kelley, Lt. J. D.
American Yachts, 1884–5, (F./27)
Cozzens, F. S. and Kelley, Lt. J. D.
Our Navy, 1897, (11″ × 15″/25)
Culin, S.
Korean Games, 1895, (4to./22)

Dahlgren, J. A. B.
System of Boat Armament of the U.S. Navy, 1852, (8vo./4 first, 13 second ed.)
Dankers, J. and Sluyter, P.
Memoirs of the Long Island Historical Society (early trips to New York City), 1867, (8vo./12)
Deems, C. F.
Chips and Chunks for Every Fireside (Victorian life), 1890, (8vo./6)
DeKay, J. E.
Zoology of New York (Part II, Birds), 1844, (4to./141)
DeKay, J. E.
Zoology of New York (Parts V, VI: Mollusca and Crustacea), 1843, (4to./53)
Delafield, J.
An Inquiry into the Antiquities of America (Mexico), 1839, (4to./10)
Deland, M.
Florida Days (scenes), 1899, (8vo./4)
Deland, M.
The Old Garden (Flowers), 1894, (12 mo.)
Delmes, L. F.
Collection of Flowers, c. 1833, (4to./9)
Delord, T.
The Flowers Personified, 1847, (4to./18)
Deming, E. W.
Indian Pictures, 1899, (17″ × 13″)
Denton, S. F.
Moths and Butterflies of the United States East of the Rocky Mts., 1900, (8vo./56)
Dickens, Charles
Boots at the "Holly Tree Inn," 1882, (4to./16) 1882, (4to./16)
Dickeson, M. W.
American Numismatic Manual, 1859. (4to./20)
Dodge, Col. R. I.
Our Wild Indians, 1882, (8vo./6)
Doughty, J. and T.
Cabinet of Natural History and American Rural Sports, 1830, 32, 33, (4to./57–54 colored) 3 vols.
Downing, A. J.
The Fruits and Fruit Trees of America, 1850, (8vo./69)
Drake, S. G.
Aboriginal Races of North America, 1860, (8vo./11)
Dumont, H.
The Floral Offering, 1856, (12mo./6)

Eastman, M. H.
The Romance of Indian Life, 1853, (8vo./12)
Eaton, D. C.
Beautiful Ferns, 1882, (4to./19)

Eaton, D. C.
The Ferns of North America, 1879–80, (4to./81), 2 vols.

Edgeworth, M.
Moral Tales, 1850, (12mo./6)

Edwards, W. H.
The Butterflies of North America, 1868–94, (4to./152 or 155 plates depending on edition), 3 vols.

Ellet, E. F.
The Charm (groups of people), 1848, (F./6)

Elliot, D. G.
A Monograph of the Phasianidae (pheasants), 1872, (F. 81), 2 vols.

Elliot, D. G.
A Monograph of the Pittidae (thrushes), 1867, (F./31), originally issued in parts, 1861–63.

Elliot, D. G.
A Monograph of the Tetraoninae (Grouse), 1865, (F./27), originally issued in parts, 1864–65.

Elliot, D. G.
The New and Heretofore Unfigured Species of the Birds of North America, 1866–69, (F./72), 2 vols.

Embury, E. C.
Nature's Gems (wildflowers), 1845, (4to./20)

Emerson, G. B.
A Report of the Trees and Shrubs Growing Naturally in the Forests of Massachusetts, 1875, (8vo./35), 2 vols.

Emory, W. H.
Report on the U. S. and Mexican Boundary Survey (scenery, botany, animals, etc.), 1857–58, (4to./37), 2 vols.

Falke, J. V. and Perkins, C. C.
Art in the House (furnishings), 1879, (4to./7)

Felter, J. D.
Morning Ramble, 1850, (12mo./8)

Field, T. W.
Historic and Antiquarian Scenes in Brooklyn and its Vicinity, 1868, (4to./11)

Fisher, A. H.
The Hawks and Owls of the United States in their Relation to Agriculture, 1893, (8to./26)

Flags
Flags of the Army of the United States carried during the War of the Rebellion, 1861–65, 1887, (87 plates)

Floral
Flora and Thalia, 1836, (16mo./24)

Floral
The Floral Alphabet, H. Hooker, 1845, (12-mo./25)

Floral
Flora's Lexicon, 1840, (8vo./4)

Floral
Floral Keepsake, ed. John Keese, *c.* 1845, (4to./30)

Floral
Floral Magazine and Botanical Repository, by D. and C. Landreth, Nursery and Seedsmen, Phila., 1832, (4to./81)

Floral
Floral Offering, Osgood, 1847, (4to./10)

Fremaux, L. J.
New Orleans Characters, 1876, (4to./16)

Frost, A. B.
Shooting Pictures, 1895, (F./12)

Furbish, J. A. M.
The Flower of Liberty (patriotic), 1866, (8vo./50)

Gambado, G.
An Academy for Grown Horsemen, 1813, (7½″ × 4½″/12)

Gentry, T. G.
Nests and Eggs of Birds of the United States, 1882, (9½″ × 12½″/54)

Gerstaecker, F.
Wild Sports of the Far West, 1859, (12mo./8)

Gibbs, M. B.
Napoleon's Military Career, 1895, (small F./20)

Gibson, W. H.
Our Edible Toadstools and Mushrooms, 1895, (8vo./30)

Girard, C.
United States Exploring Expedition, Herpetology, Vol. 20, 1858, (4to./32)

Giraud, J. P.
A Description of Sixteen New Species of North American Birds, 1841, (F./8)

Goethe
Goethe's Faust, J. Amster, 1888, (large F./10)
Good, P. P.
The Family Flora and Materia Medica Botanica, 1847, (8vo./48), later 2 vol.-sets have 96 plates
Good, P. P.
A Materia Medica Animalia, 1853, (8vo./24)
Goodale, G. L.
Wild Flowers of America, 1882, (4to./50)
Goodell
The Old and the New (Arabs in costume), 1853, (12mo./6)
Goodrich, F. B.
The Court of Napoleon Under the First Empire, 1857, (4to./14)
Goodrich, S. C.
A Winter Wreath of Summer Flowers (groups of Europeans), 1855, (12mo./12)
Gould, A. C.
Sport, or Fishing and Shooting, 1889, (atlas F./15)
Graham, E. O.
Nursery man (Garden Catalogue), *c.* 1870, ($8\frac{1}{2}'' \times 5\frac{3}{4}''$/56)

Hall, J. S.
The Book of the Feet (boots, shoes, etc.), 1847, (12mo./4)
Halliday, R. J.
Practical Camellia Culture, 1880, (12mo./5)
Halsey, R. T. H.
Picture of Early New York in Dark Blue Staffordshire, 1899, (4to./100+)
Hamilton, S.
The History of the National Flag of the United States of America, 1853, (12mo./3)
Hamlin, A. C.
The Tourmaline, 1873, (12mo./4)
Harbaugh, Rev. H.
The Birds of the Bible, 1854, (8vo./12)
Harland, M.
The Christmas Holly, 1867, (8vo./4)
Harper
Harper's Pictorial History of the War with Spain, 1899, (F./27)
Harris, W. C.
The Fishes of North America, 1893–8, (F./40)
Hart, M. E.
Stray Violets Gathered and Pictured, 1893, (8vo./16)
Harvey, G.
Harvey's Scenes of the Primitive Forests of America, 1841, (F/4)
Hawthorne, N.
The Snow Image, 1864, (8vo./6)
Hazard, W. P. (Publisher)
Animals in Costume, c. 1835, ($5'' \times 7''$/48)
Healy, M.
Report of the Cruise of the Marine Steamer Corwin in the Arctic Ocean in the Year 1885, etc., 1887, (8vo./4)
Heine, W.
Graphic Scenes in the Japan Expedition, 1856, (F./9)
Henriot
The Book-Lovers Almanac, 1893, (12mo./12)
Heraldry
American Heraldica, 1886, (F./17)
Heraldry
Dame Heraldry, 1866, (8vo./9)
Herbert, H. W. and Surtees, R. S.
Mr. Sponge's Sporting Tour, 1856, (12mo./6)
Herne, P.
Perils and Pleasures of a Hunter's Life, 1846, (12mo./12)
Herrick, F. H.
The American Lobster, 1895, (4to./8)
Hervey, A. B.
Sea Mosses, A Collector's Guide, 1881, (12mo./20)
Hill, J.
Drawing Book of Landscape Scenery, 1821 (F./12)
Hill, J.
Picturesque Views of American Scenery (painted by J. Shaw), 1819, (F./18) 20 plates in 1820 second edition
Hill, J.
A Series of Progressive Lessons (flower painting), 1818, (F./12)
Hillard, E. B.
The Last Men of the Revolution, 1864, (12mo./5)

Hoey, C.
"Yester-Year" Ten Centuries of Toilette, 1891, (8vo./28)

Hoffy, A.
Hoffy's North American Pomologist (fruits), 1860, (4to./36)

Holbrook, J. E.
Icthyology of South Carolina, 1860, (4to./28)

Holbrook, J. E.
North American Herpetology, 1836–8, (4to./111), 4 vols., second edition in 1842 with 147 plates in 5 vols.

Holden, G. H.
Canaries and Cage Birds, 1888, (8vo./8,12 plates in second ed.)

Holland, W. J.
The Butterfly Book, 1898, (8vo./48)

Homes
Homes of American Authors, 1853, (8vo./14)

Hooper, E. J.
Western Fruit Book, 1857, (12mo./4)

Hooper, L. (editor)
The Lady's Book of Flowers and Poetry, 1842, (12mo./9)

Hopkins, J. H.
The Book of Flowers, 1846, (F./10)

Horses
Celebrated Horses from Paintings by the Best Artists, 1882, (F./24)

Hovey, C. M.
The Fruits of America, Vol. 1 1852, Vol. II, 1856, (4to./96)

Howells, W. D.
Venetian Life, 1892, (12mo./18), 2 vols.

Hudson River Portfolio, engravings by J. Hill after paintings by W. G. Wall, 1825–6, (F./20)

Huestis, C. P.
Guide to Painting in Watercolors, 1845, (12mo./6)

Huggins, J. R. D.
Hugginiana or Huggins Fantasy (caricatures), 1808, (12mo./7)

Humorist
The Humorist, 1829, (16mo./14)

Humphrey, H. N.
Ocean Gardens, 1857, (12mo./12)

Huntington, D. W.
In Brush, Sage and Stubble (bird hunting), 1898, (17″ × 12½″/7)

Iris
The Iris, 1852, (8vo./12)

Jackson, H. H.
The Procession of Flowers in Colorado, 1886, (4to./12)

Jaeger, Prof. B.
North American Insects, 1854, (8vo./6)

Jasper, T.
The Birds of North America, 1878, (F./119)

Johnson, H. J.
Johnson's Household Book of Nature, 1880, (7″ × 10″/64)

Johnston, Lt. Col. J. E. et al
Reports of the Secretary of War, with the Reconnaissances of Routes from San Antonio to El Paso, 1850, (8vo./72)

Johnston, Lt. J. D.
China and Japan, 1861, (8vo./8)

Jones, H. E. and N. E.
Illustrations of the Nests and Eggs of the Birds of Ohio, 1886, (4to./68)

Keeler, C. A.
Evolution of the Colors of North American Land Birds, 1893, (8vo./19)

Kendall, G. W.
The War Between the United States and Mexico, 1851, (F./12)

Kilbourne, S. A. and Goode, G. B.
Game Fishes of the United States, 1879, (large F./20)

Kitto, J.
The Gallery of Scripture Engravings, 1856, (4to./10)

Knobel, E.
Field Key to the Land Birds, 1899, (8vo./9)

Kunz, G. F.
Gems and Precious Stones of North America, 1890, (8vo./8)

Lafayette, General
Pictorial Life of Gen. Lafayette, 1847, (8vo./8)
L'Aine, P. G.
The Timber Merchant's Guide, 1823, (8vo./30)
Lau, G. T.
Greek Vases, 1879, (4to./12)
Lewis, J. O.
Aboriginal Portfolio (Indians), 1835–6, (F./80)
Lindsay, H.
New Bedford and Fair Haven Signal Book (Flags), 1845, (8vo.)
Longfellow, H. W.
Evangeline, 1895, (8vo./10)
Lounsberry, A.
A Guide to the Wild Flowers, 1899, (8vo./64)
Lucas, F. Jr.
The Art of Coloring and Painting Landscapes in Water Colors, 1815, (6″ × 9″/10)
Lucas, F. Jr.
Lucas's Progressive Drawing Book, 1827, (F./14)
Lucas, J.
The Pleasures of a Pigeon Fancier, 1897, (8vo./3)

Magic
The Magic Lantern, 1807, (12mo./10)
Mapleson, T. W. G.
A Handbook of Heraldry, 1851, (8vo./8)
Mapleson, T. W. G.
Lays of the Western World (jousting, etc.), *c.* 1849, (8vo./34 including illuminated borders)
Mapleson, T. W. G.
Pearls of American Poetry (birds, flowers, etc.), *c.* 1853, (8vo./53 illuminated)
Marbury, M. O.
Favorite Flies and their Histories (insects), 1892, (8 vo./32)
Martyn, S. T.
Ladies' Wreath (flowers), 1848–9, Vol. II, (12mo./12)
Matthews, A. E.
Pencil Sketches of Colorado, 1866, (F./23)
Mattson, M.
The American Vegetable Practise, 1841, (8vo./24), 2 vols.
Maynard, C. J.
The Birds of Eastern North America, 1896, (4to./40)
Maynard, C. J.
The Birds of Florida, 1872–8, (4to./18)
Maynard, C. J.
The Butterflies of New England, 1886, (4to./8)
Maynard, C. J.
Eggs of North American Birds, 1890, (8vo./10)
Maynard, C. J.
Handbook of the Sparrows, Finches, etc. of New England, 1896, (12mo./17)
McCook, H. C.
American Spiders and their Spinning Work, 1889–93, (4to./no color plates in the 1889 edition, 5 in 1890, 30 in 1893 edition), 3 vols.
McIlvaine, C.
Toadstools, Mushrooms, Fungi Edible and Poisonous, 1900, (8vo./36)
McKenney, T. L.
Sketches of a Tour of the Lakes, 1827 (8vo./27)
McKenney, T. L. and Hall, J.
History of the Indian Tribes of North America 1836–38, '44, (F./120), 3 vols
Issued by four successive publishers: E. C. Biddle, F. W. Greenough, D. Rice and J. G. Clark, and then by J. M. Campbell in London.
McKenney, T. L. and Hall, J.
History of the Indian Tribes of North America 1848, 49, 50 (8vo./120) 3 vols.
McVickar, H. V.
The Boston Tea Party, 1882, (4to./29 illuminated)
Meehan, T.
Native Flowers and Ferns of the United States, 1878–9, (4to./96)
Mercier, Rev. J. J.
Mountains and Lakes of Switzerland and Italy, 1871, (4to./64)
Merrill, O. N.
True History of the Kansas Wars, 1856, (8vo./3)
Michaux, F. A.

North American Sylva, 1817–19, (8vo./156), 3 vols., printed first in France, then later in the U.S.—in subsequent editions as late as 1849, Thos. Nuttall was listed as co-author

Military
U.S. Military Magazine, issued Mar. 1839–June 1842, (8vo./81)

Military Manual
Soldier's Manual for Cavalry, Artillery, Light Infantry and Infantry, 1824, (8vo./12)

Millspaugh, C. F.
American Medicinal Plants, 1883, (4to./180), 2 vols.

Miner, H. S.
Orchids, the Royal Family of Plants, 1885, (F./24)

Moore, Rev. H. D. (editor)
The Winter Bloom, 1852, (8vo./9)

Moran, T.
The Yellowstone National Park, etc., 1876, (F./15)

Morgan, L. H.
The League of the Ho-de-no-sau-nee, or Iroquois, 1851, (8vo./21)

Moscow
Sketches of Moscow and St. Petersburg (P. Svenin), 1813, (12mo./9)

Mumford, J. K.
Oriental Rugs, 1900, (4to./16)

Munson, L. G.
Flowers from My Garden, 1864, (4to./18)

Muzzy, J. S.
A Lecture on Intemperance, 1846, (12mo./18)

Nansen, Dr. F.
Farthest North (Arctic journey), 1897, (8vo./16), 2 vols.

Navy
Uniform of the United States Navy, 1869, (F./8)

Nehring, H.
Our Native Birds of Song and Beauty, 1893, (4to./36), 2 vols.

Nelson, E. W.
Birds of Alaska, 1887, (4to./12)

Newman, J. B.
Boudoir Botany (flowers), 1847, (4to./60)

Newman, J. B.
The Illustrated Botany, 1846, (8vo./46)

New York
The New Metropolis, 1600–1900, 1899 (F./9)

Nicholson, W.
An Almanach of Twelve Sports, 1898, (4to./12)

Nott, J. C. and Glidden, G. R.
Indigenous Races of the Earth, 1857, (8vo.)

Nye, B.
Bill Nye's History of the United States, 1894, (8vo./7)

Ogden, H. A.
Regulations for the Uniform of the Army of the United States, 1888, (F./12)

Ogden, H. A.
Uniform of the Army of the United States, 1774 to 1889, (F./44)

Orchards
Orchardists Companion, 1841–2, (Quarterly), (4to./12 per part)

Orvis, C. F. and Cheney, A. N.
Fishing with the Fly, 1883, (12mo./13)

Osgood, F. S.
The Poetry of Flowers and the Flowers of Poetry, 1851, (12mo./12)

Osgood, F. S.
The Cries of New York, 1846, (8vo./14)

Otis, H.
Comic History of the United States, 1861, (12mo./43)

Owen, D. D.
First Report of a Geological Reconnoissance of the Northern Counties of Arkansas, 1858, (8vo./6)

Page, T. N.
Santa Claus's Partner, 1899, (12mo./6)

Parquin, Capt. C.
Napoleon's Victories from the Personal Memoirs of Capt. C. P. of the Imperial Guard, 1893, (4to./20)

Pears
The Illustrated Pear Culturist, 1857, (8vo.)

Pearson, L.
Diseases of Poultry, 1877, (8vo./75)

Peck, C. H.
Mushrooms, 1897, (4to./43)
Perry, Commodore M. C.
Narrative of the Expedition of an American Squadron to the China Seas and Japan, 1856, (F./109), 3 vols.
Pettrich, F.
Portraits of Distinguished Indians, 1842, (F./5)
Phillips, A. A.
The Bouquet for 1847 (women/flowers), 1847, (4to./10)
Pollard, J.
The Decorative Sisters, 1881, (8vo./16)
Pope, A. Jr.
Celebrated Dogs of America, 1880, (F./20)
Pope, A. Jr.
Upland Game Birds and Water Fowl of the United States, 1877–8, (22″ × 27″/20)
Preble, G. H.
Origin and Progress of the Flag of the United States, 1872, (8vo./12)
Proctor, E. D.
The Song of the Ancient People, 1893, (8vo./11)
Pyle, H.
The Lady of Shalott, 1881, (4to./37)
Pyle, H.
Yankee Doodle, 1881, (4to./8)

Rand, E. S., Jr.
The Rhododendron and "American Plants", 1871, (8vo./10)
Rathbun, F. R.
Bright Feathers (birds), 1880, (8vo./5)
Reigart, J. F.
The Life of Robert Fulton, 1856, (8vo./8)
Rein, J. J.
Industries of Japan, 1899, (8vo./9)
Rodenbaugh, T. F.
From Everglade to Canon with the Second Dragoons, 1875, (8vo./5)
Rosetta Stone
Report of the Committee Appointed by the Philomathean Society of the University of Pennsylvania, etc., 1858, (4to./14)

Samuels, E. A.
Ornithology and Oology of New England, etc., 1867, (8vo./4)
Samuels, E. A.
Our Northern and Eastern Birds, 1883, (8vo./6)
Say, T.
American Conchology, 1830–8, (92 plates)
Say, T.
American Entomology, 1817, (8vo./6)
Say, T.
An Entomology or Description of the Insects of North America, 1824–8, (8vo./54), 3 vols.
Schoolcraft, H. R.
Historical and Statistical Information Respecting the History, Condition and Prospects of the Indian Tribes of the United States, 1851–7, (4to./70+), 6 vols.
Schoolcraft, H. R.
Narrative Journal of Travels from Detroit, 1821, (8vo./8)
Scudder, S. H.
The Butterflies of the Eastern United States and Canada, 1889, (4to./10)
Semmes, Admiral R.
Memoirs of Service Afloat During the War Between the States, 1869, (8vo./6)
Shoberl, F.
Persia, 1828, (12mo./12)
Shoberl, F.
Turkey, 1829, (12mo./24), 3 vols.
Signals
Merchant Signals of the Port of New York, 1860, (46 small prints)
Simpson, J. H.
Journal of a Military Reconnaissance from Santa Fe, New Mexico, to Navajo Country, 1852, (8vo./34)
Skelding, S. B.
Flowers from Sunlight to Shade, 1885, (8vo./12)
Sloan, W. L.
Life of Napoleon Bonaparte, 1896, (4to./80)
Smith, F. H.
Venice of Today, 1895, (F./20+)
Smith, Sir J. E.
The Grammar of Botany, 1822, (4to./21)
Spectropia
Spectropia, or Surprising Spectral Illusions, 1864, (4to./16)

Sprague, I.
Flowers from the Field and Forest, 1882, (4to./14)

Spratt, G.
Twelve Original Designs (humorous figures), 1831, (4to/12)

Squier, E. G.
Travels in Central America, 1853, (8vo./6), 2 vols.

Steele, H. M.
Sporting Incidents, 1893–4, (F./16)

Stephens, H. L.
The Comic Natural History of the Human Race, 1851, (8vo./39)

Stevens, I. I.
Narrative and Final Report of Explorations for a Route for a Pacific Railroad, etc. (views, animals), 1860, (4to./8+), 2 vols.

Strahan, E.
Mrs. Vanderbilt's House and Collection, 1883–4, (F./33)

Strecker, H.
Lepidoptera, Rhopaloceres and Heteroceres, Indigenous and Exotic, 1872–7; 1878–1900, (4to./15+)

Strong, A. B.
The American Flora, 1848–50, (4to./240), 4 vols.

Taylor, B.
The Ballad of Abraham Lincoln, 1870, (4to./4)

Thaxter, C.
An Island Garden (flower plates by Childe Hassam), 1894, (8vo./11)

Thayer, E. H.
Wild Flowers of Colorado, 1885, (4to./24)

Thayer, E. H.
Wild Flowers of the Pacific Coast, 1887, (4to./24)

Thoreau, H. D.
Cape Cod, 1896, (12mo./2+), 2 vols.

Titford, W. J.
Hortus Botanicus Americanus, 1810, (4to./6+)

Toilet
The Toilet, 1867, (12mo./20)

Torrey, J.
Flora of the State of New York, 1843, (4to./160), 2 vols.

Townsend, J.
Ornithology of the United States of America, 1839, (8vo./4)

Trimble, I. P.
A Treatise on the Insect Enemies of Fruit and Fruit Trees, 1865, (4to./11)

Turner, L. M.
Contributions to the Natural History of Alaska (birds), 1886, (4to./10)

Tweedie, W. K.
Jerusalem and its Environs, 1860, (16mo./9)

Valentine, D. T.
Manuals of the Corporation of the City of New York, 28 vols., 1841–70 (maps, portraits, etc.), (8vo. to 16mo./annual)

Valentine, Mrs.
Shakespearean Tales in Verse, 1890, (4to./23+)

Van Lennert, H. J.
The Oriental Album, 1862, (F./20)

Van Rensselaer, Mrs. J. K.
The Devil's Picture Books (playing cards), 1890, (8vo./15)

Von Rezold, W.
The Theory of Color in its Relation to Art and Art Industry, 1876, (8vo./11)

Wade, W.
Panorama of the Hudson River from New York to Albany, 1845, (12mo./folding print 6″ wide and 12′ long)

Wagner, Lt. Col. A. L. and Kelley, Comm. J. D. J.
Our Country's Defensive Forces in War and Peace, 1899, (F./42)

Walker, Mrs. S. A.
Female Beauty as Preserved and Improved by Regimen, Cleanliness and Dress, 1846, (12mo./7)

Walters, W. T.
Oriental Ceramic Art, 1897, (F./116)

Walton, W.
Chefs-d'Oeuvre de L'Exposition Universelle de Paris (painting, tapestries, etc.), 1889, (F./32)

Warren, B. H.
Report on the Birds of Pennsylvania, 1888, (8vo./49)

Warren, J.
The Conchologist, 1834, (4to./17)

Webber, C. W.
Wild Scenes and Song Birds, 1854, (8vo./20)

Webber, C. W.
Wild Scenes and Wild Hunters of the Woods, 1852, (8vo./3)

Weik, J.
Pittoresque Scenes of American Life (semi-comic scenes), *c.* 1840, (12mo./16)

Whibley, C.
The Cathedrals of England and Wales, 1888, (F./16)

Whitefield, E.
Houses of our Forefathers, 1889, (4to./64)

Whittier, J. G.
Jack in the Pulpit, 1884, (8vo./8)

Wilcox, M.
History of the War in the Philippines, 1900, (F./25)

Wild Flowers
Wild Flowers of America, published weekly from May 22, 1894 to Sept. 11, 1894, (4to./288)

Wilkes, C.
United States Exploring Expedition, 1838, '39, '40, '41, (birds, mammals, scenes), 1858, (F./53), 2 vols.

Williams, J. L.
The Home and Haunts of Shakespeare, 1892, (F./15)

Wilson, A.
American Ornithology, 1808, 1810–1814, (4to./76), 9 vols.

Wilson, E. W.
Cruise of the Revenue Steamer Corwin in Alaska, 1882, (4to./4+)

Wirt, E. W.
Flora's Dictionary, 1837, (4to./58)

Wood, J. G.
Our Living World, 1885, (4to./42), 3 vols.

Wyatt, T.
A Manual of Conchology, 1838, (8 vo./36)

Yachting
Code of Yachting Signals, New York Yacht Club, 1874, (4to./2)

Zoology
The Zoological Garden, 1855, (8vo./16)

SELECTED BIBLIOGRAPHY

CHAPTER ONE

Adhémar, Jean. *Graphic Art of The Eighteenth Century.* McGraw-Hill, New York: 1964

Belknap, Waldron Phoenix, Jr. *American Colonial Painting.* The Belknap Press of Harvard University, Cambridge, Mass.: 1959

Bishop, J. Leander. *A History of American Manufactures from 1608 to 1860.* Edward Young and Company, Philadelphia: 1868

Cummings, Abbott Lowell, ed. *Rural Household Inventories.* The Society for the Preservation of New England Antiquities, Boston: 1964

Dunlap, William. *History of the Rise and Progress of the Arts of Design in the United States.* Dover, New York: 1969. Reprint of the 1834 edition published by George P. Scott and Company

Albrecht Dürer, Master Printmaker. Department of Prints and Drawings, Museum of Fine Arts, Boston: 1971

Dürer and his Time. An Exhibition Catalogue, The Smithsonian Institution: 1965–66

Hind, Arthur M. *A History of Engraving and Etching.* Houghton-Mifflin: 1923

Ivins, William M., Jr. *Prints and Visual Communication.* Harvard University Press, Cambridge, Mass.: 1953

Mayor, A. Hyatt. *Prints and People.* The Metropolitan Museum of Art, New York: 1971

Morse, John D., ed. *Prints in and of America.* University Press of Virginia, Charlottesville: 1970

Newhall, Beaumont. *The History of Photography.* The Museum of Modern Art, New York: 1964

Panofsky, Erwin. *The Life and Art of Albrecht Dürer.* Princeton University Press, Princeton: 1945

Papermaking. Library of Congress, Washington: 1968

Roger-Marx. Claude. *Graphic Art of the Nineteenth Century.* McGraw-Hill, New York: 1962

Senefelder, Alois. *A Complete Course of Lithography.* Da Capo Press, New York: 1968. Reprint of first English edition published in London in 1819.

Shadwell, Wendy J. *American Printmaking, The First 150 Years.* The Museum of Graphic Art: 1969.

Weiss, Harry B. "The Growth of the Graphic Arts in Philadelphia 1663–1820," *Bulletin of the New York Public Library.* LVI. Feb. 1952, March 1952, "The Number of Persons and Firms Connected with the Graphic Arts in New York City 1633–1820." op. cit. L. Oct. 1946

CHAPTER TWO

Hughes, Therle, *Prints for the Collector.* Praeger, New York: 1971

Ivins, William M., Jr. *How Prints Look.* Beacon Press, Boston: 1948

Lumsden, E. S. *The Art of Etching.* Dover, New York: 1962

Mayor, Hyatt A. *Prints and People.* Metropolitan Museum of Art, New York: 1971

Marzio, Peter C. "American Lithographic Technology Before the Civil War," *Prints in and of America to 1850.* University of Virginia Press, Charlottesville: 1970

Zigrosser, Carl and Gaehde, Christa M. *A Guide to the Collecting and Care of Original Prints.* Crown Publishers, New York: 1965

CHAPTER THREE

Cantor, J. "Prints and the American Art-Union," *Prints in and of America to 1850.* University Press of Virginia, Charlottesville: 1970

Comstock, Helen. *The Concise Encyclopedia of American Antiques.* Hawthorn Books, New York: 1965

Fielding, Mantle. *American Engravers upon Copper and Steel,* a supplement to David McNeely Stauffer, *American Engravers.* Philadelphia: 1917

Flexner, James Thomas. *That Wilder Image.* Crown, New York: 1962

Groce, George C. and Wallace, David H. *The New York Historical Society's Dictionary of Artists in America 1564–1860.* Yale University Press, New Haven: 1957

Holman, Richard B. "Seventeenth-Century American Prints," *Prints in and of America to 1850.* University Press of Virginia, Charlottesville: 1970

Shadwell, Wendy J. *American Printmaking, the First 150 Years,* an exhibition catalogue. Museum of Graphic Art, New York: 1969

Stauffer, David McNeely. *American Engravers upon Copper and Steel.* The Grolier Club of the City of New York, New York: 1907. 2 vol.

Stokes, I. N. Phelps and Haskell, Daniel C. *American Historical Prints, Early Views of American Cities.* New York Public Library, New York: 1933

CHAPTER FOUR

Dunlap, William. op. cit.

Groce, George C. and Wallace, David H. op. cit.

Morse, John D., ed. *Prints in and of America to 1850.* University of Virginia Press, Charlottesville: 1970

Norton, A. Bettina. "Edwin Whitefield, 1816–1892," *Antiques.* Vol. CII. No. 2, August 1972, pp 232–243

Peters, Harry T. *America on Stone.* Doubleday, Doran and Company, Garden City, New York: 1931

Peters. Harry T. *California on Stone.* Doubleday, Doran and Company, Garden City, New York: 1935

Ramsay, John. "The American Scene in Lithograph," *Antiques.* LX. No. 3, September 1951, 180–83

Senefelder, Alois. op. cit.
Weber, Wilhelm. *A History of Lithography.* McGraw-Hill, New York: 1966
Welsh, Peter C. "The Lithograph: a Mirror of Victorian Taste," *Antiques.* LXXX. No 3, September 1961

CHAPTER FIVE

Best Fifty Currier and Ives Lithographs/ Small Folio Size. Old Print Shop, New York: about 1934
Bland, Jane Cooper. *Currier and Ives, A Manuel for Collectors.* Doubleday, Doran and Company, Garden City, New York: 1931
Cowdrey, Mary Bartlett. "Fanny Palmer, an American Lithographer," *Prints.* Selected for the Print Council of America by Carl Zigrosser, Holt Rinehart and Winston, New York: 1962
Cunningham, Frederick C. (updated by Colin Simpkin). *Currier and Ives Prints, An Illustrated Checklist,* Crown, New York: 1970
King, Roy and Davis, Burke. *The World of Currier and Ives.* Random House: 1968
Peters, Fred J. *Clipper Ship Prints by N. Currier and Currier and Ives.* Antique Bulletin Publishing Company, New York: 1930
Peters, Fred J. *Railroad, Indian and Pioneer Prints by N. Currier and Currier and Ives.* Antique Bulletin Publishing Company, New York: 1930
Peters, Fred J. *Sporting Prints by N. Currier and Currier and Ives.* Antique Bulletin Publishing Company, New York: 1930
Peters, Harry T. *Currier and Ives, Printmakers to the American People.* New York. Vol. I: 1929; Vol. II: 1931
Peters, Harry T. *Currier and Ives, Printmakers to the American People.* Doubleday, Doran and Company, Garden City, New York: 1942
Simkin, Colin. *Currier and Ives' America.* Crown Publishers Inc., New York: 1952

CHAPTER SIX

Artist-Naturalist: Observations in the Americas. An Exhibition Catalogue, July 14–September 10, 1972. National Collection of Fine Arts, Smithsonion Institution, Washington, D.C.
Bennett, Whitman. *A Practical Guide to American Nineteenth Century Color Plate Books.* Bennett Book Studios, New York: 1949
Dunlap, William. op. cit.
Wood, Charles B., III. "Prints and Scientific Illustrations," *Prints in and of America to 1850.* University Press of Virginia: 1970

CHAPTER SEVEN

Comstock, Helen. op. cit.
Davison, Nancy R. **"The Grand Triumphal Quick Step: Or Sheet Music Covers in America,"** *Prints in and of America to 1850.* University Press of Virginia: 1970
Dow, George Francis. *The Arts and Crafts in New England 1704–1775.* The Wayside Press, Topsfield, Mass.: 1927
Gelman, Barbara. *The Wood Engravings of Winslow Homer.* Bounty Books, New York: 1969
Harris, Elizabeth. "Jacob Perkins, William Congreve, and Counterfeit Printing in 1820," *Prints in and of America to 1850.* op. cit.
Landauer, Bella C. *Early America Trade Cards.* Wm. Edwin Rudge Inc., New York: 1927

Lee, Ruth Webb. *A History of Valentines.* Studio Publications and Thomas Crowell Company, New York: 1952

CHAPTER EIGHT

Dolloff, Francis W. and Perkinson, Roy L. *How to Care for Works of Art on Paper.* Museum of Fine Arts, Boston: 1971

Kelly, Francis. *Art Restoration.* McGraw-Hill Book Company, New York: 1972

Papermaking/ Art and Craft. Exhibition Catalogue of exhibition starting April 21, 1968, Library of Congress, Washington, D.C.: 1968

Plenderleith, H. J. *The Conservation of Antiquities and Works of Art.* Oxford University Press, London: 1956

Zigrosser, Carl and Gaehde, Christa M. *A Guide to the Collecting and Care of Original Prints.* Crown Publisher Inc., New York: 1965

APPENDIX II

Comstock, Helen. op. cit.

Fielding, Mantle. op. cit.

Groce, George C. and Wallace, David H. op. cit.

Hamilton, Sinclair. *Early American Book Illustrators and Wood Engravers 1670–1870.* Vol. I and II. Princeton University Press: 1968

One Hundred Notable American Engravers, 1683–1850. Exhibition at the New York Public Library: 1928

Peters, Harry T. *America on Stone,* Doubleday, Doran and Company, Garden City, New York: 1931

Stauffer, David McNeely. op. cit.

Taft, Robert, *Artists and Illustrators of the Old West 1850–1900* Charles Scribner's Son, New York: 1953

Index